Amnesty International
Report 2006

the state of the world's human rights

This report covers the period January to December 2005.

AMNESTY INTERNATIONAL

Amnesty International is a worldwide movement of people who campaign for internationally recognized human rights to be respected and protected.

Amnesty International's vision is of a world in which every person enjoys all of the human rights enshrined in the Universal Declaration of Human Rights and other international human rights standards.

Amnesty International's mission is to undertake research and action focused on preventing and ending grave abuses of the rights to physical and mental integrity, freedom of conscience and expression, and freedom from discrimination, within the context of its work to promote all human rights.

Amnesty International is independent of any government, political ideology, economic interest or religion. It does not support or oppose any government or political system, nor does it support or oppose the views of the victims whose rights it seeks to protect. It is concerned solely with the impartial protection of human rights.

Amnesty International is a democratic, self-governing movement. Major policy decisions are taken by a two-yearly International Council made up of representatives from all national sections. The Council elects an International Executive Committee of volunteers which carries out its decisions.

Amnesty International's Secretary General is Irene Khan (Bangladesh) and International Executive Committee members elected for 2005-7 were Soledad García Muñoz (Argentina), Ian Gibson (Australia), Lilian Gonçalves-Ho Kang You (Netherlands), Petri Merenlahti (Finland), Claire Paponneau (France), Vanushi Rajanayagam (New Zealand), Hanna Roberts (Sweden; Chair), and David Weissbrodt (USA).

Amnesty International has more than 1.8 million members and supporters in over 150 countries and territories in every region of the world. It is funded largely by its worldwide membership and public donations. No funds are sought or accepted from governments for Amnesty International's work investigating and campaigning against human rights violations.

ABOUT THIS REPORT

The *Amnesty International Report 2006* documents human rights issues of concern to Amnesty International (AI) during 2005.

AI's approach to tackling human rights abuses is informed by both the challenges and opportunities for change within a given country or region. The strategic goals that AI identifies in a country or region determine AI's work. As a result, AI addresses particular issues in specific countries. Its coverage of individual issues, as reflected in the content of this report, is focused rather than comprehensive. If an issue is not covered in a country entry, this should not be taken as a statement by AI that abuses within this category did not occur. Nor can the absence of an entry on a particular country or territory be taken to imply that no human rights abuses of concern to AI took place there during 2005. In particular, the length of individual entries cannot be used as the basis for a comparison of the extent and depth of AI's concerns.

Regional maps have been included in this report to indicate the location of countries and territories, and each individual country entry begins with some basic information about the country. Neither the maps nor the country information may be interpreted as AI's view on questions such as the status of disputed territory.

©Private

PETER BENENSON (1921-2005)

"Only when the last prisoner of conscience has been freed, when the last torture chamber has been closed, when the United Nations Universal Declaration of Human Rights is a reality for the world's people, will our work be done."
Peter Benenson, founder of AI, died on 25 February 2005, aged 83.

It was a chance reading of an article in the press that led British lawyer Peter Benenson to take a stand against human rights abuses – this at a time when human rights had little protection under international law. Outraged by the case of two students in Portugal who were imprisoned for raising a toast to freedom, Peter Benenson wrote a full-page appeal in the UK newspaper, *The Observer*, prompting thousands to write letters of support.

AI was born. From a one-year campaign for the release of six prisoners of conscience, AI grew to become a worldwide human rights movement, taking up thousands of cases and inspiring millions to take action to defend human rights the world over.

Throughout his life, Peter Benenson put human rights first, whether as a student helping to bring Jewish refugees fleeing Nazi Germany to Britain, or as a co-founder of the law reform and human rights organization, Justice.

By 2005, its 44th year, AI had become the world's largest independent human rights organization, with over 1.8 million members and supporters worldwide. Its founder could not have been more prescient when he said, lighting the first candle for AI in 1961, "We have today lit such a candle as shall never be put out."

First published in 2006 by
Amnesty International USA
5 Penn Plaza
New York, NY 10001
USA

www.amnestyusa.org

© Copyright
Amnesty International Publications 2006
ISBN# 1-887204-45-8
AI Index: POL 10/001/2006
Original language: English

Printed by:
The Alden Press
Osney Mead, Oxford
United Kingdom

Cover design by John Finn

Regional maps by András Bereznay,
www.historyonmaps.com

Inside cover: All photographs appear with full
credits and captions in the report.

For more information on Amnesty International's
work in the United States of America, or for a
complete listing of AI publications with dollar
prices, write to:

Amnesty International USA
National Office
5 Penn Plaza
New York, NY 10001
USA

CONTENTS

CONTENTS

ABBREVIATIONS

The following abbreviations are used in this report:

■ UN Convention against Torture refers to the Convention against Torture and Other Cruel, Inhuman or Degrading Treatment or Punishment.

■ UN Women's Convention refers to the Convention on the Elimination of All Forms of Discrimination against Women.

■ UN Children's Convention refers to the Convention on the Rights of the Child.

■ UN Convention against Racism refers to the International Convention on the Elimination of All Forms of Racial Discrimination.

■ UN Refugee Convention refers to the Convention relating to the Status of Refugees.

■ European Convention on Human Rights refers to the (European) Convention for the Protection of Human Rights and Fundamental Freedoms.

■ European Committee for the Prevention of Torture refers to the European Committee for the Prevention of Torture and Inhuman or Degrading Treatment or Punishment.

AI Report 2006

PART 1

A YEAR IN PERSPECTIVE: A GLASS HALF FULL

BY IRENE KHAN, SECRETARY GENERAL, AMNESTY INTERNATIONAL

Krishna Pahadi, a human rights activist in Nepal, has been detained 28 times by the government. When I met him in a police detention centre in Kathmandu in February 2005, shortly after he had been arrested for the 27th time, his message was surprisingly upbeat. The more the regime locks up peaceful protesters like him, he told me, the more it strengthens the cause of human rights. Widespread political unrest and international condemnation of the Nepalese government's actions support Krishna's views. Deprived of any reading material in prison except religious books, he had finished reading the Bhagavad Gita and was about to begin the Bible, to be followed by the Qur'an. He has no doubt that his struggle and that of others like him will prevail. It is only a matter of time, he said.

Krishna is not daunted. Nor am I, despite the abuse and injustice, violence and violations across the globe documented in the *Amnesty International Report 2006*.

The human rights landscape is littered with broken promises and failures of leadership. Governments profess to champion the cause of human rights but show repressive reflexes when it comes to their own policies and performance. Grave abuses in Afghanistan and Iraq cast a shadow over much of the human rights debate, as torture and terror feed off each other in a vicious cycle. The brutality and intensity of attacks by armed groups in these and other countries grow, taking a heavy toll on human lives.

Nevertheless, a closer look at the events of 2005 gives me reason for hope. There were some clear signs that a turning point may be in sight after five years of backlash against human rights in the name of counter-terrorism. Over the past year, some of the world's most powerful governments have received an uncomfortable wake-up call about the dangers of undervaluing the human rights dimension of their actions at home and abroad. Their doublespeak and deception have been exposed by the media, challenged by activists and rejected by the courts.

I also see other signs for optimism. The overall number of conflicts worldwide continues to fall, thanks to international conflict management, conflict prevention and peace-building initiatives, giving hope to millions of people in countries like Angola, Liberia and Sierra Leone.

Institutional reform was initiated at the United Nations (UN) to strengthen the international human rights machinery, despite the attempt by a number of cynical and "spoiler" governments to block progress.

The call for justice for some of the worst crimes under international law gained greater force across the world, from Latin America to the Balkans. Although corrupt, inefficient and politically biased national judicial systems remain a major barrier to justice, the tide is beginning to turn against impunity in some parts of the world. In 2005 several countries opened investigations or conducted trials of people suspected of war crimes and crimes against humanity. Despite the opposition of the USA, support for the International Criminal Court (ICC) has grown, with Mexico becoming the 100th state party to ratify the Rome Statute of the ICC. The UN Security Council's decision to refer the situation in Darfur to the ICC set an important precedent, demonstrating the link between security and justice.

Ordinary people took to the streets to demand their rights and to seek political change. In Bolivia, the poorest country in South America, massive protests by indigenous communities, peasants and miners led to the resignation of the President and election to power of the country's first ever indigenous Head of State. Even repressive governments found themselves caught out by mass protest, and were forced to make some concessions.

There will be those who will challenge my sense of optimism. But I take strength from these developments and, most importantly, from the extraordinary display of global activism and human solidarity across borders;

Krishna Pahadi (*right*), a founding member of the Human Rights and Peace Society and former Chair of AI Nepal, with Irene Khan in London shortly after his release, 2005.

© AI

from the energy and commitment of Amnesty International (AI) members worldwide; from the huge crowds that turned out to "make poverty history" in the lead-up to the G8 Summit; and from the outpouring of support from ordinary people for the victims of the tsunami in Asia, Hurricane Katrina in the USA and the earthquake in Kashmir.

From peasant farmers protesting against land grabbing in China to women asserting their rights on the 10th anniversary of the UN World Conference on Women, the events of 2005 showed that the human rights *idea* – together with the worldwide movement of people that drives it forward – is more powerful and stronger than ever.

Torture and counter-terrorism

When suicide bombers struck at the heart of London in July 2005, the UK Prime Minister Tony Blair reacted by announcing plans that would drastically restrict human rights and show the world that "the rules of the game are changing". Lord Steyn, a retired Law Lord of the UK judiciary, responded aptly: "The maintenance of the rule of law is not a game. It is about access to justice, fundamental human rights and democratic values".

Fortunately, some of the most outrageous provisions of the legislation proposed by the UK government were thrown out by Parliament. The government was defeated twice on its counter-terrorism legislation in 2005 – the first ever parliamentary defeats for Prime Minister Blair in his nine years of office.

The judiciary also took the UK government to task. The highest court in the land, the House of Lords, rejected the government's contention that it could use information obtained by torture by foreign governments as evidence in UK courts. In another case, the Court of Appeal rejected the government's claim that UK forces in Iraq were not bound by international and domestic human rights law. It also ruled that the system for investigating deaths of Iraqi prisoners at the hands of UK armed forces personnel was seriously deficient.

In the USA there was similar questioning of the Bush Administration's claim that in its fight against terrorism it could exempt itself from the prohibition against torture and ill-treatment. A legislative amendment sought to affirm the ban on torture and cruel, inhuman and degrading treatment of all prisoners by US officials and agents, wherever they might be. Not only did the President threaten to veto the bill, the Vice President sought to exempt the Central Intelligence Agency (CIA) from the law. The CIA itself admitted to using "water-boarding" (simulated drowning) as an interrogation technique, and the Attorney-General claimed that the USA has the power to mistreat detainees abroad, so long as they are not US citizens.

In the end, it was President Bush who blinked first and was forced to withdraw his opposition to the bill. However, the bill had a serious sting in its tail, with an amendment which stripped Guantánamo detainees of the right to file habeas corpus appeals in a federal court and barred them from seeking court review of their treatment or conditions of detention. Nevertheless, the President's public climb-down was indicative of the pressure being put on the Administration by powerful divisions within the USA and increasing concern among its allies abroad.

European governments squirmed as one story after another revealed their role as junior partners of the USA in its "war on terror". There was public outcry following media reports of possible collusion between the US Administration and some European governments on "CIA black sites" – alleged secret detention centres on European territory. Increasing evidence that prisoners were being illegally transferred through European airports to countries where there was a risk they would be tortured ("extraordinary renditions") also provoked widespread public condemnation.

© EMPICS/AP

Roma in Bulgaria at an anti-discrimination rally in central Sofia, February 2005. The rally coincided with the start of the international initiative "2005-2015 Decade of Roma Inclusion" which was launched in eight south-eastern European states.

Women protest against gender discrimination in the Iranian capital, Tehran, June 2005.

© Reuters/Raheb Homavandi

The demand for the closure of the detention centre in Guantánamo Bay gained greater momentum with the UN, various European institutions, and political and opinion leaders, including prominent US figures, adding their voices to the growing pressure. What was once AI's lone voice in the wilderness has now become a crescendo of condemnation against the most blatant symbol of US abuse of power. That strengthens our own resolve to continue to campaign until the US Administration closes the Guantánamo camp, discloses the truth about secret detention centres under its control, and acknowledges the right of detainees to be tried in accordance with international law standards or be released.

The shifts I have identified do not mean that support for restrictive measures has disappeared or that attacks on human rights in the name of counter-terrorism have

diminished. The USA has not categorically rejected the use of certain forms of torture or ill-treatment. It has failed to institute an independent investigation into the role of senior US officials in the abuses committed in Iraq's Abu Ghraib prison and elsewhere, despite growing evidence of high-level involvement.

When the British courts declared the detention of foreigners without charge or trial to be unlawful, the UK government immediately introduced new legislation to hold people under virtual house arrest. It continues to seek "diplomatic assurances" to enable it to return people to countries where they could face torture.

The "export value" of the "war on terror" has not decreased either. With the tacit or explicit approval of the USA, countries like Egypt, Jordan and Yemen continue to detain, without charge or fair trial, people suspected of involvement in terrorism.

What is different about 2005 compared to past years is that the public mood is changing, thanks to the work of human rights advocates and others, which is putting the US and European governments on the defensive. People are no longer willing to buy the fallacious argument that reducing our liberty will increase our security. More and more governments are being called to account – before legislatures, in courts and other public forums. More and more there is a realization that flouting human rights and the rule of law, far from winning the "war on terror", only creates resentment and isolates those communities targeted by these measures, plays into the hands of extremists, and undermines our collective security.

Lines, however fragile, are being drawn. Voices are being raised. This offers hope for a turning point in the debate and a more principled approach to human rights and security in the future.

Contrary to the statement of the UK Prime Minister, the rules of the game have not changed. Neither security nor human rights are well served by governments who play games with these fundamental rules.

International Women's Day, Beni, North Kivu Province, Democratic Republic of the Congo, March 2005. The women are marching barefoot with their shoes on their heads in protest at widespread rape in the region.

© AI

We must continue to condemn in the strongest possible terms the cowardly and heinous attacks on civilians by armed groups. Equally strongly, we must also resist the foolish and dangerous strategies of governments who seek to fight terror with torture.

Reform initiatives

Growing disillusionment and damning criticism of the UN human rights machinery finally led governments to initiate some important reforms as part of a rethink of the UN's role in international governance.

UN member states agreed to double the budget of the Office of the UN High Commissioner for Human Rights, and to focus its work to a much greater extent on protecting human rights through presence in the field.

The member states decided to jettison the discredited UN Commission on Human Rights, and proposed to replace it with a Human Rights Council, elected by and accountable to the UN General Assembly, and able to scrutinize all states, including, first and foremost, its own members. Although a product of compromise, the proposal represents a significant opportunity to improve the UN human rights machinery. Regrettably, the future of the Council hangs in the balance as we go to press because of the refusal of the USA to support it, ostensibly on the basis that it has too many "deficiencies". One state, no matter how powerful, should not be allowed to undermine a broad, international consensus. I hope that other governments will resist US pressure, rally behind the resolution and get the Council up and running.

I am encouraged by the support that governments have shown for changes to the UN human rights machinery. This is all the more remarkable, given the way in which much of the UN Secretary-General's ambitious and forward-looking package on UN reform – including proposals to expand Security Council membership, strengthen weapons non-proliferation and better equip the UN to act effectively to halt genocide – was rejected or wrecked.

I am also heartened by some less publicized gains in the past year. The UN completed drafting an International Convention for the Protection of All

Members of the Torture Abolition and Survivors Support Coalition International demonstrate outside the White House, Washington D.C., USA, June 2005.

© Reuters/Chris Kleponis

Persons from Enforced Disappearance, to address the unacknowledged arrest, detention, torture and often death of prisoners at the hands of agents of the state. AI, which first began campaigning on behalf of the "disappeared" some 35 years ago, welcomes this important contribution to human rights protection.

The UN appointed a Special Representative on the issue of human rights and transnational corporations and other business enterprises. Although companies can be a force for positive social and economic development, the impact of some business operations on human rights are deeply damaging, as shown by the violence generated by oil and mineral interests in places like the Niger delta in Nigeria, the Democratic Republic of the Congo and Sudan, or the readiness of the information and technology industry to fall in line with China's restrictive policies on freedom of expression. Yet a powerful combination of political and business interests has managed to resist international efforts to advance the legal accountability of business

© CNDDHH

Human rights defenders outside the building where former Peruvian President Alberto Fujimori was detained in Santiago, Chile, December 2005. Alberto Fujimori has been charged in Peru with human rights violations including ordering killings and torture.

Former Iraqi President Saddam Hussein stands trial, Baghdad, October 2005.

© EMPICS/AP

for human rights. Despite considerable controversy surrounding the UN Norms on business and human rights, the issue of corporate accountability remained firmly on the international agenda. Building on the experience of the Norms, the task now will be to develop a clear set of international human rights standards and principles for corporate actors.

Rhetoric and reality

Institutions are only as strong as the political will of those who govern them. Far too often, powerful governments manipulate the UN and regional institutions to further their narrow national interests. The USA is a prime example, but unfortunately it is not alone, as is evidenced by Russia's record in the Caucasus and Central Asia, and China's expanding economic co-operation with some of the most repressive governments in Africa.

Those who bear the greatest responsibility for safeguarding global security in the UN Security Council proved in 2005 to be among the most willing to paralyze the Council and prevent it from taking effective action on human rights. This was clearly

demonstrated by the USA and the UK in relation to Iraq, and by Russia and China in the case of Sudan. They appear oblivious to the lessons of history that the road to strengthening global security lies through respect for human rights.

The hypocrisy of the G8 was particularly marked in 2005. The G8 governments claimed to put eradication of poverty in Africa high on their agenda, while continuing to be major suppliers of arms to African governments. Six of the eight G8 countries are among the top 10 largest global arms exporters, and all eight export large amounts of conventional weapons or small arms to developing countries. This should place a particular responsibility on the G8 to help create an effective system of global control on arms transfers. But, despite pressure from the UK government, the leaders of the G8 failed to agree on the need for an Arms Trade Treaty at the Gleneagles Summit in July 2005.

However, the call for a global treaty to control small arms gained support from at least 50 countries around the world. The message of the campaign, jointly led by AI, Oxfam and the International Action Network for Small Arms (IANSA), is clear: the arms trade is out of control, and must be restrained urgently.

Turning to regional institutions, I am disappointed that the European Union (EU) remains a largely muted voice on human rights. It cannot expect to maintain its credibility on human rights and occupy the moral high ground if it buries its collective head in the sand when confronted with abuses committed by its major political and trading partners, or closes its eyes to the policies and practices of its own member states towards refugees and asylum-seekers and on counter-terrorism. It must be more willing to confront Russia's appalling human rights failures in Chechnya. It must also resist pressures from business to lift its arms embargo against China. This embargo was originally

AI members from around the world take part in the march which launched the World Social Forum, Porto Alegre, Brazil, January 2005.

© AI

imposed after the brutal 1989 crackdown in Tiananmen Square in order to show the commitment of the EU to promoting human rights in China. It should not be removed until the Chinese government has made significant human rights concessions.

The African Union (AU) has developed a progressive framework on human rights, and played an important role in resolving the crisis in Togo, but it is sadly lacking the capacity and political will to deliver on its promises consistently. Hampered by logistical constraints and the refusal of the Sudanese government and armed militias to abide by international law, AU human rights monitors could not make a real difference on the ground in Darfur. It showed no stomach to tackle the appalling human rights situation in Zimbabwe. It failed to convince Nigeria or Senegal to co-operate with the efforts to bring to justice the former Liberian and Chadian presidents Charles Taylor and Hissène Habré. African leaders do a disservice to themselves and the African people when they use African solidarity to shield each other from justice and accountability.

In the face of institutional lethargy and governments' failures, public opinion, whether in Africa, Europe or elsewhere, is demanding a stronger commitment by governments to human rights at home and abroad. Thanks to human rights advocates and others, and the growing pressure of public opinion, the international community is being forced to acknowledge human rights as the framework within which security and development should be imagined and implemented. Without respect for human rights, neither security nor development can be sustained.

In both international and regional contexts, human rights are increasingly being acknowledged as a benchmark for the credibility and authority of institutions and individual states. That is one of the reasons why governments contested Myanmar becoming the chair of the Association of Southeast Asian Nations (ASEAN). That is why the EU decided in the end not to reverse the ban on arms sales to China. That is why India has put human rights considerations as a key element in its approach to Nepal.

Both on principled as well as pragmatic grounds, human rights should be seen as a critical element of sustainable global and regional security strategies, not as an optional extra for good times. There is no doubt in my mind that the events of 2005 show that the political and moral authority of governments will be judged more and more by their stand on human rights at home and abroad. Therein lies one of the most important achievements of the human rights movement in recent times.

There are clear challenges ahead. Vicious attacks by armed groups, the increased instability in the Middle East, the mounting anger and isolation of Muslim communities around the world, the forgotten conflicts in Africa and elsewhere, growing inequalities and glaring poverty — all are evidence of a dangerous and divided world in which human rights are being daily threatened. But far from being discouraged, I believe these challenges make the impetus for action even greater.

As we set our agenda for 2006, AI and its millions of members and supporters take encouragement from the remarkable achievements of the human rights movement and the faith of ordinary people in the power of human rights. We in AI do not underestimate that power. We will use it to fight those who peddle fear and hate, to challenge the myopic vision of the world's most powerful leaders, and to hold governments to account.

AMNESTY INTERNATIONAL'S COMMITMENTS

In 2006, Amnesty International is committed to:

- Resist attacks on human rights standards, in particular the absolute prohibition on torture and ill-treatment.
- Demand the closure of the Guantánamo Bay detention camp and secret detention centres, and the disclosure of "extraordinary renditions" and "ghost detainees".
- Condemn strongly deliberate attacks on civilians by armed groups.
- Fight to end impunity and to strengthen national and international justice systems.
- Expose human rights abuses committed during armed conflicts, and campaign for an international arms trade treaty to control the sale of small arms.
- Seek a universal moratorium on the death penalty as a step towards its abolition.
- Champion the right of women and girls to be free from violence and discrimination.
- Promote the protection of refugees, displaced people and migrants.
- Expose the link between poverty and human rights abuses and hold governments accountable for poverty eradication through respect for all human rights.
- Campaign to hold corporate and economic actors accountable for human rights abuses.
- Strive for universal ratification of the seven core human rights treaties fundamental for human security and dignity.
- Support human rights defenders and activists in their fight for equality and justice.

THE SEARCH FOR HUMAN SECURITY

The year 2005 posed some major challenges for governments: intractable conflicts, terrorist attacks, the relentless spread of the HIV/AIDS pandemic, the persistence of widespread extreme poverty and natural disasters.

These challenges should have been met with responses based on human rights principles. All too often they were not. Individually and collectively, governments continued to pursue policies that often sacrificed human rights for political or economic expediency.

At the same time, around the world, millions of people lent their weight to calls for greater accountability, more transparency and greater recognition of our shared responsibility to tackle these global threats collectively. From the mass mobilization around the slogan "make poverty history" to the lawyers and activists who took on powerful states in groundbreaking court cases, civil society pressed governments to deliver on their responsibilities.

The year saw a growing understanding that respect for the rule of law is essential for human security, and that undermining human rights principles in the "war on terror" is not a route to security. Similarly, the failure to respect, protect and fulfil economic, social and cultural rights was more and more widely seen as a grave injustice and a denial of human development. Whether in response to the urgent needs of people caught up in natural disasters or the plight of individual victims of government repression, the activities of ordinary people often shamed governments into action.

Human security requires that individuals and communities are safe not only from war, genocide and terrorist attack, but also from hunger, disease and natural disaster. Throughout 2005 activists campaigned for notorious human rights violators and powerful multinationals to be held more accountable, and for an end to racism, discrimination and social exclusion.

Many of the human rights abuses seen in 2005 crossed national boundaries – from torture and "renditions" to the negative impact of trade and aid policies. While borders were being dismantled in some aspects of international relations – particularly in the sphere of economic transactions – they continued to be erected in others, notably migration.

Recognition of the need for global solutions to address global threats, from terrorism to bird flu, undoubtedly grew. There were also many reminders of the necessity for UN reform. These included the continued failure of the UN Security Council to hold rogue states accountable, the exposure of high level corruption at the UN in the Oil for Food scandal, the silence which greeted the failure to meet the first of the UN Millennium Development Goals and the failure of international financial institutions to grapple with the

Kashmiri girls in a tent camp in Muzaffarabad, Pakistan. Aid was slow in reaching millions of people rendered homeless by an earthquake in October 2005.

© REUTERS/Kimimasa Mayama

Afghans in the Panjshir valley, north of Kabul, January 2005, move tanks as part of a disarmament programme. This flawed programme was followed by another to remove arms from illegal armed groups. Much of Afghanistan remained under the control of factional commanders, many accused of gross human rights abuses. Lawlessness and insecurity were widespread.

© REUTERS/Ahmad Masood

inequities of trade, aid and debt. The UN's own leadership proposed a number of far-reaching initiatives, but the limited outcomes of the UN World Summit in September revealed how the politics of narrow national self-interest continued to trump multilateralist aspirations.

Yet there was progress, notably in the area of consolidating an emerging international justice system in the form of the International Criminal Court, the ad hoc international tribunals and increased use of extraterritorial jurisdiction. After years of calls for additional resources for the Office of the UN High Commissioner for Human Rights, its budget was significantly increased. Proposals to replace the much discredited UN Commission on Human Rights with a UN Human Rights Council were under discussion. Encouraged by these moves, and above all by the growing strength and diversity of the world's human rights community, AI renewed its commitment to globalizing justice as a means of realizing rights for all in the search for human security.

TORTURE AND TERROR
The challenges that the human rights movement faced in the wake of the attacks in the USA on 11 September 2001 continued. Governments continued to promote the rhetoric that human rights are an obstacle to, rather than an essential precondition for, human security. However, thanks to the efforts of human rights activists and others, there was growing criticism of and resistance to government efforts to subordinate human rights to security concerns.

Despite the governmental resources and efforts committed to combating terrorism, the year saw a rising number of attacks by individuals and armed groups espousing a wide range of causes in many countries.

Deliberate attacks on civilians, breaching the most basic human rights principles, were seen around the world. For example, in India in October, during the run-up to the annual festival season, a series of bomb blasts in Delhi left 66 people dead and more than 220 injured. In Iraq, hundreds of civilians were killed or injured in attacks by armed groups throughout the year. In Jordan, three bombs in hotels in Amman killed 60 people in November. In the UK, bomb attacks on the public transport system in London in July killed 52 people and injured hundreds.

Some of the counter-terrorism tactics adopted by governments flouted human rights. Some governments even tried to legalize or justify abusive methods that have long been deemed illegal by the international community and can never be justified.

Thousands of men suspected of terrorism remained in US-run detention centres around the world without any prospect of being charged or facing a fair trial. At the end of 2005, some 14,000 people detained by the USA and its allies during military and security operations in Iraq and Afghanistan were still held in US military detention centres in Afghanistan, Guantánamo Bay in Cuba and Iraq. In Guantánamo, dozens of detainees staged hunger strikes to protest against the conditions of their detention and were force fed.

Terrorism suspects were held by other countries too, some of them detained for long periods without charge or trial, including in Egypt, Jordan, the UK and Yemen. Others languished in prison facing the threat of deportation to countries where torture was routine. Many detainees were subjected to torture and other ill-treatment.

During 2005, it became increasingly clear how far many countries had colluded or participated in supporting abusive US policies and practices in the "war on terror", including torture, ill-treatment, secret and unlimited detentions and unlawful cross-border transfers. Many governments faced demands for greater accountability and there were key judicial decisions in defence of basic human rights principles. Even within the US government itself, tensions emerged over the curtailment of fundamental liberties.

Information continued to emerge in 2005 that helped to expose some of the secret and abusive practices developed by states in the name of fighting terrorism. For example, further information came to light about the illegal transfer of terrorism suspects from one country to another without any judicial process — a practice known in the USA as "extraordinary renditions". It was revealed that the USA had, through this practice, transferred many detainees to countries known to use torture and other ill-treatment in interrogations, including Egypt, Jordan, Morocco, Saudi Arabia and Syria. Such transfers effectively outsourced torture.

What renditions mean in reality was highlighted in 2005 by the case of Muhammad al-Assad, a Yemeni living in Tanzania, who was arrested at his home in Dar-es-Salaam on 26 December 2003. He was hooded, handcuffed and flown to an unknown destination. It was the beginning of a 16-month ordeal of unacknowledged detention and interrogation, in which he had no contact with the outside world and no idea where he was.

He was held for a year in a secret facility where he was subjected to extreme sensory deprivation. His masked guards never spoke a word to him, but communicated their instructions in sign language. There was a constant low-level hum of white noise. Artificial light was kept on 24 hours a day. Muhammad al-Assad's father was told by Tanzanian officials that his son had been turned over to US custody, and that no one knew where he was. His family heard nothing of him until he was flown to Yemen in May 2005, where he was imprisoned, apparently at the request of the US authorities. Muhammad al-Assad was still in custody in Yemen without charge or trial at the end of 2005.

Other testimonies from former detainees collected during 2005 by AI were shockingly similar to the experience described by Muhammad al-Assad. Two other Yemeni men were transferred to Yemen by the USA in May 2005, where they remained in custody without charge or trial at the end of the year. In separate interviews with AI in June, September and October 2005, all three described being held in isolation for 16 to 18 months in secret detention centres run by US officials. The interviews conducted by AI provided strong new evidence of the US network of secret detention centres around the world.

In December 2005, after the UK Foreign Secretary said that he was not aware of any renditions flights refuelling or using other facilities in the UK since early 2001, AI published details of three flights that refuelled in the UK, hours after transferring detainees to countries where they risked "disappearance", torture or other ill-treatment. Information increasingly came to light in 2005, partly because evidence was uncovered by victims themselves and partly due to governmental inquiries, that other European countries may have been similarly involved in secret transfers. Inquiries were conducted in

Germany, Italy and Sweden into the role of government officials in specific rendition cases; in Spain, an investigation was opened by the Spanish authorities into the use of Spanish airports and airspace by aircraft operated by the US Central Intelligence Agency (CIA). In Iceland, Ireland and the Netherlands, government officials or activists called for official inquiries.

Investigations by journalists, AI and others in 2005 left little doubt that the US government was running a system of covert prisons, known as "black sites". There were persistent reports that the CIA had operated such secret detention centres in Afghanistan, Iraq, Jordan, Pakistan, Thailand, Uzbekistan and other unknown locations in Europe and elsewhere, including on the British Indian Ocean territory of Diego Garcia. About three dozen detainees deemed to have high intelligence value had "disappeared" in US custody, and were allegedly being held in black sites, completely outside the protection of the law.

In November the Council of Europe launched an investigation into reports that the network of US secret prisons and involvement in renditions included sites in Europe. AI strongly endorsed calls to European governments to investigate such allegations by officials of the Council of Europe, one of whom declared: "not knowing is not good enough regardless of whether ignorance is intentional or accidental".

At a conference jointly organized by AI and the UK-based NGO Reprieve in London in November, former detainees and families of detainees held in Guantánamo or in UK facilities testified to the human cost of indefinite detention without charge or trial. Speaking of the trauma of the families of those detained, Nadja Dizdarevic, the wife of Boudelaa Hadz of Bosnia and Herzegovina who has been held at Guantánamo for four years, said:

"It is difficult to be a mother to my children because I have not enough time for them and I am everything that they have... At night after I put my children to sleep I start my work and while the whole world sleeps in peace I tirelessly write complaints, requests, letters, learn the laws and human rights conventions so that I could continue my struggle for the life and release of my husband and the others."

Governments have over the years requested "diplomatic assurances" from countries known to use torture in order to allow them to deport people there. In 2005 the UK government sought to rely on diplomatic assurances and concluded Memorandums of Understanding with Jordan, Lebanon and Libya, and was seeking similar agreements with Algeria, Egypt and other states in the region. AI opposed the use of such "diplomatic assurances" as they erode the absolute prohibition of torture, and are inherently unreliable and unenforceable.

Evidence that many governments had been engaging in, conniving in or acquiescing to the outsourcing of torture underlined the need for greater transnational accountability in a world where human rights responsibilities do not stop at the borders of a state.

The outsourcing of torture meant that the USA and some of its European allies, which had for decades unreservedly condemned torture at all times and in all circumstances, openly defied the absolute ban against torture. The implication was that they believed that some torture and ill-treatment was justifiable in the "war on terror".

The US administration continued its attempts to redefine and justify certain forms of torture or other ill-treatment in the name of "national security" and public order. When questioned about the US position on the treatment of prisoners, the US Attorney General, Alberto Gonzales, made it clear that his government would define torture in its own way. Although the US leadership denied that the government condoned torture, evidence emerged that the CIA used "water boarding" (simulated drowning), prolonged shackling or induced hypothermia on prisoners held in secret prisons. Some people within the US administration apparently continued to believe that certain forms of torture and ill-treatment practices were acceptable if used to gather intelligence to counter terrorism. However, growing challenges to these policies both within the USA – where at the end of the year the US Senate passed legislation affirming the ban on torture and other cruel, inhuman and degrading treatment – and among the USA's allies in the "war on terror" offered hope of a more principled approach to human rights and security in the future.

Human rights abuses in the context of counter-terrorism policies were not confined to the USA and its European allies. In Uzbekistan, the authorities claimed that people taking part in a demonstration in Andizhan at which peaceful demonstrators were killed had been coerced to do so by "terrorists". Subsequently, more than 70 people were convicted of "terrorist" offences after unfair trials and sentenced to long prison terms for allegedly participating in the protest.

In China, the authorities continued to use the global "war on terror" to justify harsh repression in the Xinjiang Uighur Autonomous Region (XUAR), resulting in serious human rights violations against the ethnic Uighur community. While China's latest "strike-hard" campaign against crime had subsided in most parts of the country, it was officially renewed in the XUAR in May 2005 to eradicate "terrorism, separatism and religious extremism". It resulted in the closure of unofficial mosques and arrests of imams. Uighur nationalists, including peaceful activists, continued to be detained or imprisoned. Those charged with serious "separatist" or "terrorist" offences were at risk of lengthy imprisonment or execution. Those attempting to pass information abroad about the extent of the crackdown faced arbitrary detention and imprisonment. The authorities continued to accuse Uighur activists of terrorism without providing credible evidence for such charges.

In both Malaysia and Singapore, where national security legislation allows prolonged detention without charge of terrorism suspects, dozens of individuals remained in detention under Internal Security Acts without charge or trial.

In Kenya and certain other African countries, the rhetoric of counter-terrorism was employed to justify repressive legislation which was used to silence human rights defenders and obstruct their work.

The exposure during 2005 of the unlawful practices of governments in the name of countering terrorism mobilized and affirmed the growing demands for accountability. The determined work of human rights activists, lawyers, journalists and many others helped to lift the blanket of secrecy to expose states that

AI INTERVENES IN COURT CASES

AI continued to seek the legal implementation of international human rights standards by intervening in cases before national and international courts.

Preventing the erosion of the absolute prohibition against torture in the context of the "war on terror" was the objective of two interventions in 2005.

In a case before the UK's highest court, the Appellate Committee of the House of Lords, AI coordinated a coalition of 14 organizations in a joint intervention to challenge the admissibility as evidence in judicial proceedings of information extracted as a result of torture. The government had contended that it should be allowed to introduce into judicial proceedings information obtained from abroad allegedly as a result of torture, on the ground that no torture had been committed or supported by UK agents. The Law Lords ruled that such information was inadmissible in UK courts.

In a case before the European Court of Human Rights, AI intervened with six other NGOs to argue that the prohibition on the transfer (*refoulement*) of a person from a state party to the European Convention on Human Rights to another state where he or she would be at risk of torture or ill-treatment is and should remain absolute. Four states intervened to argue that this prohibition is not absolute, but may be subject to a "balancing" test against such interests as countering terrorism. At the end of 2005, the decision of the Court was still pending.

As part of its work against the death penalty, AI intervened in a case concerning Guatemala before the Inter-American Court of Human Rights.

Guatemala, which ratified the American Convention on Human Rights in 1978, sought to extend the use of the death penalty in 1996 to make it mandatory for kidnapping. AI argued that the death penalty could not be extended beyond the legislation applicable when Guatemala ratified the Convention and that as a result of a law passed in 2000, Guatemala had failed to guarantee the right of a convicted person to seek pardon, amnesty or commutation of sentence. In September the Inter-American Court of Human Rights ordered Guatemala to suspend the death sentence in this case, and not to execute anyone condemned to death for the crime of kidnapping under the current legislation.

Ninety people were killed and at least 100 were injured when car bombs exploded in the tourist resort of Sharm el-Sheikh, Egypt, on 23 July 2005.

transferred, detained and tortured those they suspected of terrorism.

The year 2005 also witnessed some successes in the struggle by civil society to stop the trend towards states justifying, on security grounds, the use of information extracted through torture. The year ended with a major judicial victory when the UK government lost its legal battle in the domestic courts to reverse the centuries-old ban against the admissibility of information obtained as a result of torture in judicial proceedings. AI had intervened in the case, arguing that the absolute prohibition of torture and ill-treatment under international law prevented such use.

The attempts by governments to weaken the ban on torture and other ill-treatment compromised both the moral integrity and practical effectiveness of efforts to combat terrorism. 2005 showed the absolute necessity of holding governments accountable to the rule of law, and reconfirmed that an independent and impartial judiciary plays a vital role in preventing the erosion of fundamental safeguards and securing respect for human rights.

CONFLICT AND ITS AFTERMATH

The number of armed conflicts around the world continued to fall, but the toll of human suffering did not. Continuing violence fed on a steady diet of unresolved grievances arising from years of destructive conflict and the failure to hold perpetrators of abuse to account. It was sustained by the easy availability of weaponry; the marginalization and impoverishment of entire populations; systemic and widespread corruption; and the failure to address impunity for gross violations of human rights and humanitarian law.

Millions of people faced violence and hardship in conflicts caused or prolonged by the collective failures of political leaders, armed groups and to some extent the international community. Millions more endured insecurity, hunger and homelessness in the aftermath of conflicts, without the necessary levels of support from the international community to rebuild their lives.

The failure of governments and armed groups alike to seek the political solutions needed to end conflict and to abide by negotiated settlements took a heavy toll on the human rights of ordinary people. Some governments sought advantage from conflicts in other countries, often arming one side or the other, while disclaiming responsibility. When the international community mustered enough support to put pressure on warring factions through the UN Security Council or regional bodies, the parties often failed to deliver on their commitments, as seen in Sudan and Côte d'Ivoire.

In their quest for political or economic gain, government forces and armed groups often showed total disregard for the civilian population caught in their path and even specifically targeted civilians as part of their military strategy. The large majority of casualties in armed conflicts in 2005 were civilians. Women and girls were exposed to the violence that accompanies any war and were also subject to particular, often sexual, abuse. In Papua New Guinea girls were reportedly exchanged for guns by their male relatives. In the Democratic Republic of the Congo large numbers of women and girls were abducted and raped by armed combatants. In nearly three quarters of the conflicts around the world, children were recruited as soldiers.

The world's attention focused largely on Iraq, Sudan, and Israel/Occupied Territories while prolonged conflicts in Afghanistan, Chechnya/Russian Federation, Nepal, northern Uganda and other corners of the world were largely ignored or forgotten.

In Iraq, US-led multinational forces, armed groups and the transitional government all failed to respect the rights of civilians. Armed groups deliberately attacked civilians causing great loss of life. They targeted humanitarian organizations and tortured and killed hostages. The killing of two defence lawyers involved in Saddam Hussain's trial highlighted the chronic insecurity in the country. This insecurity drastically curtailed the ability of many Iraqi women and girls to go about their daily lives in safety, and a number of Iraqi and non-Iraqi women politicians,

ARMS CONTROL

Tackling the proliferation and misuse of weapons remained a key element of AI's efforts to combat human rights violations, whether committed in the course of conflict, crime or security operations.

The Control Arms Campaign – launched in October 2003 by AI, Oxfam International and the International Action Network on Small Arms (IANSA) – achieved some notable successes in 2005.

By the end of the year, about 50 governments had declared their support for an enforceable international Arms Trade Treaty – a key demand of the Control Arms Campaign. An arms control treaty based on international human rights and humanitarian law would save lives, prevent suffering and protect livelihoods. Costa Rica, Finland, Kenya, Norway and the UK, among others, promised to back the treaty. In October, the European Union (EU) Council of Foreign Ministers called for global support for such a treaty. There was considerable backing from governments for the UK position that separate UN negotiations on a treaty that would cover all conventional arms should begin in late 2006.

At the UN, governments agreed on a global standard for marking and tracing small arms in October 2005. This went some way towards fulfilling the proposal put forward by the Control Arms Campaign for a global system to track small arms and to hold arms traders accountable. However, not only did the agreement exclude ammunition, but it was not legally binding.

© Jo Wright

A young man displays his weapons outside a *favela* (shanty town) in Rio de Janeiro, Brazil. The level of armed violence at the hands of drug gangs, police or vigilante "death squads" was extremely high, especially in the *favelas*. Although the government took steps to curb the proliferation of small arms, a referendum in October 2005 over a ban on gun sales was defeated. The result was widely attributed to popular anxiety about insecurity and lack of faith in the police's ability to provide protection.

The global arms trade remained largely unaccountable and most transfers were shrouded in secrecy. Accurate and up-to-date statistics were therefore difficult to obtain. However, the information available suggested some striking trends. Most of the world's military equipment and services were traded by a relatively small number of countries. According to an authoritative report by the US Congress, 35 countries exported some 90 per cent of the world's arms in terms of value. By 2005, more than 68 per cent of arms exports were going to countries in the global South.

Six of the eight G8 countries are among the top 10 largest global arms exporters, and all eight export large amounts of major conventional weapons or small arms to developing countries. A series of loopholes and weaknesses in arms export controls, common across most G8 countries, meant that the G8's commitments to poverty reduction, stability and human rights were undermined. Arms exports from G8 countries reached some of the world's poorest and most conflict-ridden countries. Such countries included Colombia, the Democratic Republic of the Congo (DRC), the Philippines and Sudan.

In 2005 large quantities of weapons and ammunition from the Balkans and Eastern Europe continued to flow into Africa's conflict-ridden Great Lakes region. Shipments to the DRC continued, despite a peace process initiated in 2002 and a UN arms embargo.

Weapons and ammunition supplied to the governments of the DRC, Rwanda and Uganda were subsequently distributed to armed groups and militia in the eastern DRC involved in war crimes and crimes against humanity. In addition to committing other crimes, these armed groups systematically and brutally raped and sexually abused tens of thousands of women. Arms dealers, brokers and transporters from many countries including Albania, Bosnia and Herzegovina, Croatia, the Czech Republic, Israel, Russia, Serbia, South Africa, the UK and the USA were involved in these arms transfers, highlighting once again the key importance of regulating the operations of arms brokers and dealers. By the end of 2005 only about 30 states had laws regulating such brokers.

Hundreds of thousands of people were killed using small arms in 2005. In Haiti, for example, small arms were used by armed groups and former soldiers to kidnap, sexually abuse and kill Haitians with impunity. Without disarmament and effective justice for the victims, Haiti risked sinking further into crisis.

Women paid a high price for the unregulated trade in small arms, both in their homes and in their communities. The presence of a gun in the household has been shown to vastly increase the risk that violence in the home will have fatal consequences. In 2005, the Control Arms Campaign called on governments to address inadequate firearms regulations, poor law enforcement and widespread discrimination which put women at heightened risk of violence.

Internally displaced Sudanese children from Mahli village in southern Darfur region collect rainwater to be used for drinking and cooking. In April 2005 they were living in an improvised camp without the most basic facilities.

© REUTERS/Moses Muiruri

activists and journalists were abducted or murdered. During 2005 evidence mounted that the US-led multinational forces and foreign private security guards committed grave human rights violations, including killing unarmed civilians and torturing prisoners. The failure to mount effective investigations into these abuses and to hold those responsible to account undermined claims by the occupying forces and the transitional authorities that they were restoring the rule of law in the country.

The removal of some 8,000 Israeli settlers from the Gaza Strip under the so-called disengagement plan diverted attention from Israel's continuing expansion of Israeli settlements and its construction of a 600km fence/wall in the occupied West Bank, where some 450,000 Israeli settlers lived in violation of international law. The presence of Israeli settlements throughout the West Bank was the main reason for the stringent restrictions (military checkpoints and blockades) imposed by the Israeli army on the movement of some 2 million Palestinians between towns and villages within the occupied West Bank. These restrictions on freedom of movement paralysed the Palestinian economy and curtailed Palestinians' access to their land, their places of work, and to education and health facilities. The resulting increased poverty, unemployment, frustration and lack of prospects for a predominantly young population contributed to the spiral of violence, both against Israelis and within Palestinian society, including growing lawlessness in the street and violence in the home. However, the year saw a significant reduction in the number of killings by both sides: some 190 Palestinians, including around 50 children, were killed by Israeli forces, and 50 Israelis, including six children, were killed

by Palestinian armed groups, as compared to more than 700 Palestinians and 109 Israelis killed in 2004.

Atrocities continued in Darfur, Sudan, despite considerable efforts throughout 2005 by the international community to reach a political solution to end the violence. The Sudanese government and its allied militias (Janjawid) killed and injured civilians in bombing raids and attacks on villages, raped women and girls, and forced villagers from their lands. Abuses by the opposition armed groups escalated as their command structures broke down under increased factionalism and in-fighting between rival leaders. The violations in Darfur were described by the UN Secretary-General and UN agencies as staggering in scale and harrowing in nature with widespread and systematic human rights abuses, violations of humanitarian law, forced displacement of millions of people and looming hunger. In early 2005 the UN negotiated a peace agreement, raising hopes of a "peace dividend". The African Union deployed forces, but their mandate to protect civilians was limited and they were further hampered by the relatively small number of troops deployed and the lack of logistical support. The peace did not hold. A UN Commission of Inquiry found that the government and the Janjawid militia were responsible for crimes under international law and the case of Darfur was referred by the Security Council to the International Criminal Court. Although the International Criminal Court began investigations, by the end of 2005, it had not been granted access to Sudan.

Similar patterns were seen in many other conflicts that received less international attention during 2005: targeting of civilians, sexual abuse particularly of women and girls, the use of child soldiers, and a pattern of impunity. These conflicts were fought in

INTERNATIONAL JUSTICE

2005 saw some significant developments towards bringing to justice those responsible for crimes under international law, including genocide, crimes against humanity, war crimes, torture, extrajudicial executions and enforced disappearances. However, there was also continuing widespread impunity in national courts in the states where crimes were committed, as well as only limited use of universal jurisdiction by courts in other states.

In October, the International Criminal Court (ICC) announced its first ever arrest warrants for five leaders of the Lord's Resistance Army for crimes against humanity and war crimes committed in northern Uganda. AI called on the ICC and the Ugandan government to ensure that tens of thousands of other crimes committed during the conflict were investigated and prosecuted, including crimes by government forces. AI urged the Ugandan government to repeal an amnesty law which prevents Ugandan courts from addressing these crimes.

The ICC continued to investigate crimes committed in the Democratic Republic of the Congo, but did not issue any arrest warrants during 2005. It also undertook preliminary analyses of eight other situations. However, the President and Prosecutor of the ICC suggested that resource constraints would limit its ability to undertake any new investigations until the current ones were completed.

While the UN Security Council's referral to the ICC of crimes committed in Darfur, Sudan, was a positive step in addressing impunity, it was disappointing that the Security Council, as part of a compromise to ensure US support, included in its resolution a provision to exempt nationals of states not party to the Rome Statute of the ICC (other than Sudan) from the jurisdiction of the Court. In AI's view, this provision creates double standards of justice and violates the UN Charter and other international law.

The struggle against impunity was reinforced by the work of other international and internationalized courts, notwithstanding some constraints and setbacks. The Special Court for Sierra Leone advanced in three trials involving nine suspects charged with war crimes and crimes against humanity. However, the Sierra Leone government took no steps to end an amnesty, part of the 1999 Lomé peace accord, which prevents prosecution of all others in Sierra Leone responsible for crimes under international law. Ignoring calls from the international community, Nigeria continued, with the apparent support of the African Union, to refuse to surrender former Liberian president Charles Taylor to the Special Court for Sierra Leone, where he has been charged with crimes against humanity and war crimes against the population of Sierra Leone.

Some progress was made in establishing special courts – Extraordinary Chambers – for Cambodia. These were expected to try no more than half a dozen people for crimes committed while the Khmer Rouge were in power, while tens of thousands of others continued to benefit from a national amnesty. AI was concerned about the composition of the courts and whether the Cambodian judges would have the necessary training and experience, given the serious weaknesses in the Cambodian judicial system.

National courts in a number of countries also contributed to the effort to end impunity by investigating and prosecuting crimes committed in other countries using universal jurisdiction legislation. People were convicted of crimes under international law in Belgium, France, the Netherlands, Spain and the UK. Canada opened its first case under its universal jurisdiction legislation of 2000, charging Désiré Munyaneza with genocide, crimes against humanity and war crimes committed in 1994 in Rwanda.

In September, Belgium issued a request for Senegal to extradite the former president of Chad, Hissène Habré, to face prosecution for the murder of at least 40,000 people, systematic torture, arbitrary arrests and other crimes, but Senegal referred the matter to the African Union. In November, former Peruvian president Alberto Fujimori was arrested in Chile. He had been shielded from prosecution for extrajudicial executions and "disappearances" by Japan, which refused to extradite him to Peru.

The long-awaited trial of Saddam Hussain started in Iraq in October. Although the opportunity to obtain justice for some of the crimes committed under his regime was welcome, AI had serious concerns about the lack of fair trial guarantees in the statute of the tribunal, denial of proper access to counsel and the provision of the death penalty.

Despite progress on international justice, much more remained to be done to address impunity. 2005 was the 10th anniversary of the massacre of around 8,000 Bosnian Muslims after the UN "safe area" of Srebrenica fell to the Bosnian Serb Army in 1995. While crimes committed in Srebrenica have been recognized as amounting to genocide by the International Criminal Tribunal for the former Yugoslavia, the women of Srebrenica whose husbands and sons were killed are still waiting for most of the perpetrators to be brought to justice. In June, AI voiced concerns to the UN Security Council about its efforts to close the International Criminal Tribunal for the former Yugoslavia without establishing effective national courts to deal with the tens of thousands of crimes that the Tribunal was not able to investigate and prosecute. (There were similar concerns over the future of the International Criminal Tribunal for Rwanda.)

At the international level, the courts and tribunals require the full support of states, in terms both of providing resources and of exercising the political will to hand over suspects. At the national level, obstacles to prosecutions, such as amnesties, have to be removed, and where national justice systems have been destroyed by conflict long-term rebuilding plans are urgently needed. While the increase in universal jurisdiction cases in 2005 was welcome, states still have to ensure that they do not provide a safe haven for people accused of crimes under international law.

both urban and rural settings, generally using small arms and light weaponry. Often diverse pockets of violence erupted, with little chain of command or accountability. In some cases, governments armed civilians in an effort to distance themselves from accountability or culpability for abuses.

In Colombia, after 40 years of internal armed conflict, serious human rights abuses by all parties remained at critical levels. A law was passed providing a framework for disarmament and demobilization of paramilitaries and armed groups. However, there were fears that the legislation would allow the most serious human rights abusers to enjoy impunity, while human rights violations continued to be committed in areas where paramilitaries had supposedly demobilized. In addition, government policies designed to reintegrate members of illegal armed groups into civilian life risked recycling them into the conflict.

Despite claims that the situation was normalizing, Russian and Chechen security forces conducted targeted raids in Chechnya during which they committed serious human rights violations. Women were reportedly subjected to gender-based violence, including rape and threats of rape, by Russian and Chechen soldiers. Chechen armed opposition groups committed abuses including targeted attacks on civilians and indiscriminate attacks. There was also violence and unrest in other North Caucasus republics, increasingly accompanied by reports of human rights violations.

In Nepal, the human rights situation deteriorated sharply under a state of emergency imposed in February 2005, with thousands of politically motivated arrests, strict media censorship and atrocities committed by the security forces and Maoist groups. Following a mission to Nepal in the immediate aftermath of the emergency, AI called on the governments of India, the UK and the USA, Nepal's main arms suppliers, to suspend all military supplies to Nepal until the government took clear steps to halt human rights violations. It made a similar call to other governments, including Belgium, Germany, South Africa and France (which supplied crucial components for helicopters assembled and delivered by India). However, although some governments responded positively to the appeal for a suspension of military supplies, China continued to supply arms and ammunition to Nepal.

The failure to resolve manifest injustices, to address impunity and to control the spread of arms led to continuing insecurity and violence in many countries trying to emerge from conflict. Even in countries where steps towards peace had been agreed, there was often little political will or rigour to ensure that agreements were respected and faithfully implemented.

In Afghanistan, lawlessness, insecurity and persecution continued to blight the lives of millions of Afghans. Factional commanders – many suspected of having committed gross human rights crimes in previous years – wielded public authority independently of central government control. Absence of the rule of law left many victims of human rights violations without redress, and the criminal justice system barely functioned. Thousands of civilians were killed in attacks by US and Coalition Forces and by armed groups.

In Côte d'Ivoire, where a disastrous decline in the economy precipitated a conflict in a country until recently regarded as one of the most stable in West

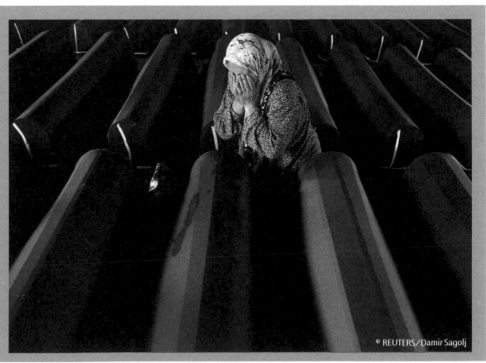

A Bosnian woman cries over the coffin of her son, who was a victim of the 1995 Srebrenica massacre by Bosnian Serb forces. On 11 July 2005, 610 identified victims were buried at a memorial ceremony. Their bodies were among those found in more than 60 mass graves around the town.

© REUTERS/Damir Sagolj

REFUGEES, ASYLUM-SEEKERS AND INTERNALLY DISPLACED PEOPLE

In recent years, the number of refugees worldwide has fallen significantly, but the reality in 2005 was more complex and far bleaker than the numbers suggested.

In 2004, the last year for which figures were available, the number of refugees recorded was the lowest in almost 25 years. The decline in refugee numbers was largely because of the numbers of refugees who returned to their countries of origin, but not all were able to return to their homes and villages of origin, and many returned in conditions that were not voluntary, safe or dignified.

In all, more than 5 million refugees were returned – not all voluntarily – to their countries of origin between 2001 and 2004. Many of the returns took place to countries such as Afghanistan, Angola, Burundi, Iraq and Liberia where their safety and dignity could not necessarily be guaranteed. Some returns breached the fundamental principle of *non-refoulement* – the cornerstone of international refugee protection – that no one should be returned against their will to a situation where they would be at risk of serious human rights abuse.

The focus on numbers by both the international community and individual governments often led to the rights of refugees being disregarded. In many countries, asylum-seekers were excluded from seeking protection, either physically or by procedures that failed to provide a fair hearing. In Greece, for example, in 2004 just 11 asylum-seekers were recognized as refugees and 3,731 were rejected. The refusal rate in fast-track asylum procedures in the UK was 99 per cent. In South Africa some asylum-seekers were arbitrarily deported because of corrupt practices at refugee reception centres and borders. In China hundreds, possibly thousands, of North Korean asylum-seekers were arrested and expelled with no opportunity to claim asylum.

While the number of people crossing international borders in search of protection fell, the number of internally displaced persons remained unchanged at 25 million in 2004, many of whom had been displaced for years. States continued to be reluctant to allow international observers to monitor the conditions and human rights situation of internally displaced people in their countries. The UN Secretary-General's March 2005 report on the implementation of the Millennium Development Goals, *In Larger Freedom*, recommended strengthening the inter-agency response to the protection and assistance needs of internally displaced people. The resulting new inter-agency "cluster approach" promised to deliver greater accountability, but it remained to be seen whether it would deliver more predictable, robust and coherent protection to the millions of internally displaced people around the world.

For refugees living in camps, conditions worsened in 2005, particularly as many faced reductions in food rations – a sign of the failure of the world's governments to fulfil their international obligations to share the responsibility of protecting and assisting refugees. This often resulted in an increase in violence against women, including domestic violence, and sexual exploitation of women who were forced to exchange sex for food rations as their only means of survival. Refugees continued to be denied freedom of movement outside camps and so were unable to earn a living, raising serious questions about the impact of long-term encampment policies on the rights and lives of refugees. In urban settings, many refugees were denied legal status and the right to work, forcing them into destitution or into a dangerous search for survival elsewhere, sometimes by travelling to other countries.

For governments keen to minimize their obligations to protect refugees, the rhetoric of the "war on terror" provided yet another excuse to increase border controls. In many countries, politicians and the media fuelled xenophobia and racism, falsely linking refugees with terrorism and criminality and whipping up hostility towards asylum-seekers.

© Refugee Solidarity Committee

A container used by the Greek authorities to detain irregular migrants, Chios island, April 2005.

The Israeli wall in al-Ram, near Jerusalem, October 2005. Palestinians were increasingly confined to restricted areas and denied freedom of movement between towns and villages within the Occupied Territories. Many were cut off from their farmlands and their workplaces, and denied access to education and health care facilities.

© REUTERS/Mahfouz Abu Turk

Africa, easy access to small arms contributed to violations of the agreed ceasefire, inter-ethnic conflict in the west of the country, xenophobia and the ongoing use of child soldiers. Despite efforts by the African Union to restore peace and security in the country, the disarmament, demobilization and reintegration process remained deadlocked. In October, AI publicized reports of small arms proliferation, re-circulation and possible new arms transfers to both sides of the conflict despite a UN-imposed arms embargo.

In several post-conflict countries the dominant culture of impunity – the failure to bring to justice those responsible for human rights abuses – fostered continued cycles of violence. In Sri Lanka, for example, the security situation deteriorated in 2005 as both the government and the armed opposition failed to make the human rights guarantees in the ceasefire agreement work. Tensions over scarce resources were exacerbated by internal displacement resulting from the conflict and the tsunami.

The struggle to overcome impunity can last for decades, or even generations. The survivors of Japan's system of military sexual slavery during World War II – the so-called "comfort women" – have persistently called for recognition and justice for more than half a century, their numbers dwindling with time. Once again in 2005 the Japanese government refused to accept responsibility, formally apologize, or provide official compensation for the suffering endured by thousands of women.

There were some exceptions to this generally grim landscape, including elections in a number of states emerging from conflict. Greater stability in Sierra Leone allowed the UN forces to leave the country. The Polisario Front, which demands independence for Western Sahara, released 404 Moroccan prisoners of war who had been held for well over two decades despite the formal cessation of hostilities 14 years ago. Efforts to overcome impunity moved forward with the prospect of Lord's Resistance Army (LRA) leaders being brought before the International Criminal Court charged with war crimes in northern Uganda.

FUELLED BY FEAR: SUFFERING DUE TO IDENTITY

The blurring of cultural boundaries often associated with globalization, far from overcoming deep divisions based on identity, was accompanied by continued, and some believe increasing, racism, discrimination and xenophobia. Across the world, people were attacked and deprived of basic human rights because of their gender, race, ethnicity, religion, sexual orientation and other similar aspects of their identity, or combinations of these identities.

In the context of the "war on terror", 2005 saw continued polarization along identity lines in an increasingly intolerant and fearful world. Many people were targeted for discrimination and violence because of their identity – Muslims, those identified as Muslims, other minorities, migrants and refugees all fell victim. Some Muslim communities in Europe and elsewhere said they felt under siege: they feared and abhorred the bombings, but also experienced growing racism, fostered in part by some governments and media broadly linking the "terrorist threat" with "foreigners" and "Muslims". On top of this, many suffered the consequences of counter-terrorism measures that were discriminatory in law and practice as young Muslim males continued to be portrayed as "typical terrorists".

In their efforts to assert their power or resist challenges to their authority, repressive regimes targeted ethnic or religious minorities. One of the most blatant examples was the treatment of Kurdish groups in Syria and Iran. Up to 21 people were reportedly killed, scores injured and at least 190 more arrested in a brutal clampdown on civil unrest in the Kurdish areas of western Iran from July onwards. The mass arrests and excessive use of force against protesters in the Kurdish areas were part of a pattern of abuse of ethnic minorities in Iran, where up to half the population is Persian and the rest is made up of other ethnic groups including Kurds, Arabs and Azeri Turks.

In Syria too, Kurds continued to suffer from identity-based discrimination, including restrictions on the use of the Kurdish language and culture. Tens of thousands of Syrian Kurds remained effectively stateless, and were consequently denied full access to education, health services and employment, as well as the right to a nationality. However, in June, at its first meeting for 10 years, the ruling Ba'th Party Congress ordered a review of a 1962 census which could result in stateless Kurds obtaining Syrian citizenship.

Challenges to mainstream religious views were severely punished in some countries. In Egypt, despite the (Emergency) Supreme State Security Court ruling at least seven times in his favour, Mitwalli Ibrahim Mitwalli Saleh remained in administrative detention for his scholarly views on apostasy and marriage between Muslim women and non-Muslim men. In Pakistan, where blasphemy laws make it a criminal offence for members of the Ahmadiyya community to practise their faith, police investigations into killings of Ahmadis were slow or did not take place at all. In just one incident in October, eight Ahmadis were shot dead and 22 injured in their mosque by men shooting from a passing motorbike. Eighteen men arrested shortly afterwards were released without charge. In China, religious observance outside official channels remained tightly circumscribed. In March, the authorities issued a new regulation aimed at strengthening official controls on religious activities, and in April a crackdown on the Falun Gong spiritual movement was renewed. A Beijing official stated that since the group had been banned as a "heretical organization", any activities linked to Falun Gong were illegal. Many Falun Gong practitioners reportedly remained in detention where they were at high risk of torture or ill-treatment.

In Eritrea, where the government cracked down on evangelical Christian churches during 2005, more than 1,750 church members and dozens of Muslims were in detention at the end of 2005 because of their religious beliefs. They were held in indefinite and incommunicado detention without charge or trial, some in secret locations. Many were tortured or ill-treated, and large numbers were held in metal shipping containers or underground cells.

A perceived lack of ethnic "purity" was used as a basis to exclude people from employment and education in Turkmenistan. Many members of ethnic

Around 300 people hold a candlelit vigil in Santa Fe, New Mexico, USA, for James Maestas, a young gay man who was beaten and badly injured in March 2005 as he left a restaurant where he had been eating with friends.

© EMPICS/AP/Jeff Geissler

minorities such as Uzbeks, Russians and Kazakhs were dismissed from their workplaces and denied access to higher education. Members of religious minority groups risked harassment, arbitrary detention, imprisonment after unfair trials and ill-treatment. Latvia ratified the Council of Europe's Framework Convention for the Protection of National Minorities during 2005, but the government's definition of a minority effectively excluded most members of the Russian-speaking community from qualifying for recognition as a minority.

In many countries, indigenous people remained an underclass and were victims of widespread human rights violations. Discussions on an international Declaration on the Rights of Indigenous People, deadlocked for almost a decade, made halting progress in 2005. This dilatory response by the international community to the urgent need to recognize and respect the rights of indigenous people was reflected at the national level. In Brazil, for example, the government's demarcation and ratification of indigenous territories fell far short of its promised goals. This contributed to insecurity and violent attacks on indigenous communities and forced evictions, aggravating already severe economic and social deprivation.

The UN Special Rapporteur on the situation of human rights and fundamental freedoms of indigenous people, who visited New Zealand in 2005, said that there were significant, and in some cases widening, disparities between Maori and the rest of the population. He said Maori considered this the result of a trans-generational backlog of broken promises, economic marginalization, social exclusion and cultural discrimination.

WOMEN'S RIGHT TO FREEDOM FROM VIOLENCE

Some 3,000 representatives from governments and women's and human rights organizations came together in New York in March 2005 to mark the 10th anniversary of the Beijing UN World Conference on Women and to assess progress towards fulfilling the Beijing Declaration and Program for Action. While governments unanimously reaffirmed the commitments they had made a decade ago, they failed to make further pledges to promote and protect women's human rights. This failure was in part the result of a retrogressive attack on women's human rights that has become evident over the past few years. This attack, especially regarding women's sexual rights and reproductive rights, was led by conservative US-backed Christian groups and supported by the Holy See and some member states of the Organization of the Islamic Conference.

The attacks on women's rights, the changed global security context and the lack of will by states to implement international human rights standards formed the backdrop against which AI continued throughout 2005 to join with women's groups around the world to promote women's human rights.

Areas of progress included new legislation in a number of countries which reduced discrimination against women. In Ethiopia, a new Penal Code removed the marital exemption for the crimes of bride abduction and associated rape. The Kuwaiti Parliament amended the electoral law to grant women the right to vote and stand for election. AI welcomed the entry into force of the Protocol to the African Charter on Human and Peoples' Rights on the Rights of Women in Africa. Women's organizations in the Solomon Islands celebrated the creation of the country's first purpose-built shelter for victims of family violence.

Despite the gains made by the global women's movement over recent years, pervasive discrimination and impunity for crimes of violence against women continued to undermine women's fundamental rights to freedom, security and justice.

AI's campaign to Stop Violence against Women concentrated during 2005 largely on violence against women in armed conflict, violence within the family and the role of women human rights defenders.

As its campaign increasingly focused on the private sphere of violence in intimate relationships, AI emphasized the duty of governments to intervene to adequately protect, respect, promote and fulfil women's human rights. AI produced reports documenting domestic violence in a number of countries including Afghanistan, Guatemala, Gulf Cooperation Council countries, India, Iraq, Israel and the Occupied Territories, Nigeria, the Russian Federation, Spain and Sweden. Reports were also issued on the impact of guns on women's lives, and on women, violence and health.

The long-term impact of violence against women was also highlighted in a major World Health Organization study published in 2005. As AI has consistently argued, violence against women causes prolonged physical and psychological suffering to women, and has repercussions for the well-being and security of their families and communities. The connection between violence against women as a human rights issue and as a public health crisis led AI to accept an invitation to join the Leadership Council of the Global Coalition on Women and AIDS.

At a conference of women human rights defenders held in Sri Lanka towards the end of 2005, organizations and individuals recognized the significant contribution of women human rights defenders to the advancement of the human rights of all people, and the serious risks to which they are exposed, including killings, abductions, rapes, "disappearances" and assaults. Those who defend and promote women's human rights and gender equality

© AI

Marisela Ortiz, co-founder of a women's support group, stands among the crosses commemorating women abducted and murdered in Ciudad Juárez, Mexico, August 2005.

are often targeted for their activism and can face marginalization, prejudice and danger. Defenders of contested rights such as environmental or sexual rights were particularly at risk in 2005 as they were seen to threaten the status quo.

The need for integrated approaches to combating violence against women was highlighted by two 2005 decisions by the UN Committee on the Elimination of Discrimination against Women. In the Mexican city of Ciudad Juárez, hundreds of poor, largely indigenous, women have been abducted and murdered in recent years without the authorities taking appropriate action. The Committee called for a thorough, systemic revision of the criminal justice apparatus, and for mass popular education to address structural discrimination against women. A Hungarian woman brought a case claiming that the authorities in Hungary had failed to protect her from a series of violent assaults by her former common law husband, despite repeated appeals for help. In this case, the Committee reaffirmed that, where government authorities fail to exercise due diligence to prevent, investigate and punish violations of rights, states themselves bear responsibility for actions of perpetrators.

DEATH PENALTY

At least 2,148 people were executed in 2005 and at least another 5,186 were sentenced to death. These figures only reflect cases known to AI; the true figures were certainly higher.

Many of those put to death had been denied a fair trial; they had "confessed" under torture, had not had proper legal representation or were not given an impartial hearing. Drug smuggling, embezzlement and fraud were some of the crimes for which capital punishment was imposed. Some people lived under sentence of death for more than 20 years before being executed, while others were executed almost immediately. Executioners used various means, including hanging, firing squad, lethal injection and beheading. Among those put to death were children and people with mental disabilities.

As in previous years, the vast majority of executions took place in only a handful of countries: 94 per cent of executions in 2005 were in China, Iran, Saudi Arabia and the USA.

In 2005 Mexico and Liberia abolished the death penalty for all crimes, bringing the number of countries that are abolitionist for all crimes to 86. In 1977, the year when the USA resumed the use of the death penalty and AI convened a groundbreaking International Conference on the Death Penalty in Stockholm, only 16 countries were abolitionist. At the end of 2005, 122 countries were abolitionist, either in law or practice.

The campaign against the death penalty gained strength in the course of 2005. The third World Day Against the Death Penalty, on 10 October, was marked in more than 50 countries and territories, including Benin, Congo, China (Hong Kong), the Democratic Republic of the Congo, France, Germany, India, Japan, Mali, Puerto Rico, Sierra Leone and Togo. Around the world there were demonstrations, petitions, concerts and televised debates to campaign against capital punishment. AI members in 40 countries participated in such events.

There was progress also at the UN level. UN Resolution 2005/59 on the question of the death penalty, passed in April 2005, came the closest yet to condemning the death penalty as a violation of human rights. The resolution affirms the right to life and declares, significantly, that abolition is "essential for the protection of this right". Resolution 2005/59 was co-sponsored by 81 UN member states, the highest number ever. The Special Rapporteur on extrajudicial, summary or arbitrary executions issued strong statements in 2005 against the use of mandatory death sentences. He said that they remove a court's freedom to exercise leniency or to take account of any extenuating or mitigating circumstances and that mandatory sentencing is entirely inappropriate in a matter of life or death.

One of the most powerful arguments against capital punishment is the inherent risk of executing the innocent. In 2005 both China and the USA released people from death row who had been wrongly

convicted: China also acknowledged that innocent people had been executed. Unfair trials have led to executions in many countries; in 2005 people were executed in Iran, Saudi Arabia and Uzbekistan, reportedly without being given the benefit of due process of law, and therefore not afforded sufficient opportunity to present evidence of their innocence.

Discrimination based on a wide range of characteristics such as ethnicity, religion and poverty manifested itself at every stage of the death penalty process.

In a large number of countries, including India, Uzbekistan and Viet Nam, information about the death penalty remained secret. Sometimes information was withheld not only from the public but even from the victims. Japan remained one of the countries where inmates are not told when they are going to be executed until a few hours before their death. Just five hours before they were beheaded, six Somali nationals put to death in Saudi Arabia in April were reportedly still unaware that they were at risk of execution.

Even members of groups protected from the death penalty by international law and standards – such as juvenile offenders and the mentally disabled – were executed in 2005. In the USA, where more than 1,000 people have been executed since the resumption of capital punishment in 1977, the person who died in the thousandth execution was borderline mentally disabled. In Iran, at least eight people were executed for crimes committed when they were less than 18 years old – at least two were children under the age of 18 when they were hanged.

In a welcome judgment on 1 March 2005 the US Supreme Court ruled that the use of the death penalty against people under the age of 18 was unconstitutional, leading to more than 70 child offenders under sentence of death having their sentences commuted. Concerns remained, however, that the Supreme Court's ruling did not apply to Guantánamo detainees who were juveniles when they were detained.

© Private

Nanon Williams, sentenced to death on flawed evidence for a crime committed when he was 17 years old. He was one of 70 child offenders on death row in the USA whose sentences were commuted in 2005 after a Supreme Court ruling.

A labourer unloads emergency supplies in north-western Niger, July 2005. Although several non-governmental organizations had been warning of the risk of famine in Niger since late 2004, international donors, including the UN and the European Union, did not react quickly to calls for urgent food aid. The UN estimated that the famine put in danger the lives of 3.5 million of Niger's 12 million inhabitants.

© REUTERS/Finbarr O'Reilly

At a time of unprecedented globalization, with barriers to the free flow of capital and goods across borders being dismantled, it was ironic that the movement of people across national boundaries became more highly regulated than ever. Migrant workers became the focus of particular attack and ill-treatment, notwithstanding the benefits that host communities derived from their presence. An estimated 200 million migrants lived and worked outside their country of origin. From Burmese agricultural workers in Thailand to Indian domestic workers in Kuwait, many migrant workers all over the world faced exploitation and abuse. Ill-treated by employers and often with alarmingly little legal protection, they had scant access to justice. When irregular migrants came to the attention of the authorities, they risked being arbitrarily detained and expelled in conditions that violated their human rights.

As in many parts of the world, in the Mediterranean region there continued to be a blatant disregard for migrants' and asylum-seekers' rights. Some of the thousands of people attempting to enter the Spanish enclaves of Ceuta and Melilla, on the north African coast, were intercepted and forcibly taken back to Morocco. Migrants and asylum-seekers fleeing extreme poverty and repression in sub-Saharan Africa were rounded up by Moroccan forces and detained. Some were deported to Algeria or taken to remote desert regions along the border with Algeria and Mauritania and left with little or no food and no means of transport. In Italy and Greece migrants and asylum-seekers continued to be detained, often in grossly inadequate conditions.

Most of the world's governments declined to commit themselves to enhancing migrants' rights — by December 2005 only 34 countries had ratified the International Convention on the Protection of the Rights of All Migrant Workers and Members of Their Families. Of the 20 countries committed to report to the UN Committee on Migrant Workers, just two had done so by the end of 2005.

Bilateral agreements between migrant-sending and migrant-receiving countries often ignored the human rights of migrants, treating human beings as commodities, "service providers" or "agents of development", regardless of the contribution of migrants to their host societies and countries of origin. Many states focused on border controls while turning a blind eye to the exploitation of migrants, including migrant workers employed in the informal economy. The important contributions made by migrants to their host societies were frequently obscured in public debates that were often overtly racist and xenophobic, encouraging a climate in which human rights abuses against migrants were overlooked or even condoned.

Women migrants were at particular risk of gender-specific human rights violations. A foreign domestic worker was sentenced by a Shari'a (Islamic law) court in the United Arab Emirates to 150 lashes for becoming pregnant outside marriage. Many women migrants were not only vulnerable to sexual exploitation by traffickers and employers, but also faced systematic discrimination in the country where they worked. A woman from India working in Kuwait who was raped and became pregnant was held in prison after giving birth; she was not allowed to leave the country without the permission of the child's father.

Discrimination and violence on grounds of gender persisted in every country in the world, as documented in several major reports released by AI during 2005 as part of its global campaign to Stop Violence against Women. In Nigeria, girls and women were left blind from beatings, doused with kerosene and set on fire, jailed for reporting that they had been raped or murdered for daring to report that their husbands were threatening to kill them. AI's report on family violence in Spain analyzed the obstacles women face when trying to escape abusive relationships. In particular, migrant women, Roma women and women with physical or mental disabilities were rarely able to gain access to shelters and financial aid for survivors of gender-based violence.

During 2005 AI campaigned for the rights of women disregarded by the criminal justice system. Hundreds of cases of women abducted and murdered in Guatemala were not adequately addressed by the authorities and the government itself reported that 40 per cent of cases were archived and never investigated. Such official inaction sent the strongest signal possible to those who perpetrated these crimes that they did so with impunity.

Despite moves towards greater legal recognition of their rights in certain countries, lesbian, gay, bisexual and transgender (LGBT) people continued to face widespread discrimination and violence, often officially sanctioned. The authorities tried to ban Latvia's first ever Gay Pride march to mark the struggle for the rights of LGBT people. Homophobic remarks made by the Latvian Prime Minister and other senior figures – who, together with religious leaders, opposed the march – were reported to have encouraged a climate of intolerance and hatred. In Saudi Arabia, 35 men were sentenced to flogging and imprisonment for attending what was described as a "gay wedding". AI's findings in a major report on the USA showed that LGBT people were targeted for human rights abuses by the police. The discrimination against them significantly restricted their access to equal protection under the law and to redress for abuses. A 60-year-old gay man arrested in St Louis, Missouri, told AI:

> "I did nothing wrong... did not hurt anyone and was targeted simply for being a gay male in a city park ... Nothing is more unfair than singling out a group and making them criminal when they are not."

Depriving a person of their rights because of a characteristic they cannot change or that is so central to their being that they should not be forced to change it, such as their race, religion, gender or sexual orientation, attacks the central premise of human rights – the conviction that every human being is equal in dignity and worth.

POOR, EXCLUDED AND INVISIBLE

During 2005 the international community's commitment to "make poverty history" became more prominent on the international agenda. However, while government leaders pronounced their intention to reduce poverty, particularly in Africa, most of the targets set under the UN's 15-year Millennium Development Goals showed little, if any, prospect of being met. The first time-bound target to achieve gender parity in primary education passed unmet with little or no protest from the international community. There was more rhetoric than real commitment to

action, and not nearly enough attention to basing strategies on human rights principles.

Action by states to relieve poverty and deprivation globally is not an optional extra – it is an international obligation. It was a measure of states' failure to fulfil this obligation that in 2005, when the world's economic output was at its highest level ever, more than 800 million people around the world were chronically malnourished. At least 10 million children died before the age of five. Over 100 million children (the majority girls) did not have access even to primary education.

The disappointing outcome of the UN World Summit, which took place in September, illustrated clearly the gap between political rhetoric and genuine commitment. A small number of countries blocked efforts to make significant progress on human rights, security, genocide and poverty reduction. Delegates had to work so hard to maintain commitments made in the past that they had little time to discuss implementation of the Outcome Document, a political declaration where governments made pledges in the four areas of development, peace and security, human rights, and UN reform.

The lack of progress on the Millennium Development Goals was particularly shocking in light of the fact that some of the Goals set levels of expected achievement lower than those that states are required to meet under international human rights law. The Goal of halving hunger, if met, would hugely increase life expectancy, health and human dignity. Yet the 152 states that have ratified the International Covenant on Economic, Social and Cultural Rights have, at the very minimum, an obligation to take the necessary action to mitigate and alleviate hunger for the whole population, even in times of natural or other disasters.

While global poverty climbed up the international agenda during 2005, it was also a year that exposed the gross economic and social inequalities within even the wealthiest of countries. The aftermath of Hurricane Katrina shocked many around the world as it revealed the underbelly of deprivation, racial inequalities and poverty within the USA, the most powerful economy in the world.

The riots in France drew attention to decades of social inequality and discrimination against migrants and French nationals of African descent. The French government responded by declaring a state of emergency, imposing curfews and allowing law enforcement officials to carry out searches without warrants, close public meeting places of any kind and place people under "house arrest". The government also announced plans to expel migrants convicted during the riots, regardless of whether they had a legal right to reside in France.

In countries of all political colours, and all levels of development, many were still unable to access even minimum levels of food, water, education, health care and housing. Deprivation in the midst of plenty could not be blamed solely on a lack of resources – it resulted from unwillingness, systemic corruption, negligence

Firefighters extinguish a car fire in Cenon, near Bordeaux, south-western France, 9 November 2005. After France's most widespread civil unrest in more than 30 years, the government ordered a state of emergency.

© Empics/AP/Bob Edme

and discrimination by governments and others, and from their failure to respect, protect and fulfil economic, social and cultural rights.

For example, millions of people living with HIV/AIDS were unable to realize their right to health not just because of poverty, but because of discrimination and stigma, violence against women, and trade and patent agreements that obstructed access to life-saving drugs. During 2005, fewer than 15 per cent of those needing anti-retroviral treatment in the developing world received it, demonstrating the failure not only of governments, but also of intergovernmental bodies and companies, to fulfil their shared responsibilities for human rights.

In a globalized economy, the failure to uphold human rights also brought to the fore the debate about the responsibilities of companies and financial institutions for human rights. The process of establishing human rights principles applicable to companies moved forward in 2005 with the appointment in July by the UN Secretary-General of a Special Representative on human rights and transnational corporations and other business enterprises. There was debate over the UN Human Rights Norms for Business and some further progress was made towards the acceptance by companies of voluntary codes of conduct. However, the need remained for common universal standards for corporate commitment on human rights and legal accountability.

Countless situations across the globe highlighted how poverty can be an aggregate violation of human rights — civil, cultural, economic, political and social rights — and how poverty, marginalization and vulnerability to violence are often inescapably linked.

In Brazil, where millions lived in poverty in *favelas* (shanty towns), the government's continued failure to address systemic levels of criminal violence and human rights violations at the hands of the police reinforced patterns of social exclusion. The state's persistent negligence over public security in *favelas* not only resulted in some of the highest homicide figures in the world, but effectively criminalized whole communities, further prejudicing access to already meagre public services such as education and health care as well as employment. For example, many *favela* residents would not be able to get a job if they gave their true address, as they were so widely seen as criminals. Armed violence was an inescapable part of daily life, either at the hands of drug gangs, police or vigilante "death squads". A police policy of military-style incursions into the *favelas* not only failed to curb violence, it endangered the lives of some of the most vulnerable people in society. In October, a referendum on a total ban on the sale of guns in Brazil was defeated. Many analysts attributed the result to people's sense of despair about the security situation and lack of faith in the police's ability to protect them.

In Haiti, high levels of violence, particularly sexual violence, were perpetrated by armed groups and vigilante groups against women in poor communities. Many women were under constant threat of attack. Given the extremely low rate of conviction in relation to crimes of sexual violence, and the lack of official, community or family support to identify and investigate perpetrators, it was not surprising that these victims did not seek justice. Law enforcement officials have consistently failed to provide adequate protection or access to justice for these women.

The people of Sri Lanka worked hard to rebuild their lives during 2005, after the devastation caused by the tsunami, but escalating violence in the north-east and human rights abuses hampered reconstruction efforts.

Roma communities across Europe were often denied basic economic, social and cultural rights such as access to education and health services, and were frequently the targets of police abuse. In Slovenia, Roma formed a significant proportion of the people unlawfully removed from the Slovenian registry of permanent residents in 1992, known as the "erased", and as a result they were not able to access basic social services.

Whether in response to natural disasters or humanitarian crises, the international community often faces criticism for failing to provide timely and adequate assistance to people in urgent need of aid. However, in some countries humanitarian efforts were hampered by governments unable or unwilling to address the needs of the poor and marginalized in their own countries. In Zimbabwe, despite overwhelming evidence of humanitarian need, the government repeatedly obstructed the humanitarian efforts of the UN and civil society groups for political reasons. One of the major factors behind the need for external support was the impact of government policies; hundreds of thousands of people were forcibly evicted from their homes and tens of thousands of people lost their livelihoods and the ability to support their families.

In 2005 there were some positive steps towards greater recognition of economic, social and cultural rights at national and international levels. These included an important Inter-American Court of Human Rights decision in the case of two Haitian girls, Dilcia Yean and Violeta Bosico, against the Dominican Republic, which had denied them access to education on the basis of their nationality. Also, steps were taken towards creating a UN mechanism for lodging complaints of violations of economic, social and cultural rights. Such a mechanism would help put economic, social and cultural rights on an equal footing with civil and political rights and end this arbitrary classification of human rights. It would strike a blow against impunity for economic, social and cultural rights violations and open a much-needed avenue for victims to claim redress.

CONCLUSION

For AI, genuine human security means that all rights — civil, cultural, economic, political and social — are realized. These are interrelated and indivisible — no security policy can ignore any one dimension. Human beings can flourish and fulfil their potential only if secure in all aspects of their lives. Human security therefore depends on the full range of interdependent human rights being respected, protected and fulfilled.

This report shows how human security, understood in this way, has often been a casualty of the national security strategies of the world's most powerful governments, and those emboldened by their example. Our collective human security will not be safeguarded through such state-centred and narrowly defined approaches to security. It requires a more comprehensive vision of what security means, as well as a collective sense of shared responsibility for protecting it within and beyond the boundaries of the state.

REGIONAL OVERVIEWS

AFRICA

The signing of several peace agreements in 2005 resulted in a decline in armed conflict across the region. However, grave human rights violations, including killings, rape and other forms of sexual violence, characterized continuing conflicts in Burundi, Chad, Côte d'Ivoire, the Democratic Republic of the Congo (DRC) and Sudan. Many places faced political instability and a serious risk of further conflict and violence. Refugees and internally displaced persons (IDPs) in camps and urban areas had inadequate access to basic needs assistance and were exposed to serious human rights abuses. Impunity for human rights violations remained widespread, despite some international and regional efforts to bring suspected perpetrators to account. Human rights defenders, journalists and political opponents continued to face harassment, assault and unlawful detention for denouncing human rights violations or criticizing their governments.

Millions of men, women and children remained impoverished and deprived of clean water, adequate housing, food, education and primary health care. This situation was exacerbated by widespread and systemic corruption and the apparent indifference of governments to providing their citizens with the most basic economic and social rights. Across the region, hundreds of thousands of families were forcibly evicted from their homes, further violating their fundamental human rights.

The Protocol to the African Charter on Human and Peoples' Rights on the Rights of Women in Africa entered into force during the year, but continuing violations of women's human rights, including female genital mutilation (FGM), domestic violence, rape, trafficking and sexual violence during conflicts, made the development nominal rather than substantive.

A series of important regional initiatives, including the Pan-African Parliament, the African Union (AU) Peace and Security Council and the African Peer Review Mechanism, became fully operational, although their overall impact on respect for human rights was difficult to measure. The AU Assembly continued to make efforts to address human rights problems in the region, but its failure to respond firmly to the human rights crisis in Zimbabwe illustrated the need for the AU to apply its human rights principles consistently.

Armed conflict

Governments and armed opposition groups continued to abuse human rights and international humanitarian law in Sudan (particularly in Darfur), northern Uganda, Chad, Côte d'Ivoire and the DRC, resulting in unlawful killings, rape and other torture, population displacements and other grave human rights violations. In Darfur, civilians were killed and injured by government troops, which sometimes bombed villages from the air, and by government-allied nomadic militias known as the Janjawid. Women were raped and some were abducted and held as sexual slaves. Many had fled conflict and extreme deprivation in the south and other parts of Darfur.

Civilians continued to be the victims of the 19-year conflict in northern Uganda. Despite peace talks, attacks by the Lord's Resistance Army increased towards the end of 2005, and some dissident militias remained active and clashed from time to time. More than 3 million IDPs and half a million refugees were expected to return to the south.

In Burundi, armed conflict continued throughout 2005 between one armed group, the PALIPEHUTU-FNL, and government forces in the provinces of Bujumbura rural and Bubanza, despite the presence of UN peacekeeping soldiers. More than 120,000 people, most of them women and children, remained internally displaced and in exile at the end of 2005.

No progress was made in demobilizing an estimated 50,000 combatants under the peace process in Côte d'Ivoire. The main obstacle to progress appeared to be a lack of trust between the government and the leadership of the New Forces (Forces nouvelles), a coalition of former armed groups. Child soldiers were used by all parties to the conflicts in Côte d'Ivoire and the DRC.

In October, Eritrea banned UN helicopter flights and other travel to UN monitors, further restricting the multinational UN Mission in Ethiopia and Eritrea, whose 2,800 personnel administered a buffer zone along the border. Both sides had rearmed since 2000 and deployed troops near the border in late 2005. The UN Security Council called on Ethiopia to implement the International Boundary Commission's judgment regarding the border areas, particularly its allocation to Eritrea of Badme town, the flash point of war in 1998, but no progress was made on this during 2005.

Illegal exploitation of natural resources continued in the DRC, Liberia and Sudan. In Liberia, former combatants occupied rubber plantations and tapped rubber, claiming it was their only means of survival. They were reportedly responsible for killings and torture, including rape, of civilians.

There was encouraging progress in peacemaking in some conflicts. In Senegal, for example, the 2004 peace agreement that ended two decades of conflict in the southern Casamance region of the country held throughout 2005.

Impunity and justice

Despite widespread and systematic violations of human rights, including war crimes and crimes against humanity, most perpetrators were not held to account. Although investigations were opened in a few cases, the justice systems in many countries continued to suffer from systemic corruption, lack of resources and inadequate training for personnel. Despite encouraging

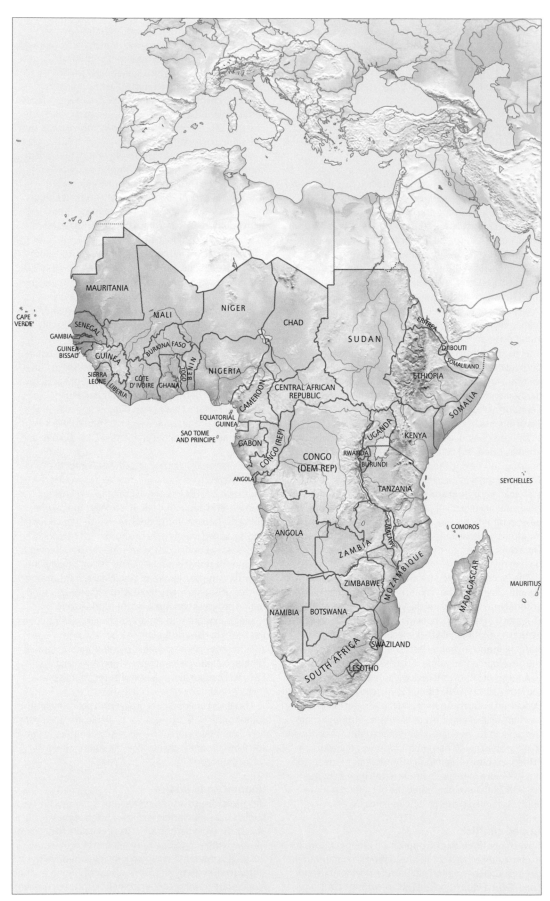

judicial pronouncements in some countries, there was little progress in creating an adequate mechanism for prosecution before domestic courts of war crimes and crimes against humanity. The AU tended to downplay the issue of accountability in the implementation of its mandate.

In Senegal, despite publicly expressed commitments by the authorities, no steps were taken to end impunity for perpetrators of human rights abuses. In January, parliament passed a law that provided an amnesty for "politically motivated" offences committed between 1983 and 2004. Senegal did not respond positively to the extradition request and international arrest warrant issued by a Belgian judge and charging Chad's former President Hissène Habré with gross human rights violations committed during his 1982-90 rule. Hissène Habré moved to Senegal after he was ousted from power in 1990. In November, the Dakar Appeal Court declared itself "not competent" to rule whether to issue an extradition order in the case. A few days later, the authorities stated that the AU should indicate who had jurisdiction to rule on the case and declared that Hissène Habré would remain in Senegal pending the AU's decision.

There were some limited steps at the international or regional level to address impunity. In January, a UN-appointed commission of inquiry reported that war crimes and crimes against humanity had been committed in Darfur, and that the Sudanese justice system was unable and unwilling to address the situation. In March, the UN Security Council passed Resolution 1593, referring the situation in Darfur to the International Criminal Court (ICC). The resolution required Sudan and all other parties to the conflict to co-operate fully with the Court. However, as a result of US pressure, a provision was inserted in the resolution to exempt nationals of states not party to the Rome Statute of the ICC (other than Sudan) from the jurisdiction of the ICC. The ICC began investigations, but by the end of 2005 had not been granted access to Sudan.

In January, the Ugandan government formally asked the ICC to investigate and prosecute war crimes and other serious human rights abuses that had occurred during the armed conflict in the north of the country. In October, the ICC issued arrest warrants for five senior leaders of the Lord's Resistance Army charged with war crimes and crimes against humanity committed in Uganda since July 2002.

Two years after the Prosecutor of the ICC announced that the Court would look into the hundreds of thousands of crimes committed in the DRC since July 2002, investigations had yet to result in any international arrest warrants. The likelihood that only a handful of suspected perpetrators would be prosecuted underlined the necessity for comprehensive action by the DRC government to reform the national justice system and end impunity.

Former Liberian President Charles Taylor continued to enjoy impunity in Nigeria despite international pressure for Nigeria to surrender him to the Special Court for Sierra Leone to face charges of crimes against humanity, war crimes and other serious violations of international law. In July, the leadership of the Mano River Union countries (Guinea, Liberia and Sierra Leone) publicly stated that some of Charles Taylor's activities in Nigeria breached the terms of his asylum.

Trials of prominent genocide suspects continued before the International Criminal Tribunal for Rwanda (ICTR) in Arusha, which held 60 detainees at the end of 2005. Five trials involving 20 defendants continued from previous years, and five new trials involving seven defendants began in 2005. Two judgments were given: one defendant received a six-year prison sentence and another received life imprisonment. One suspect surrendered himself to the ICTR and was later transferred to The Hague for detention pending his trial on charges of genocide, conspiracy to commit genocide and complicity in genocide. Another suspect was arrested in Gabon. He was charged with genocide, conspiracy to commit genocide, direct and public incitement to commit genocide, and persecution as a crime against humanity.

A report by the African Commission on Human and Peoples' Rights (ACHPR) of a fact-finding mission to Zimbabwe in 2002, which was officially made public in February 2005, concluded that human rights violations had occurred in Zimbabwe. The ACHPR made several recommendations, but by the end of the year almost nothing had been done to implement them. Zimbabwean government ministers and officials made disparaging comments about the report and the ACHPR. In December, the ACHPR adopted a resolution on Zimbabwe condemning violations of human rights. The ACHPR did not, however, make public the report of its July 2004 mission to Sudan.

Violence against women

Women remained without adequate protection in law and practice, and continued to face violence and discrimination. Women were raped and subjected to other forms of sexual violence by government agents as well as partners, employers and others. In some communities, FGM and forced marriages were still the norm. In Cameroon, approximately 20 per cent of women and girls were reported to have been subjected to FGM, which was still legal. Provisions also remained in the Penal Code that exempted a suspected rapist from judicial proceedings if he marries the victim, effectively protecting the perpetrator while subjecting the victim to further abuse.

Hundreds of thousands of women were believed to have been raped by government forces and armed political groups in conflict. In eastern DRC, rape was sometimes committed in front of the victim's children, family or community. In some cases, the girl or woman was killed or deliberately wounded. Few rape survivors had access to appropriate medical care. In Togo, security forces and militia groups allegedly raped women suspected of supporting the opposition.

Legislative reform to increase respect for women's human rights began or was completed in some countries. In Ghana, civil society organizations

©REUTERS/Mike Hutchings

An AIDS activist (*right*) counsels a young HIV positive woman and her grandmother at their home near Lusikisiki, South Africa, November 2005.

discussed reform of abortion legislation and the absence of laws prohibiting marital rape, and some members of parliament advocated tougher sentences for rape and sexual assaults against women. In Liberia, a law on rape was passed that had a broader definition of rape. However, it included the death penalty among the punishments for perpetrators, despite Liberia's commitment to abolish the death penalty. The Kenyan parliament agreed to discuss a proposed Sexual Offences Bill and discussed a draft law on rape, sponsored by women's groups. The draft law proposed broadening the definition of rape and denying bail to anyone charged with raping a minor.

In Nigeria, some states introduced legislation on violence against women in the home, but the federal government did not review discriminatory laws or amend national law to comply with the Protocol to the African Charter on Human and Peoples' Rights on the Rights of Women in Africa, which Nigeria had ratified.

Despite the lack of official statistics, it was estimated that nearly two thirds of women in certain groups in Lagos State, for example, were victims of violence in the home. Discriminatory laws and practices, dismissive attitudes within the police, and an inaccessible justice system contributed to violence against women being widely tolerated and underreported.

Economic, social and cultural rights

Many governments engaged in practices that systematically denied people their rights to shelter, food, health and education. In Zimbabwe, hundreds of thousands of people were forcibly evicted and their homes demolished as part of Operation Murambatsvina (Restore Order). The operation was carried out against a backdrop of severe food shortages. The government repeatedly obstructed the humanitarian work of non-governmental organizations (NGOs) and UN agencies, including attempts to provide shelter for the homeless.

In Nigeria, thousands of people were made homeless without due process, compensation or the provision of alternative housing.

In Niger, serious food shortages were compounded by years of drought and an invasion of desert locusts in 2004, the worst in more than a decade, which wiped out much of the country's cereal production. The UN estimated that famine put in danger the lives of over a quarter of Niger's population. The famine had a knock-on effect in neighbouring Benin, Burkina Faso, Mali and Nigeria, all of which experienced rising prices or food shortages. Despite warnings of the impending famine, international donors failed to respond quickly. In Mozambique, over 800,000 people needed food aid as a result of prolonged drought.

High death rates from AIDS-related illnesses seriously affected economic and social development in many countries of the region. The southern Africa region continued to have the highest prevalence rate of HIV in the world and severe problems in access to care and treatment. Swaziland had the highest rate globally with 42.6 per cent, and more than three quarters of people known to need antiretroviral treatment were still not receiving it. In South Africa, new figures revealed that around 6 million people had been infected with HIV by 2004, with less than 20 per cent of them receiving antiretroviral drugs. In Mozambique, approximately 200,000 people were unable to access antiretroviral drugs and other treatment for HIV infection.

Death penalty

Prisoners remained under sentence of death in Burundi, Cameroon, DRC, Guinea, Liberia, Nigeria, Somaliland, Tanzania, Uganda and Zambia.

In Uganda, the High Court in Kakamega freed four people who had been on death row since 1995 after a successful appeal against their death sentences. In a landmark judgment, the Constitutional Court of Uganda ruled in favour of ending laws that stipulate a mandatory death sentence. The Attorney General appealed against the ruling.

In the DRC, argument over abolition of the death penalty resurfaced during parliamentary debates on the new Constitution. An early draft of the Constitution proposed abolition, but a majority in the Senate and National Assembly rejected the change.

Human rights defenders

Across the region, governments remained hostile to human rights defenders, and many faced harassment, arbitrary arrest and detention, and assault.

In the DRC, Pascal Kabungulu, Executive Secretary of the human rights organization Heirs of Justice, was shot dead by three armed men in July at his home in Bukavu, South-Kivu. An official commission of inquiry failed to report its findings, and no perpetrators had been brought to justice by the end of 2005. In Zimbabwe, numerous NGOs and individual human rights defenders were harassed and intimidated by the state. In Rwanda, several members of civil society, including staff of human rights organizations, were forced to flee the country for fear of being persecuted or arbitrarily arrested. Some previously outspoken human rights activists were intimidated into silence.

In Sudan, the government launched legal proceedings against one of the leading human rights groups in the country, the Sudan Organisation Against Torture, in an apparent attempt to silence it. Its members faced more than five years' imprisonment. Prominent human rights activist Mudawi Ibrahim was arbitrarily arrested and detained without charge, including when he was trying to leave Sudan to receive an award in Ireland for human rights activism. He was later released.

In Somalia, Abdulqadir Yahya Ali, director of the Centre for Research and Dialogue, was assassinated in Mogadishu in July by unidentified assailants.

In Togo, a group of young people associated with the ruling party prevented the Togolese Human Rights League from holding a press conference. In Angola, Luís Araújo, coordinator of SOS-Habitat, a housing NGO, was briefly detained in June and November because of his activities to prevent forced evictions. The authorities in Cameroon continued to use criminal libel laws to imprison journalists in cases that appeared to be politically motivated.

In Equatorial Guinea, lawyer and human rights defender Fabián Nsué Nguema, a former prisoner of conscience, was accused of misconduct and arbitrarily suspended from the Bar Association for a year.

Many prisoners of conscience in Eritrea remained in indefinite and incommunicado detention, without charge or trial, and some were tortured or ill-treated. A new law in May imposed severe restrictions on NGOs. Human rights defenders and prisoners of conscience were also held in Ethiopia. In Mauritania, however, several NGOs were officially recognized for the first time.

AI regional reports

- Africa: Entry into force of Protocol on the Rights of Women in Africa positive step towards ending discrimination (AI Index: AFR 01/004/2005)
- African Commission on Human and Peoples' Rights: Oral statement on Item 6 – Human rights situation in Africa; Ending Impunity in Sudan (AI Index: IOR 10/001/2005)
- African Commission on Human and Peoples' Rights: Oral statement on Item 9 – Human rights situation in Africa; Human rights in Zimbabwe (AI Index: IOR 10/003/2005)
- African Commission on Human and Peoples' Rights: Oral statement on Item 9 – Human rights situation in Africa; Fight against impunity (AI Index: IOR 10/004/2005)
- African Commission on Human and Peoples' Rights: Oral statement on Item 11 – The Establishment of the African Court on Human and Peoples' Rights (AI Index: IOR 10/005/2005)
- Oral Statement by Amnesty International: Item 8 – The Establishment of the African Court on Human and Peoples' Rights (AI Index: IOR 30/011/2005)

AMERICAS

The denial of human rights continued to be a daily reality for many people in the Americas, particularly those in the most vulnerable sectors of society such as indigenous communities, women and children. However, civil society, including the human rights movement, continued to gain strength and influence in their demands for better living conditions, government transparency and accountability, and respect for human rights.

The lives of the majority of people were blighted by discrimination and poverty, both of which led to social unrest and political instability in a number of countries. Indigenous movements, representing some of the poorest and most marginalized people in the Americas, stepped up their challenge to traditional political structures, particularly in the Andean region.

Police abuse, torture and ill-treatment of detainees remained widespread. "Disappearances" continued to be reported in the context of Colombia's internal conflict. Violence against women was endemic throughout the region and the murders of hundreds of women in El Salvador, Guatemala and Mexico, as well as the apparent indifference of the authorities, caused widespread outrage. The conflict in Colombia and high levels of organized crime throughout the region, continued to adversely affect the rights of vast numbers of people.

US policies pursued in the name of security undermined human rights both within the USA and in many countries around the world.

Natural disasters, including a series of devastating hurricanes, affected countries in the Caribbean and Central America and the southern states of the USA, exacerbating already serious levels of poverty and marginalization. In many cases, such as in New Orleans and other communities in Louisiana State in the USA, the authorities did not provide adequate protection and aid provision was slow and insufficient.

National security and the 'war on terror'

Hypocrisy and a disregard for basic human rights principles and international legal obligations continued to mark the USA's "war on terror".

Thousands of detainees remained held without charge in US custody in Iraq, Afghanistan, Guantánamo Bay in Cuba, and in secret detention centres known as "black sites" believed to exist in Europe, North Africa and elsewhere. Torture and other ill-treatment continued to be reported and further evidence emerged that the US authorities "outsourced" torture by means including "rendition" — the transfer of individuals to another country without any form of judicial or administrative process, sometimes in secret.

Around 500 detainees remained in Guantánamo Bay, where they were held in conditions amounting to cruel, inhuman or degrading treatment and continued to be denied their right to challenge the lawfulness of their detention.

Despite mounting evidence that the US government had sanctioned "disappearances" as well as interrogation techniques constituting torture or other ill-treatment, there was a failure to hold officials at the highest levels accountable, including individuals who may have been responsible for war crimes and crimes against humanity.

US "war on terror" policies that undermined human rights standards were challenged during 2005. Legislation was passed prohibiting the torture and inhumane treatment of detainees anywhere in the world, despite initial objections from the Bush administration that the prohibition would hamper its ability to obtain information from detainees. However, the bill also severely limited the Guantánamo detainees' access to federal courts and called into question the future of some 200 pending cases in which detainees had challenged the legality of their detention.

The USA increased its military assistance programme in Colombia despite continued evidence of grave human rights violations by military personnel and paramilitary groups operating with their active or tacit support.

Conflict and crime

The rule of law in several countries was threatened by abusive government policies, corruption, discrimination and inequality that sparked social protest by marginalized communities, particularly in the Andean countries. Indigenous movements were again at the forefront of many of the extended protests and were increasingly vocal in demanding their rights and participation in political life. The governments in Ecuador and Bolivia were forced to resign as a result of mass discontent.

In Colombia, the rule of law was threatened by government policies in the context of the long-running conflict. All parties to the conflict continued to commit widespread human rights abuses principally against the civilian population.

Human rights and the rule of law were also under threat through high levels of violence in several countries, especially in urban areas. In some Brazilian, Central American and Caribbean cities, entire neighbourhoods were trapped between criminal, often gang-related, violence and the repressive response of the state security forces whose methods violated the rights of entire communities. Although most public attention was devoted to crime against the wealthy, it was the lives of the urban poor which, deprived of state protection, were most dominated by violence.

The trend towards militarization of law enforcement continued. In Central America the role of the armed forces was increasingly directed towards maintaining public order and combating crime.

In Haiti, illegal armed groups and police officers were implicated in the killing and kidnapping of civilians.

The proliferation of small arms remained a concern, despite attempts by some governments to restrict them. In a referendum in Brazil, 64 per cent of the electorate voted against a proposal to ban commercial sales of firearms.

Impunity and justice

Members of the security forces continued to commit widespread human rights violations with impunity. Across the region torture and other ill-treatment, sometimes resulting in deaths in custody, were reported but few of the perpetrators were punished. Victims, their relatives or those representing them when they filed complaints, as well as witnesses, members of the judiciary and investigators, were frequently intimidated, harassed, threatened with death and sometimes killed.

Many prisons were severely overcrowded and lacking in basic services. Often, the conditions amounted to cruel, inhuman and degrading treatment. This caused several riots across the region resulting in scores of deaths, mostly of young, poor men. Inefficient, corrupt and discriminatory judicial systems meant that detainees who came from poor and marginalized communities could languish for months and even years in prison without being tried and sentenced, and frequently without access to defence lawyers.

Excessive use of force by the security forces to curb crime and civil unrest were reported in Brazil, Colombia, Ecuador, Jamaica, Paraguay and elsewhere in the region. In some cases, people were killed as a result.

The lack of independence and impartiality of judicial systems in the region – because of corruption or political bias, or because of corporate interests within police and military courts – remained a serious concern and fed the cycle of impunity for human rights violations.

There was significant progress in addressing the unresolved legacy of past human rights violations in some Latin American countries. Former Chilean leader Augusto Pinochet was placed under house arrest on charges related to human rights violations. Having been stripped of his legal immunity and declared "mentally competent" to stand trial, victims and their relatives were hopeful that their quest for justice for over 30 years might be fulfilled.

Victims and relatives of more recent grave human rights violations saw their right to justice move closer to realization when the former Peruvian President, Alberto Fujimori, was arrested in Chile pending an extradition request on charges of murder, forced disappearance and torture.

The Argentine Supreme Court of Justice declared the Full Stop and Due Obedience laws null and void, opening the way towards truth and justice for thousands of victims of human rights violations committed in Argentina between 1976 and 1983.

Adolfo Scilingo, an Argentine former naval officer who had admitted to being aboard planes carrying detainees who were drugged, stripped naked and thrown into the sea during the military governments in Argentina, was tried and sentenced in Spain on charges of crimes against humanity. In another case, a ruling by Spain's Constitutional Court opened the way for former Guatemalan President Rios Montt and other former military officials to be tried for human rights violations.

However, there were also significant setbacks. In Colombia, the Justice and Peace Law threatened to guarantee impunity for members of illegal armed groups implicated in human rights abuses, including war crimes and crimes against humanity, who agreed to demobilize. In Haiti, scores of former military and paramilitary officials serving sentences for their involvement in past massacres escaped prison and some were granted unconditional release for no apparent lawful reason. Despite five years in office, the Special Prosecutor assigned to bring to justice those responsible for widespread human rights violations in Mexico in the 1960s, 1970s and 1980s achieved virtually no progress.

Gender-based violence

Violence against women continued to be one of the most pressing human rights challenges in the Americas. Countless women and girls faced violence on a daily basis and could not count on their government to provide them with the basic level of protection and security that is their fundamental right.

Governments across the region continued to ignore provisions enshrined in women's human rights treaties. Although most countries in the region had laws to prevent and protect women from violence in the home and community, police investigations into allegations of violence against women were rarely effective, criminal justice systems frequently failed to take violence against women seriously and perpetrators were rarely punished.

The number of women and girls murdered in Ciudad Juárez, Mexico, continued to rise and there was insufficient progress to end impunity for past abductions and murders both in this city and in the city of Chihuahua. The number of women killed in Guatemala rose to up to 665 compared to 527 in 2004, and the increase of sexual abuse and murders of women in El Salvador that began in 2002 continued. Little progress was made in investigating these killings and preventing future ones.

The lack of specific definitions in law to criminalize violence against women continued to be an obstacle to obtaining justice in a region where gender-based discrimination remained endemic in state institutions. However, some progress was made. In Mexico, the Supreme Court ruled that rape within marriage is a crime, ending a 15-year legal battle during which members of the judicial system argued that since the purpose of marriage was procreation, forced sexual relations by a spouse was not rape but "an undue exercise of a [conjugal] right". In Guatemala, the Constitutional Court suspended a law that allowed rapists, in certain circumstances, to escape prosecution if they married their victim.

Lesbian, gay, bisexual and transgender (LGBT) people continued to suffer discrimination and violence. In the USA a study carried out by AI indicated a heightened pattern of misconduct and abuse by police of transgender individuals and of all LGBT people of colour or who are young, immigrants, homeless or sex workers. In Nicaragua, gay and lesbian relationships continued to be criminalized and a number of sodomy laws were still in force in Caribbean countries.

Economic, social and cultural rights

According to UN studies, there were signs of a slight reduction in poverty levels in some countries in the region. However, these figures masked pockets of decline in some places, including Haiti, and in some rural areas in Guatemala, Peru and elsewhere. Income and social inequalities remained among the highest in the world, undermining the potential for overall development. Marginalized and dispossessed communities in rural and urban settings in many countries continued to live in extreme poverty with their rights to health care, clean water, a livelihood, education and shelter disregarded.

Participation of indigenous peoples in political affairs was not matched with improvements in their enjoyment of economic, social and cultural rights, despite repeated calls by international banks and others to develop help and support for indigenous peoples and afro-descendants and to invest in rural communities. A World Bank study of indigenous peoples in Bolivia, Ecuador, Guatemala, Mexico and Peru found that indigenous peoples were 13 to 30 per cent more likely to be poor than non-indigenous peoples.

The HIV/AIDS epidemic claimed an estimated 24,000 lives in the Caribbean in 2005, making it the leading cause of death among adults aged between 15 and 44. A total of 300,000 people were believed to be living with HIV in the region, including 30,000 people who became infected in 2005. In the other parts of the region, infection rates rose, especially among men. Women sex workers were also badly affected.

The conflicts over resources, such as land and water, and privatization plans were reflected by the number of human rights defenders attacked on account of their efforts to raise legitimate concerns in these areas.

A summit of Americas' governments held in Argentina in November failed to break the deadlock on long-stalled negotiations to establish a Free Trade Area of the Americas (FTAA). Some countries, led by Argentina, Brazil and Venezuela, vigorously opposed the initiative.

However, liberalized trade and investment continued to prevail in the region, through bilateral agreements or sub-regional arrangements. There were protests about the effect of such agreements on entrenching poverty in large sectors of the population and the failure of governments to ensure that human rights safeguards were built into the agreements. Human rights continued to take a back seat to economic interests, increasing the risk that irresponsible trade practices or investment decisions would undermine human rights. Areas of specific concern included labour rights, access to affordable medicines and intellectual property rights.

Death penalty

Death sentences continued to be handed down in several countries, including Belize and Trinidad and Tobago. However, the only executions in the region were in the USA. Mexico abolished the death penalty for all crimes.

In December the USA carried out its 1,000th execution since 1977, when executions resumed after a moratorium. Despite this shameful landmark, the trend towards restricting its application continued. In March, the US Supreme Court banned the execution of child offenders (those aged under 18 at the time of the crime),

©REUTERS/Eliana Aponte

Indigenous children who have fled one of many areas of conflict in Colombia take shelter in a refugee camp in San José del Guaviare, May 2005.

bringing the USA into line with international standards prohibiting such executions. Two people were released from death row on grounds of innocence. However, among the 60 people executed in 2005 were people with mental disabilities, defendants without access to effective legal representation and foreign nationals denied their consular rights.

Human rights defenders

Human rights activists across the Americas campaigned vigorously to hold governments and armed groups to their obligations to respect international and domestic human rights standards.

Women's rights activists struggled to reform antiquated laws on rape and domestic violence and were often threatened or intimidated for trying to support victims of violence and sexual abuse. Indigenous activists in Central America championed their community's rights to defend their livelihoods and the right to be consulted on issues that affect their ancestral lands, such as the extraction of natural resources or the construction of dams. AI feared that some gay, lesbian and transgender activists went underground following mounting homophobia in Jamaica and some other Caribbean countries.

The difficulties and dangers faced by activists in the Americas ranged from intimidation and restrictions on travel, to arbitrary detention and unfounded accusations of terrorism and other violent activities. The authorities often refused to take reports of violations against human rights defenders seriously, suggesting that the reports were fabricated or exaggerated. Activists working locally on rural poverty and development, often in isolated areas, and journalists covering issues such as corruption were killed in Brazil, Colombia, Guatemala and Mexico. In Ecuador, members of an NGO that campaigns to protect indigenous communities and the environment from the adverse effects of oil drilling and fumigation of coca plantations were threatened with death. In Cuba human rights activists, political dissidents and trade unionists continued to be harassed and intimidated and attacks on freedom of expression and association were frequent.

The use of the judicial system to hamper the work of human rights defenders by threatening them with investigation or detention on unfounded criminal charges was a serious problem in Colombia, Cuba, Guatemala, Haiti, Honduras and Mexico. Cases were also reported in the USA.

Government efforts to protect human rights defenders at risk were marred by extended delays by some authorities in implementing requests for precautionary measures to protect named individuals, as recommended by the Inter-American Commission of Human Rights. Some governments only managed to offer protection measures such as bullet-proof vests and were unable to muster sufficient political will to tackle deep hostility towards human rights work within their governments, or to correct legal provisions restricting the right to defend human rights.

ASIA-PACIFIC

With 56 per cent of the world's population, two emergent economic superpowers, a host of armed conflicts, a series of natural disasters and civil society organization ranging from minimal to vibrant, the Asia-Pacific region continued to provide a challenging and dynamic context for the promotion of human rights in 2005. Ongoing conflicts and security concerns persisted, heightening the vulnerability of populations and providing the context for many grave abuses.

Welcome moves in 2005 towards a greater acceptance of international human rights standards included the ratification by Afghanistan of the UN Refugee Convention, the ratification by India of the Optional Protocol to the Convention on the Rights of the Child on the involvement of children in armed conflict, and the ratification by the Indonesian parliament of the International Covenant on Civil and Political Rights and the International Covenant on Economic, Social and Cultural Rights.

National human rights institutions continued to operate in several countries, including Afghanistan, India, Indonesia, Malaysia, Mongolia, Nepal, Sri Lanka and Thailand, although not in Bangladesh, China and Viet Nam. In Pakistan, a draft bill to establish a national human rights commission was presented to parliament. There were also positive moves towards cooperation between national human rights bodies, including those in Indonesia, Malaysia, the Philippines and Thailand.

2005 saw moves towards a thawing of relations between states historically hostile to each other. There were talks and cross-border transport between India and Pakistan, and six-party discussions on North Korea progressed with an accord in which North Korea pledged to abandon its nuclear programme in return for assurances on aid and security.

Politicized religious movements impacted on the everyday reality of human rights, especially in south Asia. There were constraints on women's movement and dress as well as impediments to the ability of minority groups to practise their beliefs and live peacefully.

Asia moved centre stage in international trade and business affairs with the Global Compact and the World Trade Organization's meetings held in China and Hong Kong. India and China continued to show fast rates of economic growth. However, national indicators suggested that millions of people were living in poverty — from more than a quarter of the population in Cambodia, India, Indonesia, Laos, Mongolia, Nepal, Pakistan, Papua New Guinea and the Philippines, to around half the population in Bangladesh and Viet Nam.

Although the Internet was widely taken up, in parts of Asia it was not the tool of freedom of expression it had promised to be. In China, access continued to be heavily monitored by the state, with many websites blocked and users prosecuted for posting political opinions or information embarrassing to the government. In Viet Nam, the sharing of opinions and information on the web resulted in prosecutions for "espionage".

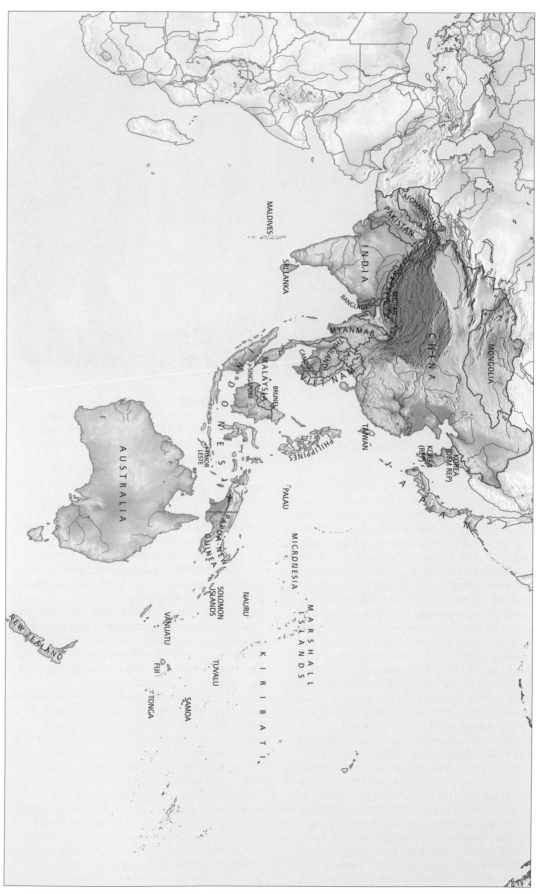

©REUTERS/Bobby Yip

People in Hong Kong protesting against the death penalty in China, July 2005.

Security concerns

Attacks against civilians by armed groups affected many parts of the region, including Afghanistan, Bangladesh, India, Indonesia, Nepal and Sri Lanka. Bombings caused carnage and robbed hundreds of people of their lives.

Some state responses to such attacks were disproportionate and at times discriminated against marginal or minority groups, reinforcing pre-existing grievances or persecution. Arbitrary arrests in the name of combating terrorism were reportedly made in Afghanistan, including by US and Coalition forces, and in Pakistan by the security forces. In China, people charged with terrorism and "state secrets" offences were tried in secret. In India, the Unlawful Activities (Prevention) Act continued to provide the state with many of the powers that had been heavily criticized in annulled counter-terrorism legislation. In Australia, detention without trial and renewable control orders were introduced through counter-terrorism legislation. New national security legislation in South Korea continued to be used against those engaged in peaceful political activities. In Malaysia, alleged Islamists had two-year detention orders renewed despite the National Human Rights Commission urging the trial or release of all Internal Security Act detainees.

The role of the USA in its "war on terror" continued in the region during 2005. Air attacks by US forces killed at least 15 civilians in Pakistan and dozens in Afghanistan. Abuses reportedly continued in US bases in Afghanistan and prompted popular unrest, during which people were killed. Men returning to Afghanistan from US custody in Guantánamo Bay, Cuba, brought home gruelling accounts of torture and ill-treatment which further fuelled local anger, anxiety and unrest.

Troubled states

In a number of states in the region, the national framework through which protection against and redress for human rights abuses could be sought was weak and ineffective.

The Afghan state continued to fail to deliver safety, security and the rule of law to its people. Warlords believed to have been responsible for human rights abuses wielded power and instilled a climate of fear in parts of the country. Fundamental flaws in the criminal justice system, the legacy of decades of conflict, and deeply embedded discrimination against women profoundly militated against the promotion of human rights and justice for past and continuing violations, particularly for women and girls.

In Nepal, the King cited the need to counter violence by Maoist groups to declare a state of emergency in February, dismiss the government and suspend civil liberties. Mass detentions followed and there was a further breakdown in security for much of the population.

In Timor-Leste, the very newness of the institutional structures meant there was a shortage of judges, prosecutors and defence lawyers. This seriously impacted on the right to a fair trial and other aspects of the criminal justice system.

Elsewhere in the region, governments in countries including Myanmar, North Korea and Viet Nam appeared to be largely impervious to pressure to uphold human rights. The authorities in Myanmar, for example, continued to violate human rights through widespread and long-term political imprisonments, forced labour, land confiscations and displacement of minorities, thereby showing utter disregard for the population and the international community.

Armed conflicts

Armed conflicts persisted in several places, including Afghanistan, parts of India, Nepal, the Philippines, Sri Lanka and southern Thailand.

Two areas of armed conflict that were affected by the December 2004 tsunami saw very different developments in the following 12 months. Indonesia underwent a process of negotiation leading to a peace agreement in Nanggroe Aceh Darussalam in August. By contrast, Sri Lanka witnessed increased violence, including the assassination of the Foreign Minister in August, growing insecurity in the east, and a marked deterioration of the situation in the north in December, shortly after the election of a new President. At the end of 2005 there was deep concern about the escalation of violence in Sri Lanka and the viability of the ceasefire agreement.

The conflict in southern Thailand continued to deteriorate in 2005 with a considerable heightening of the climate of fear and constraint. Both sides to the conflict were implicated in human rights abuses and violence. In the Philippines a ceasefire between the government and secessionist forces in Mindanao, although fragile, largely held throughout 2005.

Discrimination

States continued to fail in their duty to protect the human rights of all, both by maintaining discriminatory laws and by failing to ensure that those who suffer discrimination have adequate redress.

Ethnicity, gender, socio-economic factors and sexual identities continued to provide the backdrop for discrimination across the region. Among those targeted were *dalits* ("low caste" people) and *adivasis* (indigenous people) in India; Ahmadis in Bangladesh, Pakistan and Indonesia; Montagnards and Buddhists in Viet Nam; indigenous peoples in Australia; Karen, Mon, Rohingyas and Shan in Myanmar; Uighurs in China; and lesbian, gay, bisexual and transgender people across the region. Among the abuses such targeted groups suffered were forced labour, displacement, persecution, and restrictions on freedom of expression and the right to practise their religion.

On a positive note, a landmark ruling by a Fiji court recognized that provisions in the Penal Code used against consensual homosexual activity violated constitutional guarantees on privacy and equality.

Violence against women

Women and girls continued to suffer a vast array of forms of violence, including domestic violence, forced abortions and sterilizations, forced marriages, killings and crimes of "honour". Such abuses were systematic and carried out on a massive scale.

Violence against women continued to be closely interrelated with cultural attitudes and practices of gender discrimination, such as wanting babies to be boys, the belief that women should not leave the home and the view that women should not take decisions relating to marriage.

Gender discrimination constrained life and employment choices, thus making women and girls particularly vulnerable to trafficking – a third of all global human trafficking was estimated to originate from or be located in Asia. Many countries in the region continued to view trafficked women as illegal immigrants and failed to prosecute the traffickers.

Justice and safety often escaped women facing violence because of inadequate or non-existent state mechanisms, or because penalties for perpetrators were inconsistent or did not reflect the seriousness of the violence. As a result, many of those who perpetrated violence against women enjoyed impunity.

The need for changes in attitudes as well as legal reform meant that progress in challenging the violence was patchy and slow. Some notable efforts included the establishment of an inter-ministerial council aimed at combating violence against women in Afghanistan; the adoption or proposal of laws to protect women from domestic violence in Cambodia, Fiji and India; the introduction of legislation against sexual harassment in China; the draft before parliament of anti-trafficking legislation in Indonesia; and the establishment of the first purpose-built shelter for victims of family violence in the Solomon Islands.

The plight of the so-called "comfort women" demonstrated the low priority of delivering redress to women victims of violence. Having been victims of military systems of sexual slavery more than 50 years ago, these women continued to campaign for reparations through the courts in Japan and elsewhere, but at the end of 2005 were still waiting for justice.

Migrants and refugees

Asia continued to see significant migration flows within and beyond the region. Migrant workers and their families faced uncertainty, vulnerability and poor treatment in many countries, including Japan, Malaysia, South Korea and Taiwan. Few states in the region, particularly receiving states, had ratified the International Convention on the Protection of the Rights of All Migrant Workers and Members of Their Families.

Refugees and asylum-seekers faced marginalization, harassment and arbitrary arrest. Laws and practice in several states allowed ill-treatment of refugees, including caning of migrants and asylum-seekers in Malaysia and arbitrary detention of asylum-seekers and refugees in detention centres in Australia.

The conflicts in Sri Lanka and Nepal generated significant numbers of internally displaced people. In Nepal, an estimated 200,000 displaced people suffered a severe lack of services, including housing, health and education. In Sri Lanka, hundreds of thousands of people displaced by the conflict and the tsunami were particularly vulnerable to conflict-related violence.

Natural disasters

The region suffered devastating natural disasters in 2005, and the extent of the impact of the 2004 tsunami became clear during the year. In Indonesia, it emerged that over 700,000 people had died, were still missing or had been displaced as a result of the tsunami. In Thailand, at least 100,000 people had been affected. In Sri Lanka, 35,322 people died and 516,150 were displaced. In India, an estimated 15,000 people died and more than 112,000 were displaced.

A powerful earthquake that struck the Pakistan/India border region in October 2005 left an estimated 73,000 dead in Pakistan and at least 1,200 dead in India's Jammu and Kashmir state. Between 2 and 3 million people were made homeless. Further deaths and widespread suffering were witnessed in the severe weather conditions in the following Himalayan winter. Concerns about relief efforts after the tsunami and the earthquake centred on ongoing conflict, access to remote areas and allegations of discrimination.

Economic, social and cultural rights
India and China enjoyed considerable international attention and support for their economic growth and status as emerging players in the global economic scene. While claims of a decrease in the number of those in "absolute poverty" were contested, any parallel improvement in human rights was not manifest. Economic development did not prioritize realization of economic, social and cultural rights. In China, rural migrant labour continued to suffer dire conditions, and hundreds of thousands of peasant farmers were increasingly marginalized through land expropriation, lack of health care and the failure of the state to provide education for millions of children in rural areas. Rural-urban disparities and the growing gap between rich and poor fuelled social unrest in the countryside. In India, legislation was introduced in 2005 to guarantee minimum annual employment for the poor in selected areas.

Across the region, conflict and environmental degradation still adversely affected many communities. In Afghanistan, up to a third of the population could not rely on safe or reliable sources of food, drinkable water or shelter. In India, thousands of people were still awaiting remedies for the 1984 Bhopal disaster.

Death penalty
The Asia-Pacific region continued to have a poor profile with regard to the death penalty, although a notable minority of countries were abolitionist. The death penalty was retained in 26 countries, including Afghanistan, China, India, Japan, Pakistan, Singapore, Thailand and Viet Nam. Capital offences included tax fraud, murder, drugs smuggling, robbery and kidnapping.

In South Korea an unofficial moratorium remained in place. A death penalty abolition bill introduced in 2004 by a member of parliament and former death row inmate passed its first parliamentary hurdle, with bipartisan support, in February 2005.

China and Mongolia still refused to make death penalty statistics public and official statistics from some other countries were considered unreliable. Even so, official statistics remained high. They included at least 1,770 executions and 3,900 death sentences in China, at least 31 executions and 241 death sentences in Pakistan, at least 21 executions and 65 death sentences in Viet Nam, and at least 24 death sentences in Afghanistan.

Practices that aggravated the suffering of those awaiting execution included the sudden announcement of executions in Japan, so that those about to be killed did not have the chance to meet their families and other loved ones. In Pakistan, the unreliability of documentation relating to registration of births led to a lack of confidence that all those facing execution were adults and that a 2001 commutation order for juveniles on death row was applied to all child offenders sentenced to death.

Key abolitionist voices in the region included the President and Chief Justice to the Supreme Court in India, the Foreign Minister in Sri Lanka and the Home Minister in Japan. However, no country in the Asia-Pacific region abolished the death penalty in 2005.

Human rights defenders
Human rights activists, particularly those defending the rights of women, came under increasing attack by private individuals and groups as well as by agents of the state. Human rights defenders across the region faced threats, harassment, and arrest and assault for their work. China detained many human rights defenders, including journalists and lawyers, and some were sentenced to prison terms. Activists were also arrested during political crackdowns in Cambodia and Nepal, and human rights defenders suffered death threats in Afghanistan and Bangladesh.

Impunity for crimes against human rights defenders remained a problem, even in the most high-profile cases. In Thailand, for instance, despite pressure from the Prime Minister to resolve the "disappearance" of human rights lawyer Somchai Neelapaijit in March 2004, none of the suspects had been brought to justice by the end of 2005.

Despite the tremendous pressures facing human rights defenders, the scale of human rights activism across the region was remarkable. Human rights defenders were at the forefront of struggles to advance economic, social and cultural rights, particularly in China, India and the Philippines. Women human rights defenders began forging partnerships, including at the first-ever global gathering of women human rights defenders in Sri Lanka in December 2005. At this meeting, which brought together some 200 activists from around the world, women activists developed a range of strategies to combat the violence, discrimination and other abuses they experience specifically because of their gender and because of their work in defence of human rights.

In some cases, victims of abuse became committed human rights defenders. In Pakistan, for example, Mukhtaran Mai, a survivor of gang-rape, became an activist for the right of all women to live their lives in safety and dignity.

EUROPE/CENTRAL ASIA

Direct attacks on civilians, including in Russia, Spain, Turkey and the UK, led to loss of life and many injuries. Governments continued to attack human rights in the name of security, including through measures that undermined the universal and absolute ban on torture and other ill-treatment.

The legacy of previous conflicts, including impunity for crimes committed during them, persisted. Cyprus continued to be a divided island and no significant progress was made in resolving the status of the region's internationally unrecognized entities, situated within the borders of Azerbaijan, Georgia and Moldova but remaining outside of those states' de facto control. However, steps were taken to open talks on the final status of Kosovo.

Many countries in the region were a magnet for those attempting to escape poverty, violence or persecution. The fact that asylum is principally a human rights issue continued to be all but lost in the face of political pressure to control "illegal immigration" or to prioritize "security concerns". In breach of their international obligations, some states unlawfully detained asylum-seekers and conducted expulsions without due process, including to countries where those seeking protection were at further risk of violations. Asylum-seekers, migrants and minorities remained among those continuing to face racism and discrimination across the region.

While the process of accession to the European Union (EU) continued to encourage human rights progress in some states, institutionally the EU continued to have a minimalist concept of its domestic human rights role. Adoption of the EU's constitutional treaty, incorporating its Charter of Fundamental Rights, stalled after rejection by voters in two member states. The EU's proposed new Agency for Fundamental Rights, while potentially a significant step forward in overcoming EU complacency towards observance and fulfilment of human rights within its own borders, showed a limited and ad hoc approach to human rights policy — with abuses by member states largely excluded from its remit.

Security and human rights

Security continued to eclipse observance of fundamental human rights, to the detriment of both issues. In the UK, new measures purportedly to counter terrorism were enacted even though the country had some of the toughest anti-terrorism laws in the region. The enactment of other measures, including provisions that would undermine the rights to freedom of expression, association, liberty and fair trial, was pending at the end of the year. People previously held without charge or trial, labelled "terrorist suspects" on the basis of secret intelligence they were not allowed to know and therefore could not refute, were placed under restrictive "control orders" after their detention had, in 2004, been ruled incompatible with their human rights. Most of them were subsequently reimprisoned under immigration powers pending deportation on national security grounds: many of the men and their families suffered serious deterioration in their mental and physical health as a result of their ordeals.

The UK government also continued to undermine the universal and absolute ban on torture by trying to deport people they deemed to be terror suspects to

Uzbekistani refugees in Kara Darya, Kyrgyzstan, after fleeing violence and killings in Andizhan, Uzbekistan, May 2005.

©EMPICS/AP/Mikhail Metzel

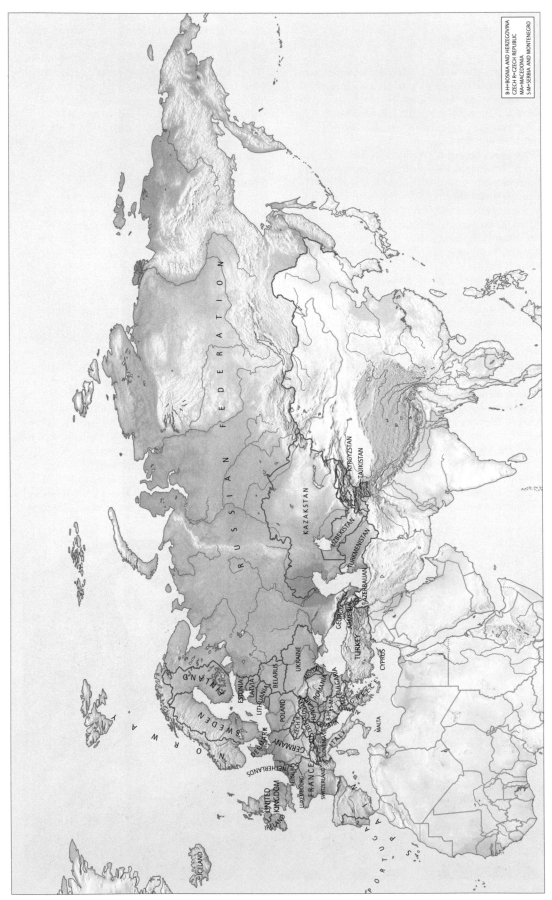

B-H=BOSNIA AND HERZEGOVINA
CZECH R=CZECH REPUBLIC
MA=MACEDONIA
S-M=SERBIA AND MONTENEGRO

countries with a history of torture or other ill-treatment. The authorities sought to rely on inherently unreliable and ineffective "diplomatic assurances" featured in Memorandums of Understanding agreed with states with a well-documented record of torture. In December the highest court in the UK delivered a landmark judgment upholding the absolute inadmissibility as evidence in legal proceedings of information extracted under torture. However, earlier in the year a German court ruled that evidence possibly obtained under torture or other ill-treatment was admissible in legal proceedings. In France, a draft anti-terrorism law would allow longer periods of incommunicado detention and so would remove safeguards against torture and other ill-treatment.

Disclosures at the end of the year suggested the involvement of a number of European states in illegal and secret transfers ("renditions") by the USA of individuals to countries where torture was rife, or to US custody in military bases and secret locations around the world. Both the Council of Europe and the European Parliament launched inquiries into allegations of secret US Central Intelligence Agency (CIA) detention centres in Europe and of CIA-chartered aeroplanes making flights in or out of European airspace said to have been used in abductions and unlawful transfers of prisoners.

In Uzbekistan, the authorities responded brutally when a group of armed men seized various buildings in the city of Andizhan in May. Witnesses reported that hundreds of people were killed when security forces fired recklessly and without warning on a mostly unarmed and peaceful crowd of demonstrators that included children.

In a disturbing development in Turkey, against a background of increasing violence between the security services and the armed opposition Kurdistan Workers' Party (PKK), there were reports of direct official involvement in the November bombing of a bookshop in the Şemdinli district of Hakkâri in which one man was killed.

Refugees, asylum-seekers and migrants
There was a consistent pattern of human rights violations linked to the interception, detention and expulsion by states of foreign nationals, including those seeking international protection. At least 13 people were killed when trying to enter the Spanish enclaves of Ceuta and Melilla from Morocco, allegedly as a result of Spanish and Moroccan law enforcement officers using disproportionate and lethal force to prevent them entering the enclaves.

Men, women and children continued to face obstacles in accessing asylum procedures. In Greece, Italy, Spain and the UK, some were unlawfully detained and others were denied necessary guidance and legal support. Many were unlawfully expelled before their claims could be heard, including from Cyprus, Greece, Italy, Kazakstan, Malta, Russia and Spain. Some were sent to countries where they were at risk of human rights violations. The fact that EU member states were among those doing this illustrated the EU's failure to

acknowledge that it faced a crisis of protection, rather than of asylum. Elsewhere, intense international pressure was placed on Kyrgyzstan to honour its obligation to offer protection to those fleeing the Andizhan events in Uzbekistan.

Racism and discrimination
Continuing racism, discrimination and intolerance were often identity-based. In many countries in the region, Jews and Muslims were among those targeted by individuals and organizations for hate crimes.

In Russia, there were hundreds of racially motivated physical assaults; at least 28 of them resulted in deaths. In France, migrants and French nationals of North African and sub-Saharan extraction, apparently enraged by discriminatory practices in employment and other areas, and the often racist and aggressive conduct of the police, began rioting in cities and towns across the country in October after the deaths of two boys in disputed circumstances. A state of emergency was declared.

Across the region Roma remained severely disadvantaged in key areas of public and private life such as housing, employment, education and health services. They were also frequently the targets of racism by law enforcement officials.

In some countries of the former Yugoslavia, discrimination on ethnic grounds in areas such as employment and housing continued to block a durable and dignified return for many people displaced by the conflict.

Others faced discrimination around issues of their legal status. Meskhetians in the Krasnodar Territory in Russia continued to be refused recognition of their citizenship on ethnic grounds, and so were unable to access a wide range of basic rights. In Greece, the authorities still refused to reissue citizenship documents to members of the Muslim population in western Thrace, with those affected thereby denied access to state benefits and institutions. In Slovenia, thousands of people unlawfully "erased" in 1992 from the registry of permanent residents, mainly people from other Yugoslav republics (many of them Roma), were still waiting for their status to be resolved. As a result of the "erasure" many were denied full access to their economic and social rights.

A climate of intolerance against the lesbian, gay, bisexual and transgender (LGBT) communities in Latvia, Poland and Romania saw local authorities actively obstructing public events organized by LGBT groups amid openly homophobic language used by some highly placed politicians. However, in Spain and the UK new laws recognized partnerships for same sex couples.

Violence against women
Domestic violence against women and girls remained widespread across the region, affecting all ages and social groups. Positive attempts to tackle it included provisions in the new Turkish Penal Code offering greater protection for women against violence in the family, and special courts established for women victims

of domestic violence in Spain. However, the law in Spain – as in other places – continued to leave the onus on the victim, not the state, to lodge a formal complaint or take the initiative in organizing protection.

Other gaps in legal protection included no specific criminalization of domestic violence in countries such as Albania and Russia. Too often, initiatives such as the opening of a shelter, the establishment of a helpline or provision of other services happened through the efforts of individuals and NGOs struggling with inadequate funding. Moscow, the capital of Russia and a city of 10 million people, remained without a single shelter for women who were victims of violence.

Poverty, lack of education, family breakdown and crime networks contributed to the continuing problem of trafficking of human beings, including of women and girls for enforced prostitution. Protection for the survivors and prosecution of the perpetrators were hindered by issues such as a failure to provide trafficked people with an automatic right to protection and assistance; the lack, or inadequate implementation of, witness protection law; failure to criminalize internal trafficking; and threats and fears of reprisals. One potentially positive step was the opening for signature in May of the Council of Europe's Convention on Action against Trafficking in Human Beings.

Abuses by officials and impunity

Torture and ill-treatment, often race-related, were reported across the region. Victims described a catalogue of abuses, including being beaten, stripped naked and threatened with death; deprivation of food, water and sleep; having plastic bags placed over their heads; and threats against their family. In some cases, detainees reportedly died as a result of such abuse or excessive use of force, including in Bulgaria, Russia and Spain.

Although there were some positive developments, including moves by new administrations in Georgia and Ukraine to tackle torture and ill-treatment, there were still obstacles in these and other countries that prevented the eradication of such abuses. The obstacles included police cover-ups, victims' fear of repercussions, lack of prompt access to a lawyer, and the lack of an effective, properly resourced and independent system to investigate complaints. Failure to conduct prompt, thorough and impartial investigations led to an overwhelming climate of impunity in Turkey, Uzbekistan and elsewhere in the region. In Russia, impunity remained the norm for serious human rights abuses in the context of the Chechen conflict.

In many countries, conditions in prisons, as well as in detention centres for asylum-seekers and irregular migrants, were inhuman and degrading.

Intense international pressure on some countries in the western Balkans produced improved cooperation with the International Criminal Tribunal for the former Yugoslavia early in the year, with the capture or apparently voluntary surrender of a number of suspects accused of crimes, including war crimes and crimes against humanity. Among those held was former Croatian Army General Ante Gotovina, although other suspects continued to evade arrest. Lack of full cooperation with the Tribunal together with insufficient efforts by domestic courts remained an obstacle to justice.

Death penalty

There was further progress towards total abolition of the death penalty in the region. Legal amendments in Moldova removed the last provisions for the death penalty from the Constitution. Similar draft constitutional amendments were proposed in Kyrgyzstan.

Uzbekistan announced that capital punishment would be abolished from 2008, but this was little comfort for all those affected by the death penalty. Dozens of people were believed to have been sentenced to death and executed during 2005 in a criminal justice system flawed throughout by corruption and which consistently failed to investigate allegations of torture. Relatives, tormented by uncertainty, were not told in advance the date of executions and were denied the bodies of their executed relatives and knowledge of where they were buried. Uzbekistan also flouted its international legal obligations by executing at least one person whose case was under consideration by the UN Human Rights Committee, at one point even assuring the Committee that the man remained alive when the death certificate indicated that he had been executed three weeks earlier. Belarus and Uzbekistan remained the region's last executioners.

Repression of dissent

Civil, political and religious dissent remained systematically and often brutally repressed in Belarus, Turkmenistan and Uzbekistan. In Uzbekistan, official attempts to block alternative reports of the many deaths in Andizhan involved widespread intimidation, beatings and detentions, including of witnesses, demonstrators, journalists and human rights defenders. In Belarus, opposition activists were imprisoned on false criminal charges. In Turkmenistan, political dissidents and members of religious minority groups were among those harassed, arbitrarily detained and tortured.

In Russia, the climate of hostility towards human rights defenders intensified and some individuals were prosecuted for exercising their right to freedom of expression. A new law affecting NGOs, requiring stricter registration rules and increased state scrutiny, threatened to further compromise the independence of civil society.

In Serbia, increasing attacks by non-state actors on human rights defenders, with the tacit support of the state, were reminiscent of the period under former President Slobodan Milošević. In Turkey a wide range of critical opinions remained open to criminalization, with writers, publishers, human rights defenders and academics among those prosecuted under a law which penalized "denigration" of Turkishness, the state and its institutions.

In spite of threats, intimidation and detention, however, human rights defenders across the region remained resolute in continuing their work, inspiring others to join them in aiming for lasting change and respect for the human rights of all.

AI regional reports

- Europe and Central Asia: Summary of Amnesty International's Concerns in the Region: January-June 2005 (AI Index: EUR 01/012/2005)
- Council of Europe: Recommendations to Strengthen the December 2004 Draft European Convention on Action against Trafficking in Human Beings (AI Index: IOR 61/001/2005)
- Human rights dissolving at the borders? Counter-terrorism and criminal law in the EU (AI Index: IOR 61/013/2005)
- Amnesty International's Statements to the 2005 OSCE Human Dimension Implementation Meeting (AI Index: IOR 30/014/2005)
- Delivering on human rights: Amnesty International's ten-point program for the UK Presidency of the European Union (AI Index: IOR 61/017/2005)
- Reject rather than regulate: Call on Council of Europe member states not to establish minimum standards for the use of diplomatic assurances in transfers to risk of torture and other ill-treatment (AI Index: IOR 61/025/2005)

MIDDLE EAST/NORTH AFRICA

At first sight, the pattern of widespread abuse that has long characterized human rights in the Middle East and North Africa remained firmly entrenched in 2005. Indeed, considering the appalling toll of abuses perpetrated by all parties to the conflict in Iraq, the continuing struggle between Israelis and Palestinians, and some of the views expressed by Iran's new President, the picture could have appeared very bleak.

Despite this and the persistence of grave violations across the region, there were some signs to suggest that 2005 might come to be seen as a time when some of the old certainties began to look less certain and a new dynamic began to take hold. The wall of impunity behind which so many perpetrators of torture, political killings and other abuses had sheltered for so long began to fracture. Former Iraqi President Saddam Hussain was brought to trial on charges relating to executions of villagers in 1982, and an unprecedented UN Security Council-mandated inquiry implicated senior Syrian and Lebanese officials in the 2005 assassination of former Lebanese Prime Minister Rafiq al-Hariri.

In Morocco, the Arab world's first truth commission shed important light on grave human rights abuses committed over a period of more than 40 years and brought acknowledgement and reparation for at least some of the victims, although not yet justice. In Libya, the authorities announced a belated investigation into the killing or "disappearance" of possibly hundreds of prisoners at Tripoli's Abu Selim Prison in 1996.

Women, for so long subject to discrimination in both law and practice, finally won the right to vote in Kuwait and achieved greater recognition of their human rights in countries such as Algeria and Morocco. Even in Saudi Arabia, the exclusion of women from participation in the country's first ever municipal elections sparked debate and growing pressure for change.

Only time will tell whether these were the first signs of real and overdue change or merely instances that bucked the trend. However, the emergence of an increasingly active and outspoken community of human rights activists was a further promising development. Using the Internet and the opportunities provided by the growth and popularity of satellite television, human rights activists were able increasingly to communicate information and share ideas unimpeded by national boundaries both within and beyond the region and to derive new strength and solidarity from the regional and global alliances to which they contributed.

However, 2005 also brought repression and misery to far too many people in the region as their human rights were abused or denied. Some were targeted because of their political views, others because of their religion or ethnicity, yet others for their sexual orientation. Throughout the region women were subject to varying degrees of discrimination and violence because of their gender. Countless others were unable to enjoy fully their economic, social and cultural rights.

Conflict, violence and crimes under international law

The persistence of armed conflict and other forms of political violence was the context for war crimes and crimes against humanity perpetrated by several parties. Thousands of children and adult civilians were killed or injured in the continuing conflict in Iraq, many of them victims of suicide bomb attacks carried out by militant groups that frequently targeted civilians. Other civilians, including Iraqis and foreign nationals, were abducted and held hostage; some were released but others were killed by their captors. Troops of the US-led multinational force and Iraqi government forces also committed widespread abuses, including torture and unlawful killings of civilians, and detained thousands of suspects arbitrarily and without access to due process. In November, the Iraq conflict spilled over to Jordan when suicide bombers apparently linked to Iraq targeted three hotels in the capital, Amman, killing 60 people and wounding many others. In Egypt, bombs that targeted civilians exploded in Cairo in April and Sharm el-Sheik in July; 90 people were killed and at least 100 were injured.

New evidence emerged of human rights violations by governments and intelligence services in the Middle East/North Africa region and those in the USA and other Western countries in their close collaboration in the "war on terror". AI interviewed detainees in Yemen who said that they had been briefly detained and tortured in Jordan and then held for many months in secret detention centres under US control, whose location they never learned, before being flown to Yemen. Yemeni authorities told AI that the detainees were being held at the behest of the US government.

There was increasing information to indicate that individuals suspected of terrorism by the US authorities had been secretly and forcibly transferred to countries, including Egypt, Morocco, Jordan and Syria, for interrogation. Senior US officials continued to proclaim their administration's opposition to torture despite such transfers ("renditions") of suspects to countries whose security services had long records of torturing detainees with impunity. Neither the USA nor any of the countries concerned disclosed the number of those transferred, where they were being held or their identities.

As a further sign of close collaboration, three countries – Lebanon, Libya and Jordan – signed bilateral agreements with the UK under which they agreed to accept individuals whom the UK authorities said were suspected of terrorism and wished forcibly to expel. All three countries, under the terms of these Memorandums of Understanding with the UK, were required to provide specific assurances that anyone returned under the agreement would not be tortured or treated inhumanely, in implicit recognition that these countries had failed to respect the guarantees against torture to which they had previously committed under international law.

Several countries invoked the "war on terror" as a justification for maintaining long-standing emergency powers, as in Egypt, or for introducing new legislation that threatened to violate human rights ostensibly in the interests of protecting national security, as in Bahrain. Scores of prosecutions on terrorism-related charges were mounted in countries that included Algeria, Egypt, Jordan, Morocco and Tunisia. In many cases, defendants appeared before special or ordinary courts whose procedures fell far short of those required by international fair trial standards. Some complained that they had been tortured and ill-treated while held in pre-trial detention and forced to "confess". However, courts rarely ordered investigations or gave credence to such claims.

Impunity, justice and accountability

With few exceptions, perpetrators of human rights abuses continued to benefit from impunity as governments failed to hold them to account and ensure justice for their victims. In many countries in the region, security and intelligence services were given free rein to detain suspects for long periods, often holding them incommunicado and without charge and exposing them to torture and ill-treatment, confident that they did so with official acquiescence and without fear of intervention by the courts. Detainees were frequently tortured in Syria in pre-trial detention. In Egypt, Iran and Tunisia, defendants frequently complained of torture when

they were eventually brought to trial only for courts to dismiss their allegations out of hand without investigation.

The problem was exacerbated by the continued prevalence of exceptional courts, including military courts empowered to try civilians. In Egypt and Syria, such courts were maintained under long-standing states of emergency. Special courts were also used to try and sentence political suspects in Lebanon and Oman. In Libya, the General People's Congress abolished the People's Court, a notoriously unfair special court that had previously sentenced many critics and opponents of the government to long prison terms or death. Despite this, neither in Libya nor in most other countries in the Middle East and North Africa could it be said that there was an independent judiciary, especially in cases having a political or security aspect.

Police and security forces also operated largely behind a shield of impunity when they used excessive force, causing deaths and injuries, whether in Iran and Yemen, where the victims were often members of religious or ethnic minorities; in Egypt and Morocco, where the targets included refugees and migrants; or in the West Bank and Gaza Strip, where Palestinian children were among those killed with impunity by Israeli troops. In Iraq, both US and other foreign forces and those of the Iraqi government used excessive force with impunity.

Killings of civilians by Israeli forces and Palestinian armed groups continued in Israel and the occupied West Bank and Gaza Strip, although on a lesser scale than in recent years. While Israel used a wide range of judicial and extrajudicial means to punish Palestinians individually and collectively for killings of Israelis, Palestinian victims were denied justice and redress. Impunity remained the rule for Israeli forces who unlawfully killed and ill-treated Palestinians. In July Israel passed a new law denying Palestinians the right to claim compensation for death, injury or damage caused by Israeli forces. The Palestinian Authority also failed to take action against Palestinian armed groups responsible for unlawful killings and abductions amid increasing lawlessness.

The issue of impunity for past grave abuses came into sharp focus during the year. In Algeria, the government held a national referendum to win support for its plan to extend an amnesty to those responsible for the thousands of political killings, "disappearances" and widespread torture that were so much a feature of the internal conflict that raged from the early 1990s.

In neighbouring Morocco, however, an Equity and Reconciliation Commission appointed by King Mohamed VI completed its inquiries into "disappearances" and other violations committed between 1956 and 1999, and at the end of the year submitted its final report. Although its statutes categorically excluded the identification of individual perpetrators, the Commission represented a unique initiative within the region, one that appeared likely to clarify a good number of cases of past abuse and ensure both official acknowledgement of, and the payment of

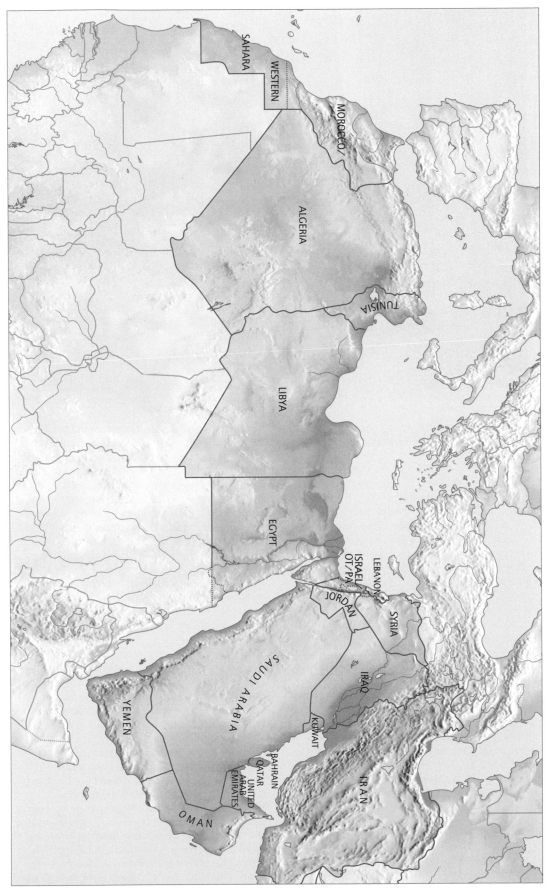

©EMPICS/AP/Hadi Mizban

Iraqi and US soldiers searching the scene after a suicide bomb attack outside Rashad police station in Baghdad, July 2005.

reparation for, some of the suffering to which victims and their relatives had been exposed. The independent Moroccan Human Rights Association, meanwhile, organized its own informal public hearings in which some victims named individuals they held responsible for past violations against them.

In Iraq, justice continued to be denied to countless victims of abuse. However, former President Saddam Hussain was finally called to account for some of the crimes committed when he was in power, crimes whose enormity was reflected following the discovery of mass graves in 2003. Facing charges related to only one of the many incidents of killings for which his government was believed responsible, it remained to be seen whether he would receive a fair trial. The initial conduct of the trial did not inspire confidence. Yet, for a once-powerful leader to have to answer to some of his victims was a breakthrough for a region in which impunity had been well-entrenched for so long.

In neighbouring Syria, senior government figures came under pressure as a UN investigation implicated them and Lebanese political leaders and security officials in the February bomb explosion that killed former Lebanese Prime Minister Rafiq al-Hariri and 22 others in Beirut. However, the killings and "disappearances" of thousands of Syrian and Lebanese nationals in past decades remained almost entirely uninvestigated.

Refugees and migrants

Most countries lacked a legal regime for the protection of refugees and asylum-seekers. Only seven – Algeria, Egypt, Iran, Israel, Morocco, Tunisia and Yemen – were parties to the UN Refugee Convention and its 1967 Protocol. Long-standing refugee communities within the region continued to face discrimination and denial of their human rights by governments in host countries. Palestinian refugees in Lebanon remained barred from working in certain professions, despite some easing of restrictions during the year, and faced other limitations severely affecting their rights to education and adequate housing. Despite the Israeli withdrawal from the Gaza Strip, the situation for Palestinian refugees there and in the occupied West Bank continued to worsen because of land acquisitions, house demolitions, closures and other controls on movement imposed by the Israeli authorities and the increasing lawlessness arising from rivalry between Palestinian armed groups.

In Egypt, a three-month demonstration by Sudanese refugees and migrants seeking improvements in their living conditions, protection from return to Sudan and resettlement in a third country came to a head in December when police used force to disperse the demonstrators. At least 27 people were killed and others were injured.

Europe's restrictive immigration policies contributed to the difficulties faced by several North African countries which refugees and migrants from further south sought to traverse in order to gain entry to Europe's southern borders. The Spanish enclaves of Ceuta and Melilla emerged as particular pressure points. Between August and October, Spanish and Moroccan police used excessive force against people, mostly from West Africa, who sought to enter Spanish territory by climbing the border fences. At least 13 people were killed.

Many others were rounded up by Moroccan police, transported to remote desert areas along the border with Algeria and dumped, left to fend for themselves without adequate water or shelter. Amid wide publicity and condemnation, both governments said they would investigate the killings, but no such investigation was known to have been started by the end of 2005.

Women's rights

Women continued to suffer legal and other forms of discrimination throughout the region, although 2005 saw a quickening process of change. In Kuwait, women for the first time became eligible to vote in the country's national elections. In Morocco, King Mohamed VI announced that citizenship would be granted to all children born of women with foreign spouses and that a discriminatory law severely limiting this right would be reformed. In Algeria too, amendments to the Family Code removed some aspects of discrimination, although not enough to give women equal status with men.

That such changes represented something of a breakthrough said a lot about how much further change is necessary before women truly achieve equal status in the region. Violence against women, including within the family, remained widespread and insufficiently addressed by governments and state authorities. In Iraq, where increasing religious sectarianism emerged as a feature of the political breakdown, women came under greater threat of violence because of how they dressed and behaved.

Economic, social and cultural rights

Many communities faced denial of or were hampered from accessing basic economic, social and cultural rights. Marginalized people were particularly vulnerable, including Bedouins in Israel, Palestinian refugees in Lebanon, members of ethnic and religious minorities in Iran, and migrants, especially women migrant workers in Gulf countries and Lebanon. For Palestinians in the occupied West Bank and Gaza Strip, Israeli policies and controls made life especially harsh. Palestinians were left without shelter by destruction of their homes; without livelihood by the seizure of land and closures; and without access to adequate health care due to road closures and checkpoints. Access to scarce water resources increasingly emerged as a likely flashpoint for the future.

Death penalty

Both Iran and Saudi Arabia continued to carry out executions – at least 94 and 88 respectively in 2005. In both countries the real totals were probably higher. Iran's victims included child offenders, while a large proportion of those executed in Saudi Arabia were foreign nationals, including some who were sentenced after trials whose proceedings they did not understand.

In September, Iraq carried out its first executions since the death penalty was restored in August 2004, and the effective moratorium on executions that had existed in the Palestinian Authority since 2002 was ended by five executions. Algeria, Israel, Morocco and Tunisia remained abolitionist in practice.

Human rights defenders

Human rights defenders continued to face a momentous task as they sought to promote wider understanding and ensure more effective protection of the rights due to all people in the region regardless of age, gender, nationality, religion, sexual orientation or other defining characteristics. They faced many obstacles and in some cases put their lives on the line to defend their own and others' fundamental rights.

Independent human rights organizations were active in a majority of countries, despite restrictive laws designed to regulate the operation of non-governmental groups. However, human rights defenders continued to be targeted for abuse or harassment, particularly in Iran and Syria. In Tunisia, the run-up to a UN-sponsored world summit in November was accompanied by an increase in state repression directed against leading human rights activists. The repression persisted through the summit itself which, ironically, aimed to advance international information exchange through the use of new technology. Sahrawi human rights defenders who documented abuses by Moroccan forces in confronting protests earlier in the year were jailed in Western Sahara.

AI regional report

- Gulf Cooperation Council (GCC) countries: Women deserve dignity and respect (AI Index: MDE 04/004/2005)

AI Report 2006

PART 2

AFGHANISTAN

AFGHANISTAN
Head of state and government: Hamid Karzai
Death penalty: retentionist
International Criminal Court: ratified
UN Women's Convention: ratified
Optional Protocol to UN Women's Convention: not signed

The government and its international partners remained incapable of providing security to the people of Afghanistan. Factional commanders secured positions of public authority, acted independently of government control and remained a major source of insecurity. Absence of rule of law, and a barely functional criminal justice system left many victims of human rights violations, especially women, without redress. Over 1,000 civilians were killed in attacks by US and Coalition forces and by armed groups. US forces continued to carry out arbitrary arrests and indefinite detentions. Refugees were pressured into returning to Afghanistan, despite continuing threats to their safety.

Background

The 2001 Bonn process culminated in the holding, in September, of elections to the National Assembly (*Wolesi Jirga*) and provincial councils. Marred by a climate of intimidation in the run up to polling, there was widespread public dismay at the number of factional leaders – many accused of human rights abuses – who stood for election.

Women were guaranteed at least a quarter of the seats in the *Wolesi Jirga* but faced social and administrative barriers. The legitimacy of the process was called into question on account of the low turnout, notably in Kabul.

In February, the UN Development Programme ranked Afghanistan at 173 of 178 in the world in terms of development, reflecting the country's severe socio-economic situation.

The flawed UN-supported Disarmament, Demobilization and Reintegration (DDR) programme ended in March. It was supplemented by the Disarmament of Illegal Armed Groups (DIAG) project. In September, the UN extended the mandate of the NATO-led International Security Assistance Force to 2006.

In February, Cherif Bassiouni, the UN Independent Expert on the Situation of Afghanistan, criticized the Afghan criminal justice system and the US detention of Afghans. The mandate of this position was, however, ended by the UN Commission on Human Rights in April, in accordance with US wishes.

Redressing past violations

In January, the Afghanistan Independent Human Rights Commission (AIHRC) issued a report examining measures to address past human rights violations. In December, the government passed the Transitional Justice Action Plan, which calls for the commemoration of victims, vetting of state employees to exclude human rights violators, the creation of a truth-seeking mechanism, the promotion of national reconciliation and the establishment of justice mechanisms for past crimes.

⌂ In July Faryadi Sarwar Zardad, a commander who had fled to the UK in 1988, was sentenced to 20 years' imprisonment in connection with human rights violations carried out by him and those under his command. The UK authorities cited their obligations under the UN Convention against Torture as the basis for prosecution.

⌂ In September, Habibullah Jalalzai and Hesamuddin Hesam, both former senior officials of KHAD, a security body during the 1980s, were sentenced to nine and 12 years' imprisonment respectively following a trial in the Netherlands.

Many regional officials and commanders – often called warlords – continued to wield power within Afghanistan. Some continued to maintain links with armed groups responsible for abuses that included war crimes committed during armed conflicts since 1979-80, including mass killings and rape. In December a national conference on truth-seeking and reconciliation was held.

Violence against women

In a climate of continued lack of public security and rule of law, women were denied enjoyment of their human rights. Women continued to face systematic and widespread violence and discrimination in public and private including discriminatory customary practices. In June the government established an inter-ministerial council aimed at combating violence against women, but by the end of 2005 few legal provisions to protect women had been promulgated, and fewer implemented.

⌂ In April, a *shura* (council), relying on customary practices, authorized the murder of a 29-year-old woman named Amina in Badakhshan. Six men, members of one family, were subsequently arrested, but it was not known if they were charged or tried.

⌂ In May, the bodies of three women were found raped and strangled on a road in Pul-e Khumri. Arrests followed but it was not known whether these resulted in trials.

Ineffective justice system

Flaws in the administration of justice remained a key source of human rights violations, especially in rural areas. All stages of the legal process were hampered by corruption, the influence of armed groups, lack of oversight mechanisms, non-payment of salaries and inadequate infrastructure. Detainees continued to be held unlawfully for prolonged periods and denied a fair trial. There were reports of inhumane conditions in prisons.

⌂ In October, prisoner of conscience Ali Mohaqqeq Nasab, the editor of a journal on women's rights, was sentenced to two years' imprisonment for "defamation" and "blasphemy". An appeal court in December suspended his sentence and he was freed.

Abuses by armed groups

Hundreds of civilians including aid workers, election officials and clerics were killed by armed groups such as the Taleban, who were resurgent in the southern region. Most of the killings resulted from suicide attacks and roadside bombs.

⬜ On 30 May, cleric Molavi Abdollah Fayyaz, who had spoken out against the Taleban, was shot dead in Kandahar. During his funeral ceremony the following day, a suicide bomber killed at least 21 people.

⬜ On 20 July, two or more unidentified gunmen in Paktika killed Hamid Mohammad Sarwar, an election worker from the Joint Electoral Monitoring Board, who was educating voters ahead of the September elections. At that stage, he was the fourth Afghan working in support of the elections to be killed.

Violations by US and Coalition Forces

US forces continued to arbitrarily detain hundreds of people beyond the reach of the courts and their own families, UN human rights experts, the AIHRC and, in some instances, the International Committee of the Red Cross (ICRC). Excessive use of force during arrest and torture and ill-treatment inside Bagram airbase and other US facilities continued to be reported. Conditions for many detainees reportedly improved in the second half of the year.

In May, reports of torture and ill-treatment in US-controlled facilities led to civil unrest across the country. In Jalalabad up to seven people died in riots. The UN called on the USA to open the detention facilities at Bagram airbase to the AIHRC.

Despite repeated calls for independent investigations into reports of torture by US forces and deaths in custody, investigations were conducted under the auspices of the US Department of Defense.

Military operations undertaken by US and Coalition Forces continued to result in civilian deaths or injury, usually following air strikes in southern areas. There were concerns that not all necessary precautions had been taken in the conduct of such attacks.

⬜ In 2005, more than 20 US military personnel were investigated in connection with the deaths in custody in 2002 of Dilawar and Habibullah, two Afghan detainees held in Bagram airbase. As of December 2005, seven low-ranking soldiers had been convicted of minor offences and received light penalties, but no one had been held directly responsible for the deaths in custody.

⬜ On 4 July, US military sources confirmed that they had killed 17 civilians in an air strike in Chichal village, Kunar province.

Hundreds of Afghans were released by the US authorities from Bagram airbase and Guantánamo Bay during 2005. Some claimed that they were ill-treated in custody.

Refugees

In response to pressure from the authorities in Iran and Pakistan, more than 100,000 refugees returned to Afghanistan during 2005.

The Iranian authorities reportedly added to restrictions imposed on Afghan refugees in recent years by refusing to issue them with identity cards. There were unconfirmed reports that Iranian authorities expelled hundreds of asylum-seekers from southern Iran.

In June it was announced that up to 90,000 Afghans had left Pakistan for Afghanistan over the preceding two and a half months. Hundreds of others had moved within Pakistan as camps were consolidated.

In August, the Minister for Refugees and Repatriation stated that 40 per cent of all returned refugees were in a vulnerable situation, "struggling between hope and hopelessness". The same month Afghanistan ratified the UN Refugee Convention.

Human rights defenders

The growing community of human rights defenders faced harassment and death threats. In November, a member of the AIHRC was the target of a grenade attack.

⬜ Shaheeda Hussain, a women's human rights defender and candidate for the *Wolesi Jirga*, was shot at in her car during the election campaign.

Death penalty

At least 24 death sentences were passed by lower and appeal courts. AI did not learn of any executions. In February, three people were sentenced to death in connection with the killing of a taxi driver. They appealed against the sentence. In May, four men were sentenced to death in connection with armed robbery and murder. In August, seven men were sentenced to death in connection with the kidnapping of election workers and, in a separate case, robbery.

AI country reports/ visits

Reports
- Afghanistan: Addressing the past to secure the future (AI Index: ASA 11/003/2005)
- Afghanistan: Women still under attack – a systematic failure to protect (AI Index: ASA 11/007/2005)
- Afghanistan: Human rights challenges facing Afghanistan's National and Provincial Assemblies – an open letter to candidates (AI Index: ASA 11/011/2005) ASA 11/011/2005)

Visit
AI visited Afghanistan in November and December to carry out research into human rights abuses in the context of the "war on terror".

ALBANIA

REPUBLIC OF ALBANIA
Head of state: Alfred Moisiu
Head of government: Sali Berisha (replaced Fatos Nano in September)
Death penalty: abolitionist for ordinary crimes
International Criminal Court: ratified
UN Women's Convention and its Optional Protocol: ratified

A number of detainees complained that they were tortured or ill-treated during arrest, in police custody or in prison. Investigations into complaints tended to be delayed and inconclusive, although in a few cases police officers were prosecuted or disciplined. Detention conditions, particularly for remand prisoners held in police stations, remained harsh. Domestic violence was common. There were arrests and prosecutions for trafficking women and children for forced prostitution and cheap labour.

Background
Poverty, unemployment and widespread corruption continued to undermine efforts to promote the rule of law. National elections in July were won by the Democratic Party and its allies, who called for a crackdown on corruption and organized crime.

Torture and ill-treatment
Police officers or prison guards allegedly beat detainees during arrest or subsequently in detention. At least six such complaints, three of them made by taxi-drivers, related to police officers attached to Korçë police station.

▭ Rrok Pepaj was arrested in Shkodër in April and charged with trafficking explosives. He subsequently filed a complaint against a named judicial police officer whom he accused of torture, forgery and "abuse of office". He alleged that following his arrest he was repeatedly kicked and beaten with truncheons by masked police officers and that while his head was crushed between two tables he was forced to sign a document that he could not see. He suffered damage to his kidneys; in October he was reportedly still urinating blood and receiving medical treatment while in pre-trial detention.

▭ In April the Ministry of Justice dismissed the director and the chief of the police guards of Tirana prison 302 after a number of remand prisoners complained that they had been physically and psychologically ill-treated. Also in April, criminal proceedings were started against two police officers at Lushnjë police station following a complaint by a detainee, Miti Mitro, that they had beaten him.

In May the UN Committee against Torture considered Albania's initial report, submitted with an eight-year delay. Among other recommendations, the Committee called on Albania to "ensure strict application of the provisions against torture and ill-treatment, adequately qualifying, prosecuting and punishing perpetrators in a manner proportionate to the seriousness of the crimes committed".

Impunity
Prosecutors did not always investigate complaints of ill-treatment or did so only after delay. Even when an investigation was formally opened, it was often inconclusive. Prosecutors were reluctant to apply provisions of the Criminal Code dealing with "torture and any other degrading or inhuman treatment", preferring to invoke lesser charges, such as "arbitrary acts", which usually resulted in non-custodial sentences. AI did not learn of any convictions for these offences, although there were several reports that police officers had received disciplinary punishments for ill-treating detainees.

▭ On 30 June Ali Shabani was allegedly beaten and injured by Korçë traffic police officers after he failed to obey their orders. He was brought to hospital with serious head injuries. Police sources denied that he had been beaten and claimed that he had injured himself. He was charged with resisting arrest. A local prosecutor reportedly declined to investigate a complaint filed by Ali Shabani, who subsequently brought a civil suit against the police.

▭ In April Elsen Gropa from Patos alleged that the investigation of a complaint he had filed 11 months previously was being deliberately delayed by the investigating and police authorities. He complained that two police officers had twice arrested him and beaten him at Fier police station in an unsuccessful attempt to force him to confess to a crime or to give them money to close the case. He said that he had supported his allegations with photographs of his injuries and a medical forensic report.

Conditions of detention
In March a new prison in Lezhë was opened as part of a plan supported by the European Union (EU) to improve the infrastructure of the penitentiary system. Despite this and certain other improvements, prison conditions continued to be marked by overcrowding and poor diet and hygiene, leading to frequent protests by prisoners. Conditions for remand prisoners in Vlorë detention centre and in pre-trial detention facilities in police stations were particularly harsh. In violation of domestic law, some convicted prisoners continued to be held together with remand prisoners and minors (under 18 years of age) sometimes shared cells with adult detainees. A 2003 government decision to transfer responsibility for all pre-trial detention facilities from the Ministry of Public Order to the Ministry of Justice had not been implemented by the end of 2005.

Violence against women
Surveys indicated that domestic violence was common, affecting up to 40 per cent of women. Intimate partner violence affected women of all ages and social groups and was often persistent. Women rarely reported such

incidents to the police, and few perpetrators were prosecuted, except in cases of serious injury or death. At least three women were convicted of killing partners whom they claimed had persistently subjected them to physical and psychological violence.

The law did not adequately protect victims of domestic violence, for whom there were limited support services provided by non-governmental organizations (NGOs). The Criminal Code did not specifically criminalize domestic violence. Local NGOs compiled a draft law aiming to introduce procedures to give victims of domestic violence legal protection, as envisaged in the 2003 Family Code.

Trafficking

Poverty, lack of education, family breakdown and crime networks at home and abroad contributed to the trafficking of women and children for sexual exploitation and cheap labour. There were reports that although the numbers of Albanian women being trafficked might be decreasing, many were being re-trafficked, sometimes as often as twice in a month.

The adoption of a witness protection law in Albania in 2004 appeared to have encouraged EU countries to deport victims of trafficking. However, difficulties in implementing the law meant that protection was in practice inadequate and victims were usually unwilling to testify against their traffickers for fear of reprisal. There were also concerns that traffickers or their families were using bribes or threats to induce relatives of those victims who did testify to persuade them to withdraw their testimony. According to official figures, 62 people were prosecuted for trafficking women for prostitution, and 13 people for child-trafficking between January and June.

In February the government approved a national strategy to combat child trafficking. In November the UN Special Rapporteur on the sale of children, child prostitution and child pornography, following a visit to Albania, welcomed the legislative measures, but called on the authorities to "develop a national child protection system aimed at combating the poverty that drives exploitation".

◻ In July the Serious Crimes Prosecutor's Office charged a man with trafficking six children to Greece. He had allegedly forced them to sell trinkets and beat them if they failed to earn enough money. The children had been returned to Albania in 2004 by the Greek authorities.

AI country reports/ visits
Report
- Albania: Obligations under the UN Convention against Torture – a gap between law and practice (AI Index: EUR 11/001/2005)
Visit
AI representatives visited Albania in October.

ALGERIA

PEOPLE'S DEMOCRATIC REPUBLIC OF ALGERIA
Head of state: Abdelaziz Bouteflika
Head of government: Ahmed Ouyahia
Death penalty: abolitionist in practice
International Criminal Court: signed
UN Women's Convention: ratified with reservations
Optional Protocol to UN Women's Convention: not signed

The government promoted a controversial plan aimed at bringing closure to the internal conflict of the 1990s amid continuing restrictions on human rights. The level of violence decreased in comparison with previous years, but hundreds of people were killed, among them dozens of civilians. Tens of thousands of cases of torture, killings, abductions and "disappearances" carried out since 1992 by the security forces, state-armed militias and armed groups had still not been investigated; this remained the key obstacle to addressing the legacy of the conflict. Torture continued to be reported, particularly in the cases of suspects accused of "belonging to a terrorist group". More than a dozen suspected members of armed groups were sentenced to death, most of them in their absence. A moratorium on executions remained in place. Changes to the law gradually improved the legal status of women, but many discriminatory provisions remained unchanged.

Background

Gas price rises at the beginning of the year sparked violent protests throughout the country. Demonstrations, strikes and violent protests erupted throughout the year over a range of social, economic and political problems, including water, job and housing shortages, public mismanagement and corruption.

An association agreement with the European Union entered into force on 1 September. The agreement, which sets out conditions for trade liberalization and security co-operation, contains a human rights clause which is binding on both parties.

The state of emergency, imposed in 1992, remained in force.

Killings

Some 400 people were killed as a result of continuing violence, including dozens of civilians. Attacks by armed groups on military targets, and to a lesser extent, civilians, continued to be reported. Dozens of people suspected of being members of armed groups were killed during operations by the security forces. There were concerns that some of these killings may have been extrajudicial executions.

Impunity

President Abdelaziz Bouteflika officially stated that some 200,000 people were believed to have been killed since

1992, but there was no commitment to establishing the truth about these killings and other gross human rights abuses, the vast majority of which had not been investigated. Instead, President Bouteflika called a referendum seeking a mandate to exonerate the security forces and armed groups, ostensibly in an effort to bring closure to the conflict of the 1990s.

A Charter for Peace and National Reconciliation was adopted by referendum on 29 September. In a speech made in late March, President Bouteflika declared that reconciliation required that families of victims of human rights abuses make sacrifices and that they might have to renounce some of their rights.

The Charter proposes clemency or exemption from prosecution for members of armed groups who give themselves up to the authorities. Armed groups have been responsible for widespread and grave abuses – such as targeted killings of civilians, abductions, rape and other forms of torture – some of which amount to crimes against humanity. Although perpetrators of certain serious abuses were not to be exempt from prosecution, no details were provided concerning the process for determining who would be eligible. Similar measures introduced in 1999 were applied arbitrarily and resulted de facto in wide-ranging impunity for abuses committed by armed groups.

The Charter denies that the security forces and state-armed militias have been responsible for serious crimes, thus conferring systematic impunity. This denial stands in stark contrast to a body of evidence which points to their responsibility for thousands of cases of torture, extrajudicial executions and "disappearances", some of which constitute crimes against humanity.

Victims of human rights abuses, human rights defenders, and others opposing the Charter were intimidated by state agents in an effort to stifle criticism. Some continued to express their anger at the authorities' failure to uphold their right to truth and justice. In the province of Blida, near the capital, Algiers, victims of abuses by armed groups and their families gathered at the cemetery on the day the referendum was held to remember the dead and bury their ballots in protest at the provisions of the Charter.

The UN Special Rapporteur on extrajudicial, summary or arbitrary executions and the UN Working Group on Enforced or Involuntary Disappearances expressed concern about the proposed measures. They urged the Algerian government not to adopt laws which would contravene its obligations under international law to ensure the right of victims of grave human rights abuses to truth and full reparations.

By the end of the year, no concrete measures had been taken to implement the provisions of the Charter.

'Disappearances'
No new cases of "disappearance" were reported during the year, but several thousand Algerians remained "disappeared" and no progress was made in clarifying their fate and whereabouts. The Charter for Peace and National Reconciliation specifically denies state responsibility for "disappearances", claiming that past wrongful acts have been punished.

At the end of March the mandate of an official commission on "disappearances", set up with a narrow mandate in 2004, expired. The head of the commission publicly excluded criminal prosecution of those responsible for the "disappearances" and proposed compensation payments to the families, many of whom continued to endure economic hardship. The commission remained silent on the state's duty to investigate serious human rights violations and to guarantee the victims' right to an effective remedy. The head of the commission told AI in May that, on the basis of complaints which families had made to the authorities, it had concluded that 6,146 individuals had "disappeared" at the hands of security officers between 1992 and 1998. However, media reports later quoted him contradicting this by saying that half of these were "terrorists", rather than victims of state abuses. The commission did not have powers to investigate cases of "disappearances". The commission's confidential report to the President had not been made public by the end of the year.

Many families of the "disappeared" feared that the compensation payments would be a substitute for long-overdue investigations. The government did not respond to the interest expressed since August 2000 by the UN Working Group on Enforced or Involuntary Disappearances to visit the country.

Torture and ill-treatment
There were further allegations that individuals arrested after protests were tortured or ill-treated in custody. The vast majority of allegations of torture made during 2005 and in previous years were not investigated. The UN Committee on the Rights of the Child expressed concern about a number of cases of torture and ill-treatment of children reported in previous years. The UN Special Rapporteur on torture was not invited to Algeria, despite repeated requests to visit the country since 1997.

In violation of national and international law, detainees accused of "belonging to a terrorist group" continued to be held in a secret location during *garde à vue* detention (the period before they are brought before the judicial authorities) and denied their right to communicate with their families, putting them at risk of torture.

Amar Saker was arrested on 19 February and reportedly tortured over a period of 15 days while held by the Department for Information and Security, an intelligence agency formerly known as Military Security. Among other things, he alleged that he was beaten until he lost consciousness, given electric shocks and suspended by his arms for three days to force him to sign a police report which he had not read. He was charged with "belonging to a terrorist group operating in Algeria and abroad" and remained in detention awaiting trial at the end of the year. The allegations of torture were not known to have been investigated, although a prison doctor had certified that his body bore traces of violence when he was transferred to prison.

Freedom of expression and assembly

Journalists, civil society activists and government critics faced harassment and intimidation and risked imprisonment. Pressure on journalists remained high. Dozens of journalists who criticized representatives of the state and security forces or reported on human rights abuses and corruption allegations faced charges of defamation, many of which were filed by public officials. Some 18 journalists were sentenced to imprisonment on defamation charges; others received suspended sentences and heavy fines. Nearly all remained at liberty pending appeals at the end of the year.

Mohamed Benchicou, former editor of the French language daily *Le Matin*, remained in prison. He had been convicted of violating exchange regulations and sentenced to two years' imprisonment in June 2004. Further prison terms and heavy fines were imposed in a series of lawsuits for defamation, but remained at appeal stage.

Independent organizations, among them human rights groups and independent trade unions, were repeatedly refused authorizations for public events.

Kamal Eddine Fekhar – a doctor, elected member of the Parliamentary Assembly in the province of Ghardaia in southern Algeria, and a member of the Socialist Forces Front and of the Algerian League for the Defence of Human Rights – was imprisoned for five months, apparently to discourage him and others from political activity. He was accused of incitement to rebellion and arson, among other things, in the wake of violent demonstrations which took place in the area in late 2004. Some of the protesters reported having been beaten on arrest and ill-treated or threatened with torture during questioning to force them to sign police reports incriminating Kamal Eddine Fekhar. Eyewitnesses reported that he had attempted to negotiate a peaceful settlement of the conflict.

The authorities stepped up pressure on families of the "disappeared" to abandon their public protests against the Charter for Peace and National Reconciliation. At least three demonstrations by families of the "disappeared" were violently dispersed by the security forces. Several relatives of the "disappeared" were summoned by security forces, questioned and threatened with legal proceedings should they continue their protests.

Belkacem Rachedi, whose father "disappeared" in 1995 and who had publicly accused members of a local militia of having arrested his father and of being responsible for his "disappearance", was sued for defamation by two of the alleged perpetrators. In one of the cases, a court in Relizane province, western Algeria, sentenced him to a six-month suspended prison term and a fine; the second case remained pending at the end of the year. The court had failed to investigate some 10 complaints lodged by the Rachedi family since 1997 in respect of the father's "disappearance".

Women's rights

In February amendments were introduced to the Family and Nationality Codes. Women were given equal rights with men in transmitting their nationality to their children. Changes to the Family Code revised some provisions discriminating against women but fell far short of offering women equal status with men. Key changes include the introduction of the same legal age for marriage for both men and women, and of a legal requirement for a divorced man to provide housing for his former wife if she has custody of the couple's under-age children. Homelessness among divorced women and their children had been recognized as a growing problem. The new law also rescinded the legal duty of a wife to obey her husband and introduced equal rights and duties for men and women during marriage.

However, numerous provisions which discriminate against women were maintained. These include polygamy and a husband's unilateral right to divorce. Discriminatory provisions governing inheritance rights remained unchanged.

Algeria maintained reservations to key articles of the UN Women's Convention, undermining its purpose. In February, the UN expert committee overseeing implementation of the Convention recommended that the government establish a binding timeline for reforming discriminatory legislation and withdrawing reservations to the Convention. The committee also expressed concern about the lack of progress in addressing the situation of female relatives of the "disappeared" and of women who had suffered physical and sexual violence by armed groups.

An unprecedented study on domestic violence was published, reflecting increasing recognition of violence against women as a problem in Algerian society. The study, which was conducted collaboratively by Algerian governmental and non-governmental bodies, revealed factors facilitating violence against women and identified needs for improving care for survivors.

AI country reports/ visits
Reports
- Algeria: Initial report of an Amnesty International delegation's visit to Algeria, 6-25 May 2005 (AI Index: MDE 28/008/2005)
- Algeria: President calls referendum to obliterate crimes of the past (AI Index: MDE 28/010/2005)

Visit
AI delegates visited Algeria in May.

ANGOLA

THE REPUBLIC OF ANGOLA
Head of state: José Eduardo dos Santos
Head of government: Fernando da Piedade Dias dos Santos
Death penalty: abolitionist for all crimes
International Criminal Court: signed
UN Women's Convention: ratified
Optional Protocol to UN Women's Convention: not signed

Hundreds of families were forcibly evicted from their homes. Police were responsible for human rights violations, including extrajudicial executions and excessive use of force. There were also reports of human rights violations by police and soldiers in Cabinda, with no prosecutions of any accused officers. Human rights defenders and political activists were threatened and briefly detained for their non-violent activities. Efforts to improve human rights increased with the appointment of a Justice Ombudsman.

Background

Hundreds of families were left homeless in Kwanza Norte province as a result of heavy rains and floods in the first quarter of 2005.

In February, Angola ratified the African Union Protocol to the Convention on the Prevention and Combating of Terrorism. In May it became the 100th country to sign an agreement with the USA, which was subsequently approved by the National Assembly, giving US troops and others immunity from prosecution before the International Criminal Court.

In March, the UN Committee on Human Rights ruled that the Angolan government had breached journalist Rafael Marques' human rights. He had been arrested and imprisoned for six months in October 1999 for criticizing President José Eduardo dos Santos and ordered to pay damages to the President. The Committee held that his conviction and sentence constituted an unlawful interference with his right to freedom of expression and urged the government to provide him with an effective remedy, including compensation. He had not been compensated by the year's end.

A Justice Ombudsman was appointed in April. The establishment of an Ombudsman Office was provided for by the Constitution of 1992 but was delayed by the civil war. The law establishing the mandate of the Ombudsman and his Office had not been approved by the end of the year

Elections were scheduled for late 2006. President José Eduardo dos Santos announced that he would stand as the presidential candidate of the ruling People's Movement for the Liberation of Angola (Movimento Popular de Libertação de Angola, MPLA). An amended electoral law was promulgated in August after the Supreme Court ruled that some of its provisions barring President dos Santos from standing were unconstitutional.

In November the country was officially declared free of the Marburg fever epidemic which, between March and July, killed 227 out of the reported 252 people infected. Most cases occurred in the northern province of Uige.

In November, the Huila Provincial Court convicted José Marques Pinto, the administrator of a ranch owned by a former minister, of the illegal imprisonment and torture of 18 villagers in 2003. He was sentenced to 28 years' imprisonment.

Forced evictions

The regulations for the implementation of a land law approved in 2004 had not beeen drafted by the end of 2005 and consultation with civil society groups had not started.

Hundreds of families were made homeless and had their property destroyed or stolen after being forcibly evicted from their homes in several Luanda suburbs. They were not given compensation. Members of the national and military police, who assisted the Luanda provincial government fiscal agents and private demolition brigades who carried out the evictions, used force. There were no investigations into allegations of police misconduct.

▢ An ongoing land dispute between the Catholic Church and about 2,000 families in the Wenji Maka neighbourhood was not resolved. Between June and November, scores of families were forcibly evicted by heavily armed police officers who beat residents and used excessive force. Dozens of residents and human rights activists were arrested and released without charge within 24 hours.

▢ Over 300 families in Cidadania neighbourhood had their houses demolished and were forcibly evicted, some for the fifth time, in September. Apparently, the land had been allocated to a former member of the government. The demolitions were carried out by a private construction firm and municipal fiscal agents, protected by about 20 heavily armed police officers.

▢ Over 600 families were forcibly evicted from their homes in Cambamba I and II in November. Police arrived at about 7am and started demolishing the houses and beating residents who opposed the evictions. Twelve people, including Luís Araújo, the coordinator of the non-governmental organization (NGO) SOS-Habitat, were arrested for allegedly inciting violence and held overnight at the local police station. The following day they appeared in court but were released for lack of evidence. The judge referred the case to the criminal investigation police.

Policing and human rights

Efforts were made to improve police respect for human rights and to combat impunity. In July the Angola National Police signed an agreement with the Association for Justice, Peace and Democracy to provide human rights and civic education to the police.

Some police officers were expelled from the force for misuse of firearms and beatings. However, no police officer was known to have been prosecuted for human rights violations, including extrajudicial executions, torture and ill-treatment or the use of excessive force during 2005.

▭ In January, a police officer extrajudicially executed Antoninho Tchsiwugo, a homeless youngster, in the city of Lobito. The officer went to the fourth floor of the abandoned building where Antoninho Tchsiwugo and other homeless young people lived, threatened them with his gun, grabbed and handcuffed Antoninho Tchsiwugo and shot him in the head at close range. The officer then removed the handcuffs and threw the body down the elevator shaft. The body was removed the next day by the police and buried without informing his family. It was not clear whether the officer was arrested. Following pressure from the local NGO, OMUNGA Project, officials from the Attorney's Office in Luanda went to Lobito in February to investigate the killing and stated that the officer had escaped from prison, with the connivance of his colleagues. In June, an official from the Ministry of the Interior stated that the officer had been arrested in March and was in prison. He had not been tried by the end of the year. Two of the witnesses to the killing received threats and were later arrested on suspicion of theft. In March, José Patrocínio, coordinator of the OMUNGA Project, received veiled threats because of his work on this case.

Police apparently used excessive force to prevent a demonstration by university students protesting against the cost of transport. The students were reportedly beaten. About 20 students, including student leader Mfuca Fualala Muzambe, were arrested and briefly held at the 3rd Police Station where they were beaten again before being released without charge.

Update
The trial of 17 people charged with disobeying the authorities in Cafunfo in 2004 resumed in July. All were acquitted. However, there was no investigation into reports that police had used excessive force.

The results of an inquiry initiated in late 2004 into five deaths in police custody in Capenda-Camulemba and the killing by the police of two demonstrators outside the police station had not been made public by the end of the year.

Human rights defenders
Human rights defenders were subjected to threats and arrest on account of their activities.

▭ Luís Araújo, coordinator of SOS-Habitat, was briefly detained in June and November because of his activities to prevent forced evictions.

Cabinda
In January the Provincial Governor reportedly admitted that there had been human rights violations in the province and that cases had been investigated and many individuals had been tried.

The first authorized demonstration was held in January to commemorate the anniversary of the

Simulambuco Treaty which incorporated Cabinda into Angola. However, further demonstrations were banned; police used force to suppress them and demonstrators were arrested.

There were unconfirmed reports of sporadic fighting in May and June between Angolan forces and the Front for the Liberation of the Cabindan Enclave (FLEC). Civil society groups accused both sides of embarking on a campaign of misinformation and called on them to enter negotiations.

The appointment in February of a Catholic bishop from outside Cabinda to the province led to violent protests. In June the police reportedly used force and tear gas to disperse a demonstration protesting at the appointment.

In November Rapid Intervention Police used firearms to disperse a reportedly peaceful demonstration in Landana and beat demonstrators. Some 25 demonstrators were arrested and briefly detained.

Political violence
There were several reports of politically motivated violence between supporters of the MPLA and the National Union for the Total Independence of Angola (UNITA). In March, one person was reportedly killed and 28 others were wounded in clashes between MPLA and UNITA supporters in the southern town of Mavinga, when UNITA members tried to raise their flag to commemorate the 39th anniversary of the organization's foundation.

AI country reports/ visits
Report
- Angola: The establishment of the Justice Ombudsman should comply with international standards (AI Index: AFR 12/002/2005)

ARGENTINA

ARGENTINE REPUBLIC
Head of state and government: Néstor Kirchner
Death penalty: abolitionist for ordinary crimes
International Criminal Court: ratified
UN Women's Convention: ratified with reservations
Optional Protocol to UN Women's Convention: signed

Thousands of prisoners were reportedly held in very poor conditions. Excessive use of force by the security forces against demonstrators and indigenous groups was reported. Important judicial decisions signalled progress in ending impunity for human rights violations by the military.

Background
Although there was some economic recovery during the year, levels of poverty remained high. Unemployment ran at 12.1 per cent and some five million people were reported to be working in the informal economy, largely without labour rights or access to social security. Demonstrations by *piqueteros* (unemployed protesters) demanding jobs, better pay and better unemployment benefits continued.

In September, the government approved a National Plan against Discrimination.

Indigenous people
In August and September indigenous representatives demanded that the national government stop violent evictions and suspend mining projects in regions inhabited by indigenous communities.

In July, 73-year-old José Galarza – leader of the Wichí indigenous people in Pozo Nuevo, Salta Province – was reportedly seriously injured when he was hit by rubber bullets fired by police as they entered indigenous land to recover a landowner's vehicle. Wichís had taken the vehicle in protest at the fencing off of land they claimed belonged to the community.

Demonstrations
In April teachers taking part in a peaceful demonstration in support of a pay demand in Salta, Salta Province, were beaten and threatened with firearms by police. Some demonstrators required medical attention and some were arrested and charged. All were subsequently released.

Prisons
Some 62,500 inmates were held in Argentine prisons during 2005. Most provincial prisons lacked basic facilities such as drinking water, adequate light and sanitation, medical facilities and rehabilitation schemes. Many prisoners experienced severe overcrowding, and ill-treatment by prison guards was reported. Seventy-five per cent of those detained were awaiting trial. Inmates in Córdoba, Coronda, Rosario, Tucumán, Mendoza and Magdalena prisons staged protests and riots in which several prisoners died.

In October at least 33 inmates died during a fire in block 16 of Penitentiary Unit 28 in Magdalena, Buenos Aires Province. The prisoners had reportedly been protesting to demand better conditions. Most of those killed died of asphyxiation. Reports indicated that prison guards locked the gates when the fire started; prisoners from a neighbouring block managed to help release some of those trapped inside. A judicial investigation was initiated but had not concluded by the end of the year.

In June, Ricardo David Videla Fernandez, an adolescent sentenced to life imprisonment, was found hanging in his cell in the maximum security block No. 2 in the Provincial jail in Mendoza, Mendoza Province. Days before, Ricardo David Videla had been held in his cell in inhuman and degrading conditions, according to a Local Commission on Penitentiary Policies.

Judicial decisions to end impunity
In June the Supreme Court ruled that the Full Stop and Due Obedience laws were unconstitutional, upholding the decision by Congress in August 2003 to declare the laws null and void. The judicial ruling cleared the way for the prosecution of members of the military suspected of human rights abuses during the military governments (1976-83).

Adolfo Scilingo
In April former naval officer Adolfo Scilingo was tried in Spain on charges of crimes against humanity, including arbitrary detention and torture, committed in Argentina during the military governments. He was sentenced to 640 years' imprisonment of which he was expected to serve 30 years. The former officer had admitted being aboard planes carrying detainees who were drugged, stripped naked and thrown into the sea.

AI country reports/ visits
Reports
- Argentina: Historical ruling opens the way for justice in the country (AI Index: AMR 13/005/2005)
- Argentina: Memorandum to the Governor of Mendoza Province (AI Index: AMR 13/008/2005)
- Argentina: Implementation of the United Nations Convention against Torture and Other Cruel, Inhuman or Degrading Treatment or Punishment (AI Index: AMR 13/001/2005)

Visit
An AI delegation visited Santiago del Estero, Salta, Jujuy and Mendoza in May.

ARMENIA

REPUBLIC OF ARMENIA
Head of state: Robert Kocharian
Head of government: Andranik Markarian
Death penalty: abolitionist for all crimes
International Criminal Court: signed
UN Women's Convention: acceded
Optional Protocol to UN Women's Convention: not signed

Conscientious objectors to compulsory military service remained in jail. A new law failed to introduce a genuine civilian alternative service despite Armenia's commitments made to the Council of Europe. The authorities reportedly ill-treated some residents who were peacefully protesting at the demolition of their homes.

Background

Opposition parties boycotted a 27 November referendum on constitutional reforms and contested official reports of an overwhelming turnout and "yes" vote. The Parliamentary Assembly of the Council of Europe concluded that although the referendum generally reflected the will of voters, serious abuses in several polling stations raised questions about official turnout claims. The authorities failed to prevent an opposition demonstration in the capital, Yerevan, on 29 November to protest that the constitutional reforms were not sufficiently far-reaching.

On 6 May the Constitutional Court ruled unconstitutional a provision in the Law on the Human Rights Defender that allowed the Ombudsperson to make recommendations to the courts to ensure the right to a fair trial. The Ministry of Justice had argued that it undermined the judiciary's independence. The Ombudsperson questioned whether the judiciary could be independent, given their direct appointment by the head of state, and said most complaints received by her Office were about unfair trials.

Conscientious objectors imprisoned

Armenia did not release jailed conscientious objectors, in defiance of its commitments to the Council of Europe. Although a law that came into force in 2004 provided for unarmed military service, this was not a genuinely civilian alternative to compulsory military service, and the authorities continued to imprison conscientious objectors.

At least six members of the Jehovah's Witnesses religious group who had begun but then abandoned unarmed military service were sentenced to prison terms of up to three years. They had objected to the service being under the control of the Ministry of Defence and not genuinely civilian. They complained of restrictions on their movements and of being forced to wear military-style uniforms.

On 3 November, four conscientious objectors who had abandoned their unarmed military service were sentenced to three years' imprisonment for being absent without leave. They had been working in a psychiatric hospital. They were reportedly detained for five months in the hospital compound, forced to shovel snow with their bare hands and locked out in freezing rain with no outdoor clothes. Their appeal was pending at the end of 2005.

Alleged ill-treatment of peaceful protesters

In August the police allegedly used excessive force against peaceful protests by residents of Yerevan over demolition of their homes for an urban renewal scheme. Those who refused to vacate their homes had parts of their houses destroyed. One resident was allegedly removed by force and severely beaten. The police forcibly removed barricades. A lawyer representing several residents, Vahe Grigorian, was arrested on 10 October, reportedly on fabricated fraud charges based on evidence obtained under duress. He was still in pre-trial detention at the end of the year. The father of one of his clients told the Ombudsperson's Office that he had been ill-treated and forced to incriminate Vahe Grigorian. The protesters said the compensation paid was not adequate and their eviction illegal – claims supported by the Ombudsperson's Office, which received more than 200 complaints.

AUSTRALIA

AUSTRALIA
Head of state: Queen Elizabeth II, represented by Michael Jeffery
Head of government: John Howard
Death penalty: abolitionist for all crimes
International Criminal Court: ratified
UN Women's Convention: ratified with reservations
Optional Protocol to UN Women's Convention: not signed

Indigenous people continued to make up a disproportionate percentage of the prison population. Major changes to immigration detention practices resulted in the release of child asylum-seekers and their families. However, the policy of mandatory detention of asylum-seekers remained unchanged. There were concerns that new counter-terrorism measures could have a negative impact on fundamental human rights.

Violence against women

Although the government extended the national awareness campaign, "Violence against Women – Australia says No", it did not provide funding in the 2005 budget for the two substantive national programmes addressing domestic and sexual violence against women (Partnerships against Domestic Violence and the National Initiative to Combat Sexual Assault). The Australian Institute for Health and Welfare found that on average 48 per cent of women fleeing domestic violence were turned away from specialist accommodation for lack of resources.

The Victorian state government abolished the partial defence of provocation to murder and amended self-defence laws in recognition of the gendered nature of these defences. Victoria and New South Wales established pilot, specialized domestic violence courts.

⛛ In August, a Northern Territory court sentenced a 50-year-old man to one month's imprisonment with two years suspended after a charge of raping a 14-year-old girl was reduced to "carnal knowledge". The man's defence argued that he had a right to sexual relations with the girl who was a "promised bride" under Aboriginal customary law. In December an appeal court found the sentence "manifestly unjust" and ordered that the man serve at least 18 months' imprisonment.

Indigenous people

The government's Productivity Commission report, Overcoming Indigenous Disadvantage: Key Indicators 2005, noted an increase in the number of indigenous Australians who reported being victims of violence. The report noted that indigenous people were 11 times more likely than other Australians to be imprisoned and that the life expectancy of indigenous people was around 17 years less than that of the population as a whole.

⛛ A coroner's inquiry into the 2004 death in custody of Cameron Doomadgee on Palm Island started in February 2005 and was continuing at the end of the year.

Refugees and asylum-seekers

In June, the government announced changes to migration legislation affecting asylum-seekers and refugees. These increased ministerial discretionary powers and resulted in the release of all children and their families from immigration detention centres into community detention. Not all those released were granted permanent visas and many still faced uncertain futures.

Public awareness of the detention of an Australian permanent resident and the forcible removal from Australia of an Australian citizen resulted in inquiries into Australia's immigration detention centres and into the operation of the Department of Immigration and Multicultural Affairs. The ensuing reports were critical of both cases and found additional instances of wrongful detention, poor case management and inadequate care of detainees' mental health.

Human rights and security

Counter-terrorism laws introduced in December contained measures with potentially negative impacts on fundamental human rights. Measures included preventative detention in secret for 14 days without charge or trial, and renewable control orders for up to 12 months; the latter could severely constrain freedom of movement and association and could limit

employment and communications. Freedom of speech was limited by new sedition laws.

Australian David Hicks entered his fourth year in detention in Guantánamo Bay, pending his trial by a US military commission which fails to meet international fair trial standards. The Australian government continued to assert such commissions would deliver fair trials. David Hicks' trial was stayed by a US court on 14 November 2005 (see United Kingdom entry). Mamdouh Habib, the other Australian detainee held by the US authorities in Guantánamo Bay, was repatriated to Australia without charge in January 2005.

AI country reports/ visits
Report
· Australia: The impact of indefinite detention – the case to change Australia's mandatory detention regime (AI Index: ASA 12/001/2005)

AUSTRIA

FEDERAL REPUBLIC OF AUSTRIA
Head of state: Heinz Fischer
Head of government: Wolfgang Schüssel
Death penalty: abolitionist for all crimes
International Criminal Court: ratified
UN Women's Convention and its Optional Protocol: ratified

There were allegations of ill-treatment by police. Austria failed to comply with a ruling by the UN Human Rights Committee. New laws on asylum and police powers contravened human rights standards and could threaten the work of human rights defenders. Overcrowding in prisons continued to worsen.

Allegations of police ill-treatment

There were continuing allegations of ill-treatment and harassment by police, particularly of foreign nationals.

⛛ In July, the trial opened of six police officers, three paramedics and a doctor charged with involuntary manslaughter under especially dangerous conditions in connection with the death in July 2003 of Mauritanian citizen Cheibani Wague in Vienna. In November, the Higher Criminal Court in Vienna sentenced the doctor and one police officer to suspended seven-month prison terms; the other defendants were acquitted. AI had repeatedly expressed concern about the circumstances surrounding the death of Cheibani Wague while being restrained by police officers and paramedics, and at what appeared to be substantial failures to conduct a prompt, independent and impartial investigation aimed at bringing those responsible to justice. Evidence produced in the trial also highlighted deficiencies within the police training system with regard to restraint methods.

🗁 In March, the Independent Administrative Tribunal concluded that the arrest, detention and beating of a young man by police in Vienna on 13 August 2004 was unlawful.

🗁 During a stop-and-search police operation against a family from Ghana in Ansfelden, in July, a woman, Mrs A., was arrested, taken to a police station and strip-searched, apparently without any legal basis. The police officers involved have not reportedly faced any criminal investigation.

Compliance with international human rights law

In violation of the requirement to ensure an effective remedy to people whose rights under the International Covenant on Civil and Political Rights (ICCPR) have been violated, the authorities refused to pay compensation to Paul Perterer, who was denied his right to a fair hearing when he was dismissed from the civil service. On 20 August 2004, the UN Human Rights Committee concluded that Austria had violated Paul Perterer's right to a fair hearing and recommended that the authorities ensure him an effective remedy, including compensation. Austria argued that neither the ICCPR (to which Austria is a state party) nor the views of the Human Rights Committee have any effect in domestic law.

Extradition

In September, the Vienna Court of Appeal confirmed a previous court decision allowing the extradition of Muhammad 'Abd al-Rahmin Bilasi-Ashri to Egypt on the basis of diplomatic assurances. Bilasi-Ashri would be at serious risk of torture and other serious human rights violations if returned to Egypt. On 18 November, the European Court of Human Rights issued an interim measure *not* to extradite Bilasi-Ashri.

New laws on asylum and foreign nationals

Several provisions in the new Asylum Act and the Aliens Police Act contravened international refugee and human rights standards. A provision penalizing people who "abet" "unauthorized habitation" could result in persecution of human rights defenders who represent asylum-seekers.

Justice sector

The Ministry of Justice failed to address deficiencies in the prison system. Prisons continued to be overcrowded, and conditions were aggravated by an increasing number of mentally ill inmates and a decrease in staff. Sixty taser guns were in use in judicial institutions as of July.

Arms control

Despite amendments, long-standing loopholes remained in the Law on War Material, allowing surplus weapons to be transferred to countries where they might be misused for human rights violations.

AI country reports/ visits
Reports
- Austria: Court delivers verdict in the case of Cheibani Wague (AI Index: EUR 13/002/2005)
- Austria: Risk of forcible return/torture: Muhammad 'Abd al-Rahmin Bilasi-Ashri (AI Index: EUR 13/001/2005)

AZERBAIJAN

REPUBLIC OF AZERBAIJAN
Head of state: Ilham Aliev
Head of government: Artur Rasizade
Death penalty: abolitionist for all crimes
International Criminal Court: not signed
UN Women's Convention and its Optional Protocol: ratified

Rights to freedom of expression and assembly were restricted. The security forces used excessive force to break up peaceful opposition demonstrations. Scores of opposition activists and journalists were beaten and detained. Seven opposition leaders were pardoned and released. Charges of attempting to overthrow the government were brought against dozens of opposition activists and state officials. Several were reportedly tortured or ill-treated in detention.

Background

Despite a presidential decree in May that the November parliamentary elections were to be held in a democratic manner, there was constant obstruction of opposition campaigning. International observers reported that the elections did not meet international standards. After the poll, opposition parties formed a new coalition, the Democratic Popular Front, announced a boycott of the new parliament, and demanded a re-run in at least 100 constituencies.

In March, Elmar Husseinov, editor of the weekly *Monitor* magazine, was killed in suspicious circumstances outside his home in the capital, Baku. His death sparked large-scale demonstrations amid opposition claims that he was murdered because of his criticism of official corruption. The authorities denied any involvement. No one had been brought to justice by the end of 2005.

Excessive use of force

Between May and December, the security forces used excessive force to break up both authorized and unauthorized demonstrations in Baku, kicking and beating protesters and journalists. Scores of demonstrators were detained, and some were reportedly beaten in custody.

🗁 The excessive force reportedly used to break up an authorized demonstration by the Democratic Popular Front in Baku on 26 November provoked criticism from the USA and the European Union. No attempt was apparently made to disperse the crowd peacefully, and opposition leaders said they were hit on the head with truncheons by the police, despite offering no resistance.

🗁 At an unauthorized demonstration organized by opposition coalition Azadlig (Freedom) on 9 October, 14 journalists were among those said to have been severely beaten. Idrak Abbasov, of the *Zerkalo* (Mirror) newspaper, was reportedly hit on the head repeatedly with baseball bats by a plainclothes police officer and other men until he lost consciousness. He was taken to hospital, where guards allegedly prevented other journalists from seeing him.

Opposition trials: update

In February the Organization for Security and Co-operation in Europe (OSCE) published its findings on the trials of 125 people charged in relation to the October 2003 post-election violence. In 2004 at least 40 men received prison sentences after unfair trials for their alleged participation in the violence. The OSCE report concluded that most of the trials fell well short of international fair trial standards, that the courts admitted evidence reportedly obtained through the use of torture, and that defendants were denied the rights to presumption of innocence and to prepare an effective defence. The report called for the release or retrial of all those denied a fair trial.

🗁 In March, seven opposition leaders imprisoned since October 2003 were pardoned by President Aliev and subsequently released. In July their convictions were quashed in court, allowing them to run in the November elections. They had been sentenced in October 2004 to prison terms of between two and a half and five years for their alleged participation in the 2003 post-election violence. The Supreme Court had turned down their appeal.

State security arrests

🗁 In August, Ruslan Bashirli, the leader of Yeni Fikir (New Thinking), a youth organization with reported links to the opposition Azerbaijani Popular Front Party (APFP), was arrested on charges of attempting to overthrow the government. He denied official accusations of accepting money from Armenia to destabilize the country. He was reportedly put under pressure to implicate APFP leader Ali Kerimli in an alleged coup plot. He was remanded in custody for three months. Pro-government demonstrators attacked his family home and APFP offices with impunity, and his father was made to resign from his job. Members of Yeni Fikir were reportedly detained, threatened, beaten, denied medical care and coerced into making statements against Yeni Fikir and APFP.

🗁 Dozens of officials, including government ministers, were arrested or dismissed following an alleged coup attempt in October. Four officials reportedly confessed on state television to conspiring with Rasul Quliev, the exiled leader of the opposition Azerbaijani Democratic Party. There were fears that their confessions had been coerced. Rasul Quliev was detained in Ukraine on 17 October after his plane was prevented from landing in Baku. Azerbaijan requested his extradition on embezzlement charges, but he was eventually released by a court in Ukraine. The authorities in Azerbaijan detained scores of his supporters, and claimed to have seized weapons. Some were later charged.

BAHAMAS

COMMONWEALTH OF THE BAHAMAS
Head of state: Queen Elizabeth II, represented by Paul Adderley (replaced Ivy Dumont in December)
Head of government: Perry Gladstone Christie
Death penalty: retentionist
International Criminal Court: signed
UN Women's Convention: ratified
Optional Protocol to UN Women's Convention: not signed

Death sentences were imposed by the courts. No executions were carried out. Detained asylum-seekers and migrants, the majority black Haitian nationals, were held in harsh conditions and reportedly ill-treated. Reports of police abuses continued.

Death penalty

The courts continued to pass death sentences. No executions took place. At the end of 2005, there were at least 39 prisoners on death row. Numerous people, including the Commissioner of Police, called for the resumption of executions in reaction to an increase in violent crime.

In April, 12 prisoners on death row at the Fox Hill Prison staged a three-day hunger strike to protest at their "inhumane" conditions. Inmates alleged inadequate sanitation, food, water and medical care. In October a new prison building was commissioned, for completion in 2007.

Police abuses

There were continued reports of police brutality.

🗁 In January a riot erupted in Nassau Village after police allegedly abused Haitian women and shot a young man aged 19 in the face. A police investigation had not concluded by the end of 2005.

Asylum-seekers and migrants

There were continued reports of abuses against asylum-seekers and other detainees at the Carmichael Detention Centre. Inmates were reportedly beaten and received inadequate medical attention, food and water. Asylum-seekers were forcibly returned to countries including Cuba and Haiti without access to a full and fair determination procedure.

Hostility increased towards Haitian immigrants, unofficially estimated at 60,000 out of a population of 300,000. In 2005, according to the Department of Immigration, 5,543 irregular immigrants – 4,504 from Haiti – were forcibly returned to their countries of origin.

AI country reports/visits
Visit
In May, AI sent a police expert to provide human rights training to members of the Royal Bahamas Police Force.

BAHRAIN

KINGDOM OF BAHRAIN
Head of state: King Hamad bin 'Issa Al Khalifa
Head of government: Shaikh Khalifa bin Salman Al Khalifa
Death penalty: retentionist
International Criminal Court: signed
UN Women's Convention: ratified with reservations
Optional Protocol to UN Women's Convention: not signed

Three people were arrested in connection with material published on an Internet website. A human rights activist appeared before a court on charges that seemed to be politically motivated. Security forces used excessive force to disperse demonstrators in the capital al-Manama.

Key developments
The government proposed a new counter-terrorism law to the National Assembly (parliament) in April under which anyone convicted of committing or planning terrorist acts would face the death penalty. Human rights activists and some members of parliament criticized the proposed law as an attempt to restrict freedoms excessively. The law was approved by the parliament in December and was due to be referred to the Shura (Consultative) Council and then ratified by the King in 2006. In July, parliament approved a new law to regulate political associations. This requires associations to be approved by the Minister of Justice who can also apply to the Supreme Court to have them

dissolved or cease their activities. Human rights and other groups criticized the new law as overly restrictive and called on King Hamad bin 'Issa Al Khalifa to cancel it. He had not done so by the end of 2005.

Human rights activists and some members of the parliament continued to urge the government to press for the release of six Bahraini nationals detained by the US military at Guantánamo Bay. Three of them were returned to Bahrain in November and released.

Political arrests
Three men were arrested in February in connection with comments published on their Internet website discussion forum (www.bahrainonline.org) which were alleged to be critical of the government and offensive to the royal family. 'Ali 'Abdul Imam, Mohammad al-Mousawi and Hussain Yousef were detained for 15 days on the orders of the Public Prosecution. The charges against them included "inciting hatred, defamation and spreading false information". The three went on hunger strike during their detention at al-Hoora police station in al-Manama. They were released on 14 March. At the end of the year it was not clear whether they were still awaiting trial.

Human rights defenders
Ghada Jamsheer, a leading human rights defender, appeared in court in June. She faced charges of insulting the judiciary; defamation and slander of a family court judge; and slander of the husband of a victim of domestic violence. The first charge arose from petitions and articles issued between October 2002 and June 2003 by the Women's Petition Committee, of which Ghada Jamsheer is the director. The group was formed in October 2002 to campaign for the reform of personal status courts and the codification of family laws. Ghada Jamsheer denied all the charges, most of which were dropped or dismissed by the courts. However, the charge of slandering a judge remained pending at the end of the year.

Lawyers acting for the Bahrain Centre for Human Rights (BCHR) filed a court case against the Ministry of Labour in January. The action contested the Minister of Labour's decision to order the closure of the Centre in September 2004 for an alleged breach of the 1989 Societies Law. The application was rejected by the High Civil Court in January. The lawyers acting for the Centre then reportedly referred the case to the Administrative Court in April, where it was believed to remain pending at the end of the year.

Excessive force
In June, the security forces were reported to have used excessive force when dispersing peaceful demonstrators calling for more job opportunities who had gathered outside the Royal Court in Rifa'a in al-Manama. Many of the demonstrators were beaten and some required hospital treatment. About 30 were arrested but released the same day without charge. In July, a further demonstration against unemployment resulted in more than 30 people being severely beaten by the security forces; some required hospital

treatment. Those assaulted included 'Abdul Hadi al-Khawaja and Nabeel Rajab, human rights activists belonging to the BCHR.

UN Committee against Torture

In May the UN Committee against Torture considered Bahrain's report on its implementation of the UN Convention against Torture. The Committee regretted the government's five-year delay in submitting the report, but noted that several positive developments had occurred in Bahrain since 2001. However, the Committee expressed concern about the continuing "lack of a comprehensive definition of torture" in Bahraini law; the "provision of blanket amnesty to all alleged perpetrators of torture and other crimes by Decree 56 of 2002"; and the "lack of redress available to victims of torture". It urged the government to adopt legislation to prevent and punish violence against women, including domestic violence, and to amend Decree 56 to "ensure there is no impunity for officials who have perpetrated or acquiesced in torture and other cruel and inhuman or degrading treatment".

Death penalty

Two Bangladeshi nationals, Jasmine Anwar Hussain and Mohammad Hilaluddin, had their death sentences upheld on appeal in December. At the end of the year it was unclear whether the case would be referred to the Court of Cassation. They had been sentenced to death for murder in November 2004.

AI country reports/ visits
Report
• Gulf Cooperation Council (GCC) countries: Women deserve dignity and respect (AI Index: MDE 04/004/2005)
Visit
In January AI held a conference in al-Manama on violence against women in the Gulf region.

BANGLADESH

PEOPLE'S REPUBLIC OF BANGLADESH
Head of state: Iajuddin Ahmed
Head of government: Begum Khaleda Zia
Death penalty: retentionist
International Criminal Court: signed
UN Women's Convention: ratified with reservations
Optional Protocol to UN Women's Convention: ratified

A rising tide of violence, much of it perpetrated by Islamist groups, affected most parts of the country. The main targets of the violence were human rights defenders, lawyers, judges, opposition activists, members of minority communities and places of worship. Police abuses, including torture, continued. Violence against women was widespread. At least three people were executed.

Background

Escalating levels of violence, including several waves of bombings, combined with lack of appropriate action by the authorities pushed Bangladesh to the edge of a human rights crisis. The government — a four-party coalition led by the Bangladesh Nationalist Party (BNP) — at first blamed the main opposition Awami League before acknowledging that it faced growing Islamist militancy. In February it banned two Islamist groups — Jama'atul Mujahideen (Assembly of the Holy Warriors) Bangladesh and Jagrata Muslim Janata (Awakened Muslim Citizens) Bangladesh.

The World Bank cancelled funding for three development projects, blaming government corruption for its decision. For the fifth consecutive year, the non-governmental organization Transparency International named Bangladesh the world's most corrupt country.

In August, the High Court declared the Fifth Amendment to the Constitution unlawful. The amendment had legitimized the imposition of martial law from 1975 to 1979. Following an appeal by the government, the Supreme Court suspended the High Court ruling.

Escalating violence

After a series of isolated bomb attacks from the beginning of the year, on 17 August hundreds of small bombs, many targeting government buildings, were detonated within a period of 30 minutes across the country. Two people were killed and hundreds injured. Jama'atul Mujahideen leaflets at the bomb sites called for the introduction of Islamic law in Bangladesh. Hundreds of people were arrested in the following weeks.

At least 25 people were killed and hundreds injured in similar attacks at other times in the year. On 29 November Bangladesh's first suicide bombings marked a significant escalation in the violence and sparked widespread criticism of the ruling coalition for failing to prevent such attacks.

Targets of attacks and other abuses
Opposition members
Opposition activists faced attack by Islamists and members of the ruling BNP.

▢ On 27 January a bomb killed five people, including former Finance Minister and leading Awami League politician Shah Abu Mohammad Shamsul Kibria, at an Awami League rally in Habiganj, north-east of the capital Dhaka. The family of the assassinated politician demanded an independent international investigation, but the government refused their demand.

▢ Hundreds of Awami League supporters were reportedly injured on 15 August when various Awami League gatherings were attacked by BNP members.

Human rights defenders
Human rights defenders continued to face abuses by the police, army and other law enforcement personnel, including arbitrary arrest and torture. They were also harassed through the filing of unsubstantiated criminal accusations against them. Many were threatened by individuals or groups linked to armed criminal gangs or political parties. Some were physically attacked. Despite the attacks, human rights defenders remained extremely active.

▢ Suresh Chandra Halder, former General Secretary of the Association for Village Advancement, a non-governmental organization in Faridpur, was arrested on 9 August, reportedly without a warrant. He remained in Faridpur jail for more than three months, and was denied medical treatment vital for his diabetes and other medical conditions. His harassment was believed to be linked to his attempts to expose corruption in the Association, which angered members of the organization linked to the government. On the orders of a court, he was released on 25 November.

Journalists
Hundreds of journalists were reportedly harassed, intimidated and attacked by state agents and non-state actors including Islamist groups.

▢ On 5 February a bomb outside the press club in Khulna seriously injured Sheikh Belaluddin Ahmed, the local bureau chief of the daily *Dainik Sangram*. He died several days later.

▢ A national conference to discuss repression of journalists planned for 11 November in Dhaka by the Federal Union of Journalists was reportedly stopped by the government two days before it was due to start.

Lawyers and judges
Islamist groups attacked courts, judges and lawyers, apparently because they practised non-Islamic law.

▢ On 3 October, two people were killed when bombs exploded in court buildings in several places around the country. Jama'atul Mujahideen appeared to have carried out the attacks. Two judges were killed on 14 November when a bomb was thrown at their car in Jhalakathi.

▢ Nine people, including two lawyers, were killed on 29 November by suicide bombers outside courts in Chittagong and Gazipur.

Attacks on minority communities
Attacks on minorities, including Hindus, Christians, Ahmadis and tribal people in the Chittagong Hill Tracts and elsewhere were carried out with apparent impunity.

▢ On 24 July, dozens of tribal villagers in the Chittagong Hill Tracts were severely beaten and otherwise abused, reportedly by soldiers, at Fakinala Nee Aung Karbari Para, Manikchari sub-district, in Khagrachari.

▢ A hate campaign against members of the Ahmadiyya Muslim Jamaat continued and involved attacks on Ahmadi places of worship. In one attack in April, more than 50 men, women and children were reportedly injured at Sundarban Bazar in Jotindryanagar by the International Khatme Nabuwat Movement Bangladesh, an Islamist group.

▢ In October, Hindu temples and houses were attacked and set on fire in Rangpur. Five people were reported to have been seriously injured.

Abuses by police
▢ Shankar Sen, aged 27, reportedly died on 14 August allegedly after being tortured by police at Ramna police station. He had been arrested six days earlier on suspicion of stealing a mobile phone. Relatives said Shankar Sen had mental health problems.

▢ On 24 August, Mokaddes Hossain, General Secretary of the Tetulbaria union of the Jubo League, died allegedly as a result of torture by police. He was arrested on his way home from attending an Awami League event.

Violence against women
According to media reports, in the first quarter of the year alone, more than 1,900 women were allegedly subjected to violence, over 200 were killed allegedly following rape, over 300 women were allegedly abused for not meeting their husbands' dowry demands and over 100 were trafficked. Acid Survivors Foundation said that at least 166 incidents of acid attacks involving 210 victims – 138 of whom were women – took place in the first nine months of the year. Social stigma, police refusal to act on most reports of violence against women, and a lack of legal and community support for the victims prevented many of them from seeking justice. However, almost all reports of acid attacks were believed to have been investigated by the police.

Death penalty
At least 217 men and one woman were sentenced to death, and at least three men were executed by hanging.

AI country reports/visits
Report
· Bangladesh: Human rights defenders under attack (AI Index: ASA 13/004/2005)
Visit
AI delegates visited Bangladesh in February/March to research human rights and to help stage a workshop for human rights defenders.

BELARUS

REPUBLIC OF BELARUS
Head of state: Alyaksandr Lukashenka
Head of government: Sergei Sidorsky
Death penalty: retentionist
International Criminal Court: not signed
UN Women's Convention and its Optional Protocol:
ratified

The government continued to restrict freedom of expression and assembly. Opposition activists were arbitrarily detained and allegedly ill-treated by police. Some were given lengthy prison sentences for exercising their right to freedom of expression. Human rights defenders and civil society organizations were subjected to further restrictions and harassment. No progress was made in investigating four cases of "disappearance". Use of the death penalty continued.

Background

The government clampdown on civil society and freedom of expression remained of concern to the international community. In February the Representative on Freedom of the Media of the Organization for Security and Co-operation in Europe (OSCE) visited Belarus. He criticized its restrictive media legislation, lack of an independent news media, and laws that criminalize libel and protect state officials from legitimate criticism. On 10 March the European Parliament adopted a resolution strongly condemning the harassment of opposition figures. The resolution called for efforts to overcome the isolation of Belarus through the creation of alternative news sources and the provision of scholarships in the European Union to Belarusian students.

Prisoners of conscience

Government critics were sentenced to prison terms or continued to serve long prison sentences for voicing their opposition to the government or its policies. Some prisoners had their sentences reduced under an amnesty declared by President Lukashenka on 5 May to commemorate the end of the Second World War.

⬠ Mikhail Marinich, an opposition leader sentenced to five years' imprisonment on 20 December 2004, had his sentence reduced to three and a half years in February. He had been convicted on trumped-up charges of abusing an official position and theft. The court of appeal granted his appeal because of his past services to the state and his deteriorating health. He had a stroke on 7 March, but the authorities failed to inform his family or lawyer, who only learned of it when a fellow-inmate was released and told a newspaper. He was transferred to a prison hospital in Minsk on 15 March and returned to the prison colony on 18 May. In July he was hospitalized again with an

eye infection. In August his sentence was reduced by a further year under the May amnesty measure.

⬠ On 31 May Nikolai Statkevich, chair of Narodnaya Gramada, a social democratic party, and Pavel Severinets, head of the Popular Front youth movement, were sentenced to three years of corrective labour by Minsk Central District Court. They had been convicted of public order offences (under Article 342 of the Criminal Code) for organizing protests in Minsk. Opposition activists were protesting at electoral irregularities in parliamentary elections in October 2004 and in a referendum in which President Lukashenka won the right to lift the constitutional limit of two presidential terms. Their sentences were immediately reduced to two years under the terms of the May amnesty.

⬠ On 10 June, Andrei Klimov, a former businessman and outspoken opposition politician, was sentenced to one and a half years of "restricted freedom" after being convicted of public order offences for organizing protests on 25 March. He started his sentence in September. Many protesters had been injured when riot police forcibly dispersed the March demonstration, which marked Freedom Day, the anniversary of the creation of the Belarusian People's Republic in 1918. On 28 March, 24 demonstrators were sentenced to jail terms of between three and 15 days for administrative offences.

Update

⬠ On 5 August, Yury Bandazhevsky was conditionally released under the May amnesty after serving four years of an eight-year sentence. Former rector of the Gomel State Medical Institute, he had been convicted in June 2001 of bribe-taking, although AI believes that the real reason for his imprisonment was that he had criticized official responses to the Chernobyl nuclear reactor catastrophe of 1986. He remained subject to restrictive conditions, among them reporting regularly to the police and being barred from any managerial or political functions. In addition he was required to pay a fine of 35 million Belarusian roubles (US$17,000), the amount he was alleged to have taken in bribes, before he was allowed to travel abroad.

Clampdown on freedom of expression

Opposition groups were harassed and threatened. Protests at the failure of investigations into the "disappearances" of four people, widely believed to have been killed by state agents, were among those that law enforcement officers suppressed with excessive force.

⬠ The youth opposition movement Zubr recorded 417 incidents of harassment, including detention, of their members by the authorities between January and December. Three members were expelled from educational establishments for their political activities.

⬠ In April police Special Forces (OMON) beat and detained peaceful demonstrators who had gathered on the 19th anniversary of the Chernobyl nuclear accident. A 14-year-old boy was allegedly pulled into a police van, so forcefully that ligaments in his hand were torn, and threatened for wearing a T-shirt bearing the slogan "Free Marinich".

On 7 July police dispersed a demonstration to commemorate the anniversary of the "disappearance" of television camera operator Dmitry Zavadsky in 2000. His wife, Svetlana Zavadskaya, was reportedly punched in the face by riot police officers.

On 16 September police attempted to disrupt a demonstration to observe the anniversary of the "disappearance" of opposition leaders Viktor Gonchar and Anatoly Krasovsky in 1999, and reportedly beat five Zubr protesters. One of them, Mikita Sasim, was treated in hospital for head injuries.

Human rights defenders

Human rights organizations, already severely hampered in their work by bureaucratic registration requirements and controversial guidelines, faced further obstructions. During the year parliament adopted a number of amendments to laws on public associations and political parties that further strengthened state control of non-governmental organizations. In July a presidential decree limited the financial support such groups could receive from Belarusian organizations and donors. In August international financial support for any activities that "aimed to change the constitutional order in Belarus, overthrow state power, interfere in internal affairs of the Republic of Belarus, or encourage the carrying out of such activities" was prohibited by amendment of a presidential decree of 22 October 2003.

In April the Belarusian Helsinki Committee, the last remaining registered human rights organization, applied for a tax exemption for financial assistance from the International Helsinki Federation. In June it was informed that the request could not be granted because the funding was not in line with the presidential decree on the acceptance of foreign financial support.

In July, Andrei Pochebut, Yusef Pozhetsky and Mecheslav Yaskevits, three prominent members of the Union of Poles of Belarus, were given prison sentences of between 10 and 15 days for protesting at government interference in the running of the Union. Police subsequently seized control of its headquarters. The three were convicted of "participating in an illegal protest" and "disobeying police orders". The government had refused to acknowledge the removal in elections of government supporters from its leadership.

Death penalty

No official statistics on the death penalty were published. According to the human rights group Viasna, at least one execution was carried out in 2005.

In July the deputy head of the presidential administration said that abolition of the death penalty could be considered "once social and economic preconditions were in place". Despite this statement from the government, there were no moves to end the use of the death penalty.

AI country reports/ visits
Report
· Europe and Central Asia: Summary of Amnesty International's concerns in the region, January-June 2005: Belarus (AI Index: EUR 01/012/2005)

BELGIUM

KINGDOM OF BELGIUM
Head of state: King Albert II
Head of government: Guy Verhofstadt
Death penalty: abolitionist for all crimes
International Criminal Court: ratified
UN Women's Convention and its Optional Protocol: ratified

Racist attacks directed against ethnic, religious and other minorities continued to be reported. Little was done to implement the National Plan of Action on Domestic Violence (2004-07). Foreign nationals, including minors, continued to be confined to airport transit zones for extended periods, in conditions often amounting to cruel, inhuman or degrading treatment. A Belgian court found two Rwandans guilty of war crimes committed in 1994 in Rwanda.

Background

During 2005, Belgium signed a number of human rights instruments including the Optional Protocol to the UN Convention against Torture and the European Convention on Action against Trafficking in Human Beings.

In October, the Belgian Council of Ministers proposed draft counter-terrorism legislation to parliament. The stated intent of the draft law was to modify the current criminal and judicial codes in order to "improve the methods of investigation in the fight against terrorism and grave and organized crime". The measures proposed included extending the hours during which a house search can be conducted; allowing suspects to be filmed without the authorization of a judge; and authorizing the creation of a confidential file to which suspects and their lawyers may be denied access. The law was awaiting approval at the end of the year.

Prison conditions

New legislation on prison conditions was not implemented and prison conditions continued to fall short of human rights standards.

On 18 March, a riot involving approximately 50 inmates took place in Ittre prison in the region of Walloon. The riot ended with three people injured and extensive material damage. On 27 March, the Council of State nullified the disciplinary proceedings initiated against some detainees thought to be responsible. Prison officers responded to this decision by going on strike for more than a week. The lawyer acting on behalf of some of the prisoners reported that the judgement of the Council of State had been ignored and her clients were being held in solitary confinement. There were also allegations that the inmates in solitary confinement were not allowed to read or write and those with an "Arab sounding" surname were denied contact with the religious counsel.

A delegation of the Council of Europe's Committee for the Prevention of Torture and Inhuman or Degrading Treatment or Punishment (CPT) carried out its fourth visit to Belgium in April.

A month-long strike by the prison guards at Antwerp prison started in September. They were protesting against overcrowding in detention facilities and the shortage of personnel. One of the consequences of overcrowding was that detainees were not allowed any daily exercise, despite a court order to reinstate daily exercise periods.

Racism and discrimination

In its annual report published in June, the Centre for Equal Opportunities and the Fight against Racism (Centre pour l'égalité des chances et de la lutte contre le racisme) expressed its concern at increasing xenophobia and racism in the country. The report highlighted employment discrimination, social discrimination and discrimination in access to public services. It also noted discrimination against people with disabilities, on the basis of sexual orientation and linked with health conditions.

Many racist incidents directed against ethnic, religious and other minorities continued to be reported in 2005.
⮑ In March, a Muslim woman resigned from her job in a food processing firm in Ledegem, western Belgium, after her employer received seven written death threats from a previously unknown organization. The threats stated that the life of the woman and the lives of her colleagues were in danger because she wore a headscarf to work. Two bullets were included in the seventh threatening letter. Despite the threats, her employer was actively supportive of her, and in April she resumed her job at the firm.
⮑ In March and May, the Juvenile Court of Louvain found three individuals guilty of a violent attack against two gay men in 2003. It was the first time a judgment by a Belgian court had referred specifically to sexual orientation and homophobia as the motivation behind a violent attack. The three men were sentenced to 100-euro fines.
⮑ In June, two trials regarding anti-Semitic acts opened in Antwerp. In the first case, a 22-year-old man was sentenced to six months' imprisonment and a fine of 550 euros on a charge of racism for threatening a Jewish man with a knife. The second case involved a 23-year-old man who was also convicted of racism for verbally abusing two Jewish youths. He received a two-month suspended sentence and a fine of 330 euros.

Violence against women

The prevalence of violence in the home remained a serious concern. According to a poll commissioned by AI in February and carried out within the French-speaking community, 29 per cent of Belgians knew of at least one household in which domestic violence had taken place.

In June, AI together with a large number of representatives of civil society — including women's organizations, unions, friendly societies and the largest employer's federation in Belgium, the Belgian Federation of Enterprises — presented the Belgian authorities with a list of principles and priorities on domestic violence.

The lack of official government statistics regarding gender violence in the home meant that the true scale of the problem was difficult to gauge. By the end of the year little had been done by the authorities to implement the National Plan of Action on Domestic Violence initiated in 2004.

Detention and deportation of foreign nationals

In February the report of an independent commission (the so-called Vermeersch II), set up by the Minister of the Interior to re-evaluate the techniques used in forcible deportations, was made public. The commission addressed some issues of concern including the need for transparency during forced removal; for asylum-seekers denied entry into Belgian territory from a transit zone to be provided with a right of appeal; and for the need to assign legal guardians for unaccompanied minors to be investigated. However, it concluded that a foreign national who resists forcible return can be detained until they abandon all resistance and can be expelled, raising concerns at the lack of a clear definition of what would constitute resistance and at the absence of a maximum period of detention.

Foreign nationals, including minors, continued to be confined to the airport transit zones for extended periods and in conditions often amounting to cruel, inhuman or degrading treatment. The UN High Commissioner for Refugees (UNHCR) stated in December, that the number of minors detained in such centres had continued to increase during the year and the length of their detention had also increased.

Universal jurisdiction

Although the law on universal jurisdiction was amended in 2003 so that victims could lodge complaints directly with an investigating magistrate only if the case had a direct connection with Belgium, a limited number of cases were pursued.
⮑ On 29 June, two Rwandans were convicted of war crimes and murder committed in 1994 in Rwanda. Half-brothers Etienne Nzabonimana, aged 53, and Samuel Ndashyikirwa, aged 43, were sentenced to 12 and 10 years' imprisonment respectively.
⮑ In September, Belgium issued an international arrest warrant against the former President of Chad, Hissène Habré. He was accused of human rights violations including torture, murder and "disappearances". Hissène Habré was arrested in November by the authorities in Senegal, where he had taken up residence. The Senegalese authorities stated that he would remain in detention until January 2006 when his extradition would be discussed at the summit of the African Union.

BELIZE

BELIZE
Head of state: Queen Elizabeth II, represented by Colville Young
Head of government: Said Musa
Death penalty: retentionist
International Criminal Court: ratified
UN Women's Convention and its Optional Protocol: ratified

There were reports of police abuse and use of excessive force. Eight people remained on death row. Children were subject to a wide range of human rights abuses.

Background

There were strikes and riots in January and April as a result of public anger over the economy.

The government expressed a desire to change the Constitution in order to accept the jurisdiction of the Caribbean Court of Justice as the final court of appeal in Belize, replacing the Privy Council.

Death penalty

One person was sentenced to death in 2005. In 2004 two death sentences were passed, but no executions were carried out. At the end of 2005, eight people were held on death row. There had been no executions since 1985.

Abuses by police

There were several reports of abuses by police, including torture, ill-treatment and arbitrary detention.

Three men, a father and his two sons, were arrested separately in July, on suspicion of withholding evidence related to a bank robbery. All three were reportedly beaten and subjected to electric shock torture before being released without charge.

Children

The UN Committee on the Rights of the Child expressed a number of concerns about abuses of children in Belize in its Concluding Observations issued in 2005, although it acknowledged that the government had made some efforts to remedy the situation. Concerns included: corporal punishment of children; discrimination against vulnerable groups of children; children without birth registration and nationality; the lack of access of non-registered children to services such as education and health; and the generally violent environment in which many Belizean children live.

BOLIVIA

REPUBLIC OF BOLIVIA
Head of state and government: Eduardo Rodríguez Veltzé (replaced Carlos Mesa Gisbert in June)
Death penalty: abolitionist for ordinary crimes
International Criminal Court: ratified
UN Women's Convention and its Optional Protocol: ratified

Peasant farmers, indigenous communities and human rights activists were threatened and violently evicted in land conflicts. Indigenous people were exploited as slave labour on farms and in homes in return for food, clothes and schooling. Judicial investigations into killings during political unrest in 2003 were delayed. Prison inmates protested at severe overcrowding and the lack of minimum facilities.

Background

There was widespread political unrest. Public demonstrations and road blockades led to the resignation of President Carlos Mesa Gisbert in June. The protests were staged mainly by indigenous communities, peasants and miners, who called for early elections and a greater role in determining economic policy. Following popular rejection of traditional political parties and of the constitutional succession of the Presidents of the Senate or Chamber of Deputies, President of the Supreme Court Eduardo Rodríguez Veltzé was appointed interim head of state.

In general elections in December, Evo Morales Ayma of the Movement to Socialism (Movimiento al Socialismo, MAS) was elected President.

Land and economic rights

Several disputes over land rights were reported, involving violent evictions. Indigenous groups, peasant farmers seeking land rights and members of non-governmental organizations representing them faced threats and assault. The economic rights of indigenous peoples were not respected.

In January members of the Association of Ranchers and Foresters of Riberalta (ASAGRI) destroyed and looted equipment at the offices of the non-governmental Centre for Legal Studies and Social Research, in Riberalta, Beni Department. The attackers also burned documents related to land ownership and threatened to burn lawyer Cliver Rocha alive. The Centre offers legal aid to indigenous and peasant communities. ASAGRI members had previously warned the Tacana people in the Miraflores area of Beni to leave communal land officially granted them in 2002, or be evicted by force.

In May, Silvestre Saisari Cruz, President of the Landless Movement of Santa Cruz Department, was beaten and kicked by men allegedly linked to a local landowner. He had denounced the burning of the community's recently harvested crops of rice and pineapples.

In August the Ombudsman called on President Rodríguez Veltzé to promote the correct implementation of Law 1715 in the Province of Guarayos, Department of Santa Cruz. Law 1715 regulates entitlements to communal land and use of natural resources by indigenous communities. In November he urged the authorities to end the exploitation and slave labour of 14,000 indigenous Guarani people in Chaco, Chuquisaca Department. Indentured labourers received food, clothes and a daily payment of under US$2, and children did farm or domestic work in exchange for a school education.

Delayed investigation into killings
Investigations into killings of civilians in October 2003 were further delayed. In October senior armed forces officers refused to testify to the court investigating the killings on the grounds that they had acted within the Constitution. In November the Supreme Court confirmed the court's request for their testimony, and President Rodríguez Veltzé, as Commander in Chief of the armed forces, authorized them to testify.

In November former head of state Gonzalo Sánchez de Lozada was served in the USA with judicial documents related to the criminal investigation in Bolivia into his responsibility for crimes committed at that time including human rights violations.

Prison overcrowding and protests
There were riots and hunger strikes as a result of overcrowding and the lack of essential facilities.
In September over 1,000 inmates of the seven prisons in Cochabamba Department started a hunger strike to press for food subsidies.
In October inmates rioted after telephone use was restricted and visits were cancelled in the women's wing of Cantumarca prison, Potosí Department.

The director of San Pedro prison, La Paz, stated in June that inmates had been forced to construct makeshift shelters inside the prison. Built for 380 people, the prison was housing 1,300.

Children's rights
Among recommendations made by the UN Committee on the Rights of the Child in January was the formulation of an action plan to eliminate the worst forms of child labour. The Committee recommended that sexual and economic exploitation and trafficking of children be made criminal offences, and that children subjected to these crimes be treated as victims and the perpetrators prosecuted. It also requested assistance for street children; the development of alternatives to imprisonment as a punishment; significant improvements in conditions for imprisoned juveniles; and ratification of the Protocol to Prevent, Suppress and Punish Trafficking in Persons Especially Women and Children, supplementing the UN Convention against Transnational Organized Crime.

AI country reports/ visits
Statements
- Bolivia: Fear for safety of Cliver Rocha and others (AI Index: AMR 18/001/2005)
- Bolivia: Fear for safety, Silvestre Saisari Cruz (AI Index: AMR 18/003/2005)
- Bolivia: The solution to the crisis lies in respect for human rights (AI Index: AMR 18/004/2005)
- Bolivia: Open letter from Amnesty International to the candidates to the Presidency of Bolivia (AI Index: AMR 18/006/2005)

BOSNIA AND HERZEGOVINA

BOSNIA AND HERZEGOVINA
Head of state: rotating presidency – Ivo Miro Jović, Borislav Paravac, Sulejman Tihić
Head of government: Adnan Terzić
President of the Federation of Bosnia and Herzegovina: Niko Lozančić
President of the Republika Srpska: Dragan Čavić
Death penalty: abolitionist for all crimes
International Criminal Court: ratified
UN Women's Convention and its Optional Protocol: ratified

Impunity for war crimes and crimes against humanity during the 1992-95 war was widespread. Thousands of "disappearances" were still unresolved. Victims and their families were denied access to justice. Lack of full co-operation with the International Criminal Tribunal for the former Yugoslavia (Tribunal), particularly by the Republika Srpska (RS), remained an obstacle to justice. Efforts to tackle impunity in proceedings before domestic courts remained largely insufficient, although some war crimes trials were conducted. The first convictions for war crimes committed by Bosnian Serbs were passed by RS courts. Of the one million refugees and internally displaced people who had returned to their homes since the end of the war, many continued to face discrimination.

Background
Bosnia and Herzegovina (BiH) remained divided in two semi-autonomous entities, the RS and the Federation of Bosnia and Herzegovina (FBiH), with a special status granted to the Brčko District.

The international community continued to exert significant influence over the country's political process, in particular through a High Representative with executive powers nominated by the Peace Implementation Council, an intergovernmental body monitoring implementation of the Dayton Peace Agreement. Approximately 6,500 troops of the European Union (EU)-led peacekeeping force EUFOR and 400 members of the European Union Police Mission remained in BiH. In November negotiations for a Stabilisation and Association Agreement (SAA) between the EU and BiH were opened.

International prosecutions for war crimes

The Tribunal continued to try alleged perpetrators of serious violations of international humanitarian law. In January, Vidoje Blagojević and Dragan Jokić, former officers of the Bosnian Serb Army (Vojska Republike Srpske, VRS), were sentenced to 18 and nine years' imprisonment respectively for their role in the killing of thousands of Bosniak men and boys after the fall of Srebrenica in July 1995.

In November Sefer Halilović, former Chief of the Main Staff of the Army of Bosnia and Herzegovina (Armija Bosne i Hercegovine, ABiH), was acquitted of the charge of murder as a war crime for the killing of non-Bosniaks in the villages of Uzdol and Grabovica. The Tribunal ruled that it had not been established beyond reasonable doubt that he had effective control over the troops when the crimes were committed.

In December Miroslav Bralo, former member of the Croatian Defence Council (Hrvatsko vijeće odbrane, HVO), the Bosnian Croat armed forces, was sentenced to 20 years' imprisonment for crimes committed in 1993 against Bosniaks in and around the villages of Ahmići and Nadioci. Miroslav Bralo had pleaded guilty to eight counts of war crimes and crimes against humanity, including persecutions, murder, torture and inhumane treatment, outrages upon personal dignity including rape, and unlawful confinement.

The trial continued of former President of the Federal Republic of Yugoslavia Slobodan Milošević, charged with war crimes and crimes against humanity for his alleged involvement in BiH, Croatia and Kosovo, and with aiding and abetting genocide in the war in BiH.

Co-operation between the RS authorities and the Tribunal remained inadequate. By the end of 2005, no suspect indicted by the Tribunal had been arrested by the RS police. A policy of "voluntary surrenders" by the RS authorities resulted in a number of transfers from the RS, or with the assistance of the RS authorities. However, the policy violated the obligation of the RS to co-operate fully by arresting and transferring indicted suspects. Six publicly indicted suspects remained at large, some of them believed to be in the RS or in Serbia and Montenegro.

Under a "completion strategy" laid down by the UN Security Council, the Tribunal was expected to conclude all cases, including appeals, by 2010. The last indictments before the closing down of the Tribunal were confirmed and unsealed between February and April.

In February former VRS officers Zdravko Tolimir, Radivoje Miletić and Milan Gvero were indicted on charges of war crimes and crimes against humanity

against the Bosniak population in the Srebrenica and Žepa enclaves. Radivoje Miletić and Milan Gvero surrendered voluntarily but Zdravko Tolimir remained at large at the end of 2005. Also in February the Tribunal indicted Rasim Delić, former Commander of the Main Staff of the ABiH, for murder, cruel treatment and rape committed in 1993 and 1995 against the non-Bosniak population. Following his indictment, he voluntarily surrendered.

Among those who surrendered voluntarily were Momčilo Perišić, former Chief of Staff of the Yugoslav People's Army, in March. He was indicted in February, charged with war crimes and crimes against humanity in BiH and Croatia, including against the civilian population during the siege of Sarajevo and against non-Serbs after the fall of Srebrenica. The indictment against former RS Interior Minister Mićo Stanišić, confirmed in February, charged him with war crimes and crimes against humanity, committed as part of a joint criminal enterprise aimed at permanently removing non-Serbs from areas under Bosnian Serb control. He voluntarily surrendered.

In May the Tribunal decided for the first time to refer one of its indictments to a national jurisdiction. Following a request by the Prosecutor, the case of former Bosnian Serb soldier Radovan Stanković, charged with the enslavement and rape of non-Serb women detained in Foča, was referred to the War Crimes Chamber of the BiH State Court (see below). The Tribunal subsequently transferred seven other suspects' cases to BiH.

In August Milan Lukić, former member of a Bosnian Serb paramilitary group indicted for war crimes and crimes against humanity including extermination, persecution, murder and inhumane acts against the non-Serb population in the Višegrad area, was arrested in Argentina by the local police. He was still held in Argentina at the end of 2005. In August former sub-commander of the RS military police and paramilitary leader in Foča, Dragan Zelenović, indicted for torture and rape committed by Bosnian Serb forces against non-Serb women detained in Foča, was arrested in the Russian Federation, where he remained in detention at the end of 2005.

Domestic prosecutions for war crimes

A War Crimes Chamber within the BiH State Court, set up to try cases referred by the Tribunal and particularly sensitive cases, became operational in March. The first trial before the Chamber started in September. In December the Prosecution at the BiH State Court confirmed indictments against 11 Bosnian Serbs suspected of involvement in the 1995 Srebrenica massacre. There remained concerns over the inadequacy of mechanisms to ensure the transfer of evidence from the Tribunal to the Chamber, and to ensure that the Tribunal's jurisprudence was consistently applied in its proceedings. The War Crimes Chamber only tried cases referred by the Tribunal and particularly sensitive cases, while a large number of cases remained to be dealt with by RS and FBiH courts.

In general, prosecutions were not actively pursued. Victims, witnesses and courts, particularly in cases before RS and FBiH courts, were not adequately protected from harassment, intimidation and threats. However, some war crimes trials opened or continued before national courts.

In January the Sarajevo Cantonal Court sentenced Veselin Čančar to four-and-a-half years' imprisonment for crimes committed against the civilian population detained by the Bosnian Serb forces in Foča. Former RS policeman Boban Šimšić, suspected of war crimes against civilians in the Višegrad area, surrendered to EUFOR troops in January. In May the War Crimes Chamber decided that he would be tried at the BiH State Court, and proceedings began in September.

In February, 11 former RS police officers were acquitted by the Banja Luka District Court of charges of illegally detaining Father Tomislav Matanović, a Roman Catholic priest, and his parents in 1995. The bodies of the priest and his parents were found in 2001 near Prijedor, with close-range gunshot wounds. Investigations into the killings reportedly continued.

In June, Tomo Mihajlović, a former RS police officer, was sentenced to four years' imprisonment by the Zenica Cantonal Court for crimes against the non-Serb population in the Teslić area in 1992. Also in June, Goran Vasić, a former member of a Bosnian Serb paramilitary group, received a six-year prison term from the Sarajevo Cantonal Court for the cruel and inhuman treatment of prisoners of war detained in the Sarajevo suburb of Nedžarići in 1992.

In July, Abduladhim Maktouf, a BiH citizen of Iraqi origin, was sentenced by the BiH State Court to five years' imprisonment for his role in the abduction of non-Bosniak civilians, who were beaten and ill-treated in a detention camp in Orašac and one of whom was beheaded. The sentence was quashed on appeal in November and a retrial ordered.

In October Konstantin Simonović was found guilty by the Brčko Basic Court for war crimes, including torture, against non-Serbs detained in the Luka camp near Brčko and sentenced to six years' imprisonment.

In November, for the first time since the end of the war, a war crimes trial of Bosnian Serb suspects before an RS court ended in convictions. The Banja Luka District Court sentenced Drago Radaković, Draško Krndija and Radoslav Knežević, former RS police officers, to between 15 and 20 years' imprisonment for the murder of six Bosniak civilians in Prijedor in 1994. In December, the Banja Luka District Court sentenced former VRS member Nikola Dereta to 13 years' imprisonment for the murder of one Bosniak civilian and the attempted murder of his father in the village of Štrbine.

Unresolved 'disappearances'
According to estimates of the International Commission on Missing Persons (ICMP), between 15,000 and 20,000 people who went missing during the war were still unaccounted for. Many of the missing were victims of "disappearances", and the perpetrators continued to enjoy impunity. In August the BiH Council of Ministers became the co-founder, with the ICMP, of a national Missing Persons Institute.

In a ceremony in July marking the 10th anniversary of the Srebrenica massacre, the remains of 610 victims were buried at the Potočari Memorial. At the end of 2005 the remains of approximately 5,000 victims had been recovered and over 2,800 victims identified.

Implementing a decision by the High Representative, the RS in January appointed a working group to study documentation produced by the Srebrenica Commission, established by the RS authorities to investigate the Srebrenica massacre, with a view to identifying those implicated. In its first report in March, the working group presented a list of 892 suspects still reportedly employed in RS and BiH institutions. The High Representative expressed concern at the failure of the RS Ministries of the Interior and of Defence to provide specific data on individuals deployed in Srebrenica in July 1995, and urged them to provide all information necessary to complete the list so that it could be forwarded to the Tribunal and the BiH Prosecutor. A further report and list were presented by the working group in September, which the High Representative deemed had met the obligations of the RS.

Right to return in safety and dignity
Since the end of the war, out of an estimated 2.2 million displaced people, more than a million refugees and internally displaced persons (IDPs) were estimated to have returned to their homes. According to the UN High Commissioner for Refugees field mission in BiH, between January and December, approximately 6,400 refugees and IDPs returned to their pre-war homes. Of these, approximately 5,800 people were registered as members of minorities.

Lack of access to employment continued to be a major factor in people's decision not to return or remain in their pre-war community. Employment opportunities were scarce in general, reflecting the weak economic situation and difficulties of economic transition and post-war reconstruction. In addition, returnees faced discrimination on ethnic grounds when trying to find work and, in some cases, ethnically motivated harassment and attacks.

AI country reports/ visits
Reports
- Amnesty International's concerns on the implementation of the "completion strategy" of the International Criminal Tribunal for the former Yugoslavia (AI Index: EUR 05/001/2005)
- Europe and Central Asia: Summary of Amnesty International's concerns in the region, July-December 2004: Bosnia and Herzegovina (AI Index: EUR 01/002/2005)
- Europe and Central Asia: Summary of Amnesty International's concerns in the region, January-June 2005: Bosnia and Herzegovina (AI Index: EUR 01/012/2005)

Visit
An AI delegate visited BiH in February.

BRAZIL

FEDERATIVE REPUBLIC OF BRAZIL
Head of state and government: Luiz Inácio Lula da Silva
Death penalty: abolitionist for ordinary crimes
International Criminal Court: ratified
UN Women's Convention: ratified with reservations
Optional Protocol to UN Women's Convention: ratified

Brazilians, especially the poor and socially excluded, continued to suffer high levels of human rights violations. There were few policy initiatives in the area of human rights, with many federal government proposals still awaiting implementation and few, if any, state authorities introducing promised public security reforms. Violations at the hands of the police, including extrajudicial executions, torture and excessive use of force, persisted across the country. Torture and ill-treatment were widespread in the prison system, where conditions were often cruel, inhuman or degrading. Indigenous peoples suffered attacks and killings as well as forcible evictions from their ancestral lands and the federal government fell short of its stated goal of demarcating all remaining indigenous lands by 2006. Human rights defenders and land activists suffered threats, attacks and killings. Impunity for human rights violations was the norm, arising from the slowness of judicial proceedings and the reluctance of some of the judiciary to prosecute such cases.

Background
The year was marked by a political crisis as evidence emerged of high-level corruption involving members of the government and of Congress. Accusations that the governing Workers' Party (Partido dos Trabalhadores, PT) had been involved in raising undeclared electoral funds, awarding government contracts dishonestly and buying votes in Congress shook the government and led to the resignation of the President's chief of staff, José Dirceu, and his subsequent expulsion from Congress. Three parliamentary inquiries into corruption were initiated and several members of Congress were under investigation by Congress' ethics committee. President Luiz Inácio Lula da Silva publicly apologized, accepting some of the charges levelled against his party, although denying any involvement.

Important efforts were made towards disarmament, with a law to control the carrying of guns introduced in 2003 apparently contributing to a national decline in homicides. However, Brazilians rejected a total ban on the sales of guns to civilians in a national referendum held in October, reflecting the public's anxiety about levels of crime. The federal authorities reported a decline of 8.2 per cent in the number of homicides nationally, the first such decline since 1992, while the state of São Paulo reported notable declines over a period of five years. These reductions were attributed to a combination of efforts to control small arms, alternative public security policies and targeted social investment at local level.

In October the UN Human Rights Committee expressed concern about a number of issues including extrajudicial executions and torture by police forces and threats to indigenous populations.

Public security and killings by the police
Reports of extrajudicial executions, excessive use of force and the systematic use of torture by state police forces persisted. Many states continued to defend tough policing policies to counter high levels of crime.

The number of people killed by police in situations officially registered as "resistance followed by death" (implying that the police had acted in self-defence) remained high in the states of Rio de Janeiro and São Paulo. Between 1999 and 2004, more than 9,000 cases of police killings, predominantly "resistance followed by death", were recorded in the two states. Investigations into these killings continued to be minimal.

There were also recurrent reports of human rights violations by federal and state police officers involved in corrupt and criminal activity, and of killings perpetrated by "death squads" involving active and former members of the police. State governments consistently failed to implement the public security reforms set out in the proposed Single Public Security System (SUSP) and the federal government focused its attention on police training rather than broader human rights-based reforms. As a result, residents of poor communities continued to suffer discriminatory, invasive and violent policing which failed to combat crime or provide any form of security.

On 31 March, 29 people were killed in the Baixada Fluminense district of Rio de Janeiro. The killings were attributed to a "death squad" of military police officers, who drove through the towns of Queimados and Nova Iguaçu shooting randomly at passers-by. Ten military police officers and one former police officer were arrested and charged with murder. The joint federal and civil police investigation linked at least 15 earlier killings to the massacre suspects, who were believed to have been involved in kidnapping and extorting money from lorry drivers.

While official statistics of police killings declined in São Paulo, human rights groups and residents of poor communities reported several multiple homicides allegedly committed by police officers.

On 22 June, five youths aged between 14 and 22 were reportedly executed by members of the civil police in the Morro do Samba community in Diadema. During a raid on the area, 35 police officers reportedly cornered the five in a house and sprayed them with machine-gun fire from the door and through the roof. Investigations into the killings were reportedly closed as the Internal Investigations Unit claimed the victims were all drug traffickers. Some family members of the dead youths were forced to leave the community for fear of reprisals.

In November the parliamentary Commission of Inquiry of the lower house of Congress published its final report on "death-squad" activity in the north-east, detailing cases from nine states. According to one of the parliamentarians responsible for the report, all involved active or former police officers. The report found links between state officials, business interests and organized crime across the north-east.

Torture and ill-treatment

Torture and ill-treatment continued to be used at the time of arrest, during interrogations and as a means of control within the detention system. There were also many reports of torture being used by law enforcement officials for criminal ends.

Impunity persisted and lack of published information about prosecutions under the 1997 Torture Law made the extent of the problem uncertain. The federal government's promised campaign against torture was finally launched in December. Proposals for Brazil to ratify the UN Optional Protocol to the UN Convention against Torture were pending before Congress.

Throughout 2005 there were reports of torture in São Paulo's FEBEM juvenile detention centres. Punishment units were reportedly staffed by guards from the adult prison system, contrary to the law. In the Vila Maria unit, which was reportedly used as a punishment centre, detainees were allegedly tortured and locked up all day. Concern was heightened by attempts by the authorities to block access to the detainees.

Riots within the juvenile detention system led to the death of at least five young detainees. In an apparent attempt to undermine the work of human rights groups, Governor Geraldo Alckmin accused two leading human rights activists — Conceição Paganele and Ariel de Castro Alvez — of inciting the riots. In November the Inter-American Commission on Human Rights ordered the Brazilian government to take measures to improve the FEBEM system.

◻ In September, the mother of a juvenile in the Vila Maria unit reported that her son had been so severely beaten by wardens that he was urinating blood. Another imprisoned juvenile showed his mother bruising and signs of torture. He told her that the director of the unit had personally ordered that his food be withheld. He was kept for four days in solitary confinement, after being dragged out of class by a guard who shot five times into the ceiling to intimidate him.

In April, two civil police officers, from Xinguara in the state of Pará, were convicted of the torture of a 15-year-old boy in 1999. The boy was severely beaten and suffered continuing psychological problems. This was the first conviction for torture in the region.

In November a video was aired on television showing veteran soldiers of an armoured infantry unit in the state of Paraná inflicting electric shocks, drowning and branding with irons during an initiation ceremony of recent recruits. The army immediately announced the suspension of the commanding officer and an internal investigation.

Prison conditions

Conditions in prisons amounted to cruel, inhuman or degrading treatment, and the prison population continued to rise. Overcrowding, poor sanitation and lack of health facilities contributed to frequent riots and high levels of prisoner-on-prisoner violence. There were also consistent reports of violent and abusive behaviour by guards, including the use of torture and ill-treatment. Special punishment regimes for prisoners found guilty of crimes within the prison system continued to be used, although in July the National Council on Criminal and Penal Policy of the Ministry of Justice described them as unconstitutional and contrary to international standards for the protection of detainees.

In Rio de Janeiro, human rights groups denounced conditions in the Polinter pre-trial detention centre. In August the unit held 1,500 detainees in a space designed for 250, with an average of 90 men per 3m x 4m cell. Between January and June, three men were killed in incidents between prisoners. Officials in the detention centre were also forcing detainees to choose which criminal faction they wished to be segregated with inside Polinter. In November the Inter-American Commission on Human Rights ordered the Brazilian government to take measures to improve the situation.

In June, during a riot in Zwinglio Ferreira detention centre in Presidente Venceslau, São Paulo state, five detainees were beheaded by other prisoners from opposing prison gangs.

In November the federal Commission of Human Rights of Congress held a public hearing on women in detention. The Commission received reports of human rights violations against women detained in São Paulo, who suffered from overcrowding, especially the 52 per cent held, many irregularly, in police holding cells.

Abuses in connection with land disputes

Thirty-seven land workers were killed between January and November, according to the Pastoral Land Commission (CPT). However, according to the CPT, even more died as a result of lack of medical or social assistance after they were evicted from land they had settled. Many land workers suffered death threats and harassment, as did homeless activists in cities and activists fighting against the constructions of dams.

In November, members of a congressional inquiry into rural violence approved a final report which called for farm invasions by land workers from the Landless Workers' Movement (Movimento dos Trabalhadores Rurais Sem Terra, MST) to be denoted "terrorist acts". They voted down a version of the report that cited the lack of land reform as the major factor in land conflict.

Reports of the use of slaves or indentured labour persisted. In December, AI delegates were informed by members of the Araquara town council that many sugar cane workers in the interior of São Paulo state had died, allegedly from exhaustion. According to these reports, workers were forced to cut several tons of sugar cane each day.

Proposed legislation that would allow the confiscation of land where slave labour is used remained in Congress. According to figures from the CPT, by August the government's campaign to combat slave labour had received reports of 173 such cases involving 5,407 people.

Indigenous peoples campaigning for land and human rights faced violent attacks and forced evictions. Many suffered extreme deprivation as a result. In Mato Grosso do Sul, long-standing demarcation processes of Guarani-Kaiowa lands were delayed by judicial proceedings, culminating in the forced evictions of Guarani-Kaiowa. While the federal government did ratify some important territories, they remained a long way from complying with their promised target of demarcating all remaining indigenous lands by 2006.

On 12 February, hired gunmen killed Sister Dorothy Stang, a nun who had long campaigned on ecological and land issues in Pará state. Two days earlier she had met the federal government's Special Secretary for Human Rights and told him of death threats against her. In December, two gunmen were convicted of the killing but those who allegedly ordered it were still awaiting trial. After this killing, the federal government sent federal police and army forces to help in investigations and to support the formation of a protected ecological area. Nevertheless, according to human rights groups, numerous land activists in the region were still under threat. A further 15 land activists were killed in the first six months of 2005 in Pará. An appeal to transfer Sister Dorothy's case to the federal judicial system was turned down by the Federal Appeals Court. This was the first case to seek to use new legislation allowing human rights crimes to be heard in the federal system.

In February, two homeless activists were shot and killed by military police officers during their forced eviction from a building in Goania, Goias state.

In June Adenilson dos Santos and his son Jorge were killed when four armed men, allegedly undercover police officers belonging to a "death squad", opened fire at a party held by the Truká community in Cabrobó, Pernambuco. The police stated that there was an exchange of fire, but Truká representatives stated that no one at the party was armed. The Truká alleged the attack was a result of their struggle for land and their opposition to organized crime and drug-trafficking organizations in their territory.

Human rights defenders

Human rights defenders, including those defending marginalized groups, opposing organized crime and corruption, and challenging vested political and economic interests, suffered defamation, threats, attacks and killings. The federal government's promised programme for the protection of human rights defenders showed little sign of implementation. In December the UN Special Representative on the situation of human rights defenders visited Brazil.

In September, military police raided the offices of Antonio Fernandez Saenz, a lawyer working with the socially deprived inhabitants of São Bernardo do Campo, south of São Paulo. The officers allegedly did not present a search warrant and took several documents containing statements by local residents accusing civil and military police of torture, extortion and sexually assaulting children. When Antonio Fernandez Saenz tried to report the incident to the civil police, he was threatened and intimidated. According to reports, he continued to receive anonymous death threats.

Impunity

The criminal justice system continued to fail those suffering human rights violations, as few perpetrators were brought to justice. There was little progress in several long-standing cases. The commanding officers convicted of the 1992 Carandiru massacre of prisoners by the military police and the 1997 Eldorado dos Carajás massacre of land activists remained at liberty pending appeals. Individual police officers in both cases were still awaiting trial.

Human rights groups expressed dismay following the government's announcement that only selected archives relating to "disappearances" and killings of political prisoners during the military government would be opened.

AI country reports/visits
Reports

- Brazil: "Foreigners in our own country"– Indigenous peoples in Brazil (AI Index: AMR 19/002/2005)
- Brazil: Briefing on Brazil's Second Periodic Report on the Implementation of the International Covenant on Civil and Political Rights (AI Index: AMR 19/021/2005)
- Brazil: "They come in shooting" – Policing socially excluded communities in Brazil (AI Index: AMR 19/025/2005)u

Visits

AI delegates visited Brazil in January, April and November/December.

BULGARIA

REPUBLIC OF BULGARIA
Head of state: Georgi Parvanov
Head of government: Sergey Stanishev (replaced
Simeon Saxe-Coburg-Gotha in August)
Death penalty: abolitionist for all crimes
International Criminal Court: ratified
UN Women's Convention: ratified
Optional Protocol to UN Women's Convention: signed

Reports of torture or ill-treatment of police detainees
continued. Discrimination against the Romani
community persisted, although legal action to
enforce anti-discrimination legislation achieved
favourable court rulings, including a landmark
decision that established the right of Romani
children to equality in education. Some residents of
care homes for people with mental disabilities
continued to live in conditions that amounted to
inhuman and degrading treatment. A court ruled
that neglect by the state caused the deaths of 13
children deprived of food and heating at a care home
in 1996 and 1997.

Political developments
After a general election in June, a coalition government
was eventually formed two months later, headed by
Sergey Stanishev of the Socialist Party. The far-right
party Ataka (Attack) saw a rapid rise in support, coming
fourth in the poll.

Bulgaria made progress towards greater respect for
human rights in an attempt to meet the criteria for
membership of the European Union (EU), scheduled for
2007. Efforts were made to observe the rights of
suspects in criminal proceedings, to end trafficking in
human beings and to fulfil health rights. However, the
European Commission expressed concerns about ill-
treatment by law enforcement officials, discrimination
against Roma and the living conditions of people with
mental disabilities in its annual report, published in
October, on Bulgaria's preparations for EU accession.

Police and prison abuses
The European Court of Human Rights gave a number of
rulings that poor conditions of detention had
amounted to cruel or degrading treatment. The Court
also found in several cases that Bulgaria had violated
the right to liberty and security of person, the right to
a hearing within a reasonable time, and the right to
fair trial.

Reports of torture or ill-treatment by law
enforcement officials continued. Failure to respect the
detainee's right to be questioned in the presence of a
lawyer often contributed to such abuse.

In 16 April Julian Krastev, aged 38 and homeless,
was reportedly beaten to death by a police sergeant in
the town of Varna. He had been living in a cupboard in
the apartment block where the officer lived.

Reportedly, the officer had been drinking alcohol and
two police colleagues witnessed the assault. The officer
was dismissed from the police and charged before the
Varna Regional Military Court.

In November, 39-year-old businessman Anguel
Dimitrov died during a police operation in Blagoevgrad,
according to the police from a heart attack during his
arrest. Following public protests by his family, who
claimed that the police were responsible for his death,
an inquest was opened. In December, the findings of an
autopsy revealed that he had died from a haemorrhage
caused by a blow to the head. Although the Interior
Ministry publicly accepted responsibility for the
wrongful actions of the police and the Blagoevgrad
police chief resigned, the Prosecutor's Office
announced that there was insufficient evidence to
bring a prosecution.

The International Helsinki Federation, a human
rights organization, reported inhuman conditions in
several detention facilities, especially in Plovdiv and
Nova Zagora. There were no effective mechanisms to
respond to complaints of ill-treatment and violence
between prisoners. Medical care in prisons was of poor
quality and was not integrated within the national
health care system.

Discrimination against Roma
The Romani community was most often targeted for ill-
treatment by law enforcement officials and
discriminatory treatment.

In July the Grand Chamber of the European Court
of Human Rights for the first time addressed the racial
element in a case involving the deprivation of life. It
upheld an earlier decision by the Court in the
landmark case of *Nachova v Bulgaria*, which involved
the 1996 killing of two unarmed Romani army
deserters by a military police officer. The Court
unanimously found the Bulgarian state responsible
for the deaths of the two men, and for the failure to
conduct an effective official investigation into
allegations that the killings were motivated by anti-
Roma racism.

In June a court in Blagoevgrad ruled against a
restaurant for refusing to serve a group of Romani
customers in March 2004 while serving non-Romani
people who had arrived later. The Romani group
brought a complaint of discrimination after waiting
for service for an hour, and the restaurant owner was
unable to show that he had not treated them
differently from others, as required under Bulgaria's
comprehensive anti-discrimination legislation.

Forced evictions in Sofia
On 31 August at least 24 Romani houses in the Hristo
Botev municipality of Sofia were demolished, leaving
some 150 Roma homeless. In September the authorities
in Vuzrazhdane municipality subsequently warned
Romani inhabitants to abandon their illegally
constructed houses in Serdika district within seven
days. However, a day before the scheduled
demolitions, the Sofia District Court ordered the
evictions to be postponed pending a decision on the
Roma's legal entitlement to remain. The authorities had

reportedly made no provision for compensation or alternative accommodation for those to be evicted.

School segregation

In October the Sofia District Court ruled that the Ministry of Education, the Sofia municipality and a Sofia school had segregated Romani children in violation of anti-discrimination legislation. It found that the school's students were all Romani, not through the choice of the students but because of failures by the authorities. The court held that substandard conditions in the school, lack of control over school attendance and lower educational requirements violated Romani children's right to equal and integrated education.

This was a landmark case for Bulgarian Roma, who faced discrimination in many spheres of public life, including education and employment. According to the European Roma Rights Centre, between 70 and 90 per cent of students in special schools for children with physical and developmental disabilities in Bulgaria were Roma.

People with mental disabilities

People with mental disabilities living in social care homes were not effectively protected from physical and mental abuse. The services they received did not meet international human rights standards or conform to best professional practice.

The situation for former residents of a care home in Dragash Voyvoda, closed in 2003 following publicity about inadequate medical care and harsh living conditions, was only slightly improved in some of the homes to which residents had been transferred. Although their material provision had in most cases improved slightly, some still lived in conditions that amounted to inhuman and degrading treatment. There was still no independent mechanism to ensure prompt, thorough and impartial investigation of reported abuses against residents of mental health institutions.

In June, Ivailo Vakarelski, aged 24, was found dead in the State Psychiatric Hospital in Karlukovo to which he had been admitted several days earlier. According to reports, his body showed extensive bruising. Hospital staff were said to have told his parents that an autopsy could only be performed if they paid for one, even though the hospital was obliged to perform an autopsy under the Health Care Act. The regional prosecutor ordered an investigation after the local prosecutor initially declined to investigate the death.

The International Helsinki Federation reported that many Bulgarian psychiatric hospitals and social care homes lacked facilities for adequate treatment or care for people with mental and developmental disabilities. Despite some improvements, food was insufficient, and treatment methods were not compatible with international obligations to provide the highest attainable level of health and life in dignity for people with disabilities.

In May the District Court of Plovdiv acquitted three members of staff from a social care home in Dzhurkovo who had been charged in connection with the deaths of 13 children from hypothermia, malnutrition and lung diseases between December 1996 and March 1997. The

court was unable to establish a causal link between the deaths and negligence by staff, but found that neglect on the part of the state had left the home without the means to pay for food and heating, resulting in living conditions that were cruel, inhuman and degrading.

AI country reports/ visits
Reports

- Bulgaria: Failings in the provision of care – The fate of the men of Dragash Voyvoda (AI Index: EUR 15/002/2005)
- Bulgaria and Romania: Amnesty International's human rights concerns in the EU accession countries (AI Index: EUR 02/001/2005)

BURUNDI

REPUBLIC OF BURUNDI
Head of state: Pierre Nkurunziza (replaced Domitien Ndayizeye in August)
Death penalty: retentionist
International Criminal Court: ratified
UN Women's Convention: ratified
Optional Protocol to UN Women's Convention: signed

Local, legislative and presidential elections were held, signalling the end of Burundi's transition period, although armed conflict continued in two provinces. Government forces committed serious human rights violations including arbitrary arrests and detentions, rape and extrajudicial executions. An opposition armed group committed abuses including unlawful killings. Sexual violence against women, including rape, persisted. The Burundi authorities forcibly returned more than 5,000 Rwandan asylum-seekers, and reportedly allowed Rwandan soldiers into the country to take them back to Rwanda. At the end of 2005, 499 detainees were under sentence of death.

Background

2005 saw a series of elections. On 28 February, a national referendum on the Constitution produced a "yes" vote of more than 90 per cent. However, negotiations between the political parties relating to the electoral code and the schedule for local and legislative elections stalled. The UN Secretary-General and regional leaders intervened, setting a deadline of August to complete the electoral process, and the President called local elections on 3 June, legislative elections on 4 July and the presidential election on 18 August.

The former armed opposition group, the CNDD-FDD, won the local elections with more than 55 per cent of the vote, and in the legislative elections gained 59 of the 118 seats in parliament. On 26 August, Pierre Nkurunziza, leader of the CNDD-FDD, became President, ending the transitional period that started in 2002.

Armed conflict continued throughout 2005 between one armed group, PALIPEHUTU-FNL, known as the FNL (Forces nationales de libération), and the government armed forces (Forces de défense nationale, FDN) in the provinces of Bujumbura rural and Bubanza, despite the presence of 5,634 UN peacekeeping soldiers serving with the UN Operation in Burundi (ONUB). The FNL still refused to negotiate a ceasefire agreement with the government.

Human rights violations

Government armed forces composed of former CNDD-FDD fighters and soldiers of the former Burundi armed forces (Forces armées burundaises, FAB) were responsible for serious human rights violations. Civilians in Bujumbura rural and alleged FNL members were subjected to abuses including arbitrary arrests and detentions, rape and extrajudicial executions.

On 14 May in the commune of Isale the FDN allegedly shot dead 17 FNL fighters who were reportedly unarmed.

After the election, the security forces and the national intelligence agency (Documentation nationale) undertook operations to secure the borders with the Democratic Republic of the Congo (DRC) and to counter the FNL. During these operations, they frequently detained Burundi and DRC nationals arbitrarily.

On 24 September, a Congolese refugee from the Banyamulenge community was arrested in the town centre of Bujumbura by intelligence agents. He was held for more than three weeks without being told the legal basis for his arrest.

During the week beginning 3 October, intelligence agents arrested two local civil servants and dozens of other people in Bujumbura for allegedly being FNL members. According to reports, several of them were beaten and injured in detention.

Human rights abuses by the FNL

Throughout 2005, the FNL threatened and intimidated the civilian population in the provinces of Bujumbura rural and Bubanza, often demanding shelter or food.

During the election period, low-level government officials and civilians suspected of collaborating with government armed forces were killed by the FNL. Between 6 March and 6 June, the FNL reportedly killed at least six local administrative staff in Bujumbura rural province and abducted three others. Several political members of CNDD-FDD were beheaded and rural families were targeted for merely speaking with soldiers.

On 16 June, a group of 11 combatants, reportedly belonging to the FNL, entered a Protestant church service in Muyaga, Muhutu commune. Once inside, they closed the doors and windows of the church and fired into the congregation. Eight people were killed and 30 others were wounded.

A single mother was attacked on 14 August at her home in the province of Bujumbura rural by armed FNL combatants who accused her of working for the government. According to her statement, to punish her, they buried her child alive, physically assaulted her and tied her to a tree. She only managed to escape after three days.

During the second half of 2005, the FNL sought to expand its activities in other provinces, notably Bubanza and Ngozi, often with the help of local officials.

Violence against women

Rape and other forms of sexual violence persisted despite the implementation of a ceasefire in most areas of the country.

On 20 August, H.A., a 16-year-old girl from the commune of Murwi, Cibitoke province, was raped. The alleged perpetrator was arrested but then immediately released.

According to the human rights department of ONUB, in 2005, only one out of every three women raped lodged a complaint. Of these, the majority dropped their case before anyone was brought to justice.

Death penalty

At the end of 2005, 499 detainees were under sentence of death. The last executions, of seven civilians, took place in 1997, but courts continued to pass death sentences.

Kassi Manlan verdict

On 3 May, the Bujumbura appeals court sentenced to death four people accused of taking part in the assassination of Dr Kassi Manlan, the representative of the World Health Organization, in November 2001: Emile Manisha, the former commandant of the public security police station; Colonel Gérard Ntunzwenayo, the assistant commissioner in charge of Documentation nationale; Aloys Dizimana, the former commandant of the Kiyange brigade; and Japhet Ndayegamiye, the official in charge of Documentation nationale. Three other men were sentenced to life imprisonment, two of whom had been in prison at the time of the murder. Two men were sentenced to 20 years in jail: Expert Bihumugani, head of a private security firm, and Athanase Bizindavyi, Director of the central prison of Bujumbura.

Administration of justice

The justice system continued to suffer from lack of resources and inadequate training for personnel. There were frequent complaints of corruption at national and local levels.

On 10 July 2005, detainees in Rumonge prison went on strike to protest against the indefinite detention of prisoners without trial. Some detainees accused of ordinary criminal offences had been waiting for more than five years for a trial.

Trials of people accused of participating in the violence which followed the 1993 assassination of former President Ndadaye continued.

National Truth and Reconciliation Commission

Legislation establishing a National Truth and Reconciliation Commission (NTRC), passed in December 2004, mandated the NTRC to establish the truth about acts of violence committed in the course of the conflict since 1962, specify which crimes had been committed, other than genocide, and identify both perpetrators and victims of such crimes. In a report published in March, the UN Secretary-General raised doubts about the credibility and impartiality of the NTRC and addressed the feasibility of establishing an international judicial commission of inquiry. It recommended amending the composition of the NTRC by including an international component (originally it was to comprise 25 members, all Burundians) and setting up a special chamber within the court system of Burundi. This chamber would be competent to prosecute those bearing the greatest responsibility for the crime of genocide, crimes against humanity and war crimes, and would be composed of national and international judges. In November, the new government designated a delegation of eight members to establish an NTRC in collaboration with the UN.

On 15 November, the authorities set up a commission to identify political prisoners. Composed of 21 members, its tasks included defining political prisoners and formulating recommendations.

Juvenile justice

In most prisons, children endured harsh and overcrowded conditions. Some child detainees reported acts of sexual abuse; many were malnourished and had lost contact with their families. Several suffered cruel, inhuman or degrading treatment.

⌐ R., aged 14, was arrested in January 2004, accused of robbery, and sentenced in May 2004 to 30 months' imprisonment. He said that during his initial six months' custody, he was beaten with a metal rod and a stick by a police officer. When AI delegates met him in January 2005, they saw the scars on his arms.

Although Burundi ratified the African Charter on the Rights and Welfare of the Child in 2004, and its national legislation includes provisions specific to children, the authorities failed to take into account children's special status. Magistrates and penitentiary authorities did not receive the necessary training on how to implement the laws that apply to children.

Refugees, returnees and the internally displaced

Between April and November, more than 10,000 Rwandans fled their country to seek asylum in Burundi (see Rwanda entry). The Burundian authorities initially registered the asylum-seekers and requested assistance from the UN High Commissioner for Refugees (UNHCR). However, at the end of April, Burundi changed this approach under pressure from Rwanda. On 27 April, in breach of its regional and international obligations, the government declared that the Rwandans would not be granted asylum, and in the following days and weeks soldiers rounded up asylum-seekers, placed them in trucks and forced them to go back to Rwanda. As early as 25 May, more than 7,000 of them had found their way back to Burundi. The Burundian authorities then reportedly allowed Rwandan soldiers to enter the country, to destroy the asylum-seekers' makeshift camps and to forcibly repatriate them once more. On 13 June, Burundian officials described these people as "illegal immigrants".

After the elections, the new government declared that there would be no forcible returns and that it would allow UNHCR to assist asylum-seekers. However, the authorities continued to refer to them as "illegal immigrants".

Between January and December, UNHCR facilitated the repatriation of some 60,000 Burundian refugees (returnees), bringing the total number to 300,000 since 2002. The lack of land available in Burundi caused problems for returnees trying to regain their former property.

⌐ Marthe Misago, a 28-year-old widow, fled Kirundo province in Burundi in 1994. She returned in 2004 with her four children. Her mother-in-law, who had taken over her land, refused to return it and threatened to kill her if she tried to recover it. Marthe Misago asked the authorities to intervene but by the end of 2005, her case was still unresolved.

At the end of 2005, more than 120,000 people still lived in internally displaced people's camps, mainly in the northern and eastern provinces. Meanwhile, the populations of Bujumbura rural and Bubanza continued to face short-term displacement. Many of them were too frightened to spend the night in their homes because of armed attacks.

AI country reports/visits

Reports

- Burundi: Refugee rights at risk – human rights abuses in returns to and from Burundi (AI Index: AFR 16/006/2005)
- Burundi: Gatumba massacre – an urgent need for justice (AI Index: AFR 16/010/2005)
- Burundi: Fragile peace at risk as refugees pressured to return (AI Index: AFR 16/008/2005)
- Burundi: Security considerations should not prejudice human rights (AI Index: AFR 16/011/2005)

Visits

AI delegates visited Burundi in January, July and October.

CAMBODIA

KINGDOM OF CAMBODIA
Head of state: King Norodom Sihamoni
Head of government: Hun Sen
Death penalty: abolitionist for all crimes
International Criminal Court: ratified
UN Women's Convention: ratified
Optional Protocol to UN Women's Convention: signed

Peaceful criticism of the government was curtailed. Immunity was lifted for three opposition parliamentarians; two were subsequently sentenced to imprisonment. Criminal charges were brought against trade union leaders and a media representative. Human rights defenders and opposition politicians faced threats. Restrictions on freedom of assembly were maintained. Vietnamese Montagnard asylum-seekers continued to arrive; some were forcibly returned.

Background
Cambodian politics continued to be pursued through the courts. Political opponents lodged numerous criminal complaints against each other, putting considerable political pressure on the judiciary.

In February a closed session of the National Assembly lifted the parliamentary immunity of three Sam Rainsy Party (SRP) members. The SRP responded by boycotting the legislative chamber until August. The boycott and a culture of declining attendance meant that parliament was repeatedly inquorate.

The agreement between Cambodia and the UN to set up a criminal tribunal to prosecute suspected major perpetrators of gross human rights violations during the Khmer Rouge rule (1975-1979) took effect in April.

In October a supplemental border agreement was signed with Viet Nam.

In November UN Secretary-General Kofi Annan announced the appointment of Professor Yash Ghai as his Special Representative on human rights in Cambodia. The appointment followed the resignation from the post of Peter Leuprecht.

Critics gagged
In a crackdown against critics of the border agreement with Viet Nam, radio manager Mam Sonando and President of the Independent Teachers Association Rong Chhun were detained and charged with defamation and incitement to commit a crime. If found guilty they could face several years' imprisonment. They were prisoners of conscience.

Court summons were issued on similar charges to at least three other union leaders and a number of public figures, several of whom sought sanctuary abroad.

Two leading human rights defenders, Kem Sokha and Yeng Virak, were arrested on 31 December for allegedly defaming the government. Their detention came nine days after opposition leader Sam Rainsy, in exile since he lost his parliamentary immunity, was convicted in absentia of defamation and sentenced to 18 months' imprisonment.

These breaches of the right to freedom of speech caused considerable tension within civil society.

In September, two Ministry of the Environment rangers were shot dead in an apparently premeditated attack in Aural Wildlife Sanctuary. The attack underscored the dangers facing defenders of natural resources and local livelihoods. Days earlier the international non-governmental organization Global Witness had closed its Cambodia office after its international staff were denied visas and its local staff were harassed.

Weak legal system
In March, Prime Minister Hun Sen launched an "iron fist" policy, purportedly to combat corruption in the judiciary. Several judges and prosecutors were removed without due disciplinary procedures, and the UN Special Representative on human rights in Cambodia warned that the policy further undermined the independence of the courts.

Two high-profile trials illustrated the corrupt and weak judicial system's failure to ensure impartiality and its disregard for the presumption of innocence.

Cheam Channy, the SRP shadow minister of defence, was arrested immediately after his parliamentary immunity was lifted. He was tried in a military court and, despite the lack of evidence, convicted in August of establishing an illegal armed force and fraud. He was sentenced to seven years in prison.

There were numerous irregularities in the trial. Military courts have no jurisdiction over civilians. The defence was barred from calling witnesses to testify and prevented from cross-examining all prosecution witnesses. No credible evidence was presented to substantiate the charges which were believed to be unfounded.

Fellow party member Khom Piseth had fled abroad after the accusations were levelled against the two in 2004 and had resettled as a political refugee. At the same trial he was sentenced to five years' imprisonment after being convicted, in absentia, of similar charges.

In August, Born Samnang and Sok Samoeun were sentenced to 20 years in prison for the murder in 2004 of trade union leader Chea Vichea following an unfair trial. The criminal investigation lacked integrity; people providing alibis for the suspects were threatened with arrest; the prosecution failed to produce evidence; and the pre-trial detention period exceeded by almost one year the legal limit under Cambodian law.

Land and housing
After a visit to Cambodia in August, the UN Special Rapporteur on adequate housing highlighted substantial land grabbing which appeared to be depriving the rural and urban poor of land. The Special Rapporteur also noted that many violent forced evictions followed inconclusive court investigations.

▭ Two hundred families in Kbal Spean village near the Thai border crossing of Poipet were forcibly evicted in March after a court battle against their village chief. Five villagers, including one man disabled in a mine accident, were shot dead and 40 wounded as armed forces implemented a court order following a questionable legal process. By the end of the year nobody had been brought to justice for the shootings. The provincial authorities endorsed the relocation of residents to an area far from the border crossing where they earn their living.

Land concessions continued to dispossess and impoverish Cambodians.

▭ In Mondulkiri province, indigenous Phnong people lost both ancestral land and farmland as a result of a land concession granted by the government in 2004. Villagers and local authorities were never consulted and no environmental or social impact studies were undertaken before the company was awarded the concession for tree plantation, which vastly exceeded the legal limit of 10,000 hectares. The company failed to comply with a government order issued in June to suspend operations.

Refugees

Montagnard refugees from Viet Nam continued to cross into Cambodia. Some were forcibly returned before they could present their asylum claims, in breach of Cambodia's obligations under the 1951 UN Refugee Convention.

Following a tripartite Memorandum of Understanding signed by Cambodia, Viet Nam and the UN High Commissioner for Refugees in January, refugees who did not wish to resettle in a third country or to return to Viet Nam were sent back to their native Central Highlands despite the absence of permanent monitoring (see Viet Nam entry). Of the several hundred people awaiting resettlement abroad in sites in Phnom Penh, some 340 were resettled, mainly in the USA.

The government warned that villagers assisting Vietnamese Montagnard asylum-seekers in the border provinces would face trafficking charges. Harassment and threats were reported against individual human rights defenders who had aided refugees.

Violence against women

In September the National Assembly adopted a law against domestic violence. The law extended the legal authority for police and local officials to respond to domestic violence, and included legal protections for victims.

In its annual Trafficking in Persons report, the US government criticized the lack of progress made by the Cambodian authorities in combating trafficking and the failure to convict public officials and others involved in people trafficking.

AI country reports/ visits
Reports
- Cambodia: Chea Vichea (AI Index: ASA 23/001/2005)
- Cambodia: Amnesty International calls on states to nominate their highest qualified judges and prosecutors to the Extraordinary Chambers of Cambodia (AI Index: ASA 23/004/2005)
- Cambodia: Sentencing of parliamentarian reflects continuing flaws in the judicial system (AI Index: ASA 23/005/2005)
- Cambodia: Open Letter to Prime Minister Hun Sen on the occasion of International Human Rights Day 2005 raising concern about the state of freedom of expression in the Kingdom of Cambodia (AI Index: ASA 23/006/2005)

Visit
An AI delegation visited Cambodia in November.

CAMEROON

REPUBLIC OF CAMEROON
Head of state: Paul Biya
Head of government: Ephraim Inoni
Death penalty: retentionist
International Criminal Court: signed
UN Women's Convention and its Optional Protocol: ratified

Human rights defenders were harassed, assaulted and detained. Individuals were unlawfully detained on account of their sexual orientation. A group of political prisoners, convicted after unfair trials and held in life-threatening conditions that have killed three of their number since 1999, continued to be denied a right of appeal. Investigations were started into a few deaths in police custody that reportedly resulted from torture, but they were not independent or open. Inmates were killed and injured in prison riots stemming from severe overcrowding and harsh discipline.

Background

The oil-rich Bakassi peninsula remained under the control of the Nigerian government, despite a 2002 ruling by the International Court of Justice in the Hague that it be handed over to Cameroon. Local leaders of Nigerian nationality urged their government not to cede sovereignty over the peninsula to Cameroon.

Human rights defenders under threat

Critics of the government's human rights record continued to be routinely harassed, detained and assaulted.

▭ Nelson Ndi, a member of the government's National Commission on Human Rights and Freedoms, was assaulted on 3 February by members of the paramilitary police Mobile Intervention Unit. He had tried to stop officers beating a group of youths near his office. No action was known to have been taken against his assailants.

Unlawful detention for sexual orientation

Eleven men, aged between 18 and 49, and two women were arrested by gendarmes on 20 and 21 May in Yaoundé, the capital. The two women were charged with public disorder and released to await trial. The men, who should have been brought before a judge within three days, were transferred to Kondengui Central Prison in Yaoundé on 13 June, where they saw a lawyer for the first time. They were subsequently charged with sodomy because of their real or perceived same-sex orientation.

Southern Cameroons National Council

In December, the Appeal Court in Yaoundé decided on appeals by imprisoned members of the Southern Cameroons National Council (SCNC) against their 1999 convictions by a military tribunal. Adelbert Ngek and Promise Nyamsai, who were serving 10-year prison terms, had their convictions quashed and were released. Three prisoners had their life sentences reduced to 25 years, and one had a 20-year term reduced to 15 years. Two prisoners had 15-year terms reduced to 10 years, and four others had 10-year terms confirmed. Two prisoners, Wilson Che Neba and Samuel Che Neba, had been released in May after serving eight-year prison terms. The prisoners who remained in custody appealed to the Supreme Court against the decision of the Appeal Court.

The prisoners had been denied an appeal for more than five years. After lawyers lodged a complaint with the African Commission on Human and Peoples' Rights on the prisoners' behalf, the Minister of Defence announced in November 2004 that they could appeal to the Appeal Court. The hearings, which started in January 2005, were repeatedly adjourned because the authorities failed to produce some of the prisoners in court or provide an interpreter for English-speaking prisoners.

The prisoners had been sentenced to between eight years and life imprisonment after an unfair trial before a special court directly controlled by the Ministry of Defence, on charges in connection with armed attacks in North West Province in 1997. Most of the prisoners who appeared before the Appeal Court looked sick and frail as a result of life-threatening prison conditions and medical neglect.

☐ Julius Ngu Ndi, who had been serving a 20-year prison sentence, died from tuberculosis in July. He had reportedly been denied adequate and prompt medical treatment for several months and was taken to hospital only days before he died.

Peaceful political activities by SCNC members were met with arbitrary and unlawful detentions.

☐ On 15 January as many as 40 SCNC supporters were detained and the group's leader, Henry Fossung, was reportedly assaulted by Mobile Intervention Unit officers in Buéa. The women detainees, who had been preparing food for a celebration at Henry Fossung's home, were released without charge the same day. The men were freed two days later. A government minister reportedly said they had been holding a clandestine meeting. Ayemba Ette Otun and about 20 other SCNC members were arrested while meeting in October and detained for up to two weeks.

Denial of freedom of expression

The authorities continued to use criminal libel laws to imprison journalists in cases that appeared to be politically motivated.

☐ Jules Koum Koum, director of *Le Jeune Observateur* newspaper, was sentenced to six months' imprisonment on 10 January for publishing articles alleging corruption among insurance company executives. Provisionally released on 9 February, he faced further charges in criminal libel cases involving an insurance company and two former government ministers.

Harsh prison conditions

Overcrowding, inadequate food and medical neglect continued to result in high mortality rates in prisons. New Bell prison in Douala, built for only 800 prisoners, held about 3,000 at the start of 2005. Prisoners were said to sleep on the ground, sometimes in the toilets and even outdoors. Prison authorities failed to ensure the safety of inmates.

☐ On 3 January, one prisoner was reportedly killed and about 20 injured in a riot in New Bell prison. The fighting between prisoners involved a group known as "anti-gang", which was accused of inflicting harsh discipline in the prison, including by beatings, at the request of the authorities. Soon after the riot was quelled, the prison director was replaced.

Torture and ill-treatment

The systematic torture continued of suspects arrested by the police and gendarmerie. Most perpetrators were not held to account, but investigations were opened in a few cases in which suspects died.

☐ In March, after months of inaction, the procuracy in Buéa initiated investigations into the death of Afuh Bernard Weriwo in hospital on 10 July 2004. A senior police officer had allegedly been involved in assaulting and setting fire to him after he was arrested at his home in Ikiliwindi town on suspicion of stealing a bicycle. In October the High Court in Kumba sentenced him to five years' imprisonment for torturing and causing the death of Afuh Bernard Weriwo. A key witness for the prosecution reportedly received death threats for testifying against the officer.

☐ On 8 February, Emmanuel Moutombi died from injuries sustained after he was detained in Douala in mid-January following accusations of embezzlement. A postmortem revealed severe swelling and injuries to his entire body. Six gendarmes and the victim's former manager were implicated in the death and were on trial before the Douala military tribunal at the end of 2005.

☐ Eleven people arrested in September 2004 in connection with the killing of John Kohtem, a leader of the opposition Social Democratic Front, remained in custody without trial. A member of parliament implicated in the killing remained free on bail.

Violence against women

Women remained without adequate protection in law against violence. Approximately 20 per cent of women and girls were reported to undergo female genital mutilation (FGM), which continued to be practised primarily in the far north and the south-west and was still not prohibited in law. Provisions also remained in the Penal Code that exempted a rapist from judicial proceedings if he married his victim, effectively protecting the perpetrator while subjecting the victim to further abuse.

Death penalty
No death sentences were known to have been passed or executions carried out. By the end of 2005 the authorities had still not made public how many prisoners under sentence of death had benefited from a presidential decree issued on 29 December 2004. Under the decree, death sentences were commuted to life imprisonment, except in some specified cases, including the killing of a child. The numbers of prisoners still awaiting execution remained unknown.

AI country reports/ visits
Visits
The government continued to deny AI representatives access to the country, as it has done for over a decade.

CANADA

CANADA
Head of state: Queen Elizabeth II, represented by Michaëlle Jean (replaced Adrienne Clarkson in September)
Head of government: Paul Martin
Death penalty: abolitionist for all crimes
International Criminal Court: ratified
UN Women's Convention and its Optional Protocol: ratified

Indigenous women and girls continued to suffer a high level of discrimination and violence. There were concerns that counter-terrorism practices did not conform to human rights obligations.

Background
Canada ratified in September the Optional Protocol to the UN Children's Convention on the sale of children, child prostitution and child pornography, and in November the Second Optional Protocol to the International Covenant on Civil and Political Rights, aiming at the abolition of the death penalty.

Violence against Indigenous women
High levels of discrimination and violence against Indigenous women continued. Federal and provincial governments announced initiatives to address these problems, but officials failed to advance a comprehensive national strategy. Crucially, police responses to threats against Indigenous women's lives were inconsistent and often inadequate.

Police abuses
There were reports of excessive use of force involving taser guns. During the year, four men died after being subdued by police using a taser, bringing the number of such deaths to 13 since April 2003.

Security and human rights
A public inquiry continued into Canada's role in the case of Maher Arar, a Canadian-Syrian national who was deported in 2002 from the USA to Syria where he was detained without charge for a year and tortured.

There were concerns about three other dual Canadian nationals who had been detained and tortured abroad: Abdullah Almalki, of Syrian origin, held in Syria for nearly two years; Ahmad Abou El-Maati, of Syrian origin, held in Syria and Egypt for over two years; and Muayyed Nureddin, of Iraqi origin, held in Syria for one month. The government refused to hold a public inquiry into the cases.

Four Muslim men remained in detention pending deportation and a fifth was released on strict bail restrictions, all pursuant to security certificates issued under the 2001 Immigration and Refugee Protection Act. The men faced a serious risk of torture if deported. Under security certificate proceedings, detainees only have access to summaries of evidence and no opportunity to challenge key witnesses.

There were reports that Canadian forces in Afghanistan were handing over detainees to US forces without reliable assurances that the detainees would not be subjected to the death penalty, and would be treated in a manner consistent with international humanitarian law and human rights obligations.

Omar Khadr, a Canadian national arrested by US forces in Afghanistan in July 2002 when he was a minor, remained in US custody in Guantánamo Bay, Cuba, where he had been since November 2002. In August an interim injunction was granted by the Federal Court of Canada prohibiting Canadian officials from questioning Omar Khadr unless this directly related to providing him with consular assistance.

Refugee protection
Under the 2004 Canada/USA "safe-third country" deal, most refugee claimants arriving in Canada via the USA were restricted to making refugee claims in the USA, where there were concerns that some faced human rights violations.

The government announced in November that it would not enact provisions under the Immigration and Refugee Protection Act to establish a full appeal of decisions denying refugee status.

Other concerns
In October, Rwandan national Desire Munyaneza, who had been denied refugee status in Canada, became the first person charged under the Crimes against Humanity and War Crimes Act.

There were no further negotiations with the Lubicon Cree in Alberta. In November the UN Human Rights Committee called on Canada to make every effort to resolve the long-standing land dispute, to consult with the Lubicon before licensing any economic exploitation of the disputed lands, and to ensure that the human rights of the Lubicon are not jeopardized by such activities.

AI country reports/ visits
Report
· 2005 UN Commission on Human Rights: Recommendations to the government of Canada on the occasion of its election on the Bureau of the Commission on Human Rights (AI Index: AMR 20/001/2005)
Visit
In October AI's Secretary General visited Canada and met federal government officials to discuss a range of human rights issues.

CENTRAL AFRICAN REPUBLIC

CENTRAL AFRICAN REPUBLIC
Head of state: François Bozizé
Head of government: Elie Dote (replaced Célestin-Leroy Gaombalet in June)
Death penalty: abolitionist in practice
International Criminal Court: ratified
UN Women's Convention: ratified
Optional Protocol to UN Women's Convention: not signed

Hundreds of women who were raped in late 2002 and early 2003 by combatants remained without redress, although the government asked the International Criminal Court (ICC) to investigate allegations of war crimes committed during the period. Members of the security forces suspected of being responsible for human rights violations enjoyed impunity. Journalists who published information unfavourable to the government received death threats. Thousands of civilians fled to Chad to escape human rights abuses during clashes between armed gangs and government forces.

Background
Although most of the country was politically stable, insecurity persisted in the north. Repeated clashes between armed gangs and members of the security forces caused more than 10,000 civilians to flee to southern Chad. Armed gangs were reported to have looted property and food from the local population and to have raped women. In October, members of a peacekeeping force backed by the Economic and Monetary Community of Central Africa (Communauté économique et monétaire d'Afrique centrale, CEMAC) were deployed in the north-eastern province of Haute Kotto to restore security in the region. The mandate of the CEMAC peacekeepers was extended for six months in June, and they were still deployed in the country at the end of 2005.

In January, President François Bozizé signed a decree promoting himself from the rank of Major General to that of General. His promotion had been recommended by the 2003 National Dialogue.

In January, seven opposition presidential candidates and their supporters called for the dissolution of the Transitional Constitutional Court, which in December 2004 had disqualified them from standing. Following mediation by Gabonese President Omar Bongo, the candidates were reinstated. However, exiled former President Ange-Félix Patassé was still banned from standing on the grounds that he was under investigation for atrocities committed before he was overthrown in March 2003.

After elections on 13 March, there was no outright winner among the presidential candidates. On 16 March President Bozizé dismissed the Vice-President, Abel Goumba, who had stood as a presidential candidate. President Bozizé defeated former Prime Minister Martin Ziguélé in the second round on 8 May. In June Prime Minister Célestin-Leroy Gaombalet resigned and was replaced by Elie Dote. On 24 June the Central African Republic was readmitted to the African Union's Peace and Security Council, from which it had been suspended after the overthrow of President Ange-Félix Patassé.

Impunity
The judiciary failed to investigate the rape of hundreds of women and other human rights abuses which occurred during the armed conflict in late 2002 and early 2003, as well as those that took place after President Bozizé took power in March 2003. However, in January the government formally requested the ICC to investigate and prosecute war crimes and other human rights abuses which occurred in the country during the armed conflict. The ICC had not started investigations by the end of 2005.

Five soldiers sentenced to five years' imprisonment after being convicted of raping a woman in custody were reported to have been freed by early 2005, without completing their sentence or having their conviction reviewed by a court. A government minister claimed to be unaware of the release of the soldiers, but no action was known to have been taken to re-arrest them.

Reports of unlawful killings, mainly by members of the presidential guard, remained uninvestigated.
🗁 In January, Jules-Aimé Gaboua was killed by members of the presidential guard in Bangui. No action was known to have been taken to identify the perpetrators and bring them to justice.

◻ A military officer accused of several unlawful killings and arrested in September 2004 was freed without charge or trial at the start of 2005. He reportedly attempted to kill an employee of the US Embassy in January. He was believed to have remained at large throughout 2005, despite written protests by local human rights activists.

Freedom of expression

Although there were no further arrests of journalists following the press law passed in 2004, several independent media journalists were threatened with death after they reported electoral malpractices, including intimidation of voters by members of the security forces.

◻ After the second round of presidential elections in May, Zéphirin Kaya and Patrick Akibata of *Ndeke Luka* radio station were reportedly threatened with death by President Bozizé's supporters and members of his presidential guard. Similar threats were reportedly made against Alexis Maka Gbossokotto, editor of *Le Citoyen* newspaper.

Continued detention of a government opponent

Virtually all government opponents still held at the end of 2004 were released during 2005. However, Simon Kulumba, who had been briefly released due to ill-health, was re-arrested and remained in custody without trial. He had been arrested in 2003 and accused of colluding with former President Patassé to embezzle funds from the sale of fuel donated by Libya. Those freed included General Ferdinand Bomba Yeke, former President Ange-Félix Patassé's head of security, who was released in October after being pardoned by President Bozizé. General Bomba Yeke had been in custody without charge or trial since November 2003.

AI country reports/ visits

Statement

• Central African Republic: Referral to the International Criminal Court should be accompanied by judicial reforms to address impunity (AI Index: AFR 19/001/2005)

Visit

AI delegates visited the Central African Republic in April to gather information about the human rights situation, particularly the progress of investigations into violence against women during the armed conflict.

CHAD

REPUBLIC OF CHAD
Head of state: Idriss Déby
Head of government: Pascal Yoadimnadji (replaced Moussa Faki Mahamat in February)
Death penalty: retentionist
International Criminal Court: signed
UN Women's Convention: ratified
Optional Protocol to UN Women's Convention: not signed

Freedom of expression remained under threat, and journalists faced politically motivated and arbitrary arrest, prolonged detention and imprisonment. Thousands of refugees arrived from the Central African Republic. The legal framework governing the construction of an oil pipeline undermined the rights of those living and working in the vicinity.

Background

A new constitution was approved allowing President Déby to stand for re-election by removing the previous two-term limit. It was approved after a referendum in June which was boycotted by the opposition and human rights organizations.

A peace agreement was signed in August between the authorities and the Movement for Democracy and Justice in Chad (Mouvement pour la démocratie et la justice au Tchad, MDJT), one of the Chadian armed opposition groups which had been active in Tibesti, northern Chad. A dissident group of the MDJT rejected the agreement and said that it would carry on fighting.

In October, a group of soldiers including military officers deserted their posts in N'Djaména and fled to the eastern part of the country. The deserters called on President Déby to step down and to free political prisoners. President Déby then dissolved the presidential guard and created a new unit drawn from the army and the police.

In November, the opposition coalition refused to appoint representatives to the electoral commission for the 2006 legislative and presidential elections. The opposition asked for the contested census, which was closed in January, to be reopened.

In September, gunmen on horseback from Sudan attacked the village of Madayouna, eastern Chad. Dozens of people were killed, including villagers and members of the assailant group. In a radio interview, President Déby accused the Janjawid militia group of being behind this attack.

In December the town of Adré, in eastern Chad close to the Sudanese border, was attacked. The Rally for Democracy and Liberty (Rassemblement pour la démocratie et la liberté, RDL), a new armed opposition group, claimed responsibility for the attack. The Chadian authorities blamed Sudan which denied any involvement in the attack.

Refugees

Around 200,000 Sudanese refugees remained in Chad, nearly half of them living in the south-eastern region of Goz-Beida. Thousands of refugees fleeing human rights abuses in the Central African Republic arrived in Chad.

Freedom of expression under attack

Freedom of expression came under attack throughout 2005. Journalists faced politically motivated and arbitrary arrest, prolonged detention and imprisonment. Between July and September, at least four journalists were sentenced to prison terms. They were released in September on appeal.

In July, Samory Ngaradoumbé, El Hadj Garonde Djarma and Koumbo Singa Gali of the weekly L'Observateur were sentenced to prison terms after the publication of articles critical of the authorities. Samory Ngaradoumbé was sentenced to three months' imprisonment and a fine after his newspaper published an open letter asking President Déby to release prisoners. Garonde Djarma was sentenced to three years' imprisonment after he criticized the constitutional amendment allowing President Déby to stand for re-election. Koumbo Singa Gali was sentenced to one year's imprisonment after her newspaper published an interview with imprisoned journalist Garonde Djarma.

In August, Michael Didama, editor of the weekly Le Temps, was convicted on charges of defamation and incitement to hatred after the publication of articles on the activities of armed opposition groups in eastern Chad. He was sentenced to six months' imprisonment.

In September the N'Ddjaména Court of Appeal overturned the convictions of Garonde Djarma and Koumbo Singa Gali because of procedural irregularities. The court also overturned the conviction of Samory Ngaradoumbé. Michael Didama's conviction was upheld but his sentence was reduced to the time he had already served. All the journalists were freed.

Impunity

In August, the authorities dismissed at least six people who had served under deposed President Hissène Habré. It was unclear whether any formal charges were brought against people suspected of committing human rights violations.

Few steps were taken to bring Hissène Habré to justice for human rights violations committed during his time in power. In November, the Dakar Appeal Court in Senegal declared itself "not competent" to rule on whether to issue an order for Hissène Habré's extradition to Belgium. In a press interview, President Déby appealed to the Senegalese President to extradite Hissène Habré (see Senegal entry).

Chad-Cameroon pipeline

In September, AI published a report on the Chad-Cameroon pipeline project, a World Bank supported project. The report detailed concerns that contracts signed between the governments of Chad and Cameroon and an Exxon Mobil-led oil company consortium undermined the ability of Chad and Cameroon to fulfil their obligations under international human rights law. The report said that the contracts created risks for all human rights, ranging from civil and political to economic, social and cultural rights. For example, some clauses in the contracts made it difficult or impossible for Chad to regulate the activities of the oil consortium, including to protect the safety and health of workers or the rights to food and water for people living near the oil development areas. AI called for the contracts underpinning this project to be amended to guard against the risks to human rights. AI also urged project lenders to institute policies to ensure that such contracts would not obtain funding in the future.

In November, the authorities substantially modified the Revenue Management Law, which governs the proceeds of the pipeline project. This law originally sought to ensure that revenue from the project was used for the benefit of local populations, through health and education spending for example, and for future generations. The government's amendment would allow revenues to be diverted to military and security spending. In December the President of the World Bank expressed serious concerns about the proposed amendment to the Revenue Management Law.

AI country reports/ visits

Report

- Contracting out of human rights: The Chad-Cameroon pipeline project (AI Index: POL 34/012/2005)

CHILE

REPUBLIC OF CHILE
Head of state and government: Ricardo Lagos
Death penalty: abolitionist for ordinary crimes
International Criminal Court: signed
UN Women's Convention: ratified with reservations
Optional Protocol to UN Women's Convention: signed

The prosecution of Augusto Pinochet for human rights violations committed under his military government took a significant step forward. However, the 1978 Amnesty Law was used to acquit five former secret service agents of involvement in a 1974 "disappearance". Prisoners were injured in fighting over the minimal facilities provided in prisons.

Background
Presidential elections in December produced no outright winner. The two candidates who obtained the highest votes – Michelle Bachelet of the Coalition for Democracy and Sebastian Piñera of the Alliance for Chile – were set to contest the second round of the elections in January 2006.

Provisions for the appointment of "designated" senators and according others lifetime tenure were removed in August when the 1980 Constitution, introduced under the military government (1973-90), was amended by Congress. The amended Constitution also allowed Chile to ratify the Rome Statute of the International Criminal Court, although ratification had not taken place by the end of 2005. In June, Chile signed the Optional Protocol to the UN Convention against Torture.

In November, former Peruvian President Alberto Fujimori was arrested in Santiago and held in preventive detention pending an extradition request by Peru on charges of corruption and human rights violations.

Ill-treatment in prisons
Detainees continued to suffer overcrowding, lack of medical care, deficient sanitary conditions and poor infrastructure. In March, 30 prisoners were injured in fighting over sleeping space at the Detention Centre (former Penitentiary) in Santiago Sur. Severe overcrowding – 400 inmates held in an area designated for 76 – forced 120 detainees to sleep in the open.

Past human rights violations
In January the Supreme Court upheld the December 2004 indictment and house arrest of Augusto Pinochet on nine charges of kidnapping and one of murder during "Operation Cóndor", a joint plan by Southern Cone military governments in the 1970s and 1980s to eliminate opponents. However, in June the Santiago Appeals Court ruled that he was too ill to stand trial for the kidnappings and murder. The same court, in a separate ruling, allowed his prosecution on charges of tax evasion and other financial crimes to proceed. In November, Augusto Pinochet was charged and placed under house arrest. The charges against him included the murder of 119 people and the "disappearance" of 15 others in 1975 as part of "Operation Colombo". Other charges included homicide, torture, kidnapping, money laundering, tax evasion and falsifying documents. This was the first time prosecutors in Chile had successfully cleared all the legal hurdles and indicted him.

In January the Supreme Court put a time limit of six months on judicial investigations into "disappearances" and other human rights violations by the military government, but suspended the ruling in May. This allowed investigation to continue into more than 150 cases of human rights violations.

In June, five former secret service agents were acquitted under the 1978 Amnesty Law of involvement in the "disappearance" of Diana Arón Svigilsky in 1974. Although the Amnesty Law – introduced by military decree but still in force – contravenes Chile's duties under international law, it was invoked to absolve the accused.

AI country reports/ visits
Statements
- Chile: Dangerous and illegal Supreme Court decision on cases involving human rights violations (AI Index: AMR 22/002/2005)
- Chile: Probes of Pinochet-era crimes face shut down – Ensure mandate of special judges to continue their investigations (a joint release by AI, Human Rights Watch and the International Commission of Jurists) (AI Index: AMR 22/003/2005)
- Chile: A call to protect human rights in Chile – An open letter from the Secretary General to the presidential candidates (AI Index: AMR 22/004/2005)

CHINA

PEOPLE'S REPUBLIC OF CHINA
Head of state: Hu Jintao
Head of government: Wen Jiabao
Death penalty: retentionist
International Criminal Court: not signed
UN Women's Convention: ratified with reservations
Optional Protocol to UN Women's Convention: not signed

Limited legal and judicial reforms did little to improve human rights protection. Tens of thousands of people continued to be detained in violation of their human rights and were at risk of torture or ill-treatment. Thousands of people were sentenced to death or executed. The authorities frequently resorted to the use of force against growing social unrest. There was a renewed crackdown on the media and Internet controls were tightened. The Uighur community in the Xinjiang Uighur Autonomous Region (XUAR) continued to face severe repression as part of the authorities' "war on terror". Freedom of expression and religion continued to be severely restricted in Tibet and other Tibetan areas. China's arms sales to Sudan raised concerns that its actions were contributing to human rights violations in other countries. China continued a limited dialogue with selected members of the international community on human rights issues. However, human rights defenders at home continued to be arbitrarily detained and some were sentenced to prison terms.

International community
Uncontrolled arms exports from China continued to fuel massive human rights violations in Sudan. The Chinese government opposed the strengthening of the UN Security Council arms embargo on Sudan.

The European Union (EU) resisted lobbying from the Chinese government to lift its arms embargo on China, imposed after the crackdown on the pro-democracy movement in June 1989.

The government continued to engage with UN human rights mechanisms, although it largely failed to implement their recommendations. The UN High Commissioner for Human Rights and the UN Special Rapporteur on torture visited China in August and November. In September, China and the Russian Federation spearheaded a move to block the creation of an effective new Human Rights Council at the UN.

Human rights defenders
Individuals continued to use China's petitioning system, and sometimes the courts, in an attempt to obtain redress for various abuses. However, fundamental weaknesses in both systems left many without redress, fuelling an increase in social protests throughout the country. New regulations were introduced in May in a stated attempt to provide better

protection for the interests of petitioners but these appeared to have little impact on resolving complaints.

Informal networks of rights defenders publicly lobbied the authorities and the international community about various abuses. However, the authorities continued to use broadly defined national security offences to prosecute and imprison activists, including lawyers, petitioners and housing rights advocates. Civil society organizations continued to grow in number and effectiveness. However, controls were tightened to curtail the activities of those who challenged official policies.

▢ Hou Wenzhuo, director of the non-governmental Empowerment and Rights Institute, was subjected to numerous abuses in connection with her human rights activities, including eviction from her home and office in Beijing and arbitrary detention by the police in southern China. Her work included investigating reports of illegal land expropriation from farmers in Foshan, Guangdong province. She fled China in October in fear of further arbitrary detention by the police.

Journalists and Internet users
The authorities became increasingly intolerant of reporting which covered sensitive issues or questioned government policies. There was a renewed crackdown on journalists and the media. Those reporting on sensitive issues or who challenged the status quo were at risk of dismissal, arbitrary detention or imprisonment. Broadly defined "state secrets" offences continued to be used to prosecute journalists and reporters. Restrictions on Internet use were tightened and dozens of people remained behind bars for accessing or circulating politically sensitive information on-line.

▢ Journalist Shi Tao was sentenced to 10 years in prison in April for leaking "state secrets". He had posted to an overseas website Communist Party instructions on how journalists should handle the 15th anniversary of the crackdown on the 1989 pro-democracy movement.

Violations in the context of economic reform
Forced evictions in urban areas as well as land requisition and high taxes in the countryside were increasingly the focus of local protests and social unrest. Disturbances were often met with violence, sometimes by criminal gangs, allegedly backed or hired by local authorities or enterprises.

Despite ongoing reforms to the Household Registration (*Hukou*) System, migrants from rural to urban areas remained vulnerable to discrimination in the cities, including denial of access to health care and other social services.

General working conditions in factories, mines and other enterprises remained poor. The rights of freedom of expression and association of workers' representatives continued to be severely curtailed and independent trade unions remained illegal.

▢ Xu Zhengqing, an activist who had campaigned against land grabs and evictions in Shanghai, was sentenced to three years in prison in October for "disrupting public order" when he travelled to Beijing in January in an attempt to commemorate deceased former Premier Zhao Ziyang.

Violence against women

Despite laws prohibiting such practices, many women continued to be subjected to forced abortions and sterilizations by local authorities attempting to comply with strict family planning policies.

Prohibition of sex identification of foetuses appeared to have little effect on the sex imbalance. Trafficking in women and children, especially girls, continued to be reported.

Some provinces adopted regulations aimed at preventing domestic violence but abuses reportedly remained widespread.

Women in detention remained at risk of sexual abuse and other forms of torture or ill-treatment.

In August the authorities amended the Law on the Protection of Women's Rights and Interests specifically to prohibit sexual harassment of women and strengthen women's rights to lodge complaints.

▢ Chen Guangcheng, a blind, self-trained lawyer, was harassed, beaten and arbitrarily detained at his home in September after he attempted to sue the local authorities in Linyi city, Shandong province, for conducting forced sterilizations and abortions in pursuit of birth quotas. He remained held at the end of the year.

Repression of spiritual and religious groups

Religious observance outside official channels remained tightly circumscribed. In March, the authorities promulgated a new Regulation on Religious Affairs aimed at strengthening official controls on religious activities.

The crackdown on the Falun Gong spiritual movement was renewed in April. A Beijing official clarified that since the group had been banned as a "heretical organization", any activities linked to Falun Gong were illegal. Many Falun Gong practitioners reportedly remained in detention where they were at high risk of torture or ill-treatment.

Unregistered Catholics and Protestants associated with unofficial house churches were also harassed, arbitrarily detained and imprisoned.

▢ In November, prominent defence lawyer Gao Zhisheng was forced to close down his law firm for a year after he refused to withdraw an Open Letter to the President and Premier calling on the authorities to respect religious freedom and to stop the "barbaric" persecution of Falun Gong. The order came shortly after he had filed an appeal on behalf of underground Protestant pastor Cai Zhuohua who had been sentenced to three years in prison for illegally printing bibles.

Death penalty

The death penalty continued to be used extensively and arbitrarily, at times as a result of political interference. People were executed for non-violent crimes such as tax fraud and embezzlement as well as drug offences and violent crimes. Based on public reports available, AI estimated that at least 1,770 people were executed and 3,900 people were sentenced to death during the year, although the true figures were believed to be much higher.

Several miscarriages of justice in death penalty cases published in the Chinese press in the first half of the year caused considerable public disquiet and increased momentum towards reform. In September, a senior Supreme Court official announced that the Court was establishing three branch courts to review death sentences. Previously this had been delegated to lower courts, reducing safeguards against unfair proceedings. Officials anticipated that the reform would lead to a 30 per cent reduction in executions. However, national statistics on death sentences and executions remained classified as a state secret, making analysis and monitoring of the death penalty problematic.

▢ Wang Binyu, a migrant worker from Gansu, was sentenced to death in Ningxia in June for stabbing to death his foreman and three others during a violent dispute about unpaid wages. He reportedly needed the money to pay for an operation for his father. He was executed in October despite calls for leniency from academics and members of the public in the Chinese media.

Torture, arbitrary detention and unfair trials

Torture and ill-treatment continued to be reported in a wide variety of state institutions. Common methods included kicking, beating, electric shocks, suspension by the arms, shackling in painful positions, and sleep and food deprivation. Restricted access to the outside world for detainees and a failure to establish effective mechanisms for complaint and investigation continued to be key factors allowing the practice to flourish.

In May the authorities announced a pilot project allowing police interrogation of criminal suspects in front of video cameras and lawyers in three regions. In July the authorities announced that they were accelerating their campaign to prosecute police who extract confessions through torture, adding that 1,924 officials had been prosecuted since the campaign was launched in May 2004.

▢ Gao Rongrong, a Falun Gong practitioner, died in custody in June after being detained in Longshan Re-education through Labour facility in Shenyang, Liaoning province. Officials had reportedly beaten her in 2004, including by using electro-shock batons on her face and neck, which caused severe blistering and eyesight problems, after she was discovered reading Falun Gong materials in the facility.

A proposed new Law on the Rectification of Illegal Behaviour was reportedly being discussed by legislators as a replacement for Re-education through Labour — a system of administrative detention used to detain hundreds of thousands of people for up to four years without charge or trial. Officials indicated that the new law would probably reduce terms of detention. However, elements that contravene international fair trial standards potentially remain unchanged.

A campaign aimed at improving the conduct of the police and eradicating torture was initiated, but few efforts were made to introduce the fundamental legal and institutional reforms necessary to prevent such abuses in practice.

People accused of political or criminal offences continued to be denied due process. Detainees' access to lawyers and family members continued to be severely restricted and trials fell far short of international fair trial standards. Those charged with offences related to state secrets or terrorism had their legal rights restricted and were tried in camera.

North Korean asylum-seekers

People continued to flee across the border into China to escape the acute food shortages in North Korea. Hundreds, possibly thousands, of North Koreans were arrested and forcibly returned by the Chinese authorities who considered them to be economic migrants and denied them access to any refugee determination procedures, in breach of the UN Refugee Convention. Unconfirmed reports suggested that at least five South Korean nationals of North Korean origin were abducted in China and forcibly taken to North Korea.

Xinjiang Uighur Autonomous Region (XUAR)

The authorities continued to use the global "war on terror" to justify harsh repression in the XUAR, resulting in serious human rights violations against the ethnic Uighur community.

While China's latest "strike-hard" campaign against crime had subsided in most parts of the country, it was officially renewed in the XUAR in May to eradicate "terrorism, separatism and religious extremism". Repression resulted in the closure of unofficial mosques and arrests of imams.

Uighur nationalists, including peaceful activists, continued to be detained or imprisoned. Those charged with serious "separatist" or "terrorist" offences were at risk of lengthy imprisonment or execution. Those attempting to pass information abroad about the extent of the crackdown faced arbitrary detention and imprisonment.

The authorities continued to accuse Uighur activists of terrorism without providing credible evidence for such charges.

▢ Rebiya Kadeer, a prisoner of conscience released in March, became a key target in an apparent attempt to counter her influence as a Uighur activist abroad.

▢ Writer Nurmuhemmet Yasin was sentenced to 10 years' imprisonment in a closed trial in February after he published a short story entitled "Wild Pigeon" about a trapped bird that commits suicide in captivity – apparently seen by the authorities as an allegory for Uighurs living in China.

Tibet Autonomous Region and other ethnic Tibetan areas

Freedom of religion, expression and association continued to be severely restricted and arbitrary arrests and unfair trials continued. Some prisoners of conscience were released at the end of their sentences, but dozens of others, including Buddhist monks and nuns, remained behind bars where they were at risk of torture or ill-treatment.

▢ Tashi Gyaltsen and four other monks were assigned to between two and three years' Re-education through Labour in Xiling, Qinghai province, in February for publishing a newsletter which contained poems and articles deemed to be politically sensitive.

Hong Kong Special Administrative Region

In April the Hong Kong Court of Final Appeal overturned all remaining convictions against eight Falun Gong practitioners for obstructing and assaulting the police during a demonstration in March 2002. Some charges against them had already been quashed on appeal in 2004.

In September, the Coroner's Court's verdict on the death of Kim Shuk-ying and her two daughters at the hands of her husband accelerated the process of revising the Domestic Violence Ordinance, which narrowly defines domestic violence as physical violence between couples.

Human rights activists protested against a decision by the Hong Kong authorities to commission the Society for Truth and Light, a conservative Christian group which opposes gay rights and "excessive use" of human rights, to educate school teachers on human rights and anti-discrimination.

Police used pepper spray, tear-gas and bean-bag rounds against protesters during ministerial meetings of the World Trade Organization (WTO) in December, prompting accusations by human rights monitors of excessive use of force. More than 1,000 protesters were detained, and several claimed to have been ill-treated in police custody. All were later released, but 14 were charged with unlawful assembly and released on bail. Their trial had not taken place by the end of the year.

▢ William Leung, a 20-year-old gay man, successfully challenged a law which prohibits sex between consenting men under 21. A court of first instance ruled that the law was discriminatory and a violation of human rights. The Hong Kong authorities vowed to appeal against the ruling, but the appeal had not been heard by the end of the year.

AI country reports/ visits
Reports
- People's Republic of China: Human Rights Defenders at risk (AI Index: ASA 17/002/2005)
- People's Republic of China: The Olympic countdown – three years of human rights reform? (AI Index: ASA 17/021/2005)
- People's Republic of China: Briefing on EU concerns regarding human rights in China (AI Index: ASA 17/027/2005)

Visits
AI delegates attended an EU-China Human Rights Dialogue Seminar in June and a UN Workshop of the Framework on Regional Cooperation for the Promotion of Human Rights in the Asia Pacific Region in August, both held in Beijing. AI's Secretary General and two

other delegates attended a meeting of the UN Global Compact, a voluntary international corporate responsibility network, in Shanghai in November.

COLOMBIA

REPUBLIC OF COLOMBIA
Head of state and government: Álvaro Uribe Vélez
Death penalty: abolitionist for all crimes
International Criminal Court: ratified
UN Women's Convention: ratified
Optional Protocol to UN Women's Convention: signed

Although the number of killings and kidnappings in some parts of the country fell, serious human rights abuses committed by all parties to the conflict remained at critical levels. Of particular concern were reports of extrajudicial executions carried out by the security forces, killings of civilians by armed opposition groups and paramilitaries, and the forced displacement of civilian communities. Paramilitaries who had supposedly demobilized under the terms of a controversial law ratified in July continued to commit human rights violations, while armed opposition groups continued to commit serious and widespread breaches of international humanitarian law. Individuals who may have been responsible for war crimes and crimes against humanity were not brought to justice.

Background
President Álvaro Uribe ratified the Justice and Peace Law on 22 July. The law, which provides a legal framework for the demobilization of members of paramilitary and armed opposition groups, fails to respect international standards on the right of victims to truth, justice and reparation and threatened to exacerbate Colombia's endemic problem of impunity. By the end of 2005, negotiations between the government and the paramilitary umbrella organization, the United Self-Defence Forces of Colombia (Autodefensas Unidas de Colombia, AUC), led to the reported "demobilization" of more than half of the country's estimated 20,000 AUC-linked paramilitaries. However, paramilitaries in supposedly demobilized areas continued to commit violations, and evidence of links between paramilitaries and the security forces remained strong. There were also fears that government policies designed to reintegrate members of illegal armed groups into civilian life risked recycling them into the conflict.

Efforts to negotiate a prisoner exchange with the main armed opposition group, the Revolutionary Armed Forces of Colombia (Fuerzas Armadas Revolucionarias de Colombia, FARC), failed to achieve concrete results. However, "talks about talks" with the smaller National Liberation Army (Ejército de Liberación Nacional, ELN) resumed in December. The FARC and ELN were responsible for serious and widespread breaches of international humanitarian law, especially kidnappings, hostage-taking and killings of civilians.

On 1 April, Colombia ratified the Inter-American Convention on Forced Disappearance of Persons.

The Justice and Peace Law: paramilitary demobilization
The Justice and Peace Law grants significantly reduced prison sentences to members of illegal armed groups under investigation for human rights abuses who agree to demobilize. Although most of the beneficiaries were expected to be paramilitaries, by the end of 2005 the law had reportedly only been applied to around 30 alleged FARC prisoners. Because of the problem of impunity, few members of illegal armed groups were under investigation for human rights offences. Most demobilized paramilitaries thus benefited from de facto amnesties granted under Decree 128, promulgated in 2003.

The Justice and Peace Law gives judicial investigators strict time limits to investigate each case, with little incentive for potential beneficiaries to collaborate with investigators. The participation of victims in legal proceedings is limited, and there are no provisions to expose third parties, such as the security forces, who have played an integral part in coordinating human rights violations carried out by paramilitaries.

The law was criticized by the Office in Colombia of the UN High Commissioner for Human Rights, and the Inter-American Commission on Human Rights (IACHR) and Inter-American Court of Human Rights of the Organization of American States (OAS).

All paramilitaries were supposed to demobilize by the end of 2005. However, the process stalled in October after the government transferred paramilitary leader Diego Fernando Murillo Bejarano, alias "Don Berna", to prison for his alleged involvement in the 10 April killing of legislator Orlando Benítez, and over rumours about his possible extradition to the USA on drug-trafficking charges. The demobilization process resumed in December after an agreement was reached in November between the government and the AUC extending the timescale for demobilization.

More than 2,750 killings and "disappearances" were attributed to paramilitaries between the announcement by the AUC of a ceasefire in 2002 and the end of 2005. Because of its limited mandate, the Mission to Support the Peace Process in Colombia, set up by the OAS in 2004 to verify the ceasefire, could not take action against paramilitaries who failed to abide by the ceasefire nor comment on government policy.

The government encouraged demobilized paramilitaries to work in intelligence-related activities, such as the civilian informer network, as auxiliaries in security force operations, as "civic police", and as private security guards. This raised fears that the mechanisms that led to the creation of paramilitary groups were being replicated and threw into doubt the government's commitment to reintegrate combatants fully into civilian life.

There were reports that paramilitary groups were still recruiting members after they had supposedly demobilized. On 25 August, the IACHR wrote to the government asking for clarification of reports that paramilitaries were still recruiting minors in Medellín, despite having supposedly demobilized in 2003.

There were numerous reports of human rights violations committed by paramilitaries in areas where they had supposedly demobilized, including Medellín, and evidence of collusion between paramilitaries and the security forces.

▭ On 29 January, paramilitaries reportedly killed seven peasant farmers in El Vergel, San Carlos Municipality, Antioquia Department. Members of the armed forces were allegedly patrolling in El Vergel from 26 to 31 January. Just before the killings, the army had reportedly been searching for one of the victims, who they labelled a subversive.

▭ On 9 July, paramilitaries allegedly killed six civilians in Buenaventura, Valle del Cauca Department. The police, who had been patrolling the area, reportedly withdrew hours before the killings. The paramilitary group, the Calima Bloc (Bloque Calima), which operated in Buenaventura, supposedly demobilized in December 2004.

Impunity

Impunity for human rights abuses remained the norm. High-ranking military personnel, and paramilitary and guerrilla leaders, continued to evade justice.

Action was taken in very few cases. In July, an army lieutenant, three soldiers and a civilian were formally charged for the August 2004 killing of three trade unionists in Arauca Department, while the Office of the Attorney General ordered the arrest of six soldiers for the killing in April 2004 of five civilians, including a baby, in Cajamarca Municipality, Tolima Department. However, criminal investigations into the possible involvement of more senior officers in these killings did not advance.

In January, the Supreme Court dismissed a case against former Rear Admiral Rodrigo Quiñónez regarding his role in the 2001 Chengue massacre, in which at least 26 people were killed by paramilitaries, operating in collusion with the armed forces. The Procurator General's Office criticized this decision, calling on the Office of the Attorney General to press forward criminal investigations into the massacre.

On 15 September, the Inter-American Court of Human Rights ruled that the Colombian state must pay compensation to the families of 49 peasant farmers killed by paramilitaries in 1997 in Mapiripán, Meta Department. Paramilitary leader Salvatore Mancuso, now officially demobilized, and several army officials, including retired general Jaime Humberto Uscátegui, have been implicated in the killings.

The military justice system continued to claim jurisdiction over cases of potential human rights violations committed by members of the security forces, despite the 1997 ruling of the Constitutional Court that such cases must be investigated by the civilian justice system.

▭ In April, the military justice system absolved 12 army soldiers of responsibility in the killing of seven police officers and four civilians in Guaitarilla Municipality, Nariño Department, in March 2004.

Killings by the security forces

There were continuing reports of extrajudicial executions by the security forces, with some estimates suggesting at least 100 fatalities. These killings were often falsely described as "guerrillas killed in combat". Although the military justice system claimed jurisdiction over most such cases, and then archived many of them, the civilian justice system was sometimes able to intervene.

▭ In July, the Office of the Attorney General ordered the arrest of eight soldiers for the killing of Reinel Antonio Escobar Guzmán and brothers Juvenal and Mario Guzmán Sepúlveda in Dabeiba Municipality, Antioquia Department, on 8 May. The army had alleged that the three men were FARC guerrillas killed in combat.

Civilians were reportedly killed by the police anti-riot unit (Escuadrón Móvil Antidisturbios, ESMAD) during protests. ESMAD agents carry no visible individual identification.

▭ On 1 May, at least eight ESMAD agents allegedly beat 15-year-old Nicolás David Neira during a May Day march in Bogotá. A week later he died of his injuries.

▭ On 22 September, Jhony Silva Aranguren died and several other students were injured after allegedly being shot by ESMAD agents during a protest at a university in Cali.

Abuses by armed opposition groups

On 12 September, ELN leader Gerardo Bermúdez, alias Francisco Galán, was released from prison for a limited period to help restart the peace process. As a result, exploratory talks between government and ELN representatives took place in Cuba from 16 to 22 December.

The FARC and ELN continued to commit serious and repeated breaches of international humanitarian law, including hostage-taking and civilian killings.

▭ On 15 August, the ELN killed two priests and two other civilians on the Teorema-Convención highway in Norte de Santander Department.

▭ On 23 August, the FARC allegedly killed 14 peasant farmers in Palomas, Valdivia Municipality, Antioquia Department.

The FARC also carried out disproportionate and indiscriminate attacks which resulted in the deaths of numerous civilians.

▭ On 20 February, three civilians and three soldiers died, and 13 civilians and 11 soldiers were injured, when a bomb exploded in a hotel in Puerto Toledo, Meta Department.

On 3 October, a bomb killed three members of an indigenous community, including two children, in Florida Municipality, Valle del Cauca Department.

Violence against women

Women and girls continued to be killed, tortured and kidnapped by both sides in the conflict.

On 24 May, a woman and her husband were detained by the army in Saravena Municipality, Arauca Department. The woman was reportedly handed over to a paramilitary who raped her.

On 9 August, an indigenous woman was allegedly raped by a soldier in Coconuco, Cauca Department.

The body of Angela Diosa Correa Borja was found on 15 September in San José de Apartadó, Antioquia Department. She had allegedly been killed by the FARC after they accused her of collaborating with the police.

Kidnappings

In November, the government announced plans to set up an "international commission" to help negotiate the release of FARC hostages. However, repeated speculation about a possible prisoner exchange failed to yield results by the end of 2005. The FARC and ELN continued to hold numerous hostages, including high-profile politicians such as former presidential candidate Ingrid Betancourt, kidnapped by the FARC in 2002. There were more than 751 kidnappings in 2005, compared to 1,402 in 2004, of which 273 were reportedly carried out by armed opposition groups and 49 by paramilitaries. Responsibility could not be attributed in 208 cases.

On 23 January, the ELN allegedly kidnapped community leader Héctor Bastidas in Samaniego Municipality, Nariño Department. He had not been released by the end of 2005.

On 31 March, the FARC kidnapped five human rights activists working with the Afro-descendant communities of Jiguamiandó and Curvaradó in Chocó Department. They were released on 8 April.

On 30 August, paramilitaries abducted at least 11 children and 13 adults in El Carmen Municipality, Norte de Santander Department, during an attack in which three people were killed and a woman was allegedly sexually abused. The 24 were subsequently released. Paramilitary units operating in this region supposedly demobilized at the end of 2004.

Attacks on civilians

Civilians continued to bear the brunt of the conflict, with trade unionists, human rights defenders and community activists, as well as indigenous, Afro-descendant and displaced communities, and those living in areas of intense conflict, at particular risk. At least 70 trade unionists and seven human rights defenders were killed in 2005. At least 1,050 civilians were killed or "disappeared" in non-combat situations during the first half of 2005.

More than 310,000 civilians were internally displaced in 2005, compared to 287,000 in 2004. Economic blockades imposed by combatants and clashes between the parties to the conflict created serious humanitarian crises in different parts of the country.

About 1,300 members of the Awá indigenous community were forced to flee their homes in June because of clashes between the army and FARC in Nariño Department.

The Peace Community of San José de Apartadó, Antioquia Department, which insists on the right of civilians not to be drawn into the conflict, was again attacked. Over 150 of its members have "disappeared" or been killed since 1997, mostly by paramilitaries and the security forces, but also by the FARC. On 21 February, eight community members, including community leader Luis Eduardo Guerra, were killed by men who witnesses claimed were army troops. The community has often been labelled as subversive by the army and paramilitaries, while the FARC accuses it of siding with its enemies. On 20 March, President Uribe publicly accused some Peace Community leaders of being FARC auxiliaries.

Members of the Jiguamiandó and Curvaradó Afro-descendant communities also continued to be threatened by the security forces and the paramilitaries.

On 24 October, the body of Afro-descendant activist Orlando Valencia was found in Chirigorodó Municipality, Antioquia Department. He had been abducted by alleged paramilitaries on 15 October, hours after being detained by police who accused him of being a FARC member.

Clashes resulting from attacks by the FARC on 14 and 17 April against security force units in the indigenous community of Toribío, Cauca Department, resulted in the death of 10-year-old Yanson Trochez Pavi, and injuries to 19 civilians. The FARC reportedly used gas cylinders in the attacks, while the security forces allegedly used aerial strafing in their response.

Freedom of expression

Freedom of expression was undermined by continued threats, kidnappings and killings of journalists.

On 11 January, journalist Julio Palacios Sánchez was killed by unknown assailants in Cúcuta, Norte de Santander Department.

On 20 February, the FARC detonated a car bomb outside the Cali headquarters of the RCN television and radio station, injuring two people.

On 16 May, journalists Hollman Morris, Carlos Lozano and Daniel Coronell, who have repeatedly denounced human rights violations by paramilitaries, received death threats in the form of funeral wreaths.

US military aid

In 2005, US assistance to Colombia was some US$ 781 million, with military aid accounting for around 80 per cent of the total. The US Congress again required that the US Secretary of State certify progress in specific human rights categories before the final 25 per cent could be transferred. Given the lack of progress on several human rights categories, the US State Department withheld its certification for several months before granting it. US financial assistance to the paramilitary demobilization process was approved, albeit with certain human rights conditions. In August, the State Department announced it would cease security assistance to the XVII Brigade of the Colombian army, due to accusations of human rights violations, including the February killings in San José de Apartadó. Assistance was not to be renewed until the accusations were "credibly addressed".

Intergovernmental organizations

The UN Commission on Human Rights expressed concern at violations of human rights and international humanitarian law, recognizing the responsibility of armed opposition groups, paramilitaries and the security forces. It deplored reports of extrajudicial executions attributed to members of the security forces and other public servants and reports of arrests and mass searches carried out without appropriate legal foundations. It also expressed concern about collusion of state agents with paramilitaries. It condemned violence against women committed by all parties to the conflict and the impunity which prevailed.

AI country reports/ visits

Reports

· Colombia: Justice is the only way forward for the Peace Community of San José de Apartadó (AI Index: AMR 23/004/2005)
· Colombia: Amnesty International condemns attacks against the population of Toribío (AI Index: AMR 23/011/2005)
· Colombia: The paramilitaries in Medellín — demobilization or legalization? (AI Index: AMR 23/019/2005)
· Colombia: The Justice and Peace Law will benefit human rights abusers (AI Index: AMR 23/030/2005)

Visits

AI delegates visited the country in February, April and October.

CONGO
(DEMOCRATIC REPUBLIC OF THE)

DEMOCRATIC REPUBLIC OF THE CONGO
Head of state and government: Joseph Kabila
Death penalty: retentionist
International Criminal Court: ratified
UN Women's Convention: ratified
Optional Protocol to UN Women's Convention: not signed

Slow progress was made in building security, justice and respect for human rights after nearly a decade of war. Tens of thousands of people died in continuing conflict or from preventable disease and starvation. Extrajudicial executions and other unlawful killings, arbitrary arrests, unlawful detentions, acts of torture or ill-treatment, and life-threatening prison conditions were reported across the country. The security forces used indiscriminate or excessive force to break up political protests. Ethnic tensions were manipulated for political ends in politically or militarily strategic areas, including Katanga and North-Kivu provinces. Insecurity persisted in eastern Democratic Republic of the Congo (DRC), where war crimes were committed by Congolese armed factions and foreign armed groups from Rwanda and Uganda, including unlawful killings, rape, torture and the use of child soldiers. The government and the international community largely failed to address the immense humanitarian needs of a population brought about by insecurity, displacement and lack of access to humanitarian and medical care.

Background

The transitional power-sharing government, created in 2003 and including members of the former government, major armed groups, opposition political parties and civil society, made little progress towards unification and a transition to democratic rule. Serious delays in the passing of electoral laws and the organization of elections planned for June 2005 resulted in the transition being extended to June 2006.

Factionalism and mistrust within the government contributed to continued tension and occasional armed conflict between military units supposed to be part of a unified national army. Integrating tens of thousands of members of former armed groups and the former army into the new army started in early 2005, as did the disarmament, demobilization and reintegration into civilian life of tens of thousands of other fighters. Former belligerents remained reluctant to dismantle their military structures, and integration was resisted in some areas. In North-Kivu hundreds of soldiers deserted before being persuaded to return to their units. The integration process was under-resourced, with no or minimal payment of salaries, and insufficient supplies of food, water and medical equipment to integration sites. Coordination was poor between the integration of fighters into the new army, led by the military, and the reintegration of demobilized fighters into civilian life, led by a civilian government body. Projects to support re-entry into civilian life, involving thousands of child soldiers, were still not fully identified or functional. In Ituri, a voluntary Disarmament and Community Reinsertion programme had disarmed over 12,500 combatants from former armed groups by the end of 2005 out of an estimated, but disputed, total of 15,000. However, most community projects to facilitate reinsertion into civilian life were considerably delayed or not undertaken at all, leaving thousands of demobilized militia members without access to alternative forms of employment. Thousands of other combatants, opposed to demobilization, were still at large.

The peacekeeping force of the UN Organization Mission in the Democratic Republic of the Congo (MONUC), with only some 16,000 troops at the end of 2005, continued to be overstretched. The governments of Uganda and Rwanda allegedly continued to channel support to armed groups, or factions of armed groups, that opposed the transitional government.

Unlawful killings

All armed forces and groups were responsible for unlawful killings, which were reported on an almost daily basis.

Government security forces used excessive and sometimes lethal force to break up public demonstrations. In January, scores of people in Kinshasa were killed or seriously injured by army and police units during protests at the postponement of the elections.

▭ On 30 June, the notional end date of the transition, 10 protesters in a number of cities were reportedly shot dead by the security forces.

North-Kivu

Armed groups that failed to engage in the military integration process continued to commit almost daily killings and other grave human rights abuses in North-Kivu, particularly in Rutshuru territory. Information emerged that hundreds of civilians had been killed, raped or tortured in Nyabiondo, in Masisi territory, and Buramba, in Rutshuru territory, in December 2004, following fighting between rival forces not integrated into the new army. Many abuses appeared to be ethnically motivated.

South-Kivu

Thousands of civilians were killed, raped and abducted, and child soldiers continued to be used, especially in the Walungu and Kabare territories of South-Kivu where Rwandan insurgents operated.

▭ On 9 and 10 July around 40 civilians, mainly women and children, were killed in Ntulumamba locality, reportedly by a group of armed Rwandan fighters.

Government forces were also responsible for killings, rapes and looting during counter-insurgency operations.

Ituri

Despite a significant improvement in security around Bunia town, the Ituri district was still affected by violence. On 25 February, nine UN peacekeepers were killed in Kafe, a region believed to be the stronghold of

several ethnic and political armed militias. Murder, rape and looting by the militias drove over 80,000 civilians from their homes to camps for the internally displaced, despite the presence of three integrated army brigades in parallel or joint security operations with MONUC forces.

Katanga

Katanga province experienced heightened instability and a sharp increase in killings, rapes, abductions and looting, mainly by mayi-mayi militia. In the north, frequent fighting between mayi-mayi and government forces resulted in massive population displacement. During an ethnic and political leadership contest, at least 65 people were detained incommunicado in April and May by military intelligence agents in connection with an alleged secession plot. A number were reportedly tortured or severely ill-treated. Most were released without charge. Others were still in detention in Kinshasa at the end of 2005.

Violence against women

Large numbers of women and girls continued to be subjected to rape and other forms of sexual violence by government forces and armed groups. In eastern DRC, girls under five and women over 70 were not spared. Rape was sometimes committed in front of the victim's children, family or community, and was often accompanied by other extreme forms of torture. In some cases, the girl or woman was killed or deliberately wounded. Few rape survivors had access to appropriate medical care.

▭ Bitombo Nyumba, a 56-year-old widow and mother of four children, died from her injuries and inadequate medical treatment in June 2005 after seven soldiers tortured and raped her in Fizi territory, South-Kivu.

Attacks on human rights defenders

In most areas the authorities remained hostile to human rights defenders. A number of prominent defenders were physically attacked, illegally detained or threatened.

▭ Pascal Kabungulu, Executive Secretary of the human rights organization, Heirs of Justice (Héritiers de la Justice), was shot dead by three armed men on 31 July at his home in Bukavu, South-Kivu. An official commission of inquiry failed to report its findings, and no suspected perpetrators had been brought to justice by the end of 2005.

Torture and ill-treatment

Torture and ill-treatment continued of detainees in the custody of the military, police and other security forces. It was frequently facilitated by the use of incommunicado detention. Among practices reported were sustained beatings, often with sticks, lengths of metal or rifle-butts; death threats or mock executions; prolonged suspension by the arms or legs from walls or doors; and the forcing of detainees to stare for long periods into strong sunlight.

Conditions in many prisons and detention centres, which were often overcrowded, insanitary and life-threatening, amounted to cruel, inhuman or degrading treatment. Deaths from malnutrition or untreated medical conditions were common. In some prisons, little effort was made adequately to separate children from adult inmates, or women from men. In many cases detainees were refused access to lawyers, family members or medical care, especially in pre-trial detention.

Impunity and lack of access to justice
Despite systematic violations of human rights, hardly any suspected perpetrators were brought to justice. No effort was made to exclude individuals suspected of grave human rights abuses from the new army, and people allegedly responsible for crimes under international law and other human rights abuses assumed key positions in the army and transitional institutions.

Victims of human rights abuses were blocked from pursuing legal action against the perpetrators by failings in the justice system. Few had the confidence in the system to lodge a legal complaint. They had to pay for the costs of summons and court proceedings. Authorities failed to protect victims and witnesses from intimidation or reprisals. Rape survivors, many of them living in the same communities or areas as their attackers, were particularly affected by the lack of access to justice, and lived in fear of further assault.

Justice officials operated with limited resources, without office equipment or even basic legal texts. Non-payment of police and judicial salaries had a demoralizing and corrupting effect. Pre-trial detainees languished in prisons for want of funds to bring them to trial, including their transport to court. Political interference and pressure, sometimes accompanied by threats or dismissal, were exerted on judges, prosecutors and police officers.

Despite the introduction in 2002 of a revised military penal code, military courts and tribunals sometimes failed to respect international fair trial standards. In summary trials before such courts, defendants did not have full or adequate legal representation.

International justice
Two years after the prosecutor of the International Criminal Court announced that the Court would investigate crimes committed in the DRC since July 2002, investigations have yet to result in any international arrest warrants. The likelihood that only a handful of suspected perpetrators would be prosecuted underlined the necessity for comprehensive action by the DRC government to reform the national justice sector and take steps to end impuntiy, including by enacting appropriate legislation to implement the Rome Statute of the International Criminal Court.

Death penalty
Death sentences continued to be passed, mainly by military courts. Hundreds of prisoners remained under sentence of death, nearly all of them convicted after unfair trials by military courts. No executions were reported.

In March argument over abolition of the death penalty resurfaced during parliamentary debates on the new national Constitution. An early draft of the Constitution proposed abolition, but a majority in the Senate and National Assembly rejected the change.

Repression of freedom of expression
In advance of national elections, and as dissatisfaction with the transitional government grew, politically motivated harassment and detentions were used in an attempt to silence government critics. Members of human rights organizations, journalists and opposition activists were arbitrarily detained for denouncing human rights violations or criticizing the authorities. More than 40 journalists were detained, and many were charged with defamation. Others were threatened. Journalist Franck Ngyke Kangundu and his wife were shot dead in unexplained circumstances outside their home on 3 November. Dozens of opposition activists and some high-profile figures perceived as a political threat were harassed or detained.

AI country reports/visits
Reports
- Democratic Republic of the Congo: Arming the East (AI Index: AFR 62/006/2005)
- Democratic Republic of the Congo: North-Kivu — Civilians pay the price for political and military rivalry (AI Index: AFR 62/013/2005)
Visits
In February and March, AI delegates visited North and South-Kivu, Oriental province and Kinshasa, and organized a workshop in Bukavu, South-Kivu, to support initiatives by local non-governmental organizations and address the issue of sexual violence against women. In November, delegates from AI and Front Line, an international foundation for the protection of human rights defenders, jointly visited North and South-Kivu and Kinshasa to assess the protection needs of human rights defenders.

CONGO
(REPUBLIC OF THE)

REPUBLIC OF THE CONGO
Head of state and government: Denis Sassou-Nguesso
Death penalty: abolitionist in practice
International Criminal Court: ratified
UN Women's Convention: ratified
Optional Protocol to UN Women's Convention: not signed

More than 20 people were arrested in January and February in connection with an alleged plot against the government; more were arrested later in the year. Several of them were granted provisional release, but most remained in custody without trial at the end of the year. A trial of 15 serving members of the security forces and a civilian charged with genocide and crimes against humanity ended in August. All 16 were acquitted, but the court held the government responsible for the "disappearance" of at least 80 returning refugees in 1999.

Background

The 2003 peace agreement between the government and the armed opposition National Resistance Council (Conseil national de résistance, CNR) was not implemented and armed clashes were reported. In March the government announced a programme of demobilization, disarmament and reintegration of some 450 former CNR fighters but the armed group did not participate.

There were reports during the year of looting and lawlessness by CNR combatants. In one incident in April they attacked a UN humanitarian delegation visiting the Pool region and stole the delegates' property. On 13 October, three gendarmes, two policemen and a Chinese trader were killed during clashes between members of the security forces and CNR combatants in Brazzaville. The combatants were occupying a house allocated by the government to CNR leader Frédéric Bitsangou as part of the 2003 peace accord. On 19 October government forces attacked the combatants and drove them out of Brazzaville.

In July the Congolese Human Rights Observatory (Observatoire congolais des droits de l'homme, OCDH), a local independent human rights group, pulled out of the government-sponsored National Human Rights Commission. The OCDH accused the Commission of failing to act on human rights abuses and of lack of independence.

Former Prime Minister Bernard Kolelas, who had been sentenced to death in absentia in May 2000, returned home in October to bury his wife. Parliament granted him an amnesty in November.

Congo remained suspended from the Kimberley process, which traces the origin of diamonds, although officials said that they were doing all they could to rejoin the process.

Impunity

In July the trial of 15 members of the security forces and a civilian began before the Brazzaville criminal court. The men were charged with genocide and crimes against humanity for their alleged role in the "disappearance" in mid-1999 of more than 350 refugees returning from the neighbouring Democratic Republic of the Congo (formerly Zaire). Members of the security services were not suspended from their positions before or during the trial. When the trial concluded in August, the court found the state responsible for the "disappearance" of at least 80 people but acquitted all the defendants on the grounds that they bore no responsibility for the "disappearances". The court failed to specify who had carried out the "disappearances" but ordered the state to pay unspecified compensation to the families of the victims. Local and international human rights organizations expressed concern that the criminal court had only pursued the case to prevent the trial of the alleged perpetrators by an independent foreign court.

Detention without trial

In January, at least eight gendarmes and four civilians accused of involvement in the theft of arms from Bifouiti gendarmerie were arrested in Brazzaville and detained at the headquarters of the Central Directorate of Military Intelligence (Direction centrale des renseignements militaires, DCRM).

In February, more than 20 members of the security forces and civilians accused of plotting against the government were arrested in Pointe-Noire and detained by the security services. They were transferred to Brazzaville in March. Most of them were detained at the DCRM headquarters; others were held at the military academy, north of Brazzaville.

While in military custody without charge or trial, the detainees were held incommunicado and denied the right to see their defence counsel or their relatives. AI delegates visiting Brazzaville in April were also denied permission to meet the detainees. In May the detainees were transferred to Brazzaville's central prison and were allowed visits thereafter.

In September they were charged with endangering the security of the state. They had not been tried by the end of the year. At least four of the detainees, including Magoud Beconith Cotody and Jean Romain Tsiba, were granted provisional release in September.

AI country reports/ visits
Visit
AI delegates visited the Republic of the Congo in April.

CÔTE D'IVOIRE

REPUBLIC OF CÔTE D'IVOIRE
Head of state: Laurent Gbagbo
Head of government: Charles Konan Banny (replaced Seydou Diarra in December)
Death penalty: abolitionist for all crimes
International Criminal Court: signed
UN Women's Convention: ratified
Optional Protocol to UN Women's Convention: not signed

The postponement of presidential elections in October, despite intense diplomatic efforts by the African Union and pressure from the UN and the international community, resulted in political deadlock. In December a transitional government and prime minister were appointed. A resumption of hostilities was averted by international efforts to find a peaceful solution to the crisis and the presence of 10,000 peacekeeping troops. Both government security forces and the New Forces (Forces Nouvelles), a political coalition of former armed opposition groups in control of the north, continued to commit human rights abuses. People suspected of supporting the opposition forces were reportedly killed in the custody of the security forces. The death of a foreign national detained by opposition forces was believed to be the result of torture or other ill-treatment. Inter-ethnic tensions were stirred up by xenophobic propaganda. No progress was made in demobilizing forces under the peace process. Freedom of expression was under constant attack by both sides.

Background
In February a pro-government militia attacked a New Forces position in the first renewal of hostilities since forces loyal to President Laurent Gbagbo bombed rebel-held towns in November 2004, shattering an 18-month ceasefire.

In April, following mediation by South Africa's President Thabo Mbeki, both sides signed an agreement (Pretoria I) declaring an official end to the war, and pledged to demobilize, disarm and reintegrate all forces enlisted since the start of the insurgency in September 2002. Following ethnic clashes in the west in May and June, all the parties further agreed in June (Pretoria II) to African Union sanctions against forces that failed to implement peace agreements. In July, President Gbagbo adopted legal amendments identified in the peace accords as pre-conditions for presidential elections in October, but the New Forces and other opposition parties claimed the amendments were not in line with the Pretoria agreements.

In July tensions increased after attacks by unidentified armed groups on guard posts in two towns close to Abidjan, the economic capital, in which at least five military policemen were killed. In August, General

Mathias Doué, a former Army Chief of Staff, threatened to use "any means" to oust President Gbagbo, saying he was an obstacle to peace.

In October, following postponement of the presidential elections, the African Union proposed that President Gbagbo remain in power until October 2006, 12 months beyond his term of office, while conditions were created to hold fair elections. Under this proposal, which was endorsed by the UN, a new Prime Minister "acceptable to all Ivorian parties" was appointed in December as a result of the mediation of Presidents Thabo Mbeki of South Africa and Olusegun Obasanjo of Nigeria. Prime Minister Charles Konan Banny and a new government that included members of all Ivorian political parties were appointed for a transitional period until October 2006 to prepare future presidential elections.

The UN Security Council and Secretary-General continued to raise the possibility of sanctions against those undermining the peace process. In October, after a visit to Côte d'Ivoire, the head of the UN Sanctions Committee said that the international community would impose "measures" against political factions if they failed to reach a peace agreement.

Deaths in detention and unlawful killings
The security forces were responsible for the extrajudicial execution of detainees suspected of supporting the armed elements of the New Forces.
◻ In April, Samassi Abdramane, Touré Adama and Nimba Kah Hyacinthe were arrested by the police on suspicion of being "rebels". They were denied access to their lawyer, although their families were able to visit them at police headquarters in Abidjan some days after their arrest. A few days later, their bodies were found in the morgue at Anyama, 20km north of Abidjan. Despite a judicial investigation, by the end of 2005 no significant progress appeared to have been made in identifying their killers.
◻ In July, following an attack by unidentified armed men on police stations in the towns of Abgoville and Anyama, the security forces arrested dozens of civilians as suspects. A number were reported to have been extrajudicially executed, including Koné Gaoussou, a driver, and Diarra Lacény, an apprentice driver. No investigation was known to have been opened into these deaths.

Abuses by the New Forces
Armed New Forces units continued to be responsible for human rights abuses, including arbitrary detention, torture and ill-treatment.
◻ In March, Brian Hamish Sands, a New Zealand national, was arrested on suspicion of being a mercenary and detained incommunicado in Bouaké, the New Forces stronghold. He died three weeks later, according to the New Forces from natural causes. However, autopsy findings appeared to exclude this possibility. Other reports suggested that he had been tortured or might have committed suicide. There was no independent investigation into the circumstances surrounding his death.

☐ Also in March, some 35 men accused of being pro-government fighters were arrested by the New Forces. They were transferred to Korhogo, where they were allegedly detained for months incommunicado, without charge or trial and at risk of torture.

Extrajudicial executions by French peacekeeping forces

In May, soldiers of the French peacekeeping force Licorne killed Firmin Mahé, an alleged highway gang leader wanted for murder and rape. He suffocated while being transferred to hospital on the road between Bangolo and Man in the west. In October, three members of the French forces – including General Henri Poncet, former commander of the peacekeeping force – were suspended and reprimanded over their role in covering-up the killing. French investigators subsequently launched a military investigation and a criminal investigation into voluntary manslaughter.

Ethnic clashes in the west of the country

In the west, antagonism between the indigenous population and farmers from other regions or neighbouring countries such as Burkina Faso continued to provoke ethnic clashes. Xenophobic rhetoric by politicians and the news media aggravated the conflict.

☐ In May and June, more than a hundred people were killed, many with machetes and cudgels, in two separate incidents in Duékoué, 500km north-west of Abidjan. The conflict took place in a region under government rule, alongside the "confidence zone" controlled by French soldiers and the peacekeeping force of the UN Operation in Côte d'Ivoire (UNOCI).

Demobilization at a standstill

The stalling of the demobilization, disarmament and reintegration programme constituted one of the most obvious failures of the peace process. An estimated 50,000 combatants enlisted since the start of the insurgency in September 2002 were supposed to enter the programme. They included armed elements of the New Forces, pro-government militia members, and women and child soldiers. However, none of the measures anticipated in the timetable had been implemented by the end of 2005, in particular the preparation of sites designated for demobilized combatants. The main obstacle to progress appeared to be a lack of mutual confidence between the government and the New Forces leadership.

Child soldiers

As in previous years, child soldiers were recruited by both parties to the conflict.

☐ In February, two children aged 10 and 11, apparently of Liberian origin, took part in an attack on the western town of Logoualé by a pro-government militia, the Movement for the Liberation of Western Côte d'Ivoire (Mouvement de Libération de l'Ouest de la Côte d'Ivoire). The two children were placed under the protection of UNICEF, the UN Children's Fund.

Freedom of expression under attack

Journalists and media organizations were harassed and attacked by the security forces and pro-government militias.

☐ In July, members of the Young Patriots (Jeunes Patriotes), a loosely defined movement professing support for President Gbagbo, destroyed copies of opposition newspapers including *Le Patriote* and *Le Nouveau Réveil*.

☐ Also in July, the National Council for Radio and Television Broadcasting suspended broadcasts of *Radio France Internationale* in Côte d'Ivoire, and accused the station of unprofessional and biased coverage. Its broadcasts were still suspended at the end of 2005.

☐ In August, General Philippe Mangou, the Army Chief of Staff, threatened to ban newspapers that were "not working in the interests of the country".

AI country reports/visits
Reports
· Côte d'Ivoire: Stop the use of child soldiers (AI Index: AFR 31/003/2005)
· Côte d'Ivoire: Threats hang heavy over the future (AI Index: AFR 31/013/2005)
Visit
In January and February an AI delegation visited Côte d'Ivoire to investigate reports of human rights abuses during clashes in November 2004, including the alleged use of excessive force by French peacekeeping forces against civilian supporters of President Gbagbo in Abidjan.

CROATIA

REPUBLIC OF CROATIA
Head of state: Stjepan Mesić
Head of government: Ivo Sanader
Death penalty: abolitionist for all crimes
International Criminal Court: ratified
UN Women's Convention and its Optional Protocol: ratified

The legacy of the 1991-95 war continued to overshadow human rights in Croatia. Many of those responsible for human rights violations during the conflict continued to evade justice. The Croatian judicial system failed to address wartime human rights violations, regardless of the ethnicity of the victims or of the perpetrators. Of at least 300,000 Croatian Serbs displaced by the conflict, approximately 120,000 were officially registered as having returned home.

Background

In March the European Union (EU) Council decided to postpone the beginning of accession talks, because of the failure of the Croatian authorities to fully co-operate with the International Criminal Tribunal for the former Yugoslavia. In October, after the Tribunal's Prosecutor assessed that Croatia was fully co-operating with the Tribunal, the EU Council decided to open membership talks with Croatia. The EU Council agreed that less than full co-operation with the Tribunal at any stage would affect the overall progress of the negotiations and could be grounds for their suspension.

War crimes and crimes against humanity
International prosecutions

▭ In December former Croatian Army General Ante Gotovina was arrested in Spain, apparently after the Croatian authorities had provided the Tribunal with information on his whereabouts. He was subsequently transferred to the Tribunal's custody. Ante Gotovina was indicted by the Tribunal on seven counts: persecution; murder — including the murder of at least 150 Croatian Serbs; plunder; wanton destruction of cities, towns and villages; deportation and forced displacement; and other inhumane acts.

▭ In January Pavle Strugar, a former Lieutenant-General in the Yugoslav People's Army (Jugoslovenska narodna armija, JNA), was sentenced to eight years' imprisonment for his role in attacks on civilians and the destruction of cultural property during the shelling of Dubrovnik's Old Town in December 1991.

▭ In February the Tribunal indicted Momčilo Perišić, former JNA Chief of Staff, for war crimes and crimes against humanity committed during the wars in Croatia and Bosnia and Herzegovina (BiH), including his alleged role in the shelling of Zagreb in 1995.

▭ In June the Tribunal Prosecutor withdrew her application to refer the "Vukovar Three" case to a domestic jurisdiction in the former Yugoslavia, citing its highly sensitive nature and the fact that any decision to transfer it would provoke "deep resentment in one or the other country considered for the transfer". The accused, Mile Mrkšić, Miroslav Radić and Veselin Šljivančanin, who remained in the Tribunal's custody, are all former JNA officers indicted for their alleged involvement in the removal and execution of more than 250 non-Serbs from Vukovar hospital, after Vukovar fell to the JNA and Croatian Serb forces in 1991. The trial started at the Tribunal in October.

▭ In November the case of Rahim Ademi and Mirko Norac was officially transferred to Croatia. The Prosecution had requested the transfer in 2004. Mirko Norac was already serving a prison sentence in Croatia after being convicted in 2003 by the Rijeka County Court of war crimes against non-Croat civilians. The accused are former Croatian Army commanders charged with crimes against humanity and war crimes, including murder and persecutions, committed against Croatian Serbs during military operations in the so-called "Medak pocket" in 1993.

Domestic prosecutions

Trials for war crimes and crimes against humanity continued or started before local courts, often in absentia. In some cases these trials did not meet internationally recognized standards of fairness. In general, ethnic bias continued to affect the investigation and prosecution by the Croatian judiciary of wartime human rights violations. There continued to be widespread impunity for crimes allegedly committed by members of the Croatian Army and police forces.

▭ In February, three former Croatian police officers and one serving police officer, accused of having killed six captured JNA reservists in 1991, were acquitted by the Varaždin County Court. In May 2004 the Croatian Supreme Court had quashed a previous acquittal in this case by the Bjelovar County Court and ordered a retrial.

▭ In April proceedings against 27 Croatian Serbs, Roma and Ruthenians, 18 of whom were being tried in their absence, reopened at the Vukovar County Court, in what was reportedly the biggest war crimes trial ever held in Croatia. The defendants, who faced charges of genocide, were suspected of crimes against the civilian population of the village of Mikluševci, near Vukovar, in 1991 and 1992. The trial initially started in 2004 on the basis of an indictment issued in 1996 against 35 suspects. It was suspended when it was ascertained that eight of the accused had died.

▭ In May proceedings started at the Zagreb County Court against five former members of a Croatian Ministry of the Interior unit. In September, three received prison sentences of between five and 10 years for the murder of a member of the Croatian Army in 1991. The other two defendants were sentenced to two and four years' imprisonment for abducting and detaining three Croatian Serbs living in Zagreb who were later killed by unknown perpetrators in Pakračka poljana. Two of the accused went into hiding the day after the verdict was issued and were still at large at the end of 2005.

▭ In July an investigation was launched into murders and "disappearances" of Croatian Serb civilians in Osijek in 1991 and 1992. In October two suspects, reportedly former members of the Croatian Army, were arrested on suspicion of involvement in the wartime murder of four Croatian Serbs. In December Anto Đapić, President of the Croatian Party of Rights and Mayor of Osijek, reportedly disclosed to the media the names of 19 potential witnesses who could testify about crimes committed against Croatian Serbs in Osijek, leading to concerns about their safety and their willingness to testify in court.

▭ In September the retrial started at the Split County Court of eight former members of the Croatian Military Police, accused of having tortured and murdered non-Croat detainees in Split's Lora military prison in 1992. Four of the accused were tried in their absence. An initial trial held in 2002 ended with an acquittal verdict, subsequently overturned by the Croatian Supreme Court.

▭ In September the trial restarted at the Karlovac County Court of a former member of the Croatian special police on charges of having killed 13 disarmed

JNA reservists in 1991. Two earlier acquittal verdicts had been overturned by the Croatian Supreme Court.

Right to return/ attacks against Croatian Serbs
At least 300,000 Croatian Serbs were displaced by the 1991-95 conflict, of whom approximately 120,000 were officially registered as having returned home. One of the greatest obstacles to sustainable return was the failure of the Croatian authorities to provide adequate housing for Croatian Serbs who were stripped of their rights to socially owned flats during and after the war.

Cases of violence and harassment by private individuals against Croatian Serbs appeared to have increased in 2005. These included racist graffiti, threats and assaults. The most serious incident saw the apparently ethnically motivated killing in May of an elderly Croatian Serb man in Karin, near Zadar. The investigation into this murder was continuing at the end of 2005. Also in May, there were three bomb attacks on municipality buildings in the predominantly Croatian Serb towns of Borovo and Trpinja and in the premises of a Croatian Serb party in Vukovar. In August a bomb was thrown into the yard of a house owned by a Croatian Serb in the Imotski region, damaging the building. In October and November two Croatian Serb returnees were killed by explosive devices in a wood in the village of Jagma, Lipik municipality. The incidents raised particular concern since both occurred, in similar circumstances, in an area that was not considered to be affected by mines. The Croatian authorities were still investigating the incidents at the end of the year.

Violence against women
In February the UN Committee on the Elimination of Discrimination against Women expressed, among other things, its concern over the high incidence of domestic violence, the limited number of shelters available for victims of violence and the lack of clear procedures for law enforcement and health care personnel dealing with domestic violence. The Committee also expressed concern at the high incidence of trafficking in women.

AI country reports/ visits
Reports
- Amnesty International's concerns on the implementation of the "completion strategy" of the International Criminal Tribunal for the former Yugoslavia (AI Index: EUR 05/001/2005)
- Europe and Central Asia: Summary of Amnesty International's concerns in the region, July-December 2004: Croatia (AI Index: EUR 01/002/2005)
- Europe and Central Asia: Summary of Amnesty International's concerns in the region, January-June 2005: Croatia (AI Index: EUR 01/012/2005)

CUBA

REPUBLIC OF CUBA
Head of state and government: Fidel Castro Ruz
Death penalty: retentionist
International Criminal Court: not signed
UN Women's Convention: ratified with reservations
Optional Protocol to UN Women's Convention: signed

Restrictions on freedom of expression, association and movement continued to cause great concern. Nearly 70 prisoners of conscience remained in prison. The US embargo continued to have a negative effect on the enjoyment of the full range of human rights in Cuba. The economic situation deteriorated and the government attempted to suppress private entrepreneurship. More than 30 prisoners remained on death row; no one was executed.

Background
There was increasing international concern about Cuba's failure to improve civil and political rights. In April, in a highly politicized process, the UN Commission on Human Rights condemned Cuba once again for its human rights record.

The government maintained a tight control on those who criticized it, and detained several human rights defenders and political dissidents. However, in May the Assembly to Promote Civil Society — a coalition of more than 350 independent non-governmental organizations (NGOs) — held an unprecedented meeting of dissidents in Cuba.

The authorities launched an energetic campaign to tackle informal economic activities and widespread corruption in the state sector.

Prisoners of conscience
Prisoners of conscience continued to be arrested and sentenced for their peacefully held views. Some were released for health reasons.
- René Gómez Manzano and Julio César López Rodríguez were detained, along with several others, in the capital Havana after participating in a peaceful anti-government demonstration on 22 July. René Gómez Manzano, a member of the Assembly to Promote Civil Society, and eight others remained imprisoned awaiting trial.
- On 13 July around 20 people were detained while participating in a peaceful event in Havana. They were commemorating the "*13 de Marzo*" tugboat disaster of 1994, in which some 35 people were killed while attempting to flee Cuba when their boat was reportedly rammed by the Cuban authorities. Six remained in detention without charge and one was sentenced to one year's imprisonment for "*peligrosidad predelictiva*" defined as "a person's special proclivity to commit offences as demonstrated by conduct that is manifestly contrary to the norms of socialist morality".

⬜ Prisoner of conscience Mario Enrique Mayo Hernández, sentenced to 20 years' imprisonment in 2003, was conditionally released on health grounds on 1 December.

Restrictions on freedom of expression, association and movement

Human rights activists, political dissidents and trade unionists were harassed and intimidated. Such attacks were frequently perpetrated by quasi-official groups, the rapid-response brigades, allegedly acting in collusion with members of the security forces.

Freedom of expression and association continued to be under attack. All legal media outlets were under government control and independent media remained banned. Independent journalists faced intimidation, harassment and imprisonment for publishing articles outside Cuba. Human rights defenders also faced intimidation and politically motivated and arbitrary arrests.

The laws used to arrest and imprison journalists, relating to defamation, national security and disturbing public order, did not comply with international standards. According to the international NGO Reporters Without Borders, 24 journalists were imprisoned at the end of 2005.

⬜ Oscar Mario González Pérez, an independent journalist, was arrested on 22 July after covering a demonstration. He remained in prison without charge.

Dissidents continued to face restrictions when attempting to travel abroad.

⬜ Miguel Sigler Amaya, a member of the unofficial Alternative Option Movement (Movimiento Independiente Opción Alternativa), was detained at Havana International Airport when he and his family were about to board a plane to the USA even though they had exit visas as political refugees. He and his family were released several days later and finally left Cuba on 5 October. Miguel Sigler Amaya's brothers, Guido and Ariel, both prisoners of conscience, continued to serve sentences of 20 and 25 years respectively.

⬜ In December, representatives of Ladies in White (Las Damas de Blanco), a group of prisoners' female relatives who had marched every Sunday since March 2003 demanding the release of their husbands, brothers and sons, were not given official permission to travel to attend the award ceremony in Strasbourg, France, to receive the European Parliament's Sakharov Prize for Freedom of Thought.

AI country reports/ visits
Report
- Cuba: Prisoners of conscience – 71 longing for freedom (AI Index: AMR 25/002/2005)

CYPRUS

REPUBLIC OF CYPRUS
Head of state and government: Tassos Papadopoulos
Death penalty: abolitionist for all crimes
International Criminal Court: ratified
UN Women's Convention and its Optional Protocol: ratified

Foreign nationals were reported to have been unlawfully expelled, arbitrarily detained and ill-treated in police custody. The police allegedly used excessive force against demonstrators and journalists at a picket by striking lorry drivers. State policies failed to provide protection, support, justice or redress to victims of violence in the family.

Background

The de facto separation of the north and south parts of the island persisted, with the northern part remaining unrecognized by the international community. The Committee of Missing Persons, which reconvened in 2005 in an attempt to discover the fate of about 2,000 people missing in ethnic strife since 1963, held further meetings but made little progress.

Detention and deportation of foreign nationals

Experts from the European Union Network of Independent Experts in Fundamental Human Rights expressed concern in January that foreign nationals arriving in Cyprus in 2004 had been deported without being offered access to the asylum process. They cited cases of individuals who had been detained for prolonged periods pending deportation, even in cases where deportation orders could not be carried out or where detainees' asylum applications were under consideration.

Foreign detainees at the Central Prison in Nicosia complained that prison staff mocked them and made racist comments, the Ombudsperson reported in February. She also reported that foreign nationals who had filed asylum applications were being detained in police stations around the country.

In May there were reports that foreign detainees had been beaten while held in poor detention conditions in Limassol police station.

In July the Ombudsperson reported receiving complaints from foreign nationals applying for asylum who said they had been detained in police stations, ill-treated and forced to sign declarations withdrawing their requests for asylum. In one case, an Iranian asylum-seeker was arrested in February, detained for three months in Limassol police station and subsequently expelled to Iran. He had been arrested after he visited the police station to inform the Cypriot authorities that his address had changed. In her report, the Ombudsperson said that his arrest and detention were arbitrary, and that the expulsion was in violation of the principle of *non-refoulement* which states that those seeking asylum should not be forcibly returned to countries where they risked serious human rights abuses.

Excessive use of force

On 18 July members of the special police Mobile Immediate Response Unit were alleged to have used excessive force against demonstrators and journalists at a picket by striking lorry drivers. In response to a complaint by the Union of Journalists, the Ombudsperson carried out an investigation. She concluded that the police had exhibited "unpardonable negligence" and failed to inform the strikers about their "intention to ensure, using any possible means, including violence, lorry access across the picket line". The Ombudsperson also concluded that "the situation [which led to the beating and arrest of one cameraman in particular] was not of an intensity or gravity and did not bear a serious or direct danger such that would justify the involvement of the police officer in charge [as was the case]". Her report recommended that the police reconsider their role in policing future demonstrations to ensure that the public's right to freedom of information was not compromised and that their actions during the policing of such demonstrations were not excessive.

Domestic violence

Cyprus had not formulated a National Action Plan to combat domestic violence, according to the Swedish organization Kvinnoforum (Women's Forum) in a report in March. Experts from the local Mediterranean Institute of Gender Studies identified a number of failures in state policies on violence in the home. These included limited psychological support to victims; a lack of coordination between police and the judiciary; the absence of training for lawyers and judges; the lack of information in foreign languages to assist non-Cypriot victims; and the non-existent legal protections for lesbian, gay, bisexual or transgender people.

CZECH REPUBLIC

CZECH REPUBLIC
Head of state: Václav Klaus
Head of government: Jiří Paroubek (replaced Stanislav Gross in April)
Death penalty: abolitionist for all crimes
International Criminal Court: signed
UN Women's Convention and its Optional Protocol: ratified

Roma continued to suffer discrimination at the hands of public officials and private individuals. There were continuing reports of police ill-treatment.

Discrimination against Roma

Roma continued to face discrimination in employment, housing and education. They also suffered frequent violent attacks by racist individuals.
Housing
Discriminatory practices in public and private rental markets meant that in practice Roma could frequently not obtain housing, even if they were able to present financial guarantees, and as a result lived in segregated substandard housing. Ostensibly neutral eligibility requirements, such as an adequate education level for all members of the family applying for housing, disproportionately affected Roma whose level of education was often lower than that of ethnic Czechs.
In June, the municipality in the northern town of Bohumin issued eviction orders to the predominantly Romani residents of a hostel that it decided to convert into flats. The municipality offered no feasible plan to provide the low-income residents with alternative accommodation. Instead, it proposed to segregate the men from the women and children, and move them into a shelter for single mothers. Most of the residents left, while the remaining 15 appealed against the eviction orders. By November a regional court had ordered them to leave the hostel, without instructing the authorities to provide alternative accommodation. They appealed, and pending a decision, the town authorities were prohibited from evicting them.
Education
In May the European Court of Human Rights in Strasbourg decided to admit a complaint filed by 18 schoolchildren of Romani origin against the Czech Republic. The complaint alleged racial discrimination in education. The applicants claimed that their placement in "special schools" for mentally disabled children on the basis of their ethnic origin constituted racial discrimination and contravened international human rights principles.

Police ill-treatment

Reports of ill-treatment by the police continued, particularly of Roma, but also of other vulnerable groups, such as homeless people, people with substance abuse problems and foreigners. There was no mechanism, totally independent from the Interior Ministry, for investigating complaints about the actions of law enforcement officials.

🗀 The League of Human Rights, a local non-governmental organization, reported that on 1 February an 18-year-old Roma youth, R.B., was assaulted by municipal police in the city of Krupka. He was stopped on the street by the police and taken in a patrol car to a bar where he had allegedly earlier broken a window. He was reportedly kicked in the body and head in front of several witnesses, and required treatment for extensive injuries. The League of Human Rights filed a complaint on behalf of R.B. with the state police but, despite witness testimonies, the case was closed.

🗀 On 20 April, brothers Jan M. and Jozef M., both minors, were reportedly ill-treated after being taken into custody by police in a Prague street on suspicion of illegally pasting posters. In the car, Jan M. was hit by a policeman. At the police station in Prague 3 (Žižkov), the boys were made to strip naked and do push-ups in front of three policemen. During the interrogation, Jan M. was reportedly hit on the head so hard that his ear and nose bled and he had concussion. Relying on the testimony of the three policemen and despite a medical report on one of the youngsters, the case was not taken forward by the Inspectorate of the Interior Ministry. The League of Human Rights appealed against the decision of the inspectorate and, as of November, the case was under investigation by the state attorney.

🗀 On 30 July police intervened to disperse some 5,000 people gathered in a field near the village of Mlýnec, West Bohemia, for a music festival known as "CzechTek", which was allegedly unauthorized and causing damage to private property. Police in riot gear reportedly shot tear gas grenades and used water cannons to end the festival. More than 80 people were injured, and around 20 members of the public and five police officers sought medical attention. In November, the Ombudsman's office stated that the intervention was legal but that police failed to take adequate preventive measures that might have helped to avoid the later use of force.

Mental health issues

Despite the banning of cage beds in psychiatric institutions under the Ministry of Health, their use was still permitted in social care centres under the Ministry of Labour and Social Affairs. These centres housed children and adults with mental disabilities and people with substance abuse problems.

In May, parliament adopted an amendment to the law on social care on the use of restraint in all social care institutions, including cage beds. Regularization of restraint use was cited as the objective of the law, although in fact it legalized the use of restraints. The amendment allows employees of social care homes who are not qualified physicians to make decisions regarding restraint use. Moreover, the amendment does not provide for supervision of the restraint order, time limits on restraint, or a complaint mechanism for victims.

Forced sterilization of women

In late 2004, the Ministry of Health established a panel to review the files of alleged victims of forced sterilization, to facilitate investigation of the issue and to respond to queries from the Ombudsman. The Ombudsman was conducting an independent investigation into approximately 80 complaints against hospitals that allegedly sterilized women without their informed consent. In December, the Ombudsman produced a final report, stating that in most cases of forced sterilization, women were not able to give informed consent because they did not understand the procedure, because of lack of time (sometimes the procedure was carried out within a few minutes of their agreeing to it, or after labour had started) or because of misleading information on the part of hospital personnel about the nature and consequences of the sterilization procedure. A number of these cases were transferred to the state attorney and the police for investigation.

🗀 The Group of Women Harmed by Sterilization, a victim advocacy group, lodged formal complaints in cases of Romani women sterilized under coercion. In November, the Ostrava District Court indicated that it would uphold the complaint of Helena Ferencikova, who was sterilized in an Ostrava hospital in 2001 while giving birth to her second child by caesarean section. The court was expected to rule that, in violation of the rules on informed consent, the doctors secured her consent when she was deep in labour and did not fully understand the consequences of her actions.

DOMINICAN REPUBLIC

DOMINICAN REPUBLIC
Head of state and government: Leonel Fernández Reyna
Death penalty: abolitionist for all crimes
International Criminal Court: ratified
UN Women's Convention and its Optional Protocol: ratified

Large numbers of Haitians and Dominicans of Haitian origin were forcibly expelled. Many were beaten and some killed in a climate of xenophobic hostility. Women continued to suffer domestic violence.

Discrimination against Haitians
Expulsions

There were mass expulsions of Haitians and Dominicans of Haitian origin across the border to Haiti. Although officials stated that the round-ups and deportations were to combat illegal immigration, Haitians with a legal right to remain in the Dominican Republic and black Dominicans were among those forcibly expelled.

◻ In May, more than 3,000 Haitians and black Dominicans were forcibly expelled in three days. They were reportedly rounded up in the early hours of the morning, forced onto buses and left at the Haitian border. Many were unable to collect their belongings and some were allegedly separated from family members.

Access to nationality
◻ In October, the Inter-American Court of Human Rights ruled in the case of *Dilcia Yean and Violeta Bosico v Dominican Republic*. The two girls of Haitian descent were born on Dominican territory and lived there all their lives but were denied Dominican nationality in contravention of the country's Constitution. As a result, they could not obtain birth certificates or enrol in school, and remained vulnerable to expulsion. The Court found that the Dominican Republic's application of nationality laws and regulations was discriminatory and therefore contravened international human rights standards.

Assaults
Haitians faced an increasing climate of xenophobic hostility, particularly after the murder in May of a Dominican shop owner in the north of the country, allegedly perpetrated by Haitian migrants. Incidents of lynching were reported, often after the murder or rape of a Dominican, and several Haitians were killed. The security forces failed to intervene to halt attacks.

◻ In August, three Haitians were lynched and burned alive following an alleged argument with a group of Dominicans.

Killings by security forces
There was an increase in the number of people killed in shoot-outs ("intercambios de disparos") with members of the security forces, apparently in the context of anti-crime operations. Between January and August, 348 people were killed in this way, according to official statistics, compared with 360 such deaths during the whole of 2004. Uncorroborated reports suggested that a number of these fatal shootings may have been extrajudicial killings. Fifty-five members of the security forces were reportedly killed in the same eight-month period.

Torture and ill-treatment
In August, five inmates from the prison in the city of Mao were reportedly tortured by police personnel from the prison, leaving them with broken ribs, arms and legs. They had allegedly helped another inmate to escape. The escaped prisoner was eventually shot dead by prison guards. According to press reports, the Chief of the National Police ordered the local police commander to open an investigation into the prisoners' allegations of torture.

Violence against women
Violence against women continued to be widespread, affecting women from all backgrounds. During the first six months of 2005, the Care Centre for Battered Women reported 386 cases of sexual violence in which 205 women were beaten.

Human rights defenders
Father Pedro Ruquoy, a Belgian Catholic priest, received death threats in September apparently because of his work on behalf of Dominican peasants and Haitian migrants working in sugar cane plantations. As a result of the threats and other intimidation, Father Ruquoy was forced to leave the Dominican Republic in November after 30 years of missionary work in the country. According to reports, other human rights defenders working on behalf of Haitians and Dominicans of Haitian origin also had to flee the country.

AI country reports/visits
Statement
- Dominican Republic: Fear for safety/death threat — Father Pedro Ruquoy, human rights defender (AI Index: AMR 27/001/2005)

ECUADOR

REPUBLIC OF ECUADOR
Head of state and government: Alfredo Palacio (replaced Lucio Gutiérrez Borbua in April)
Death penalty: abolitionist for all crimes
International Criminal Court: ratified
UN Women's Convention and its Optional Protocol: ratified

The independence of the judiciary was threatened by the sacking of Supreme Court judges. There were clashes between demonstrators and the security forces during protests in the capital, Quito, in April, and the provinces of Sucumbíos and Orellana in May and August. Critics of the government were threatened. Cases of torture and ill-treatment by the police continued to be tried in police courts.

Background
The political atmosphere remained unstable. Following public protests over interference in the appointment of Supreme Court judges, first by Congress and later by President Gutiérrez, Congress ousted and replaced the President on 20 April. In October, when he returned from Colombia, he was arrested and charged with corruption and undermining the security of the state.

The number of refugees fleeing the internal armed conflict in Colombia grew, asylum applications reportedly reaching 20,000 by October. Colombian state forces and armed opposition groups reportedly entered Ecuador's increasingly militarized border areas.

The appointment of the Human Rights Ombudsman in July was criticized by human rights defenders for apparently flouting procedures aimed at ensuring the involvement of civil society. The candidate supported by civil society organizations was denied the opportunity to be considered for the position.

Judicial independence attacked

In March, the UN Special Rapporteur on the independence of judges and lawyers said that the replacement by Congress of most Supreme Court judges in December 2004 had been unconstitutional. Also in March, the new Court withdrew corruption charges against three former heads of state in a move that appeared to favour their political affiliations. In April, President Gutiérrez sacked the Court in an attempt to avert an impending constitutional crisis. A new Court was appointed at the end of November.

Attacks on human rights defenders

There were continued reports of individuals working to protect human rights, and people who criticized the authorities, being threatened and harassed.

▭ In July, María Teresa Cherres Mesías, a community leader from Orellana province, was threatened and intimidated apparently because of her work defending the labour rights of oil company workers in the region.

Ill-treatment of oil protesters

In May and August, the government declared a state of emergency in response to demonstrations, strikes and occupations in the provinces of Sucumbíos and Orellana. Protesters were demanding greater local investment of revenues from oil exploitation in the area. Amid reports of violence by protesters, dozens of people, including minors, were detained by police, and some were reportedly ill-treated in custody. No investigation was opened.

Torture and impunity

In November the UN Committee against Torture expressed concern at the high level of allegations of torture and ill-treatment, including of indigenous peoples, women, and lesbian, gay, bisexual and transgender people. The Committee expressed serious concern that complaints of human rights violations by the security forces continued to be tried in police and military courts, which were neither independent nor impartial.

▭ On 2 February, Juan Carlos Pesantes Umatambo was detained at a police roadblock for not carrying identity papers, and reportedly forced to strip, hosed with cold water and beaten with a metal bar. An investigation was opened in a civil court, and the judge ordered the arrest of a police officer. However, a parallel investigation was conducted in a police court. The arrested officer was remanded in police, not prison, custody. Reportedly, none of the other officers

accused of involvement was suspended from duty. By the end of 2005 no decision had been made as to whether the civil or police court would be granted jurisdiction over the case.

Economic, social and cultural rights

Many women and children from marginalized communities still did not have access to health care guaranteed them under 1998 legislation. In some provinces, health centre and hospital staff were reportedly not even aware of the legislation.

Children

In June, the UN Committee on the Rights of the Child expressed concern at continued discrimination against indigenous and Afro-Ecuadorian people, including children; the limited enjoyment of the rights to education and health by poor indigenous children; the lack of policies on widespread abuse and violence within the family; and the high levels of child labour and commercial sexual exploitation of children.

AI country reports/ visits
Statements
- Ecuador: It is essential for the intimidation of government critics to stop if respect for human rights is to be safeguarded (AI Index: AMR 28/004/2005)
- Ecuador: Respect for human rights must be the top priority of the political agenda (AI Index: AMR 28/010/2005)

Visit
AI delegates visited Ecuador in February.

EGYPT

ARAB REPUBLIC OF EGYPT
Head of state: Muhammad Hosni Mubarak
Head of government: Ahmed Nazif
Death penalty: retentionist
International Criminal Court: signed
UN Women's Convention: ratified with reservations
Optional Protocol to UN Women's Convention: not signed

Ninety people were killed and more than 100 injured in bomb attacks in Cairo in April and Sharm el-Sheikh in July. Scores of people were arrested in connection with the attacks and at least 14 people, including several police officers, were killed in shoot-outs between police and alleged suspects. Peaceful demonstrations calling for political reform were violently dispersed. Non-governmental organizations (NGOs) continued to operate under a restrictive law introduced in 2002. Hundreds of members of the banned Muslim Brothers organization were arrested;

scores of them remained held awaiting trial at the end of the year. Thousands of suspected supporters of banned Islamist groups, including possible prisoners of conscience, remained in detention without charge or trial; some had been held for years. Torture and ill-treatment in detention continued to be systematic. Deaths in custody were reported. In the majority of torture cases, the perpetrators were not brought to justice. At least two people were sentenced to death; no executions were known to have taken place.

Background

The nationwide state of emergency imposed in 1981 remained in force despite calls by human rights groups and others for it to be lifted.

President Muhammad Hosni Mubarak began a fifth term of office following an election in September, when for the first time other candidates were allowed to stand against him after the government amended Article 76 of the Constitution. The amendment was first proposed by President Mubarak in February and then approved by a national referendum in May, which some opposition parties sought to boycott. Nine candidates stood against the President in September, but he was returned by a large margin. There were some allegations of electoral fraud. In December Ayman Nour, leader of the al-Ghad party who came second in the election with less than 10 per cent of the poll, was prosecuted and jailed for five years, allegedly for fraudulently obtaining signatures to support his application to legalize his party. The prosecution provoked widespread international and national criticism.

Elections for a new parliament were held in three stages in November and December. They were marred by serious irregularities and by violence, including police shootings of voters, which left at least 11 dead and many others injured. Many supporters of candidates associated with the Muslim Brothers were detained by police, and many others were violently attacked by supporters of the ruling National Democratic Party (NDP) who were allowed to act with impunity. While the NDP kept its majority in parliament, the Muslim Brothers won 88 seats, six times more than they held in the previous parliament.

Egypt's government-sponsored National Council for Human Rights (NCHR) issued its first report in April, covering February 2004 to February 2005. It called for the abolition of the state of emergency, drew attention to continuing human rights violations, notably torture and ill-treatment, and made a number of recommendations.

In September, the European Union and Egypt began negotiating an Action Plan for Egypt within the framework of the European Neighbourhood Policy. Twenty-five Egyptian NGOs called for a stronger human rights agenda to be considered during negotiations.

Human rights violations in the 'war on terror'

New information emerged about Egypt's role in connection with the international "war on terror".

While visiting the USA in May, Prime Minister Ahmed Nazif stated that more than 60 people had been forcibly transferred to Egypt by US forces since September 2001. However, no Egyptian or US officials provided further details of the individuals concerned or their fate. In addition, the Egyptian authorities continued actively to seek the forcible return of alleged members of Islamist groups from abroad.

Scores of people detained following the bomb attacks on civilians at Taba and Nuweiba in October 2004 were released during 2005, but more than 100 others were still detained at the end of the year, many of them apparently held under administrative detention powers. Many of those released alleged that they had been tortured in detention.

Ahmed Abdallah Raba', who was arrested in November 2004 in al-'Arish, was detained without charge for three and a half months, mostly without contact with his relatives or a lawyer. For most of that time, he was held at Istiqbal Tora prison. However, he was taken twice to the State Security Intelligence (SSI) headquarters in Cairo for interrogation where, he alleged, he was repeatedly tortured for a week by being beaten, hung by his wrists and ankles in contorted positions and subjected to electric shocks while all the time naked and with his eyes covered by a blindfold. He said that a doctor regularly checked on the health of torture victims while he was at the SSI headquarters.

Further arrests were made following the bomb attacks in Cairo in April and in Sharm el-Sheikh in July. Again, many of those detained were reportedly tortured and there were at least two deaths in custody in circumstances suggesting that torture or ill-treatment were contributory factors.

Muhammad Suleyman Youssef and Ashraf Sa'id Youssef, two cousins, both died soon after being detained. Following the former's death on 29 April, his family was reportedly pressured by the authorities into signing a medical report which attributed his death to natural causes. Ashraf Sa'id Youssef, who was detained on the day that his cousin died, was held incommunicado for 13 days and his relatives only learned of his whereabouts when he was transferred to al-Minyal University Hospital with serious head injuries on 11 May. He died six days later. The Public Prosecutor said he caused his own injuries by repeatedly banging his head against his cell wall. No proper investigation was known to have been carried out.

The authorities generally failed to conduct prompt, impartial and thorough investigations into allegations of torture, especially in cases having a political or security aspect, where officials responsible for carrying out investigations were allowed to commit abuses with impunity. By contrast, there were several prosecutions of police officers accused of torturing, ill-treating or causing the deaths of suspects in ordinary criminal cases. There were reports that some torture victims had received compensation.

Defendants facing charges relating to national security or terrorism were frequently tried before courts established under emergency legislation or military courts, even when the defendants were civilians. These courts fail in many respects to satisfy international standards for fair trial; for example, they provide for no right of full judicial review before a higher tribunal.

◻ Muhammad Abdallah Raba' and Muhammad Gayiz Sabbah went on trial before the (Emergency) Supreme State Security Court at Ismailia in July, accused in connection with the Taba and Nuweiba bomb attacks of October 2004. Both defendants alleged at the trial's opening session, which AI observed, that they had been tortured by the SSI to force them to confess. They were then referred for medical examination, but a subsequent report dismissed their allegations and the court failed to order a thorough, impartial investigation. Although arrested in October 2004, they first had access to their lawyers only on the opening day of the trial.

Violence against women
In July, a coalition of 94 organizations and civil associations from various governorates launched a national campaign to criminalize all forms of domestic violence against women in Egypt. The launch was declared during a conference organized by the Nadim Centre for the Psychological Treatment and Rehabilitation of Victims of Violence in the presence of a number of human rights and women activists.

Restrictions on freedom of expression, association and assembly
Restrictions on freedom of expression, association and assembly persisted. NGOs continued to operate under a restrictive 2002 law; some faced obstacles at the Ministry of Social Affairs when seeking to register and obtain legal status. For example, the Ministry turned down the Egyptian Association Against Torture's application to register, a decision subsequently upheld by an administrative court.

Journalists continued to be threatened, beaten or imprisoned because of their work. A Bill introduced by President Mubarak in February 2004 that would abolish prison terms for publishing offences was not made law.

On several occasions, police used excessive force against people demonstrating against government policies or to assert their basic rights. At other times, police stood back and took no action when supporters of the ruling NDP physically assaulted opposition supporters.

◻ Scores of demonstrators advocating a boycott of the May referendum to amend the Constitution and journalists working for opposition newspapers were assaulted, reportedly by NDP supporters. Some of the assaults allegedly took place in the presence of police who failed to intervene. The Public Prosecutor ordered an investigation into the assaults but closed it in December on the grounds that there was insufficient evidence to prosecute.

◻ During the December parliamentary elections, police fired live ammunition, rubber bullets and tear gas into crowds seeking to vote at polling stations that police had closed or cordoned off in al-Daqahlia,

al-Sharqia and other areas. At least 11 people were killed in the violence. No official investigation was known to have been held.

Refugees and migrants
In December, 27 Sudanese refugees and migrants were killed and others injured when police brutally dispersed what had been for three months a peaceful sit-in close to the offices of the UN High Commissioner for Refugees in Cairo. Police were said to have aimed water cannons at protesters and subjected them to indiscriminate beatings. The demonstrators, whose numbers had swelled to around 2,500 by December, were calling for improvements in their living conditions, protection from return to Sudan, and resettlement in Europe or North America.

Prison conditions
In September, up to 2,000 prisoners were released for health and humanitarian reasons, reportedly following recommendations by the NCHR. Thousands of other detainees were held in prisons where conditions amounted to cruel, inhuman or degrading treatment. Hundreds held in administrative detention were reportedly suffering from illnesses including tuberculosis, skin diseases and paralysis, which were common because of lack of hygiene and medical care, overcrowding and poor food quality. Scores of them went on hunger strikes in May and June to protest against their ill-treatment and lack of adequate medical care.

◻ Relatives of hundreds of administrative detainees held a sit-in at the Lawyers' Syndicate's building in Cairo for several months prior to the September presidential elections. They were protesting against the continued detention of their relatives and the conditions of detention, which had caused health problems. They also demonstrated in October outside the Ministry of the Interior building in Cairo's Lazoghly Square to call for the release of their relatives, some of whom were thought to have been detained for more than a decade.

AI country reports/ visits
Statements
- Egypt: Mixed signals — arrests of political opponents amidst talks of political reform (AI Index: MDE 12/016/2005)
- Egypt: Continuing arrests of critics and opponents "chill" prospects for reform (AI Index: MDE 12/021/2005)
- Egypt: Intimidation and assault on journalists and peaceful demonstrators must stop (AI Index: MDE 12/025/2005)
- Egypt: Amnesty International condemns bomb attacks in Sharm el-Sheikh (AI Index: MDE 12/030/2005)
- Egypt: Human rights should be at centre of election agenda (AI Index: MDE 12/032/2005)
- Egypt: Amnesty International concerned about mass arrests and violent attacks (AI Index: MDE 12/037/2005)

- Egypt: Police killings of voters requires urgent, independent investigation (AI Index: MDE 12/039/2005)

Visit
In June/July AI delegates met victims of torture and their families, families of administrative detainees, human rights activists, lawyers, and NCHR and government officials.

EL SALVADOR

REPUBLIC OF EL SALVADOR
Head of state and government: Elías Antonio Saca
Death penalty: abolitionist for ordinary crimes
International Criminal Court: not signed
UN Women's Convention: ratified with reservations
Optional Protocol to UN Women's Convention: signed

Impunity for past human rights violations, including "disappearances", persisted. Reports of violence against women increased but investigations remained inadequate. There were threats against human rights defenders.

Background
Criminal violence increased during the year by around 34 per cent, according to the National Civil Police. There were 3,761 murders, 82 per cent committed with firearms. The harsh government initiatives of previous years against *maras* (gangs) did not bring the improvements in the security situation predicted by the authorities. Instead, the prison population increased, causing greater overcrowding and protests. Prisons designed for 7,000 held around 12,000 inmates.

Natural disasters hit El Salvador, particularly affecting the poor. In October a volcanic eruption killed two peasant farmers and displaced over 5,000 people. Later, Hurricane Stan caused extensive damage and casualties. The authorities were criticized for failing to provide prompt relief to the victims.

'Disappeared' children
In March the Inter-American Court of Human Rights ruled that the state of El Salvador, by failing to carry out an effective and timely investigation into the "disappearance" of three-year-old Ernestina and seven-year-old Erlinda Serrano Cruz in June 1982 during a military operation in Chalatenango, had violated their human rights and those of their family. The ruling compels the state to determine the whereabouts of the girls, investigate and bring those responsible to justice and, among other things, to set up a National Search Commission to trace "disappeared" children. Only some of the Court's recommendations had been implemented by the end of 2005.

Three more cases of children who "disappeared" during the armed conflict were admitted by the Inter-American Commission on Human Rights in November.

Violence against women
There was a sharp rise in the number of women murdered. According to the National Civil Police, 323 women and girls were killed between January and November, a rise over the corresponding period in 2004. The incidence of domestic violence also increased. In the first six months of the year, the emergency system of the National Civil Police received nearly 12,000 calls reporting incidents of domestic violence and 24 women were killed by partners or family members.

The report of the 2004 visit of the UN Special Rapporteur on violence against women was published in February. She recommended that the government prevent, investigate and punish acts of violence against women, whoever the perpetrator, and prioritize ending impunity for these crimes. The authorities apparently took no steps to comply with the recommendations.

No progress was made in investigating cases of women who had been killed and, in some cases, raped in previous years. AI called on the authorities to properly investigate such cases, but no progress was evident by the end of 2005.

Human rights defenders
Four officials from the Human Rights Procurator's Office were arrested in April on charges of having committed "arbitrary acts" while monitoring the procedures followed in the deportation of an Ecuadorian doctor. He had been living in El Salvador for several years and was married to a Salvadorean citizen, and denied allegations that he had participated in political activities. The Human Rights Procurator's Office considered the arrests to be harassment of its officials, an obstruction to their lawful activities and a demonstration of the government's opposition to the institution's work. The four officials were released after three days.

EQUATORIAL GUINEA

REPUBLIC OF EQUATORIAL GUINEA
Head of state: Teodoro Obiang Nguema Mbasogo
Head of government: Miguel Abia Biteo Borico
Death penalty: retentionist
International Criminal Court: not signed
UN Women's Convention: ratified
Optional Protocol to UN Women's Convention: not signed

Suspected political opponents were arbitrarily detained without charge or trial. At least 20 detainees, including prisoners of conscience, were still in custody after being detained in 2003 and 2004. There were reports of torture, in at least one case resulting in death. Two people were alleged to have been killed unlawfully by soldiers. Four government opponents reportedly "disappeared" in custody following their abduction from neighbouring countries. Conditions at Black Beach prison in the capital, Malabo, were life-threatening. Over 20 soldiers and former military personnel were given long prison sentences for an alleged attempted coup after an unfair military trial. Six Armenian nationals sentenced to long prison terms after an unfair trial in 2004 were released. Two young boys were unlawfully charged and detained.

Background
In January, Equatorial Guinea signed the Protocol to the African Charter on Human and Peoples' Rights on the Rights of Women in Africa.

Despite high levels of economic growth and oil production, poverty remained widespread. Shortages of drinking water in the main cities, sometime lasting for several weeks, were frequent. According to the UN Development Programme's Human Development Index, life expectancy decreased from 49.1 years in 2001 to 43.3 years in 2005.

In September a High Court in the United Kingdom dismissed a claim for damages brought by President Teodoro Obiang Nguema against several British businessmen and an Equatorial Guinean exile who were accused of financing an alleged coup attempt in March 2004.

Arbitrary detention
At least 20 people arrested in 2003 and 2004, including some 12 prisoners of conscience, continued to be held without charge or trial. Interrogation of the detainees by the investigating judge started in late December 2005.

Dozens of suspected political opponents were arbitrarily detained, some of them briefly. Others were still in prison, without charge or trial, at the end of 2005. Most appeared to be prisoners of conscience.

Vidal Bomabá Sirubé, Marcelino Barila Buale and Deogracias Batapa Barila were arrested in January, apparently on suspicion of being members of the Movement for the Self-determination of Bioko Island (Movimiento para la autodeterminación de la isla de Bioko, MAIB). They were still held without charge or trial in Black Beach prison at the end of 2005. Vidal Bomabá Sirubé, a lawyer resident in Spain, received no medication for a chronic kidney ailment.

In April, 75-year-old Anastasia Ncumu was arrested and briefly detained after she took food to her son in Bata prison, apparently because she had criticized President Obiang.

Death in detention, torture and ill-treatment
Police tortured or ill-treated detainees with impunity. At least one detainee was reported to have died as a result of torture. Those responsible were not brought to justice.

In March taxi driver Mariano Esono "Nenuco" died in the Mondoasi police station in Bata, a week after his arrest for allegedly not repaying a debt to his employer. He was reportedly burned with an iron and subjected to electric shocks on his genitals and face. He was taken to court, where a judge was said to have ordered immediate hospital treatment. However, police officers allegedly returned him to the police station, where he died soon afterwards, then tried to hide his body by burying it on a beach, where they were observed by passers-by. They then returned the body to his family.

In May Prosper Diffo, a Cameroonian car mechanic, was held for four hours at police headquarters in Bata. He was reportedly beaten with batons and kicked because he had refused to work on the Provincial Governor's car. He required two days' treatment in hospital and could not work for a month. He received no compensation, and those responsible were not brought to justice.

'Disappearances'
The authorities failed to disclose the whereabouts of detainees who "disappeared" following their arrest in late 2004. A further four people "disappeared" in 2005.

Former Navy Commander Juan Ondó Abaga, a refugee in Benin since 1997, was allegedly abducted by Equatorial Guinean security personnel in February. Lieutenant-Colonel Florencio Bibang Elá, soldier Felipe Esono Ntumu "Pancho" and civilian Antimo Edú were arrested in April in Lagos, Nigeria, and transferred to the capital, Abuja. In July, Equatorial Guinean security personnel reportedly abducted them from Nigerian custody after bribing prison officials. After being returned to Equatorial Guinea, all four men were imprisoned incommunicado in Black Beach prison, where they were allegedly tortured and denied medical care. They subsequently "disappeared". The three members of the armed forces were tried in their absence in September on charges of attempting a coup in October 2004, and sentenced to 30 years' imprisonment. The state-controlled radio said that they were outside the country. No official announcement was made about the fate of Antimo Edú.

Unlawful killings
Soldiers who killed two people in Bata were not brought to justice.

🗀 Plácido Ndong Anvam died in January, a few days after being beaten in the street by soldiers who appeared to be drunk.

🗀 In May, Miguel Ángel Ndong Ondó died from his injuries 10 days after a soldier allegedly ordered him to raise his hands and shot him at close range. He had been returning home with a woman friend in the early hours of the morning, when they were followed by the soldier and there was a brief fight.

Unfair political trials
Further arrests took place in January of people accused of involvement in an alleged coup attempt in October 2004. Of the 70 prisoners who were tried by a military court in Bata in September, on charges of treason and undermining the security of the state, 20 soldiers and former soldiers were convicted and sentenced to prison terms of between six and 30 years. The rest of the accused were acquitted. The trial was unfair. The defendants were held incommunicado before the trial and reportedly convicted on the basis of confession statements they said were extracted under torture. They bore scars consistent with their allegations. There is no right of appeal from a military court.

Update
In June, six Armenian nationals, sentenced to long prison terms in November 2004 for their alleged participation in an alleged coup attempt in March 2004, were released under a presidential pardon. Two Equatorial Guineans sentenced in the same case were also released in August, having completed their sentences.

Harassment of a human rights defender
🗀 In June, lawyer and human rights defender Fabián Nsué Nguema, a former prisoner of conscience, was arbitrarily suspended from the Bar Association for a year, for alleged misconduct. The suspension order did not specify the nature or source of the complaint against him, and he was given no opportunity to refute any accusation. His suspension appeared to be politically motivated and related to his work as a lawyer for people tried for alleged coup attempts, including a group of South African nationals convicted after unfair trials in 2004, and to his criticisms of the government.

Prison conditions
Prison conditions were life-threatening as a result of overcrowding, lack of medical treatment and insufficient food.

🗀 Prisoners in Black Beach prison were at risk of starvation, particularly those without families to support them. Food rations, reduced to one or two bread rolls a day in late 2004, were cut again in late February, with prisoners receiving no food at all for days at a time. The situation improved in late April. Prisoners were held incommunicado from February to September, when limited family visits were again allowed.

Unlawful arrest of children
Two 12-year-old boys were unlawfully arrested, detained and charged in February in Malabo. They were held in a police station for three days on charges of killing another child three years earlier, before being taken before a judge to have their detention legalized. The judge ordered their detention at Black Beach prison, which has no facilities for juveniles. They were released two weeks later to await trial. The trial had not started by the end of 2005. Under national law, the age of criminal responsibility is 16 and there is no juvenile justice system.

AI country reports/ visits
Report
· Equatorial Guinea: A trial with too many flaws (AI Index: AFR 24/005/2005)

ERITREA

ERITREA
Head of state and government: Issayas Afewerki
Death penalty: retentionist
International Criminal Court: signed
UN Women's Convention: ratified
Optional Protocol to UN Women's Convention: not signed

Several thousand prisoners of conscience, many held because of their religious beliefs and others for political reasons, were in indefinite and incommunicado detention without charge or trial, some in secret locations. Many detainees were tortured or ill-treated, and large numbers were held in metal shipping containers or underground cells.

Background
The government took no steps to establish a multi-party democratic system as required by the 1997 Constitution. The ruling party, the People's Front for Democracy and Justice (PFDJ), was the sole party allowed and no opposition activity or criticism was tolerated.

Two thirds of the population were dependent on international emergency food aid. They included 70,000 people living in internally displaced people's camps since the war with Ethiopia in 1998-2000, and refugees who had returned from Sudan. Many donors suspended development aid programmes because of the government's failures in democratization and human rights.

Human rights defenders were not allowed to operate. A new law in May imposed severe restrictions on non-governmental organizations (NGOs), allowing them only to work on relief and rehabilitation projects through government structures. International NGOs had to deposit US$2 million in Eritrean banks and local NGOs US$1 million. No local NGOs were able to register.

The government continued to support two Ethiopian armed opposition groups fighting inside Ethiopia, the Oromo Liberation Front and the Ogaden National Liberation Front. The Sudan-based armed opposition Eritrean Democratic Alliance was supported by Ethiopia, although it was not clear that it had carried out any armed activities inside Eritrea during 2005.

Fears of a new war with Ethiopia

The UN Security Council called on Ethiopia to implement the International Boundary Commission's judgment regarding the border areas, particularly its allocation to Eritrea of Badme town, the flashpoint of war in 1998. Ethiopia refused to agree to border demarcation, instead calling for negotiation over certain issues. Eritrea demanded UN action against Ethiopia to enforce the border judgment.

In October, Eritrea banned UN helicopter flights and other travel to UN monitoring posts, further restricting the multinational UN Mission in Ethiopia and Eritrea (UNMEE), whose 2,800 personnel administered a buffer zone along the border. Both countries had re-armed since 2000 and deployed troops near the border in late 2005. The UN Security Council threatened sanctions against either side if it started a new war.

Religious persecution

A 2002 ban on religions other than the Eritrean Orthodox Church, the Catholic and Lutheran Churches and Islam remained in force. Minority religions were ordered to register and provide details of their members and finances, which many refused to do, fearing reprisals. Those that applied received no response, and remained banned.

The government cracked down on evangelical Christian churches such as the Kale Hiwot (Word of Life) and Mullu Wengel (Full Gospel) churches. More than 1,000 believers from some 35 churches were arrested by police in at least 23 incidents during 2005 in Asmara and other towns, while worshipping in their homes or at weddings. They were detained without charge or trial, tortured or ill-treated, and usually were only released if they agreed to stop attending religious gatherings. Parents of detained children were forced to sign guarantees that their children would stop worshipping.

At least 26 pastors and priests, and over 1,750 church members, including children and 175 women, and dozens of Muslims, were in detention at the end of 2005 as prisoners of conscience because of their religious beliefs. Jehovah's Witnesses and members of new groups within the Eritrean Orthodox Church and Islam were also detained on account of their beliefs.

◻ In January, Pastor Ogbamichael Haimanot of the Kale Hiwot church was detained in Asmara. He suffered a mental breakdown in Sawa army camp on account of prolonged solitary confinement, forced labour and denial of medical treatment. He was released in October.

◻ In July, Semere Zaid, an agriculture lecturer at the University of Asmara who had been detained for a month in January on account of worshipping in the Church of the Living God, was rearrested. He was detained in the Karchele security prison, then moved to Sembel civil prison to serve a secretly imposed prison term of two years.

In August, Patriarch Antonios, head of the Eritrean Orthodox Church, who had apparently opposed government interference in church affairs, was reportedly stripped of his authority by the government and restricted in his movements. The government denied undermining him.

Prisoners of conscience and political prisoners

Few details were available about prisoners of conscience arrested for their political opinions. Three trade unionists – Tewelde Gebremedhin, Minassie Andezion and Habtom Woldemichael – were detained in Asmara in March and were still detained without charge at the end of 2005.

Thousands of prisoners of conscience detained in previous years remained in incommunicado detention throughout 2005, some of them in secret locations. No political prisoners were brought before a court.

Prisoners of conscience included 11 former government ministers detained in secret since a September 2001 crackdown on people calling for democratic reforms. They were publicly accused of treason but never charged. They included Haile Woldetensae and Petros Solomon, both former Foreign Ministers, and Mahmoud Ahmed Sheriffo, a former Vice-President.

Dozens of women prisoners of conscience were held. They included Aster Fissehatsion, a former PFDJ central committee member arrested in 2001, and Aster Yohannes, the wife of Petros Solomon, who had returned voluntarily from the USA in 2003 to be with her children. She was detained on arrival at Asmara airport, despite a previous government guarantee of her safety.

Other prisoners of conscience were former leaders of the Eritrean People's Liberation Front (now the government), such as Bitwoded Abraha, an army major general detained almost continuously for the past 13 years and reportedly mentally ill as a result; civil servants and professionals; and some 300 asylum-seekers forcibly returned by Malta in 2002 and by Libya in 2003.

During 2005 several prisoners of conscience were illegally sentenced to prison terms in their absence by a secret security committee. They were denied the right to present a legal defence or to appeal to a higher court.

Military conscription

Military service was compulsory for all men aged between 18 and 40, although the upper age limit for women's conscription was reduced to 27. The internationally recognized right of conscientious objection was denied.

◻ Six Jehovah's Witnesses were detained in 2005 for refusing military service, bringing the total number to 22. They included Paulos Iyassu, Negede Teklemariam and Isaac Moges, detained incommunicado in Sawa army camp since 1994.

Several hundred youths fled the country to avoid military service, and many conscripts escaped from military service to seek asylum abroad. In July and November, relatives of conscription evaders were detained in the southern Debub Region.

Journalists

Two prisoners of conscience were released. Saadia Ahmed, a television reporter for the government's Arabic-language service, detained in 2002, was freed in early 2005, and Aklilu Solomon, a reporter for the *Voice of America* international radio station, detained in 2003, was freed in mid-2005.

Ten other journalists arrested in 2001 when the entire private press was shut down, and two others arrested in 2002, were still detained without charge or trial at the end of 2005. They were held incommunicado and in secret without charge or trial.

🗀 Dawit Isaac, owner and editor of *Setit* newspaper and a Swedish citizen, detained in 2001, was released for a few days' medical treatment in November, then returned to prison.

Torture and ill-treatment

People detained on account of their political opinions or religious beliefs were tortured in military custody. They were tied up in painful positions for hours or days, particularly in a method nicknamed "helicopter", and beaten. Conscript soldiers were also punished in this manner.

Religious and political prisoners were often held in harsh conditions with little or no medical treatment and inadequate food and sanitation. Some were held in underground cells or metal shipping containers.

AI country reports/ visits

Report
- Eritrea: Religious persecution (AI Index: AFR 64/013/2005)

ESTONIA

REPUBLIC OF ESTONIA
Head of state: Arnold Rüütel
Head of government: Andrus Ansip (replaced Juhan Parts in April)
Death penalty: abolitionist for all crimes
International Criminal Court: ratified
UN Women's Convention: ratified
Optional Protocol to UN Women's Convention: not signed

A report published by the European Committee for the Prevention of Torture (CPT) documented a number of positive developments, but some areas of concern remained. The Council of Europe's Advisory Committee on the Framework Convention for the Protection of National Minorities issued a report also noting progress, while continuing to express concerns about the treatment of non-nationals and national minorities in Estonia. Many residents continued to live in the country without citizenship and as a result often faced discriminatory practices, particularly in the fields of education and labour and language rights.

Torture and ill-treatment

In April, the CPT published a report based on the findings of a visit to the country by a CPT delegation in 2003.

The CPT delegation recorded that it had received very few reports of ill-treatment in detention. However, there were a number of allegations that people had been punched, kicked or hit with batons at the time of detention. The CPT recommended that "no more force than is reasonably necessary" should be used during apprehension.

The CPT report expressed concern about conditions of detention which could amount to inhuman or degrading treatment at the Kohtla-Järve and Narva detention centres. Detainees were locked up for 24 hours a day in cells that were generally dirty, badly lit and ventilated, and overcrowded.

Other concerns raised by the CPT included: the absence of special provisions for detaining juveniles and the failure to house them separately from adults; the absence in national law of an explicit legal right of detainees to notify a third party of their detention; and the lack of prompt medical screening of detainees on arrival in detention facilities.

In response to reports of beatings of inmates in the Tartu prison by masked members of a special squad in May 2003, the CPT recommended independent monitoring of any future activity by special intervention squads in prisons.

Ethnic minorities

In February, the Council of Europe's Advisory Committee on the Framework Convention for the Protection of National Minorities noted that Estonia had taken certain legal and administrative steps to make the naturalization process more accessible and streamlined, and that the rate of naturalization had recently increased. However, it also noted that 150,536 people were living in Estonia without citizenship at the end of 2004, a figure which the Committee described as disconcertingly high.

The Committee noted that non-citizens were not properly protected under current legislation and recommended that Estonia introduce anti-discrimination laws which included adequate legal safeguards for non-citizens. It also encouraged the authorities to make naturalization more accessible. Such measures would include pursuing the proposals to exempt elderly applicants from language requirements under the Citizenship Act.

The Committee expressed concern that national minorities did not have a legal right to communicate with the authorities in a minority language free of charge. It also pointed out that regulations only allowed written documentation to be submitted in a minority language in local government units where more than half of the population belonged to a national minority. The Committee considered this to be an excessively high threshold.

The Committee recommended that teaching of Estonian in secondary schools should be pursued in a way that did not harm the quality of education provided to members of national minorities or limit their access to higher education.

The Committee also expressed concern that members of national minorities, especially young women, experienced higher levels of unemployment than other groups. The Committee called on authorities to ensure that national minorities were not subjected to direct or indirect discrimination in the labour market. The Committee also recommended that the authorities review the suitability of existing language proficiency requirements in all sectors of employment to ensure that they were realistic and proportionate and did not have a discriminatory effect.

ETHIOPIA

FEDERAL DEMOCRATIC REPUBLIC OF ETHIOPIA
Head of state: Girma Wolde-Giorgis
Head of government: Meles Zenawi
Death penalty: retentionist
International Criminal Court: not signed
UN Women's Convention: ratified with reservations
Optional Protocol to UN Women's Convention: not signed

Opposition candidates and supporters were arrested, beaten and intimidated in the run-up to elections. Some 9,000 opposition supporters were detained in June for several weeks following protests at alleged fraud in elections in which soldiers killed at least 36 people. In November, police killed at least 42 people after peaceful protests turned violent. Over 10,000 opposition supporters and demonstrators were detained. Ten new members of parliament, 15 journalists, several human rights defenders and prisoners of conscience were among 86 detainees later charged with treason, genocide and other offences. Civilians were killed and arbitrarily detained in the context of armed conflicts in the Oromia and Somali regions, with thousands remaining in detention without charge or trial. Several Oromo community activists were prisoners of conscience. Journalists and human rights defenders were detained and threatened with prosecution for criticizing the government. Death sentences were passed but no executions carried out.

Background
Seven million people were dependent on emergency food aid, with a critical drought and food shortages in the Somali region in eastern Ethiopia.

The government faced armed opposition from the Oromo Liberation Front (OLF) and the Ogaden National Liberation Front (ONLF), both based in Eritrea. Ethiopia continued to support the Sudan-based armed Eritrean opposition group, the Eritrean Democratic Alliance, although it was not clear that it had carried out any armed activities inside Eritrea during 2005.

The UN Security Council called on Ethiopia to implement its acceptance in principle of the International Boundary Commission's judgment regarding the border areas, particularly its allocation to Eritrea of Badme town, the flashpoint of war in 1998. Ethiopia refused to agree to border demarcation, instead calling for negotiation over certain issues. Eritrea demanded UN action against Ethiopia to enforce the border judgment.

In October, Eritrea banned helicopter flights and other travel by the UN Mission in Ethiopia and Eritrea (UNMEE), which administered a buffer zone along the border. Both sides had re-armed since 2000 and deployed troops near the border in late 2005. The UN Security Council threatened sanctions against either side if it started a new war.

Elections

In the months preceding parliamentary and regional assembly elections in May, there were arrests, beatings and intimidation of candidates and supporters from the two main opposition groupings, the Coalition for Unity and Democracy (CUD) and the United Ethiopian Democratic Front (UEDF). Election observers from Ethiopian non-governmental organizations were only allowed after they won a court case against the National Election Board.

Provisional results in June gave the ruling Ethiopian People's Revolutionary Democratic Front (EPRDF) a narrow majority. The opposition complained about election fraud in over half the constituencies. European Union election observers reported numerous election irregularities. In re-runs in 31 constituencies, several government ministers regained their seats after opposition candidates withdrew, alleging intimidation and violence.

In the final results in September, including from the delayed Somali region elections in August, the EPRDF and affiliated parties won two thirds of the 527 seats. Most CUD elected members of parliament and regional assemblies did not take their seats, in protest at alleged election fraud and at new procedural rules that disadvantaged the opposition. Parliament withdrew their parliamentary immunity.

Post-election killings and arrests

On 8 June soldiers shot dead at least 36 opposition supporters and wounded dozens of others in initially peaceful demonstrations in Addis Ababa at alleged election fraud by the EPRDF. In the weeks following, police arrested some 9,000 people allegedly involved in violent protests, including 2,000 Addis Ababa University students, some 120 opposition party officials, and six human rights defenders. The detainees were initially held incommunicado, and many beaten or ill-treated. They had all been released without charge by the end of July.

▭ Two air force officers who fled to Djibouti at the beginning of the protests were forcibly returned and detained after being denied access to asylum procedures. They were reportedly tortured on their return to Ethiopia, and still detained incommunicado without charge or trial at the end of 2005.

After the final election results, CUD called for non-violent protests and stay-home strikes. On 31 October, 30 taxi drivers were arrested after drivers in Addis Ababa protested by sounding their horns. On 1 November peaceful street protests were followed by shootings and violence. Riot police killed at least 42 protesters and wounded about 200 others, some at their homes. Police admitted 34 deaths, and said seven police officers were killed and others injured.

In the weeks following 1 November police arrested most CUD leaders, including 10 members of parliament, 15 journalists, human rights defenders, lawyers and a teachers' union leader. The Prime Minister accused them of treason and organizing a violent uprising. They were taken to court, allowed access to lawyers and relatives, and remanded in custody for investigation. In December,

131 defendants (86 of whom were in custody) were charged with the mostly capital offences of treason, inciting armed uprising and genocide against an ethnic group and members of the ruling party. Several thousand school and college students were detained and beaten by police in late December in Addis Ababa and towns in Amhara region for demonstrating in support of the release of the CUD leaders.

▭ The accused included 55 CUD party leaders and others earlier arrested or declared "wanted", such as Berhanu Negga, an economics professor and newly elected Mayor of Addis Ababa; Birtukan Mideksa, a former judge; and Yacob Hailemariam, a former UN prosecutor in the Rwanda genocide trial in Tanzania. Also charged, in their absence, were 30 government opponents living abroad, mostly in the USA. Many of the accused were prisoners of conscience. They denied calling for violent protests, and on 28 November began a hunger strike that lasted some weeks.

Other detentions and killings

Thousands of people remained in indefinite and mainly incommunicado detention without charge or trial in connection particularly with the armed conflicts in the Oromia and Somali regions, and arrests continued throughout the Oromia region. Thousands of Oromo school students were detained – and many ill-treated and some killed – in demonstrations in November and December throughout the Oromia region in support of the release of Oromo detainees and other political demands.

▭ Diribi Demissie, President of the Mecha Tulema Association, an officially registered Oromo community welfare organization, was arrested in February with three other members. He had been released on bail in November 2004. The four were charged with armed conspiracy and membership of the OLF, along with 24 others, including university students and two state television journalists arrested in May 2004, Dabassa Wakjira and Shifferaw Insarmu. All denied the charges. They were all acquitted by the High Court in June but were immediately re-arrested after the prosecution appealed to a different bench of the High Court. They remained in custody at the end of 2005, with the 24 other co-accused.

▭ Some 900 alleged government opponents, all members of the Anuak ethnic group, remained in detention without trial in the south-west Gambela region throughout 2005. Most had been arrested for political reasons during the killings by the army and civilian mobs in December 2003 in Gambela. Fifteen of them, including former regional president Okello Nyigello, were acquitted and freed in December. Following a Commission of Inquiry into the killings, seven soldiers were charged with murder. They had not been tried by the end of 2005. Government soldiers reportedly killed and arbitrarily detained Anuak civilians on several occasions in 2005, including after an attack by an armed Anuak group on a prison in Gambela in November.

Human rights abuses were committed with impunity by government forces against civilians, including the reported killing of over 20 civilians and political prisoners in Kebri Dahar town in the Somali region in November.

Violence against women
In May the revised Criminal Code made female genital mutilation a new criminal offence punishable by up to 10 years' imprisonment. It also increased the punishment for the traditional practice of bride abduction for the purpose of marriage from three to up to 10 years' imprisonment, and made the offence liable for punishment as rape, removing the impunity previously allowed to suspects who married the rape victim.

Women's organizations campaigned against harmful traditional practices affecting women's rights and against domestic violence.

Freedom of the media
The private press, which often criticized the government, remained under pressure. The Ministry of Justice instigated further court action in 2005 against the Ethiopian Free Press Journalists Association (EFJA), aiming to replace its leadership with a pro-government group. A court ruled in favour of the EFJA, but in December its president, Kifle Mulat, was charged with treason in his absence, together with other journalists. Most of the private press was shut down.

⮡ In December, three journalists were given prison terms ranging from three to 15 months because of articles published some years previously. Dozens of other journalists and publishers arrested in previous years were on bail awaiting trial on charges under the 1992 Press Law.

⮡ Three journalists were briefly detained during the elections and released on bail.

⮡ Fifteen journalists were arrested in the November round-up of opposition leaders (see above) and charged. Nearly all had previously been imprisoned after unfair trials under the 1992 Press Law.

A new harsh Press Law, proposed by the government in 2003, was still under consideration but not yet enacted.

Human rights commission
A National Human Rights Commission, originally proposed by the government in 1997 and finally established in 2004, did not begin functioning in 2005. In March its work plan contained no objective to monitor human rights or to co-operate with local or international human rights defenders.

Human rights defenders
In early 2005, the Ministry of Justice finally registered the Human Rights League, an Oromo human rights defenders group, some of whose founding members had spent four years in prison before being acquitted of violent conspiracy. However, human rights defenders remained at risk of imprisonment.

⮡ Three investigators from the Ethiopian Human Rights Council (EHRCO), Yared Hailemariam, Cherinet Tadesse and Berhanu Tsige, and three EHRCO branch officials were detained for a month in the mass round-up of early June.

⮡ Three prominent human rights defenders were detained in the November arrests and charged with treason: Professor Mesfin Woldemariam, the 75-year-old founder and former president of the Ethiopian Human Rights Council, who was in poor health; and anti-poverty campaigners Daniel Bekelle, a senior official of ActionAid, and Netsanet Demissie, president of the Organisation for Social Justice in Ethiopia.

Dergue trial update
The trial continued of 33 former senior government officials on charges of genocide, torture and other crimes. They had been in detention for 14 years. Other trials continued in the absence of the defendants, including former President Mengistu Hailemariam, whose extradition had been refused by the Zimbabwe government.

The series of trials of less senior officials was still not completed at the end of 2005. Over a dozen former officials were under sentence of death at the end of 2005. Mekonnen Dori, 72, a prominent member of a southern Ethiopia opposition party arrested in 1993, who appeared to be a prisoner of conscience, was acquitted of genocide and released in December.

Death penalty
Several death sentences were imposed, but no executions were reported. There were dozens of people reportedly in prison after being sentenced to death in previous years.

AI country reports/ visits
Report
- Ethiopia: The 15 May 2005 elections and human rights — Recommendations to the government, election observers and political parties (AI Index: AFR 25/002/2005)

Visit
AI representatives visited Ethiopia in March.

FIJI

REPUBLIC OF THE FIJI ISLANDS
Head of state: Ratu Josefa Iloilovatu Uluivuda
Head of government: Laisenia Qarase
Death penalty: abolitionist for ordinary crimes
International Criminal Court: ratified
UN Women's Convention: ratified
Optional Protocol to UN Women's Convention: not signed

Legislation supposed to reconcile groups involved in and affected by the May 2000 coup instead provoked further political schisms. A landmark High Court ruling upheld the right to privacy and equality for lesbian and gay people under the Constitution. Legislative reforms were proposed to improve prison services and provide protection against domestic violence.

Reconciliation and Unity Commission
Political power struggles continued among the civilian and military elites. The government proposed legislation to establish a Reconciliation and Unity Commission with the power to recommend amnesty for "politically motivated" crimes committed in connection with the May 2000 coup and to grant compensation to those affected by such crimes. The proposed legislation promoted impunity for human rights violations and acts of treason, and was opposed by the military, the political opposition, and many areas of civil society on this basis. In late 2005 a parliamentary committee recommended that the amnesty proposal be amended to reflect constitutional principles.

Coup trials
Trials of individuals charged with offences relating to the May 2000 coup continued. Sentences passed during 2005 ranged from four months' to two years' imprisonment, with the two-year sentence suspended. A number of those convicted, including former government senators, were given community-based punishments or released early on health grounds. Former government minister Ratu Lalabalavu was sentenced to eight months' imprisonment in April, served most of the sentence out of prison, and was then appointed Minister of Transport. There was at least one report that state witnesses in coup-related trials received threats.

In August the Court of Appeal ordered the retrial of 20 soldiers convicted of participating in a November 2000 mutiny because their trial had not been fair. Their retrial by court martial was delayed, in part by failures to deliver all the accused to the courtroom and by the President's temporary removal of the presiding judge advocate appointed by the military. No progress was made in investigating the beating to death of four mutineers by soldiers suppressing the November mutiny.

Landmark ruling on discrimination
In April, two men were sentenced to two years' imprisonment for homosexual acts. In August the High Court overturned their conviction. It also declared provisions in the penal code discriminatory and unconstitutional in violating guarantees on privacy and equality to the extent that they penalized consensual sexual acts between males. The state appealed against the ruling.

The Methodist Church held a rally in June against same-sex marriages, but two further applications for large-scale marches were refused on the grounds that they could encourage hate crimes.

Violence against women
There was a 70 per cent increase in reported rapes and attempted rapes since 2004, police said in November. Where convictions were obtained for rape, prison terms of up to 20 years were imposed.

In a report in November 2005 the Fiji Law Reform Commission recommended a comprehensive overhaul of civil and criminal law responses to domestic violence. It proposed improving prosecutions, strengthening protection and services for victims, and adopting a national strategy to combat domestic violence.

Law reform
Reform of the Prison Act was also among recommendations made by the Fiji Law Reform Commission, which proposed a draft Corrections Bill to bring prison services into line with international human rights standards.

FINLAND

REPUBLIC OF FINLAND
Head of state: Tarja Halonen
Head of government: Matti Vanhanen
Death penalty: abolitionist for all crimes
International Criminal Court: ratified
UN Women's Convention and its Optional Protocol: ratified

Seven conscientious objectors to military service were imprisoned; they were prisoners of conscience. Little coordinated action was taken to combat widespread violence against women.

Conscientious objection to military service

The length of alternative civilian service remained punitive and discriminatory. Conscientious objectors were obliged to perform 395 days of civilian service, 215 days longer than the usual military service. In addition, the option of alternative service was restricted to peacetime. Conscientious objectors imprisoned for refusing to do civilian service because of its punitive length were prisoners of conscience.

AI continued to urge the authorities to reduce the length of alternative civilian service in line with internationally recognized standards and recommendations. The Labour Minister proposed shortening the alternative service, but in June the government decided not to amend the law.

◻ Seven conscientious objectors were known to have been imprisoned during the year. They received sentences of between 126 and 197 days for refusing to perform alternative civilian service. The length of their sentences equalled half of their remaining civilian service time.

Violence against women

Violence against women continued to be widespread. The last extensive study on the issue, conducted in 1998, showed that 40 per cent of women in Finland had been victims of physical or sexual violence or threats of violence by men, and 22 per cent of married women and women cohabiting with men had been victims of physical or sexual violence or threats of violence by their partner. The government failed to follow up effectively on a national project on the prevention of violence against women that was carried out between 1998 and 2002.

During 2005 AI and 18 other non-governmental organizations called for an inter-ministry action plan for the prevention of violence against women and submitted detailed recommendations. A reply received in February from the Prime Minister implied that there was no overall action plan but that the issue of violence against women was being included in other government programmes. In November AI reiterated its call for an overall action plan.

AI also conducted a survey of the work of Finnish municipalities on eradication of violence against women. It found that in general this work lacked political will, coordination, expertise and resources, although a few municipalities were doing pioneering work.

Unfair residence permit procedures

The immigration authorities reportedly refused to grant some residence permits solely on the basis of information provided by Finland's Security Police (Suojelupoliisi, SUPO). The applicants were not allowed to see the information, which they could therefore not contest.

◻ Qari Muzaffar Iqbal Naeemi, a Pakistani national resident in Finland since May 1997, remained uncertain of his future. He had been denied a renewal of his residence permit in September 2002 and issued with a deportation order in March 2003 on the basis of secret information supplied by SUPO. In April, AI raised his case with the authorities, but it had still not been resolved by the end of the year.

FRANCE

FRENCH REPUBLIC
Head of state: Jacques Chirac
Head of government: Dominique de Villepin (replaced Jean-Pierre Raffarin in May)
Death penalty: abolitionist for all crimes
International Criminal Court: ratified
UN Women's Convention and its Optional Protocol: ratified

Following serious unrest in many cities and towns throughout France, the government declared a state of emergency in November. Immediate expulsions of people involved in the riots were also announced by the Minister of Interior. Developments in law and administrative regulations restricted the right to seek asylum and to have the asylum claim considered on its merits. An AI report demonstrated a 10-year pattern of racist ill-treatment and killings by the police, and of failures in the judicial system to hold those responsible to account. Racism within the police and other law enforcement bodies was targeted at people of Muslim or minority ethnic origin. A draft anti-terrorism law would allow longer periods in incommunicado detention, removing safeguards against torture and ill-treatment and reinforcing the effective impunity of law enforcement officials. New regulations curtailed domestic asylum law by cutting the time in which asylum applications could be made, and requiring applications to be made in French.

State of emergency declared

Frustration at discriminatory practices in areas such as employment among communities of French nationals of North African and sub-Saharan extraction, as well as migrants, coupled with anger at the often racist and aggressive conduct of the police, boiled over into rioting in many cities and towns throughout France after the disputed deaths of two boys in October. On 9 November the government declared a state of emergency in the whole metropolitan territory and imposed specific additional measures in some areas and cities, including Paris, under a law passed in 1955 and applied only once since then. The law allows *Préfets* (high-level civil servants who represent the state at the local level) to take measures needed for the maintenance of public order. The measures included curfews within certain areas and times, and allowed law enforcement officials to carry out searches without warrants, close public meeting places of any kind and limit freedom of movement.

On the same day, the Minister of Interior announced that he had ordered the *Préfets* to proceed with the immediate expulsion of people convicted of criminal acts during the riots, whether their status was regular or irregular, and regardless of whether they had residence permits.

The state of emergency, initially due to last only 12 days, was later extended until 21 February 2006.

Impunity for police abuses

In April, AI published a report demonstrating a 10-year pattern of racist ill-treatment and killings by the police. The report highlighted failures in the judicial system to hold those responsible to account, and to provide victims of human rights violations with the right to redress and reparations. The report concluded that the government's continued failure to address these violations had led to a climate of impunity for law enforcement officers, resulting in a "two-speed" approach by officials which ensured that the prosecution of cases brought by police officers proceeded more quickly than those brought by the victims of police abuse. The vast majority of such cases involved foreign nationals or French nationals of foreign origin.

On 17 May, two policemen were given suspended prison sentences after being convicted of the serious assault and racial abuse in 2002 of Karim Latifi, a computer consultant. The High Court in Paris gave them suspended three- and four-month prison sentences, and acquitted two other law enforcement officers in the same case. A civil lawsuit for damages was still pending. In 2002 the case had been closed after investigation by the Services General Inspectorate, the police complaints body for the Paris area, and judicial proceedings were pursued only because Karim Latifi initiated a private prosecution.

On 31 August, Brice Petit and Jean-Michel Maulpoix, both writers and teachers, were convicted of defamation and fined 3,000 euros each. Brice Petit was acquitted of insulting public officials. He had been roughly handled and detained for 12 hours after challenging police treatment of a suspect restrained on the ground in Montpellier in April 2004. He and others subsequently published information about the case on the Internet. He and an eyewitness testified in court that he had not called the officers "Nazis" or "anti-Semites", as alleged, but had peacefully protested that the force used to arrest an unarmed man for a minor public order offence was unacceptable.

Racism and discrimination

In February and March, the UN Committee on the Elimination of Racial Discrimination considered periodic reports by France on implementation of the UN Convention against Racism. The Committee welcomed legislative measures to combat racial discrimination, including laws adopted in June 2004 to ban the spread of racist messages on the Internet and in December 2004 to establish an official body to investigate and take action against discrimination. However, the Committee recommended further preventive measures, impartial investigation of all complaints, punishments proportionate to the gravity of the crimes, and the publicizing of complaints and compensation procedures.

In a report in February the Council of Europe's European Commission against Racism and Intolerance (ECRI) acknowledged that France had taken steps to combat racism and intolerance. These included the establishment of a free telephone helpline for reporting racial discrimination and schemes to facilitate the integration of newly arrived immigrants; improvements in immigrant children's access to education; and the creation of an independent police and prison oversight body, the National Commission on Ethics and Security. However, the ECRI pointed to persistent complaints of violence, humiliation, racist verbal abuse and racial discrimination by police and gendarmerie officers, prison staff and personnel working in reception centres or holding areas for refugees and asylum-seekers.

A 38 per cent rise in complaints of police violence (97 in 2004, compared with 70 in 2003) was reported in April by the National Commission on Ethics and Security. In a third of cases, the violence was said to be manifestly racist in character.

In March, the National Consultative Human Rights Commission (CNCDH) published its annual report, according to which the number of racist and anti-Semitic attacks had almost doubled in 2004 compared with the previous year. The CNCDH expressed its concern that anti-Semitism had become "rooted" in society.

Anti-terrorism measures
Draft anti-terrorism law

A new anti-terrorism law proposed to the Council of Ministers in October would remove safeguards against torture or ill-treatment. Under the draft, the period in which people suspected of terrorism could be detained for interrogation before being brought before a judge (*garde à vue*) was to be extended from four to six days. The Minister of Interior, Nicolas Sarkozy, was reported as saying that such detainees would have access to a lawyer only after 72 hours in police custody. Combined with the continued failure to videotape the interrogation of adult suspects, such measures risked contributing to the effective impunity of law enforcement officials for the torture or ill-treatment of detainees.

Other measures in the draft law were an expansion of video and telephone surveillance; the monitoring of public transport records; and new powers of official access to connection data held by Internet cafés and to data on identity cards, passports, driving licences, car registration documents, residence permits for non-nationals and other personal records. The draft law would also raise the sentence for heading a terrorist organization from 20 to 30 years' imprisonment and, under its provisions, people who had become nationals through naturalization in the previous 15 years could have their French nationality withdrawn and be expelled from the country (previously the limit was 10 years).

The proposed law was approved by both chambers of parliament in December. It was then sent to the Constitutional Council for approval.

Deportations
In separate cases in July and August, four Algerian nationals were deported to Algeria where they were at risk of torture or ill-treatment. The men were reportedly suspected of a range of offences, including promoting violence and religious hatred in mosques in the Lyon and Paris areas. Three of them had served prison sentences in France after being convicted on charges including unauthorized entry to the country; having links with terrorist networks; providing paramilitary training to young Islamist activists; and an attempted attack on a train.

Asylum rights curtailed
In April a three-year process of increasing restrictions on asylum, included under a new asylum law in December 2003, concluded with the implementation of administrative measures. New regulations allowed less time for submitting asylum applications: asylum-seekers were to be issued temporary residence permits but had to complete their applications and submit them in French within 21 days (previously within a month).

A new list of 12 "safe" countries was adopted in June. Under the new regulations the claims of people from these countries are examined under a fast-track procedure that lacks basic elements of protection. Asylum-seekers are not granted a residence permit, do not receive any support from the state, and have only two weeks to submit their application in French. They must be given a decision within two weeks, and may be deported before any appeal is heard.

Under the new regulations, individuals held in a detention centre and awaiting expulsion had only five days to make an asylum application (previously they had 12 days). The European Court of Human Rights condemned Turkey for a similar procedure in 2000, on the grounds that such a short time limit denied the possibility of adequate scrutiny of the asylum-seeker's case.

A decree in May legalized the practice – already implemented in certain prefectures from the beginning of 2005 – of denying language interpretation free of charge to asylum applicants in detention centres. Several administrative courts subsequently ruled that it was essential to provide interpreters, given that asylum applications had to be submitted in French. In July AI and other non-governmental organizations filed an appeal to overturn the decree before the State Council. At the close of 2005 AI had still not received a response. Domestic asylum law requires that applicants be given the means to support their claim and that decisions and information are communicated in a language the applicant understands, whether in writing or through an interpreter.

Ineffective domestic remedies
On 27 January the European Court of Human Rights ruled on the case of Ilich Ramírez Sánchez (often known as "Carlos the Jackal"). He was held in solitary confinement after his arrest in 1994, was sentenced to life imprisonment for murder in 1997 but remained under investigation for other alleged crimes. He had lodged an application with the Court in July 2004. The Court was unanimous that the prisoner had been unable to challenge his prolonged solitary confinement because of the lack of any remedy in domestic law, although it held that this did not violate the prohibition of torture.

AI country reports/ visits
Report
- France: The search for justice – The effective impunity of law enforcement officers in cases of shootings, deaths in custody or torture and ill-treatment (AI Index: EUR 21/001/2005)

Visit
AI delegates visited France in April.

GEORGIA

GEORGIA
Head of state: Mikhail Saakashvili
Head of government: Zurab Noghaideli (replaced Zurab Zhvania in February)
Death penalty: abolitionist for all crimes
International Criminal Court: ratified
UN Women's Convention and its Optional Protocol: ratified

Reports of torture and ill-treatment by law enforcement officers continued, despite efforts by the authorities to address the issue. Some perpetrators of attacks on religious minorities were imprisoned but hundreds of others remained unpunished. Chechens sought by the Russian Federation on terrorism charges and a Kurd wanted by Turkey were at risk of expulsion or extradition. The judiciary appeared to be unduly influenced by the government. There were allegations of government interference with freedom of the media in particular in relation to television. The internationally unrecognized breakaway areas of South Ossetia and Abkhazia retained the death penalty.

Torture and ill-treatment

The authorities took a number of measures to tackle torture and ill-treatment and several key government officials publicly stated their commitment to fight such abuses. The measures included legal amendments and extensive monitoring of detention facilities, in particular by the office of the Public Defender of Georgia (Ombudsman). Eleven perpetrators of crimes amounting to torture or ill-treatment were serving prison terms handed down since the "Rose Revolution" in November 2003. In June Georgia recognized the competence of the UN Committee against Torture to consider individual complaints and in August it acceded to the Optional Protocol to the Convention against Torture.

Nevertheless, reports of torture and ill-treatment continued. The methods allegedly included putting plastic bags over the detainee's head; placing a gun in the detainee's mouth and threatening to shoot; beatings, including with gun butts; kicking; and threats against the detainee's family.

Most injuries inflicted by police were reportedly sustained at the time of arrest. In some cases detainees were reportedly tortured or ill-treated in police vehicles, in police stations, and in the Ministry of Internal Affairs. One detainee alleged that he was ill-treated during a court hearing.

Many cases did not come to light because police covered up their crimes and detainees were often afraid to complain or identify the perpetrators for fear of repercussions. There were shortcomings in the implementation of legal safeguards aimed at preventing torture and ill-treatment, such as prompt access to a lawyer.

Impunity for torture and ill-treatment remained a problem, and no victims of torture or ill-treatment were known to have been awarded compensation. According to the Human Rights Protection Unit of the General Procuracy, 151 criminal cases or preliminary investigations were opened and charges were brought against 31 law enforcement officers during 2005. However, procurators did not open investigations into all potential torture and ill-treatment cases in a systematic manner. In dozens of cases where the procuracy opened investigations the perpetrators were not brought to justice. Many investigations were not carried out in an impartial and independent manner.

In March the UN Special Rapporteur on torture issued a list of recommendations to the authorities aimed at eradicating torture and ill-treatment, after visiting Georgia in February. He recommended: that judges and prosecutors should routinely ask detainees how they had been treated; that any public official indicted for abuse or torture should be suspended from duty and prosecuted; and compensation, medical treatment and rehabilitation for victims.

The European Committee for the Prevention of Torture (CPT) stated in its report issued in June that in Georgia, "criminal suspects ran a significant risk of being ill-treated by the police, and that on occasion resort may be had to severe ill-treatment/torture".

In November AI urged the authorities to set up a body independent of the police, procuracy and the justice system to review investigations into allegations of torture and ill-treatment and judicial proceedings in such cases. Such a body should have the authority to present findings and make recommendations to the relevant authorities and to issue public reports. The organization also called on the authorities to pay special attention to ending torture and ill-treatment in the regions of Georgia outside Tbilisi. AI called for masks and other clothing that hides officers' personal identities to be prohibited, other than in exceptional circumstances when each officer should be identifiable by such means as an identification number.

Givi Janiashvili was arrested by more than 30 masked special unit police officers at his home in the town of Rustavi on 12 May. He was unarmed, and said that he put up no resistance. He was reportedly beaten severely in front of his wife, his 11-year-old child and several neighbours. A forensic expert who examined him four days later found injuries consistent with his account. Tbilisi city procuracy did not open an investigation into the allegations of ill-treatment until 29 June.

In many cases investigations were not opened promptly after complaints of torture or ill-treatment by law enforcement officers.

Alexander Mkheidze, a 27-year-old architect, was detained by police in the village of Tsqneti near Tbilisi on 6 April. He alleged that he was beaten and kicked while he was being taken to the building of the Ministry of Internal Affairs in the centre of Tbilisi, and that police continued to beat him there. Later that day he was transferred to a detention facility, where the doctor who examined him found that his skin was "slightly red" on his legs but diagnosed him as "healthy". Two days later he was transferred to an investigation-isolation prison, where Alexander Mkheidze reiterated his allegations and a doctor recorded bruising on his legs. Two weeks later he was examined by a forensic expert who found bruises and abrasions caused by a heavy blunt object consistent with his allegations.

Religious minorities

There were several instances where members of religious minorities were beaten and harassed by supporters of the Georgian Orthodox Church. In some cases, it was alleged that the attacks were incited by Georgian Orthodox priests. Several perpetrators of violent attacks on religious minorities in recent years were imprisoned during 2005. However, hundreds continued to enjoy impunity. Some of those who were convicted were not tried for all the attacks they were believed to have been involved in.

On 31 January Vake-Saburtalo district court in Tbilisi sentenced Basil Mkalavishvili, Petre Ivanidze and Merab Korashinidze to six, four and one year's imprisonment respectively on charges including "illegal interference with the execution of religious rites or other religious rules and habits", "beatings" and "arson". Other supporters of Basil Mkalavishvili – Avtandil Donadze, Avtandil Gabunia, Akaki Mosashvili and Mikheil Nikolozashvili – were given three-year suspended prison sentences. In October a higher court in Tbilisi turned down an appeal by Basil Mkalavishvili and Petre Ivanidze.

Risk of expulsion

Chechen refugees sought by the Russian Federation on terrorism charges and an ethnic Kurd wanted by Turkey, who was allegedly a member of the Kurdistan Workers' Party (PKK), faced being forcibly returned to a country where they would be at risk of serious human rights violations.

In March, three young Russian citizens, Shengeli Tsatiashvili and his younger brothers Suleiman and Sosran, were reportedly detained in the Ministry of Refugees and Accommodation in Tbilisi by officers of the Interior Ministry's anti-terrorism group. They had gone to the building to register an asylum claim for the two younger men; the older brother had applied for asylum in December 2004. They were reportedly first taken to the offices of the anti-terrorism group for questioning and then to the Red Bridge on the border with Azerbaijan. They were left in the territory between Georgia and Azerbaijan but managed to return to Georgia. They returned to the Ministry of Refugees and Accommodation, accompanied by representatives of the Ombudsman's office and the UN Association of Georgia, and registered the asylum claim. Reportedly, there was no extradition request for the three brothers and they were expelled although the authorities had not yet considered their asylum applications.

Abkhazia and South Ossetia

The status of the internationally unrecognized breakaway regions of Abkhazia and South Ossetia remained unresolved. Both retained the death penalty in law. While in South Ossetia a de facto moratorium on death sentences and executions was believed to be in force, Abkhazia had a de facto moratorium on executions only.

In February, as part of his visit to Georgia, the UN Special Rapporteur on torture visited South Ossetia and Abkhazia. In Abkhazia he visited a man and a woman held on death row, and in March he called for the death penalty to be abolished there.

AI country reports/visits
Reports
- Europe and Central Asia: Summary of Amnesty International's concerns in the region, January-June 2005: Georgia (AI Index: EUR 01/012/2005)
- Georgia: Torture and ill-treatment – Still a concern after the "Rose Revolution" (AI Index: EUR 56/001/2005)

Visits
AI conducted research in Georgia from March to June and in October, visiting Tbilisi, the western town of Zugdidi and the internationally unrecognized region of South Ossetia.

GERMANY

FEDERAL REPUBLIC OF GERMANY
Head of state: Horst Köhler
Head of government: Angela Merkel (replaced Gerhard Schröder in November)
Death penalty: abolitionist for all crimes
International Criminal Court: ratified
UN Women's Convention and its Optional Protocol: ratified

In breach of the absolute ban on torture under international human rights law, a court ruled that evidence that could have been extracted under torture or ill-treatment was admissible in legal proceedings.

Torture concerns

On 14 June the Hamburg Supreme Court ruled that evidence possibly obtained under torture or cruel, inhuman or degrading treatment was admissible in legal proceedings, a ruling that breached international human rights law. In the retrial of Mounir al-Motassadeq, who stood accused of membership of a "terrorist group" and aiding the attacks in the USA on 11 September 2001, the court accepted statements as evidence that had been provided by US authorities. The court argued that it could not be proven that the statements were obtained through torture or other ill-treatment, apparently ignoring the widespread evidence of torture and other ill-treatment in the network of detention centres around the world used by US authorities to hold terror suspects. The statements reportedly comprised summaries of interrogations of three people held by US authorities — Ramzi Binalshibh, Mohamed Ould Slahi and Khalid Sheikh Mohammed.

In November, 13 of the 16 Länder (regional states) agreed to the ratification of the Optional Protocol to the UN Convention against Torture, while Niedersachsen (Lower Saxony), Sachsen (Saxony) and Sachsen-Anhalt (Saxony-Anhalt) refused to give their required approval.

Public debate continued on whether there are circumstances, including the threat of terrorism, that justify the use of torture by law enforcement officials.

Refugees at risk

The Federal Agency for Migration and Refugees continued to withdraw refugee status from individuals, in particular refugees from Afghanistan, Iraq and Kosovo. When considering withdrawal of refugee status, the Agency looked only at whether the situation in the country of origin had changed. It did not consider, as required by the UN Refugee Convention, issues such as whether the authorities in the country of origin could offer the returning refugees effective protection. After refugee status had been withdrawn, the residence permits of the individuals concerned were often cancelled, putting them at risk of deportation to their country of origin.

This policy began in 2004, when up to 16,800 refugees had their status withdrawn. In the first half of 2005, some 5,897 refugees lost their status, a slight drop on the rate of the previous year, but 7,346 cases were pending. In November the policy was confirmed by a Federal Administration Court decision.

The German authorities continued to deport foreigners to countries where the human rights situation was extremely fragile. The German Aliens Act allows authorities to stop deportations to certain countries or regions if the human rights situation is generally insecure. However, this provision was rarely implemented. There were deportations to places such as Afghanistan, Chechnya and Togo as well as deportations of members of ethnic minorities to Kosovo.

Racist attacks

According to official statistics, the number of xenophobic and racist acts of violence continued to be high.

Anti-discrimination legislation passed by the Federal Parliament (Bundestag) on 17 June was rejected by the Federal Council (Bundesrat). The legislation was intended to incorporate European Union anti-discrimination guidelines into German law, the deadline for which was in 2003.

AI country reports/visits
Report
- Germany: Hamburg court violates international law by admitting evidence potentially obtained through torture (AI Index: EUR 23/001/2005)

GHANA

REPUBLIC OF GHANA
Head of state and government: John Agyekum Kufuor
Death penalty: retentionist
International Criminal Court: ratified
UN Women's Convention: ratified
Optional Protocol to UN Women's Convention: signed

The government released the final report of the National Reconciliation Commission with plans for implementing some of its recommendations. The President granted amnesty to 1,317 prisoners on humanitarian grounds. Violence against women continued to be widespread without progress in law reform.

The National Reconciliation Commission

On 22 April, the report of the National Reconciliation Commission, investigating past human rights abuses during Ghana's periods of unconstitutional government between 1957 and 1993, was made public by the government, together with a white paper accepting some of the recommendations and promising that a reparation and rehabilitation fund would be operational before the end of 2005. No recommendations had been implemented by the end of the year. The government issued an apology to all those who had been wronged by past governments.

The report concluded that the majority of human rights abuses were attributed to the unconstitutional governments. The recommendations included reparation for and rehabilitation of victims, and paid particular attention to rape and other sexual violence against women. Specifics included a formal presidential apology to victims of abuses by state agents, financial compensation, restitution of property, medical care, and the creation of trauma and counselling centres in hospitals. The report also recommended reconciliation and institutional reforms such as training on human rights for the police, judges and prison officials.

Violence against women

Violence against women continued to be widespread, with violence in the family thought to affect one in three women. Civil society organizations discussed reform of abortion legislation and laws permitting marital rape, and some members of parliament advocated higher sentences for rape and defilement of women. However, no progress was made in passing the Domestic Violence Bill into law.

The Human Trafficking Law was passed by parliament in June; it had not received presidential assent by the end of the year. Ghana had not yet ratified the Protocol to the African Charter on Human and Peoples' Rights on the Rights of Women in Africa.

GREECE

HELLENIC REPUBLIC
Head of state: Karolos Papoulias (replaced Constantinos Stephanopoulos in March)
Head of government: Constantinos Karamanlis
Death penalty: abolitionist for all crimes
International Criminal Court: ratified
UN Women's Convention and its Optional Protocol: ratified

Migrants, refugees and members of minority groups suffered human rights violations, including denial of access to asylum procedures, ill-treatment in detention and discrimination. Romani homes were targeted for demolition in ways that breached international standards, and Roma faced discrimination and racist attacks. A new law improved the situation for conscientious objectors to military service, but still provided for punitive alternative civilian service.

Denial of refugee protection
The government continued to fail to comply with its obligations under international law in relation to providing access to asylum procedures and the prohibition of *refoulement*. On several occasions groups of people arriving in Greece seeking asylum were forcibly expelled without being given access to asylum procedures. Cases were reported on Greece's coastline and some islands, and at the border area of Evros. During meetings with government officials, AI was told that such practices would be stopped, but further cases were subsequently reported.

🗁 On 1 April, 106 people who said they were Palestinians, but whom the government maintained were Egyptians, landed on the island of Crete seeking asylum. They were reportedly expelled to Egypt 12 days later without being given an opportunity to file asylum claims. The group arrived in the Palaiochora area of Crete after their boat sank just off the coast. They were escorted by police to a hotel, where they were detained for 10 days. The local police chief and the Deputy Minister of Public Order initially refused to allow

human rights activists and lawyers to meet the group and said that all 106 would be immediately expelled. However, a meeting with a lawyer present was allowed on 7 April, during which the detainees said they wanted to seek asylum in Greece. On 10 April they were escorted by police onto a ship bound for Athens. On arrival, they were detained at the Attica Aliens Department and other police stations in Attica. AI representatives who visited them on 12 April witnessed poor conditions of detention and heard allegations of ill-treatment by police. Later that day all 106 detainees were put on a ship bound for Egypt.

🗁 A group of 141 people shipwrecked on Crete on 23 October were expelled to Egypt on 4 November, reportedly without being given access to refugee protection or lawyers.

Detention and ill-treatment of irregular migrants and asylum-seekers
Asylum-seekers and people without legal permission to be in the country (irregular migrants), including unaccompanied minors, were arbitrarily detained, often in poor conditions which may have amounted to cruel, inhuman and degrading treatment. Asylum-seekers and irregular migrants alleged that they were ill-treated by police officers and in detention centres.

Several irregular migrants who arrived on the island of Chios in April were detained in conditions that amounted to cruel, inhuman and degrading treatment, including being held in a metal container close to the island's main harbour. On 19 April, human rights activists on the island demonstrated against the use of the metal container to hold migrants.

Police ill-treatment
On 13 December in the case of *Bekos and Koutropoulos v Greece*, the European Court of Human Rights found that Greece had violated provisions of the European Convention on Human Rights (ECHR) which prohibit torture and other ill-treatment, and discrimination in the enjoyment of ECHR rights. The two applicants, Greek Roma who were arrested in 1998, were taken to Mesolonghi police station where police officers beat them with a truncheon and iron bar, slapped and kicked them, threatened them with sexual assault, and verbally abused them. The police officers in question were cleared of ill-treatment by both the internal police inquiry and the trial that ensued. In its judgment, the European Court of Human Rights found that the two Roma had suffered inhuman and degrading treatment at the hands of the police, that the authorities failed to conduct an effective investigation into the incident, and that the authorities failed to investigate possible racist motives behind the incident.

Update: the killing of Vullnet Bytyçi
On 5 June the police officer charged with fatally wounding Vullnet Bytyçi was found guilty of manslaughter and received a suspended prison sentence of two years and three months. Vullnet Bytyçi, an 18-year-old Albanian national, was shot as he tried to cross the Greek-Albanian border in September 2003. The court also sentenced in absentia

one of the five Albanians who had attempted to cross the border with Vullnet Bytyçi to three months' imprisonment, suspended for three years, for illegal entry, and fined him.

Discrimination against minorities

Romani families continued to be targeted for eviction and demolition of their homes in ways that contravened international human rights standards, including the International Covenant on Economic, Social and Cultural Rights and anti-discrimination laws.
▱ On 23 and 24 June, during a "cleaning operation" by Patras local municipality, 11 of around 20 homes belonging to Albanian Roma legally residing in Greece were demolished, including one that still contained the family's belongings. There were also reports of arson attacks against the Romani settlement in Patras on 21, 23 and 24 June. No investigation into the attacks appeared to have been initiated by the end of the year.

In October, according to the Greek Helsinki Monitor, parents of Romani children attending the elementary school of Psari, outside Athens, were pressured by local and education authorities to sign declarations asking for their children to be moved to segregated, all-Romani education facilities far from the Romani settlement. The reports followed racist protests by parents of non-Romani pupils demanding the removal of Romani children from the school.

The authorities continued to refuse to re-issue citizenship documents to members of the Muslim population of western Thrace. According to legal provisions abrogated in 1998, Greek citizens who were not of ethnic Greek origin could have their citizenship withdrawn if they were believed by the authorities to have emigrated to another country. People from this minority were classified as "non-citizens": some of them had lost their citizenship because they had left the country at some point in their lives. In most cases, the authorities did not take adequate steps to ensure that the people concerned were informed of the decision to withdraw their citizenship in time to appeal against these decisions. Such people continued to be denied access to state benefits such as security benefits and pension allowances.

Conscientious objection to military service

In November parliament approved an amended law on military service, which revised the conditions of alternative civilian service for conscientious objectors. The new law allowed people who have lost their claim to conscientious objection status to reapply. However, the length of alternative civilian service remained punitive and the law still fell short of international standards. In particular, the board responsible for granting conscientious objection status was not under a civilian authority; professional soldiers were not allowed to change their views and become conscientious objectors; conscientious objectors were not allowed to vote or form unions; and the right to conscientious objection could be suspended during war.
▱ In August the military court of Xanthi convicted conscientious objector Boris Sotiriadis to three and a half years in prison for disobedience. He was consequently imprisoned between 22 August and 20 September but was released pending appeal. The appeal had not been heard by the end of the year. On 9 November the military court of Ioannina found him not guilty of a further charge of disobedience.

Violence against women

Inter-ministerial efforts to combat trafficking in human beings continued. Several initiatives were started, including the establishment of shelters offering protection to victims of trafficking. However, the shelters remained empty, reportedly because of the difficulties experienced by victims of trafficking in obtaining official designation as such. In order for victims to access shelter protection, they needed to have filed complaints against their traffickers and could only be designated "victims of trafficking" by the prosecutor to whom the complaint was addressed.

In December the government presented non-governmental organizations (NGOs) with a draft law on domestic violence, expected to pass through parliament in 2006. Successive governments had worked on domestic violence legislation for three years. While the draft contained a provision criminalizing marital rape, the proposed law failed to define "violence between family members" or to recognize it as a form of discrimination against women. It also failed to provide for the establishment and organization of institutions for the protection of victims of domestic violence (including shelters and medical care); to make training on domestic violence compulsory for police and judicial personnel; or to allow NGOs to file suits in domestic violence cases. The law also failed to allocate funding for activities aiming to combat and prevent domestic violence.

AI country reports/visits
Reports
- Greece: Punished for their beliefs – how conscientious objectors continue to be deprived of their rights (AI Index: EUR 25/007/2005)
- Greece: Out of the spotlight – the rights of foreigners and minorities are still a grey area (AI Index: EUR 25/016/2005)
Visits
AI delegates visited Greece in January and October.

GUATEMALA

REPUBLIC OF GUATEMALA
Head of state and government: Óscar Berger Perdomo
Death penalty: retentionist
International Criminal Court: not signed
UN Women's Convention and its Optional Protocol: ratified.

Record numbers of women were killed; the government's response remained ineffective and inadequate and there were few successful prosecutions of those responsible. Human rights defenders faced repeated threats and intimidation, especially at times of nationwide protest against government economic policies. Hundreds of cases of disputes between rural communities and landowners remained unresolved. Those responsible for past human rights violations, including genocide, committed during the internal armed conflict, were not brought to justice.

Background

In March, Congress ratified a free trade agreement (known as CAFTA) with the USA, the Dominican Republic and other Central American states. This and other economic policies, such as the expansion of mining activities by foreign companies and proposed privatization of parts of the public sector, caused significant protest nationwide. At least two demonstrators were killed, allegedly by members of the security forces, and many were injured during demonstrations.

The government issued public apologies in four cases of past human rights violations committed during the internal armed conflict. One public apology, for the 1982 Plan de Sánchez massacre of more than 250 indigenous villagers by state forces, had been ordered by the Inter-American Court of Human Rights.

An Office of the UN High Commissioner for Human Rights was established in September.

More than 650 people died in Guatemala in the wake of Hurricane Stan which caused extensive damage and casualties in Central America in October.

Efforts to make progress on a UN-backed proposal to establish a commission to investigate illegal organizations and clandestine groups failed to materialize despite previous government assurances. The proposed commission had been rejected by Congress in 2004.

Violence against women

According to police figures, up to 665 women were murdered in Guatemala, an increase from the 527 killed in 2004. The attacks were often accompanied by sexual violence and extreme brutality. Little progress was made in bringing those responsible to justice. In January cases were transferred to a new investigating

agency with more resources, but this did not result in successful prosecutions.

A law which considers sexual relations with a female minor a crime only if the woman is "honest" remained in force. However, a law which allowed rapists, in certain cases, to escape prosecution if they marry their victim, was suspended in December by the Constitutional Court, the country's highest court.

Nineteen-year-old Claudina Velázquez's body was found on 13 August. She had died from a gunshot wound to the head. There were bruises on her cheek and knee and traces of semen were found. There were serious concerns about the effectiveness of the investigation. For example, tests on the principal suspects, to ascertain if they had fired a gun, were not carried out and the investigating prosecutor attempted to return her clothes to the family, who insisted that they be kept as a potential source of future evidence.

Economic, social and cultural rights

Twenty-two evictions of rural communities were reported to have been carried out in 2005. The authorities showed undue partiality towards individual, normally wealthy, landowners in issuing eviction orders. The evictions themselves were characterized by destruction of homes and excessive use of force which sometimes resulted in injuries.

Threats and intimidation

During 2005, 224 attacks on human rights activists and organizations were reported. The timing and nature of many of these attacks suggested the involvement of illegal clandestine groups.

The Rapporteur for Guatemala of the Inter-American Commission on Human Rights visited in July and noted the difficult situation faced by human rights defenders. While commending the government's public declaration of support for defenders, the Rapporteur concluded that impunity was a structural problem and little progress was being made in investigating present and past human rights violations against activists.

In January, Makrina Gudiel, a campaigner against corruption and the daughter of a prominent human rights defender who was murdered in December 2004, was attacked. Her car was drenched in gasoline in an attempt to burn her alive. She managed to escape and remained in hiding for most of 2005.

In May, the office of a national rural workers' organization was raided. Computers were taken containing important information on the organization's work and members, while many other objects of value were left behind. The organization had been active in opposing CAFTA and forced evictions of rural communities.

Impunity

There was no progress in trying past cases of genocide or crimes against humanity in Guatemala.

In February, the Constitutional Court halted a trial in the case of the 1982 massacre in Dos Erres, in which over 200 people were killed by the Guatemalan Army.

The Court determined that due process had been violated. The case was pending at the end of the year.

⌂ In September, the Spanish Constitutional Court ruled that the case for alleged genocide against Guatemalan General Rios Montt, military ruler of Guatemala between 1981-82, and other officers, could proceed in Spain.

Death penalty

In April President Berger announced he would seek to abolish the death penalty. Legislation was presented to Congress in May where it remained pending at the end of the year.

In two separate cases in June and September, the Inter-American Court of Human Rights ruled that articles of the Criminal Code relating to the application of the death penalty for murder and kidnapping were unclear and therefore could not be applied. The Court ordered a reprieve for the two prisoners who presented their cases and for a further 18 prisoners condemned to death for kidnapping. If implemented, the judgments could reduce those on death row from the current 29 to nine.

No executions took place in 2005.

AI country reports/ visits
Reports
- Guatemala: Memorandum to the Government of Guatemala: Amnesty International's concerns regarding the current human rights situation (AI Index: AMR 34/014/2005)
- Guatemala: No protection, no justice – killings of women in Guatemala (AI Index: AMR 34/017/2005)
- Amicus Curiae Brief before the Inter-American Court of Human Rights in the matter of Ronald Ernesto Raxcacó Reyes (AI Index: IOR 62/003/2005)

Visits
AI delegations visited Guatemala in August and in September.

GUINEA

REPUBLIC OF GUINEA
Head of state: Lansana Conté
Head of government: Cellou Dalein Diallo
Death penalty: retentionist
International Criminal Court: ratified
UN Women's Convention: ratified
Optional Protocol to UN Women's Convention: not signed

Several people were arrested following an attempt to assassinate the head of state in January. Police used excessive force to disperse a protest march. Freedom of expression remained under threat. Death sentences continued to be imposed; no executions were reported.

Background

In January, an unidentified group wearing military uniforms attempted to assassinate President Conté. The authorities said that the attackers escaped after gunshots were fired at a presidential convoy. Several people, including military officers, were arrested.

In September, following clashes between different ethnic groups in Nzérékoré that left several people injured, the authorities imposed a curfew and arrested at least 20 people.

The opposition, which had boycotted presidential elections in 2003, took part in local elections in December 2005. The ruling Party for Union and Progress won most urban districts and rural development communities. Opposition parties accused the authorities of rigging the polls.

Excessive use of force

In November, police allegedly used excessive force against high-school students during a protest march over a lack of teachers in Télémélé, 250km north of the capital Conakry. Two students were killed and a third person who was shot died later in hospital.

Detention without trial

Around 11 military officers, including Amadou Diallo and Alama Condé, held since November 2003 on suspicion of plotting to overthrow President Conté, were still in detention without charge or trial at the end of the year. It was learned during 2005 that Moussa Touré, a military officer arrested in 2003, had died in detention in September 2004 and had been denied medical care.

Attacks on freedom of expression

In August, the authorities ended the state monopoly on broadcasting. A new law allows private citizens and organizations to broadcast, but not political parties or religious movements. Freedom of expression continued to be curtailed, with journalists, lawyers and others who criticized state representatives at risk of beatings, arrests and imprisonment.

⮒ Sotigtui Kaba, a journalist with *Le Lynx* newspaper, was beaten in February while covering a protest march by truck drivers who were demanding better working conditions.

⮒ Mohamed Lamine Diallo, known as Ben Pepito, editor-in-chief of the weekly *La Lance*, was detained for three days in February on unknown charges. He had been investigating the case of Antoine Soromou, a member of the opposition, who had been detained for more than two weeks in January.

⮒ In November, Louis Espérant Célestin, editor of *Guinée Actuelle* newspaper, was detained for more than 48 hours after he published an article about Prime Minister Cellou Dalein Diallo that was considered defamatory.

Death penalty

In August the Minister of Security signalled a tougher approach to crime and announced that "whoever kills deliberately will also be killed". A wide range of offences, including murder, carry a mandatory death sentence; execution is by firing squad.

⮒ In August a diamond merchant, Malick Condé, and a policeman, Cléophace Lamah, were sentenced to death for murder. They said they would appeal. Two co-defendants were sentenced to four years' imprisonment.

GUINEA-BISSAU

REPUBLIC OF GUINEA-BISSAU
Head of state: João Bernardo "Nino" Vieira (replaced Henrique Pereira Rosa (interim) in October)
Head of government: Aristide Gomes (replaced Carlos Gomes Júnior in November)
Death penalty: abolitionist for all crimes
International Criminal Court: signed
UN Women's Convention: ratified
Optional Protocol to UN Women's Convention: signed

The risks of conflict and instability remained high. Political tension increased in the run-up to presidential elections in July, and the election of former President João Bernardo "Nino" Vieira failed to calm the situation. The police used firearms to disperse a demonstration, killing four people and injuring several others. There was no investigation into this incident.

Background

Economic and social conditions remained dire and continued to threaten the stability of the country, ranked the sixth poorest in the world. In January, a locust invasion threatened the cashew nut harvest, the country's main cash crop. Following a donors' conference in February, the government relied on international donors to pay salary arrears, especially to the armed forces, and to finance elections. International donors also pledged assistance to restructure the armed forces.

In March, a UN delegation visited the country to assist in efforts to combat the proliferation of illegally circulating small arms, estimated at around 175,000.

Former President João Bernardo "Nino" Vieira was sworn in as President in October having won the second round of presidential elections in July. The elections were declared free and fair by international observers. The delay in taking office arose because his opponent, Malam Bacai Sanhá, of the ruling African Party for the Independence of Guinea-Bissau and Cape Verde (Partido Africano da Indepêndencia da Guiné e Cabo Verde, PAIGC), contested the results and demanded a recount of the votes.

At the end of October the new President dismissed the government. Three days later he appointed Aristide Gomes as Prime Minister. Aristide Gomes had been expelled from the PAIGC in May for supporting President Vieira in the presidential election. The PAIGC rejected the appointment as unconstitutional. The dismissed Prime Minister refused to hand over office and demonstrators in Bissau protesting against the new appointment burned tyres and caused some material damage. There were no arrests.

In October the government declared that it had fulfilled its obligations under the Ottawa Convention by destroying its stockpile of about 5,000 landmines. However, several minefields remained to be cleared.

There was conflict between Muslim groups in the city of Gabú in the east in February. A month later, the authorities accused the Muslim group *Ahmadi* of failing to co-operate with other Muslim groups and banned it from carrying out its activities. The group had been banned and arbitrarily expelled from the country in 2001 by then President Kumba Ialá, but in January 2005 the ban had been lifted following a court order.

Political violence and impunity

Political tension heightened around the presidential elections and the army was placed on high alert. Tension was exacerbated by the Supreme Court's delay in making a decision to allow two former presidents to stand in the elections. Kumba Ialá of the Social Renewal Party (Partido da Renovação Social, PRS) was overthrown from power in September 2003 and banned from seeking political office for eight years. João Bernardo "Nino" Vieira, a refugee in Portugal since being ousted in 1999, was forbidden to seek political office by the Constitution. Kumba Ialá threatened to seize power if his candidacy was rejected. In May, the Supreme Court ruled that the two could stand. Opposition parties criticized the ruling as politically motivated. Despite the ruling, Kumba Ialá declared himself President and occupied the presidential palace for a few hours. The army broke up a demonstration by PRS supporters and pledged loyalty to the government.

In June, Kumba Ialá rejected the results of the first ballot. The PRS organized a demonstration in his support, which led to violence in which people lost their lives. The Rapid Intervention Police reportedly beat demonstrators and used tear gas and live ammunition to disperse them, killing four and injuring about six others. There were reports that some of the demonstrators were armed with sticks, stones and guns. About 50 people were reportedly arrested, including Artur Sanhá, Secretary General of the PRS. All were released uncharged after two days, pending an investigation. However, no investigation was carried out by the end of 2005.

A week before the second ballot, in July, a group of armed men wearing military uniforms attacked the Ministry of Interior. Two police officers were killed and several people were injured in the attack. Twenty people were reportedly arrested. The Army Chief of Staff blamed the attack on people acting outside the military command structure. No investigation into this incident was known to have taken place.

Similarly, there was no investigation into the killing in September 2004 of the Chief-of-Staff of the Armed Forces. Soldiers arrested in 2002 and released in 2004 pending trial were not tried.

Freedom of expression

In September the government dismissed the directors of the national television and radio stations. There were reports that the dismissals were politically motivated and related to the two men's alleged support for the President-elect, João Bernardo "Nino" Vieira.

GUYANA

REPUBLIC OF GUYANA
Head of state: Bharrat Jagdeo
Head of government: Samuel Hinds
Death penalty: retentionist
International Criminal Court: ratified
UN Women's Convention: ratified
Optional Protocol to UN Women's Convention: not signed

There were reports of killings by a "death squad" allegedly involving serving and former police officers. The criminal justice system failed to bring vast numbers of cases of sexual violence against women to trial.

Death penalty

No executions took place but 21 people remained on death row – 19 men and two women.

Guyana formally adopted the Caribbean Court of Justice, inaugurated in April, as its highest appellate court. Since independence in 1970, the Court of Appeal of Guyana had been the final court of appeal.

'Death squad'

In April a Presidential Commission found that there was no evidence of "a credible nature" linking the Home Affairs Minister to the activities of an alleged "death squad". In June, following international pressure, the Minister resigned. According to reports, several witnesses failed to appear before the Commission because of fears for their safety.

In August a high court overturned the decision of a lower court to charge an alleged hit-woman with the June 2004 murder of George Bacchus. He was shot dead days before he was due to testify in a trial related to "death squad" killings.

The separate killings of five people between August and September were attributed in the news media to "death squad" activities.

Violence against women

According to a report by the Guyana Human Rights Association, in only nine out of 647 rapes reported from 2000 to 2004 was the perpetrator convicted. The report detailed a rise of some 30 per cent in the incidence of sexual violence against women, and a 16-fold increase in statutory rape cases from 2000 to 2004. Only three per cent of rape cases filed over the five-year period resulted in a trial. The report pointed to "deficiencies and weaknesses in the justice system".

HAITI

REPUBLIC OF HAITI
Head of state: Boniface Alexandre
Head of government: Gérard Latortue
Death penalty: abolitionist for all crimes
International Criminal Court: signed
UN Women's Convention: ratified
Optional Protocol to UN Women's Convention: not signed

Excessive use of force by police officers continued and there were reports of extrajudicial executions. No proper investigations were carried out, reinforcing the climate of impunity. Unlawful killings and kidnappings by illegal armed groups escalated, exacerbating political tensions ahead of elections. Clashes between UN soldiers and illegal armed groups continued throughout 2005. Violence against women persisted and officials failed to take adequate steps to prevent and punish it. The justice system remained dysfunctional and scores of people remained imprisoned without charge or trial. Impunity for past human rights violations prevailed.

Background

2005 was marked by instability and violence, particularly in Port-au-Prince, the capital. The large quantity of small arms in circulation fuelled criminal activities and human rights abuses. The number of kidnappings for ransom increased dramatically with over 1,000 cases between March and December. All sectors of society were targeted, along with foreign nationals. Among the victims was one of Haiti's best-known journalists and poets, Jacques Roche, who was kidnapped and murdered in July. Many children were abducted to extort money from their parents. At least 20 Haitian National Police (HNP) officers were arrested for taking part in kidnappings.

The security situation improved generally across the country, although armed gangs in the capital, particularly in the Cité Soleil district, continued to defy both the HNP and soldiers from the UN Stabilization Mission in Haiti (MINUSTAH). Clashes between armed gangs and MINUSTAH military and HNP officers continued throughout 2005 – most of those killed and injured were unarmed civilian men, women and children, although several gang leaders were also killed. Reports of unlawful killings, rape, extortion and arson continued to be frequent in the impoverished neighbourhoods controlled by armed gangs.

MINUSTAH had its mandate extended until February 2006 and its strength increased to more than 8,000 military personnel and UN police officers. In March, MINUSTAH forces reclaimed two police stations in Petit Goâve and Terre-Rouge that had been occupied since 2004 by former officials of the Haitian Armed Forces (FADH), disbanded in 1995, and former rebels. MINUSTAH

acknowledged responsibility for the deaths of civilians during military operations carried out in Cité Soleil in July.

In April, Remissainthe Ravix, the self-proclaimed leader of the demobilized armed forces, was killed in a clash with police. Disarmament of the ex-FADH officers and former rebels was not implemented by the end of 2005. Former members of the FADH pressed the interim government to pay them compensation for their demobilization in 1995 and to reinstate their pension fund. The interim government agreed to pay US$28 million in compensation to the ex-FADH officers, without making the payment conditional on implementing a disarmament and demobilization programme. In addition, hundreds of ex-FADH officers were incorporated into the HNP without proper vetting of their past human rights record.

Delegations from the UN Security Council and the Inter-American Commission on Human Rights visited Haiti in April. Both delegations raised concerns about the human rights situation. The UN Security Council strengthened MINUSTAH's mandate to give it a more vigorous role in professionalizing the HNP, after numerous reports of human rights violations by police officers. In June the Minister of Justice resigned and the Director of Police was dismissed after criticism from the international community over the administration of justice and the failures of the HNP to comply with international standards of policing.

Local, legislative and presidential elections were initially scheduled for October and November but were postponed on four occasions until early 2006. Shortcomings in organizing the ballot and delays in registering more than 4 million potential voters, particularly those living in impoverished neighbourhoods and rural areas, gave rise to serious concerns over the capability of the interim government and the Provisional Electoral Council (Conseil Electoral Provisoire, CEP) to organize the elections according to international standards. The CEP endorsed 43 political parties and 35 presidential candidates, only one of them a woman.

There was continued concern about the independence of the judiciary after the interim government dismissed five members of the Supreme Court following their decision to allow a candidate with US and Haitian nationality to stand for president.

Violence against women

Gender-based violence, in particular rape of women by gang members, was reported increasingly frequently in impoverished neighbourhoods of the capital.

Long overdue reforms to the Criminal Code to address flaws in the criminalization of gender-based violence, including rape, were finally introduced in October by a Presidential decree. Under the amended Criminal Code rape was defined as a criminal offence – previously it was considered a moral offence – punishable by up to 10 years' forced labour. However, the majority of rapes were not reported to the authorities for fear of reprisal or because of lack of confidence in the authorities and the justice system.

The interim government failed to combat the culture of tolerance of violence against women and to provide assistance for victims of sexual violence.

Killings and attacks by illegal armed groups

Illegal armed groups or gangs killed dozens of civilians. Twelve police officers were also killed during 2005. Gangs allegedly supporting former President Jean-Bertrand Aristide committed most of the killings. Inter-gang warfare decreased after a gang leader linked to the Lavalas opposition was killed in February.

☐ On 31 May, an armed group allegedly supporting the Lavalas party attacked Têt-Boeuf public market in Port-au-Prince and set it on fire. More than 15 people reportedly died in the attack.

☐ On 10 August, groups armed with machetes (widely known as *"attachés"*), allegedly acting in collusion with HNP officers, reportedly killed at least 10 people in the Delmas 2 and Bel-Air neighbourhoods of the capital.

Excessive force and unlawful killings by police

The HNP continued to use excessive force and there were several allegations of extrajudicial executions. The victims included criminal suspects, a journalist and Lavalas supporters.

☐ On 14 January, HNP officers allegedly killed Abdias Jean, a Miami-based radio reporter, while he was covering a police operation in Village de Dieu, Port-au-Prince. The police denied the killing. Local residents claimed that Abdias Jean was killed because he was investigating the deaths of four alleged bandits killed during the police operation. According to witnesses, he identified himself to the police officers as a journalist before he was shot dead.

☐ On 27 April, HNP officers opened fire on a peaceful demonstration in front of MINUSTAH headquarters. Five people were killed and several others wounded.

☐ On 20 August, the HNP interrupted a football match attended by about 5,000 people in the Martissant stadium. According to reports, HNP officers ordered everyone to lie down while *"attachés"* belonging to a group called the Small Machetes Army (Lame Ti manchèt) attacked people identified by the police as criminal suspects. The stadium was surrounded by police officers and *"attachés"* who shot or hacked to death those who attempted to flee. Nine people were killed and four injured. At least 13 police officers were arrested in connection with the killings.

Prisoners of conscience, political prisoners

Scores of detainees were held for long periods without legal basis and denied a fair trial. In November, Louis Joinet, the UN Independent Expert on Haiti, expressed concern about the lack of transparency of the justice system and the unjustifiable delays in bringing detainees to trial. He called for the release of all political prisoners.

The UN Security Council and other international bodies urged the interim government to expedite the cases of political prisoners, in particular that of former Prime Minister Yvon Neptune.

☐ Former Prime Minister Yvon Neptune, imprisoned since June 2004, staged a hunger strike in March and April in protest at his prison conditions and detention without trial. In June, the investigative magistrate finally indicted Yvon Neptune and 30 other individuals for their involvement in an alleged massacre at La Scierie in February 2004. At the end of 2005, he was still awaiting trial.

☐ On 21 July, Father Gérard Jean-Juste, a Catholic priest and Aristide supporter, was taken into police custody after a mob attacked him outside the church where journalist Jacques Roche's funeral took place. Considered a potential presidential candidate for the Lavalas party, Father Jean-Juste was illegally arrested and held on trumped-up charges. He was a prisoner of conscience.

☐ Annette Auguste (known as Sò Ann), a grass-roots organizer and folk singer, remained imprisoned without having been formally charged. The 65-year-old woman was arrested on 11 May 2004 by US Marines, part of the Multinational Interim Force deployed in Haiti hours after former President Aristide went into exile. Annette Auguste was handed over to the Haitian authorities, who imprisoned her in the Pétion-Ville Penitentiary. The reason for her initial detention was unclear but she remained imprisoned without trial on suspicion of inciting Lavalas supporters to attack university students in December 2003.

Journalists under attack

Journalists were harassed and subjected to abuse throughout 2005. In September the Council of the Wise (Conseil des Sages), a body of notable citizens created to guide the interim government, publicly threatened to prosecute journalists who broadcast the views of opposition leaders advocating the return to Haiti of former President Aristide.

☐ On 14 January, *Le Nouvelliste* newspaper reporters Claude Bernard Serrat and Jonel Juste were assaulted by mobs in Bel-Air, a stronghold of Aristide supporters. The mobs reportedly accused the press of contributing to the ousting of the former president.

☐ Kevin Pina, a US journalist and film maker, and Jean Ristil, a Haitian journalist working for the *Associated Press*, were arrested on 9 September while monitoring a search at Father Jean-Juste's church (see above). They were accused of showing disrespect to the magistrate executing the warrant, but were released without charge four days later.

☐ On 3 October, President Boniface Alexandre's security guards attacked Guyler C. Delva, a *Reuters* correspondent, and Jean Wilkens Merone, a *Radio Metropole* reporter. Both journalists were covering a ceremony marking the beginning of the judicial year when they were dragged into a courthouse and severely beaten.

Impunity

There was no effective system to administer justice, uphold the rule of law and provide impartial protection of human rights. Abuses committed by HNP officials were committed with impunity. Investigations into most police violations, when conducted, did not meet international standards. Prosecutions and convictions for human rights violations were non-existent.

The authorities also failed to address human rights violations committed in previous years, including long-standing cases of political killings and massacres. Former military leaders accused of human rights violations during the 1991-1994 military government continued to enjoy impunity. Investigations into the cases of murdered journalists Brignol Lindor and Jean Dominique were at a standstill.

◻ In May, the Supreme Court overturned the sentences passed in the Raboteau massacre trial on the grounds of a technical error. The court argued that the trial, in 2000, should not have taken place before a jury. Thirty-four former members of the military and paramilitary groups had been sentenced to prison terms of two to 10 years. The Raboteau trial was considered by human rights organizations as a milestone in fighting impunity in Haiti. Most of those convicted in the case had escaped from prison in early 2004.

◻ In August, Louis Jodel Chamblain, former second in command of a paramilitary group during the 1991-1994 military government, was freed from jail without any legal grounds. He was awaiting his second trial for the Raboteau massacre. He had been sentenced in absentia in 2000 and he turned himself in after President Aristide was ousted in 2004. According to Haitian law, those sentenced in absentia face a re-trial once they return to Haiti.

Disarmament
Little progress was made towards disarmament. A National Commission on Disarmament was created in February but only became operational in July. Repeated calls from the UN Security Council to implement without delay a disarmament programme remained unheeded. Lack of political will to disarm illegal armed groups undermined efforts to establish peace and a secure environment throughout the transition process. MINUSTAH initiated small-scale disarmament programmes as pilot projects at a community level, but faced opposition from sectors of Haitian society.

AI country reports/visits
Reports
- Haiti: Disarmament delayed, justice denied (AI Index: AMR 36/005/2005)
- Haiti: Arms proliferation fuels human rights abuses ahead of elections (AI Index: AMR 36/011/2005)
- Haiti: Obliterating justice – overturning of sentences for Raboteau massacre by Supreme Court is a huge step backwards (AI Index: AMR 36/006/2005)

HONDURAS

REPUBLIC OF HONDURAS
Head of state and government: Ricardo Maduro
Death penalty: abolitionist for all crimes
International Criminal Court: ratified
UN Women's Convention: ratified
Optional Protocol to UN Women's Convention: not signed

The killing, torture, imprisonment on fabricated criminal charges and harassment of human rights defenders and indigenous community activists continued. Complaints of violence against women in the family continued to soar.

Background
In November elections, Manuel Zelaya of the opposition Liberal Party was elected President.

In June, Honduras had over half its external debt written off as part of a programme for heavily indebted poor countries. Some 64 per cent of the population lived in poverty, and Honduras ranked 116 out of 177 countries in the UN Human Development Index. Hurricanes left dozens dead, thousands homeless and crops destroyed.

Attacks on human rights defenders
Activists defending the environment and the rights of indigenous people were among those killed, tortured and imprisoned. The government showed little political will to end the abuses, instigated in most cases by powerful landowners or logging interests.

◻ Edickson Roberto Lemus, regional coordinator of a leading peasant farmer organization, the National Union of Farm Workers, was killed on 24 May. An unidentified individual shot him on a bus. He was on his way to visit the peasant group Renacer (Rebirth) in the community of El Pajuiles, Yoro department, which had been served with an eviction order on 19 May. The authorities had reportedly said they could provide no protection after he received threats. By the end of 2005 no one had been identified or detained in relation to his killing.

◻ Feliciano Pineda, a community leader in the municipality of Gracias, Lempira department, was attacked and seriously injured in June. He was handcuffed and arrested on his arrival at hospital, and subsequently imprisoned before he could receive proper medical treatment. Criminal charges brought against him were reportedly fabricated. In December he was acquitted of the charge of homicide but remained in prison on other lesser charges, despite the fact that the time limit for bringing him to trial on these charges had lapsed.

◻ The case of convicted indigenous community leaders Marcelino and Leonardo Miranda, who were attempting to have 25-year prison sentences overturned, was still before the courts. They were convicted after a politically motivated trial because of their work to resolve local land disputes and defend indigenous rights. Both men were repeatedly tortured in pre-trial detention. An appeal on procedural defects submitted to the Supreme Court in 2004 was rejected in August. In October a new appeal, on defective application of the law, was submitted to the Supreme Court. A decision was pending at the end of 2005.

Violence against women

Special domestic violence courts were reportedly overwhelmed with growing numbers of complaints, said to total over 30,000 between 2000 and mid-2005. According to the Special Prosecutor for Women's Affairs, three out of 10 women who submitted complaints were eventually killed by their attacker. In August, Deputy Attorney General Omar Cerna was reported as acknowledging that allegations of violence in the family were not taken seriously enough.

In January, Marta Beatriz Reyes died after being set on fire while she slept, reportedly by her estranged husband. Taken to hospital in San Pedro Sula with second and third degree burns to 40 per cent of her body, she died 11 days later. After enduring years of violence, she had left her husband. Although she submitted several complaints to the police, they failed to protect her or take action.

Children and young people

A high level of killings of children and young people persisted, with 431 deaths in 2005. Government initiatives to investigate and bring those responsible to justice, promised in previous years, did not materialize, and the perpetrators continued to enjoy impunity.

The case of four young people who were killed in 1995 in Tegucigalpa was submitted to the Inter-American Court of Human Rights in February following failure by the government to act on recommendations made by the Inter-American Commission on Human Rights. The four were among around 120 people detained by the police in September 1995. Their bodies were found two days later in different parts of the city; each had been shot several times in the back of the head. The case was representative of thousands of similar cases that the authorities have failed to investigate.

HUNGARY

REPUBLIC OF HUNGARY
Head of state: László Sólyom (replaced Ferenc Mádl in June)
Head of government: Ferenc Gyurcsány
Death penalty: abolitionist for all crimes
International Criminal Court: ratified
UN Women's Convention and its Optional Protocol: ratified

Racist attacks on Roma and other minorities, and discrimination against Roma in all sectors of public services, continued. There was official acknowledgement that segregation in schools had increased for Romani children, a quarter of whom were being taught separately despite anti-discrimination legislation. In education, health care and housing, the Romani population continued to face deprivation and discrimination. Legislation to tackle violence against women in abusive relationships was delayed.

Racism and discrimination

Racist attacks and other racially motivated crimes continued to target Romani and Jewish communities. Public statements by senior political figures and the news media fostered racism and intolerance. Prime Minister Ferenc Gyurcsány apologized after referring to the Saudi Arabian football team as "full of terrorists" in February. The Vice-Chairman of Parliament's Human Rights Commission, Zsolt Semjén, also came in for criticism in February for a homophobic jibe at a rival political party.

In February the Constitutional Court declared provisions in a housing decree to be discriminatory and unconstitutional. The decree declared people ineligible for social housing if they had previously occupied accommodation without legal entitlement. The Court held that the decree had a disproportionately negative effect on Roma, and conflicted with local government obligations to house the socially deprived. Romani families reportedly received eviction notices even during a moratorium on winter evictions.

By denying two Romani men entrance to a disco bar in Nagyhalasz, its owners had violated their dignity and infringed legal requirements of equal treatment, the Szabolcs-Szatmár-Bereg County Court held in June. Under comprehensive anti-discrimination legislation from 2003, the Court awarded 150,000 Hungarian forints (US$695) to each man as victims of racial discrimination. The disco bar was ordered to refrain from further discrimination against Roma.

In September, the European Roma Rights Centre based in Budapest, the capital, issued a report on Romani children's rights in Hungary, in advance of a periodic review of Hungary's obligations by the UN Committee on the Rights of the Child in January 2006. The report described how Romani children experienced segregation in education, health care and housing, and said that disproportionately high numbers were removed from their families by the state. More than half of Romani households did not have access to hot running water, and 17 per cent of the Romani population lived in settlements where there is no doctor.

In November the Commissioner for Integration of Disadvantaged and Roma Children at the Hungarian Ministry of Education confirmed that the segregation of Romani children remained a serious problem. At least 3,000 elementary school classes and 178 schools were predominantly made up of Romani students, and 25 per cent of Romani students were being taught in a segregated environment.

The police reportedly downplayed the discriminatory motivation of physical assaults on Roma and other minorities, and this reluctance was claimed to have led to punishments for the perpetrators of violent crimes that did not reflect the gravity of the offence.

▭ The case of 15-year-old Roma József Patai, who was stabbed on a bus in Budapest in May, was initially treated as a racist crime. However, after it emerged that the perpetrator was himself Roma, the police became reluctant to consider racism as a motive in subsequent crimes.

Domestic violence

A resolution on the development of a national strategy to prevent and effectively address domestic violence, passed by parliament in 2003 in response to public concerns, remained largely unimplemented. The draft Law on the Order of Protection, requiring an abusive partner to temporarily leave jointly owned premises, was delayed. The only crisis centre in Budapest for women experiencing violence in the home remained partially closed, and no new shelters were established.

A new law to protect victims of domestic violence was being drafted. However, it still required a court to issue an order to restrain an abuser from approaching a victim, making immediate intervention by the police impossible. In addition, the draft law did not provide for extension of the 10-to-30-day limit of a restraining order, and imposition of such an order remained virtually impossible unless the victim was able or willing to testify against the abuser.

In January the UN Committee on the Elimination of Discrimination against Women found in a landmark case that Hungary had not provided effective protection from domestic violence. In a case brought before the Committee, an applicant who had been subjected to regular and severe violence, and whose partner had threatened both her and the children, was not admitted to a government shelter as none was equipped to accept her with her children, one of whom had severe disabilities. Neither protection nor a legal restraining order was available under national law. Legal proceedings initiated by the applicant herself were slow and ineffective, and a domestic court ordered that she share ownership of their apartment with her partner. The Committee ordered immediate measures to guarantee the physical and mental

integrity of the woman and her family, and to ensure that all victims of domestic violence were accorded the maximum protection of the law.

INDIA

REPUBLIC OF INDIA
Head of state: A.P.J. Abdul Kalam
Head of government: Manmohan Singh
Death penalty: retentionist
International Criminal Court: not signed
UN Women's Convention: ratified with reservations
Optional Protocol to UN Women's Convention: not signed

Perpetrators of human rights violations continued to enjoy impunity, particularly in Gujarat, which witnessed widespread violence in early 2002. There were reports of human rights violations in the context of unrest in several states, including Jammu and Kashmir and some north-eastern states. The government repealed security legislation which had been used to facilitate arbitrary arrests, torture and other grave human rights violations. However, some of the provisions allowing these violations were transferred into existing laws, a move widely criticized by human rights organizations. Socially and economically marginalized groups, including women, *dalits* and *adivasis* (tribal people), continued to face systemic discrimination and serious doubts remained about whether moves to enact new laws could achieve the intended aim of protecting their rights. Some states in central and eastern India, where traditional *adivasi* habitations are located, witnessed an increase in violence involving armed groups and state forces.

Background

Ongoing peace talks between India and Pakistan ensured the resumption of bus services across the divided Himalayan region of Kashmir after 58 years. In October and November, transport lines were opened at five points along the Line of Control in Kashmir to facilitate the delivery of aid to people affected by the earthquake in October. However, with issues at the core of the conflict yet to be taken up, relations between the two countries improved at only a slow pace.

During the year, government and foreign agencies were engaged in the relief efforts for those affected by the 26 December 2004 tsunami which killed an estimated 15,000 people and displaced more than 112,000 others in the southern states of Tamil Nadu, Kerala and Andhra Pradesh and the union territories of Pondicherry and Andaman and the Nicobar Islands.

In Andhra Pradesh, peace talks between the state government and the Maoist (naxalite) People's War Group (PWG) collapsed after eight months, signalling a return to a series of attacks during which civilians were routinely targeted. Similar incidents were witnessed in several central and eastern states, putting members of already marginalized rural and *adivasi* populations at increased risk.

In the north-east, talks between the Union government and a section of the National Socialist Council of Nagaland remained inconclusive. There were moves to initiate talks between the Union government and the United Liberation Front of Assam. The region also witnessed sporadic clashes between members of tribal communities during which civilians were targeted.

The United Progressive Alliance (UPA) government introduced a draft bill to prevent communal violence, following widespread criticism of its predecessor for failing to halt the 2002 communal violence in Gujarat targeting the Muslim minority. However, some of the bill's provisions were criticized as repressive.

Proceedings regarding the 1992 demolition of Babri Mosque at Ayodhya, in which senior leaders of the Bharatiya Janata Party (BJP) were facing trial, made little progress during the year.

Following a vigorous civil society campaign, the Indian parliament passed landmark legislation guaranteeing the right to information. However, it was unclear whether various union and state government agencies would fully enforce this legislation.

Violence against women

In an effort to stem increasing abuses against girls and women, including dowry deaths, sexual assault and acid attacks, parliament in August passed the Protection of Women from Domestic Violence Bill (2005), which legislates for comprehensive protection of women from all forms of domestic violence.

Traditional preference for boys has led to thousands of female foetuses being aborted despite the prohibition of pre-natal sex determination for this purpose. In May the Health Minister stated that there had not been a single conviction for breaking the ban since it was introduced eight years earlier.

Many of the abuses suffered by Muslim women in Gujarat in 2002 fell outside the definition of rape in national law, thereby hampering victims' quest for justice.

The Supreme Court in October objected to a 2003 order of the Madhya Pradesh High Court reducing a 10-year sentence for rape to nine months' imprisonment. It held that an inadequate punishment for rape was an "affront to society".

The personal law of specific communities became a political issue after the All India Muslim Personal Law Board confirmed Muslim clerics' *fatwa* concerning the marriage of Imrana Ilahi. Imrana Ilahi alleged rape by her father-in-law in June in Muzzaffarnagar, Uttar Pradesh; the Board subsequently annulled her marriage and pressed for her rape allegation to be re-framed as a charge of adultery. Imrana Ilahi and her husband defied the directive but the local village council continued to put pressure on them to withdraw their charge of rape.

A petition seeking to prevent the establishment of a parallel Muslim judicial system and binding *fatwas* issued by Muslim clerics or organizations was pending in the Supreme Court at the end of the year.

Jammu and Kashmir

Politically motivated violence slightly decreased but torture, deaths in custody and "disappearances" continued to be reported. At least 38 people were reported to have died in custody. In January, the Minister of State for Home Affairs stated that some 600 people, including 174 foreigners, were held under the Public Safety Act (PSA), a preventive detention law. In October 44 detainees were released but new detentions were reported. Several people had been held under the PSA for over 10 years under successive PSA detention orders.

⌑ Farooq Ahmad Dar was detained in November under his ninth consecutive PSA order. He had been in continuous detention under the PSA since 1991.

Civilians were repeatedly targeted by state agencies and armed groups.

⌑ In May, armed fighters threw a grenade just as children were leaving their school in Srinagar, killing two women who had come to pick up children and injuring 50 others, including 20 pupils.

⌑ In July, four juveniles aged between 11 and 15 were shot dead by paramilitary Rashtriya Rifles in Kupwara district. Local people said that the boys had participated in a marriage party and gone for a stroll but ran away when ordered to stop. They said that the army had been informed of possible movements of people attending the party late at night.

In September, the State Human Rights Commission, which had registered 3,187 cases of human rights violations since its inception in 1991, reiterated its earlier complaint that government departments failed to implement its recommendations.

Gujarat

Survivors of targeted killings and sexual violence in 2002, some of which had amounted to crimes against humanity, continued to be denied justice and reparations. Key cases relating to these killings and sexual assaults of Muslim women in which complainants had sought transfers to courts outside the state, were still pending in the Supreme Court at the end of the year. In December a mass grave containing the remains of Muslim victims was found.

Impunity

Members of the security forces continued to enjoy impunity for human rights violations.

⌑ Nine years after the "disappearance" and killing of human rights lawyer Jalil Andrabi in Srinagar, Jammu and Kashmir, an army major identified as responsible by a special investigation team had still not been brought to justice. Army representatives asserted that they had not been able to locate him.

More than two decades after the anti-Sikh riots in Delhi and elsewhere in the aftermath of Prime Minister Indira Gandhi's assassination, a judicial commission concluded that there was credible evidence pointing to the involvement of two leaders of the Congress party heading the ruling UPA. Both were forced to resign from their official posts. Several others belonging to the same party were cleared of charges, leading to criticism by human rights organizations. Prime Minister Manmohan Singh offered a public apology to the Sikh community and the government promised to reopen some of the riot cases.

In Punjab, the vast majority of police officers responsible for serious human rights violations during the period of civil unrest in the mid-1990s continued to evade justice, despite the recommendations of several judicial inquiries and commissions. In response to 2,097 reported cases of human rights violations during this period, the National Human Rights Commission (NHRC) had ordered the state of Punjab to provide compensation in 109 cases concerning people who died in police custody. The NHRC did not address issues of liability; the culture of impunity developed during that period prevailed. Reports of abuses including torture and ill-treatment persisted.

▢ Six policemen were convicted of the abduction and murder of human rights defender Jaswant Singh Kalra in 1995. Kalra had exposed large-scale violations in Punjab.

Human rights defenders

Human rights defenders in many parts of the country continued to be harassed and attacked. Among them were activists working on behalf of marginalized communities including *dalits* and *adivasis* who faced systemic discrimination.

Abuses by armed groups

There were reports of abuses – including torture, attacks and killings of civilians – by armed groups in Jammu and Kashmir, the north-east and several central and eastern states where left-wing armed groups were becoming increasingly active. (See Jammu and Kashmir above.)

▢ In November, during elections in Bihar, Maoists (naxalites) attacked the Jehanabad prison. More than 340 prisoners, including key Maoist leaders, were freed. Eight prisoners belonging to a private army of dominant landed castes, Ranvir Sena, were killed and 20 others kidnapped.

Following the upsurge in the activities of left-wing armed groups in several states, the government set in motion plans for joint inter-state anti-naxalite operations. These initiatives raised concerns over the rights and safety of *adivasi* populations who traditionally inhabit the area.

In July, there was an attack on the disputed religious site at Ayodhya. Later in October, during the run-up to the annual festival season, Delhi was rocked by a series of blasts which left 66 people dead and more than 220 injured.

Death penalty

At least 77 people were sentenced to death during the year; no executions took place. No comprehensive information on the number of people under sentence of death in each state was available.

President Kalam and the newly-appointed Chief Justice to the Supreme Court expressed themselves in general against the death penalty. The President sought from the Indian parliament a comprehensive policy to deal with clemency petitions from those under sentence of death.

Security legislation

More than a year after the repeal of the Prevention of Terrorism Act (POTA), cases of all those held under the Act had not been fully reviewed within the stipulated period. In addition, a number of state governments had not taken action on the recommendations of a judicial committee set up to review the cases.

Human rights organizations continued to express concern over amendments made to the Unlawful Activities (Prevention) Act which granted special powers to the state, similar to those previously provided by the POTA. Although the 1958 Armed Forces Special Powers Act (AFSPA) was under review, there was concern over its continued enforcement in "disturbed areas", including large parts of the north-east.

▢ Syed Geelani, a Kashmiri lecturer sentenced to death under the POTA for conspiring, planning and abetting the attack on the parliament building in New Delhi in December 2001 and acquitted on appeal in 2003, was shot and injured in February outside his lawyer's office. The inquiry into the shooting was entrusted to the very police force that Syed Geelani alleged had harassed him since his release. An appeal filed by police against his acquittal was dismissed by the Supreme Court in September.

Economic, social and cultural rights

Despite positive economic gains in recent years, approximately 300 million people remained mired in poverty.

Following persistent reports over increasing rural unemployment and campaigns to empower the rural poor, the UPA government enacted legislation to guarantee minimum annual employment for all poor households in selected rural areas. However, guidelines for its implementation had not been fully framed by the end of the year.

Twenty-one years after the Union Carbide Corporation's (UCC) pesticide plant in Bhopal leaked toxic gases that took a heavy toll on lives and the environment, survivors continued to struggle for adequate compensation, medical help and rehabilitation. The plant site had still not been cleaned and toxic wastes continued to pollute groundwater. UCC and Dow Chemicals (which took over UCC in 2001) had publicly stated that they had no responsibility for the leak or its consequences. AI joined a year-long campaign by the Bhopal survivors and other organizations to call for an immediate clean-up of the pollutants from the site and the affected surroundings as well as a full remedy for the victims, and for those responsible to be brought to justice.

Other issues

There was grave concern at the intensification of social, political, cultural and economic discrimination, oppression and violence against *dalits*. Data suggested that few cases under the Scheduled Caste and Scheduled Tribes (Prevention of Atrocities) Act 1989 had resulted in convictions.

Adivasi communities in several states continued to face great pressure from dam and mining development projects, expansion of modern forms of agriculture and settlements. Legislation aimed at recognizing and guaranteeing the rights of these communities to access forest areas and resources was under debate in the Indian parliament at the end of the year.

AI country reports/ visits

Reports

- Justice the victim: Gujarat state fails to protect women from violence in 2002 (AI Index: ASA 20/002/2005)
- India: Union Carbide Corporation, DOW Chemicals and the Bhopal communities in India – the case (AI Index: ASA 20/005/2005)se nx: ASA 20/005/2005).
- Briefing on the Armed Forces Special Powers Act (Manipur) (AI Index: ASA 20/025/2005)
- The death penalty in India: briefing for the EU-India Summit, 7 September 2005 (AI Index: ASA 20/034/2005)

Visits

AI delegates, including AI's Secretary General, visited India in February and met government officials, NHRC representatives and civil society organizations.

AI representatives met government officials and activists in December.

INDONESIA

REPUBLIC OF INDONESIA
Head of state and government: Susilo Bambang Yudhoyono
Death penalty: retentionist
International Criminal Court: not signed
UN Women's Convention: ratified with reservations
Optional Protocol to UN Women's Convention: signed

Although the general situation in Nanggroe Aceh Darussalam (NAD) improved after a peace agreement was signed in August by the government and the Free Aceh Movement (Gerakan Aceh Merdeka, GAM), impunity for serious human rights violations remained a concern. In Papua, cases of torture and arbitrary detention were reported. Across the country, the police used excessive force against demonstrators, and ill-treatment in detention facilities and police lock-ups was widespread. At least two people were executed by firing squad and at least 10 people were sentenced to death. Freedom of expression remained severely curtailed and at least 18 people were detained for criticizing the government.

Background

For the first time a representative of Indonesia chaired the annual session of the UN Commission on Human Rights in Geneva. In September parliament took the necessary steps to approve ratification of the International Covenant on Civil and Political Rights and the International Covenant on Economic, Social and Cultural Rights.

Various religious minority groups came under threat. Members of the Ahmaddiya community were targeted for attacks, sometimes forcing them to flee. The Liberal Islam Network was also attacked, and several Christian churches were forced to close in Java. In Maluku and Central Sulawesi, ethnic and religious tensions continued to result in violence.

On 1 October bomb attacks in Bali killed 23 people.

Nanggroe Aceh Darussalam

On 15 August a Memorandum of Understanding between the government and GAM was signed setting out a framework to end peacefully the 29-year conflict in NAD. Over 200 monitors from European Union and Association of South East Asian Nations (ASEAN) countries were deployed to monitor compliance with the agreement. By the end of the year over 30,000 police and army personnel had left the province and the fourth phase of the decommissioning of GAM's weapons had been completed. There was hope that the peace process would hold. Preparations for local elections were well under way.

In January human rights monitors, humanitarian aid agencies and journalists were allowed to operate in NAD for the first time since martial law was declared in

May 2003. Their presence, although mainly restricted to areas affected by the 2004 tsunami, contributed to an enhanced feeling of security in the province.

In May, as part of the government's post-tsunami reconstruction and rehabilitation efforts, the Civil Emergency status in NAD was downgraded to Civil Order status. This had little impact in practice as military operations continued. However, as a result of the peace agreement in August the human rights situation improved significantly.

Despite considerable human and financial investment in the reconstruction effort, there was widespread criticism of the aid agencies' lack of local consultation and coordination. In November over 130,000 people were still living in tents or temporary barracks waiting for permanent housing. There were concerns that many were living in facilities that did not meet basic needs.

In August more than 1,400 political prisoners and at least two human rights activists were released from prisons in NAD and Java as part of an amnesty granted to alleged GAM combatants and their supporters. In October, concerns were raised that 115 GAM prisoners had not been released. During the military and civil emergencies, suspected GAM members and supporters faced unfair trials. Many suspects were denied full access to lawyers and were convicted on the basis of confessions reportedly extracted under torture.

According to local human rights organizations, during the Civil Emergency period alone (May 2004-May 2005) 80 civilians were killed: three died as a result of torture; 64 were assassinated; six were abducted and killed; and seven were killed during shootings. There were concerns that past human rights violations would not be prosecuted and that impunity could undermine prospects for a lasting peace. Despite provisions within the Memorandum of Understanding that a human rights court would be set up, the government announced that the court would not have powers to hear cases from the past.

Papua

In March, the military announced plans to increase troop numbers in Papua by 15,000. There were concerns that this might lead to more human rights violations in the province. Hundreds of additional military troops were reportedly sent to Merauke in October. Concerns were also expressed that troops withdrawn from NAD could be deployed in Papua.

Tight restrictions on access to Papua by international human rights monitors, as well as harassment and intimidation of local activists, hampered independent human rights monitoring. At least two peaceful supporters of Papuan independence were sentenced to long jail sentences. There were reports of arbitrary arrests, torture and ill-treatment.

In April, prisoners of conscience Yusak Pakage and Filep Karma were sentenced to 10 and 15 years in prison respectively for having raised the Papuan flag in December 2004. Both were imprisoned in Jayapura, Papua province, and had lodged appeals to the Supreme Court by the end of the year.

Security legislation

Between April and June, at least 64 civilians were arrested under the Law on Combating Criminal Acts of Terrorism. Concerns about the legislation remained, including the inadequate definition of acts of "terrorism"; provision for up to six months' detention without access to judicial review; and provisions allowing capital punishment. There were reports that 36 of those arrested were arbitrarily arrested and four of them were ill-treated.

In June, four peasant farmers — Jumaedi, Jumeri, Mastur Saputra and Sutikno — who were arrested in relation to a bomb attack in Tentena, Sulawesi district, in May, were reportedly beaten by police during interrogation. An internal investigation was initiated by the police but there were fears that it would not lead to full prosecution of those found responsible.

Excessive use of force

Members of the police used excessive force on numerous occasions, including against demonstrators and detainees.

In September, 37 people were reportedly wounded when the police shot into a crowd of around 700 peasant farmers in Tanak Awuk, Lombok island. The gathering was organized to commemorate National Peasants' Day and to discuss land issues. The police said they were responding to people attacking them. The National Human Rights Commission (Komnas HAM) sent a team to investigate the incident in October.

Torture and cruel, inhuman or degrading treatment

According to a survey conducted by a local non-governmental organization, over 81 per cent of prisoners arrested between January 2003 and April 2005 in Salemba detention centre, Cipinang prison and Pondok Bambu prison, all in Jakarta, were tortured or ill-treated. About 64 per cent were tortured or ill-treated during interrogation, 43 per cent during arrest and 25 per cent during detention.

For the 12th consecutive year, the request by the UN Special Rapporteur on torture to conduct research in the country was not granted.

At least 29 men convicted of gambling and two women were caned under local Sharia (Islamic law) in NAD.

Impunity

The Human Rights Courts proved unable to bring perpetrators of serious human rights violations to justice, including those in Tanjung Priok, Timor-Leste and Abepura.

In a report submitted to the UN Security Council, a Commission of Experts (CoE) appointed by the UN Secretary-General to review the prosecution of serious violations of human rights in Timor-Leste (then East Timor) in 1999 concluded that the judicial process before the Indonesian ad hoc Human Rights Court for Timor-Leste was "manifestly inadequate with respect to investigations, prosecutions and trials". The CoE pointed to provisions in the terms of reference of the Truth and Friendship Commission, officially established by the governments of Indonesia and Timor-Leste in March to reveal the truth about the 1999 events, which "contradict international standards on denial of impunity for serious crimes". In particular, the CoE stated that the Truth and Friendship Commission should not allow amnesties for cases of genocide, crimes against humanity and other grave human rights violations. Despite such criticism, the Truth and Friendship Commission was set up in August without appropriate changes to its mandate.

In July, an Appeals Court overturned the decision by the ad hoc Human Rights Court in Jakarta to convict 12 military officials of charges arising from the detention, torture and killing of Muslim protesters in Tanjung Priok, Jakarta, in 1984. No one has been held to account for these crimes.

In September, two police officers were acquitted by the Human Rights Court in Makassar and victims were denied reparations. The officers were charged with command responsibility for the killing of three people and the torture of many others in Abepura, Papua, in 2000. The initial investigation was marred by allegations of witness intimidation. The trial suffered severe delays in both the investigation and trial stages. The victims and their families lodged an appeal.

Investigations into other human rights violations were stalled. The report submitted in September 2004 by Komnas HAM to the Attorney General's Office suggesting that security forces had committed crimes against humanity in Wasior in June 2001 and Wamena in April 2003 were not acted upon during the year.

Freedom of expression

At least 19 prisoners of conscience were sentenced to prison terms during the year and three others sentenced in previous years remained in jail. They included peaceful political and independence activists, members of religious minorities, students and journalists. Defamation suits were also used against human rights activists, sending a chilling message to the human rights community.

In September Rebekka Zakaria, Eti Pangesti and Ratna Bangun were each sentenced by the Indramayu District Court, West Java, to three years' imprisonment for having violated the 2002 Child Protection Act. The three women, all prisoners of conscience, were accused by a chapter of the Indonesian Council of Muslim Clerics of enticing children to participate in a Sunday school programme and trying to convert them to Christianity. The trial was marred by Islamists who made threats inside and outside the courtroom to kill the accused. In November the High Court confirmed the sentence.

Death penalty

At least 10 people, including two convicted of terrorism-related charges, were sentenced to death, bringing to at least 82 the total number of people known to be under sentence of death.

At least one woman, Astini, and one man, Turmudi bin Kasturi, were executed by firing squad. Both were convicted of murder.

Violence against women

Women's organizations expressed concern about the lack of implementation of the 2004 Law on Domestic Violence. In November, the commission on violence against women reported that the Law had not contributed to reducing the high number of domestic violence cases, and that the lack of clarity of the definitions and regulations pertaining to the Law hampered full enforcement by local police and judges.

AI country reports/visits
Reports
- Recommendations to the Government of Indonesia on the occasion of the election of Ambassador Makarim Wibisono as Chair of the United Nations Commission on Human Rights (AI Index: ASA 21/001/2005)
- The role of human rights in the wake of the earthquake and tsunami: A briefing for Members of the Consultative Group on Indonesia, 19-20 January 2005 (AI Index: ASA 21/002/2005)
- A briefing for EU and ASEAN countries concerning the deployment of the Aceh Monitoring Mission to Nanggroe Aceh Darussalam Province (AI Index: ASA 21/017/2005)

Visits
In February, AI delegates attempted to investigate conditions facing internally displaced people in tsunami-affected areas in NAD, but were not granted the necessary authorization by the authorities.

AI delegates visited Jakarta in September and October.

IRAN

ISLAMIC REPUBLIC OF IRAN
Head of state: Leader of the Islamic Republic of Iran: Ayatollah Sayed 'Ali Khamenei
Head of government: President: Dr Mahmoud Ahmadinejad (replaced Hojjatoleslam val Moslemin Sayed Mohammad Khatami in August)
Death penalty: retentionist
International Criminal Court: signed
UN Women's Convention and its Optional Protocol: not signed

Scores of political prisoners, including prisoners of conscience, continued to serve prison sentences imposed following unfair trials in previous years. Hundreds more were arrested in 2005, mostly in connection with civil unrest in areas with large minority populations. Internet journalists and human rights defenders were among those detained arbitrarily without access to family or legal representation, often initially in secret detention centres. Intimidation of the families of those arrested persisted. Torture remained commonplace. At least 94 people were executed, including at least eight who were under 18 at the time of their alleged offence. Many sentences of flogging were imposed. The true number of those executed or subjected to corporal punishment was believed to be considerably higher than the cases reported.

Background
The political stalemate of the previous year continued until the election of a new president in June. Over 1,000 presidential candidates were excluded from the election by the Council of Guardians, which reviews laws and policies to ensure that they uphold Islamic tenets and the Constitution. All 89 women candidates were excluded on the basis of their gender under discriminatory selection procedures known as *gozinesh*. There were reports of arrests of people demonstrating against the elections. Up to 10 people were killed in separate pre-election bomb attacks in Ahvaz and Tehran, and six others were killed in a bomb attack in Ahvaz in October. The authorities faced armed opposition from Kurdish and other groups.

The election as President of former Revolutionary Guard Special Forces member Dr Mahmoud Ahmadinejad, who took office in August, completed the marginalization of pro-reform supporters from the political process and led to a concentration of power in the Office of the Supreme Leader, Ayatollah Sayed 'Ali Khamenei. In October, the Supreme Leader delegated some of his supervisory powers over the government to the Expediency Council, headed by defeated presidential candidate Hojjatoleslam AliAkbar Hashemi Rafsanjani.

Relations with the international community remained strained over human rights and Iran's nuclear programme, particularly after Iran announced in August that it was resuming uranium enrichment for civilian purposes. Iran accused foreign governments, particularly those of the USA and UK, of instigating unrest in border areas; the UK accused Iran of aiding anti-UK insurgency activities in Iraq. The European Union-Iran human rights dialogue was suspended because of diplomatic tensions.

In December, the UN General Assembly passed a resolution condemning the human rights situation in Iran.

Repression of minorities
Discriminatory laws and practices remained a source of social and political unrest and of human rights violations, particularly against Iran's ethnic and religious minorities. In July the UN Special Rapporteur on the right to adequate housing visited Iran. He found discrimination in the distribution of resources, and in access to and quality of housing, water and sanitation in areas populated by minorities.

Arabs
In April, at least 31 Arabs were killed and hundreds injured during clashes with the police following demonstrations in Ahvaz and elsewhere in Khuzestan province. Hundreds of other people were detained. The demonstrators were protesting against a letter allegedly written by a presidential adviser, who denied its authenticity, which set out policies for the reduction of the Arab population of Khuzestan. Waves of arrests continued throughout the year, particularly following bomb explosions in Ahvaz in June and October and attacks on oil installations in September and October.

▢ At least 81 people were arrested in November while attending an Arab cultural gathering called *Mahabis*. Those arrested included Zahra Nasser-Torfi, director of the Ahwaz al-Amjad cultural centre, who was reportedly tortured in detention, including with beatings and threats of execution, rape and other sexual abuse, before being released on bail to await trial.

Azeris
At the end of June, scores of ethnic Azeris participating in an annual cultural gathering at Babek Castle in Kalayber were arrested. At least 21 were later sentenced to prison terms of between three months and one year, some of which were suspended. Some were also banned from entering Kalayber for 10 years.

▢ Abbas Lisani, an Azeri butcher, was arrested during the Babek Castle event. He was released on bail in July and was sentenced in August to one year's imprisonment to be spent in internal exile after conviction of "spreading propaganda" and "disturbing public opinion". He was believed to have appealed against his sentence.

Kurds
In June, clashes between security forces and Kurds celebrating events in Iraq led to injuries to police officers and the arrest of dozens of demonstrators. In July, after Iranian security forces shot dead a Kurdish opposition activist, Shivan Qaderi, and reportedly dragged his body through the streets behind a jeep,

thousands of Kurds took to the streets to protest. Security forces reportedly killed up to 21 people, injured scores more and arrested at least 190. In further clashes in October and November, at least one person, Shoresh Amiri, was killed, several people were injured and others were arrested.

⌷ Dr Roya Toloui, a women's rights activist, and two journalists, Ajlal Qavami and Sa'id Sa'edi, were among the Kurds arrested in August. All were released on bail in October and were reported to be facing political charges that can carry the death penalty.

Religious minorities
Members of Iran's religious minorities were detained solely in connection with their faith.

⌷ Hamid Pourmand, who had converted to Christianity from Islam over 25 years previously, was sentenced in February by a military court to three years' imprisonment on charges of deceiving the Iranian armed forces about his religion and "acts against national security". In May he was acquitted of apostasy.

⌷ At least 66 Baha'is were detained and two remained held at the end of the year. Mehran Kawsari and Bahram Mashhadi were sentenced to three years and one year in prison respectively in connection with an open letter sent to President Khatami in November 2004.

Human rights defenders

The registration process for independent non-governmental organizations remained a barrier to their effective operation, and individual human rights defenders remained at risk of reprisal for their work.

⌷ In July, Abdolfattah Soltani, a lawyer and co-founder of the Centre for Defenders of Human Rights, was detained. He was reportedly accused of releasing "secret and classified national intelligence" in connection with his work defending an espionage case. He remained in detention at the end of the year with limited access to his family and no access to his lawyer.

⌷ Prisoner of conscience Akbar Ganji, an investigative reporter who uncovered the involvement of government officials in the murder of intellectuals and journalists in the 1990s, continued to serve a six-year prison sentence imposed after he was convicted of vaguely worded charges including "acting against national security". Following a hunger strike in protest at being denied independent medical treatment outside prison, accompanied by considerable domestic and international protests, he was temporarily released for medical treatment in July. He was returned to prison in September and placed in solitary confinement for over six weeks. His wife said he had been beaten by security forces in hospital.

Torture and cruel, inhuman and degrading punishments

Torture continued to be routine in many prisons and detention centres. At least five people died in custody. In several cases, torture or ill-treatment may have been a factor. Denial of medical treatment to put pressure on political prisoners emerged as an increasingly common practice.

In July a report by the judiciary detailed human rights violations, including torture, of prisoners and detainees. It stated that measures had been taken to address the problems, but gave no details.

⌷ In September, Arezoo Siabi Shahrivar, a photographer, was arrested along with up to 14 other women, at a ceremony commemorating the 1988 "prison massacre" in Evin prison, Tehran, in which thousands of political prisoners were executed. In detention she was suspended from the ceiling, beaten with a wire cable and sexually abused.

⌷ A man from Shiraz sentenced to 100 lashes in 2004 for homosexual activities alleged that he had been tortured and threatened with death by security forces.

At least three amputations were carried out. It remained common for courts to hand down sentences of flogging.

Update: Zahra Kazemi

In November the Appeals Court upheld the acquittal of an Intelligence Ministry official accused of killing Canadian-Iranian photojournalist Zahra Kazemi in custody in July 2003. A new investigation into the killing was announced.

Death penalty

At least 94 people were executed in 2005, including at least eight aged under 18 at the time of the crime. Scores more were reported to have been sentenced to death, including at least 11 who were under 18 at the time of the offence. The true figures were probably much higher. Death sentences continued to be imposed for vaguely worded offences such as "corruption on earth".

⌷ In October, a woman was reportedly sentenced to death by stoning, despite a moratorium on the use of this punishment introduced in 2002.

In January, the UN Committee on the Rights of the Child urged Iran to suspend immediately the execution of people aged under 18 at the time of the crime, and to abolish the death penalty for people who commit crimes before they are 18. Despite Iran's statement that there was a moratorium on the use of the death penalty against juvenile offenders, Iman Farrokhi was executed on the very day that Iran's report was considered by the Committee. He was 17 when he allegedly killed a soldier in a fight.

Following domestic and international protests, the death sentences of some women and of men aged under 18 at the time of their alleged offence were suspended or lifted.

Freedom of expression and association

Freedom of expression and association remained severely curtailed. Journalists and webloggers were detained and imprisoned and some newspapers were closed down. Relatives of detainees or those sought by the authorities remained at risk of harassment or intimidation.

Press Courts were reintroduced in October comprising a panel of three judges and a jury selected by the judiciary. Some journalists' organizations criticized the composition of the juries.

Mohammad Reza Nasab Abdolahi, a student campaigner for human rights and a newspaper editor, was sentenced in January to six months' imprisonment and a fine for "insulting the country's leader and making anti-government propaganda". He was released in August. His pregnant wife, Najameh Oumidparvar, was detained in March for 24 days after posting a message on her weblog that her husband apparently wrote before his arrest.

Women's rights

The UN Special Rapporteur on violence against women visited Iran in January and February. She criticized the arbitrary arrest, torture and ill-treatment of women, including women human rights defenders, and called on Iran to adopt a national action plan to promote and protect human rights that would eliminate violence against women. She also expressed particular concern at discriminatory laws and failures in the administration of justice which result in impunity for perpetrators and perpetuate discrimination and violence against women.

The UN Special Rapporteur on the right to adequate housing noted discrimination against women in relation to housing and a lack of safe houses for women who are victims of violence.

AI country reports/ visits

Statements
- Iran: Prisoner of Conscience Appeal Case – Hamid Pourmand: Imprisonment due to religious belief (AI Index: MDE 13/060/2005)
- Iran: Medical Action – Akbar Ganji (AI Index: MDE 13/036/2005)

IRAQ

REPUBLIC OF IRAQ
Head of state: Jalal Talabani (replaced Shaikh Ghazi al-Yawar in April)
Head of the interim government: Ibrahim al-Ja'fari (replaced Iyad 'Allawi in April)
Death penalty: retentionist
International Criminal Court: not signed
UN Women's Convention: ratified with reservations
Optional Protocol to UN Women's Convention: not signed

Both the US-led Multinational Force (MNF) and Iraqi security forces committed grave human rights violations, including torture and ill-treatment, arbitrary detention without charge or trial, and excessive use of force resulting in civilian deaths. Armed groups fighting against the MNF and the Iraqi government were responsible for grave human rights abuses, including the deliberate killing of thousands of civilians in bomb and other attacks, hostage-taking and torture. Dozens of people were sentenced to death by criminal courts and at least three were executed. Former President Saddam Hussein and seven others were brought to trial. Women and girls continued to be harassed and lived in fear as a result of the continuing lack of security.

Background

Elections for the Transitional National Assembly (TNA), Iraq's interim parliament, held on 30 January, saw a high turn-out in the south and in Iraqi Kurdistan. However, most Sunnis boycotted the polls, apparently in support of calls by Sunni religious and political figures opposed to holding elections while the MNF remained in Iraq; others did not vote because they feared reprisals from armed groups. A Shi'a alliance received the majority of votes and won 140 of the 275 seats in the assembly. A Kurdish alliance won 75 seats, and a coalition led by outgoing Prime Minister Iyad 'Allawi won 40 seats.

After weeks of deadlock, an agreement between the Shi'a and Kurdish alliances led to the formation of a new government in May. It was headed by Ibrahim al-Ja'fari, leader of the al-Da'wa Party and member of the Shi'a alliance, and included several Sunnis. Jalal Talabani, leader of the Patriotic Union of Kurdistan (PUK), was appointed President.

Further protracted negotiations occurred before the Constitution Drafting Committee agreed a new draft Constitution in late August, two weeks after the deadline set under the Transitional Administrative Law. On 15 October, the new Constitution was put to a national referendum and approved overall by a three to one margin, although it was rejected by a two to one margin in two provinces with majority Sunni populations, al-Anbar and Salahuddin. It was agreed that the new parliament would establish a committee to consider possible amendments.

Elections for the new Council of Representatives — a 275-seat parliament which is to hold office for a four-year term — were held on 15 December and contested by Sunni as well as Shi'a and Kurdish parties. There was a high turn-out, officially estimated at 70 per cent, with most votes cast along ethnic and religious lines. A new government had yet to be formed by the end of the year. Against this political backdrop, grave abuses, including war crimes and crimes against humanity, were committed by armed groups, the MNF and the Iraqi security forces.

Abuses by armed groups

Armed groups fighting against the MNF and Iraqi security forces were responsible for grave human rights abuses. Hundreds of Iraqi civilians were reportedly killed or injured in attacks by armed groups. Some, including translators, drivers and others employed by the MNF, were attacked apparently because they were considered "collaborators"; others, including civil servants, government officials, judges and journalists, were singled out because of their links to the Iraqi administration. Many others were targeted because they belonged to specific religious and ethnic groups. Civilians were also killed and injured in indiscriminate car bombings and suicide attacks by armed groups targetting Iraqi police and government forces, and military convoys and bases of the MNF.

Armed groups were also responsible for abducting dozens of Iraqis as well as foreign nationals and holding them hostage. Many of the hostages were killed. Most were civilians.

▢ On 25 January, a judge, Qais Hashem al-Shamari, the secretary of Iraq's Council of Judges, was shot dead together with his son in an ambush by armed men in a car. The judge and his son had just left home and were driving in eastern Baghdad. The armed group Ansar al-Sunna claimed responsibility for the killings.

▢ On 28 February, at least 118 people were killed and 132 injured in a suicide car bomb attack near a police station and a busy market in al-Hilla, south of Baghdad. The victims included people queuing outside a health clinic to receive medical certificates which would enable them to apply for jobs in the army and police. Many other victims were at the market across the road. In a statement posted on the Internet a group called al-Qa'ida of Jihad Organization in the Land of Two Rivers claimed responsibility for the attack.

▢ On 14 September, a suicide bomber drew scores of people to his van with promises of work and then detonated a bomb in al-'Uruba Square in al-Kadhimiya, a predominantly Shi'a district of Baghdad. At least 114 civilians, including children, were killed and scores injured.

▢ On 26 November, four human rights defenders, members of the Christian Peacemaker Teams — Tom Fox, Norman Kember, James Loney and Harmeet Singh Sooden — were abducted in Baghdad. An armed group, Swords of the Truth, claimed responsibility and demanded the release of all Iraqi prisoners. The four men were still held at the end of the year.

Detention without charge or trial

Thousands of people were held without charge or trial by the MNF. Most were Sunnis arrested in the so-called Sunni Triangle where armed groups opposed to the MNF and the Iraqi government were especially active. Most were denied access to lawyers and families for the first two months of detention.

US military forces continued to control four main detention centres: Abu Ghraib Prison in Baghdad; Camp Bucca in Um Qasr, near Basra in the south; Camp Cropper near Baghdad International Airport; and Fort Suse, near Suleimaniya in the north. At the end of November, more than 14,000 detainees were being held in these detention centres; more than 1,400 had been held for more than a year. Among those held were nine women detained in Camp Cropper.

▢ 'Ali 'Omar Ibrahim al-Mashhadani, a 36-year-old cameraman, was detained by US forces on 8 August. He was arrested after a search of his home in al-Ramadi following a shooting in the city. His brother, who was arrested with him and then released, said that the soldiers arrested both of them after they saw film material taken by 'Ali 'Omar Ibrahim al-Mashhadani. At the end of the year 'Ali 'Omar Ibrahim al-Mashhadani was still held without charge or trial at Camp Bucca.

Thousands of detainees were released including some 500 security detainees who were released by the MNF in October, a few days before the start of the holy month of Ramadan.

▢ Two Palestinian students, Jayab Mahmood Hassan Humeidat and Ahmad Badran Faris, both aged 22, returned to their homes in the West Bank after they were released at the end of August. They had been detained without charge or trial by US forces for 28 months in Camp Bucca.

Torture and ill-treatment

There was evidence of widespread torture and ill-treatment by the Iraqi security forces. Methods of torture included hanging by the arms, burning with cigarettes, beatings, the use of electric shocks on different parts of the body, strangulation, the breaking of limbs and sexual abuse. Torture and ill-treatment were reported in secret detention centres, police stations and official detention centres in different parts of the country as well as in buildings in Baghdad under the control of the Interior Ministry.

▢ In February, three alleged members of the Badr Organization died in custody after being arrested by Iraqi police at a police checkpoint. The bodies of the three men, Majbal 'Adnan Latif, his brother 'Ali 'Adnan Latif, and 'Aidi Mahassin Lifteh, were found three days later, bearing marks of beatings and electric shocks.

▢ In February, a 46-year-old housewife from Mosul, Khalida Zakiya, was shown on the Iraqi TV programme "Terrorism in the Grip of Justice" alleging that she had supported an armed group. However, she later stated that she had been coerced into making a false confession. She reported that during her detention by Interior Ministry forces she had been whipped with a cable and threatened with sexual abuse.

◻ In July, 12 men were detained by the Iraqi police in Baghdad's al-'Amirya district. Nine of the 12 suffocated to death after being confined in a police van. The Iraqi authorities suggested that the 12 were members of an armed group who had engaged in an exchange of fire with US or Iraqi forces. However, other sources claimed they were a group of bricklayers who were arrested as suspected insurgents and then tortured by police commandos before being confined in a police van in extremely high temperatures for up to 14 hours. Medical staff at the Yarmouk hospital in Baghdad, where the bodies of those who died were taken on 11 July, were reported to have confirmed that some of them bore signs of torture, including electric shocks.

◻ In November, US forces announced that they had found 173 detainees confined secretly in a building controlled by the Interior Ministry. Many had been tortured, ill-treated and were malnourished. Shortly thereafter, the Iraqi government launched an investigation into these and other allegations of torture.

There were also reports that the MNF tortured or ill-treated detainees.

◻ In September, several members of the US National Guard's 184th Infantry Regiment were sentenced to prison terms in connection with torture or ill-treatment of Iraqis. The detainees had reportedly been arrested in March following an attack on a power plant near Baghdad. According to media reports, an electric stun gun had been used on handcuffed and blindfolded detainees.

Death penalty
Dozens of people were sentenced to death by Iraqi criminal courts during the year. The first executions since Iraq re-imposed the death penalty in August 2004 were carried out in September. At the end of the year dozens of people remained on death row.

◻ Ahmad al-Jaf, Jasim 'Abbas and 'Uday Dawud al-Dulaimi, who were believed to be members of the armed group Ansar al-Sunna, were sentenced to death in May by a criminal court in the town of al-Kut, about 170km south-east of Baghdad. The three men were found guilty of kidnapping, rape and murder. They were executed in September by hanging.

Unlawful attacks
MNF forces used excessive force, resulting in civilian casualties. There were reports that they failed to take necessary precautions to minimize risk to civilians.

◻ In August, US troops shot dead Walid Khaled, an Iraqi sound engineer working for the *Reuters* news agency, and wounded his colleague, Haidar Kadhem. The soldiers fired at the car in which the men were travelling to the scene of an earlier insurgent attack on an Iraqi police convoy in the al-'Adel district in Baghdad. A US official later claimed that US soldiers had taken "appropriate action" according to their rules of engagement.

◻ On 16 October, some 70 people were killed near al-Ramadi in a US air raid. Local Iraqi police said that about 20 of those killed were civilians, including children who had gathered around wreckage of a

military vehicle. US military officials initially said that those killed were "terrorists". However, two days later they reportedly stated that they would investigate allegations that civilians had been killed.

Trial of Saddam Hussein and other former officials
Former President Saddam Hussein was brought to trial on 19 October together with seven others, including former Vice-President Taha Yassin Ramadhan and Barzan Ibrahim al-Tikriti, the former head of the intelligence service (Mukhabarat). They were on trial before the Supreme Iraqi Criminal Tribunal (SICT), formerly the Iraqi Special Tribunal. They were accused in connection with the executions of 148 people from al-Dujail, a predominantly Shi'a village, following an assassination attempt against Saddam Hussein when he visited the village in 1982.

The trial was held in Baghdad's heavily fortified Green Zone amid concern for the safety of those participating and was marred by procedural irregularities. For example, the names of prosecution witnesses were withheld from the defence and the court's name and procedures were amended immediately before the proceedings opened. The defendants, all of whom could face death sentences if convicted, denied the charges and questioned the legitimacy of the court.

On 20 October, defence lawyer Sa'dun al-Janabi was abducted from his office in Baghdad by armed men and murdered. A second defence lawyer, 'Adil al-Zubeidi, was killed in November when gunmen opened fire at the car in which he was travelling. The trial was continuing at the end of the year.

Violence against women
Women and girls continued to face threats, attacks and harassment. Their freedoms were severely curtailed as a result of the lack of security on the streets. Many women and girls were under pressure to wear the hijab or Islamic veil and change their behaviour. Women were killed and abducted by armed groups.

◻ On 20 February, Ra'ida Mohammad al-Wazzan, aged 35, a journalist and news presenter for *al-'Iraqiya*, the Iraqi state television channel, and her 10-year-old son were abducted by gunmen. The boy was released three days later but Ra'ida Mohammad al-Wazzan's body was found on a street in Mosul on 25 February. She had been shot in the head. She had previously been threatened by armed men who demanded that she quit her job.

Northern Iraq
Human rights abuses were also reported from areas of northern Iraq controlled since 1991 by the Kurdistan Democratic Party (KDP) and the Patriotic Union of Kurdistan (PUK).

◻ On 7 September, security forces in Kalar, a town in the PUK-controlled area, killed one person and injured some 30 others when they fired on protesters demonstrating outside the governor's office against fuel shortages and poor public services.

▭ Kamal Sayid Qadir, a Kurdish writer with Austrian citizenship, was arrested in October in Arbil by members of Parastin, the KDP's intelligence service. In December, he was sentenced to 30 years' imprisonment for defamation after an unfair trial. He had published articles on the Internet which were critical of the KDP leadership.

AI country reports/ visits
Reports
- Iraq: Decades of suffering, now women deserve better (AI Index: MDE 14/001/2005)
- Iraq: Iraqi Special Tribunal – fair trials not guaranteed (AI Index: MDE 14/007/2005)
- Iraq: In cold blood – abuses by armed groups (AI Index: MDE 14/009/2005)
- Iraq: The new Constitution must protect human rights (AI Index: MDE 14/023/2005)

Visit
In October an AI delegation observed the opening session of the trial of former President Saddam Hussain and seven others.

IRELAND

IRELAND
Head of state: Mary McAleese
Head of government: Bertie Ahern
Death penalty: abolitionist for all crimes
International Criminal Court: ratified
UN Women's Convention: ratified with reservations
Optional Protocol to UN Women's Convention: ratified

There were concerns about the treatment of people with mental disabilities. Police ill-treatment and abuses of power were reported. New counter-terrorism legislation raised concerns about potential violations of fundamental human rights. There were continuing concerns about the effectiveness of attempts to address discrimination and about the prevalence of violence in the family.

Background
The bill published in 2003 to incorporate the Rome Statute of the International Criminal Court into Irish law had still not been enacted by the end of the year.

In October the Irish Human Rights Commission published its annual report. The report raised serious concern about the Commission's lack of resources and the "democratic deficit" in parliamentary procedures for scrutinizing legislation with human rights implications.

Treatment of people with mental disabilities
The first annual report of the Inspector of Mental Health Services, published in July, found unacceptable levels of care in some services, and inadequate facilities and services for children.

Procedures for the compulsory detention of people in mental health facilities, and independent tribunals to review decisions, provided for under the Mental Health Act (2001) had not come into force. Procedures under 1945 legislation continued to operate, in breach of international standards in relation to the deprivation of liberty.

Policing
The *Garda Síochána* (Police) Act (2005) set out for the first time in statutory form the functions of the police (Garda) and provided for the establishment of a Code of Ethics for the service. The Act also established an independent Garda Ombudsman Commission to investigate complaints against members of the police service. However, it adopted a narrow definition of serious cases which would automatically come under the jurisdiction of the Ombudsman Commission.

In April the police service published an audit of its compliance with international human rights standards. The audit documented abuse of powers, ill-treatment, institutional racism and unaccountability within the service.

▭ The Tribunal of Inquiry into complaints against Garda officers in the Donegal Division issued its second report in June, revealing systematic violations of the rights of the McBrearty family at the centre of the inquiry. The tribunal found gross negligence at senior levels of the service amounting to criminal negligence, and corruption and a lack of objectivity at lower levels.

Counter-terrorism
There were mounting concerns that the government had not satisfactorily investigated allegations that Shannon airport may have been used as a transit point in the transfer of terrorism suspects, with the involvement of the USA or its agents, in circumstances that put them at risk of torture or cruel, inhuman or degrading treatment (extraordinary rendition).

The Criminal Justice (Terrorist Offences) Act (2005), adopted to give effect to the European Union Framework Decision on Combating Terrorism, significantly expanded law enforcement powers. Its provisions contained such broad and vague definitions that there were concerns that it could lead to violations of the rights of association, peaceful assembly and freedom of expression.

Places of detention
The annual report of the Inspector of Prisons and Places of Detention published in July noted that prison conditions fell below international standards, with overcrowding and a lack of adequate sanitation facilities. Mentally ill prisoners continued to be held in prisons rather than in specialized mental health facilities. A report published by the Probation and

Welfare Service highlighted the unnecessary incarceration of homeless people or people with mental illness.

Asylum-seekers and migrants

A process of public consultation began on government proposals for consolidating and reforming immigration legislation. These included commitments to address trafficking and to provide protection for migrant women experiencing domestic violence. Proposals did not address the inappropriate use of prisons for holding immigration detainees.

The UN Committee on the Elimination of Racial Discrimination expressed concern about the treatment of asylum-seekers and the failure to prevent the exploitation of migrant workers, and called on the government to review its policy of dispersal of asylum-seekers.

It urged the Irish government to incorporate the UN Convention against Racism into Ireland's domestic legislation.

Discrimination

The first National Action Plan Against Racism was launched in January. However, there was concern that it lacked effective accountability mechanisms and failed to address institutional racism within government bodies.

The UN Committee on the Elimination of Racial Discrimination questioned the effectiveness of government measures to improve access by the Traveller community to economic and social rights, and rejected the government's contention that Travellers were not a distinct ethnic minority group.

The Committee urged the government to introduce in criminal law a provision that committing an offence with a racist motivation or aim constitutes an aggravating circumstance, allowing for a more severe punishment; establish an effective monitoring mechanism to carry out investigations into allegations of racially motivated police misconduct; consider expanding the scope of equality legislation so as to cover the whole range of government functions and activities; review its security procedures and practices at entry points with a view to ensuring that they are carried out in a non-discriminatory manner; and take measures with regard to the special needs of women belonging to minority and other groups at risk.

Women

There were concerns that the government had taken insufficient measures to identify, combat and redress violence against women.

In July, the UN Committee on the Elimination of Discrimination against Women expressed its concern at the prevalence of violence against women and girls in Ireland; the low prosecution and conviction rates of perpetrators; high withdrawal rates of complaints; and inadequate funding for organizations that provide support services to victims. It also criticized the state's failure to address trafficking of women and children.

The Committee was also critical of the persistence of traditional stereotypical views of the social roles and responsibilities of women, reflected in the Constitution, in women's educational choices and employment patterns, and in women's low participation in political and public life.

Children

Children continued to be detained in adult prisons. The Ombudsman for Children, in her first annual report, was concerned that the statutory exclusion of certain groups of children, in particular those detained in prisons and Garda stations, from her Office's investigatory remit, conflicted with the UN Convention on the Rights of the Child, and could preclude her Office from executing effectively its role and functions.

The report on clerical sex abuse in the diocese of Ferns (the Ferns Inquiry) published in October was critical of Catholic Church authorities, the Garda and the health authority in their handling of more than 100 allegations of child sexual abuse made between 1962 and 2002. It highlighted ongoing gaps in child protection, and the need to place government guidelines on mandatory reporting of child abuse on a legislative basis.

ISRAEL AND THE OCCUPIED TERRITORIES

STATE OF ISRAEL
Head of state: Moshe Katzav
Head of government: Ariel Sharon
Death penalty: abolitionist for ordinary crimes
International Criminal Court: signed but declared intention not to ratify
UN Women's Convention: ratified with reservations
Optional Protocol to UN Women's Convention: not signed

Israel withdrew its settlers and troops from the Gaza Strip and dismantled four small settlements in the northern West Bank. However, it continued to build and expand illegal settlements and related infrastructure, including a 600km fence/wall, on Palestinian land in the occupied West Bank. Military blockades and restrictions imposed by Israel on the movement of Palestinians within the Occupied Territories continued to cause high unemployment and poverty among the Palestinian population.

There was much less violence between Israelis and Palestinians, although attacks by both sides continued. Some 190 Palestinians, including around 50 children, were killed by Israeli forces, and 50 Israelis, including six children, were killed by Palestinian armed groups. Israeli forces carried out unlawful attacks and routinely used excessive force against peaceful demonstrators protesting against the destruction of Palestinian agricultural land and the Israeli army's construction of the fence/wall. Israeli settlers frequently attacked Palestinian farmers, destroying orchards and preventing cultivation of their land. Israeli soldiers and settlers responsible for unlawful killings and other abuses against Palestinians and their property generally had impunity. Thousands of Palestinians were arrested by Israeli forces throughout the Occupied Territories on suspicion of security offences. Israeli conscientious objectors continued to be imprisoned for refusing to serve in the army.

Background
Following negotiations between the Palestinian Authority (PA), Egyptian mediators and the main Palestinian armed groups early in the year, the latter declared an open-ended *tahadiyeh* (quiet), a pledge not to initiate attacks against Israel. The Israeli army likewise announced that it would refrain from attacking Palestinian targets. Despite this, both sides carried out new attacks, claiming these were in response to attacks by the other. Nevertheless, the year saw a marked reduction in attacks and killings by both sides.

The removal of Israeli settlers and troops from the Gaza Strip under Prime Minister Sharon's "disengagement plan" sharply divided the governing Likud party. In November, Prime Minister Sharon resigned from Likud and formed a new party, prompting early elections, scheduled for March 2006.

Israeli forces and Palestinian armed groups committed acts that were part of a pattern of war crimes and crimes against humanity.

Killings and attacks by the army
Some 190 Palestinians, including around 50 children, were killed by the Israeli army in the Occupied Territories. Many were killed unlawfully, in deliberate and reckless shootings, shelling and air strikes in densely populated residential areas, or as a result of excessive use of force. Some were extrajudicially executed and others died in armed clashes with Israeli soldiers. Hundreds of others were injured.

▭ Seven children aged between 10 and 17 were killed and five others seriously wounded in an Israeli air strike as they were picking strawberries in the northern Gaza Strip town of Beit Lahiya on 4 January. Those killed included six members of the Ghaben family – Rajah, Jaber, Mahmoud, Bassam, Hani and Mohammed – and Jibril al-Kaseeh.

▭ On 27 October, Karam Mohammed Abu Naji, 14, Salah Said Abu Naji, 15, and Rami Riyad Assaf, 17, were killed when the Israeli army launched an air strike on a car travelling near the Jabalya refugee camp in the Gaza

Strip. As well as the three child bystanders, all four people in the car were killed. Nineteen other bystanders, including seven children, were injured. Two members of a Palestinian armed group were believed to be the intended target.

▭ On 3 November, 12-year-old Ahmed al-Khatib was fatally wounded by Israeli soldiers during a raid in Jenin refugee camp and died three days later. The army stated that he had been playing with a toy gun and soldiers had mistaken him for a gunman.

Killings and attacks by Palestinian armed groups
Palestinian armed groups killed 41 Israeli civilians, including six children, in suicide bombings, shootings and mortar attacks in Israel and the Occupied Territories. Most of the attacks were carried out by al-Aqsa Martyrs Brigades, an offshoot of Fatah, and Islamic Jihad. Nine Israeli soldiers were also killed by Palestinian armed groups, most of them in the Occupied Territories.

▭ On 12 July, Rachel Ben Abu and Nofar Horowitz, both aged 16, Julia Voloshin, 31, Anya Lifshitz, 50, and Corporal Moshe Maor, 21, were killed in a suicide bombing carried out by Islamic Jihad in a shopping mall in Hasharon, near Natania.

▭ Palestinian gunmen shot dead Oz Ben-Meir, 15, Matat Rosenfeld-Adler, 21, and Kineret Mandel, 23, at the Gush Etzion Junction in the West Bank on 16 October. A 14-year-old boy, another civilian and a soldier were also injured in the attack. Al-Aqsa Martyrs Brigades claimed responsibility for the killings.

Attacks by Israeli settlers in the Occupied Territories
Israeli settlers in the West Bank repeatedly attacked Palestinians and their property. They destroyed crops, cut down or burned olive trees, contaminated water reservoirs and prevented farmers from cultivating their land, in order to force them to leave. Such attacks increased during the olive harvest months of October and November.

▭ In March and April, Israeli settlers spread toxic chemicals in fields around Palestinian villages in the southern Hebron Hills and near Salfit. The chemicals were spread in areas where Palestinian farmers graze their sheep, effectively depriving them of their livelihood. The farmers were forced to quarantine their flocks and stop using the milk, cheese and meat during the productive season.

▭ On 16 October some 75 acres of olive groves belonging to Palestinian villagers near Salem in the northern West Bank were burned by Israeli settlers. Much of the villagers' land was cut off from the village by a settlers' road leading to the nearby Elon Moreh settlement. For years, Israeli settlers from Elon Moreh had prevented Palestinian villagers from accessing their land under threat of attacks.

Israeli settlers also attacked Israeli and international peace activists and human rights defenders who sought to document their attacks on Palestinians.

▭ On 26 September settlers from the Havat Ma'on

settlement outpost assaulted Israeli peace activists and a film crew. Ra'anan Alexanderovitch was severely beaten and injured by a settler armed with an M16 assault rifle, and some of the crew's equipment was stolen by the attackers.

Israeli soldiers and police at times intervened to stop settlers attacking Palestinians, often when Israeli or international peace activists were present. However, in most cases they failed to intervene and often responded to settlers' attacks by imposing further restrictions on the local Palestinian population, as demanded by the settlers.

Administration of justice and impunity

The Israeli army detained hundreds of Palestinians. Many were released without charge but hundreds were charged with security offences. Trials before military courts often did not meet international standards of fairness, with allegations of torture and ill-treatment of detainees inadequately investigated. Some 1,000 Palestinians were detained administratively without charge or trial during the year. Family visits for Palestinian detainees were severely restricted and in many cases forbidden as relatives were denied permits to enter Israel, where thousands of Palestinians were imprisoned.

In July Israel passed a discriminatory law denying Palestinian victims compensation for abuses inflicted by Israeli forces.

Israeli soldiers, police and settlers who committed unlawful killings, ill-treatment and other attacks against Palestinians and their property commonly did so with impunity. Investigations were rare, as were prosecutions of the perpetrators, which in most cases did not lead to convictions. By contrast, Israel used all means at its disposal, including assassinations, collective punishment and other measures that violate international law, against Palestinians who carried out attacks against Israelis or who were suspected of direct or indirect involvement in such attacks. Palestinians convicted of killing Israelis were usually sentenced to life imprisonment by Israeli military courts, whereas in the exceptional cases when Israelis were convicted of killing or abusing Palestinians, light sentences were imposed.

▢ In August, Israeli soldier Taysir Hayb was sentenced to eight years' imprisonment for the killing of UK peace activist Tom Hurndall in the Gaza Strip in 2003. He was convicted of manslaughter, not murder, as well as obstruction of justice, providing false information and unbecoming conduct.

▢ In November an Israeli army company commander was acquitted of all charges in relation to the killing of a 13-year-old girl, Iman al-Hams. She had been shot dead by Israeli soldiers in October 2004 in Rafah in the southern Gaza Strip while walking near a fortified Israeli army tower opposite her school. According to an army communication recording of the incident, the commander had stated that "anything that's mobile, that moves in the zone, even if it's a three-year-old, needs to be killed". Neither the commander nor any other soldier was charged with the girl's murder as the court accepted that the commander had not breached regulations on when to open fire. The court focused on whether he had acted improperly by repeatedly shooting at the child as she lay injured or dead.

▢ In September, Yehoshua Elitzur, an Israeli settler, was convicted of killing Sayel Jabara, a 46-year-old Palestinian, near the West Bank village of Salem in September 2004. Even though Yehoshua Elitzur was armed with an M16 assault rifle and shot dead an unarmed man, the court contended that there was no proof that he intended to kill Sayel Jabara. It convicted him of manslaughter, not murder. He remained free as he had been released on bail within a day of his arrest and did not appear in court for his verdict.

Imprisonment of conscientious objectors

Several Israelis who refused to serve in the army because they opposed Israel's occupation of the Occupied Territories and refused to serve there were imprisoned for up to four months. They were prisoners of conscience.

Expansion of settlements and construction of the fence/wall

While international attention focused on the Gaza "disengagement plan", Israel continued to expand illegal Israeli settlements and stepped up construction of a 600km fence/wall through the West Bank, including in and around East Jerusalem. The construction compounded the military blockades and other stringent restrictions imposed by the Israeli army on the movement of the Palestinian population throughout the Occupied Territories, including measures which increasingly cut off East Jerusalem from the rest of the West Bank.

Israel seized and destroyed large areas of Palestinian land to build roads for Israeli settlers, military checkpoints and the fence/wall through the West Bank. Palestinians were increasingly confined to restricted areas and denied freedom of movement between towns and villages within the Occupied Territories. Many Palestinians were cut off from their farmland, their main source of livelihood, and others were prevented from accessing their workplaces, education and health facilities, and other services.

Israeli government officials repeatedly reiterated their determination to strengthen most of the Israeli settlements in the West Bank, where some 450,000 Israeli settlers live, and to build new ones, notably in and around East Jerusalem. The Israeli government took no steps to fulfil its commitment to dismantle settlement outposts established since 2001 in the West Bank. In March former State Prosecutor Talia Sasson published a report, commissioned by the government, which noted that unauthorized settlement outposts continued to be established and expanded by the authorities, contrary to the government's promise to dismantle them.

Restrictions on movement and violations of economic and social rights

Restrictions on the movement of people and goods remained the primary cause of high unemployment and poverty in the Occupied Territories, with about

50 per cent of Palestinians living below the poverty line and forced to depend on charity. The restrictions hindered the access of Palestinians to hospitals, schools and jobs. Cases of malnutrition and other health problems resulted from the extreme poverty.

With few exceptions, Palestinians were not allowed to move between the West Bank and the Gaza Strip and had to obtain special permits from the Israeli army to move between towns and villages within the West Bank. Travel on main roads in the West Bank, which were freely used by Israeli settlers living in illegal settlements, was forbidden to Palestinians or restricted. Such restrictions were increased in reprisal for attacks by Palestinian armed groups and during Jewish holidays.

Increasing restrictions were also imposed by the Israeli army on the movement of Israeli and international peace activists to prevent them from participating in peaceful demonstrations and other solidarity activities with Palestinian villagers in the West Bank.

During and after its withdrawal from the Gaza Strip, Israel closed the Gaza-Egypt border, the sole point of exit and entry for Palestinians living in the Gaza Strip. The border was allowed to reopen at the end of November under the supervision of a European Union force. Israel maintained control of the Gaza Strip's sea and airspace, and of the passage of goods in and out of the Gaza Strip.

Destruction of homes and properties

Although far less extensive than in previous years, destruction of Palestinian homes and land by Israeli forces continued. Large areas of agricultural land were seized and destroyed, and thousands of trees uprooted, to make way for the fence/wall and for settlers' roads through the West Bank. Israeli settlers also destroyed Palestinian farmland in order to open new roads to connect recently established settlement outposts. Even though these outposts contravened government policy, the army rarely intervened to prevent such actions.

Scores of Palestinian homes were demolished by the Israeli army and security forces in the West Bank, including in and around East Jerusalem, on the grounds that they were built without a building permit. The Israeli authorities denied permission to Palestinians to build on their own land in large areas of the West Bank, and at the same time continued to approve the construction and expansion of illegal Israeli settlements on Palestinian land.

◻ On 5 April the Israeli army destroyed the Zaatreh family home in the East Jerusalem suburb of 'Azariya to make way for the fence/wall, which was built on the ruins of the house. The demolition left 29 members of the family homeless, including 16 children. Although the land belongs to the family, they could not obtain a building permit so their house was demolished.

◻ During the week beginning 4 July the Israeli army demolished some 35 stone and metal structures/shacks in the village of Tana, near Nablus, in the northern West Bank. Fourteen of the structures were home to the villagers and the rest were used to store fodder or shelter sheep and goats, which provide the main source of livelihood for the village. A school, which had been built in 2001 and had served the village's children since then, was also demolished, along with two water reservoirs. The army took advantage of the absence of the villagers, who live a semi-nomadic life and spend the hottest months of July and August in nearby Beit Furik, to destroy much of their habitat. The reason given for the destruction was that the structures had been built without a permit.

Violence and discrimination against women

The UN Committee on the Elimination of Discrimination against Women examined Israel's report in July. It expressed concern about laws governing personal status which are based on religion and about the 2003 law which bars family unification for Israelis who marry Palestinians from the Occupied Territories. It called on the Israeli government to intensify efforts to combat trafficking in women and girls; to take measures to improve the status of Israeli Arab women, especially in the fields of education and health, and to eliminate discrimination against Bedouin women; and to enforce adherence to the minimum age of marriage.

AI country reports/ visits
Reports
- Israel: Briefing to the Committee on the Elimination of Discrimination against Women (AI Index: MDE 15/037/2005)
- Israel and the Occupied Territories: Conflict, occupation and patriarchy – Women carry the burden (AI Index: MDE 15/016/2005)016/2005)

Visits
AI delegations visited Israel and the Occupied Territories in March and April.

ITALY

ITALIAN REPUBLIC
Head of state: Carlo Azeglio Ciampi
Head of government: Silvio Berlusconi
Death penalty: abolitionist for all crimes
International Criminal Court: ratified
UN Women's Convention and its Optional Protocol:
ratified

Refugee rights were threatened by implementation
of a new immigration law, the failure to legislate
specifically to protect those seeking asylum, and
reports of plans by Italy to build detention centres for
migrants in Libya. The expulsion of more than 1,425
migrants to Libya throughout the year took place in
defiance of international refugee law. Officials and
civilian personnel convicted of physical assault and
racial abuse at a detention centre for migrants
received suspended prison sentences. The trials
proceeded of police officers charged with assault
and other offences in 2001 at the time of mass
demonstrations in Naples and during the G8 Summit
in Genoa. Italy failed to take action to address the
impunity enjoyed by law enforcement officials,
including by setting up an independent police
complaints and accountability body, making torture
a specific crime under the penal code, or requiring
police officers to display prominently some form of
identification.

Refugee rights under threat

Italy still lacked a specific and comprehensive law on
asylum, despite being a party to the UN Refugee
Convention. In practice, asylum was regulated under
the 1990 immigration law, as amended in 2002 by the
Bossi-Fini law, the implementing rules of which came
into force on 21 April 2005. The law established
Identification Centres to detain asylum-seekers and
an accelerated asylum determination procedure for
detainees, raising concerns about access to asylum
procedures, the detention of asylum-seekers in
violation of international refugee law standards, and
violation of the principle of *non-refoulement* – that
those seeking asylum should not be forcibly returned
to countries where they risked serious human rights
abuses.

There were fears that many of the thousands of
migrants and asylum-seekers arriving in Italy by boat,
mainly from Libya, were forcibly returned to countries
where they were at risk of human right violations. At
least 1,425 people were deported to Libya between
January and October.

Between 13 and 21 March, 1,235 foreign nationals
arrived at the Italian island of Lampedusa. A request on
14 March by the Office of the UN High Commissioner for
Refugees (UNHCR) for access to the detention centre on
Lampedusa was refused on security grounds. On 16
March the Minister of the Interior informed parliament

that Libyan officials had been allowed into the centre to
identify people traffickers. The following day, 180
people were allegedly expelled, escorted on the flight
by Italian law enforcement officers, to the Libyan
capital, Tripoli. On 18 March, UNHCR expressed
concern that, if any Libyan asylum-seekers had been in
the centre during the visits by Libyan officials, such
visits would have contravened basic refugee protection
principles. On 14 April, the European Parliament
expressed concern at the expulsion of migrants from
Lampedusa between October 2004 and March 2005. On
10 May the European Court of Human Rights ordered
the Italian authorities to suspend the planned
expulsion of 11 migrants who arrived in Lampedusa in
March.

Thousands of foreign nationals without residence
rights were detained in Temporary Stay and Assistance
Centres (CPTA), amid reports from some of these
centres that law enforcement officers and supervisory
staff assaulted inmates. There were also reports of
overcrowded and unhygienic living conditions;
inadequate medical care and the excessive and abusive
administration of sedatives; and difficulties for inmates
in accessing legal advice and asylum procedures.
Similar conditions were reported in the newly
established Identification Centres where hundreds of
asylum-seekers were held.

Updates

In July, a court in Lecce convicted 16 people charged in
connection with the physical assault and racial abuse of
inmates of the Regina Pacis CPTA in the Puglia region in
November 2002. The director of the centre, a Roman
Catholic priest, and two of the *carabinieri* (military
police) who provided security at the centre were given
suspended sentences of 16 months' imprisonment. The
other accused, six members of the administrative staff,
two doctors and five other *carabinieri*, also received
suspended sentences, of between nine and 16 months.

Detention by proxy

Italy's decision to build three detention facilities in
Libya – one in Gharyan, close to Tripoli, a second in
Sheba, in the desert, and a third in Kufra, close to
Libya's borders with Egypt, Sudan and Chad – was
unofficially reported during the year. There were
fears that the human rights of migrants could be at
serious risk. Libya had not ratified the UN Refugee
Convention or its Protocol, and did not acknowledge
the presence of refugees and asylum-seekers in the
country or recognize the official status of the UNHCR.

Police brutality

Italy still failed to make torture, as defined in the UN
Convention against Torture, a specific crime within its
penal code. It also took no steps to establish an
independent national human rights institution, or an
independent police complaints and accountability
body. Policing operations were not brought in line with
the European Code of Police Ethics, for example by
requiring officers to display prominently some form of
identification, such as a service number, to ensure they
could be held accountable.

Updates: policing of 2001 demonstrations

Trials of police officers continued in relation to policing operations around the mass demonstrations in Naples in March 2001 and during the G8 Summit in Genoa in July 2001.

⬜ The trial of 31 police officers on charges ranging from abduction to bodily harm and coercion in connection with the Naples demonstration, which began in December 2004, continued in 2005.

⬜ In March public prosecutors in Genoa set out evidence of verbal and physical abuse of detainees in the Bolzaneto temporary detention facility through which over 200 detainees passed during the G8 summit. Detainees were reportedly slapped, kicked, punched and spat on; subjected to threats, including of rape, and to verbal abuse, including of an obscene sexual nature; and deprived of food, water and sleep for lengthy periods. On 16 April, a total of 45 police officers, *carabinieri*, prison guards and medical personnel were committed for trial on various charges. The trial began on 11 October.

⬜ On 6 April the trial began of 28 police officers, including several senior officers, involved in an overnight police raid on a school in Genoa during the demonstrations in 2001. During the raid, nearly 100 people were injured and three were left in a coma. The officers were charged with various offences, including assault and battery, falsifying and planting evidence, and abusing their powers as officers of the state. None had been suspended from duty. Scores of other law enforcement officers believed to have participated in assaults could apparently not be identified.

Ill-treatment in prisons

Chronic overcrowding and understaffing persisted in prisons, along with high rates of suicide and self-harm. There were many reports of poor sanitary conditions and inadequate medical assistance. Infectious diseases and mental health problems persisted.

Criminal proceedings, involving large numbers of prison staff, were under way into alleged ill-treatment of individual prisoners and sometimes large groups of prisoners. Some trials were marked by excessive delays. Charges related to the alleged psychological and physical abuse of prisoners, in some cases said to have been carried out systematically and at times amounting to torture.

International scrutiny

In January the UN Committee on the Elimination of Discrimination against Women found the measures taken by Italy to address the low participation of women in public life to be inadequate. It recommended that a definition of discrimination against women be included in relevant legislation, to bring Italy in line with the UN Convention on the Elimination of All Forms of Discrimination against Women.

On 28 October the UN Human Rights Committee, in its response to a report by Italy on its implementation of the International Covenant on Civil and Political Rights, recommended the establishment of an independent national human rights institution. It pressed for increased efforts to ensure that reported ill-treatment by state agents was subject to prompt and impartial investigation, and to eliminate domestic violence. The Committee raised concerns about the right to apply for asylum, and requested detailed information regarding re-admission agreements concluded with other countries, including Libya. It urged Italy to ensure the judiciary remained independent of the executive power, and highlighted concerns about overcrowding in prisons.

International Criminal Court

Despite Italy's major role in drafting the Rome Statute of the International Criminal Court, and its ratification of the Statute in 1999, by the end of 2005 the authorities had still not enacted implementing legislation that would allow investigation and prosecution of crimes under international law in national courts or co-operation with the International Criminal Court in its investigations.

AI country reports/visits
Reports

- Italy: Temporary stay, permanent rights – The treatment of foreign nationals detained in "temporary stay and assistance centres" (AI Index: EUR 30/004/2005)
- Italy: Lampedusa, the island of Europe's forgotten promises (AI Index: EUR 30/008/2005)
- Italy: Law reform needed to implement the Rome Statute of the International Criminal Court (AI Index: EUR 30/009/2005)
- Europe and Central Asia: Summary of Amnesty International's concerns in the region, July-December 2004: Italy (AI Index: EUR 01/002/2005)

JAMAICA

JAMAICA
Head of state: Queen Elizabeth II, represented by
Howard Felix Cooke
Head of government: Percival James Patterson
Death penalty: retentionist
International Criminal Court: signed
UN Women's Convention: ratified with reservations
Optional Protocol to UN Women's Convention: not signed

Reports of police brutality continued. A number of police officers were charged and tried after unlawful killings, but none was convicted. At least 168 people were killed by the police, many in circumstances suggesting they were extrajudicially executed. Conditions of detention frequently amounted to cruel, inhuman or degrading treatment. At least two people were sentenced to death; there were no executions.

Background
Jamaica continued to suffer from increasing levels of violence; 1,674 people were reportedly murdered during 2005, an increase on previous years. At least 13 police officers were killed. In May, three police officers were killed within hours of each other in apparently coordinated attacks.

Unlawful killings and impunity
At least 168 people were allegedly killed by members of the police, an increase over the previous year.

For the sixth consecutive year, no police or army officers were convicted of unlawful killings committed while on duty. Investigations into alleged extrajudicial executions remained inadequate. Police officers often failed to protect crime scenes, and statements from officers were often taken only after long delays.

Numerous police officers charged with unlawful killings fled from justice, including the officer charged with the murder of 10-year-old Renee Lyons in 2003 in Kingston.

▢ In February, six police officers were acquitted of the 2001 murder of seven young men in Braeton despite overwhelming evidence that the seven had been extrajudicially executed. The judge ruled that the prosecution had failed to present sufficient evidence for the case to continue.

▢ In August, six police officers were charged with the murder while on duty of two elderly men killed when police officers opened fire on their taxi in the Flankers area in October 2003. The trial had not taken place by the end of 2005.

▢ In December, the trial of six police officers charged with the murder of two men and two women in Crawle in 2003 resulted in acquittals. In July, two police officers were charged with intending to pervert the course of justice and other offences in connection with the killings. It was alleged that the officers had attempted to alter the crime scene to make it appear that the victims had fired at the police. The investigation was not completed by the end of 2005.

▢ In December, three police officers were acquitted of the murder of 15-year-old Jason Smith in 2003 in Kingston.

In October, a law was passed to establish a police Civilian Oversight Authority. However, the law did not mandate the Authority to play any major role in investigating alleged unlawful killings by police but related to matters such as the efficient use of resources.

In November, the Inter-American Commission on Human Rights issued a report critical of Jamaica's handling of the case of Michael Gayle, who was allegedly beaten to death by members of the security forces in 1999. No one was ever charged with the killing.

Death penalty
New sentencing hearings were held following the 2004 decision by the Judicial Committee of the Privy Council that mandatory death sentences were unconstitutional. At least four prisoners were re-sentenced to death and at least 11 had their sentences commuted to terms of imprisonment.

Throughout 2005, high levels of crime led to calls for the resumption of executions. There were discussions between the government and the opposition regarding changes to the Constitution to facilitate executions.

Torture and ill-treatment in detention
Conditions in prisons and other places of detention were reported to be harsh and in many cases amounted to cruel, inhuman or degrading treatment.

In April, one prisoner and one guard were shot dead and other prisoners beaten during an attempted escape from the Tower Street Correctional Centre. A government-appointed Board of Inquiry investigated the incident and found numerous violations of prisoners' human rights, including one prisoner beaten to death by guards and another dying because he was not given timely medical attention after being injured. There were no reported criminal charges brought in connection with the abuse of prisoners.

Violence against women
According to government figures, in the first eight months of 2005 there were 835 reported sexual assaults against women and girls, of which 67 per cent were against girls, and 16 per cent were at gunpoint. Most injuries to women were inflicted by an intimate partner. Rates of HIV infection among women and girls were rising, and people living with HIV faced systematic discrimination.

Routine investigations of sexual assaults were reported to be inadequate, and despite the special units set up to work with victims of sexual assault, police investigations were often returned to the regular constabulary.

Amendments to reform and update the Offences against the Person Act and the Incest (Punishment) Act, submitted to parliament in 1995, were still awaiting approval. Marital rape was still not a criminal offence. In sexual assault cases only, judges were required to warn juries that women and young girls sometimes told lies.

In November Jamaica ratified the Inter-American Convention on the Prevention, Punishment and Eradication of Violence against Women (Convention of Belém do Pará).

Gay men and lesbians

Gay men and lesbians continued to face violence and discrimination on a daily basis. In August, two men were convicted of buggery and sentenced to two years' imprisonment with hard labour, suspended for two years. During previous hearings, the two men had been insulted by crowds gathered outside the courthouse. In September, popular musician Buju Banton was charged with assaulting six men who he alleged were homosexuals. His song lyrics repeatedly advocated violence against gay men and lesbians. In November, AIDS activist Steven Harvey was murdered, allegedly because of his homosexuality.

AI country reports/ visits
Visits
In April and November delegations visited Jamaica to hold talks with non-governmental organizations addressing violence against women in Jamaica. In November, a delegation observed the trial of six police officers on charges of murder.

JAPAN

JAPAN
Head of government: Koizumi Junichiro
Death penalty: retentionist
International Criminal Court: not signed
UN Women's Convention: ratified
Optional Protocol to UN Women's Convention: not signed

One man was executed and 78 prisoners remained on death row. The authorities continued to deny reparations to victims of Japan's system of sexual slavery during World War II. A new law governing the treatment of prisoners was adopted in May. Increased punishments for trafficking in persons came into effect in July. A Bill to establish a national human rights commission was debated but not adopted.

Background
Elections in September increased the majority of the ruling party. The deployment of Japanese troops as overseas peacekeepers renewed public debate on whether to revise Article 9 of the Constitution which defines Japan as pacifist.

In November, the former President of Peru, Alberto Fujimori, left Japan for Chile where he was arrested at the request of the Peruvian authorities, pending an extradition request.

The 60th anniversary of the end of World War II, and renewed efforts by the government to secure a permanent seat on the UN Security Council, increased tensions in the east Asia region. The government was criticized for its continued failure to apologize adequately and provide full reparations for wartime crimes against humanity such as forced sexual slavery, and for the way Japanese history textbooks portray its past aggressions.

The Diet (parliament) debated but did not adopt a Bill first submitted in 2003 to establish a national human rights commission.

The government indicated that it would accede to the Rome Statute of the International Criminal Court by 2009.

Death penalty
Kitagawa Susumu was executed in secret by hanging in September, while the Diet was in recess. A former police officer, Kitagawa Susumu was sentenced to death in 1994 for the murder of two women, in 1983 and 1986. His appeal had been rejected by the Supreme Court in 2000.

The Japan Federation of Bar Associations held a joint international conference against the death penalty in December, reiterating calls for a moratorium. On his appointment in October, the Minister of Justice, Sugiura Seiken, acknowledged the worldwide trend towards abolition of the death penalty and announced that he would not personally sign any execution order. He immediately retracted this commitment.

Treatment of prisoners
A new Penal Facilities and Treatment of Prisoners Law was adopted in May, replacing the 1908 law. It provides for a monitoring body to inspect prisons, improved access to the outside world for prisoners and human rights education for prison staff. It does not, however, cover conditions in pre-trial detention or for prisoners sentenced to death.

In November, two guards at Nagoya prison received suspended sentences for killing a prisoner in 2001. Otomaru Mikio was sentenced to three years in prison, suspended for four years, for aiming water from a high-pressure hose at a naked prisoner, causing internal injuries. Takami Masahiro received a 14-month prison term, suspended for three years, for assisting in the attack.

In June, a pregnant detainee in Tokyo Detention Centre was handcuffed in hospital during her delivery, and prevented from seeing her newborn baby. She had also been required by the detention centre to have the birth induced to fit the hospital schedule. In October, the Minister of Health and Labour stated that births should be induced only when a clear medical need was established by a doctor.

Violence against women
Survivors of Japan's system of sexual slavery — before and during World War II — continued to be denied full

reparations. Survivors were also denied a remedy in the Japanese courts. In February the Supreme Court rejected a compensation claim by seven Taiwanese survivors (the case had begun with nine but two died). A Tokyo High Court also rejected a case by Chinese survivors in March.

Courts continued to argue that compensation claims were settled by post-war treaty arrangements. Contrary to international law, some applied statutes of limitation. In June a US federal appeals court rejected, for the second time, a damages suit filed by 15 survivors. The court cited Japan's immunity from such lawsuits in the USA.

Trafficking in persons
Amendments to the Criminal Code increased punishments for unlawfully detaining or buying trafficked persons. Related amendments were made to the Immigration Law and Criminal Procedure Code but none adequately addressed the protection of victims of trafficking. The government's commitment to ratify the UN Protocol to Prevent, Suppress and Punish Trafficking in Persons, Especially Women and Children (the Palermo Protocol) was not fulfilled by the end of 2005.

Restrictions on freedom of expression
The Tokyo High Court reinstated the convictions for trespass against three people detained in 2004 for distributing pamphlets within a residential military compound, opposing Japanese involvement in Iraq. They were fined between 100,000 and 200,000 yen and appealed to the Supreme Court.

Refugees
Revisions to the Immigration and Refugee Recognition Law effective from May increased time limits for filing asylum claims from 60 days to six months from arrival in Japan. Revisions also established an expert committee to give confidential recommendations to the Minister of Justice on appeals against rejected asylum claims. Appointed by the Ministry of Justice, most of the 18 members were former officials and only a few were refugee law experts.

The number of people recognized as refugees under the limited provisions of Japan's refugee law rose to at least 46. More than 40 others were granted special permission to stay for humanitarian reasons. Some individuals were released on condition they did not take up employment, but without basic livelihood assistance. Conditions in immigration centres remained harsh with inadequate medical care.

⌷ On 18 January Ahmet Kazankiran and his son, recognized as refugees by the UN High Commissioner for Refugees (UNHCR) in October 2004, were forcibly repatriated to Turkey in contravention of Japan's obligations under international law and in spite of appeals from UNHCR and human rights groups.

AI country reports/visits
Report
- Still waiting after 60 years: Justice for survivors of Japan's military sexual slavery system (AI Index: ASA 22/012/2005)

Visits
AI delegates, including AI's Secretary General, visited Japan in May/June. Delegates met senior government officials, as well as local human rights groups, and a wide range of people in civil society.

JORDAN

HASHEMITE KINGDOM OF JORDAN
Head of state: King 'Abdallah II bin al-Hussein
Head of government: Ma'arouf Bakhit (replaced Adnan Badran in November, who replaced Faisal al-Fayez in April)
Death penalty: retentionist
International Criminal Court: ratified
UN Women's Convention: ratified with reservations
Optional Protocol to UN Women's Convention: not signed

Scores of people were arrested for political reasons, including on suspicion of terrorism. Many were brought to trial before the State Security Court (SSC), whose procedures fall short of international fair trial standards, and alleged that they had been tortured to "confess". There were continuing restrictions on freedom of expression and assembly. Women were still subject to legal and other discrimination and inadequately protected against violence within the family. At least 11 people were sentenced to death and 11 were executed. Bomb attacks, apparently carried out to protest against Jordanian government policy on Iraq, targeted civilians.

Background
Suicide bombings at three Amman hotels in November, claimed by an armed Iraqi-based group led by Jordanian national Abu Mus'ab al-Zarqawi, killed 60 people and injured many others. Sajida Mubarak Atrous al-Rishawi, an Iraqi national arrested in connection with the attacks, stated on television that she had sought unsuccessfully to blow herself up with her husband at one of the hotels. After the attacks the government announced its intention to introduce new anti-terror laws that would include holding suspects under interrogation for indefinite periods. The authorities said that 12 Iraqi nationals were arrested in connection with the bombings but unofficial sources reported that scores of people were detained for questioning.

In November King 'Abdallah announced that the Director of National Security, Ma'arouf Bakhit, would replace Adnan Badran as Prime Minister and form a new government that would tackle Islamist "militants" and proceed with reforms including enhancing democracy in Jordan.

In August, Jordan finalized a Memorandum of Understanding with the UK according to which Jordanian authorities provided assurances that any people suspected of terrorism who were forcibly returned to Jordan from the UK under the terms of the agreement would not be treated inhumanely or tortured.

A separate bilateral agreement between Jordan and the USA, under which Jordan would undertake not to surrender US nationals on its territory to the International Criminal Court to face charges of genocide, crimes against humanity or war crimes, was ratified by parliament.

King 'Abdallah told an Italian newspaper in November that Jordan could soon abolish the death penalty.

Restrictions on freedom of expression and assembly

The authorities continued to censor newspapers and other publications that criticized the government. Under the Public Assemblies Law, they reportedly denied permission for demonstrations against Israel, the war in Iraq and rising oil prices.

The government proposed a new law that would restrict the activities of the Professional Associations Council (PAC), an umbrella organization representing members of 12 professional bodies which has criticized government policies. The law would require the PAC to restrict its discussions to "professional" issues and to obtain advance written approval from the Interior Ministry before it could hold public gatherings or meetings. The draft law was pending before parliament.

☐ 'Ali Hattar, a PAC member, lost his appeal in May against a three-month prison sentence imposed on 24 April. He was prosecuted for slandering the government after he delivered a lecture in December 2004 entitled "Why We Boycott America". The sentence had not been enforced by the end of the year.

☐ Three men were charged in September with belonging to the outlawed Islamist group Hizb al-Tahrir al-Islami (Islamic Liberation Party) and distributing leaflets. They were arrested in July, apparently while at a conference on Islam in Amman. In all, 28 members were reported to have been arrested during the year and remained in detention, two of them for trying to organize a demonstration in a Palestinian refugee camp.

Abuses in the context of the 'war on terror'

There were persistent reports that Jordan permitted the US government to maintain a secret detention and interrogation centre on its territory. The Jordanian authorities denied this.

Scores of people were arrested on suspicion of involvement in terrorism. Most were detained incommunicado by the General Intelligence Department (GID), the main security service responsible for the arrest of political detainees. More than a hundred people appeared before the SSC, whose proceedings fall far short of international fair trial standards and whose judges are invariably military officers, even when the accused are civilians.

Dozens of security-related or political cases were heard by the SSC in 2005. In many of these, defendants reportedly told the court that they had been tortured to extract "confessions". In no case known to AI did judges instigate an independent investigation into allegations of torture.

☐ Sheikh Abu Muhammad al-Maqdisi was rearrested in July, four days after he was released from six months' detention without charge or trial, on suspicion of contacting "terror" groups. At the end of the year he was still held incommunicado at an unknown location.

☐ AI was informed in 2005 by two Yemeni nationals that they had been detained and tortured for several days each by the GID in October 2003 before being flown out of Jordan in a military airplane to a secret detention camp run by US officials. Muhammad Faraj Bashmilah said he was arrested when he travelled to Amman from Indonesia to meet his mother. Salah Nasser Salim was arrested in Indonesia, where he lived, then flown to Jordan and tortured by the GID, including by being hung upside down and beaten on the soles of his feet.

Torture and ill-treatment

In June the government-funded National Centre for Human Rights said it had received 250 reports of torture between June 2003 and December 2004. It also pointed to the difficulties faced by criminal and SSC defendants in proving torture allegations. However, in one case, 10 police officers were sentenced in March to prison terms of up to 30 months after they were convicted of involvement in the death of 'Abdallah al-Mashaqbeh, who died in September 2004 in Jweideh prison.

Discrimination and violence against women

Amendments to the Personal Status Law, which would give women rights to divorce without their husband's consent, remained pending before parliament.

Article 98 of the Penal Code continued to be invoked as a defence by men being tried for killing female relatives. The Article allows for reduced sentences where killings are committed in a "fit of rage" caused by "unlawful" or "dangerous" acts on the part of the victim. In July 2004 the Justice Ministry proposed raising the minimum sentence for crimes committed in a "fit of rage" to five years' imprisonment, but no progress on this was evident in 2005. At least five men who said they had committed killings in defence of their family's "honour" benefited from Article 98 during the year, and at least 12 women and one man were reported to have been victims of family killings.

Dozens of women were administratively detained without charge or trial. Some of them, including victims of rape, women who had become pregnant outside marriage and women accused of extramarital sexual relations or of being prostitutes, were believed to be held to protect them from their family and community members. Some were detained after serving prison sentences; others had not been convicted of any offence. In the past, women have been killed by relatives after they were released from "protective" custody, including in cases where their relatives had signed a guarantee not to harm them.

In June, activists launched the Jordanian Coalition to Help Women in Protective Custody, which the Interior Minister promised to support.

Death penalty

At least 11 people were sentenced to death and 11 were executed. On 16 November an Italian newspaper quoted King 'Abdallah saying that "Jordan could soon become the first country in the Middle East without capital punishment."

⌢ In May, Zuheir Ahmed al-Khatib was sentenced to death for three murders including one for which another man, Bilal Musa, was executed in 2000. Bilal Musa had also been convicted of 10 other murders but alleged at his trial that he was tortured while held incommunicado by the Criminal Investigation Department (CID). His wife, who received a 15-year prison sentence but subsequently died, had also alleged that she was tortured. No judicial investigation was conducted into their torture allegations. Zuheir Ahmed al-Khatib was executed by hanging at Swaqa prison on 8 November for two murders – his conviction and sentence for the third murder had been overturned on appeal in September.

AI country reports/ visits
Report
· USA/Jordan/Yemen: Torture and secret detention – Testimony of the "disappeared" in the "war on terror" (AI Index: AMR 51/108/2005)

KAZAKSTAN

REPUBLIC OF KAZAKSTAN
Head of state: Nursultan Nazarbaev
Head of government: Danial Akhmetov
Death penalty: retentionist
International Criminal Court: not signed
UN Women's Convention and its Optional Protocol: ratified

Asylum-seekers and refugees from Uzbekistan were at risk of detention and forcible return. At least eight men were forcibly returned to Uzbekistan. An opposition party was closed down and some members briefly detained. A jailed opposition leader was recommended for early release.

Background

The Organization for Security and Co-operation in Europe (OSCE) said the December 2005 presidential election, which saw incumbent President Nursultan Nazarbaev win over 90 per cent of the votes, fell far short of OSCE and Council of Europe standards. The Constitutional Council had brought forward the election date by a year in August, and opposition parties and independent news media complained of harassment and intimidation by the authorities.

Political imprisonment

⌢ In January a court ordered the closure of the opposition Democratic Choice of Kazakstan (DVK) party, in response to an application by the Prosecutor General's office which accused it of "inciting social tension" and "extremism". Police reportedly broke up an unauthorized demonstration in Almaty organized by the DVK and detained eight DVK members, reportedly for using the slogan "Terror of the state against its citizens". Seven were subsequently brought before a court.

⌢ In November the Ministry of Justice recommended the early release of Galimzhan Zhakianov, a leading DVK member. On 14 December, a court decided to grant him early release. He had been sentenced to seven years' imprisonment in 2002 for "abuse of office" and financial crimes, but the real reason for his imprisonment appeared to be his peaceful opposition activities.

Fear of forcible return

Refugees from Uzbekistan were not effectively protected and risked being forcibly returned to Uzbekistan and subjected to serious human rights violations there. Some had fled to Kazakstan after the security forces fired indiscriminately on a crowd in Andizhan, Uzbekistan, on 13 May, killing hundreds of people. Others were suspected members of banned Islamic parties or movements. The Uzbekistani authorities have frequently targeted suspected sympathizers of such organizations or independent Muslims in the name of national security.

⌢ Lutfullo Shamsuddinov, a prominent human rights defender, fled Uzbekistan with his wife and five children. His eyewitness testimony of the events in Andizhan, quoted by the international media, differed from the official account. Although recognized as a refugee by the UN High Commissioner for Refugees (UNHCR) on 27 May, he was arrested by the Kazakstani police on 4 July at the request of the Uzbekistani authorities, who said that he faced charges of "terrorism", a capital offence, and spreading information to cause panic. Despite pressure from Uzbekistan, the Kazakstani authorities eventually handed him over to UNHCR, which flew him and his family to another country.

⌢ On 24 and 27 November, 10 Uzbekistani nationals were allegedly detained by the National Security Committee (KNB), the security services, and held incommunicado in the southern city of Shymkent. They were reportedly wanted for "participation in a banned religious organization" and "attempting to overthrow the constitutional order". According to reports, at least eight of them were forcibly returned to Uzbekistan early in the morning of 29 November. One man escaped into hiding in Kazakstan, and the whereabouts of another were unclear. Of the eight deportees, two were given access to lawyers and their place of detention in Uzbekistan was known, but the location of the remaining six was still unclear at the end of 2005. Reportedly, four of the eight men were holding asylum-seeker certificates issued by the UNHCR Office in Kazakstan.

KENYA

REPUBLIC OF KENYA
Head of state and government: Mwai Kibaki
Death penalty: abolitionist in practice
International Criminal Court: ratified
UN Women's Convention: ratified
Optional Protocol to UN Women's Convention: not signed

There was increased intimidation and harassment of the media and journalists by the authorities. Violence against women, including rape and domestic violence, remained a serious concern. The work of human rights defenders was obstructed.

Background

The protracted constitution-making process ended after a referendum on 21 November in which 57 per cent of voters rejected the draft constitution. Campaigning was marred by violence, with at least eight people killed in Kisumu and Mombasa. Following the referendum, President Kibaki sacked the entire cabinet, announcing a new cabinet on 7 December.

The proliferation of illegal weapons remained a serious concern. In July, the authorities burned 3,786 small arms recovered by police. According to police estimates, over 20,000 crimes were committed in the country annually using small arms.

In early June, four men charged with murder following the bombing of a hotel in Kikambala near Mombasa in November 2002 were acquitted after the trial judge ruled there was no evidence to connect them to the murders. One of them was rearrested and charged with illegal possession of arms. His application for bail was rejected. On 27 June, Nairobi's Chief Magistrate acquitted another three men charged with conspiracy to commit murder in the November 2002 hotel attack, saying that the prosecution had failed to prove its case.

More than 300,000 people continued to be internally displaced in Kenya. Conflict along borders and over access to scarce resources such as water and grazing lands, as well as inter-communal hostility aggravated by political rivalry, were among the main causes of internal displacement.

In March, Kenya ratified the Rome Statute of the International Criminal Court (ICC). Kenya did not sign the Article 98 exemption that would give US citizens on Kenyan soil immunity from prosecution by the ICC.

Kenya presented its second periodic report for consideration by the UN Human Rights Committee in March, after an 18-year delay.

Attacks on freedom of the media

There was increased intimidation and harassment of the media and journalists as the authorities took aggressive measures to silence investigative or critical voices.

 Criminal libel charges were brought against Kamau Ngotho, an investigative journalist, arising from an article about corruption published in the *Standard* in January. Following a public outcry, the charges were dropped.

 In September, David Ochami of the *Kenya Times* was arrested and charged with "publishing alarming information" for writing an article critical of the President. His trial started in November.

 The wife of the President went to the premises of the Nation Media Group on 2 May, accompanied by bodyguards, allegedly to complain about criticisms of her. She reportedly assaulted a cameraman, Clifford Derrick Otieno, who was filming the scene. He complained to police, but no further action was taken, and the Attorney General terminated a private prosecution that he initiated.

Violence against women

Women and girls continued to face widespread violence and discrimination. However, data on the prevalence of acts of violence against women, including domestic violence and rape, was inadequate. According to figures quoted in parliament, police recorded 2,300 rapes in 2004. However, statistics from health facilities and non-governmental organizations suggested that the number of unreported rapes in Kenya could be as high as 16,000 a year.

In April, parliament agreed to discuss a proposed Sexual Offences Bill.

Human rights defenders and demonstrators

The work of human rights defenders was obstructed. They were subjected to harassment and ill-treatment. During protests and demonstrations, demonstrators and their leaders were arrested and charged.

 Scores of anti-globalization activists were arrested in early March in Mombasa. They were protesting against unfair trade practices while officials from 33 countries met to discuss trade negotiations ahead of the World Trade Organization (WTO) meeting in Hong Kong in December. The activists were charged with "conducting an unlawful procession".

 Before the opening of parliament in March, police in Nairobi used tear gas and water cannons to disperse some 200 people demonstrating peacefully to demand a referendum on the draft constitution. Seven people were arrested and detained. Two of them, injured during the arrest, were reportedly denied access to medical care.

 At least one person was killed by the police in further demonstrations over the draft constitution in

July. About 20 people were detained and charged with "creating disturbance and malicious damage".

⬭ On 10 August, 22 activists demonstrating against irregular allocation of public land to private investors in Kitale Town were arrested and detained. On 12 August, Father Gabriel Dolan, a well-known human rights defender who had taken part in the demonstration, was arrested when he visited those in custody. Father Dolan was charged with "incitement to violence, malicious damage of property by a rioting assembly group and taking part in unlawful assembly".

Torture and unlawful killings

There were continuing reports of torture and unlawful killings by state agents.

A survey commissioned by the Kenya Human Rights Commission to establish the level of public awareness of human rights disclosed that people were reluctant to report torture.

In March, human rights groups condemned a statement by the Minister for Internal Security calling for police to shoot to kill anyone found with illegal firearms. Human rights defenders argued that while they deplored the level of insecurity in the country, shooting in such conditions would amount to unlawful killing.

There were several reports of unlawful killings perpetrated by law enforcement officials. Few such cases were investigated or prosecuted, encouraging impunity for such acts. No statistics were available on the number of people killed by police.

Protection of refugees and asylum-seekers

Approximately 240,000 refugees and asylum-seekers lived in Kenya. Refugees lived in designated refugee camps – Dadaab had about 138,000 refugees, predominantly from Somalia, and Kakuma had about 87,100 refugees, the majority from Sudan. There were also substantial numbers from Ethiopia, Eritrea and neighbouring countries in the Great Lakes region. An estimated 15,000 to 60,000 refugees were living without the necessary documents in Nairobi and other towns.

In April, the Minister for Immigration, Registration of Persons and Refugees stated that non-citizens who did not possess necessary registration documents would be deported to their countries of origin. The deadline for registration was fixed for 30 June, later extended to 15 August 2005. Large numbers of people turned up at the Office of the UN High Commissioner for Refugees in Nairobi in June in order to register an asylum claim. Many would be at risk of serious human rights violations in their countries of origin if they were arrested and deported. The process of refugee status determination was still under way at the end of the year.

In March, the authorities released former Iraqi air force pilot, Adel Mohammed Al-Dahas, after four years in detention in a police cell in Nairobi despite the fact that he was granted refugee status in 2001. By the end of 2005, his request for resettlement to a third country had not yet been granted.

Death penalty

In March, the Minister of Justice and Constitutional Affairs declared at the UN Commission on Human Rights that his government was committed to abolishing the death penalty and that in the meantime all death sentences would be commuted to life imprisonment. At the end of the year, however, this process had not been completed.

In April, the High Court in Kakamega freed four Ugandans who had been on death row since 1995 after a successful appeal against their death sentences. The four were members of the February Eighteen Movement, which allegedly aimed to overthrow the former government in Kenya.

Impact of 'anti-terrorism' operations on human rights

Human rights violations were committed during "anti-terrorism" operations conducted since the 2002 bombing of a hotel near Mombasa that killed 15 people. The violations included: the use of torture and other ill-treatment during detention including physical abuse; detention of suspects without charge in undisclosed locations and without access to a lawyer or relatives; the holding of suspects in degrading and unsanitary conditions without access to medical care; harassment of family members and arbitrary detention of relatives to put pressure on suspects to hand themselves in; and the failure of police to show warrants when arresting individuals or conducting searches of property.

AI country reports/ visits
Reports/statements
- Kenya: The impact of "anti-terrorism" operations on human rights (AI Index: AFR 32/002/2005)
- Kenya: Abolition of the death penalty is essential for a Constitution that respects human rights (AI Index: AFR 32/005/2005)
- Kenya: The Government must respect the rights of refugees under international law (AI Index: AFR 32/007/2005)

Visit
AI delegates visited Kenya in March to meet government officials and launch the report *Kenya: The impact of "anti-terrorism" operations on human rights.*

KOREA
(DEMOCRATIC PEOPLE'S REPUBLIC OF)

DEMOCRATIC PEOPLE'S REPUBLIC OF KOREA
Head of state: Kim Jong-il
Head of government: Pak Pong-ju
Death penalty: retentionist
International Criminal Court: not signed
UN Women's Convention: ratified
Optional Protocol to UN Women's Convention: not signed

Fundamental rights including freedom of expression, association and movement continued to be denied. There were reports of public executions, widespread political imprisonment, torture and ill-treatment. Access by independent monitors continued to be restricted.

Background
In March, North Korea declared itself a nuclear power. In September, the fourth round of six-party talks in Beijing (involving North Korea, South Korea, China, Japan, Russia and the USA) reached a breakthrough accord in which North Korea pledged to abandon its nuclear programmes in exchange for aid and security assurances. However, there was no further progress on implementing the agreement.

International scrutiny
In April the UN Commission on Human Rights expressed concern about the human rights situation in North Korea, the third such resolution in three years.

In November, for the first time, the UN General Assembly passed a resolution expressing concern about the human rights situation in North Korea.

In August, the UN Special Rapporteur on the situation of human rights in the Democratic People's Republic of Korea (DPRK) reported that there was evidence of torture, detention without trial, public executions and capital punishment for political dissidents.

In July, the UN Committee on the Elimination of Discrimination against Women considered North Korea's initial periodic report. The Committee expressed concern about the government's lack of awareness of the extent of domestic violence, the absence of legislation to deal with violence against women, including domestic violence, and the lack of prevention and protection measures for victims. The Committee also expressed concern that the government had not given sufficient information on the impact of the famine and natural disasters on women and young girls. The Committee was concerned that in such circumstances, they might become vulnerable to trafficking and other forms of exploitation, such as prostitution.

Denial of access
Information and access continued to be highly controlled. Despite repeated requests, the government continued to deny access to independent human rights monitors including the UN Special Rapporteur on the situation of human rights in the DPRK and the UN Special Rapporteur on the right to adequate food.

Death penalty
There were renewed reports of executions of political opponents in political prisons, and of executions of people charged with economic crimes, such as stealing food. Unconfirmed reports suggested that people operating underground churches had been executed.

☐ In February, there were unconfirmed reports that about 70 North Korean defectors had been executed in public in January after being forcibly repatriated from China.

☐ Video footage emerged showing two people being shot in a public execution. The execution reportedly took place on 1 March in Hoeryang, a north-eastern city, after a public trial of 11 people charged with trafficking in people and aiding unauthorized visits to China. The footage also showed an execution which reportedly took place on 2 March in the nearby city of Yuson.

Torture and ill-treatment
Hundreds of North Koreans forcibly returned from China faced detention, torture or ill-treatment, and up to three years' imprisonment in appalling conditions.

Prisoners reportedly died from malnutrition in labour camps for political prisoners and in detention centres, which were severely overcrowded. Prisoners charged with breaking prison rules had their food cut even further.

Women in detention
Women detainees continued to be subjected to degrading prison conditions. Prisons lacked basic facilities for women's needs. There were unconfirmed reports that pregnant women detainees were forced to undergo abortions after being forcibly returned from China. Women detainees stated that during pre-trial detention male guards humiliated them and touched them inappropriately. Women who attempted to protest were reportedly beaten. All women, including those who were pregnant or elderly, were forced to work from early morning to late at night in fields or prison factories.

Freedom of expression
Severe restrictions on freedom of expression and association persisted.

☐ In July, 64-year-old Moon Sung-Jun was reportedly arrested on suspicion of leading an underground church in Shinuiju, North Pyongan province. At least 80 local residents, including eight of Moon Sung-Jun's siblings were reportedly detained and questioned on suspicion of attending the church.

North Koreans in Asia
Hundreds of North Koreans were forcibly returned by the Chinese authorities to North Korea. Many tried to enter foreign-run schools in Beijing and foreign

diplomatic missions to seek permission to leave China. At the end of 2005, more than 100 were awaiting decisions in diplomatic missions.

North Korean women in China were reportedly exploited sexually, including through forced marriages and trafficking into the sex industry. The authorities in Viet Nam, Laos and Cambodia reportedly increased forcible repatriations of North Korean refugees who were attempting to reach South Korea.

People assisting North Koreans in China were targeted by the North Korean authorities.

In March, Kang Gun, who had settled in South Korea, was reportedly abducted by North Korean agents from Longjing in Jilin province in China, where he was helping North Koreans who had fled to China as a result of the food crisis. He was apparently held in a National Security Agency prison in Pyongyang.

The right to food

A national nutrition survey conducted by the government, the World Food Programme (WFP) and the UN Children's Fund (UNICEF) was published in March. It found that 7 per cent of children were severely malnourished; 37 per cent were chronically malnourished; 23.4 per cent were underweight; and one in three mothers was malnourished and anaemic. The study found that the plight of the most vulnerable had been aggravated by an economic adjustment process initiated in mid-2002 that led to steep increases in the market prices of basic foods, and sharply lower incomes for millions of factory workers made redundant or employed part-time. Market prices of cereals, which tripled in 2004, continued to rise.

In September the government called for more development aid and an end to humanitarian aid, citing good agricultural harvests in 2005. It also called for WFP monitors to be expelled, raising concerns about the monitoring of food aid. Reports in September suggested that up to half of bilateral food aid supplied by China and South Korea did not reach the intended recipients.

At the government's request, the WFP shut down five regional offices and 19 food factories in North Korea in December.

KOREA
(REPUBLIC OF)

REPUBLIC OF KOREA
Head of state: Roh Moo-hyun
Head of government: Lee Hae-chan
Death penalty: retentionist
International Criminal Court: ratified
UN Women's Convention: ratified
Optional Protocol to UN Women's Convention: not signed

Refugee recognition procedures did not take into account the threats faced by asylum-seekers. A draft bill to abolish the death penalty was introduced. At least 63 prisoners remained under sentence of death. At least eight prisoners of conscience sentenced under the National Security Law (NSL) were released. The NSL, which allowed the imprisonment of prisoners of conscience, remained in use. At least 200,000 irregular migrant workers faced detention and deportation. Despite improved protections for migrant workers, poor working conditions and discrimination in wages and access to justice continued. At least 1,090 conscientious objectors remained imprisoned for refusing to do military service.

Refugees and asylum-seekers

Refugee recognition procedures lacked transparency and failed to take into account threats faced by asylum-seekers. Refugee status was granted to as few as 40 applicants between February 2001 — when asylum was granted for the first time under the UN Refugee Convention — and the end of 2005, 15 of them in 2005. Detention policies for asylum-seekers were vague and arbitrary.

In May new guidelines under the Immigration Law required that asylum-seekers who had not possessed valid residence visas for over three years be detained and fined before their applications were considered. Applicants were not informed of the grounds for decisions on their cases. They did not receive sufficient protection or support, including from qualified interpreters, and were not allowed to work.

In March the authorities rejected asylum applications made by nine Myanmar nationals in May 2000. In April the men were ordered to leave the country within five days. On appeal in July, they were allowed to stay until April 2006. They were reportedly active in opposition political activities in Myanmar and South Korea that put them at risk of serious human rights violations if they returned to Myanmar. Although no interpreters were present during the interviews, applicants' signatures had been added to the transcripts of their testimonies. The lawyers complained that transcripts of their interviews appeared to have been either omitted or distorted.

Migrant workers

Basic rights of migrant workers appeared to be strengthened after the Employment Permit System Act came into effect in August 2004. However, migrant workers continued to face widespread discrimination in wages and in access to justice. Many worked in dangerous conditions, were not paid regularly or did not receive severance pay. In December, there were over 200,000 undocumented migrant workers liable to immediate detention pending deportation.

◻ In May, Anwar Hossain, head of the new Migrants Trade Union that had not been recognized by the government, was arrested by over 30 immigration and police officers and reportedly assaulted. The day before his arrest, he had criticized government policy towards irregular migrant workers in a national newspaper. He was still held at the Chonju Immigration Detention Centre at the end of 2005.

Death penalty

There were no executions. At least 63 prisoners remained under sentence of death. A bill to abolish the death penalty, proposed by 175 members of the 299-member National Assembly in December 2004, was introduced in the Legislation and Judiciary Committee of the National Assembly in February.

National Security Law

Under a presidential amnesty in August, at least eight prisoners of conscience sentenced under the NSL were released. At least two long-term prisoners were serving sentences imposed under the NSL.

◻ Kang Tae-woon, aged 75, sentenced to six years' imprisonment in August 2003 for espionage, was reportedly in poor health. His sentence was reportedly reduced by half in August.

The NSL, in force since 1948, allowed for long prison sentences or the death penalty for non-violent political activities, including vaguely termed offences such as "benefiting the enemy" or "anti-state" activities. Despite growing support for repeal of the NSL, including from President Roh Moo-hyun and the National Human Rights Commission, the government did not amend or repeal it.

Conscientious objectors

At least 1,090 conscientious objectors, most of them Jehovah's Witnesses, were in prison at the end of 2005 for their refusal to carry out compulsory military service. The government gave no consideration to introducing an alternative civilian service.

Update

Lim Tae-hoon was released in June. He had been arrested in February 2004 and sentenced to 18 months' imprisonment in July 2004 for refusing to perform military service because of his pacifist beliefs and discrimination against gay, bisexual and transsexual people by the military.

AI country reports/ visits

Statement

· South Korea: Death penalty abolition – historic opportunity (AI Index: ASA 25/003/2005)

KUWAIT

STATE OF KUWAIT
Head of state: al-Shaikh Jaber al-Ahmad al-Sabah
Head of government: al-Shaikh Sabah al-Ahmad al-Sabah
Death penalty: retentionist
International Criminal Court: signed
UN Women's Convention: ratified with reservations
Optional Protocol to UN Women's Convention: not signed

Women gained the right to vote and stand for political office. Clashes between armed groups and security forces resulted in 12 deaths. At least 30 people were detained for alleged links to armed groups; one died in custody and others, when brought to trial, alleged torture. Fourteen people were charged with trying to form a political party. Migrant workers faced a wide range of abuses. At least 15 people were sentenced to death and at least seven people were executed.

Women's rights

Women gained the right to vote and stand for political office under a new electoral law which took effect on 16 May. Under the law, women are required to abide by Sharia (Islamic law) when voting or standing for election.

In June, the government appointed two women to the 16-member Municipal Council, and women's rights activist Massouma al-Mubarak became Minister of Planning and Minister of State for Administrative Affairs.

Political arrests and imprisonment

The authorities detained 14 people in May for questioning about their links to the Ummah Party, which was formed in January despite the ban on political parties and apparently advocates pluralism and peaceful political change. They were released but reportedly charged with establishing a political party to promote a change of government, punishable by up to 15 years' imprisonment. Their trial had not taken place by the end of the year.

At least 29 prisoners continued to serve sentences imposed in 1991 after manifestly unfair trials before Martial Law and State Security Courts for "collaborating" with Iraqi forces during their occupation of Kuwait. Sentences ranged from 15 years to life imprisonment.

Abuses in the context of the 'war on terror'

Gun battles in January between security forces and Islamist armed groups left 12 people dead.

In February, the authorities detained at least 30 people for suspected links to al-Qa'ida and related groups. Amer Khlaif al-Enezi, the alleged leader, died in custody eight days after his arrest in unclear circumstances; the Interior Minister later denied that he had been tortured. Others were among 37 people brought to trial in May, including 11 in absentia, on terrorism-related charges. They were accused of belonging to the Peninsula Lions Brigade, allegedly linked to al-Qa'ida, calling for war against the state and attempting to kill members of Kuwait's security forces and other "friendly forces". Some defendants said they had confessed under torture and showed the court what they said were torture injuries. Following repeated requests by defence lawyers, the court appointed an independent medical commission to probe the torture allegations. On 27 December, six were sentenced to death, one was sentenced to life imprisonment, others received prison terms of between four months and 15 years, and seven were acquitted.

Twenty-four suspected militants arrested in previous years were tried on charges of recruiting people to join terrorist groups, including groups fighting US-led forces in Iraq. One received an eight-year prison sentence, 19 received three-year terms and four were fined and released.

Six of 12 Kuwaiti nationals held for over three years in the US prison camp at Guantánamo Bay, Cuba, were released and returned to Kuwait, where they were detained. Nasser Najd al-Mutairi, aged 28, was acquitted by the Lower Court on 15 June of belonging to al-Qa'ida, seeking to take up arms against a friendly state, and possessing weapons. The Appeals Court overturned the verdict on 2 November and sentenced him to five years' imprisonment. The other five were being detained pending trial.

Abuse of migrant workers

Migrant workers, who constitute a large part of Kuwait's workforce, protested against working conditions, non-payment of wages, arbitrary pay cuts, ill-treatment, unsatisfactory living conditions, and non-renewal of residence permits. The authorities said they were considering changes to the country's labour laws to improve conditions for migrant workers. In October it was announced that a new contract stipulating a minimum wage for domestic workers would come into effect at the start of 2006.

Women migrant workers in domestic service were especially vulnerable to abuse because of discriminatory legislation and practices, and the exclusion of domestic workers from the protection of labour laws. They suffered gender-based violence, including rape by employers or their associates, and had little recourse given the prevailing climate of impunity for perpetrators of crimes against migrant domestic workers.

AI country reports/visits
Reports
- Gulf Cooperation Council (GCC) countries: Women deserve dignity and respect (AI Index: MDE 04/004/2005)
- Kuwait: Time to release the remaining prisoners of the 1991 unfair trials (AI Index: MDE 17/003/2005)

KYRGYZSTAN

KYRGYZ REPUBLIC
Head of state: Kurmanbek Bakiev (replaced Askar Akaev in March)
Head of government: Feliks Kulov (replaced Kurmanbek Bakiev in July, who replaced Nikolai Tanaev in March)
Death penalty: retentionist
International Criminal Court: signed
UN Women's Convention and its Optional Protocol: ratified

Hundreds of people fled to Kyrgyzstan after security forces reportedly fired on thousands of mainly unarmed and peaceful demonstrators in neighbouring Uzbekistan in May. Four Uzbekistani men were forcibly returned to Uzbekistan in June, and the Uzbekistani security forces pursued refugees and asylum-seekers on Kyrgyzstani territory, in some cases with the co-operation of the authorities in Kyrgyzstan. Many were unable to access asylum procedures. Kyrgyzstani citizens among those who fled Uzbekistan were not protected from being pursued illegally in Kyrgyzstan by the Uzbekistani security forces.

Background
In February elections to a new unicameral parliament sparked widespread protests amid allegations of fraud and vote-rigging. On 24 March opposition supporters stormed government buildings in the capital, Bishkek, and a loose coalition of political groups took power. President Askar Akaev formally resigned on 4 April after talks in Moscow.

Feliks Kulov, leader of the opposition Ar-Namys (Dignity) party and former Minister of National Security, was released from prison — where he was serving a 17-year sentence for abuse of office and embezzlement after an allegedly political trial — and was asked by parliament to take charge of national security and restore order. Kurmanbek Bakiev, a leading opposition member and a former Prime Minister, was named acting Prime Minister and President by parliament. The old parliament disbanded on 28 March and recognized the legitimacy of the newly elected parliament. In April the Supreme Court overturned Feliks Kulov's convictions on charges of embezzlement and corruption. In presidential elections on 10 July, Kurmanbek Bakiev was elected President. He appointed Feliks Kulov Prime Minister.

A law enacted in August to outlaw extremism appeared to threaten freedom of expression and, in particular, freedom of the media because of its broad definition of extremist activities and extremist materials.

Tensions increased in September and October. More than 20 inmates were killed in widespread prison riots, which were reportedly in response to harsh prison conditions and collusion between prison authorities and jailed criminal leaders. Tynychbek Akmatbaev, a member of parliament (MP), two of his assistants, and Ikmatullo Polotov, a senior prisons official, were killed while visiting one of these prisons on 20 October. Demonstrations in Bishkek led by the MP's brother, Ryspek Akmatbaev, who was awaiting trial on murder charges in a separate case, accused Feliks Kulov of complicity in the deaths. However, the demonstrations were called off a week later after President Bakiev agreed to meet a delegation. On 1 November more violence erupted when government forces tried to regain control of prisons left without guards and administrators following the October riots.

A moratorium on executions was extended for another year. Draft amendments to the Constitution included the permanent and full abolition of the death penalty.

Refugees from Uzbekistan at risk

Over 540 men, women and children crossed into Kyrgyzstan in the early hours of 14 May following the reported killings of hundreds of demonstrators in Andizhan, Uzbekistan, on 13 May (see Uzbekistan entry). Initially in a makeshift camp near the border, their safety could not be guaranteed and the Office of the UN High Commissioner for Refugees (UNHCR) moved them to a camp at Besh-Kana on 4 June. However, Kyrgyzstani officials allegedly handed over lists of their names and home addresses to the Uzbekistani security services, who put pressure on relatives to persuade refugees to return voluntarily — including by transporting the relatives in buses to the camp — and reportedly infiltrated the camp. Uzbekistani media reports described it as a "terrorist" camp run by "dangerous criminals", and the local population reportedly threatened to force the refugees out. On 29 July, UNHCR airlifted 439 refugees to a holding centre in Romania, pending resettlement.

Extraditions and threat of forcible return

Kyrgyzstan came under pressure from Uzbekistan to extradite a large number of the refugees. Although President Bakiev gave UNHCR guarantees of temporary protection for an initial group of over 540 refugees, on 9 June the authorities forcibly returned four of them to Uzbekistan in contravention of their international obligations. On 16 June the Uzbekistan Prosecutor General's Office said it was seeking the extradition of 131 refugees who were "direct participants in the acts of terrorism [in Andizhan]".

On 22 June the Prosecutor General of Kyrgyzstan reportedly described as "criminals" 29 refugees who had been transferred from the Besh-Kana camp to detention, indicating they would be returned to Uzbekistan within a week. On 24 June he reportedly called for the detention of a further 103 refugees. He later said Kyrgyzstan would abide by its international obligations to protect refugees, and that the 29 in detention would not be sent back to Uzbekistan until their refugee determination had been completed. Fourteen of the 29 were evacuated to Romania for resettlement in July and a further 11 of them were resettled to other European countries in September.

The status of the other four was disputed. The Uzbekistani authorities said that one had been convicted of narcotics offences and the others were wanted for the killing of the Andizhan city prosecutor on 13 May. UNHCR recognized one as a refugee, a decision rejected by the Kyrgyzstani authorities. The Kyrgyzstani authorities initially did not allow the other three to apply for asylum, and a court upheld the men's appeal against this decision, referring the cases back for reconsideration.

Lack of access to asylum procedures

Of the hundreds of people who fled Uzbekistan after 13 May, some were reportedly denied entry or were forcibly returned to Uzbekistan. Others were said to have stayed with relatives or friends, or lived without proper registration, since effective opportunities to legalize their presence in Kyrgyzstan did not exist. Little or no information was readily accessible to them on how to lodge an asylum claim. Although UNHCR registered asylum claims independently, the Kyrgyzstan authorities did not provide physical protection from the Uzbekistani authorities.

⌁ In late June, Bakhodir Sadikov, an asylum-seeker from Uzbekistan hiding in Osh region, registered his asylum claim with UNHCR but was detained on his way from the office for having no registration papers. He was on a list of criminal suspects published by the Uzbekistani authorities in June. Two days later he was reportedly in a transit prison with another Uzbekistani asylum-seeker, Hadir Ulmas, who had also been hiding in Osh. Both were believed to have been subsequently sent back to Uzbekistan.

Failure to protect nationals of Kyrgyzstan

As many as 50 Kyrgyzstani men, in Andizhan for professional or private reasons, fled with the refugees after 13 May. However, in Kyrgyzstan they were put in a refugee camp; no notification was sent to their families; and there was no record of their arrival in search of protection or of their protection needs. The camp authorities transferred them directly to a temporary detention centre, where they were held for up to 15 days on administrative charges.

Families reported that law enforcement officers systematically extorted large sums of money to allow them to visit their relatives in the camp or to have relatives released from the camp or from detention. The details of 37 of the Kyrgyzstani men were included in the list of wanted criminal suspects published by the Uzbekistani authorities in June. To avoid being seized and forcibly transferred to Uzbekistan, those on the list went into hiding.

⌁ Relatives asked the local authorities in Osh for information about the whereabouts of four young men from Kyrgyzstan who went missing after the Andizhan events. Two days later a car with Uzbekistani number plates came to their house after dark, and well-built men who presented no identification papers or legal warrant, and who they suspected were from the Uzbekistani security services, questioned them about every member of the household.

AI country reports/ visits
Reports
- Kyrgyzstan: Refugees in need of a safe haven
  (AI Index: EUR 58/008/2005)
- Kyrgyzstan: Uzbekistan in pursuit of refugees in
  Kyrgyzstan – A follow-up report (AI Index: EUR
  58/016/2005) A f58/016/2005)
Visits
In February an AI delegate visited Kyrgyzstan. AI
representatives also visited Kyrgyzstan to interview
refugees from Uzbekistan in May, June and July.

LAOS

LAO PEOPLE'S DEMOCRATIC REPUBLIC
Head of state: Khamtay Siphandone
Head of government: Bounyang Vorachit
Death penalty: retentionist
International Criminal Court: not signed
UN Women's Convention: ratified
Optional Protocol to UN Women's Convention: not
signed

The internal armed conflict with predominantly
ethnic Hmong rebel groups continued. The fate of
hundreds of Hmong civilians who surrendered to the
authorities was not known. At least four prisoners of
conscience remained in detention and one long-term
political prisoner died in prison. Reports of torture
and ill-treatment continued. An increasing number of
death sentences were handed down, but no
executions were known to have been carried out. Two
people were sentenced to prison terms for refusing to
renounce their religion, and suppression of religious
practice continued in several provinces.

Background
Assessment of the human rights situation was
hampered by continuing restrictions on freedom of
expression and severe limitations on access by
independent observers and human rights monitors to
the country.

The UN Committee on the Elimination of
Discrimination against Women recommended in
January that domestic violence and rape be made
criminal offences in Laos.

In June Laos ratified two International Labour
Organization (ILO) Conventions for ending child labour.
However, Laos still did not ratify the International
Covenant on Civil and Political Rights and the
International Covenant on Economic, Social and
Cultural Rights, which it had signed in December 2000.

The World Bank gave the final go-ahead to the Nam
Theun 2 dam project, despite continuing concerns
raised by environmental groups on its possible impact
on the thousands of people needing resettlement and
the livelihoods of many others.

Opium poppy cultivation and opium production
continued to decline substantially, as Laos moved
towards the goal of becoming opium-free by the end of
2005. However, concerns arose that this had resulted in
an estimated 65,000 members of upland Lao
communities being displaced to areas where their basic
needs were not met.

Ethnic Hmong conflict
Covert visits by international journalists to rebel areas
occasionally highlighted the plight of ethnic Hmong
rebels and their families in the decades-old internal
armed conflict. Attacks by the Lao military on rebel
groups and their families were reported.

Groups of ethnic Hmong civilians, including women,
children and elderly people, surrendered to the
authorities throughout 2005 because they were unable
to find food in the jungle and lacked basic medical care.
It was unclear what became of them. In June a group of
173 surrendered to the authorities at Chong Thuang
village in Xieng Khouang province. The surrender was
witnessed by two US nationals from the US-based Fact
Finding Commission and two ethnic Hmong US nationals
supporting the Hmong. The four were subsequently
arrested and deported. The surrendering civilians were
taken away by soldiers and their fate and whereabouts
remained unknown. In October it was reported that two
individuals in Chong Thuang village were arrested and
tortured and another was unlawfully killed by Lao
military and police in connection with the surrender.

Despite a public statement by UN Secretary-General
Kofi Annan that the UN was ready to provide
humanitarian assistance to such groups, the authorities
made no requests, and UN agencies were not given
access.

In October, 242 Hmong people in around 43 families
surrendered in Bolikhamxay province. They reportedly
received virtually no humanitarian assistance. The
authorities denied that surrenders of people from ethnic
Hmong rebel groups had taken place, claiming that they
were local people not connected to rebel groups.

The internal conflict continued to cause hundreds of
ethnic Hmong to flee to Thailand, where they joined
other Hmong refugees. At the end of 2005 more than
6,000 Lao Hmong were living in Phetchabun province.

In February a long overdue report from Laos was
considered by the UN Committee on the Elimination of
Racial Discrimination (CERD). The Committee reiterated
calls for the authorities to allow UN agencies access to
areas where members of ethnic Hmong groups in conflict
with the authorities have taken refuge, and to provide
emergency humanitarian assistance.

Political imprisonment
Prisoners of conscience Thongpaseuth Keuakoun and
Seng-aloun Phengphanh remained in detention in
Samkhe prison. They were among five members of the

Lao Students' Movement for Democracy arrested in October 1999 for attempting to hold a peaceful demonstration in Vientiane and were reportedly sentenced to 10 years' imprisonment. The identity of two other members of the group, Keochay and Bouavanh Chanhmanivong, continued to be disputed by the authorities; they were reportedly sentenced to five years' imprisonment and due for release in October 2004. However, there was no confirmation of their release. The fifth group member died in detention in 2001 following torture by prison guards.

Pangtong Chokbengboun, who was seriously ill but denied appropriate medical treatment by the authorities, died in detention in March. His co-detainee Sing Chanthakoummane remained in detention in harsh conditions. Both men were arrested in 1975 and detained without charge or trial for 17 years for "re-education" before being sentenced to life imprisonment after an unfair trial in 1992.

Freedom of religious practice

Despite the constitutional guarantee of freedom of religion, several denominations faced varying degrees of harassment and persecution, particularly evangelical Christian groups. There were reports of Christians being subjected to harsh treatment and forced to renounce their faith.

▭ Eleven men from the ethnic Bru minority were arrested in Houeihoy Neua village, Muong Phine district of Savannakhet Province, while taking part in Easter celebrations in March. Nine were released after signing renunciations of their faith. They had reportedly spent 48 hours in a rice plantation with their hands tied and without food or water. Two others — Khamchanh, a former village chief and local Communist Party member, and Vanthong — were subsequently sentenced to three years' imprisonment on charges of possessing illegal weapons. The real reason for their imprisonment appeared to be their refusal to renounce their faith.

Death penalty

Laos retained the death penalty for a wide range of offences and an increasing number of death sentences were imposed. Twenty-six people, including one woman, were sentenced to death for drug trafficking offences, bringing the number of people on death row to at least 60.

No executions were known to have taken place.

LATVIA

REPUBLIC OF LATVIA
Head of state: Vaira Vike-Freiberga
Head of government: Aigars Kalvītis
Death penalty: abolitionist for ordinary crimes
International Criminal Court: ratified
UN Women's Convention: ratified
Optional Protocol to UN Women's Convention: not signed

In July, the Prime Minister made derogatory comments regarding lesbian, gay, bisexual and transgender (LGBT) people and the Riga City Council temporarily withdrew permission for a Gay Pride march. A report published by the European Committee for the Prevention of Torture (CPT) highlighted several worrying practices and made recommendations for improvements.

Background

In June, Latvia ratified the Council of Europe's Framework Convention for the Protection of National Minorities. However, the Latvian government's definition of a minority in practice excluded most members of the Russian-speaking community in Latvia from qualifying as a minority.

LGBT rights under attack

On 20 July, the executive director of the Riga City Council, Ēriks Škapars, withdrew permission for the gay and lesbian community to hold a Gay Pride march on 23 July. Ēriks Škapars' decision came after the Prime Minister stated on television that he could not "accept that a parade of sexual minorities takes place in the middle of our capital city next to the Dom Cathedral. This is not acceptable. Latvia is a state based on Christian values. We cannot advertise things which are not acceptable to the majority of our society."

The organizers of the march subsequently made an official complaint to the Riga administrative court regarding the decision to ban the march. On 22 July the administrative court decided to annul Ēriks Škapars' decision to withdraw permission for the march. On 23 July the march went ahead as originally planned.

Organizers and news media covering the event estimated that approximately 300 people participated in the march. Meanwhile, over a thousand people had gathered to stage a protest against the march. Some of the protesters tried to block the march, while others used tear gas and threw eggs at the marchers.

In July the European Commission's Employment, Social Affairs and Equal Opportunities unit published its 2005 annual report on equality and non-discrimination. According to the report, Latvia was the only country in the European Union which had not fully transposed the requirement of the Employment Equality Directive and did not explicitly ban discrimination on grounds of sexual orientation in employment.

Torture and ill-treatment

In May the CPT published a report based on findings from a visit to Latvia in 2002. The report highlighted several worrying practices and made recommendations for improvement.

The CPT's delegation said that it had received a considerable number of credible allegations of physical ill-treatment by law enforcement agencies throughout Latvia. Most of the allegations of ill-treatment related to events at the time of detention. However, many of the allegations also concerned ill-treatment during police questioning. The forms of ill-treatment reported to the CPT included "asphyxiation with a plastic bag, strangulation, very severe beating, infliction of electric shocks, submerging the head of the suspect in the water of a lake." Some of this ill-treatment was so severe that it could be considered to constitute torture.

The CPT also remarked on the poor conditions of detention in police establishments. It stated that "the situation was particularly bad at Daugavpils, Liepaja and Ventspils Police headquarters, where persons were being held 24 hours per day in overcrowded cells, which were humid, dirty and poorly lit and ventilated." The CPT further recommended that all those who were deprived of their liberty by law enforcement authorities, regardless of the circumstances, be granted, from the very outset of their deprivation of liberty, the right to notify a close relative or third party of their choice about their situation. Concern was also expressed about the fact that some people in police custody needed urgent medical attention, but that this had not been provided.

AI country reports/ visits
Statement

- Latvia: Leading politicians make remarks which may have incited to verbal and physical attacks (AI Index: EUR 52/001/2005)

LEBANON

LEBANESE REPUBLIC
Head of state: Emile Lahoud
Head of government: Fouad Siniora (replaced 'Najib Mikati in June, who replaced 'Umar Karami in April)
Death penalty: retentionist
International Criminal Court: not signed
UN Women's Convention: ratified with reservations
Optional Protocol to UN Women's Convention: not signed

Former Prime Minister Rafiq al-Hariri and more than 30 other people were killed in bomb attacks against civilians. A UN inquiry suggested that senior Lebanese and Syrian officials were implicated in the attack on Rafiq al-Hariri. Several people were arrested for their alleged connections with a banned political party. Tens of prisoners, including some sentenced after unfair trials in previous years, were freed under an amnesty law in July. Palestinian refugees resident in Lebanon continued to face discrimination and to be denied access to adequate housing and certain categories of employment. The law continued to discriminate against women. Protection against violence in the home was inadequate; women migrants employed as domestic workers were particularly at risk of abuse. Mass graves were exhumed in November and December.

Assassination of Rafiq al-Hariri

Former Prime Minister Rafiq al-Hariri and 22 others were killed by a car bomb in Beirut on 14 February.

Rafiq al-Hariri's murder sparked popular protests and the government resigned after losing a confidence vote in parliament in February. Subsequent elections, held between 29 May and 19 June, were won by the Future Movement Block, led by Saad al-Hariri, son of the assassinated former Prime Minister.

Speculation that the Syrian authorities were involved in the assassination prompted new demands from within Lebanon and internationally for Syria to withdraw its military forces from Lebanon, in accordance with UN Security Council Resolution 1559 of September 2004. In May the UN confirmed that Syria had withdrawn its forces from Lebanon.

UN investigation

The UN Security Council sent a fact-finding team, with the agreement of the Lebanese government, to investigate the killings. The team's findings led the UN Security Council to establish the UN International Independent Investigation Commission (UNIIIC).

Four former heads of Lebanese intelligence and security services – General 'Ali al-Hajj (Internal Security Forces), General Raymond Azar (Military Intelligence), Brigadier General Jamil al-Sayyed (Sûreté Générale) and Mustafa Hamdan (Presidential Guard) – were arrested on 30 August and remained in detention at the end of the year. An interim report by UNIIIC published in October implicated senior officials of both the Lebanese and Syrian security services in the assassination and a fifth former Lebanese security official, Ghassan Tufeili, was arrested in November after he was named in the report. On 15 December, a second UNIIIC report requested that Syria detain several suspects. It also stated that Syria had hindered the investigation and that further investigation was necessary. On 15 December the UN Security Council endorsed a six-month extension of the investigation, but did not vote on the Lebanese authorities' request to establish an international court to try suspects in the case.

Other politically motivated killings

Rafiq al-Hariri's assassination was followed by 13 other bombings of civilian targets in which 12 people were killed and at least 100 injured. Among those targeted were critics of Syria's military presence in Lebanon.
▢ Samir Qasir, an academic, journalist and well-known critic of human rights abuses by the Lebanese and Syrian governments, was killed by a car bomb on 2 June in Beirut.
▢ George Hawi, former leader of the Lebanese Communist Party, was killed by a car bomb in Beirut on 21 June.
▢ Gibran Tueni, a journalist and politician well known for his criticism of Syrian interference in Lebanon, was killed with two others in a car bomb explosion in Beirut on 12 December.

In November, six Lebanese men were reported to have been charged with mounting attacks at the behest of a Syrian intelligence officer who had been based in Beirut. They had not been brought to trial by the end of 2005.

Earlier, tens of Syrian nationals working in Lebanon were reported to have been killed and others injured in attacks by Lebanese, apparently in reaction to Rafiq al-Hariri's assassination; it was not clear whether there was an investigation or any prosecutions.

'Disappearances'

A new joint Syrian-Lebanese committee was established in May to investigate the fate of more than 600 Lebanese who "disappeared" during and after the 1975-1990 Lebanese civil war, apparently while in the custody of Syrian forces. The findings of two previous Lebanese investigations were never fully disclosed and no perpetrators were ever prosecuted. Concerns about the new committee's independence and powers suggested that it would be no more effective.

A mass grave inside the Lebanese Ministry of Defence compound at al-Yarze, reportedly containing 20 bodies, was discovered in November. Another mass grave, reportedly containing 28 bodies, was exhumed in December at 'Anjar, in the Beqa' Valley, near the former Syrian military intelligence headquarters in Lebanon. During and after the Lebanese civil war, mass human rights abuses were committed with impunity. Abuses including killings of civilians; abductions and "disappearances" of Lebanese, Palestinian, and foreign

nationals; and arbitrary detentions were carried out by various armed militias and Syrian and Israeli government forces. In 1992 the Lebanese government stated that a total of 17,415 people "disappeared" during the 1975-1990 civil war, but no criminal investigations or prosecutions had been initiated by the end of 2005.

Arrests and releases

Samir Gea'gea and Jirjis al-Khouri, respectively the leader and a member of the Lebanese Forces, were freed under an amnesty law approved by parliament in July. Both were serving life sentences, imposed after unfair trials, for their alleged involvement in politically motivated killings. They had been held in solitary confinement since 1994 at the Ministry of Defence Detention Centre in Beirut.

The amnesty law also resulted in the release of at least 25 men detained for several years following violent clashes with Lebanese army troops in 2000 in the northern Dhinniyeh area. They had been charged with involvement in "terrorism" and other security offences. At the time of their release they were on trial before the Justice Council in proceedings that did not meet international standards. Some said they had been tortured and coerced into making false confessions.

Ten detainees from Majdel 'Anjar arrested in September 2004 were also released in the amnesty. Several of the men, who had not been charged or tried, were reported to have been tortured.

The authorities arrested 15 people in September for their alleged involvement with Hizb al-Tahrir (Islamic Liberation Party). All were released. Three — Sherif al-Halaq, Muhammad al-Tayesh and Bassam al-Munla — were convicted of membership of a banned organization and were awaiting sentencing at the end of the year.

Conditions in prisons and detention centres

The authorities continued to refuse the International Committee of the Red Cross (ICRC) unfettered access to all prisons despite a presidential decree in 2002 authorizing such access for the ICRC. There was particular concern about lack of ICRC access to centres operated by the Ministry of Defence where detainees have been tortured and ill-treated.

Human rights defenders

Many human rights groups operated freely but some human rights defenders were harassed or faced threats to their lives.
▢ Muhamad Mugraby, a lawyer and human rights defender, was detained for 10 hours in February. He was later charged with "slander of the military establishment" for criticizing Lebanon's military court system in a speech to the Mashrek Committee of the European Parliament in November 2003. He was due to appear before the Military Court in Beirut in January 2006.

Palestinian refugees

According to the UN, some 400,000 Palestinian refugees were resident in Lebanon. They remained subject to wide-ranging restrictions on access to housing, work and rights at work despite the Minister of Labour's decision in June to allow Palestinian refugees to work in some sectors that had previously been barred to them by law. However, Palestinian refugees continued to be excluded from the medical, legal and other professions regulated by professional syndicates.

Discrimination and violence against women

Women continued to be discriminated against and inadequately protected from violence in the family. Discriminatory practices were permitted under personal status laws, nationality laws and laws contained in the Penal Code relating to violence in the family.

In July, the UN Committee on the Elimination of Discrimination against Women recommended that Lebanon withdraw its reservations to Articles 9 and 16 of the UN Women's Convention concerning nationality and marriage rights and address inequalities which allow children to obtain Lebanese nationality only through their father and permit only men to divorce their spouse.

Women migrants employed as domestic workers faced multiple discrimination on grounds of their nationality, gender and economic and legal status. Their contracts effectively restricted exercise of their rights to freedom of movement and association by forbidding them from changing employers. They also faced exploitation and abuse by employers, including excessive hours of work and non-payment of wages. Hundreds were reported to have suffered physical and sexual abuse at the hands of employers.

The UN Special Rapporteur on trafficking in persons drew attention to the plight of migrant domestic workers during a visit to Lebanon in September, stating that they were denied basic human rights and were inadequately protected by law. The Minister of Labour said new legislation to improve conditions for migrant workers would be proposed by October 2005. However, no progress appeared to have been made on this by the end of the year.

AI country reports/ visits
Report
· Lebanon: A human rights agenda for the parliamentary elections (AI Index: MDE 18/005/2005).
Visits
AI delegates visited Lebanon several times during 2005.

LIBERIA

REPUBLIC OF LIBERIA
Head of state and government: Charles Gyude Bryant
Death penalty: abolitionist for all crimes
International Criminal Court: ratified
UN Women's Convention: ratified
Optional Protocol to UN Women's Convention: signed

Sporadic outbreaks of violence continued to threaten prospects of peace. Former rebel fighters who should have been disarmed and demobilized protested violently when they did not receive benefits. Slow progress in reforming the police, judiciary and the criminal justice system resulted in systematic violations of due process and vigilante violence against criminal suspects. Laws establishing an Independent National Commission on Human Rights and a Truth and Reconciliation Commission were adopted. Over 200,000 internally displaced people and refugees returned to their homes, although disputes over land and property appropriated during the war raised ethnic tensions. UN sanctions on the trade in diamonds and timber were renewed. Those responsible for human rights abuses during the armed conflict continued to enjoy impunity. The UN Security Council gave peacekeeping forces in Liberia powers to arrest former head of state Charles Taylor and transfer him to the Special Court for Sierra Leone if he should return from Nigeria, where he continued to receive asylum. Liberia made a commitment to abolish the death penalty. A new law on rape, which initially proposed imposition of the death penalty for gang rape, was amended to provide a maximum penalty of life imprisonment.

Background
Implementation of the Comprehensive Peace Agreement remained on track. The registration of 1.3 million voters was completed in May. Some members of the Mandingo community were denied registration or faced discrimination in establishing their Liberian nationality during the registration process.

In the lead-up to presidential and parliamentary elections in October, the peacekeeping forces of the UN Mission in Liberia (UNMIL) were increased in strength. Ellen Johnson-Sirleaf emerged as victor in the presidential ballot, after a second round of voting in November. There were some protests at polling irregularities by supporters of a rival candidate, football star George Weah. International observers considered the elections to have been free and fair.

The International Contact Group on Liberia, a grouping of donor governments, proposed measures to address corruption. In September the transitional government signed up to a Governance and Economic Management Assistance Programme, which ensures that the revenue generated from the resources of Liberia are used to impove the living standards of

Liberians. The programme required checks and balances on government spending and a transparent and functioning state bureaucracy.

The UNMIL human rights and protection section focused on failures to observe due process by the police, judiciary and prisons; provided support to the Truth and Reconciliation Commission; and made progress in drafting a National Human Rights Action Plan to fulfil Liberia's obligations under international human rights treaties.

Among the 103 international treaties Liberia acceded to in September was the Second Optional Protocol to the International Covenant on Civil and Political Rights, aiming at the abolition of the death penalty.

A new law in June provided for the establishment of a Truth and Reconciliation Commission to investigate human rights violations from 1979 to 2003. Five men and four women were selected as commissioners in October.

The return continued of refugees and people internally displaced by the war; the total number was estimated to be at least 300,000. However, there were complaints that the return programme was poorly organized although the situation improved later in the year. No arrangements were made for hundreds of thousands of refugees, who were not able to return in time for the elections, to vote. Liberian refugees in Ghana were reported to have been assaulted by the Ghanaian police in November and to have fled their refugee camp.

Incomplete demobilization
Incomplete demobilization and reintegration of former combatants resulted in several violent incidents.
◻ Former combatants rioted several times over failures to provide reintegration benefits or resettlement allowances – in January in Bong County and on three occasions in May in Nimba County.

The fragile peace process in Côte d'Ivoire affected UNMIL efforts to stabilize Liberia. Liberian children and adults in border areas continued to be recruited by armed groups, including for continuing conflict in Côte d'Ivoire. Illegal exploitation of natural resources also continued. Former combatants occupied rubber plantations and tapped rubber, claiming it was their only means of survival. They were reportedly responsible for killings and torture, including rape, against the civilian inhabitants. UNMIL subsequently took action to remove former combatants from the plantations.

By September close to 26,000 former combatants had still not entered reintegration programmes. In September the UN Secretary-General announced a US$18.5 million shortfall in international funding for reintegration and rehabilitation. This was partially met by funding made available later in the year.

Funding shortfalls contributed to delays in restructuring the armed forces. Troops demonstrated violently in June in response to late payment of their salaries. The demobilization of both regular and irregular armed forces was scheduled for completion by the end of 2005, so that the vetting, recruiting and training of a new 2,000-strong army by DynCorp, a consultancy firm based in the USA, could begin.

Ethnic tensions
A commission of inquiry into four days of violence in and around Monrovia in October 2004, in which some 20 people died and 200 were injured, reported its findings in June. It concluded that ethnic tensions and discrimination against the Mandingo population were the primary cause of the violence. No action was taken to implement the commission's recommendations for further investigation and to bring those responsible to justice.

Ethnic tensions and disputes over land and property seized during the war remained a cause of concern for internally displaced people and refugees returning home. In Lofa and Nimba Counties, the Mandingo population said they had been driven from their homes during the war and their property taken over by members of the Lorma community.

Delayed reforms
The slow pace of reform of the criminal justice system resulted in continued failures of the police and the courts to respond effectively to crime. Communities took justice into their own hands, and criminal suspects were sometimes assaulted or killed where there were suspicions of ineffective policing or of injustice or corruption in the courts.

Police involvement was minimal in traditional matters such as ritual killings, trials by ordeal or witchcraft, or vigilante action against people suspected of being witches. Most such cases occurred in Grand Bassa, Grand Gedeh and River Cess Counties. Ritual killings – killings committed in the context of religious beliefs, often in pursuit of political gain – sometimes provoked popular protests. In Bong County in July, a crowd destroyed the property of a person suspected of performing ritual killings and shots were fired. The unrest was brought under control by UNMIL forces. Ritual killings reportedly increased in the period before the elections.

During a visit to Liberia in July, the UN High Commissioner for Human Rights said that strengthening the justice sector should be the highest priority, a recommendation subsequently endorsed by the UN Independent Expert on the situation of human rights in Liberia.

Police
By the end of 2005, 1,800 police officers should have been trained and deployed. Full deployment was not achieved, especially in remote areas, because of shortfalls in funding and lack of equipment. Training was provided by the UN Civilian Police (CIVPOL). A special police unit was set up to deal with violence against women and children.

Judiciary
Judicial officials systematically failed to uphold the rule of law. Ignorance of the law, poor court management, bribery and lack of accountability remained major concerns. In January a Circuit Court judge in Grand Gedeh County unfairly tried three men for murder and sentenced them to death. The UNMIL human rights section intervened and the case was subsequently dismissed for lack of evidence. In September judges and

magistrates were deployed to courts around the country. However, a shortage of judges remained, linked closely to their poor conditions of service.

Prisons

Conditions in the majority of prisons and detention centres remained well below minimum standards. Delays in processing the cases of remand prisoners through the courts resulted in overcrowding. A UN corrections team, the International Committee of the Red Cross, the World Food Programme and other partners provided prisoners with meals, blankets and mattresses. By mid-2005, 28 corrections officers had gone through a vetting and training process, and were deployed throughout the country.

Juvenile justice

Standards set by the Juvenile Justice Procedure Code were not observed. The police had a poor record of investigating reports of sexual crimes against children, and irregularities were reported in the handling of cases in which children and juveniles were brought before the courts.

Violence against women

A law on rape, sponsored by women's groups, was debated in parliament in November and passed. The law broadened the definition of rape and denied bail to anyone charged with raping a minor. The law also increased sentences for the most serious offences, allowing life imprisonment to be imposed for the rape of a minor and for gang rape.

UNMIL worked with civil society groups and the UN Development Programme on a one-year campaign to end violence against women, to start in early 2006.

Independent National Commission on Human Rights

In March a law to establish an Independent National Commission on Human Rights, provided for in the Comprehensive Peace Agreement, was passed by the National Assembly. Its members had been appointed by the head of state before the law was passed. The independent and effective functioning of the Commission was hampered by conflicts of interest and a lack of understanding of the Commission's mandate. Civil society groups continued to call for the reappointment of the commissioners in a transparent process.

Impunity

No progress was made in creating an adequate mechanism for prosecution before the domestic courts of war crimes and crimes against humanity. People suspected of such crimes were among those elected to the National Assembly in October.

UN sanctions

Sanctions on the trade in diamonds and timber were renewed by the UN Security Council in June to reinforce measures against government corruption. Several individuals who were subject to the travel ban and freezing of assets by the UN won seats in the parliamentary elections. They included Jewel Howard, Charles Taylor's wife, who was elected to the Senate in

Bong County, and Edwin Snowe, a close associate of Charles Taylor, who was elected to the House of Representatives. The UN Sanctions Committee banned the foreign travel of five men formerly associated with warring factions for destabilizing the peace process.

Charles Taylor

In July, Liberia demanded that Nigeria provide a copy of the agreement under which Charles Taylor had been allowed to leave Liberia and seek asylum in Nigeria in August 2003. On 28 July, the leadership of the Mano River Union countries (Guinea, Liberia and Sierra Leone) stated that some of Charles Taylor's activities in Nigeria breached the terms of his asylum.

In November the UN Security Council authorized UNMIL to apprehend Charles Taylor and transfer him to the jurisdiction of the Special Court for Sierra Leone if he returned to Liberia.

AI country reports/visits

Report

- Liberia: Violence, discrimination and impunity (AI Index: AFR 34/003/2005)

LIBYA

SOCIALIST PEOPLE'S LIBYAN ARAB JAMAHIRIYA
Head of state: Mu'ammar al-Gaddafi
Death penalty: retentionist
International Criminal Court: not signed
UN Women's Convention: ratified with reservations
Optional Protocol to UN Women's Convention: ratified

The People's Court was abolished. The conviction of 85 members of the banned Libyan Islamic Group – also known as the Muslim Brothers (MB) – who had been sentenced to death or long prison terms in 2002 after an unfair trial was overturned by the Supreme Court. Their retrial before a newly established ad hoc court was ongoing at the end of the year. Five prisoners of conscience who had been held since 1998 were released but many other political prisoners, including prisoners of conscience, were believed to be held and several new arrests were reported. There was still no clarity regarding the fate of suspected government opponents who "disappeared" in previous years. Freedom of expression and association remained severely restricted and one journalist was killed in circumstances suggesting official complicity. At least six people, all foreign nationals, were executed. The rights of asylum-seekers and refugees were abused.

Background

Libya's relations with the USA and other Western countries continued to improve. In October Libya and the UK agreed a Memorandum of Understanding, according to which Libya gave diplomatic assurances that it would not torture Libyan nationals suspected of terrorism by the UK if they were returned to Libya. In September the USA waived some defence export restrictions on Libya to allow US companies to participate in destroying Tripoli's chemical weapons' stockpile and to refurbish eight transport planes.

Human rights reforms

The government continued the process of reform. The People's Court, before which many political suspects had received grossly unfair trials, was formally abolished in January. The authorities said that suspects would be tried before the ordinary criminal courts in future. However, an ad hoc court was reportedly established in September to retry the case of 85 MB members whose sentences had been overturned by the Supreme Court. In August, Saif al-Islam al-Gaddafi, head of the Al-Gaddafi International Foundation for Charitable Associations (GIFCA) and son of Libya's head of state, Colonel Mu'ammar al-Gaddafi, told *Al-Jazeera* TV that Libya wished to establish an independent judiciary after dispensing with revolutionary and people's tribunals and that new legislation was being prepared to create "a free environment that is suitable for a normal political life in Libya".

In April, the authorities announced that a committee had been established to investigate an incident at Tripoli's Abu Selim Prison in June 1996 when an undisclosed number of prisoners were killed or "disappeared". Estimated figures for those killed ranged from tens to hundreds. AI called for the committee to have full powers to investigate and to recommend prosecutions of perpetrators and compensation for victims or their families, and for its findings to be made public.

In November the authorities, responding to the entry on Libya in *Amnesty International Report 2005*, stated that both Libyan law and the Constitutional Declaration contained human rights safeguards. They also denied that the country held prisoners of conscience and said that the existence of 57 "associations actively involved in different walks of life" indicated that the rights to freedom of opinion and expression were respected.

Political prisoners

Five prisoners of conscience held since 1998 were released in September, a few weeks after Saif al-Islam al-Gaddafi told *Al-Jazeera* TV that 131 political prisoners could soon be released. Ramadan Shaglouf, Tariq al-Dernawi, Tawfiq al-Jehani, Ali Be'aou and Musa al-Ziwi were all serving long prison terms for their alleged membership of the banned Islamic Alliance Movement. They reportedly pledged that they would not again become involved in politics as a condition of their release.

Despite these releases, scores of other political prisoners, including prisoners of conscience, continued to be held.

□ Fathi el-Jahmi remained in detention following his arrest in March 2004. A prisoner of conscience, he was detained after he criticized Libya's head of state and called for political reform in international media interviews. He was held by the Internal Security Agency (ISA), reportedly at a special detention facility on the outskirts of Tripoli.

□ Abdurrazig al-Mansouri, a writer and journalist, was sentenced to 18 months' imprisonment in October for possessing an unlicensed pistol. The gun was apparently found the day after he was arrested in January at his home in Tobruk. The real reason for his imprisonment was believed to be critical articles about politics and human rights in Libya that he had published on a website shortly before his arrest.

Among others who continued to be imprisoned were the 85 members of the MB, whose retrial before an ad hoc court was ongoing at the end of the year. The sentences imposed on them in 2002, which included two death sentences and long prison terms, were overturned by the Supreme Court in September. Dozens of members of other political groups, including the Libyan Islamic Fighting Group, were still serving prison sentences imposed after unfair trials in previous years.

Several new arrests were reported, including of long-term government critics who returned to Libya after apparently receiving official assurances that they would not be arrested.

□ Mahmoud Mohamed Boushima was detained in Tripoli two weeks after he returned to Libya in July from the UK, where he had been resident since 1981. The authorities denied him access to his family and did not disclose the reasons or legal basis for his detention or where he was being held, raising concern about his safety and treatment. He was still held by the ISA at the end of 2005.

□ Kamel el-Kailani was detained by the ISA when he flew to Tripoli from the UK in July. A dual UK-Libyan national, he had reportedly been assured by Libyan diplomats in London and by GIFCA that he would not be arrested if he returned to Libya. He was still held at the end of the year and the authorities had not disclosed the reason or legal grounds for his detention.

Freedom of expression and association restricted

The authorities maintained strict controls on freedom of expression and there were no independent domestic human rights organizations. The state-owned media was closely controlled and legislation continued to prohibit the formation of independent newspapers outside the existing political system. Journalists and writers who criticized the authorities were arrested or otherwise harassed.

□ On 2 June, Dhaif al-Gazzal's mutilated body was found near Benghazi 12 days after he was reported to have been detained by two men who identified themselves as ISA officials. He had been shot in the head. In March, he had left his job as a journalist on *al-Zahf al-akhdar* (The Green March), the official newspaper of the Revolutionary Committees, apparently because of his concern about corruption, but had continued to denounce corruption and call for political reform, including on the Internet. In July, the authorities said that an official investigation into the murder was in progress.

Death penalty

The death penalty continued to be used despite Colonel al-Gaddafi's stated opposition, but it was not clear how many death sentences were passed or executions carried out. At least six foreigners, two Turkish and four Egyptian nationals, were executed in July.

The death sentences imposed in May 2004 against five Bulgarian nurses and a Palestinian doctor were overturned in December by the Supreme Court, which ordered a retrial in a lower court. The six had been sentenced after being convicted by the People's Court of deliberately infecting 426 children with HIV while working at a hospital in Benghazi. They alleged that they were tortured in pre-trial detention. A case was brought against eight police officers, a military doctor and a translator, who were accused of being responsible for the alleged torture. All 10 were acquitted in June. The six medical workers remained in detention awaiting trial at the end of the year. The Bulgarian government and many others, including AI, had criticized deficiencies in the trial of the six.

Past 'disappearances'

No progress was made in establishing the fate or whereabouts of prisoners who "disappeared" in previous years although it was hoped that the Abu Selim investigation would result in clarification of some cases. One case, that of Iranian-born Shi'a religious leader Imam Musa al-Sadr, who reportedly "disappeared" while visiting Libya in 1978, was the subject of legal action in Lebanon, where he had been resident. A Lebanese examining magistrate called for Colonel al-Gaddafi and other Libyan officials to appear before his court in March, but they declined to do so.

Migrants and asylum-seekers

Libya continued to treat asylum-seekers inhumanely and deny them minimum protection. In August around 300 Eritreans were detained in the south-east of the country, near the border with Sudan, without being given access to lawyers or representatives of the UN High Commissioner for Refugees.

In November the UN Committee on Economic, Social and Cultural Rights expressed concern that Libya did not have a law on asylum-seekers and refugees and that the effective guarantee of their rights was "seriously undermined".

AI country reports/ visits
Statements
- Libya: Abolition of People's Court is an important step (AI Index: MDE 19/001/2005)
- EU-Libya cooperation: No safeguards for refugees (AI Index: MDE 19/044/2005)

LITHUANIA

REPUBLIC OF LITHUANIA
Head of state: Valdas Adamkus
Head of government: Algirdas Brazauskas
Death penalty: abolitionist for all crimes
International Criminal Court: ratified
UN Women's Convention and its Optional Protocol: ratified

Trafficking in women and girls remained a serious and increasing problem. The government introduced programmes to counter violence in the family and trafficking in women and children.

Domestic violence

Lithuanian law did not specifically define domestic violence as a crime, although changes in the Criminal Process Law which came into force late in 2004 allowed the authorities to remove a domestic offender from the household and to keep the offender separate from the victim or other family members.

During the year, the National Programme of Prevention of Violence against Children and of Support for Children for 2005-2007 was established. The Programme aimed to reduce violence against children, raise public awareness of the problem and increase children's ability to recognize different forms of abuse and so better protect themselves.

Trafficking of women and girls

According to a survey issued by the International Organization for Migration (IOM), the number of people being trafficked to work in the sex trade increased following Lithuania's entry into the European Union (EU) in 2004. About 2,000 women and girls were taken abroad illegally. Nearly a quarter ended up in the UK where about 15 Lithuanian women a month aged between 18 and 25 were sold, according to Interpol.

The IOM survey also highlighted a marked increase in internal trafficking and a rise in the trafficking of minors. Organizations working with trafficked women and girls who had returned to Lithuania were believed to be reaching only 10 per cent of those affected.

Trafficking-related convictions and sentences increased in 2005, but the overall effort to investigate and prosecute allegations of trafficking still remained inadequate. Recent amendments to the Penal Code raised the maximum punishment for trafficking in human beings to 12 years' imprisonment if victims were adults and to 15 years if the victims were children.

On 24 May, the Lithuanian government adopted a new Programme on Control and Prevention of Trafficking in Human Beings for 2005-2008, under the coordination of the Minister of the Interior. This programme aimed to reintegrate victims of trafficking, providing medical, legal and psychological support. It further intended to provide counselling and occupational training as part of the rehabilitation programme.

Equal treatment

On 1 January, the Law on Equal Treatment came into force, implementing the prohibition of any direct or indirect discrimination on the grounds of age, sexual orientation, disability, racial or ethnic origin, religion or beliefs. While this was a welcome step, concerns remained about the vague definition of equal treatment in Article 2 of the Law.

MACEDONIA

THE FORMER YUGOSLAV REPUBLIC OF MACEDONIA
Head of state: Branko Crvenkovski
Head of government: Vlado Buckovski
Death penalty: abolitionist for all crimes
International Criminal Court: ratified
UN Women's Convention and its Optional Protocol: ratified

Investigations were opened into allegations that the Macedonian authorities unlawfully transferred a German national into US custody in Afghanistan. Two people were imprisoned after a "terrorism" trial conducted in camera. The International Criminal Tribunal for the former Yugoslavia (Tribunal) indicted two former officials for war crimes committed in 2001 and decided to return four cases involving former leaders of the Albanian National Army (ANA) to the Macedonian authorities for trial. Three former officials were acquitted by domestic courts in connection with the extrajudicial execution of seven migrants in 2002. Violence against women remained widespread but prosecutions were rare.

Background

Although the Albanian minority were increasingly represented in the police force and municipal authorities, reforms to tackle discrimination against minority communities, agreed under the Ohrid Agreement following the 2001 conflict, proceeded slowly.

Elections in March in 80 municipalities created in August 2004 failed to guarantee universal and equal suffrage or ensure the secrecy of the ballot. The Organization for Security and Co-operation in Europe urged investigations of those suspected of electoral offences. Many ethnic Albanian women were reportedly denied the right to vote.

On 9 November Macedonia's 2004 application to join the European Union (EU) was received positively, although no date was set for talks at the London summit on 15 December.

Unemployment and poverty levels remained high. According to official figures, about 18 per cent of the population was unemployed. The World Bank reported in November that some 22 per cent of the population lived in "absolute poverty".

In January a National Strategy for Roma was launched. However, Romani women were denied education, employment and health care rights because they were not Macedonian citizens, according to reports in July to the UN Committee on the Elimination of Discrimination against Women.

The EU police force tasked with advising the Macedonian police left the country on 15 December.

Indictments for war crimes

On 14 March indictments were made public by the Tribunal against former Minister of Internal Affairs Ljube Boshkovski and Jovan Tarchulovski, a police officer, who were transferred to the Tribunal's custody on 24 March and 16 March respectively. Ljube Boshkovski was charged with criminal responsibility for murder, destruction of houses and cruel treatment in the predominantly ethnic Albanian village of Ljuboten in August 2001.

In April the Tribunal's Chief Prosecutor informed the Macedonian authorities that the remaining four cases, in which the Tribunal had gained primacy over national courts in a ruling on 4 October 2002, would be returned to Macedonia for trial. On 20 June the Macedonian Public Prosecutor was reported to be still awaiting a date from the Tribunal for a joint review of war crimes cases under the Tribunal's jurisdiction involving suspects who may not have benefited from a 2002 amnesty. A March 2002 law amnestied those whose offences in the 2001 conflict came under national jurisdiction. No review had taken place by the end of 2005.

Political trials

The presence in a Skopje suburb of an armed group of ethnic Albanians, including former ANA leader Agim Krasniqi, continued despite negotiations in late 2004. On 5 June, four police officers were handcuffed, beaten and detained for two hours after they went to arrest Agim Krasniqi, indicted on seven criminal charges. He voluntarily surrendered to the court in August, and proceedings opened in October.

In April, Rajmonda Malecka, a journalist from Albania, was arrested after she visited Kondovo to interview Agim Krasniqi. Her father, Bujar Malecka, was also arrested. Video tapes allegedly showing the ANA conducting exercises were found in their possession. On 13 May they were convicted of "preparation for terrorism" in a trial conducted in camera at Skopje District Court, and each sentenced to five years' imprisonment. On 23 September the Court of Appeal annulled the conviction on the grounds that the verdict was "unclear and incomprehensible" and that no link had been established between the activities of the defendants and the charge on which they had been indicted. It returned the case for retrial to the Skopje court, which on 8 November confirmed the original verdict. There were concerns that the prosecution was politically motivated and the trial unfair.

The 'disappeared' and abducted
There was little progress in discovering the fate of 20 missing people – 13 ethnic Macedonians, six ethnic Albanians and one Bulgarian citizen – who "disappeared" or were abducted during the 2001 conflict.

▭ Despite the appearance of former ANA commander Daut Rexhepi "Leka" at a public election meeting in Tetovo in February, he was not arrested until September. An arrest warrant had been issued in September 2004 in connection with the abducted ethnic Macedonians. His trial began in October.

No indictments in connection with the "disappeared" ethnic Albanians had been issued by the end of 2005.

Extrajudicial executions in Rashtanski Lozja
On 22 April, Skopje District Court acquitted three former police commanders and a businessman charged with killing one Indian and six Pakistani nationals in March 2002 in Rashtanski Lozja. The judge found insufficient evidence that the seven migrants were unlawfully killed on the pretext that they were international terrorists. Former Minister Ljube Boshkovski, also indicted, remained in the Tribunal's custody (see above).

The authorities had acknowledged in 2004 that the seven had been extrajudicially executed, despite earlier claims that they were Islamic militants connected to ethnic Albanian insurgents and had fired on the authorities.

Key witnesses, including two special police officers among the original suspects arrested, withdrew in court statements made during the initial pre-trial investigation. Both the Macedonian Public Prosecutor and the Foreign Ministry of Pakistan indicated they would appeal against the acquittal.

'War on terror'
In November, state prosecutors in Germany opened investigations into allegations that Lebanese-born Khaled el-Masri, a German national, had been unlawfully transferred into US custody in Afghanistan. He was reportedly detained by Macedonian police officers on 31 December 2003, repeatedly questioned about Islamic organizations, handed over on 24 January 2004 to the US Central Intelligence Agency (CIA) and – outside any judicial process – flown to an airbase in Afghanistan for further interrogation. He was sent to Albania in May 2004. In December 2005 the US authorities said he was one of five people detained on the basis of mistaken identity.

Prisoner of conscience Zoran Vranishkovski
On 23 June, the Bitola Court of Appeal confirmed the conviction of Zoran Vranishkovski, a bishop of the Serbian Orthodox Church in Macedonia in Ohrid. In

August 2004 he had been sentenced to 18 months' imprisonment for allegedly inciting religious and ethnic hatred through his support for ecclesiastical control of the Macedonian Orthodox Church by the Serbian Orthodox Church. He was arrested on 26 July to serve his sentence as a prisoner of conscience.

Violence against women
In proceedings against a previously convicted trafficker in March, mechanisms to protect witnesses were ineffective. A witness protection law was introduced in May. On 1 November, a national referral mechanism was launched that would provide assistance and protection to those affected by trafficking.

Domestic violence against women remained widespread but prosecutions were rare.

▭ Of 100 incidents reported to the Tetovo police by August, criminal proceedings were brought in 10 cases, only one of which resulted in a conviction.

Refugees and internally displaced people
According to the UN High Commissioner for Refugees (UNHCR), 831 registered internally displaced people remained after the 2001 conflict in Macedonia. Some 160 registered people who were unable to return to their homes reportedly had their status withdrawn.

According to UNHCR, there were some 2,114 refugees from Kosovo, predominantly Roma, Ashkali or Egyptiani, 1,234 of whom were under "temporary protection". Few were granted asylum, and some were reportedly threatened with return to Kosovo. In May the government opened discussions with the Kosovo authorities on protocols for their voluntary return.

AI country visits/reports
Reports
- Amnesty International's concerns on the implementation of the "completion strategy" of the International Criminal Tribunal for the former Yugoslavia (AI Index: EUR 05/001/2005)
- Europe and Central Asia: Summary of Amnesty International's Concerns in the Region, July-December 2004: Macedonia (AI Index: EUR 01/002/2005)

MALAWI

REPUBLIC OF MALAWI
Head of state and government: Bingu wa Mutharika
Death penalty: retentionist
International Criminal Court: ratified
UN Women's Convention: ratified
Optional Protocol to UN Women's Convention: signed

The food crisis intensified during 2005. Prison conditions remained a significant concern. There were instances where freedom of expression was threatened. The government began investigations into child prostitution.

Background

Following a split within the ruling United Democratic Front (UDF), the President left the UDF to form the Democratic Progressive Party (DPP). Opposition parties were drawn into this conflict, distracting government and legislators from national priorities such as the hunger crisis. This culminated in October in moves to impeach the President. The impeachment did not proceed. This political insecurity appeared to fuel a disturbing tendency to crack down on critics of the government.

Policing

Torture and ill-treatment of suspects in police custody were reported.

▭ On 6 June, 12-year-old Mabvuto Bakali, who was detained on suspicion of theft, died in police custody following severe beatings at Ngabu Police post. When villagers confronted police, live ammunition was used to disperse the crowd, killing 16-year-old Anock Sande. A police investigation into the deaths had not been completed by the end of the year.

Police arrested individuals critical of those in the President's immediate circle.

▭ In October, members of parliament instrumental in the impeachment process were arrested on charges of falsifying documents in what the President described as "tit for tat" arrests.

Prisons

Conditions in prisons remained a serious concern. According to official figures, on average more than 14 people died every month in an average prison population of 9,700 people.

The International Committee of the Red Cross (ICRC) considers that more than 15 deaths per month in a prison population of 10,000 in sub-Saharan Africa requires urgent remedial measures. Many of the deaths were HIV-related, but many were treatable and avoidable. Overcrowding, poor diet and poor sanitary facilities in prisons exacerbated AIDS-related conditions and other illnesses. The prison authorities continued to work within severe resource constraints.

Freedom of expression

In March, two journalists were arrested in Blantyre in connection with an article about the President's fear of ghosts in *The Nation* newspaper and broadcast on BBC World Service. They were transferred to the capital and detained for two nights before being released without charge by the Inspector General of Police.

Women's rights

Child prostitution remained widespread. Girls, including many under the age of 13 which is the legal age of consent, were "bought" from their parents for as little as US$3 on the promise of working as waitresses and then in effect indentured in brothels. The Ministry of Gender and Children's Affairs initiated investigations.

Food

Malawi faced severe food shortages after an extremely poor harvest. Despite repeated warnings by the World Food Programme of an imminent food crisis, by the end of the year food aid pledges for Malawi still fell far short of need. Concern was expressed by civil society and faith-based groups that the continuing political feud between the UDF and President wa Mutharika's DPP diverted attention and national resources from the food crisis.

MALAYSIA

MALAYSIA
Head of state: Raja Tuanku Syed Sirajuddin
Head of government: Abdullah Ahmad Badawi
Death penalty: retentionist
International Criminal Court: not signed
UN Women's Convention: ratified with reservations
Optional Protocol to UN Women's Convention: not signed

The government pledged to implement wide-ranging recommendations for police reform. At least 71 suspected Islamist activists remained detained without charge or trial under the Internal Security Act (ISA). Restrictive laws curtailed freedom of expression, association and assembly. Many people were imprisoned and caned after unfair trials for immigration offences, and some of those held pending deportation were ill-treated and held in poor conditions. At least 58 people were arrested for alleged religious "deviancy". Death sentences were imposed. Hundreds of convicted prisoners, mostly undocumented migrant workers, were caned.

Police reform

In May the independent Royal Commission of Inquiry examining the conduct and management of the police released its report. Acknowledging reports of corruption and human rights violations by police, the Commission called for legislative, procedural and disciplinary reform. Recommendations included the establishment of an independent police complaints commission with investigatory powers, stronger custodial safeguards and increased resources and training.

The government agreed in principle to implement all 125 recommendations, but the full scope and timing of the implementation process remained unclear at the end of 2005.

◻ In November, three women of Chinese nationality complained of being physically assaulted and stripped while in police detention.

◻ In December, an inquiry was established after circulation of a video clip showing a naked Malay woman detainee being required by police to perform squats while holding her ears.

Detention without trial under the ISA and Emergency Ordinance

The ISA continued to allow for detention without trial for up to two years, renewable indefinitely, of anyone considered by the authorities to be a potential threat to national security or public order.

ISA detainees were at risk of physical intimidation, humiliation and intense psychological pressure, at times amounting to torture, while held incommunicado during an initial police investigation period of up to 60 days. Complaints of abuse by ISA detainees were not effectively investigated.

◻ In a rare case, the High Court heard a civil suit lodged by Abdul Malek Hussin against police for allegedly torturing him in ISA detention in 1998.

At least 71 alleged Islamist activists reportedly remained in detention under the ISA at the end of 2005. They included 65 detainees accused of association with al-Qa'ida and Jemaah Islamiyah (JI), as well as three alleged members of the Malaysia Mujahidin Group (Kumpulan Mujahidin Malaysia, KMM). At least 38 men were also in ISA detention for alleged passport forgery or other offences.

In March, the National Human Rights Commission (Suhakam) urged the government to review the cases of all ISA detainees, calling for them to be tried or released.

◻ In March, five students detained in 2003 following their arrest in Pakistan on suspicion of links to al-Qa'ida and JI were released. They remained subjected to restriction orders curtailing their freedom of movement.

◻ In October, three alleged KMM supporters were released. Two remained under restriction orders. The three were among six detainees arrested in 2001 who had detention orders extended in September.

In September opposition parties and civil society groups called for the abolition of the Emergency (Public Order and Prevention of Crime Ordinance) Ordinance, which allows for detention without trial of those believed by police to be "hardened" criminals.

At least 700 suspected criminals, including 105 minors aged between 14 and 21, were reportedly detained under two-year renewable detention orders at the Sempang Renggam detention centre. They were held under the Emergency Ordinance or the Dangerous Drugs (Special Preventive Measures) Act, which also allows for detention without trial.

Restrictive laws

Restrictive laws continued to be used to impose unjustified curbs on the rights to freedom of expression, association and assembly of opposition figures, journalists, students and other members of civil society.

◻ In April, a magistrate's court acquitted seven students charged in 2001 with illegal assembly under the Police Act for staging a peaceful protest against the ISA. The prosecution lodged an appeal. Under the Universities and University Colleges Act (UCCA) the students had been suspended from university since 2001.

◻ In October, at least 10 students were charged under UCCA disciplinary rules for taking part in peaceful protests against disputed campus elections. In November, riot police were called to disperse a protest outside Universiti Putra Malaysia (UPM) against the disciplinary actions.

Migrant workers, refugees and asylum-seekers

In March the authorities launched mass arrest and deportation operations against people suspected of being undocumented migrant workers. There were periodic reports of abuses and the authorities failed to provide adequate medical care, food and clean water in some detention centres and police cells. In May the operations were scaled back.

Hundreds of migrant workers prosecuted under the Immigration Act were imprisoned and caned. Failure to ensure fair trial standards led to repeated miscarriages of justice.

◻ In March, Mangal Bahadur Gurung, a Nepali migrant worker, was convicted, imprisoned and whipped under the Immigration Act. In July the courts, given evidence of a valid work permit, set aside his conviction and ordered his immediate release.

The authorities failed to distinguish consistently between people seeking asylum (mostly from Myanmar and Indonesia) and undocumented migrant workers. Asylum-seekers and refugees were therefore at risk of arrest, detention and forcible return.

In July the authorities announced that recognized refugees would be permitted to work, but implementation of this policy remained slow.

◻ In June, 68 Burmese refugees and asylum-seekers were arrested after holding a peaceful pro-democracy protest outside the Myanmar embassy. Most were charged with illegal assembly and immigration offences.

Freedom of religion: growing intolerance

While Islam is the official religion of multi-ethnic Malaysia, the religious freedom of non-Malay ethnic groups is constitutionally protected. Sharia (Islamic law), which applies to ethnic Malays who by definition must be Muslim, imposes criminal sanctions on those who seek to follow other faiths (apostasy), and on those found to hold heretical beliefs that "deviate" from Sunni Islam. In June the authorities labelled 22 religious sects as "deviant".

In July a mob of unidentified men set fire to the commune of the Sky Kingdom religious sect in Terrenganu state, which calls for a peaceful synthesis of all faiths. Following the attack, 58 sect members, including women and children, were detained. Forty-five people were subsequently charged with offences under Sharia law, including practising "deviant" Islamic beliefs. There were no prosecutions of those responsible for the attack.

◻ In July Kamariah Ali and Daud Mamat, both Malay members of the Sky Kingdom religious sect arrested after the attack on their commune, filed a petition to test constitutional guarantees of freedom of religion. Charged with apostasy under Sharia law, they were released on bail before their petition was heard.

Death penalty and corporal punishment

Death sentences were imposed, mostly for drug trafficking offences. No executions were reported.

Caning, a cruel, inhuman or degrading punishment, was carried out throughout 2005 as an additional punishment to imprisonment. Hundreds of people found guilty of breaches of the Immigration Act were among those caned.

AI country reports/ visits

Report
- Malaysia: Towards human rights-based policing (AI Index: ASA 28/001/2005)

Visits
AI delegates visited Malaysia in April and November.

MALDIVES

REPUBLIC OF MALDIVES
Head of state and government: Maumoon Abdul Gayoom
Death penalty: abolitionist in practice
International Criminal Court: not signed
UN Women's Convention: ratified with reservations
Optional Protocol to UN Women's Convention: not signed

Promises of wider political freedoms were undermined by the mass arrest of people attending political gatherings and the continued imprisonment of prisoners of conscience after unfair and politically motivated trials. Flaws in the judicial system persisted. Dozens of detainees were subjected to torture or ill-treatment, and complaints of violations by security personnel remained without prompt, thorough or independent investigation.

Background

In June, parliament removed legal barriers to the functioning of political parties for the first time in the 27-year presidency of Maumoon Abdul Gayoom.

In July, parliament passed a bill to establish a Human Rights Commission. Facing mounting concerns that the Commission had been given insufficient powers, President Gayoom indicated that it would be revised.

In September, Maldives signed the Optional Protocol to the UN Convention against Torture.

International scrutiny of the human rights situation continued. The International Committee of the Red Cross visited detention centres in April and August. A delegation of British lawyers, visiting Malé in September, found that defendants were denied fundamental rights of defence, and that "the judiciary and legal system lack[ed] the basic capacity, competency and necessary independence to deliver a fair trial".

Prisoners of conscience

August and succeeding months saw a wave of arrests of opposition activists and human rights defenders.

◻ More than 100 political activists, including Ahmed Abbas, Latheefa Umar, Ahmed Mohamed Fomy, Ali Riyaz and Aminath Shareef, were arbitrarily and unlawfully detained in August after they attended a political gathering. They were held without charge or trial for periods of up to several weeks, were denied regular access to lawyers and families, and had no recourse to the courts to challenge the legality of their detention.

◻ Jennifer Latheef, a film maker and human rights defender, was sentenced on 18 October to 10 years' imprisonment on charges of terrorism, and was removed to Maafushi prison. A former prisoner of conscience, she had been arrested in September 2003 after she was among thousands of mostly peaceful protesters who demonstrated in the streets of Malé at the cover-up of a prisoner's death. She was released in December 2003 to await trial. Her trial was marked by irregularities including an arbitrary dismissal of defence witnesses. Although some acts of violence occurred during the protest, the government provided no substantive evidence to prove her involvement. Re-detained in August 2004, she was reportedly assaulted and sexually molested in custody, then held under house arrest until late 2004. Her and other detainees' complaints to the authorities of torture and ill-treatment by security personnel remained without investigation.

◻ Naushad Waheed and Ahmed Ibrahim Didi remained under house arrest, serving long sentences imposed in 2002 after unfair political trials. Two of the prisoners convicted with them, Fathimath Nisreen and Mohamed Zaki, were released in May and August respectively.

Political trials
The government in 2004 acknowledged flaws in the judicial system and promised reform, but unfair political trials continued in 2005.

◻ Prominent politician Mohamed Nasheed was arrested during a peaceful protest in mid-August. Charged with terrorism and sedition, he was remanded in custody until 1 November when he was transferred to house arrest. Under international pressure, the government allowed an international legal observer at his trial, which started on 28 August.

◻ In October, four people were sentenced to between 10 and 11 years' imprisonment on charges of involvement in violence during the mass protests in September 2003. Their trials appeared to have fallen short of internationally accepted fair trial standards.

Torture and ill-treatment
There were consistent reports that dozens of detainees were beaten and otherwise ill-treated at the time of their arrest. These reports were not investigated.

◻ Imran Zahir, a photojournalist and human rights defender, was arrested on 4 September while taking photographs of police dismantling loudspeakers at a public gathering of the opposition Maldivian Democratic Party. Officers pushed him into a police van and beat him severely. He was accused of assault, reportedly on the basis of a complaint made after his arrest, but was released without charge in early October.

AI reports/ visits
Reports
- Maldives: Human rights violations in the context of political reforms (AI Index: ASA 29/001/2005)
- Maldives: Human rights defender Jennifer Latheef should be released immediately and unconditionally (AI Index: ASA 29/006/2005)

MALTA

REPUBLIC OF MALTA
Head of state: Edward Fenech-Adami
Head of government: Lawrence Gonzi
Death penalty: abolitionist for all crimes
International Criminal Court: ratified
UN Women's Convention: ratified with reservations
Optional Protocol to UN Women's Convention: not signed

Asylum-seekers continued to be detained in contravention of international law and subjected to procedures which fell short of international standards. Harsh conditions, ill-treatment and brutality by law enforcement officials were reported from detention centres holding asylum-seekers.

Asylum and immigration
The policy of mandatory detention for up to 18 months of irregular migrants continued throughout 2005. Although the UN High Commissioner for Refugees (UNHCR) has stated that no country should justify using detention as a form of deterrence against irregular migration, the Maltese government confirmed its commitment to continue this practice in a policy paper issued in January.

The government explored options for returning irregular migrants to Libya; the Libyan authorities claimed to have stopped 40,000 people migrating from their territory in 2005. During the year several dozen people drowned while trying to reach Malta by sea; untold numbers more were feared to have also been lost at sea.

On 13 January, individuals housed in the Hal-Safi Detention Centre held a demonstration to protest at the conditions at the centre, the length of their detention and the lack of information about the progress of their applications for refugee status and humanitarian protection. Eyewitnesses reported that soldiers attacked the peaceful protesters in a violent assault. Twenty-six people were taken to hospital, several with serious injuries. On 12 December, the Maltese Board of Inquiry published the results of its investigation into the events at the Hal-Safi Detention Centre. The inquiry found that members of the armed forces applied excessive force — "exaggerated and out of proportion in the circumstances" — in their attempts to force the protesters back into the detention centre. There were reports that members of the armed forces beat migrants after they had been subdued and were lying on the ground.

In November, the government enacted an amendment to Article 10 of the Refugees Act which would allow Malta to deport asylum-seekers while their appeal against the rejection of their application for asylum was still pending.

Prohibition on torture
On 25 August, the European Committee for the Prevention of Torture (CPT) published a report on Malta

following a visit to the country in January 2004. The delegation was particularly concerned about certain physical conditions in detention facilities, such as a lack of appropriate heating and clothing for people detained at the centres. The temperature in the Hal-Safi Detention Centre was reported to drop as low as 6°C during winter nights.

The CPT delegation reported allegations of deliberate physical ill-treatment of foreign nationals, including kicks, punches and blows with batons. The report noted that cases of self-mutilation, suicide attempts, hunger strikes, vandalism and violence were relatively common and that none of the detention facilities visited had its own health care staff. Medical members of the CPT's delegation observed that the situation had a detrimental impact on the physical and psychological state of health of the detainees.

Women's rights
In late 2005, the government passed the Domestic Violence Act (2005), which defines domestic violence as "any act of violence, even if only verbal, perpetrated by a household member upon another household member". The act contains some important protective measures, such as the inclusion of harassment, both physical and verbal, as a crime and terms providing for restraining orders physically restricting the perpetrator from the areas where the victim lives and works. However the bill excludes stalking as a crime. Under the provisions of the new bill, charges may be filed by anyone – not just the victim – but the victim may ask the court to dismiss the proceedings, leaving the door open for the abuser to put pressure on the victim to drop the charges.

The act contains provisions for a court to issue Treatment Orders requiring perpetrators of violence to undergo treatment for their behaviour. Prior to this, it was estimated that on average, less than 5 per cent of men responsible for abuse sought help voluntarily to correct their behaviour. The act also calls for the establishment of a Commission on Domestic Violence to give expert advice to the government about domestic violence issues.

AI country reports/ visits
Reports
- Protection Gaps: Amnesty International's concerns to UNHCR'S Standing Committee 8-11 March 2005 (AI Index: IOR 42/001/2005)
- Malta: Alleged ill-treatment of asylum-seekers must be investigated (AI Index: EUR 33/001/2005)
- Malta: Investigation of incidents at Hal-Safi Detention Centre finds excessive use of force and ill-treatment of detainees by armed forces (AI Index: EUR 33/002/2005)

MAURITANIA

ISLAMIC REPUBLIC OF MAURITANIA
Head of state: Colonel Ely Ould Mohamed Vall (replaced Maaouyia Ould Sid 'Ahmed Taya in August)
Head of government: Sidi Mohamed Ould Boubacar (replaced Sghaïr Ould M'Bareck in August)
Death penalty: abolitionist in practice
International Criminal Court: not signed
UN Women's Convention: ratified with reservations
Optional Protocol to UN Women's Convention: not signed

Dozens of people, including prisoners of conscience, were detained during the year. Scores of people arrested in connection with alleged plots to overthrow the government in previous years were sentenced to varying terms of imprisonment after an unfair trial. All were released under a general amnesty announced in September following a coup the previous month that toppled the President. There were reports of torture, none of which appeared to have been independently investigated. The practice of slavery persisted.

Background
In August a bloodless military coup headed by Colonel Ely Ould Mohamed Vall deposed President Maaouyia Ould Taya while he was in Saudi Arabia. President Taya had been in office since 1984. The coup was welcomed by most Mauritanians but was condemned by the international community, including the UN and the African Union (AU). A Military Council for Justice and Democracy led by the new President issued a charter for governing the country. An interim government was formed charged with organizing legislative and presidential elections within two years. In September President Vall granted a general amnesty for political prisoners.

Prisoners of conscience
Dozens of political prisoners, including prisoners of conscience, were detained. Some were held for months before being provisionally released. Others were detained incommunicado at an unknown location in the capital, Nouakchott. Several arrests appeared to be part of a campaign of intimidation against religious figures and the opposition.

◻ Jemil Ould Mansour and two other prisoners were provisionally released from Nouakchott central prison in February. They were prisoners of conscience, detained solely for their religious beliefs and peaceful political activities. They had been detained in November 2004 and held incommunicado for 14 days at an unknown place on charges of "complicity in fabrication and forgery of documents that might cause a disturbance of public order and prejudice internal and external security". They were then transferred to Nouakchott civil prison.

◻ Cheick Mohamed El Hacen Ould Dedew and 20 other people, who were arrested between April and

July, were provisionally released in August after a court dismissed the case against them. They were held incommunicado at an unknown location in Nouakchott. The police stated that the 21 men were accused of "planning acts of terrorism" and of being in contact with a group allied to al-Qa'ida.

Another group of 21 political detainees, including Abdallahi Ould Eminou and two Algerian nationals, were still detained at the end of the year. The solicitor general appealed against a court decision to release them.

Unfair trial

In February about 100 civilians and military officers, including 50 tried in absentia, were convicted of threatening the security of the state in connection with a failed coup in June 2003 and alleged coup plots in August and September 2004. They were sentenced to various terms of imprisonment ranging from 18 months to life. They were among 195 defendants whose trial began in November 2004 before the criminal court in Ouad Naga. The rest were acquitted, including former President Mohamed Khouna Ould Haidalla, leader of the Rally of Democratic Forces, and Ahmed Ould Daddah.

The trial fell short of international standards. Defence lawyers did not have access to their clients' files before trial and faced serious intimidation by the President of the court. The prosecution case was based mainly on statements obtained by torture, which were admitted as evidence by the court without any scrutiny of the torture allegations.

Torture and ill-treatment

Torture and ill-treatment continued to be widespread and systematic in police stations as well as during arrests. Detainees were reportedly tied in excruciating positions and subjected to the "jaguar" technique, which involves suspending the victim from a metal bar and beating the soles of the feet. Several detainees tried in Ouad Naga (see above) said they had been tortured, including by the "jaguar" technique.

Mahfould Ould Hamed Ould Idoumou, who was arrested in May, was reportedly kept in handcuffs and leg irons for 25 days at a police training centre. Other detainees who were arrested between April and June were held naked and were beaten during interrogation.

Harsh prison conditions and health concerns

There were continuing concerns about the health of many prisoners. Some were reportedly denied access to appropriate medical attention and were held in harsh conditions, which reportedly contributed to their illnesses. The food was reportedly poor quality and did not meet the special needs of detainees.

Saleh Ould Hannena and Abderahamane Ould Mini were detained in solitary confinement in cells without windows. They were handcuffed and held in leg irons for 24 hours a day for several days. Both were released under the September amnesty.

Recognition of human rights organizations

Several Mauritanian non-governmental organizations (NGOs), including SOS Esclaves and the Mauritanian Human Rights Association, were officially recognized in June. Although recognized by international human rights bodies, including the African Commission on Human and Peoples' Rights, these and several other NGOs had remained illegal for years under Mauritanian law and had operated with great difficulty.

Slavery

Although slavery was officially abolished in 1981, further evidence emerged about the persistence of this practice. Those denouncing slavery remained at risk of harassment.

In March, Mohamed Lemine Ould Mahmoudi, a freelance journalist, was arrested after investigating a case of domestic slavery in Mederdra, south-west Mauritania. He was arrested with two other people, including the wife of an opposition senator, when he was transcribing the story of Jabhallah Mint Mohamed, who had recently fled an estate in Abokak, 20km from Mederdra, where she had been all her life. Mohamed Lemine Ould Mahmoudi was accused of harming national security and Mauritania's economic and diplomatic interests by publishing "false information". All three were released provisionally after a month.

AI country reports/ visits
Statements

- Mauritania: Health concern – six inmates in Ouad Naga prison (AI Index: AFR 38/004/2005)
- Mauritania: 2005 UN Commission on Human Rights – Recommendations to the government of Mauritania on the occasion of its election on the Bureau of the Commission on Human Rights (AI Index: AFR 38/005/2005)
- Mauritania: Fear of torture or ill-treatment (AI Index: AFR 38/006/2005)

MEXICO

UNITED MEXICAN STATES
Head of state and government: Vicente Fox Quesada
Death penalty: abolitionist for all crimes
International Criminal Court: ratified
UN Women's Convention and its Optional Protocol: ratified

President Fox's government maintained that it was committed to the implementation of international human rights treaties and standards. Nevertheless, domestically there was little advance in ending human rights violations and impunity, particularly at state level. A National Human Rights Programme was initiated but appeared to have little impact. Proposed reforms to the Constitution and criminal justice system did not progress. Presidential and congressional elections scheduled for 2006 increasingly dominated the political agenda, as did concerns over public security and violent crime. There were continuing reports of arbitrary arrest, ill-treatment and torture. The number of young women murdered in Ciudad Juárez rose again and the response to violence against women remained inadequate. The judicial system continued to be a key source of human rights violations, failing to protect the rights of victims of crime and suspects. Its failings had a disproportionate impact on the poorest and most disadvantaged sectors of society. A number of journalists were killed or threatened. Human rights defenders working in local communities faced threats and attacks. Efforts to hold those responsible for past human rights violations accountable failed. Many members of the most socially excluded communities, particularly indigenous peoples, continued to suffer discrimination and limited access to economic, social and cultural rights.

Background
Mexico ratified the Rome Statute of the International Criminal Court and resisted pressure to sign an unlawful bilateral immunity agreement with the USA. It also ratified the Optional Protocol to the UN Convention against Torture and submitted a number of overdue reports to UN thematic mechanisms. The government also played a positive role in promoting UN reform to strengthen human rights protection.

In April the Attorney General of the Republic resigned amid increasing political pressure in the wake of Congress' decision to allow the prosecution of the Mayor of Mexico City, Andrés Manuel López Obrador. The indictment of Andrés López Obrador, the presidential candidate for the Party of the Democratic Revolution (Partido de la Revolución Democrática, PRD) would have led to his disqualification from the presidential elections. The prosecution, which was abandoned in May, had been widely perceived as politically motivated.

According to reports, at least 440 undocumented migrants died while trying to cross the border into the USA. The USA proposed that a border wall be constructed. This raised concerns that more migrants would attempt to cross in the most dangerous desert regions, resulting in increased fatalities.

Judicial reform
Congress amended the Constitution and the Military Penal Code, abolishing the death penalty for all crimes. Important reforms were also initiated regarding juvenile justice. However, Congress failed to agree other major human rights reforms.

In response to the failure to secure changes at federal level, some states proposed changes to their local justice systems, but by the end of the year it was unclear what the effects of these initiatives were.

No action was taken to limit the application of military justice to ensure that military personnel accused of committing human rights violations are investigated and tried in the civil judicial system.

A National Human Rights Programme was initiated. However, it did not receive new resources and lacked an effective national plan. An evaluation committee was established in November involving some human rights organizations.

A new representative was assigned to the Office of the UN High Commissioner for Human Rights in Mexico City. Despite a number of valuable projects, there were few advances in the implementation of recommendations proposed by the UN Office.

Impunity
Little progress was made in bringing to justice those responsible for grave human rights violations committed during the "dirty war" in the 1960s, 1970s and 1980s. Despite four years of work, only seven arrest warrants against former state officials were executed. In the hundreds of other cases, either the Special Prosecutor did not file charges, or charges were rejected by the courts.

In July, in breach of international law, the Supreme Court ruled that genocide committed before 2001 was bound by the statute of limitations. This led to the collapse of the prosecution of nine people for the murder of students in a 1971 protest known as "Corpus Cristi".

The prosecution of former head of state Luis Echeverría and former interior minister Mario Moya, for genocide in relation to the same case, also collapsed when a federal judge ruled there was insufficient evidence to file charges. In September a judge also rejected charges, including genocide, against the former president and seven others in relation to the murder of students in demonstrations in Tlatelolco, Mexico City, in 1968. At the end of the year, a ruling by the Supreme Court was awaited on the appeal against this decision filed by the Special Prosecutor.

Violence against women
Women and young girls, particularly from the poorest sectors of society, continued to suffer discrimination

and violence in the home and community. Official statistics indicated that nearly half of all women over the age of 15 had suffered some form of violence during the previous year. Efforts by the authorities to prevent and punish such crimes were frequently inadequate, despite increasing public awareness of the problem. The Supreme Court ruled that marital rape was a crime.

The pattern of killings of women and girls in Ciudad Juárez, Chihuahua state, continued with at least 28 murders. Although the state authorities appeared to be more committed to tackling the crimes, officials responsible for failings in the original investigations were not held to account and there was little progress in bringing to justice those responsible for past abductions and murders both in Ciudad Juárez and the city of Chihuahua. The Special Federal Prosecutor's Office in Ciudad Juárez failed to guarantee accountability and the post remained vacant at the end of the year. The Commission for the Prevention and Eradication of Violence against Women in Ciudad Juárez and the National Human Rights Commission both issued reports containing serious criticisms of federal and state efforts to secure justice for the women of Ciudad Juárez.

◻ Seven-year-old Airis Estrella Enríquez Pando and 10-year-old Anahí Orozco Lorenzo were brutally murdered in Ciudad Juárez in May. Separate suspects were detained for both crimes and were on trial at the end of the year.

◻ In June the body of Minerva Torres was formally identified by her family, after being kept by the authorities for two years despite clear evidence as to her identity. Minerva Torres was 18 years old when she was abducted in Chihuahua city in 2003. The family filed charges against state authorities for illegal concealment of a body.

Public security
High levels of violence related to drug crime and kidnapping kept public security high on the political agenda. The government extended the military's involvement in policing functions in a number of states with the initiative "Secure Mexico", leading to more than 5,000 arrests.

◻ In May, three young men and a federal police agent were reportedly unlawfully killed in Reynosa, Tamaulipas state, by members of the Federal Preventive Police, a police force primarily made up of military personnel. Police reportedly opened fire on the victims' vehicles without provocation or warning. Families were denied information about the official investigation which was repeatedly delayed.

Unfair justice system and discrimination
A number of factors contributed to undermining the right to a fair trial, including a failure to ensure immediate access to defence counsel and a lack of effective oversight of the prosecution service and judicial police. In May the recently founded National Council to Prevent Discrimination published a national survey illustrating the patterns of discrimination faced by socially disadvantaged groups.

◻ In September Felipe Arreaga, a human rights defender and prisoner of conscience known for his environmental activism, was acquitted of murder charges after his defence demonstrated that the prosecution case had been fabricated as a reprisal for his activism.

◻ Nicolasa Ramos was released from prison in Baja California on appeal for lack of evidence. She had served nearly three years in prison on the basis of reportedly fabricated criminal charges of stealing water from the local authority on behalf of the long-standing squatter community of Maclovio Rojas, Tijuana.

◻ In June human rights defender and gay activist Octavio Acuña was murdered in Querétaro. He and his partner had filed a complaint against local police officers for discrimination in 2004 and had complained of homophobic harassment prior to the murder. Despite this, official investigators reportedly ignored evidence that the killing was motivated by homophobia.

Arbitrary detention, torture and ill-treatment
Reports of arbitrary detention and torture remained common. The authorities failed to investigate many reports of arbitrary detention or torture. The National Human Rights Commission issued a report highlighting the widespread practice of torture across the country.

◻ In June, Teodoro Pérez Pérez, an indigenous Tzotzil man from Yabteclúm, was allegedly tortured by members of the Chiapas State Police. They reportedly beat him, threw hot water on his chest, forced him to undress and threatened him with rape. He was released the following morning without charge. He was reportedly threatened after filing a complaint.

◻ At least 12 people were convicted of involvement in violent demonstrations in Guadalajara, Jalisco state, in May 2004, many reportedly on the basis of evidence extracted under torture. The state authorities refused to investigate well-founded allegations of torture or reports of irregularities in the presentation of prosecution evidence and police conduct.

◻ In June excessive force was reportedly used against protesters in Cancún resulting in 34 detentions and a number of injuries. The authorities failed to investigate complaints of ill-treatment and torture.

Journalists and human rights defenders
At least four journalists were killed, apparently in reprisal for their work exposing corruption and organized crime. Many others were harassed, threatened and assaulted. The government promised to assign a special prosecutor to investigate cases. Human rights defenders working in local communities also faced intimidation, threats and judicial harassment.

◻ Obtilia Eugenio Manuel, a human rights defender in Ayutla de los Libres, Guerrero state, received death threats against herself and her family. She had highlighted abuses committed by the military in the region, including the reported rape of two indigenous women in 2002. The federal authorities provided some protection but the state authorities reportedly failed to conduct an effective investigation.

In December, journalist and women's rights defender Lydia Cacho was arrested and taken to Puebla, where she was held for 30 hours and charged with defamation. She was released on bail and was awaiting trial at the end of the year.

Southern states
Chiapas
In April police used excessive force to break up a protest in the town of Tila. They arrested 49 people, many of whom were reportedly detained arbitrarily and held incommunicado for several days.

In June various families were forced to flee their homes in Sabanilla municipality after reported threats from members of a paramilitary group, Peace and Justice (Paz y Justicia).

In October Hurricane Stan left many poor rural communities in extreme hardship and the response of the authorities was reportedly inadequate. New state legislation restricting press freedom was invoked to detain and question the editor of a local newspaper which alleged corruption in the official response to the natural disaster.

In July the Zapatista National Liberation Army, an armed opposition group, announced plans to initiate alternative political activism.

Oaxaca
There was a crisis in the rule of law and the protection of human rights. In an apparent attempt to deter opposition, the new state government executed several questionable old arrest warrants, mounted politically motivated prosecutions and undermined freedom of expression.

Agustín Sosa, a grassroots political activist, was charged and remanded in custody, initially accused of murder. Despite winning federal appeals on the grounds of insufficient evidence, local prosecutors brought further unfounded charges. National and international concern at the worsening human rights situation in the state led to his release along with the majority of other detained activists.

Staff of the opposition newspaper *Noticias* were harassed and threatened during the year, particularly by members of a trade union linked to the local governing party. The state authorities failed to take steps to investigate or punish threats against staff and attacks on the newspaper's premises. In October the Inter-American Commission on Human Rights granted precautionary measures in favour of the director and staff of *Noticias*.

Guerrero
Environmental activists were harassed and attacked.

In June gunmen in Petatlán reportedly tried to kill environmental activist Albertano Peñalosa. Two of his sons were killed and two others injured in the ambush which was apparently carried out in reprisal for his efforts to save the local forests.

In September, after two years of campaigning by local human rights organizations, legislation was passed criminalizing forced disappearance.

The manner in which the authorities sought approval for the proposed construction of the hydroelectric La Parota dam continued to cause division and communal violence.

Economic, social and cultural rights
Denial of rights to basic services remained a primary concern in many poor sectors of society, particularly indigenous communities. The impact of government programmes to alleviate poverty and marginalization remained limited.

In Chiapas and Guerrero, two of the states with the largest indigenous populations, there were insufficient health care professionals available to meet the minimum needs of the population.

Access to clean water was an increasing concern, reportedly giving rise to 413 community conflicts across the country.

AI country reports/ visits
Report
· Open letter to Mexican political parties (AI Index: AMR 41/031/2005)
Visits
In August AI's Secretary General visited Mexico and met senior government officials. AI delegates also visited the country in March.

MOLDOVA

REPUBLIC OF MOLDOVA
Head of state: Vladimir Voronin
Head of government: Vasile Tarlev
Death penalty: abolitionist for all crimes
International Criminal Court: signed
UN Women's Convention: ratified
Optional Protocol to UN Women's Convention: not signed

Torture and ill-treatment in police custody were widespread. There were restrictions on freedom of expression and attempts to silence opposition politicians. The death penalty was completely abolished in law. Men, women and children were trafficked for forcible sexual and other exploitation. Two men continued to be arbitrarily detained in the self-proclaimed Dnestr Moldavian Republic.

Background
In March the ruling Communist Party of President Vladimir Voronin won parliamentary elections. The elections generally met standards set by the intergovernmental Organization for Security and Co-operation in Europe, election observers reported, but

access to the media and to campaigning facilities favoured the government party. In February a joint Moldova Action Plan was signed with the European Union, setting objectives for further moves towards European integration.

Torture and ill-treatment in custody

On 30 June parliament amended the Criminal Code to make torture a criminal offence. Poor conditions of detention and ill-treatment in pre-trial detention facilities continued to be reported.

◻ Stela Draghici, who is registered blind, was transferred from a temporary detention centre operated by the police Department for Combating Organized Crime in Chişinău to a detention centre in Beltsy, a northern town. No allowances were made for her disability in either facility, for example in assisting her to the shower or toilets, resulting in bullying by other inmates. Repeated appeals by lawyers for an improvement to her detention conditions were ignored.

◻ Mikhail Kaldarar, Vasilii Kodrian, Anna Kodrian and Vyacheslav Pleshko were detained without charge or trial in the weeks following an armed police raid in the town of Yedintsy on 18 July to investigate a multiple murder in Chişinău. More than 30 Romani men and boys were allegedly arrested and beaten to force them to confess and to incriminate others. Mikhail Kaldarar was arrested on 18 July and detained for more than six weeks despite an order for his release by an appeal court in Beltsy on 25 July. Vasilii Kodrian was arrested on 5 August and detained without charge for over a month, allegedly because his son was a suspect. His wife, Anna, was arrested on 18 August and briefly detained. Vyacheslav Pleshko was arrested in Ukraine by Ukrainian and Moldovan police in late July or early August, forcibly returned to Moldova without any extradition proceedings, and detained at a temporary holding facility in Yedintsy until 4 September. All four were released without charge.

In a resolution adopted on 4 October, the Parliamentary Assembly of the Council of Europe called on Moldova to continue the reform of law enforcement agencies and to considerably improve conditions of detention.

Freedom of expression

The threat of heavy fines for "moral damage" or "insulting the honour and dignity" of an individual (Article 16, Civil Code) was used in defamation cases brought against journalists and the media for publishing criticisms of politicians and officials.

◻ In April, Iurie Roşca, head of the Christian-Democrat People's Party and Deputy Speaker of Parliament, sued the *Timpul de dimineaţa* and *Jurnal de Chişinău* newspapers under Article 16 for 50,000 and 62,000 euros respectively in damages. They had published articles criticizing him.

◻ In October the European Court of Human Rights ruled that there had been a violation of the right to freedom of expression in the case of Julieta Saviţchi, a correspondent of the *Basapress* news agency. She had

been prosecuted for defamation for publishing an article about corruption in the traffic police.

Opposition politicians prosecuted

In its 4 October resolution, the Parliamentary Assembly of the Council of Europe called for an investigation into the high number of court cases against leading opposition figures.

◻ Mihail Formuzal, Mayor of Ceadar Lunga in the Gagauz autonomous region, Chair of the opposition People's Republican Party, and a rival contestant to a ruling party incumbent for the regional governorship, faced criminal charges twice. In July he was tried for alleged abuse of office and acquitted. In October he was charged with misuse of funds.

◻ Georghe Straisteanu, a former member of parliament, founder of the first private television company in Moldova, and a well-known critic of government attacks on media freedoms, was detained with an employee on 22 July. He was charged with a series of large-scale thefts from cars, punishable by up to 25 years' imprisonment (Article 195, Criminal Code). His employee testified for the prosecution after allegedly being tortured. Acquitted and released on 18 August by the Central District Court of Chişinău, Georghe Straisteanu was reported to have been immediately redetained by police officers in defiance of a further court order on 19 August for his release. He remained in pre-trial detention until 17 November when he was released on bail on condition that he remain at his place of residence. At the end of 2005, the car thefts trial was still pending.

Death penalty

Moldova took further steps towards abolition of the death penalty in law. In September the Constitutional Court approved two amendments to the provision in the Constitution that had previously allowed for the death penalty in certain cases. Parliament was due to take a final decision in 2006.

Violence against women

In May, Moldova signed a Council of Europe declaration agreed by member states at a summit meeting in Warsaw that included a commitment to fight domestic and other forms of violence against women and children. Also in May, Moldova signed the Council of Europe Convention on Action against Trafficking in Human Beings. On 20 October the Moldovan parliament adopted a law on trafficking.

Although Moldova reportedly increased the number of convictions for trafficking in human beings, protection for the victims of trafficking remained inadequate and the government did not implement a 1998 witness protection law. The main destinations were Cyprus, Russia, Turkey and the United Arab Emirates, according to a local human rights organization, La Strada. In most cases women were trafficked for sexual exploitation, but also sometimes for forced labour. Trafficked women were mainly seeking work abroad because of unemployment and domestic violence. Increasing numbers of children and men were trafficked.

Self-proclaimed Dnestr Moldavian Republic

The status of the Dnestr Moldavian Republic (DMR), an internationally unrecognized breakaway region, remained unresolved.

⬭ Tudor Petrov-Popa and Andrei Ivanțoc were still in detention in Tiraspol at the end of 2005, despite a July 2004 judgment by the European Court of Human Rights, which did not recognize their conviction by a court of the DMR and which found their detention to be arbitrary and in breach of the European Convention on Human Rights. They were members of the "Tiraspol Six", who were sentenced to prison terms in 1993 for "terrorist acts", including the murder of two DMR officials. The four men convicted with them were released in 1994, 2001 and 2004.

The Criminal Code of the DMR retained the death penalty for six offences, but a moratorium on its use continued.

AI country reports/ visits

Report
- Europe and Central Asia: Summary of Amnesty International's concerns in the region, January-June 2005: Moldova (AI Index: EUR 01/012/2005)

MONGOLIA

MONGOLIA
Head of state: Enkhbayar Nambaryn (replaced Bagabandi Natsagiin in June)
Head of government: Elbegdorj Tsakhiagiin
Death penalty: retentionist
International Criminal Court: ratified
UN Women's Convention and its Optional Protocol: ratified

Prisoners held in police stations, pre-trial detention facilities and on death row were at risk of torture or ill-treatment in harsh living conditions. The application of the death penalty remained highly secretive.

Torture and ill-treatment

Torture and ill-treatment persisted and beatings were systematic in police stations and pre-trial detention facilities.

⬭ In May, Monkhbayar Baatar died eight days after being released from Gants Hudag detention centre. At the time of his release, he had severe bruising on his body and repeatedly vomited blood.

Detention conditions remained harsh. Prisoners typically suffered from overcrowding, a high incidence of tuberculosis, inadequate nutrition and extremes of hot and cold temperatures in cells. Those serving special 30-year "isolation sentences" were subjected to extreme physical and mental suffering by being deliberately isolated from other prisoners and denied visits from families and lawyers.

Despite a new unit in the Prosecutor's Office to combat abuses by law enforcement officials, impunity remained a problem. Mechanisms to receive and investigate allegations of ill-treatment were ineffective. The Criminal Code contained no definition of "torture" in line with the UN Convention against Torture. Compensation or rehabilitation was not available to torture victims.

The UN Special Rapporteur on torture visited Mongolia in June and highlighted the unimpeded impunity enjoyed by those responsible for torture and other ill-treatment.

Human rights defenders at risk

⬭ Prisoner of conscience and lawyer Lodoisambuu Sanjaasuren was reportedly denied access to his doctor in prison from May onwards despite a worsening heart condition. In a closed trial, he had been convicted of revealing state secrets and sentenced to 18 months' imprisonment in November 2004 after his client, Enkhbat Damiran, described on television being abducted from France and tortured by Mongolian security agents. Lodoisambuu Sanjaasuren was released in August after serving half his sentence.

Death penalty

The government failed to make available statistics on death sentences and executions. Human rights workers were denied access to prisoners on death row. Three prisoners under sentence of death reportedly killed themselves in Gants Hudag detention centre in November and December because of the harsh conditions and to ensure that their bodies were returned to their families for burial. The UN Special Rapporteur on torture found conditions on death row to be so poor as to amount to cruel treatment.

Alleged violence against protesters

The authorities reportedly failed to investigate allegations of assaults on peaceful protesters by the security personnel of a private company.

⬭ In May and July, private security forces employed by the Mongol Gazar Mining Company in Arkhangai province allegedly dispersed unarmed demonstrators with tear gas, batons and shots fired in the air. Activists were protesting that mining would harm water resources and destroy ancestral burial grounds. Security agents were said to have thrown one woman to the ground and kicked her; struck and injured other protesters with batons, handcuffs and rifle butts; and wrecked a television reporter's camera.

Trafficking of women

Trafficking of women increased from the early 1990s, according to a study by the non-governmental organization, the Asia Foundation. Most at risk were young, single women, lured by recruiters with promises of education or high-paying jobs. Most were trafficked to China, including Macao, and South Korea as well as to European countries, including Poland and Hungary, for commercial sexual exploitation. The Criminal Code continued to lack clear and comprehensive anti-trafficking provisions.

AI country reports/ visits
Statement
· Mongolia: Medical/legal concerns/prisoner of conscience – Lodoisambuu Sanjaasuren (AI Index: ASA 30/001/2005)

MOROCCO/ WESTERN SAHARA

KINGDOM OF MOROCCO
Head of state: King Mohamed VI
Head of government: Driss Jettou
Death penalty: abolitionist in practice
International Criminal Court: signed
UN Women's Convention: ratified with reservations
Optional Protocol to UN Women's Convention: not signed

The Equity and Reconciliation Commission completed its work and submitted its report to King Mohamed VI. It recommended that compensation be paid to more than 9,000 people who had suffered human rights abuses between 1956 and 1999, but it was not permitted to name perpetrators. New allegations surfaced about Morocco's role in the US-led "war on terror". Eight Sahrawi human rights defenders were imprisoned after protests which originated in Western Sahara and to which police responded with excessive force. At least 13 migrants were shot dead at the border between Morocco and the Spanish enclaves of Ceuta and Melilla. The Polisario Front released the last of the Moroccans it had held as prisoners of war; some had been held for almost 20 years.

Background
From May until December, the territory of Western Sahara, particularly the town of Laayoune, was rocked by a series of demonstrations. In many of them, demonstrators expressed their support for the Polisario Front, which calls for an independent state in the territory and had set up a self-proclaimed government-in-exile in refugee camps in south-western Algeria, or called for independence from Morocco. The continuing deadlock in attempts to

resolve the dispute between Morocco and the Polisario Front over Western Sahara appeared to have been a major factor behind the protests.

Equity and Reconciliation Commission
The groundbreaking Commission, the first truth commission in the Middle East and North Africa region, completed its work in November and reported its findings to King Mohamed VI. Since it was inaugurated in January 2004 with a remit to inquire into grave human rights violations committed between 1956 and 1999, the Commission had received information from more than 16,000 people. Many had appeared in person before the Commission. Several dozen had spoken about their experiences at seven televised hearings held in six regions of Morocco. A planned hearing in Laayoune, Western Sahara, was cancelled without official explanation. AI co-operated with the Commission, providing it with hundreds of documents from its archives, including details of several hundred cases of "disappearance" and arbitrary detention.

The Commission placed particular emphasis on finding ways of providing reparations. It ruled that over 9,000 individuals should receive financial compensation, and recommended assistance for those in need of medical attention or rehabilitation as a result of the violations they had suffered. The Commission also made a series of proposals for institutional and legislative reform.

The Commission's final report announced that it had resolved 742 "disappearance" cases and that 66 outstanding cases would be investigated further by a follow-up committee. The Commission indicated, however, that it had often not obtained the testimonies and documents it had requested from state officials, who were under no compulsion to co-operate with it. Many families of the "disappeared" were consequently disappointed.

Under its statute, the Commission was precluded from assigning responsibility to individuals for violations and, in its final report, made no proposals for suspected perpetrators to be brought to account. Impunity for past crimes remained a serious concern, particularly since some alleged perpetrators continued to be members, or even high-ranking officials, of the security forces. The independent Moroccan Human Rights Association, one of the Commission's main critics on this issue, organized its own public hearings, in which some victims named individuals they held responsible for violations against them.

Abuses in the context of the 'war on terror'
New allegations surfaced about Morocco's role in the US-led "war on terror". In December a Council of Europe investigator said that he believed some prisoners previously held by the USA in Europe had been moved to North Africa, possibly Morocco, a month earlier. Morocco denied the claim. However, the allegation echoed previous reports that the USA had sent detainees to Morocco for interrogation.
🖾 Information emerged about the case of Benyam Mohammed al-Habashi, an Ethiopian national. He was

arrested and detained in April 2002 by Pakistani officials in Pakistan, and said that he was handed over to US officials in July 2002 and then flown to Morocco. He alleged that he was held incommunicado there for the next 18 months and systematically tortured at the behest of US authorities, before being taken to Afghanistan and then to the US naval base at Guantánamo Bay, Cuba, where he remained held at the end of the year.

Dozens of suspected Islamist activists were arrested and prosecuted in Morocco during the year. This brought the total number of those arrested since bomb attacks in Casablanca in May 2003 to over 3,000 and the total of those prosecuted to over 1,500, according to official statements. Many of those prosecuted were sentenced to prison terms on charges based on a broad and unspecific definition of terrorism. At least four were sentenced to death.

Protests in Western Sahara
Popular protests which rocked Western Sahara, particularly Laayoune, from May until December were met with a police response that included excessive use of force. Scores of people, mostly demonstrators but also including police, were injured. Hundreds of people were arrested. Two men died allegedly after being beaten by police on arrest.

⌐ Hamdi Lembarki, aged in his thirties, died on 30 October as a result of a head injury, according to an autopsy. Witnesses said that several Moroccan police officers had arrested him during a demonstration in Laayoune, taken him to a nearby wall, surrounded him and repeatedly beat him with batons on the head and other parts of his body. An investigation was launched by the authorities into his death.

Dozens of those held in custody alleged that they were tortured or ill-treated, either to force them to sign confessions, to intimidate them from protesting further or to punish them for their pro-independence stance. In July the Justice Ministry told AI that all complaints it received were treated seriously and that, on the basis of three complaints, investigations had been opened into allegations of torture and ill-treatment.

Dozens of people were charged with inciting or participating in violence in the demonstrations. Over 20 were later convicted and some were sentenced to several years in prison. Among those sentenced were seven long-standing human rights defenders who were monitoring and disseminating information on the crackdown by the security forces. Two alleged that they had been tortured during questioning. An eighth human rights defender was detained awaiting trial at the end of the year. All eight were possible prisoners of conscience.

Freedom of expression
Continuing restrictions on freedom of expression were reported, particularly on issues related to the monarchy and the Western Sahara dispute. Several journalists from independent newspapers and magazines, such as *Tel Quel*, were sentenced to suspended prison terms or heavy fines in this regard. In an unprecedented move, the Moroccan authorities blocked access to the Internet sites of several international associations advocating independence for Western Sahara.

⌐ Ali Lmrabet, a journalist and former prisoner of conscience, was banned from working as a journalist for 10 years in April and given a heavy fine after he was convicted of violating both the Penal Code and Press Code. The case arose from a report he wrote after becoming the first Moroccan journalist to visit the refugee camps run by the Polisario Front in south-western Algeria. He stated that the Sahrawis there were refugees, not held as captives as the Moroccan authorities had long contended. This led to his being accused of defaming the spokesperson of a Moroccan organization that campaigns for the "release" of the Sahrawis in the camps.

Legal reform
Torture
Legal safeguards against torture were strengthened. A law defining torture as a criminal offence, punishable by long prison terms, was approved by parliament in October. At the international level, Morocco recognized the competence of the UN Committee against Torture to investigate complaints submitted by individuals.
Women's rights
Women continued to face discrimination despite the introduction of the reformed Family Code in 2004. In July, however, King Mohamed VI announced that one more element of discrimination was to be removed, declaring that the 1958 Citizenship Act would be reformed to allow children of Moroccan mothers and foreign spouses to be eligible for Moroccan citizenship on the same basis as children of Moroccan fathers with foreign spouses.

Refugees and migrants
Thousands of migrants, many of them from countries in west and central Africa and including an unknown number of refugees and asylum-seekers, sought to gain access to countries of the European Union from Morocco. Many congregated close to the Spanish enclaves of Ceuta and Melilla and made efforts to gain entry to the enclaves by various means, including by climbing over border fences. This came to a crisis point between late August and early October when both Spanish and Moroccan security forces resorted to excessive and, in some cases, lethal force against the migrants. At least 13 were killed as a result, some being shot dead while they were reportedly scaling fences but posing no risk to the lives of security force personnel or others. Moroccan officials told AI in October that judicial authorities were investigating the deaths of people whose bodies were found on the Moroccan side of the border.

From September Moroccan authorities forcibly removed hundreds of migrants from their informal camps close to the enclaves. They arrested some and transported others to remote desert areas close to Morocco's border with Algeria, where they were dumped without adequate water, food or shelter, reportedly resulting in further deaths. Hundreds of migrants and dozens of asylum-seekers were subsequently held in military bases without access to legal counsel and other rights guaranteed to them under Moroccan law, such as the right to appeal against their custody. Many of the migrants were then repatriated, while the asylum-seekers had their claims assessed by representatives of the UN High Commissioner for Refugees after being denied access to them for several weeks.

Polisario camps

In August, the Polisario Front released the last prisoners of war that it was holding in its camps in south-western Algeria. Some 404 prisoners were handed into the care of the International Committee of the Red Cross and repatriated to Morocco; some had been held for almost 20 years.

In November the Polisario Front committed to a total ban on the use of anti-personnel mines by signing the Deed of Commitment of Geneva Call, an international humanitarian organization dedicated to engaging armed non-state actors to respect humanitarian norms.

Those responsible for human rights abuses in the camps in previous years continued to enjoy impunity. The Polisario Front took no steps to address this legacy.

AI country reports/ visits
Report
· Morocco/Western Sahara: Sahrawi human rights defenders under attack (AI Index: MDE 29/008/2005)
Visits
AI delegates visited Morocco in January for meetings with the Equity and Reconciliation Commission, government authorities and local associations, and in October to investigate abuses against migrants and asylum-seekers seeking access to the Spanish enclaves of Ceuta and Melilla. An AI observer visited Western Sahara in November to attend a trial of Sahrawi human rights defenders.

MOZAMBIQUE

REPUBLIC OF MOZAMBIQUE
Head of state: Armando Guebuza
Head of government: Luisa Diogo
Death penalty: abolitionist for all crimes
International Criminal Court: signed
UN Women's Convention: ratified
Optional Protocol to UN Women's Convention: not signed

Over 800,000 people needed food aid as a result of prolonged drought. Some 200,000 people were still unable to access anti-retroviral drugs and other treatment for HIV infection. High death rates from AIDS-related illnesses seriously affected economic and social development. Police officers were charged with extrajudicial executions, ill-treatment of suspects and extortion, and were imprisoned to await trial. However, others accused of using excessive force against protesters were not subject to independent investigation or brought to justice. Violence between supporters of ruling and opposition parties led to deaths and the destruction of homes. Restrictions on freedom of the press remained, and journalists faced harassment and assault.

Background

Armando Guebuza was sworn in as the new President in February. He pledged to consolidate national unity, to promote human rights and democracy, and to fight poverty, corruption and crime. In March, the new government launched a five-year programme aimed at good governance, transparency in public services management, and public security.

The judiciary remained seriously understaffed, with just over 1,000 officials, including 184 judges, serving a population of nearly 19 million. As a result, people often took justice into their own hands.

Steps to combat drug trafficking, acts of terrorism and other organized crime included the deployment of special police anti-terrorist brigades in all airports from July. However, efforts to curb rising crime were undermined by the deaths each year of around 1,000 police officers from AIDS-related illnesses.

Efforts to combat corruption included the upgrading in September of the Anti-Corruption Unit to a Central Office for Combating Corruption, with increased staffing and resources. The Anti-Corruption Unit, an investigation unit independent of the police, had proved its effectiveness in the investigation and subsequent prosecution of several high-profile cases.

In December Mozambique ratified the Protocol to the African Charter on Human and People's Rights on the Rights of Women in Africa and the protocol establishing the African Court of Justice.

Food shortages and HIV infection

Poverty remained widespread, with over half the population reported to be living on less than one US dollar a day. Over 800,000 people were affected by food shortages and in need of food aid. Severe drought in central and south Mozambique caused widespread crop failures and inflated prices.

The rate of HIV infection among people aged between 15 and 49 was 15.6 per cent, the National Statistics Institute announced in June. Only one per cent of children with HIV had access to anti-retroviral or other drugs.

Police abuses

There were fewer allegations of police torture of detainees than in previous years. Some action was taken to discipline or prosecute police officers, particularly in Manica province. There, following an investigation by the provincial Procurator in November, 14 police officers were charged with various offences, including the assault and extrajudicial execution of suspects, extortion and theft. At least five extrajudicial executions occurred in the first half of 2005. The officers were imprisoned to await trial. According to reports, one was charged with attempted murder for trying to shoot the Procurator during an interrogation session. The trial, set for December, was postponed and had not started by the end of 2005.

▭ After a robbery at a national electricity premises in Chimoio in April and an exchange of fire with the police, two suspects were reportedly captured and killed in police custody. Four police officers were arrested in August and subsequently charged with stealing proceeds from the robbery that had been recovered but later went missing. In November, two of them were also charged with the killing of the suspects.

▭ In August officers of the Rapid Intervention Police and the public order police harassed and beat people in the Munhava area of Beira, a stronghold of the Mozambique National Resistance (Renamo) party, allegedly for not carrying identity cards.

▭ In June municipal police officers in Maputo assaulted and briefly detained two photojournalists who took pictures for the *Zambeze* newspaper of officers chasing street vendors and seizing their goods. The police commander later apologized publicly and promised to punish those responsible.

The force used by the police to break up protests appeared to be excessive, and no investigations were conducted into whether force and firearms were appropriately used.

▭ In July the Rapid Intervention Police and other police units used tear gas to disperse a peaceful demonstration in the Xipamanine market in Maputo against the removal of unauthorized traders.

▭ In September the police beat and opened fire on vendors in the Limpopo market in Xai-Xai, Gaxa province, who were marching to the municipal offices to complain about conditions in the market. Two people were arrested for throwing stones at the police.

▭ Rapid Intervention Police officers reportedly assaulted striking students who set up barricades at the Eduardo Mondlane University in Maputo to protest at

new scholarship regulations. Eleven students were said to have required medical treatment for fractures and other injuries.

Political violence

Politically motivated violence erupted in Mocimboa da Praia, Cabo Delgado province, between supporters of the ruling Front for the Liberation of Mozambique (Frelimo) and the Mozambique National Resistance-Electoral Union (RUE) over disputed municipal elections won by Frelimo in May. RUE accused Frelimo of rigging the elections and in September installed a parallel local authority, prompting three days of violence. Twelve people, including a police officer, were killed; 47 were injured; and nearly 200 houses were burned in Mocimboa da Praia and the nearby town of Muindumbe. Thirty-six people were subsequently arrested. There was no official inquiry into the incident. The Mozambican Human Rights League concluded that both parties had been responsible for the violence.

Press freedoms restricted

Journalists faced harassment and official impediments to their work.

▭ In March the news media were denied access to a trial for criminal libel, an offence punishable by up to one year's imprisonment. The accused were Teodoro de Abreu, former editor of the *Demos* newspaper, and Momad Assi Satar, the author of an open letter to the Attorney General and in prison since being convicted of the murder in 2000 of Carlos Cardoso, a journalist investigating fraud and corruption. The open letter, published by *Demos* in August 2004, said the Attorney General was complicit in delaying investigations into allegations that the son of former President Joaquim Chissano was implicated in the murder. In March the libel trial was suspended in response to a defence complaint that the Attorney General was represented in court by one of his subordinates. It had not resumed by the end of 2005.

▭ In August journalist Isaías Natal said that he had been threatened with death by a Frelimo official in Sofala province after the *Zambeze* newspaper published an article about the defection of two Frelimo members to another party.

MYANMAR

UNION OF MYANMAR
Head of state: Senior General Than Shwe
Head of government: General Soe Win
Death penalty: retentionist
International Criminal Court: not signed
UN Women's Convention: ratified with reservations
Optional Protocol to UN Women's Convention: not signed

Over 1,100 political prisoners were arrested or remained imprisoned. They included hundreds of prisoners of conscience, held for peaceful political opposition activities. At least 250 political prisoners were released. The army continued to commit serious human rights violations, including forced labour, against ethnic minority civilians during counter-insurgency activities. The International Labour Organization (ILO), other UN agencies and international aid organizations faced increasing restrictions on their ability to assist vulnerable populations.

Background
The National Convention, reconvened in 2004 by the ruling State Peace and Development Council (SPDC) to draft a constitution, met in February and December. The National League for Democracy (NLD) and several other political parties did not participate, although some ceasefire groups did. The SPDC selected all the delegates, whose freedom of movement and speech were restricted.

The Karen National Union (KNU), an armed opposition group, and the government failed to agree a ceasefire amid continued fighting in the Kayin State. Conflict persisted between the Shan State Army-South (SSA-South) and government forces in the Shan State. The SPDC demanded that some armed groups in the state, which had agreed ceasefires, give up their weapons. Other smaller, ethnically based armed opposition groups continued to engage SPDC forces in the Chin and Kayah States.

All NLD offices except its headquarters in Yangon, the capital, remained officially closed on SPDC orders.

In May bombs in Yangon killed an unknown number of people.

Political imprisonment
Over 1,100 people arrested for political reasons remained in prison. The NLD and other opposition political parties faced severe restrictions, harassment and intimidation.

▢ Daw Aung San Suu Kyi, NLD General Secretary, and U Tin Oo, NLD Vice Chairman, remained under house arrest and incommunicado.

Following arrest, political prisoners were denied access to relatives and in some cases their lawyers.

▢ In February, U Khun Htun Oo, a member of parliament (MP)-elect from the Shan Nationalities

League for Democracy, and other Shan political representatives were arrested, reportedly because of their discussions about the National Convention. In November, they were sentenced in a secret trial to between 70 and 106 years' imprisonment for treason. Some had been denied access to their families since their arrest. One of the group, 82-year-old U Shwe Ohn, was held under house arrest.

Often lengthy prison sentences were imposed on scores of individuals convicted in political trials, including for the possession of published materials that had been authorized by the state censor, or on trumped-up criminal charges.

▢ Three NLD MPs-elect, U Kyaw San, U Kyaw Khin and U Saw Hlaing, arrested in February and March, were sentenced to seven, 14 and 12-year prison terms respectively – U Saw Hlaing for distributing political leaflets. U Kyaw Khin and U Kyaw San had been released in late 2004 and early 2005 from earlier prison sentences.

▢ U Kyaw Min, a National Democratic Party for Human Rights MP-elect and member of the Committee to Convene People's Parliament, was sentenced to 47 years' imprisonment, and his wife, son and two daughters to 17 years' imprisonment, reportedly for living in Yangon without official permission.

▢ NLD local officials and members were sentenced to prison terms of up to 10 years for possessing political leaflets and a video of Daw Aung San Suu Kyi visiting party members.

▢ U Sao Oo Kya, a Shan political representative related to U Khun Htun Oo, was arrested in August and sentenced to 13 years' imprisonment for reportedly infringing tour guide regulations.

Individuals who took action to end forced labour were imprisoned for their legitimate activities.

▢ U Aye Myint, a lawyer, was released from prison in January after serving a sentence imposed in part for contacting the ILO about forced labour. He was re-arrested in September and sentenced to seven years' imprisonment in October under legislation penalizing the circulation of false information. He had helped farmers lodge an official complaint to the ILO about land confiscations by the local authorities.

Releases
Some 50 political prisoners were released in January and more than 200 in July.

▢ Those released included Dr Khin Zaw Win, a dentist and NLD member arrested in 1994; Sein Hla Oo, an NLD MP-elect arrested in 1994; and Ohn Kyaing, journalist and NLD MP-elect arrested in 1990.

▢ At least seven prisoners, who were held under administrative detention laws after their sentences expired, were released. Among them were student leaders Ko Ko Gyi and Zaw Min, arrested in 1991, and Democracy Party leaders U Htwe Myint and U Thu Wai.

Torture and ill-treatment
Reports of torture in pre-trial detention and prisons persisted.

▢ An unknown number of former Military Intelligence personnel, some of whom were reportedly tortured during interrogation, received lengthy terms of imprisonment following their convictions on corruption and other charges during the year. They had been detained after Prime Minister General Khin Nyunt was deposed and arrested in October 2004. He was reportedly sentenced for corruption in July to 44 years' imprisonment. The sentence was suspended but he was restricted under house arrest.

□ Prisoners who took part in a hunger strike over conditions in Insein Prison in May were reportedly beaten and held in cells designed for military dogs.

Prison conditions remained harsh and political prisoners were denied proper medical treatment.

□ Four political prisoners reportedly died in custody, including Ko Aung Hlaing Win, an NLD Youth Wing member. It was feared that torture or inadequate health care might have contributed to some of the deaths.

□ U Win Tin, a journalist and NLD leader arrested in 1989, was one of three prisoners of conscience who remained imprisoned despite serious multiple health problems. In January and February respectively, detention orders were extended by a year on Dr Than Nyein and Dr May Win Myint, NLD MPs-elect arrested in 1997, sentenced to prison terms, and held under administrative detention orders after completing their sentences in 2004.

Ethnic minorities

Members of ethnic minorities, including the Karen, Mon, Shan and Rohingya, continued to be subjected to forced labour and other violations at the hands of the military, especially in counter-insurgency areas in the Mon, Shan, Kayah and Kayin States, and in Bago and Tanintharyi Divisions. Hundreds of thousands of civilians in these areas were still displaced from their homes, mostly because of counter-insurgency activities. They were generally cut off from international aid organizations and UN agencies, restricting their access to health care and food. Several thousand civilians in northern Kayin State and eastern Bago Division were reportedly displaced as a result of SPDC efforts to break up imputed links with the KNU. Government troops continued land confiscations, extortion and restrictions on freedom of movement in the Shan State, and abducted civilians for portering and other forced labour in the Mon State. The Rohingyas, a Muslim ethnic minority in Rakhine State, were increasingly forced to do sentry duty and to maintain roads, military camps and farms.

International developments

In July the SPDC announced that it would postpone taking up the chair of the Association of Southeast Asian Nations (ASEAN), planned for July 2006, amid widespread reports that other ASEAN member states had urged a delay. The USA and the European Union renewed sanctions against Myanmar. The UN Commission on Human Rights adopted a resolution in April, expressing grave concern at "ongoing systematic violations of human rights" and renewing the mandate of the Special Rapporteur on Myanmar. In November the UN General Assembly adopted a similar resolution. The Special Rapporteur and the UN Secretary-General's Special Envoy continued to be denied access to the country by the SPDC. The UN Security Council held a closed session to discuss the situation in December.

In February senior ILO officials visited Myanmar but were not permitted to meet Senior General Than Shwe. In June the Committee on the Application of Standards of the International Labour Conference meeting recalled its 2000 resolution instructing all members and international organizations to ensure that their relations with the SPDC did not promote forced labour, foreign direct investment, or relations with state or military-owned enterprises. Mass rallies organized by SPDC-supported groups in mid-year called for the SPDC to withdraw from the ILO. In October the ILO reported the SPDC's stated intention to withdraw from the ILO, and the 21 death threats received by its Liaison Officer in Yangon. In November the ILO Governing Body expressed grave concern about the degradation of the situation in Myanmar.

In August the World Food Programme reported that about 40 per cent of children were malnourished, despite Myanmar's rich resources. The SPDC imposed increased restrictions on the activities and access to vulnerable populations of UN and international aid organizations, including the UN High Commissioner for Refugees, the UN Development Programme and the ILO. In August the Global Fund to Fight AIDS, Tuberculosis and Malaria announced that it would withdraw its programme by the end of 2005 partly because of these difficulties.

AI country reports/ visits
Reports
- Myanmar's political prisoners – a growing legacy of injustice (AI Index: ASA 16/019/2005)
- Myanmar: Leaving home (AI Index: ASA 16/023/2005)
- Myanmar: Travesties of justice – continued misuse of the legal system (AI Index: ASA 16/029/2005)

NAMIBIA

REPUBLIC OF NAMIBIA
Head of state and government: Hifikepunye Pohamba
(replaced Samuel Nujoma in March)
Death penalty: abolitionist for all crimes
International Criminal Court: ratified
UN Women's Convention and its Optional Protocol:
ratified

The discovery of several mass graves near the
Angolan border led to renewed calls for a truth and
reconciliation commission. After President
Hifikepunye Pohamba took office, there were fewer
instances of government hate speech. Violence
against women and children remained pervasive.

Background
In March President Pohamba succeeded Samuel
Nujoma, who had been head of state since
independence in 1990. Former President Nujoma
remained the President of the ruling party, SWAPO.

Mass graves
A series of mass graves, believed to contain the remains
of SWAPO members from the 1966-89 liberation war,
were uncovered in the north of the country. While
opposition and civil society groups called for a truth
and reconciliation commission, the government
maintained that those who had information about such
graves should come forward because the policy of
national reconciliation would protect them from
recrimination. SWAPO has rejected calls for a truth and
reconciliation commission since independence.

Hate speech
There was less official hate speech after President
Pohamba took office. However, former President
Nujoma and Deputy Minister of Home Affairs and
Immigration Teopolina Mushelenga did verbally attack
gays and lesbians. Regular verbal attacks on minorities
had been a hallmark of former President Nujoma's rule.

Trial of Caprivi detainees
Most of the 120 people on trial in connection with a
separatist uprising in the Caprivi region in 1999 spent
their sixth year in detention. The trial, which started in
2004 after years of procedural delays, was postponed
for much of 2005 after a prosecuting lawyer was killed
and two of her colleagues seriously injured in a car
accident in March. Police officers accused of torturing
suspects detained in the wake of the uprising have yet
to face any formal charges or disciplinary action.

Violence against women and children
A high level of violence against women and children
was evident from police bulletins, although no official
figures were released. The particularly brutal murder of
21-year-old Juanita Mabula provoked popular outrage.

Her beheaded body was found dumped on the outskirts
of Windhoek in September. No one had been arrested
for the murder by the end of the year.

NEPAL

KINGDOM OF NEPAL
Head of state: King Gyanendra Bir Bikram Shah Dev
Head of government: King Gyanendra Bir Bikram Shah
Dev (replaced Sher Bahadur Deuba in February)
Death penalty: abolitionist for all crimes
International Criminal Court: not signed
UN Women's Convention: ratified
Optional Protocol to UN Women's Convention: signed

The human rights situation deteriorated sharply
after King Gyanendra seized direct power and
declared a state of emergency. Civil liberties were
undermined, with thousands of politically motivated
arrests, strict media censorship and harassment of
human rights defenders. The security forces –
operating with impunity – unlawfully arrested,
tortured and killed civilians and suspected
Communist Party of Nepal (CPN) (Maoist) cadres.
CPN (Maoist) forces abducted civilians and
committed unlawful killings and torture. Thousands
of people were displaced by the conflict, while
strikes, insecurity and displacement prevented many
people from enjoying their economic and social
rights. Women and children were particularly
vulnerable to violence and human rights violations.

Background
On 1 February King Gyanendra seized power, taking
direct control of government, declaring a state of
emergency and suspending fundamental human rights.
Strict media censorship was imposed and freedom of
information was severely restricted. Human rights
defenders were threatened and arrested. Political
parties and civil society organizations staged pro-
democracy protests and many participants were beaten
or arrested. Although the state of emergency was lifted
at the end of April, fundamental rights were not fully
restored and human rights organizations and the media
faced continued restrictions. Demonstrations for the
restoration of human rights and democracy continued
throughout the year.

Some countries, including India, the UK and the USA,
suspended most military assistance to Nepal in
response to the King's takeover, although some "non-
lethal" supplies were resumed once the state of
emergency was lifted.

Fighting between the Royal Nepalese Army (RNA)
and the CPN (Maoist) escalated in the first half of the

year, with large numbers of people killed, including many civilians. On 3 September, the CPN (Maoist) announced a unilateral three-month ceasefire, which was later extended until the end of the year. The main political parties formed a pro-democracy alliance and engaged in dialogue with the CPN (Maoist). In November the political parties and the CPN (Maoist) announced a 12-point agreement that established a framework for co-operation, with the shared aim of holding elections for a constituent assembly.

It was estimated that as many as 200,000 people remained displaced by the conflict, many of whom were living in severe poverty.

Under significant international pressure during the March-April session of the UN Commission on Human Rights (CHR), Nepal signed a memorandum of understanding with the UN High Commissioner for Human Rights providing for the establishment of an office in Nepal. The new office began work in May but was not fully staffed until November. The CHR adopted a resolution in April that called on all parties to the conflict to respect human rights and international humanitarian law, condemned abuses committed by the CPN (Maoist) and urged the government to take specific measures to abide by its international obligations.

Political arrests

Following the King's takeover, thousands of political activists, human rights defenders, students, trade unionists and journalists were arrested. Many were held in preventive detention under the Public Security Act (PSA) and some were reportedly tortured. The leaders of Nepal's main political parties were placed under house arrest. Although the majority of these prisoners of conscience were released by April, political arrests continued throughout the year.

People suspected of involvement with the CPN (Maoist) were also arrested. They were held in preventive detention under the Terrorist and Disruptive Activities Ordinance (TADO). Many were held in RNA barracks and were reportedly tortured.

In February King Gyanendra established a powerful Royal Commission on Corruption Control (RCCC), prompting fears that it would be used to discredit political opponents. In April, in a case that was widely seen as politically motivated, the RCCC sentenced former Prime Minister Sher Bahadur Deuba to two years' imprisonment for misappropriating funds.

Student leader Gagan Thapa was arrested on 26 April. The Supreme Court ordered his release but he was immediately rearrested under a 90-day detention order. He was released on 25 May after another Supreme Court intervention. He was arrested again in July, accused of shouting anti-monarchist slogans at a demonstration. In August he was charged with sedition before the Special Court in Kathmandu but released on bail.

Rule of law undermined

The security forces operated with impunity and disregard for the rule of law. Judges and lawyers faced intimidation and harassment by the security forces, and military and civilian authorities obstructed judicial processes. In particular, many people freed by the courts were immediately rearrested.

On 19 September, 11 detainees suspected of involvement in CPN (Maoist) activity were rearrested by members of the security forces from the premises of the Kanchanpur District Court following a Supreme Court order for their release. This was the third time security forces had arrested the group despite repeated court orders for their release on the grounds that the government had not provided sufficient evidence to justify their preventive detention. The detainees were considered to be at risk of torture or ill-treatment.

'Village defence forces'

The emergence of "village defence forces" – civilian militias apparently supported by the state – led to an increase in civilian casualties and significantly worsened the human rights situation. Vigilante attacks also threatened to exacerbate ethnic and communal tensions. Some villagers reported being pressured into joining the militias, including by being beaten or accused as Maoist sympathizers if they refused. Militias were frequently accused of harassing women during home searches and while conducting guard duties. It was reported that the government provided funds and training for "village defence forces" and there were joint military/"village defence force" patrols. CPN (Maoist) forces attacked people suspected of participating in "village defence force" activities.

In February the abduction of two local men in Kapilvastu district by the CPN (Maoist) and the subsequent killing of one of them sparked massive violence led by "village defence forces" operating reportedly with the support of the state and security forces. Between 17 and 23 February, 31 people were reportedly killed, two women and one young girl raped, and 708 houses burned down in the district. Eleven other people were reportedly victims of revenge killings by the CPN (Maoist).

Unlawful killings

Security forces were reportedly responsible for extrajudicial executions of civilians and suspected CPN (Maoist) members in their custody, as well as unlawful killings of armed Maoists who could have been taken into custody.

Extrajudicial executions were most commonly reported during search operations in villages when local people were taken into custody, interrogated and beaten, then taken to a secluded place and shot. Most such killings were reported outside Kathmandu. Some people were killed by security forces for providing food, shelter or money to the CPN (Maoist), even though they may have done so under duress.

Torture and ill-treatment

There were frequent reports of torture and ill-treatment by security forces, particularly to extract confessions and information.

In September the UN Special Rapporteur on torture visited Nepal and concluded that torture and ill-treatment were systematically practised by the police, armed police and RNA to extract confessions and obtain intelligence. In November the UN Committee against Torture expressed grave concern at reports of the widespread use of torture and ill-treatment by law enforcement personnel and at the prevailing climate of impunity for torture.

Human rights defenders

The human rights community was directly targeted in the crackdown that accompanied the state of emergency. Scores of human rights activists were arrested, and many faced harassment by the security forces and the civil authorities. In an apparent effort to limit human rights monitoring, a number of human rights defenders were prevented from leaving Kathmandu in February and March. Some human rights defenders left the country fearing for their safety. Even after the lifting of the state of emergency, human rights defenders continued to face harassment and obstruction.

Krishna Pahadi, founding chairman of the Human Rights and Peace Society and former chair of AI Nepal, was arrested in Kathmandu on 9 February for planning a demonstration. He was held under the PSA for five months.

The National Human Rights Commission (NHRC), which had since its inception faced serious obstruction, was prevented from carrying out many of its core functions following the King's takeover. In violation of its mandate, some NHRC staff and Commissioners were prevented from travelling outside Kathmandu and from visiting detainees. When the sitting Commissioners' terms expired in May, the statutory procedure for appointing Commissioners was changed by Royal Ordinance and new Commissioners were appointed, although the existing Chairman remained in place. There was widespread concern that the process used to appoint new Commissioners jeopardized the independence and credibility of the NHRC.

In November the government adopted a code of conduct to regulate the activities of non-governmental organizations (NGOs) which placed sweeping restrictions on freedom of expression and association. There was widespread concern that the code of conduct could be used to suppress legitimate dissent by civil society. However, in December the Supreme Court issued a stay order on the code of conduct.

The media were particular targets for suppression, with the introduction of censorship in February, a ban on news broadcasting by FM radio stations and the arrest and harassment of journalists. On 9 October the government promulgated a severely restrictive Media Ordinance that further contravened the right to freedom of expression.

On 27 November police raided *Radio Sagarmatha* and terminated broadcasting, seized broadcasting equipment and detained staff.

Abuses by the CPN (Maoist)

CPN (Maoist) forces carried out indiscriminate attacks and attacks on civilians. They also abducted, tortured and killed civilians accused of "spying" and other crimes. Captured soldiers, their families and those who had left the CPN (Maoist) movement were killed in particularly brutal ways.

On 15 April, CPN (Maoist) cadres surrounded Bargadwa village, Nawalparasi district, and rounded up villagers. They then reportedly separated all the boys and men aged between 14 and 40 and killed 10 men and one boy.

Lila Singh, aged 23 from Mahendranagar, Kanchanpur district, was reportedly abducted by CPN (Maoist) cadres from her home on 29 April, allegedly on suspicion of spying.

Six family members of soldiers, including three women and a one-year-old child, were abducted by Maoists in Kailali district in mid-June. Their bodies, reportedly badly mutilated, were found two days later.

Children

Children faced human rights abuses from both sides of the conflict. There were reports of children being detained and tortured by security forces, as well as being abducted and recruited by the CPN (Maoist). Children were also killed in indiscriminate attacks and were particularly at risk from improvised explosive devices planted by the CPN (Maoist) in civilian areas. Many children died from poverty and disease, exacerbated by the conflict.

Many schools were forcibly closed by the CPN (Maoist) and thousands of schoolchildren abducted for "political education" sessions. While most of the abducted children returned home after a few days, a few did not and may have been recruited into CPN (Maoist) forces.

On 20 February, in Kapilvastu district, an 11-year-old girl was raped by three members of an anti-Maoist militia amid widespread violence led by vigilante groups. Her family was reportedly too frightened to seek justice.

Five children were killed and three injured on 22 April when an explosive device left by Maoists at a public tap exploded in Dalsing, Rukum.

Women

There were many reported incidents of trafficking, rape and other sexual violence as a result of the conflict, which also exacerbated existing discrimination against women. Widows and single women were particularly at risk of violence and harassment from parties to the conflict, as well as from within their families and communities. The breakdown in local government and law enforcement, and scarcity of shelter and other support services for women, meant there was little recourse for survivors of domestic violence.

Nepali women mobilized to claim their rights. Conflict widows worked to support each other and called for an end to the violence, while wives and mothers of those who had "disappeared" at the hands of the security forces demanded accountability.

Economic, social and cultural rights

The impact of the conflict severely reduced people's ability to enjoy their economic, social and cultural rights.

Frequent strikes (*bandhs*) imposed by the CPN (Maoist), which stopped all trade and traffic, had a severe effect on people's livelihoods and ability to travel.

Both the Maoists and the RNA disrupted the work of NGOs in deprived rural areas, exacerbating food shortages and preventing access to medical care.

AI country reports/ visits

Reports

- Nepal: Killing with impunity (AI Index: ASA 31/001/2005)
- Nepal: A long ignored human rights crisis is now on the brink of catastrophe (AI Index: ASA 31/022/2005)
- Nepal: Human rights abuses escalate under state of emergency (AI Index: ASA 31/036/2005)
- Nepal: Open letter from Amnesty International, Human Rights Watch and the International Commission of Jurists to the leader of the Communist Party of Nepal (Maoist) (AI Index: ASA 31/046/2005)
- Nepal: Military assistance contributing to grave human rights violations (AI Index: ASA 31/047/2005)
- Nepal: Children caught in the conflict (AI Index: ASA 31/054/2005)
- Nepal: Fractured country, shattered lives (AI Index: ASA 31/063/2005)
- Nepal: Open letter to the leader of the Communist Party of Nepal (Maoist) (AI Index: ASA 31/086/2005)

Visits

AI's Secretary General visited Nepal in February and met the King, Foreign Minister, Home Minister, Chief of Army Staff and representatives of civil society. AI delegates also visited Nepal in March, May, June and November.

NETHERLANDS

KINGDOM OF THE NETHERLANDS
Head of state: Queen Beatrix
Head of government: Jan Peter Balkenende
Death penalty: abolitionist for all crimes
International Criminal Court: ratified
UN Women's Convention and its Optional Protocol: ratified

There were concerns about the treatment of asylum-seekers and migrants and about the extension of counter-terrorism legislation.

Migration issues

On 26 January, the Royal Dutch Constabulary (RDC) failed to intervene in the expulsion from the USA of a Syrian man, Abd-al Rahman al Musa, so that he could file an asylum request. Subsequently, Abd-al Rahman al Musa was detained upon his arrival in Syria. In the wake of this case, the RDC announced that it would amend its policy and respond to non-governmental organizations and lawyers intervening to prevent *refoulement* of asylum-seekers in future.

On 27 October, there was a fire in the temporary detention centre at Schiphol Airport in which 11 irregular migrants (people who did not have legal permission to remain in the country) perished. Approximately 350 people were being held in the complex when the fire broke out. The centre, which held both prisoners and irregular migrants, had caught fire on two previous occasions, the first being shortly before it was opened in 2003 and the second in 2004. According to some reports, previous recommendations by fire prevention officials had not been implemented. Survivors said that there was a delayed reaction by centre staff to cries for help from the detainees. On 27 October, the Safety Investigation Council launched an investigation into the fire. While the nature and extent of the investigation were not made public, the Safety Investigation Council indicated the investigation should be concluded within a year. The National Agency for Correctional Institutions was charged with collating all relevant materials for use by the Safety Investigation Council. Additionally, the Forensic Science Service was also conducting its own investigation on behalf of the Public Prosecution Service.

Counter-terrorism

In January, the government announced the introduction of new counter-terrorism measures, including the criminalization of "incitement to terrorism". The measures were announced shortly after the murder in November 2004 of film maker Theo van Gogh by Mohammed B., a member of the Hofstad Network, which was considered a "terrorist group" by the Dutch government.

The draft proposal on counter-terrorism measures would also criminalize glorifying, condoning, trivializing and denying other serious crimes, including war crimes, crimes against humanity and genocide. The draft legislation stated that in order to be found guilty, a person must have known or reasonably expected that their utterance(s) could seriously disturb public order. Although the draft bill was circulated to advisory bodies in July, it had not been submitted to parliament by the end of the year.

A separate draft bill, introduced in parliament in June, included measures raising the maximum period of pre-trial detention for terrorist offences.

In December, the Hague Court of Appeal overturned a decision of the District Court and permitted the extradition to the USA of Mohammed A., a Dutch national of Egyptian origin accused of crimes involving fraudulent phone cards which may have been used to facilitate contact between members of al-Qa'ida. His lawyers argued against extradition, fearing he would be treated as an enemy combatant if he were extradited to the USA. The Court of Appeal allowed the extradition after receiving the assurance of the USA that he would be prosecuted "before a Federal Court in accordance with the full panoply of rights and protections that would otherwise be provided to a defendant facing similar charges". The USA further guaranteed Mohammed A. would not face prosecution by a military commission, be criminally prosecuted in any tribunal or court other than a US Federal Court, and that he would not be treated or designated as an enemy combatant.

NICARAGUA

REPUBLIC OF NICARAGUA
Head of state and government: Enrique Bolaños
Death penalty: abolitionist for all crimes
International Criminal Court: not signed
UN Women's Convention: ratified
Optional Protocol to UN Women's Convention: not signed

Violence against women remained a serious concern. People suffering from health problems reportedly linked to the use of pesticides on banana plantations sought redress from multinational companies and state support. Excessive use of force by police was reported.

Background
Civil unrest and political tensions intensified in 2005. There were efforts to strip the executive of powers and corruption scandals implicating government officials at the highest levels. Large-scale demonstrations took place in several towns against the rising cost of fuel, food and public transport.

Violence against women
High levels of violence against women and the inadequate response by the authorities remained a major concern. According to press reports, 25 women and girls were killed between January and August as a result of domestic or sexual violence.

☐ Xiomara Obregón Hondoy was shot dead by her partner on 12 April. She had reported his violent and abusive behaviour on a number of occasions to the authorities but they had failed to take appropriate action to protect her.

Right to health: state and corporate accountability
Banana workers formerly employed by US multinational companies intensified their struggle for compensation for health problems. They alleged that these were caused by the pesticides used on the banana plantations during the 1960s, 1970s and early 1980s. Health problems reported included skin and breast cancer; liver, pancreas and kidney problems; nervous disorders; and miscarriages. About 22,000 former workers and family members were estimated to be affected. By the end of 2005, over 1,000 former banana workers had reportedly died from pesticide related diseases. There were protests at the government's failure to comply with a March 2004 agreement in which commitments were made regarding medical and legal assistance for those affected. A new agreement was signed in August, setting out a legislative agenda to address the workers' demands, in particular around access to health care.

At the end of the year, court orders against several multinational companies in Nicaragua and the USA were still awaiting implementation or were the subject of appeals by the companies.

Indigenous peoples
In June the Inter-American Court of Human Rights ruled in favour of the indigenous group Yabti Tasba Masraka Nanih Asla Takanka (YATAMA) on the grounds that their right to judicial guarantees had been violated, leading to their exclusion from participating in the 2000 municipal elections.

In May the Awas Tingni indigenous community sought the intervention of the Inter-American Court of Human Rights with a new request for additional reparations. The Nicaraguan government had failed to comply with the Court's 2001 ruling ordering Nicaragua to provide reparations to the Awas Tingni indigenous community and demarcate and title their lands. The case had been brought after the state granted an exploration licence to a foreign-based logging company in 1994 in the community's ancestral territory without its consent and in breach of national and regional legislation.

Excessive use of force by police
According to press reports, police officers used excessive force against protesters during at least two demonstrations. In February, three people who had

occupied the Pañoleta farm in Chinandega were reportedly killed by police officers as they were forcibly evicted.

Lesbian, gay, bisexual and transgender (LGBT) people

Nicaragua continued to criminalize gay and lesbian relationships. The LGBT community was reportedly prevented from filing complaints and subjected to arbitrary detention and abuse of authority by police officers.

NIGER

REPUBLIC OF THE NIGER
Head of state: Mamadou Tandja
Head of government: Amadou Hama
Death penalty: abolitionist in practice
International Criminal Court: ratified
UN Women's Convention: ratified with reservations
Optional Protocol to UN Women's Convention: ratified

Niger suffered devastating food shortages because of repeated cycles of droughts and an invasion of desert locusts in 2004. Several leaders of civil society were arbitrarily detained.

Famine and belated international response

Serious food shortages were compounded by years of drought and an invasion of desert locusts in 2004, the worst in more than a decade, which wiped out much of the country's cereal production. Although several non-governmental organizations (NGOs) had been warning about the risk of famine in Niger since late 2004, international donors, including the UN and the European Union, did not react quickly to calls for urgent food aid. In June, thousands of people demonstrated in the capital, Niamey, to demand the distribution of free rations. Their demand was refused by the authorities who said that they could not distribute for free the little food they had. In July, following renewed calls from NGOs, the international community, including UN agencies, began to send emergency food aid, which slightly improved the situation.

The UN estimated that the famine put in danger the lives of 3.5 million of Niger's 12 million inhabitants. No official figures were released for how many people died as a result of the food shortages. The famine in Niger had a knock-on effect in neighbouring countries: in Benin and Nigeria, rising prices and a plague of crop-eating birds threatened food supplies, and in Burkina Faso and Mali food shortages were reported.

Arbitrary arrests

Leaders of civil society organizations were arbitrarily detained.

◻ In March, five leaders of the anti-poverty Fairness/Equality Coalition against the High Cost of Living were arrested. They included Kassoum Issa, Secretary of the national teachers' trade union, Nouhou Arzika, Moustapha Kadi, Morou Amadou and journalist Moussa Tchangari. All five were charged with "plotting against state security" after the coalition called for a general strike against a new tax on basic goods such as flour and milk. They were provisionally released 10 days later and by the end of the year no further legal action against them was known to have been taken.

◻ In May, Ilguilas Weila, President of the anti-slavery organization Timidria, and five other people working with him were arrested and charged with "attempted fraud". They were accused of seeking to defraud international lenders by soliciting funds to organize a ceremony marking the liberation of slaves. The six men were provisionally released in June and by the end of the year no further legal action was known to have been taken against them. The arrests took place against a background of attempts by the authorities to muzzle Timidria and prevent it from denouncing slavery, a practice punishable in law in Niger since 2003.

NIGERIA

FEDERAL REPUBLIC OF NIGERIA
Head of state and government: Olusegun Obasanjo
Death penalty: retentionist
International Criminal Court: ratified
UN Women's Convention and its Optional Protocol:
ratified

Death sentences continued to be handed down, but no executions were carried out. While one government commission recommended a moratorium on the death penalty or its abolition, others called for its continued use against juveniles and, reportedly, the execution of death row prisoners to decongest the prisons. The security forces in the Niger Delta killed people and razed communities with impunity to prevent disruption to oil production and in response to community protests. Violence against women, including in the family, was still widespread. Although some states introduced legislation on violence in the home, the federal government did not review discriminatory laws or amend national law to comply with the Protocol to the African Charter on Human and Peoples' Rights on the Rights of Women in Africa. Outrage over six extrajudicial executions by the police in Abuja, the capital, prompted investigation and the prosecution of suspect officers. However, few human rights abuses were investigated or their perpetrators held to account. The findings of a judicial commission of inquiry into human rights violations between 1966 and 1999 were finally made public, but the government did not announce plans to implement its recommendations. Human rights defenders and journalists continued to face harassment and unlawful detention. Over 3,000 people were made homeless without adequate prior notice, alternative accommodation or compensation in a mass forced eviction. Killings increased throughout the country in violence between and within political parties.

Death penalty

No executions were carried out. However, at least four death sentences were handed down by Sharia (Islamic law) courts in northern Nigeria. Appellate courts overturned one death sentence passed by Sharia courts.

Trials by Sharia courts – since 1999 empowered across northern Nigeria under new Sharia penal legislation to impose floggings and the death penalty on Muslims for *zina* (sexually related offences) – were in general grossly unfair. They frequently denied the poor and vulnerable basic rights of defence such as the right to a lawyer.

◻ Two men in Katsina State were arrested and charged with "sodomy" in June, and faced death by stoning if convicted. On 6 December a Sharia court acquitted the two men for lack of evidence.

◻ On 24 May the Bauchi State Sharia Court of Appeal upheld an appeal filed by Umar Tori after he was sentenced to death by stoning for *zina*, and ordered his retrial before the Upper Sharia Court in Kobi. He had been convicted by the Upper Sharia Court in Alkalere on 29 December 2004.

◻ On 10 November the Upper Sharia Court of Yankaba district, Kano State, sentenced two men to death by hanging for murder under the state Sharia Law of 2000.

The government did not make public its response to recommendations for a moratorium on the death penalty by the National Study Group on the Death Penalty, which submitted its report in October 2004. In July a committee of the National Political Reform Conference, whose representatives met from February onwards to debate a new Constitution, recommended that minors should be executed when they committed "heinous offences such as armed robbery and cultism". A presidential committee set up in March 2004 to review death row prisoners reportedly recommended that they could be executed to decongest Nigeria's prisons. In March the UN Special Rapporteur on freedom of religion or belief, during a fact-finding mission to Nigeria, raised human rights concerns about the introduction of legal systems and a mandatory death penalty based on religion. The UN Special Rapporteur on extrajudicial, summary or arbitrary executions, whose mandate includes the death penalty, also visited Nigeria in June and July.

Injustice, oil and violence

The exploration and production of oil continued to result in deprivation, injustice and violence in the oil-producing Niger Delta region. The proliferation of small arms – reportedly part-financed by oil thefts – and the government's inadequate disarmament programmes compounded the violence. The security forces razed communities and killed and injured people with impunity. Community activists who protested in pursuit of rights and resources, sometimes against oil companies, faced violence and arbitrary detention. The security forces often responded with disproportionate, including lethal, force. Whole communities were targeted for allegedly hindering oil production or harbouring criminal groups.

Oil spills and gas flaring continued to contribute to environmental degradation and affect health and livelihoods. In a historic judgment, all oil companies were ordered to stop gas flaring by the High Court in Benin state on 14 November, on the grounds that it contravened human rights including the right to life. However, access to justice for the victims of most human rights abuses remained out of reach because of expensive and lengthy litigation processes.

◻ On 4 February soldiers fired tear gas and later live ammunition to disperse as many as 300 protesters at the Chevron Nigeria-operated Escravos oil terminal in Delta State. One demonstrator, fisherman Bawo Ajeboghuku, was shot and later died, and at least 30 others were injured. The protesters from the Ugborodo community said that Chevron Nigeria had not provided the jobs and development projects promised in return for a "non-disruptive operating environment" in a 2002 agreement between the company and the community. No thorough or independent investigation was known to have been conducted by the federal government or Chevron Nigeria.

📁 On 19 February soldiers invaded the community of Odioma in Bayelsa State, killing at least 17 people and razing about 80 per cent of the buildings. Two women were reportedly raped and community leaders said they were beaten and forced to eat sand. The purpose of the raid was to arrest leaders of an armed vigilante group allegedly responsible for killing 12 people in January. The findings of a state-level judicial commission of inquiry was not made public .

Violence against women

Women were raped and subjected to other forms of sexual violence by government agents as well as partners, employers and others. In some communities, female genital mutilation and forced marriages were still practised. The numbers of women killed, injured, raped and beaten by their partners remained high. Despite the lack of official statistics, nearly two-thirds of women in certain groups in Lagos State, for example, were estimated to be victims of violence in the home. Discriminatory laws and practices, dismissive attitudes within the police, an inaccessible justice system and the lack of shelters for victims contributed to violence against women being widely tolerated and underreported.

📁 "Folake" was remanded in prison after accusing her former employer of rape. Although medical examination supported her case, she was charged with slander. The material evidence of the crime, handed over to the police, was later said to have disappeared. The alleged perpetrator was not brought to justice.

By the end of 2005, national law had not been amended in line with the Protocol to the African Charter on Human and Peoples' Rights on the Rights of Women in Africa, which had been ratified by Nigeria in December 2004. A committee set up to review discriminatory legislation had its first meeting at the end of 2005.

The first state-level laws on domestic violence were passed by state legislators in Ebonyi State and Cross River State. In Lagos State, a draft domestic violence law made slow progress, despite pressure from human rights organizations.

Impunity

Protests at police killings of five Igbo traders and one female companion, allegedly suspected of being armed robbers, on 8 June in Abuja prompted an investigation and the prosecution of eight officers on murder charges. However, in most cases, the security forces continued to commit human rights violations with impunity.

Where abuses were the subject of commissions of inquiry, the findings were generally not made public. The report of investigations into human rights violations between 1966 and 1999 by the Human Rights Violations Investigation Commission, known as the

Oputa Panel, was published by civil society organizations before it was made available to members of the National Political Reform Conference.

Charles Taylor

Resolutions by the European Parliament in February and by the US House of Representatives in July called on the Nigerian government to hand over former Liberian President Charles Taylor to the Special Court for Sierra Leone to face charges of crimes against humanity, war crimes and other serious violations of international law. The government neither handed over Charles Taylor nor brought charges against him in the Nigerian courts.

In November a federal High Court ruled admissible a legal challenge to the Nigerian government's decision to grant asylum to Charles Taylor in 2003. The case had been brought in 2004 by two Nigerian nationals who had had limbs amputated by an armed group backed by the Liberian government during the conflict in Sierra Leone.

Journalists under threat

Newspaper editors and journalists were harassed by the security police, and sometimes detained incommunicado for several days, after criticizing the federal government, exposing corruption, or reporting the activities of secessionist or armed opposition groups. Activists faced arrest and violence when trying to investigate oil spills and human rights violations in the Niger Delta.

📁 On 2 May police arrested Omo-Ojo Orobosa, publisher of the weekly *Midwest Herald*, in Lagos, and detained him incommunicado and without charge until 13 May at an interrogation centre. He appeared to have been detained because his paper had reported allegations that relatives of President Obasanjo would benefit from the sale of government-owned flats.

📁 On 1 and 2 August, three men were arrested and detained without charge until 4 August. The reason for their arrest appeared to be that they were printing materials for the international Campaign Against Impunity coalition of human rights groups, and had copies of the Interpol arrest warrant for Charles Taylor.

📁 On 11 October, Owei Kobina Sikpi, publisher of the *Weekly Star* newspaper, was arrested and charged with "false publication" after an article in his paper accused the Governor of Rivers State of money laundering.

Following a visit to Nigeria in May, the UN Special Representative on human rights defenders said that the return to civilian rule in 1999 had given human rights defenders greater freedom to operate, but that access to official information and to sensitive sites — of forced evictions, oil spills or intercommunal violence, for example — remained too restricted.

Forced evictions

In a number of mass forced evictions, thousands of people were made homeless without adequate notice, compensation or the provision of alternative housing.

📁 During three days in April approximately 3,000 residents were evicted from Makoko in Lagos. The

Lagos State administration engaged police officers to execute a court order to restore the area to its owners, but failed to give adequate notice or provide alternative accommodation to people living on the land. The police reportedly used tear gas, and beat and kicked residents, including five young children, to force them from their homes. The many buildings demolished included a church and a medical centre.

AI country reports/ visits
Reports
- Nigeria: Unheard voices – Violence against women in the family (AI Index: AFR 44/004/2005)
- Nigeria: Ten years on – Injustice and violence haunt the oil Delta (AI Index: AFR 44/022/2005)
Visits
AI delegates visited Nigeria in April and May to conduct research and meet government officials, and in June to launch a report on violence against women.

OMAN

THE SULTANATE OF OMAN
Head of state and government: Sultan Qaboos bin Said
Death penalty: retentionist
International Criminal Court: signed
UN Women's Convention and its Optional Protocol: not signed

Scores of people were arrested in January in connection with calls for political reform. Most were released without charge; 31 were tried and sentenced to prison terms but released under an amnesty. A death sentence imposed in 2004 for murder was commuted by the head of state.

Political arrests
Security forces arrested up to 100 people, including academics, religious leaders and others, in January in response to growing calls for political reform. Many of the arrests were carried out at night and computer equipment and documents were seized. Most of the detainees were released after several days or weeks in custody, but 31 of them were charged with threatening national security and tried in May before the State Security Court (SSC) in Muscat, the capital. All were convicted and sentenced to prison terms ranging from one to 20 years, but then released on 9 June under a royal pardon granted by the Sultan of Oman.

Other government critics who also called for political reform were arrested during the year, including two prisoners of conscience.

Taiba al-Mawali, a leading human rights activist and one of a number of women nominated for the Nobel Peace Prize, was arrested in June soon after she had acted as an observer at the trial of the 31 defendants brought before the SSC in Muscat. In July, a Lower Court in Muscat sentenced her to 18 months' imprisonment in connection with SMS messages that she had sent through mobile phones and the Internet. The Court of Appeal cut her sentence to six months in August but she was still held at the end of the year.

Abdullah al-Riyami, a writer and activist, was arrested on 12 July and held incommunicado for one week before being released without charge. While detained, he was questioned before a judge for over four hours about articles in which he had criticized the government and research he had conducted into torture in police stations in Oman. When released, he was reportedly warned that he would be recalled by police if he persisted in criticizing the government.

Death penalty
In January, the Sultan of Oman commuted the death sentence imposed on US national Rebecca Thompson to 15 years' imprisonment. She had been convicted of murder in 2004.

Women's rights
Omani laws and practices continued to discriminate against women in a number of important respects, including personal status, employment and participation in public life. Domestic violence remained a concern.

AI country reports/ visits
Report
- Gulf Cooperation Council (GCC) countries: Women deserve dignity and respect (AI Index: MDE 04/004/2005)

PAKISTAN

ISLAMIC REPUBLIC OF PAKISTAN
Head of state: Pervez Musharraf
Head of government: Shaukat Aziz
Death penalty: retentionist
International Criminal Court: not signed
UN Women's Convention: ratified with reservations
Optional Protocol to UN Women's Convention: not signed

Dozens of people were arbitrarily arrested and detained in the context of the "war on terror". Several of them "disappeared" and some were handed over to US custody. "Disappearances" were also reported from Balochistan province. Blasphemy laws continued to be used to persecute members of religious minorities. The state took no action to prevent "honour" crimes or to punish perpetrators. The Juvenile Justice System Ordinance, which provides protection for children within the justice system, was temporarily reinstated. At least 241 people were sentenced to death and 31 were executed.

Background

The government vacillated between seeking to control and appeasing religious groups and parties. In March, it reintroduced a "religious column" in national passports, in breach of earlier promises to minority groups. In July, following bomb attacks in the UK by men of Pakistani origin, at least 900 members of religious groups and religious school students were arrested. Most were released within weeks but some continued to be held under preventive detention legislation. The government announced that all foreign students of religious schools would be expelled and that such schools needed to register. However, after protests by religious groups, these directions were not fully implemented. In July, the Hasba (accountability) Bill was passed in the North West Frontier Province. It provided for an ombudsman empowered to "reform society in accordance with Islam". The Supreme Court, in August, declared sections of the bill unconstitutional. In the tribal areas on the border with Afghanistan, civilians suffered abuses during an ongoing security operation.

A draft bill to establish a national human rights commission was presented in May but was not passed by the end of 2005.

Arbitrary arrests and 'disappearances'

Dozens of suspects, Pakistanis as well as foreign men, women and children, were arbitrarily arrested on suspicion of terrorist activities and of contact with al-Qa'ida. Several "disappeared" in custody and some were handed over to US custody, apparently without legal process.

◻ Abu Faraj Al Libbi, a Libyan national alleged to be the operational commander of al-Qa'ida, was arrested on 2 May in Mardan, near the border with Afghanistan. The Interior Minister stated that he would be tried in an anti-terrorism court for attempting to assassinate the President. He was held incommunicado at an undisclosed location. At the end of May Al Libbi was handed over to US custody, apparently without legal process. By the end of the year, nothing was known of his whereabouts or the whereabouts of more than 12 other suspects arrested in connection with him.

The non-governmental Human Rights Commission of Pakistan investigating the situation in Balochistan province found evidence of arbitrary arrests and detention, extrajudicial executions, torture and "disappearances" committed by security and intelligence agencies. On 9 December, 18 labour union leaders from Balochistan "disappeared" in Karachi where they had gone to negotiate with the management of their company. Their whereabouts remained unknown.

◻ Several members of the Balochistan Student Organization (BSO) "disappeared" during 2005. BSO chairman Dr Imdad Baloch was arrested on 25 March along with five others in Karachi. He and three others were released on bail two months later facing politically motivated criminal charges. He reported that they had been tortured and held blindfolded, in iron shackles and threatened with death if they did not give up politics. The other two remained in custody.

Failure to protect minorities

The state failed to protect members of religious minorities from abuse by private individuals. At least 72 people were charged and arrested under blasphemy laws, including laws that make it a criminal offence for members of the Ahmadiyya community to practise their faith. Among the accused were 39 Muslims, 26 Ahmadis, four Hindus and three Christians.

◻ In October, eight Ahmadis were shot dead and 22 injured in their mosque by men shooting from a passing motorbike. Eighteen men arrested shortly afterwards were released without charge.

◻ Mohammad Younus Shaikh was sentenced to life imprisonment in August on charges of blasphemy for writing about religious matters in a book. He was held in solitary confinement in Karachi Central Prison after fellow prisoners threatened him. No action was taken against those threatening violence.

Violence against women

"Honour" killings and mutilations of girls and women, and to a lesser extent of boys and men, continued. Successful prosecutions for "honour" killings were rare. Legal changes introduced in late 2004 failed to curb the authority of the victim's heirs to forgive the perpetrators, allowing them to escape conviction.

◻ In September Amna Abbas had her nose and lips cut off by her brother-in-law near Dera Ghazi Khan, Punjab province, after she filed for divorce. He was reportedly not arrested.

◻ Mukhtaran Mai's attempt to secure justice after being gang-raped on the orders of a council of elders in Meerwala, Punjab province, led to her suffering further threats. In March the Lahore High Court reversed the August 2002 trial court's decision to sentence six men to death. It commuted the death sentence imposed on one to life imprisonment and acquitted and released five. On a request by Mukhtaran Mai, who feared for her life, the Punjab government held the five for three months in preventive detention. In June, a review board ordered their release. The Supreme Court took up the appeal against the acquittals and ordered all the original accused to be held in judicial custody. The appeal was pending at the end of 2005. Mukhtaran Mai, who had been invited to the USA to speak on women's rights, was prevented in June from leaving the country and placed under virtual house arrest.

Women's rights activists were under increased threat. Police tore the clothes and pulled the hair of women activists participating in a mixed gender marathon in Lahore in May. About 40 were detained until evening.

Children's rights

In February, the Supreme Court suspended the Lahore High Court judgment of December 2004 which had revoked the Juvenile Justice System Ordinance, 2000 (JJSO), as unconstitutional. The JJSO provides protection for children in the criminal justice system. This latest decision meant that the JJSO was reinstated, but only temporarily, pending a still awaited decision on the constitutionality of the law by the Supreme Court.

In several cases courts rejected applications for cases to be retried in juvenile courts.

▭ The Lahore High Court in February dismissed a petition that Muhammad Hayat was a juvenile at the time of a murder for which he was sentenced to death in 1995, arguing that he had not raised the point in earlier hearings. His brother asserted that they had been ignorant of legal safeguards for juveniles.

The JJSO, although formally extended to the tribal areas, was not implemented there. In the Federally Administered Tribal Areas, dozens of children, some under the age of five, were imprisoned on three-year sentences under the collective responsibility clause of the Frontier Crimes Regulation for crimes allegedly committed by members of their families.

Death penalty

At least 241 people were sentenced to death. At least 31 people were executed, the majority for murder. Many well-off convicts were able to escape punishment under provisions of the Qisas and Diyat Ordinance that allow heirs of murder victims to accept compensation and pardon the offender. In other cases convicts remained on death row for long periods while seeking pardon from the heirs of victims. In January the Supreme Court ruled that the person convicted of murder could have the sentence reduced only if all the legal heirs agreed to forgive the offender.

▭ Six members of the same family sentenced to death for murder in 1989 had their executions postponed for a third time in August as they negotiated a settlement with the heirs of the victims.

In the tribal areas two men were executed by firing squad immediately after a tribal council – which has no powers to adjudicate criminal cases – convicted them of murder. They had had no legal counsel and no chance to appeal.

Earthquake relief

A massive earthquake hit northern Pakistan in October leaving some 73,000 people dead and two million people in need of relief and rehabilitation. International humanitarian assistance was inadequate, coordination between relief agencies lacking and distribution hampered by difficulties of access. Adequate health care, including trauma counselling, shelter and protection against exploitation including trafficking was lacking, particularly for injured and orphaned children and homeless women.

AI country reports/ visits
Reports
- Pakistan: Recommendations for an effective National Human Rights Commission (AI Index: ASA 33/019/2005)
- Pakistan: Protection of juveniles in the criminal justice system remains inadequate (AI Index: ASA 33/021/2005)
- Pakistan: Amnesty International's comments on the Lahore judgment of December 2004 revoking the Juvenile Justice System Ordinance (AI Index: ASA 33/026/2005)

PALESTINIAN AUTHORITY

PALESTINIAN AUTHORITY
President: Mahmoud Abbas (replaced Rawhi Fattouh in January)
Prime Minister: Ahmad Quray
Death penalty: retentionist

Inter-factional violence within the Palestinian Authority (PA) and its security forces, and between political factions and armed groups, caused a further deterioration in security in the West Bank and Gaza Strip. Armed confrontations, attacks and abductions by Palestinian armed groups increased, and scores of Palestinians were killed amid growing lawlessness. Killings of Israelis by Palestinian armed groups diminished significantly compared to previous years. Impunity remained widespread as PA security forces were unable or unwilling to prevent killings and attacks or to apprehend the perpetrators. Members of PA security forces also participated in attacks, abductions and other abuses. Five Palestinians convicted of murder were executed, ending a three-year de facto moratorium on executions.

Background

After the election in January of President Mahmoud Abbas, Palestinian armed groups agreed to an indefinite *tahadiyeh* (quiet), during which they would refrain from attacking Israelis, and the Israeli authorities announced a suspension of offensive attacks against Palestinians in the Occupied Territories. Attacks by both sides continued nonetheless, but to a lesser extent than in previous years of the Palestinian intifada (uprising) that began in 2000. In 2005, Israeli forces killed some 190 Palestinians, many of them unlawfully and including some 50 children (see Israel and the Occupied Territories entry). Palestinian armed groups killed 50 Israelis, most of them civilians and including six children, both in the Occupied Territories and inside Israel. Most attacks against Israelis were claimed by the al-Aqsa Martyrs Brigades (an offshoot of Fatah) and Islamic Jihad. Hundreds of Palestinians and Israelis were injured in attacks by both sides. Palestinian armed groups also launched mortar attacks from the Gaza Strip towards nearby Israeli towns.

In August and September Israel removed all its 8,000 settlers and all its troops from the Gaza Strip. However, the Israeli army retained control of the airspace, territorial waters and land borders of the Gaza Strip. Israel imposed a closure at the Rafah crossing between the Gaza Strip and Egypt, the only point for Palestinians to leave or enter the Gaza Strip, from September to November.

Blockades and stringent restrictions imposed by the Israeli army throughout the West Bank continued to hinder or prevent Palestinians' access to their agricultural land, workplaces and education and health facilities. The Israeli army also carried out frequent raids into Palestinian towns and villages and stepped up its construction of a 600km fence/wall and major checkpoints throughout the West Bank, including in the East Jerusalem area, cutting off towns and villages from one another. Such restrictions continued to prevent economic recovery and caused high unemployment and extreme poverty in the West Bank and Gaza Strip, where more than half of Palestinians were obliged to rely on international aid for subsistence.

Municipal elections, which began the previous year, were held in several locations in the West Bank and Gaza Strip. Parliamentary elections, scheduled for July, were postponed to January 2006.

Increased lawlessness and impunity

The PA took some steps to reform its security services, which had been repeatedly targeted and largely destroyed by the Israeli army in previous years. In April President Abbas replaced some security forces' chiefs, but the security and judicial institutions remained dysfunctional, beset by factional fighting and power struggles, and unable or unwilling to restore law and order. Rare attempts by security forces to confront political and criminal armed groups invariably resulted in armed clashes, with the security forces often being forced to retreat. Several PA officials were attacked by armed groups. In other cases PA security forces' members participated in attacks and abuses alongside armed groups. Some armed groups and security forces' members used the call for PA reforms and accountability to justify their own attacks and abuses. The Israeli army continued to prevent PA security forces from operating in much of the West Bank, including by refusing to allow them to be present or to carry weapons in many areas. Faced with PA security forces and judicial institutions perceived as powerless or unwilling to address their grievances, many people sought the protection or mediation of armed groups to resolve their problems.

The proliferation of armed groups, the absence of the rule of law and systematic impunity compounded the atmosphere of insecurity. Scores of bystanders, including children, were killed and injured in clashes between armed groups and security forces, and by reckless use by Palestinian armed groups of weapons and explosive devices. Palestinian mortars aimed at nearby Israeli towns often missed their targets and landed in Palestinian residential areas in the Gaza Strip. Armed groups continued to use children to carry out attacks and transport explosives or weapons. Several Palestinian children were arrested by the Israeli army for their alleged involvement in such activities. The main armed groups reportedly disavowed the use of children and some blamed such abuses on local cells acting on their own initiative.

On 2 October, two bystanders, a PA police chief and a security forces' member were killed during armed clashes between PA forces and Hamas gunmen in Gaza City and in an attack by a previously unknown armed group, the Popular Army, in the southern Gaza Strip town of Khan Younis. Armed clashes broke out when PA security forces attempted to enforce a PA-imposed ban on armed groups carrying weapons in populated areas. Several bystanders and dozens of Hamas supporters and PA security forces' members were also wounded in the clashes.

Abductions

More than 20 Palestinians and foreign nationals, including journalists and aid workers, were abducted in the Gaza Strip by Palestinian armed groups. In many cases the groups demanded jobs or protested against PA policies or actions. Those abducted were generally released unharmed within hours.

Two staff members of the UN Development Programme (UNDP) were abducted in Gaza City on 29 July by relatives of a senior member of the PA Intelligence, who had been abducted the previous day by gunmen affiliated to Fatah. The three were released unharmed by their respective kidnappers a few hours later.

On 8 August gunmen abducted three staff members of the UN Relief and Work Agency (UNRWA) in Khan Younis. The three were released after a few hours. The gunmen demanded the release of a Fatah official detained the previous day by PA security forces.

Unlawful killings and targeting of suspected 'collaborators'

Well over 100 Palestinians were killed in political inter-factional fighting, family feuds and score-settling, and several were killed or attacked by armed groups who accused them of "collaborating" with Israeli security services. Most of the killings were attributed to the al-Aqsa Martyrs Brigades and other Fatah splinter groups.

☐ Major-General Musa Arafat, PA national security adviser and former chief of military intelligence, was killed on 7 September in Gaza City. Gunmen dragged him out of his house, shot him dead and abducted his son. His son was subsequently released. PA security forces from a nearby police station did not intervene.

☐ In September Farid Manasra was abducted in the West Bank village of Beni Na'im by gunmen who tortured him for four days. The gunmen, who allegedly included members of PA security forces, accused him of "collaborating" with Israeli forces and demanded money to release him and the publication of a communiqué. When he refused to pay, they shot him in the foot and stole his money, before releasing him.

☐ In October, two Palestinians were abducted in the Gaza Strip by the Knights of the Tempest, a previously unknown Fatah splinter armed group. After the abduction the gunmen held a press conference, displaying the two men hooded and bound, and accusing them of "collaborating" with Israel. The group's spokesman said they had seized the two because PA security forces had failed to bring "collaborators" to justice. The two were shot in the legs before being released several days later.

Death penalty

In June President Abbas authorized the execution of four prisoners who had been convicted of murder between 1995 and 2000. These were the first executions to be carried out by the PA since August 2002. A fifth execution was carried out in July. At the end of June, President Abbas ordered the retrial of those who had been sentenced to death by the State Security Court, which was disbanded in 2003. Some 50 Palestinians were believed to be under sentence of death.

Illegal detentions

In May the PA released several detainees who had been held for several years in Gaza City Prison without trial or in spite of court orders for their release. Other detainees continued to be held for prolonged periods without trial or beyond expiry of their sentences.

Violence against women

Palestinian women, especially those in the Occupied Territories, suffered particularly because of the conflict, including from the impact of home demolitions, movement restrictions that impeded their access to health services and education, and increased poverty. At the same time there were increased demands on women as carers and providers. The high level of conflict-related violence contributed to increased family and societal violence, and many women faced grave abuses in their homes. At least four women were known to have been killed by male relatives in so-called "honour" crimes. In February the UN Special Rapporteur on violence against women called on the PA to enact legislation to provide for the punishment and redress for the wrongs caused to women victims of violence.

AI country reports/ visits
Report
· Israel and the Occupied Territories: Conflict, occupation and patriarchy — Women carry the burden (AI Index: MDE 15/016/2005)
Visits
AI delegates visited areas under the jurisdiction of the PA from March to May and met PA officials.

PAPUA NEW GUINEA

PAPUA NEW GUINEA
Head of state: Queen Elizabeth II, represented by Paulias Matane
Head of government: Michael Somare
Death penalty: abolitionist in practice
International Criminal Court: not signed
UN Women's Convention: ratified
Optional Protocol to UN Women's Convention: not signed

Law and order problems continued to impact on the enjoyment of fundamental rights and access to basic services. Police proved unable or unwilling to prevent or effectively investigate most incidents of violence in the home and general community. Public confidence in the police was further undermined by numerous allegations of police abuses, including torture. Women and children were particularly vulnerable to violence.

Background

Celebrations in September to mark 30 years of independence were tempered by concerns over the development challenges facing the country. Access to basic services remained poor, literacy rates were low, and corruption was endemic. The HIV/AIDS epidemic posed a major threat to growth and stability.

Women continued to be grossly underrepresented in national and provincial parliaments, the police force, judiciary, village courts and other decision-making bodies.

The mandate of the UN Observer Mission in Bougainville expired in June. This followed the installation of a newly elected autonomous government led by former separatist leader Joseph

Kabui. Under the UN-brokered peace deal, a referendum on independence for Bougainville will be held within 15 years.

Law and order problems

Although police reported a decrease in the crime rate relative to 2004, the number of reported crimes, including rapes and murders, remained high. Port Moresby and the Western Highlands were worst affected. The resultant fear, especially among women, restricted freedom of movement and limited access to basic services.

Police were generally ineffective in addressing crime and often cited resource constraints for their failure to investigate complaints properly. Escapes from police custody and prisons were common. In January and February alone, 131 prisoners escaped in three separate mass breakouts.

Conflict over land and resources often fuelled violence. Tribal fighting was reported in at least six provinces and resulted in deaths, destruction of property and displacement.

In response to growing concern over the use of illegal firearms, many originating from police, military and corrective services armouries, the government conducted a public awareness campaign and held a summit in June. A report recommending a series of legislative and policy reforms was presented to government in November.

Australian police deployed under a 2004 bilateral agreement were withdrawn in May when the Supreme Court ruled that laws granting them immunity from prosecution were unconstitutional. Plans were agreed for a smaller contingent to return with a more limited mandate.

Violations by the police

In response to reports that police continued to use excessive force during arrests, and engaged in torture, including rape, against suspects, both the Internal Security Minister and Police Commissioner conceded that police brutality occurred. The Minister promised reform, while the Commissioner cited figures demonstrating that officers were disciplined when complaints could be substantiated. Nonetheless, there was little public confidence in existing accountability mechanisms, which lacked independence and transparency and had failed to deter police violence.

⌁ In November at least one person was killed and at least 18 students were injured when police opened fire on students at a school near Porgera. Police were reportedly at the school to arrest the headmaster when students began to throw stones. A criminal investigation into the shootings was initiated.

⌁ No police officers were known to have faced criminal proceedings for their role in the rape and cruel, inhuman and degrading treatment of women and girls arrested during a raid on Three Mile Guest House in Port Moresby in March 2004.

Violence against women

Information gathered from women's organizations, hospitals and police indicated that domestic violence and rape were widespread. Counselling and health care facilities for victims of violence, particularly outside major towns, were generally non-existent. The widespread violence exacerbated women's vulnerability to HIV/AIDS.

Weaknesses in the formal justice sector and male-dominated "traditional" justice mechanisms severely limited women's access to redress. Only a small percentage of cases of violence against women progressed through the formal justice system. Most incidents, including gang-rapes, were not reported or investigated and many were resolved privately with the payment of compensation to the victim's family.

AI country reports/visits
Visit
An AI delegate visited Papua New Guinea in October.

PARAGUAY

REPUBLIC OF PARAGUAY
Head of state and government: Nicanor Duarte Frutos
Death penalty: abolitionist for all crimes
International Criminal Court: ratified
UN Women's Convention and its Optional Protocol: ratified

Violent evictions of peasant farmers and threats to human rights defenders over land issues were reported. There were calls for greater efforts to protect children from abuse. Prisons remained overcrowded and violent.

Background

There were renewed calls for the reintroduction of the death penalty after the discovery in February of the body of Cecilia Cubas, daughter of a former President. She had been kidnapped in September 2004.

More than 40 per cent of the rural population was reported to live in poverty. There were frequent protests over land reform and other socio-economic issues.

Land issues

Conflicts over land rights led to excessive use of force by the authorities. Human rights defenders working to promote peasants' rights were harassed and threatened.

⌁ Two people were shot dead and at least five injured during a violent eviction in Tekojoja, Vaqueria, Caaguazu Department, on 24 June. According to reports, armed civilians shot unarmed bystanders while police destroyed crops, burned down homes and beat and detained dozens of peasant families, including children. The detained peasant farmers were subsequently released and a judicial investigation was opened into the incident.

🗀 Two Roman Catholic nuns – Juana Antonia Barua and Clara Nimia Insaurralde – and a community leader, José Bordón, received death threats in August. The threats were apparently linked to their work in Naranjito, San Pedro Department, promoting peasant farmers' rights and environmental concerns.

In June the Inter-American Court of Human Rights ruled in favour of the Yakye Axa indigenous community, which had been expelled from its ancestral lands. The Court ordered the Paraguayan state to demarcate the ancestral territory of the Yakye Axa community and hand it back within three years.

Abuses against children

The UN Special Rapporteur on the sale of children, child prostitution and child pornography, who had visited Paraguay in 2004, called for more intensive efforts to protect children, including stronger legislation, action against police corruption, cross-border co-operation, the segregation of young people from adults in prisons, programmes to reduce poverty and social exclusion, and the eradication of the practice of using children to perform domestic tasks in exchange for board, lodging or a basic education. In the area near the border with Brazil and Argentina the government set up a new office to combat the sexual exploitation of children, including sex trafficking.

🗀 The case of a servant girl who had reportedly been physically and sexually abused by her employer from the age of 12 was one of the few cases of child abuse to reach the courts. However, although legal complaints were filed in 2002, no judge had been appointed to hear the case by the end of 2005.

Prison conditions and ill-treatment

Reports indicated that prisons were grossly overcrowded, with inadequate sanitation, medical facilities and education and rehabilitation activities. There were reports that inmates, including juveniles, were ill-treated.

🗀 In May, 30 juveniles held in the regional penitentiary of Ciudad del Este began a hunger strike in protest at an alleged assault by a prison guard on a 17-year-old inmate. After police restored order, a forensic doctor reported that two juveniles had sustained injuries.

UN Human Rights Committee

In October the UN Human Rights Committee made a number of recommendations including that the authorities take appropriate measures to combat domestic violence and ensure that those responsible are brought to trial and receive an appropriate punishment. It also called for the conscription of child soldiers to be eradicated and for all complaints of ill-treatment and deaths of conscripts to be investigated and compensation awarded to the victims.

AI country reports/ visits
Statements
- Paraguay: Human rights should not be disregarded in the name of security (AI Index: AMR 45/001/2005)
- Letter to the Minister of the Interior: Amnesty International's concerns on human rights violations during evictions in Paraguay (AI Index: AMR 45/004/2005)

PERU

REPUBLIC OF PERU
Head of state and government: Alejandro Toledo Manrique
Death penalty: abolitionist for ordinary crimes
International Criminal Court: ratified
UN Women's Convention and its Optional Protocol: ratified

Some of the Truth and Reconciliation Commission's recommendations were implemented, but progress on bringing perpetrators to justice remained slow. Human rights defenders, prosecutors and witnesses were subjected to threats and attacks. Military and police officers accused of torture and ill-treatment continued to be charged with lesser offences. There were concerns about access to health care, especially for low-income families.

Background

2005 saw social unrest and increasing demands for better living and working conditions. A 30-day state of emergency was declared in Apurímac department after a group of former army reservists calling for the resignation of President Toledo seized a police station in Andahuaylas. Four police officers held as hostages and one reservist were reportedly killed. There were reports of violent clashes with security forces and the possible use of excessive force by police and military during protests against mining projects in Piura and Huaraz departments.

Small cells of the armed opposition group Shining Path (Sendero Luminoso) reportedly continued to operate in some areas in Huallaga, Huánuco department, Ayacucho department, and Satipo, Junín department. Shining Path's leaders, who had been tried in military courts in the 1990s, were put on trial again, this time in civil courts.

In November, former President Alberto Fujimori, who was accused of human rights violations, was detained while in Chile pending an extradition request from the Peruvian authorities.

Draft legislation to reform the military and police justice systems failed to comply with a 2004 ruling by the Constitutional Court. The draft law did not define the term offences "committed in the line of duty" or integrate military and police courts into the civilian judicial system.

A permanent Human Rights Ombudsman was appointed by Congress, four years after the last permanent post-holder left office.

In December, the first ever National Human Rights Plan was agreed. However, there were concerns that the plan, which covers the period 2006 to 2010, does not address discrimination on the basis of sexual identity or orientation.

Past human rights violations
The government failed to fulfil the commitment made in 2001 to comply with recommendations of the Inter-American Commission on Human Rights regarding 165 cases of human rights violations. The recommendations included establishing the truth, bringing those responsible to justice and compensating victims and their relatives.

Congress passed legislation establishing a Comprehensive Reparations Plan and a single register of people whose human rights had been violated during the internal armed conflict. President Alejandro Toledo made a commitment to fund collective reparations and to consider individual reparations. Remembrance events and memorials were organized to mark the second anniversary of the publication of the Final Report of the Truth and Reconciliation Commission (TRC). Investigations were opened into 26 of the 59 cases of human rights violations documented by the TRC and the Ombudsman's Office. Some trials began during 2005, but no cases had been resolved by the end of the year. There were concerns that detention orders against military and police officers accused of past human rights violations were not being enforced. Some of these cases continued to be tried in military courts. In some cases, the Ministry of Defence had reportedly not co-operated with civilian courts investigating military officers accused of past violations.

Threats and intimidation
Local human rights organizations registered 46 cases of threats and intimidation of human rights defenders, witnesses, victims and their relatives, judges, prosecutors and forensic experts involved in the investigation and trial of past human rights violations documented by the TRC. According to an Ombudsman's report, those who were threatened and intimidated had been provided with inadequate or no protection at all.

The legacy of the counter-insurgency
Three prisoners of conscience were released, but there were concerns that dozens of prisoners of conscience and possible prisoners of conscience unfairly charged with terrorism-related offences remained in jail.

Torture and ill-treatment
There were reports of torture and ill-treatment of detainees by members of the police and of military officers and conscripts by higher-ranking officers.

Legislation introduced in 1998 to criminalize torture remained largely ineffective and suspected perpetrators continued to be charged with lesser offences.

Prison conditions
In February, the government stated that the national prison system was in crisis because of overcrowding, inadequate infrastructure and insufficient staff to guarantee security. The government announced increased funding, up to 400 new prison staff, the opening of a new prison and construction of two more in Lima department, and the enlargement of other centres in Ica and Piura departments.

Following sustained national and international pressure, all inmates at Challapalca prison, located more than 4,600m above sea level in an extremely isolated area, were transferred to other prisons.

Violence against women
The Ombudsman expressed concern that the legislation prohibiting violence against women was still not being implemented by some police officers and judges and that only a small number of perpetrators had been convicted. Delays in the investigation and trial of these cases was also a concern.

Women's organizations expressed concerns about the lack of resources provided to the Human Rights Prosecutor's Office investigating forced sterilizations under the former government of Alberto Fujimori.

Economic, social and cultural rights
The World Health Organization reported that maternity and child mortality rates remained high. Despite legal provisions on the right to health and measures taken in recent years to improve access to free maternity and child health care for people on low income, there were concerns that this was not reaching people in the most vulnerable communities.

According to a report by the Ombudsman, more than 25 per cent of people lacked adequate access to drinking water; in rural areas this rose to 38 per cent.

AI country reports/ visits
Reports
- Peru: Free the "innocent prisoners" now! (AI Index: AMR 46/001/2005)
- Peru: Amnesty International calls for guarantees that human rights will be respected during the protests in Piura and Cajamarca (AI Index: AMR 46/008/2005)
- Peru: Close Challapalca Prison! (AI Index: AMR 46/011/2005)
- Chile/Peru: Chilean courts must extradite or try Alberto Fujimori (AI Index: AMR 46/012/2005)
- Peru/Chile: Fujimori facing justice – the victims' right (AI Index: AMR 46/015/2005)

Visits
AI delegates visited Peru in February and July.

PHILIPPINES

REPUBLIC OF THE PHILIPPINES
Head of state and government: Gloria Macapagal
Arroyo
Death penalty: retentionist
International Criminal Court: signed
UN Women's Convention and its Optional Protocol:
ratified

Scores of leftist activists were killed by unidentified assailants, often reportedly linked to the armed forces. Peace talks between the government and armed groups – Muslim separatists in Mindanao and communist rebels – made limited or no progress. Arbitrary arrests, unlawful killings, torture and "disappearances" were reported in the context of military counter-insurgency operations. Armed groups were responsible for abuses including hostage-taking. Complaints procedures, investigations and criminal prosecutions of suspected perpetrators of human rights violations were often ineffective. Criminal suspects in custody, including women and children, were at risk of torture or ill-treatment by police. Death sentences were imposed but no executions were carried out.

Background
In June, allegations that President Arroyo was linked to vote-rigging and corruption during the 2004 elections heightened political tensions. In July, amid calls for mass public protests, 10 members of her Cabinet resigned. President Arroyo denied the allegations and, responding to the crisis, called for constitutional reforms including change from a presidential to a federal parliamentary system. In September an opposition motion to impeach the President was defeated in Congress.

Communist insurgency and the peace process
Peace talks between the government and the National Democratic Front (NDF), representing the Communist Party of the Philippines (CPP) and its armed wing, the New People's Army (NPA), remained suspended. In order to resume talks, the NDF called on the government to work for the removal of the NPA's designation as a "Foreign Terrorist Organization" by the USA and its allies. With the peace process stalled, the Joint Monitoring Commission (JMC), set up to examine complaints of human rights abuses and breaches of humanitarian laws by both sides, failed to make significant progress. Previous government pledges to release listed political prisoners remained only partially implemented. At least 251 political prisoners detained within the context of anti-insurgency operations were reported still held.

NPA attacks on government targets and clashes between the Armed Forces of the Philippines (AFP) and NPA units continued throughout 2005. Suspected NPA

members and their supporters were subjected to arbitrary arrests, torture, extrajudicial executions and "disappearances".

 In March, Angelina Bisuna Ipong, a 60-year-old woman, was abducted by armed men wearing face masks in Misamis Occidental province, Mindanao. Blindfolded and transferred between military camps, she was held incommunicado for eight days. She complained of torture and ill-treatment during interrogation, including sexual abuse and physical assaults. She was charged after reportedly being forced to admit being a senior regional CPP leader.

 In April, four farmers in Compostela Valley province, Mindanao – Adreano and Joseph Otida, Malaquias Sampan and Joshua Bustillo – were arrested by the AFP and reportedly accused of being NPA members. Their complaints of torture during military detention included being punched, kicked in the face, chest and abdomen, and hit with rifles and stones.

 In June, Elmer Osila, a senior NPA member, was arrested by soldiers at a checkpoint in Albay province, Luzon. He reported being tortured during interrogation, including by suffocation with a plastic bag and electric shocks. Three days after his arrest, investigators from the Philippine Commission on Human Rights recorded marks consistent with torture on his body.

Increased killings of leftist activists
The number of attacks on leftist activists and community workers rose sharply, with at least 66 fatal shootings reported during 2005. Most of the attacks were carried out by unidentified assailants on motorcycles, at times wearing face masks, who were often described as "vigilantes" or hired killers allegedly linked to AFP members.

As well as suspected CPP-NPA members, those most at risk included members of legal leftist political parties, including Bayan Muna (People First) and Anakpawis (Toiling Masses), other human rights and community activists, priests, church workers and lawyers regarded by the authorities as sympathetic to the broader communist movement. Increased killings in particular provinces were reportedly linked to the public labelling of leftist groups as NPA "front" organizations by local AFP commanders.

A climate of impunity shielding the perpetrators of such killings deepened as ineffective investigations failed to lead to the prosecution of those responsible. In many cases witnesses were reportedly too frightened to testify.

 In March, Felidito Dacut, a lawyer and a Bayan Muna regional coordinator, was shot dead by two unidentified men on a motorbike in Tacloban city, Leyte.

 In May, Reverend Edison Lapuz, a Church minister and a Bayan Muna member, was shot dead by unidentified men in San Isidro, Leyte. He had participated in a fact-finding mission into the killing of Felidito Dacut.

At least 25 alleged "disappearances" of leftists and others were also reported.

Mindanao peace process

Despite periodic breaches, the ceasefire agreement between the government and the Muslim secessionist Moro Islamic Liberation Front (MILF), monitored by military observers from Malaysia and Brunei, was maintained in Mindanao. Intermittent informal peace talks continued.

In August, the MILF boycotted local elections for the five-province Autonomous Region of Muslim Mindanao (ARMM), set up in 1996 following a peace agreement with the Moro National Liberation Front (MNLF). Former MNLF members and members of the Muslim separatist armed group Abu Sayyaf were reportedly involved in periodic clashes with the AFP. Fighting on Jolo island in February led to the displacement of over 25,000 civilians.

Reports indicated that Abu Sayaff and renegade MNLF and MILF members were involved in kidnappings for ransom.

Administration of justice

Public confidence in the ability of the authorities to conduct prompt, thorough and impartial investigations of human rights violations and other crimes, and to deliver justice, remained fragile.

Implementation of fair trial and custodial safeguards remained weak, and criminal suspects were at risk of ill-treatment or torture by the Philippine National Police (PNP) during extended periods of "investigative" detention. Intimidation, aggravated by a lack of effective witness protection programmes, undermined the ability of victims of human rights abuses to gain redress, especially when they were members of poor or marginalized communities.

Lack of confidence in the criminal justice system contributed to an apparent public tolerance of killings of suspected criminals, including alleged petty thieves and street-children, by unidentified "vigilantes" allegedly linked to municipal authorities and the PNP. More than 90 such killings were reported in Cebu city and at least 100 in Davao city.

Journalists were also at risk of armed attacks with at least seven killed by unidentified assailants, reportedly because of their work. In November, in a rare conviction, a policeman was found guilty and given a life sentence for murdering a radio broadcaster in 2002.

Despite an array of legislative and procedural safeguards, minors in detention continued to be at risk of physical or sexual abuse and poor prison conditions. Children were at times detained with adults in overcrowded facilities and exposed to abuse from other prisoners.

Inhumane prison conditions also affected adult male and female prisoners and incidents of excessive use of force by the authorities were reported.

🗀 In March, 26 prisoners, mostly members of Muslim armed groups, were killed as police stormed the Bagong Diwa prison, Bicutan, after an escape attempt and prison revolt. Prisoners were reportedly shot after attempting to surrender. Three prison wardens and a police officer were also killed.

Death penalty

Amid continuing concerns about failures to uphold fair trial standards, death sentences were imposed throughout 2005. A total of 1,214 inmates were under sentence of death at the end of 2005. No executions took place as President Arroyo continued to issue a series of reprieves for prisoners whose sentences had been confirmed by the Supreme Court and were facing imminent execution. Bills calling for the repeal of death penalty legislation were considered by Congressional committees.

Despite continuing reviews of their sentences by the lower courts, at least 22 young offenders remained under sentence of death for offences committed when they were under the age of 18, even though the law makes clear that child offenders cannot be sentenced to death or executed.

AI country reports/ visits
Report
- Philippines: Sharp rise in "vigilante" killings as human rights activist's death remains unsolved (AI Index: ASA 35/001/2005)

POLAND

REPUBLIC OF POLAND
Head of state: Lech Kaczyńzki (replaced Aleksander Kwaśniewski in December)
Head of government: Kazimierz Marciniewicz (replaced Marek Belka in October)
Death penalty: abolitionist for all crimes
International Criminal Court: ratified
UN Women's Convention and its Optional Protocol: ratified

Racism and intolerance towards minorities was reported in both the private and public spheres. No action was taken against public figures whose statements appeared to incite intolerance. Police reportedly used excessive force against non-violent demonstrators.

Background

2005 was a year of significant political changes. After general elections in September and a presidential election in October, the Law and Justice party (Prawo i Sprawiedliwość, PiS) came to power. Before the elections, the PiS criticized gay rights campaigners and expressed support for the death penalty. Following Lech Kaczyński's election as President, the European Commission issued a formal warning to Poland, saying that it could lose its European Union (EU) voting rights if the President continued to oppose gay rights and sought to introduce the death penalty.

One of the first decisions of the new government was to abolish the Office for Gender Equality, making Poland the only EU country without a statutory equality watchdog.

Identity-based discrimination
Members of sexual minorities continued to face discrimination and restrictions on their right to freedom of expression and assembly. In June, Lech Kaczyński, then mayor of Warsaw, refused for the second year to authorize the Equality Parade, holding that such an event would be "sexually obscene" and offensive to other people's religious feelings. An improvised parade still took place on 10 June, gathering more than 2,500 participants. Less than a week later, the mayor authorized the so-called Normality Parade, allowing an extremist homophobic grouping known as All Polish Youth (Młodzież Wszechpolska) to mobilize on the streets of Warsaw.

In November the mayor of Poznań banned a gay parade, ostensibly because of security concerns. However, the parade's organizers claimed that the Poznań municipality had earlier indicated that there were no reasons to ban the parade, and that the mayor had given in to the demands of the conservative political parties Law and Justice and the League of Polish Families (Liga Polskich Rodzin). An unauthorized parade which took place on 19 November was met with physical attacks and verbal abuse from members of All Polish Youth. As a protest, demonstrations in support of tolerance and equality took place throughout Poland on 27 November. In December an administrative court in Poznań annulled the authorities' decision to ban the parade.

There was no action against public statements inciting intolerance against sexual minorities, such as that made by a then Member of the European Parliament from the League of Polish Families: "After the elections, we will illegalize all homosexual organizations and we will attack paedophiles who are statistically the most numerous among them."

Racism
In its third report on Poland, released in June, the European Commission against Racism and Intolerance (ECRI) expressed concern that the authorities rarely investigated and prosecuted cases of racial hatred, and allowed anti-Semitic material to freely circulate on the market. ECRI pointed out that in investigating violent attacks against ethnic minorities, such as Roma or migrants, the police often did not take into account the racist motivation of crimes, which resulted in a lighter sentence for the perpetrator, if convicted. Moreover, there was still no comprehensive body of legislation prohibiting racial discrimination in all fields of life.

PORTUGAL

PORTUGUESE REPUBLIC
Head of state: Jorge Fernando Branco de Sampaio
Head of government: José Sócrates Carvalho Pinto de Sousa (replaced Pedro Santana-Lopes in March)
Death penalty: abolitionist for all crimes
International Criminal Court: ratified
UN Women's Convention and its Optional Protocol: ratified

Reports of ill-treatment by police officers continued to give rise to concern about Portugal's failure to comply with international law and standards. Law enforcement training in the use of force and firearms and operational guidelines reportedly continued to be insufficient. At least 33 women were reported to have been killed as a result of violence against women in the family.

Policing concerns
Ill-treatment by police officers continued to be reported, including one case in which a man subsequently died in police custody.

In March, José Reis was arrested for causing a public disturbance in the city of Lagos. A witness reported seeing six or seven policemen beating him at the time of his arrest. He was taken to the local police station at around 4am, and was found hanging in his cell, dead, at 5.20am. The coroner's report concluded his death was suicide, but the Judiciary Police and the General Inspectorate of the Internal Administration (IGAI), the Interior Ministry's police oversight body, opened investigations into the circumstances of his death.

Training and operational guidelines for the police, including in the use of force and firearms, reportedly remained inadequate. Officers reportedly received initial training in the use of firearms, and could then have further training only once every three to four years.

At least three people died as a result of lethal force during the year, again raising long-standing concerns about the possible unnecessary or disproportionate use of force.

In March an unnamed 48-year-old man was shot dead by a member of the Republican National Guard (Guarda Nacional Republicana, GNR). An officer reportedly fired shots at the man's vehicle after he allegedly stole petrol, tried to get away and hit an officer with his car, causing him minor injuries. An investigation into the killing was opened, but the officer concerned was not suspended from duty.

Also in March, João Martins, aged 17, was fatally wounded when a GNR officer fired at his car during a police chase. The bullet passed through the car, hitting him in the chest. No official investigation was known to have been carried out into the killing.

Violence against women

Violence against women in the family remained a major concern, despite Portugal's record since 1990 of specific legislation, amendments to the penal codes and national plans against domestic violence to prevent and punish acts of violence against women, and to provide support and redress to the victims.

Thirty-three women were reported to have been killed as a result of violence against women in the family. Of these, 29 were killed by their husband, former boyfriend or partner, and four by other relatives.

PUERTO RICO

COMMONWEALTH OF PUERTO RICO
Head of state: George W. Bush
Head of government: Aníbal Acevedo-Vilá (replaced Sila María Calderón Serra in January)
Death penalty: abolitionist for all crimes

Killing in suspicious circumstances

There was concern about the circumstances of the fatal shooting by US Federal Bureau of Investigation (FBI) agents of prominent independence activist Filiberto Ojeda Ríos in September. A member of the nationalist group "Los Macheteros" (Cane Cutters) accused of involvement in a 1990 robbery in the USA, Filiberto Ojeda Ríos was shot after agents surrounded the farmhouse in which he and his wife were staying. His family accused the FBI of initiating the shooting, then leaving him to die. Separate investigations were being carried out by the US Department of Justice and the Puerto Rico Justice Department with the results still pending at the end of the year.

Federal death penalty

The second death penalty trial in Puerto Rico for more than 75 years took place in March, resulting in life sentences for Hernando Medina Villegas and Lorenzo Catalán Román, who had been convicted of the murder of a security guard. Pursuit of the death penalty in the case by the US federal authorities sparked protests in Puerto Rico which has been abolitionist since 1929. The US federal authorities said that they would continue to seek the death sentence for federal capital crimes in Puerto Rico.

QATAR

STATE OF QATAR
Head of state: Shaikh Hamad bin Khalifa Al-Thani
Head of government: Shaikh Abdullah bin Khalifa Al-Thani
Death penalty: retentionist
International Criminal Court: not signed
UN Women's Convention and its Optional Protocol: not signed

Up to 6,000 members of a Qatari tribe were arbitrarily deprived of Qatari nationality. Women faced discrimination under a range of laws and practices. At least 19 people remained under sentence of death.

Background

A new Constitution, which came into force in June, provides for hereditary rule by the Al-Thani family through the male line and contains various human rights guarantees, including some that continued to be ignored in practice.

One man was killed and at least 12 people were injured in March when a suicide bomber, believed to be an Egyptian national, exploded a car close to an English-language school in Doha.

The Interior Ministry established a human rights unit to monitor and respond to human rights issues raised by international human rights organizations and to consider complaints. In July the Ministry opened a shelter for victims of crime, labour abuse and human trafficking.

Abuses in the context of the 'war on terror'

Security forces carried out a number of arrests following the March bombing in Doha. At least 17 people, including foreign nationals, were still detained without charge or trial at the end of 2005.

▭ Mohamed Naseem Abdel Latif Hijazi, an Egyptian graphic designer, was arrested at his workplace on 21 March. He was detained without charge or trial in solitary confinement at the State Security prison in Doha until November, when he was released.

Deprivation of citizenship

As many as 6,000 members of the Al-Ghufran branch of the Al-Murra tribe were deprived of Qatari nationality between October 2004 and June 2005 on grounds, believed to be spurious, that they were nationals of other countries. Some were reportedly forced to leave Qatar to seek resettlement in neighbouring countries, or detained to induce them to do so, despite guarantees in the new Constitution against the deportation of Qatari nationals.

Women's rights

Article 35 of the new Constitution bans all discrimination "on grounds of sex, race, language, or religion". In practice, however, women remained subject to gender discrimination under a range of laws and practices, such as laws concerning marriage contracts that favour men. Women must also obtain approval from their husband or guardian before travelling, and children of Qatari women who marry foreign nationals do not qualify for Qatari citizenship, unlike children born to Qatari fathers and foreign mothers.

◻ Hamda Fahad Jassem Ali Al-Thani, a member of the ruling family, was reportedly confined to her home in Doha because her father disapproved of her choice of husband, and ill-treated. She was allegedly abducted from Egypt and forcibly returned to Qatar by Qatari security officials in November 2002. She was detained in secret in Doha for five months until April 2003, and then transferred to the offices of the state's Special Security Directorate in Doha, where she was detained until November 2003. She was then handed over to her family, who confined her against her will.

Death penalty
At least 19 people remained under sentence of death for their part in a failed coup attempt in 1996. Two others, Hamad bin Jassem bin Hamad Al-Thani and Bakhit Marzouq al-Abdullah, were pardoned by the Emir, Shaikh Hamad bin Khalifa Al-Thani, and released.

AI country reports/ visits
Report
· Gulf Cooperation Council (GCC) countries: Women deserve dignity and respect (AI Index: MDE 04/004/2005)

ROMANIA

ROMANIA
Head of state: Traian Băsescu
Head of government: Călin Popescu-Tăriceanu
Death penalty: abolitionist for all crimes
International Criminal Court: ratified
UN Women's Convention and its Optional Protocol: ratified

Discrimination and attacks against Roma continued. The situation in mental health institutions remained unsatisfactory. Deaths of individuals in psychiatric institutions were not investigated effectively and impartially. Members of the lesbian, gay, bisexual and transgender (LGBT) community experienced discrimination and intolerance.

Background
The European Commission noted in October that Romania had made progress towards greater respect for human rights in an attempt to meet the criteria for membership of the European Union, accession to which is scheduled for 2007. The Commission said that steps had been taken to ensure the independence of the judiciary, guarantee greater media freedom and promote the rights of the child. It said further efforts were needed to combat ill-treatment in police custody, prevent trafficking in human beings and ensure the effective integration of the Roma minority with regard to their economic and social rights.

Roma and racism
Discrimination against Roma continued despite Romania's commitment to the Decade of Roma Inclusion, a campaign to eliminate marginalization of Roma that started in 2005. According to the Open Society Foundation, which works to promote human rights, 75 per cent of Romanians do not want to live near Roma.

In July, the European Court of Human Rights ruled on the Hădăreni case, an incident in 1993 when three Roma were killed and more than 170 others were forced to abandon their homes in the town of Hădăreni and flee after a night of racial violence. Following a row between three Roma men and another villager, in which one ethnic Romanian was killed, a crowd of Romanians and ethnic Hungarians had vandalized 14 Romani houses beyond repair. Following the attack, the concerned Roma families were forced to live in degrading conditions as the government failed to provide them with adequate remedies.

The European Court of Human Rights found Romania in violation of numerous provisions of the European Convention on Human Rights, including the right to a fair hearing, the right to respect for family and private life, and the right not to be discriminated against. The Court obliged Romania to pay compensation to the Roma affected by the 1993 attacks.

In August a court in Romania moved to comply with the ruling, ordering the seizure of property from perpetrators of the Hădăreni attacks to finance compensation for the victims. After police arrived in Hădăreni to execute the court ruling, there was an outpouring of racist speech directed at Roma by the media and politicians.

There was an increase in racist remarks in the Romanian media. The Mayor of the southern city of Craiova was fined twice by the National Council for Combating Discrimination for expressing racist views in public. Although he was made to resign as vice-president of the Social Democrats, a national political party, he remained the Mayor of Craiova.

The procedural rules for the government's National Council for Combating Discrimination, did not allow for a speedy, independent investigation of complaints that would provide effective and proportionate remedies for victims of discrimination. Public debate to change the rules to make the work of the Council more effective was ongoing.

A draft law on national minorities adopted by the government in May was rejected by parliament in October. The law aimed to prevent discrimination against all minorities in Romania, and guarantee the right to cultural autonomy, religious freedom, freedom of expression, and the right to use minority languages. The law was supported by the Hungarian and Romani minorities in Romania.

Concerns about mental health care

Following the tragedy in Poiana Mare psychiatric hospital in 2004 when 17 patients died of malnutrition and hypothermia, the prosecutor initiated criminal investigations into the events. Having found "no causal link" between the deaths and the involvement of staff, the prosecutor closed the investigations in February 2005. After campaigning by local and international human rights organizations, the investigation was reportedly reopened in August. In November the Minister of Health announced a plan to close down Poiana Mare hospital and transfer its patients to more appropriate and centrally located institutions.

In February the UN Special Rapporteur on the right of everyone to the enjoyment of the highest attainable standard of physical and mental health released a report on Romania. He stressed that "the enjoyment of the right to mental health care remains more of an aspiration rather than a reality for many people with mental disabilities in Romania." The Rapporteur recommended that an independent mental health commissioner be established urgently.

Inadequate investigations of ill-treatment of minors

Several cases involving ill-treatment of minors were not properly investigated or the results of investigations were not made public. They included the cases of I.G., who was beaten by the police in 2003; I.M., who was ill-treated by police in 2003; F.F., who was beaten by a policeman in 2004; C.B., who was ill-treated by police in 2004; and D.N., who was beaten by a policeman with a rubber truncheon in 2004. In many cases the authorities said that the children either inflicted the injuries on themselves or had the injuries prior to their arrest. Such claims contradicted the victims' statements.

LGBT community under attack

Although homosexuality was decriminalized in 2001, reportedly more than 40 per cent of the population continued to believe that homosexuals should be removed from the country. The GayFest parade on 28 May was opposed by the Orthodox Church and the local authorities. The municipal authorities of Bucharest, who initially agreed to provide logistical support for the march, later withdrew this offer. They said they could not provide enough cover to keep people safe and that the time of the parade was inappropriate. Authorization for the parade was finally granted after the President of Romania intervened in an emergency meeting with the Mayor of Bucharest. The parade subsequently passed without incident.

In February the non-governmental organizations (NGOs) Accept and the Centre for Legal Resources won a case against the state-owned airline TAROM which illegally excluded a homosexual couple from a Valentine's Day sale. The National Council for Combating Discrimination declared that TAROM had been "restricting the free access, under equal conditions, to public services and places" and ordered TAROM to pay a US$180 fine, which it did without delay. Following the decision, the NGOs filed an administrative complaint against the fine, which they believed was nominal and not sufficient to have a dissuasive effect against further such actions. Having lost the administrative appeal, the NGOs were preparing a court appeal at the end of the year.

RUSSIAN FEDERATION

RUSSIAN FEDERATION:
Head of state: Vladimir Putin
Head of government: Mikhail Fradkov
Death penalty: abolitionist in practice
International Criminal Court: signed
UN Women's Convention and its Optional Protocol: ratified

Hostility towards human rights defenders increased and some were prosecuted for their peaceful exercise of the right to freedom of expression. Racist attacks, some of them fatal, continued, despite a small increase in convictions for racially motivated crimes. Domestic violence was widespread and the state failed to provide adequate protection. Prisoners conducted mass protests about ill-treatment in prison colonies. Serious human rights abuses including "disappearances" and abductions, torture, killings and arbitrary detention continued in the context of the conflict in Chechnya. Impunity remained the norm for those committing human rights violations. People seeking justice faced intimidation and death threats; some were killed or "disappeared".

Background

There were mass protests across the country at the beginning of the year against social welfare reform. In September the UN Committee on the Rights of the Child highlighted a wide range of concerns relating to children in Russia. In November the Federal Migration Service announced their intention in 2006 to grant amnesties and give work permits to around 1 million migrant workers from former Soviet countries working in Russia without official permission. In Chechnya, separatist leader Aslan Maskhadov was killed in the village of Tolstoi-Yurt on 8 March, during an operation by federal security forces. According to official information, these forces had attempted to detain him but he had refused to surrender. Chechen parliamentary elections were held in November in which the pro-Kremlin United Russia party gained over 60 per cent of the vote. A Council of Europe representative stated that the elections took place in an "atmosphere of fear" and Russian and international human rights groups declared that free and fair elections had not been possible given the security situation and the climate of impunity in Chechnya.

Conflict in the North Caucasus

Serious human rights violations, including war crimes, continued to be committed in Chechnya by Chechen and federal forces. Chechen security forces under the command of Ramzan Kadyrov, the First Deputy Prime Minister of Chechnya, and divisions of federal forces staffed by ethnic Chechens were increasingly implicated in arbitrary detention, torture and "disappearances" in Chechnya. High-level officials, including the President of Chechnya, Alu Alkhanov, were reported to have admitted to the involvement of federal and Chechen forces in "disappearances" in Chechnya. People were also held incommunicado, sometimes in unacknowledged detention centres. Relatives of "disappeared" people demonstrated in Chechnya for information about the fate of their loved ones. Reportedly, women continued to be subjected to gender-based violence, including rape and threats of rape, by members of the federal and Chechen security forces. Chechen armed opposition groups reportedly committed war crimes including direct attacks on civilians.

There was violence and unrest in other North Caucasus republics, increasingly accompanied by reports of human rights abuses such as arbitrary detention, torture, "disappearances" and abductions.

Over 30,000 people remained internally displaced by the Chechen conflict in neighbouring regions of the north Caucasus, in particular in Ingushetia and Dagestan. Conditions in camps in Ingushetia varied but were generally cramped and unsuitable. There remained other displaced populations in the North Caucasus from other conflicts.

⌂ In June, 11 men "disappeared" and at least one, 77-year-old Magomaz Magomazov, was reportedly killed during a raid, allegedly by the Vostok (East) battalion of the Russian federal forces, on the village of Borozdinovskaia, Chechnya. The raid prompted a mass exodus over the border to neighbouring Dagestan of around 1,000 villagers. One member of the Vostok battalion was convicted of "exceeding official authority", and given a three-year suspended sentence in October.

⌂ In March security forces carried out a passport check in a district of Nazran, Ingushetia. The following day a group of armed men in camouflage and wearing masks reportedly returned to the district and searched the family home of Vakha Matuev and took him away. His wife told AI in September that the authorities in Ingushetia had not opened a criminal investigation and that she had not received any information as to the whereabouts of her husband.

⌂ Adam Gorchkhanov was reportedly detained at his home in the Republic of Ingushetia on 23 May by unidentified security services and taken away. He was reportedly detained in a pre-trial detention centre and the headquarters of the Regional Organized Crime Squad in Vladikavkaz, North Ossetia, before being transferred to a hospital in Vladikavkaz with a serious head injury. He died in hospital on 30 May 2005. His medical certificate gave the cause of death as having "jumped from the third floor". According to a relative, by September there had been no further investigation into Adam Gorchkhanov's death as the cause of death had been "established".

Armed raid in Kabardino-Balkaria

On 13 October a group of up to 300 gunmen launched attacks on government installations in and near

Nalchik, the capital of Kabardino-Balkaria, including the building of the Federal Security Service (FSB), police stations, the TV centre and the airport. There were reports that gunmen took at least two civilians hostage. More than 100 people, including at least 12 civilians, were reported to have been killed during the ensuing shooting between law enforcement officials and the gunmen; many were wounded. The raid was reportedly in response to months of persecution of practising Muslims in the region, including arbitrary detention and torture by law enforcement officials, and wholesale closure of mosques. Following the raid, law enforcement officials detained dozens of people; many of the detainees were reportedly tortured. At least one person was reported to have "disappeared" following the raid.

◻ Former Guantánamo prisoner Rasul Kudaev was detained on 23 October by law enforcement officials at his home in Kabardino-Balkaria and taken to the headquarters of the Organized Crime Squad in Nalchik, where he was reportedly tortured, before being transferred to a pre-trial detention centre. He remained in detention at the end of the year, charged with terrorism-related offences. His mother was unable to visit her son or pass on to him sufficient medication for his serious health conditions, which according to the family had rendered him bed-ridden. A lawyer who had tried to complain about his treatment was suspended from the case and replaced with another state-appointed lawyer, a move thought to be against Rasul Kudaev's wishes.

Impunity

AI was aware of only two convictions during 2005 for serious human rights violations committed in Chechnya. The majority of investigations into alleged violations were ineffective and the prosecution of the handful of cases that came to court was flawed. Applicants to the European Court of Human Rights faced serious reprisals including intimidation, death threats, killing and "disappearance".

◻ In March a court in the Chechen capital, Grozny, found Sergei Lapin, a member of a special federal police unit (OMON), guilty of torturing Zelimkhan Murdalov, and sentenced him to 11 years' imprisonment. Zelimkhan Murdalov had been detained by police officers in Grozny in January 2001 and subsequently "disappeared". In November a criminal case was opened against the OMON unit commander and his deputy who were implicated in Zelimkhan Murdalov's torture and "disappearance", together with Sergei Lapin. The whereabouts and fate of Zelimkhan Murdalov remained unknown.

◻ In May, a court in Rostov-on-Don found four members of a special Russian military intelligence unit not guilty for a second time of the murder of six civilians from Dai village, Chechnya. Although the four admitted to the killings, the court ruled that their actions were not punishable as they had been following orders. This decision, like the previous acquittal in April 2004, was widely criticized and subsequently quashed by the Military Collegiate of the Russian Supreme Court in August 2005. A third trial started in November.

Council of Europe

In February the European Court of Human Rights released its judgments in the first six cases from the Chechen Republic to reach the Court. The Court ruled that in these cases the Russian government had violated the right to life, the prohibition of torture, the rights to an effective remedy and the peaceful enjoyment of possessions. The cases brought by the European Human Rights Advocacy Centre concerned the Russian federal forces' indiscriminate aerial bombing of a civilian convoy of refugees fleeing Grozny in October 1999; the "disappearance" and subsequent extrajudicial execution of five individuals in Grozny in January 2000; and the indiscriminate aerial and artillery bombardment of the village of Katyr-Yurt in February 2000.

In June, the Parliamentary Assembly of the Council of Europe (PACE) examined Russia's progress in honouring the obligations and commitments it undertook on joining the Council of Europe in 1996. PACE passed a resolution which stated that while Russia had made progress in some areas of human rights, there had been very little progress in relation to the obligation to bring to justice those responsible for human rights violations, notably in relation to events in Chechnya. The resolution called on the Russian authorities to "take effective action to put an immediate end to the ongoing 'disappearances', torture, arbitrary detentions, incommunicado detention in illegal and secret detention facilities, and unlawful killings" reported in Chechnya. The resolution also highlighted the lack of progress on the commitment formally to abolish the death penalty and to withdraw Russian troops from Moldova.

Violence against women

According to the Russian governmental newspaper *Rossiiskaia Gazeta* up to 80 per cent of all violent crimes in Russia were committed in the private sphere. Non-governmental organizations (NGOs) remained concerned that women were the main victims of such violence. While no official statistics were available, independent research showed that about 70 per cent of married women had been subjected to some form of violence from their husbands. There were no measures under Russian law which specifically addressed violence against women in the family. The Ministry for Health and Social Development stated that there were 23 state-run crisis centres for women in the Russian Federation. However, women's human rights organizations were concerned that government support for crisis centres and hotlines was on the decline. According to these organizations, there was only one shelter place for every 9 million women in Russia.

Human rights defenders

The climate of hostility towards some NGOs grew, spurred on by statements by President Putin that foreign financing of political activity by NGOs was unacceptable. Human rights defenders, activists and independent journalists working on human rights issues, in particular on Chechnya, were harassed, prosecuted and in some cases subjected to arbitrary detention and "disappearance". In some cases the prosecution of activists under anti-extremism and anti-racial hatred laws amounted to a violation of the right to the peaceful exercise of freedom of expression. The human rights organization Russian Chechen Friendship Society (RCFS) was subjected to administrative harassment from the tax authorities and the registration department of the Ministry of Justice.

Possible prisoners of conscience

In March a Moscow court found Yuri Samodurov, director of the Andrei Sakharov Museum and Public Centre in Moscow, and Ludmila Vasilovskaia, curator at the centre, guilty of charges relating to incitement to national and religious enmity, and fined them. A third defendant, artist Anna Mikhalchuk, was found not guilty of similar charges. The three had organized an exhibition called "Caution, Religion!" in January 2003, in which artists exhibited artwork using religious symbols.

In November Stanislav Dmitrievskii, Executive Director of the RCFS and editor-in-chief of the *Pravo-zashchita* (Rights Defence) newspaper, went on trial on charges of incitement to racial hatred, for his decision to publish articles written by a former Chechen separatist leader and his envoy. However, both articles were critical of Russian government policy rather than expressing any criticism of ethnic Russians, and contained calls for a peaceful resolution to the Chechen conflict. The charges are punishable by up to five years' imprisonment.

Investigation into murder of Galina Starovoitova

In June the St Petersburg City Court convicted two men of the 1999 murder of Duma Deputy and leader of the Democratic Russia Party, Galina Starovoitova, and the attempted murder of her assistant, Ruslan Linkov. However, the person who ordered the murder had not been identified or prosecuted. The verdict recognized the political character of the killing. Galina Starovoitova had been an outspoken critic of corruption and an advocate of human rights.

Legislation and non-governmental organizations

In June an amendment to the tax code came into force increasing the list of areas for which grants could be given tax free, to include the defence of human rights, which was welcomed by human rights groups. However, a draft law on civil society organizations was passed by the State Duma at the end of the year which raised serious concerns about freedom of association. The draft law provided for much greater scrutiny of the activities and funding of NGOs by the authorities. The proposals threatened to open the door to arbitrary decisions by the authorities, potentially compromising the independence of civil society organizations.

Racism, xenophobia and intolerance

Foreign nationals from all around the world, including asylum-seekers, refugees, students and migrant workers, were victims of racially motivated physical assaults, some of which were fatal. The Sova Information-Analytical Centre reported that there were at least 28 murders and 365 assaults across the country which had been motivated by racial hatred. Citizens of the Russian Federation were also targeted, in particular Chechens and other North Caucasus ethnic groups, Jews, Roma and practising Muslims. In some cases a lack of trust in the police prevented victims from reporting the attack. Meskhetians living in Krasnodar Territory continued to be refused Russian citizenship on grounds of ethnicity, resulting in discrimination in almost every aspect of daily life. Anti-racist protest marches and initiatives took place in cities notorious for attacks, including Voronezh, St Petersburg, Tiumen and Moscow.

Peruvian student Enrique Arturo Angelis Urtado was beaten and stabbed to death in October in the city of Voronezh, and two other students were badly injured. A number of people were detained in connection with the attack.

There were suspected arson attacks and robberies on Roma homes in the town of Iskitim, Novosibirsk region, and Roma were subjected to threats and assaults. The Novosibirsk regional procuracy stated that it was investigating the incidents.

In October a jury in St Petersburg started to hear evidence in the case of Khursheda Sultonova, a nine-year-old Tajik girl who was killed in February 2004. Seven people, aged between 14 and 21 when the crime was committed, faced charges of hooliganism, punishable by seven years' imprisonment, and one youth, aged 14 when the crime was committed, faced charges of murder of a person in a helpless state, motivated by racial hatred, as well as hooliganism and robbery.

Fair trial concerns

In May former associates of the oil and gas company YUKOS Mikhail Khodorkovskii and Platon Lebedev were found guilty of charges including tax evasion and fraud and sentenced to nine years' imprisonment. The convictions followed an investigation and trial that included violations of fair trial standards. Many believed the prosecutions to be politically motivated. The cases highlighted serious problems in Russia's criminal justice system relating to the independence of the judiciary; access to effective legal counsel; conditions of detention; and the use of torture and ill-treatment in order to extract confessions. The prosecution and conviction of Mikhail Khodorkovskii was seen as having a chilling effect on freedom of expression and political pluralism in Russia.

Arbitrary detention, torture and conditions of detention

Violations of Russian and international law relating to detention, including arbitrary detention and torture, were reported. Conditions in some overcrowded pre-trial detention facilities were so poor that they amounted to cruel, inhuman or degrading treatment. Prisoners serving life sentences lived in conditions that amounted to ill-treatment and in some cases possibly torture. Prisoners in regions including Kursk, Ulyanovsk, Smolensk and Mordovia conducted organized protests, including hunger strikes and mass self-harm, against conditions and ill-treatment.

In May and June, Senyo Adzokpa, a Ghanaian living in Moscow, was reportedly tortured in a pre-trial detention centre in Ivanovo. He was allegedly beaten repeatedly and coerced into signing a confession by being placed in a punishment cell and threatened with rape. He was also subjected to racist abuse.

Former Guantánamo detainees Airat Vakhitov and Rustam Akhmiarov were arbitrarily detained in Moscow in August by Moscow and Tatarstan law enforcement officials, transferred to Tatarstan and held in detention with access only to a state-appointed lawyer until their release six days later. A court in Tatarstan ruled on the legality of the two men's detention in their absence, in violation of Russian and international law, which require detainees to be present for such hearings. Rustam Akhmiarov and Airat Vakhitov were simply handed a copy of the court decision to detain them further.

Mikhail Trepashkin was denied urgently needed health care while in detention in prison colony IK-13 in Sverdlovsk oblast. On 20 October he was medically examined and the doctor recommended that he be admitted to hospital for monitoring and treatment. However, according to his lawyers, the prison administration refused to allow him to be transferred to hospital and failed to provide adequate medical care.

Refoulement

The Russian authorities forcibly returned at least one person to a country in former Soviet Central Asia despite a serious risk of torture and other grave human rights violations.

Student Marsel Isaev was forcibly deported from the Russian Republic of Tatarstan to Uzbekistan in October, despite the fact that his application for asylum was under consideration by the Russian authorities. In his asylum application he had stated that he feared that in Uzbekistan he could face torture as a suspected member of the banned organization Hizb-ut-Tahrir.

AI country reports/ visits

Reports
- Russian Federation: Violations continue, no justice in sight — a briefing paper on human rights violations in the context of the armed conflict in the Chechen Republic (AI Index: EUR 46/029/2005)
- Russian Federation: Torture, "disappearances" and alleged unfair trials in Russia's North Caucasus (AI Index: EUR 46/039/2005)
- Russian Federation: Nowhere to turn to — violence against women in the family (AI Index: EUR 46/056/2005)

Visits
AI delegates visited the Russian Federation in February, March, September and December.

RWANDA

REPUBLIC OF RWANDA
Head of state: Paul Kagame
Head of government: Bernard Makuza
Death penalty: retentionist
International Criminal Court: not signed
UN Women's Convention: ratified
Optional Protocol to UN Women's Convention: not signed

Human rights organizations were prevented from working freely and activists were harassed and attacked. Journalists continued to face intimidation. Trials continued of people suspected of involvement in the 1994 genocide: some 36,000 of the more than 80,000 detainees awaiting trial were provisionally released in August. There were concerns about the fairness of some of the trials.

Background

During the first half of the year, Rwanda deployed peacekeeping troops in Sudan. In mid-2005, several prominent figures from various countries visited Kigali to pay tribute to the recovery of Rwanda after the genocide. Their statements were accompanied by new financial pledges. The UK announced plans in November to provide up to US$83 million to assist the government in the areas of education, land reform and health. However, the international depiction of Rwanda contrasted greatly with the human rights situation on the ground.

Rwanda's relations with neighbouring Burundi, Uganda and the Democratic Republic of the Congo (DRC) improved slightly, despite the government's continued support for armed opposition groups operating in eastern DRC. Rwanda also continued to be responsible for arms trafficking to the DRC. Several multilateral meetings indicated that an unofficial agreement was emerging between leaders of the region to control, at least on a temporary basis, the activities of armed groups responsible for numerous human rights abuses.

Human rights work hampered

The humanitarian responsibility to prevent a recurrence of genocide or any other acts of ethnic hostility or violence was given by the authorities as the principal motive for putting into effect measures that suppressed individuals or bodies critical of government policy. A politically motivated report endorsed by parliament in 2004 adversely affected the work of human rights organizations. The parliamentary commission report had accused several institutions, including national and international non-governmental organizations (NGOs) and individuals, of supporting genocide or disseminating its principal tenets. Following the report several members of civil society, including staff of human rights organizations such as the League for the Promotion and Protection of Human Rights in Rwanda and the League for the Protection of Human Rights in the Great Lakes region, were forced to flee the country for fear of being persecuted or arbitrarily arrested.

During the year the Senate began disseminating a questionnaire to Rwandans and international organizations asking them to denounce any foreign individual or organization suspected of promoting "divisionism" or an "ideology of genocide". This, along with other government measures, continued to create a climate in which any criticisms or opposition were discredited.

Some human rights organizations were only able to work in extremely difficult conditions and under close scrutiny by the authorities. Their freedom was also affected by the law relating to non-profit associations, which stipulates that all NGOs in Rwanda must obtain an annual "certificate of registration" renewable from the Ministry of Local Government, Good Governance, Community Development and Social Affairs (Ministère de l'Administration Locale, Bonne Gouvernance, Développement Communautaire et Affaires Sociales, MINALOC). This certificate is granted on the basis of the organization's mission statement and annual report. The process allows the authorities to monitor the activities of NGOs and control their publications.

A MINALOC official told AI representatives that a Batwa association had its application rejected because it said it represented the Batwa community and therefore breached the law against "divisionism". In light of such rulings, some organizations censored themselves to obtain a certificate.

Human rights organizations were often told that they could not obtain certification because of slow administrative processes, even though other groups were successful within days.

The acquisition of a certificate did not ensure that human rights organizations could work independently. If they intended to address sensitive issues, they had to go through another process of authorization at the ministerial or local level. A local human rights organization working on land issues in the province of Kibungo did not receive the necessary authorization from the provincial authorities, even though MINALOC had issued it with a certificate of registration. The issue of land sharing remained one of the most sensitive in Kibungo. Similar difficulties were reported by an international NGO working in the same field.

Freedom of expression under attack

Despite the declaration by the Minister of Information in November that the press was free to work in Rwanda, journalists continued to face intimidation and harassment for articles criticizing government policy.

On 7 September, Jean Léonard Ruganbage, a journalist for *Umuco*, an independent newspaper, was detained because of his investigation into the justice system and the gacaca, a community-based system of tribunals established by the government in 2002 to try people suspected of crimes during the 1994 genocide (see below).

Bonaventure Bizumuremyi, editor of *Umuco*, was detained several times after September and his newspaper seized. He had published articles that criticized the governing party Rwandan Patriotic Front (Front Patriotique Rwandais) for coercing local co-operatives to fund it.

Human rights activists who spoke out faced physical and verbal attacks, and anonymous telephone calls accusing them of being "traitors". As a result, some were intimidated into silence, a phenomenon that was becoming increasingly widespread.

Genocide trials

At the beginning of 2005, more than 80,000 detainees awaited trial for their alleged participation in the 1994 genocide. The authorities had predicted that it would take several decades to process all the cases given the capacity of the judicial system. In August, 36,000 of the detainees were provisionally released on the grounds that they had confessed their involvement in the genocide. The decision to release some detainees was made in part to relieve the overcrowded conditions in the prison system, and in part to try detainees before gacaca tribunals where they would have to provide further information on the crimes of other perpetrators.

The gacaca system officially began in 2005 to gather information on crimes committed between 1 October 1990 and 31 December 1994. The department of gacaca jurisdiction declared that more than 760,000 people could be prosecuted (one in four of the adult population) and that the process should be completed by 2007. This intention to process cases as quickly as possible increased suspicion about the fairness of the gacaca system. Some decisions made by gacaca tribunals cast doubt on their impartiality.

Guy Theunis, a Belgian Catholic priest, was arrested on 6 September at Kigali Airport for his alleged role in the 1994 genocide and was taken before a gacaca court within five days. He was accused of inciting ethnic hatred and masterminding killings in a church in Kigali. After weeks of diplomatic negotiations with the Belgian authorities, Guy Theunis was transferred to Belgium on 20 November and the Belgian judicial authorities began investigating charges brought against him in Rwanda.

There was widespread distrust of the gacaca system. Some Rwandans feared being exposed for their involvement in the genocide by the gacaca tribunals. Others feared that the tribunals could be used by individuals to resolve personal conflicts or to make economic gain.

Refugees

Thousands of Rwandans fled to neighbouring countries, apparently for reasons including fear of the gacaca system, suspicion of the authorities and rumours of politically motivated "disappearances". In April, on the 11th anniversary of the genocide, thousands of Rwandans fled to Burundi and Uganda. At the end of the year, more than 7,000 Rwandans remained in exile in Burundi (see Burundi entry).

International Criminal Tribunal for Rwanda

Trials of prominent genocide suspects continued before the International Criminal Tribunal for Rwanda (ICTR), which held 60 detainees at the end of 2005.

Five trials involving 20 defendants continued from previous years, and five new trials involving seven defendants began in 2005. Two judgments were given: one defendant received a six-year prison sentence and another received life imprisonment.

One suspect surrendered himself to the ICTR in Tanzania and was later transferred to the Hague for detention pending his trial on charges of genocide, conspiracy to commit genocide and complicity in genocide. Another suspect was arrested in Gabon. In addition to the same crimes, he was charged with direct and public incitement to commit genocide and persecution as a crime against humanity.

The ICTR continued to work under a UN Security Council deadline to finish trials by the end of 2008 and appeals by 2010. The Tribunal may transfer some case files to the Rwandan authorities to meet this deadline. The ICTR's President estimated that 65-70 cases would have been completed by 2008.

Update: Augustin Cyiza and Léonard Hitimana

Augustin Cyiza, a former military officer and a prominent member of civil society, and Léonard Hitimana, a member of parliament, were among opposition activists who "disappeared" in 2003 in the run-up to elections. The authorities continued to state that the men left the country to join the Democratic Liberation Forces of Rwanda (Forces Démocratiques de Libération du Rwanda), an armed group operating in the DRC. No investigation into their "disappearance" was opened and the authorities continued to ignore requests for information from the UN High Commissioner for Human Rights and the Inter-Parliamentary Union. It appears that the two men were abducted and killed in Rwanda.

AI country report/ visits
Statement
• Rwanda: Human rights organization forced to close down (AI Index: AFR 47/001/2005)
Visits
AI delegates visited Rwanda in May to investigate the issue of land restitution for refugees and internally displaced persons, and in November to monitor the human rights situation.

SAUDI ARABIA

KINGDOM OF SAUDI ARABIA
Head of state and government: King Abdullah Bin 'Abdul 'Aziz Al-Saud (replaced King Fahd Bin 'Abdul 'Aziz Al-Saud in August)
Death penalty: retentionist
International Criminal Court: not signed
UN Women's Convention: ratified with reservations
Optional Protocol to UN Women's Convention: not signed

Killings by security forces and armed groups escalated, exacerbating the already grim human rights situation. Scores of people were arrested for suspected links with armed opposition groups but little information was available about their legal status or conditions in detention. Women remained subject to extensive discrimination in law and practice, and inadequately protected against violence in the home, but there were some signs of reform. Migrant workers also faced discrimination and abuse. At least 86 men and two women were executed, almost half of them foreign nationals.

Background
Crown Prince Abdullah became King and Head of State following King Fahd's death on 1 August and named Prince Sultan, the Defence Minister, as the new Crown Prince. The accession of King Abdullah raised hopes of political reform, including in the area of women's rights, but progress was slow.

In April, the government announced plans to reform the judicial system, introduce specialized labour, commercial and criminal courts, and establish a Supreme Court. In September, the government created a national human rights commission to "protect human rights and spread awareness about them... in keeping with the provisions of Islamic law".

Saudi Arabia's first-ever municipal elections were held in three stages from February to April to fill half of the 600 seats on the country's 178 municipal councils. The other half are filled by government appointees. Women were excluded from the elections, provoking much controversy. Women's rights activists called on the government to appoint women to some of the unelected seats.

Armed clashes and killings
Armed men allegedly aligned to al-Qa'ida engaged in armed confrontations with security forces in which scores of people from both sides were killed. Such clashes occurred in Riyadh, al-Madina, al-Dammam and elsewhere as the government intensified a "campaign for fighting terrorism" announced by the Interior Ministry in February.

▢ In early April, security forces were reported to have killed 15 armed men and injured others in fighting at al-Ras, near Riyadh. Among the dead were men whose names appeared on a list of 26 wanted men published by the government in late 2003, and a member of the security forces.

☐ In September, according to reports, five armed men were killed and others were injured when government forces, two of whom were also killed, stormed a house in al-Dammam.

Abuses in the context of the 'war on terror'

The government took various measures to counter the activities of groups suspected of links to al-Qa'ida. It hosted an international counter-terrorism conference in February which recognized that human rights abuses were one cause of terrorism and recommended that specific codes of conduct be devised to assist law enforcement agencies in combating terrorism while respecting human rights. Later, King Abdullah renewed his call for members of armed groups to surrender to the authorities.

Government forces arrested scores of suspected Islamists but disclosed little information about those detained, not even their names. The Interior Ministry reportedly stated that many of those arrested would be tried. However, the secrecy that surrounds the criminal justice system meant that no trials were reported. There was concern that those prosecuted would not receive fair trials.

Some of those arrested were among those named in a new list of 36 "most wanted" suspects, many of them foreign nationals, issued by the government in June. They included Faiz Ayoub, who reportedly handed himself in to the authorities on 1 July.

Among others arrested were at least five Chadian nationals who were detained in June, and Mohamed al-'Ameri and four people believed to be Saudi Arabian nationals who were reportedly detained in al-Madina on 25 July.

Other security suspects were returned to or received from other countries. In February and March, 27 Yemeni nationals were deported to Yemen, where they may have been detained, while Yemeni authorities returned 25 Saudi Arabian nationals to Saudi Arabia on 28 March. Further exchanges of such prisoners between the two countries, and between Saudi Arabia and other countries, were believed to have occurred, but few details were available.

☐ Salem al-Baloushi was returned in April to the United Arab Emirates (UAE), having been detained incommunicado without charge since February 2003. He was immediately detained in the UAE.

☐ Ahmed Abu 'Ali, aged 23 and a US national, was returned in February to the USA where he was tried and convicted of conspiring to assassinate US President George W. Bush and other offences. He had been arrested in Saudi Arabia in June 2003 and alleged that he was tortured and ill-treated while held incommunicado for two months and that US officials were aware of this. He also said that US Federal Bureau of Investigation (FBI) officials had participated in his interrogation in Saudi Arabia and threatened him with transferral to Guantánamo Bay, Cuba, or trial in Saudi Arabia where he would not have the right to representation by a lawyer.

Women's rights

Women remained subject to discrimination in law and practice and were not adequately protected against domestic and family violence. However, the government expressed commitment to improving the status of women and was reported in March to be preparing legislation to grant women the right to become permanent members of the Shura (Consultative Council).

The Ministry of Labour announced that it wished to increase the number of women in paid employment. However, it said this would only happen with consideration of "the need of the woman for work, the need of the society for her work, the approval of her legal guardian" and issues of "decency", including dress, and that a woman's work should not be at the expense of her family life or "lead to social or moral problems". Women's rights activists said it was such constraints that resulted in no more than 5 per cent of Saudi Arabian women being in paid employment.

The exclusion of women from participation in the municipal elections was widely criticized by women's rights activists. The government said that there were not enough qualified women to administer women-only registration centres and that not all women had identification cards needed for voting. In response to the criticisms, the Head of the Elections Committee said that he expected that women would participate in future elections.

In April, the Grand Mufti issued a statement banning the practice of forcing women to marry against their will and called for the imprisonment of those who persisted in such practice. However, cases of forced marriages continued to be reported.

☐ J.A., aged 29, reportedly remained at risk and confined to the family home where she had suffered serious violence since she was 14 years old.

☐ Rania al-Baz, whose case was widely publicized after she was severely beaten by her former husband, reportedly fled from Saudi Arabia and settled in France.

Repression of freedom of expression and religion

☐ Mohamed al-'Oshen, editor-in-chief of *al-Mohayed* newspaper, was detained in January, reportedly after he published articles critical of the government, but he was believed to have been released without charge later that month.

☐ One woman and 14 men were sentenced in January to prison terms ranging from two to six months and to between 100 and 250 lashes for demonstrating in December 2004 in Jeddah on behalf of the Movement for Islamic Reform. At least six others were said to be awaiting trial.

☐ In April, police and members of the Committee for the Propagation of Virtue and Prevention of Vice reportedly stormed a house in Riyadh and arrested 40 people of different nationalities, including Pakistani and Filipino migrant workers, for practising Christianity. The detainees were later released.

Political prisoners

Peaceful critics of the state as well as suspected members or sympathizers of armed groups were detained during the year. The exact number of those detained was unclear.

▢ Dr Sa'id Bin Zu'air, a possible prisoner of conscience held at al-Ha'ir prison in Riyadh, was released in August following a pardon by King Abdullah. Two of his sons, Mubarak Bin Sa'id Bin Zu'air and Sa'ad Bin Sa'id Bin Zu'air, who were detained after they campaigned for their father's release, were freed, the former at the beginning of 2005 and the latter in July.

Several prisoners of conscience were released under a royal pardon declared by King Abdullah on 8 August.

▢ Dr Matrouk al-Falih, Dr 'Abdullah al-Hamid and 'Ali al-Deminy were released under the pardon. They had been held since March 2004 and were serving sentences of up to nine years' imprisonment imposed in May after a closed session by the Cassation Court in Riyadh. The charges against them included "sowing dissent and disobeying the ruler". Their lawyer, 'Abdel Rahman al-Lahem, who had been in custody since November 2004, was also released following a pardon by the King.

Migrant workers

In August, the government announced plans to reform the country's labour law to improve protection of foreign workers' rights. It warned employers and employment agencies that they could be punished, including with prison terms, if they mistreated workers. The authorities said that new guidelines would be given to migrant workers explaining their rights under Saudi Arabian law and that complaints' mechanisms would be strengthened. It urged abused workers to submit complaints.

Despite these positive initiatives, there continued to be reports of abuses against migrant workers.

▢ Nour Miyati, an Indonesian woman employed as a domestic worker, was taken by her employer to a Riyadh hospital suffering from serious injuries which necessitated amputation of her fingers. She apparently alleged that her employer had tied her up for a month in a bathroom and assaulted her. According to reports, after she made the allegations she was charged with making false statements against her employer, removed from the hospital and detained for two days by police. She was then released by order of the Governor of Riyadh and handed into the care of a charitable organization.

Judicial corporal punishment

Flogging remained a routine corporal punishment imposed by courts as a main or additional sentence for a wide range of offences, including in cases involving prisoners of conscience.

▢ Hamza al-Muzaini, an academic, was sentenced to 75 lashes and two months' imprisonment in March for allegedly criticizing a cleric in an article. Crown Prince Abdullah intervened and annulled the sentence.

▢ Four men who attended a "gay wedding" in Jeddah were sentenced to two years' imprisonment and 2,000 lashes in April; 31 others were sentenced to 200 lashes and between six months and one year in prison. They were prisoners of conscience.

▢ Twelve Nigerian men were sentenced to seven-year prison terms and 700 lashes in May for assault after they were convicted following an unfair trial.

Death penalty

At least 86 men and two women were executed. Almost half of them were foreign nationals.

▢ Six Somali men were executed on 4 April even though they had served their prison sentences and been subjected to corporal punishment. Neither they nor their families were aware that they were at risk of execution, and they had not had access to consular or legal assistance.

▢ Suliamon Olyfemi, a Nigerian, remained under sentence of death. He had been convicted of murder after a trial in November 2004 during which he had no legal representation or translation services from Arabic, which he did not understand.

The authorities did not disclose the number of death sentences, which may have significantly exceeded those known by AI. Defendants in capital cases often do not have legal representation and are not informed of the progress of the proceedings. There was concern that some defendants were convicted and sentenced to death solely or largely on the basis of confessions obtained under duress, torture or deception.

AI country reports/ visits
Report

· Gulf Cooperation Council (GCC) countries: Women deserve dignity and respect (AI Index: MDE 04/004/2005)

SENEGAL

REPUBLIC OF SENEGAL
Head of state: Abdoulaye Wade
Head of government: Macky Sall
Death penalty: abolitionist for all crimes
International Criminal Court: ratified
UN Women's Convention and its Optional Protocol:
ratified

Fighting came to a halt in the southern Casamance region. Reconstruction work and demining allowed refugees and displaced farmers to return home. Threats to freedom of expression continued and several journalists and political opponents were arrested. Impunity continued with the adoption of an amnesty law on past politically motivated offences.

Background

Following the December 2004 peace agreement, which ended two decades of conflict in Casamance, reconstruction work and demining began in the region. This allowed refugees, former fighters and displaced farmers to return home. In February negotiations began on the implementation of the peace agreement but were hampered by divisions within rival factions of the Democratic Forces of Casamance Movement (Mouvement des forces démocratiques de Casamance, MFDC). Following the arrest of former Prime Minister Idrissa Seck in July (see below) and repeated intimidation of journalists and political opponents, President Wade faced increasing waves of protests from civil society groups and some political parties.

Arrest of Idrissa Seck

In July former Prime Minister Idrissa Seck was arrested and charged with threatening state security, an accusation that appeared to be politically motivated and unfounded. He was then charged with embezzlement of funds. He remained in prison and some of his defence rights were initially not respected, including the right to meet his lawyers in private. Several other people were briefly arrested or interrogated in connection with this case.

Threats to freedom of expression

Journalists and political opponents continued to be harassed and intimidated in an attempt to restrict freedom of expression.

In May, Abdourahim Agne, the leader of the opposition Reform Party, was detained and charged with inciting the population to insurrection after he urged people to follow Ukraine's example and hold peaceful protests to drive President Wade out of office. Abdourahim Agne was provisionally released in June.

In October, police shut down *Sud FM*, one of the major private radio stations, and detained about 20 staff after the station broadcast an interview with Salif Sadio, a military leader of the MFDC in which he called for the separation of Casamance from Senegal. The Minister of Information said the action had been taken because the interview might "threaten the security of state". All the *Sud FM* staff were released a few hours later and the radio broadcast signals re-established.

Impunity

Despite public commitments by the authorities, no steps were taken to end impunity for human rights perpetrators. In January parliament passed a law that provides an amnesty for "politically motivated" offences committed between 1 January 1983 and 31 December 2004.

Hissène Habré case

Senegal did not give a positive answer to the extradition request and international arrest warrant issued by a Belgian judge and charging Chad's former president, Hissène Habré, with gross human rights violations committed during his 1982-90 rule. Hissène Habré has lived in Senegal since he was ousted from power in 1990. In November the Dakar Appeal Court declared itself "not competent" to rule whether to issue an extradition order in the case. A few days later, the authorities announced that the African Union (AU) should indicate who had jurisdiction to rule on this and declared that Hissène Habré would remain in Senegal pending the AU's decision.

AI country reports/ visits
Statement
- Senegal: Government must immediately arrest and extradite Hissène Habré to Belgium to face crimes against humanity charges (AI Index: AFR 49/001/2005)

SERBIA AND MONTENEGRO

SERBIA AND MONTENEGRO
Head of state: Svetozar Marović
Head of government: Vojislav Koštunica (Serbia), Milo Đukanović (Montenegro)
Death penalty: abolitionist for all crimes
International Criminal Court: ratified
UN Women's Convention and its Optional Protocol:
ratified

Serbia's co-operation with the International Criminal Tribunal for the former Yugoslavia (Tribunal) improved in the first half of the year under intense international pressure, with the apparent voluntary surrender of 11 suspects indicted by the Tribunal.

However, in December the Tribunal's Chief Prosecutor reported that co-operation had deteriorated. The Prime Minister of Kosovo was indicted and surrendered to the Tribunal in March. Domestic trials and retrials of Serbs and Kosovo Albanians accused of war crimes continued. In Serbia trials continued of former officials accused of complicity in previous political crimes. Police torture and ill-treatment continued. Roma were deprived of many basic rights. Trafficking of women and girls for forced prostitution remained a serious concern.

Background

Serbia and Montenegro (SCG) continued to operate with separate governments and legal systems. On 3 October the European Union (EU) Council of Ministers authorized the European Council to start talks with the Union of SCG. These started on 7 November aimed at a Stabilization and Association Agreement with the EU. In October, a revised criminal code and a law on the police and on the Protector of Citizens (ombudsperson) were introduced, but legislative reform remained slow. The EU, through the Venice Commission, set out conditions for the Montenegrin independence referendum planned for April 2006.

The UN Interim Mission in Kosovo (UNMIK) continued to administer Kosovo. Some further competencies were transferred to the Provisional Institutions of Self-Government (PISG), and measures were taken towards decentralization. The presence of uniformed opposition groups was reported. The Self-Determination Movement organized non-violent demonstrations against UNMIK in which at least 186 people were arrested; some were reportedly ill-treated by the police. In October, the UN Secretary-General appointed a Special Envoy to Kosovo to conduct talks on the future status of the province.

War crimes: international prosecutions

The trial by the Tribunal of former President Slobodan Milošević, accused of responsibility for war crimes in Croatia, Bosnia and Herzegovina (BiH), and Kosovo, continued. In June the prosecution presented the court with footage of members of a Serb paramilitary unit (the "Scorpions") executing six Bosniak prisoners from Srebrenica on Mount Treskavica in BiH in July 1995. The "Scorpions" were alleged to be under the control of the Serbian authorities when the crimes were committed. In December, the Tribunal amended the indictment against Jovica Stanišić and Franko Simatović to include further charges related to this incident. Proceedings also opened on 20 December at the Belgrade war crimes court against five members of the "Scorpions" in relation to these executions.

The Serbian authorities failed to seek out and arrest suspects indicted by the Tribunal. However, under pressure from the EU and the US government, they adopted a policy of "encouraging" voluntary surrender and affording suspects official support.

In January, former commander of the Priština Corps Vladimir Lazarević surrendered to the Serbian authorities; he was transferred to the custody of the Tribunal. He had been indicted along with three other former senior officers and government officials for individual criminal responsibility and for command responsibility for crimes against humanity and violations of the laws or customs of war in Kosovo in 1999. Two others — Sreten Lukić, former police general in Kosovo and later assistant Serbian Interior Minister, and Nebojša Pavković, former commander of the Armed Forces of the Federal Republic of Yugoslavia — voluntarily surrendered in April and May. The fourth man, Vlastimir Đorđević, former Assistant Minister of the Interior, was believed to remain at large in Russia.

Between February and April, eight suspects indicted by the Tribunal for charges including war crimes, crimes against humanity and genocide in connection with the war in BiH, surrendered to the Serbian authorities and were transferred to the Tribunal. They included former Bosnian Serb Army officers Drago Nikolić, Vinko Pandurević, Ljubomir Borovčanin and Vujadin Popović, all of whom were indicted in connection with the killing of more than 8,000 Bosniak civilians in Srebrenica in July 1995 (see Bosnia and Herzegovina entry).

In October Tribunal Prosecutor Carla Del Ponte reported "complete satisfaction with Belgrade's co-operation" for the first time. However, neither Radovan Karadžić nor Ratko Mladić had surrendered by the end of the year. In December she reported that co-operation had deteriorated.

Ramush Haradinaj, former prime minister of Kosovo and Kosova Liberation Army (KLA) commander, resigned in March and surrendered to the Tribunal. He was indicted, with Lahi Brahimaj and Idriz Balaj, on 37 counts of crimes against humanity and war crimes against the Serb, Roma, Ashkali and "Egyptian" populations.

On 5 May, Beqa Beqaj was convicted and sentenced to four months' imprisonment for contempt of the Tribunal in connection with the intimidation of witnesses in the Limaj case. In November, in the same case, Haradin Bala was convicted of torture, cruel treatment and murder of prisoners in the Llapushnik (Lapušnik) area and prison camp in 1998. He was sentenced to 15 years' imprisonment. Two others were found not guilty.

Serbia
War crimes: domestic prosecutions

Of those indicted in connection with the Ovčara massacre near Vukovar in Croatia in 1991, 14 were convicted of war crimes by the special War Crimes Panel within the Belgrade District Court in December.

In a case investigated by the Tribunal and transferred to Serbia in 2004, nine men were indicted in August for the detention and torture of at least 174 Bosniak civilians and the murder of at least 15 men at Čelopek in BiH, and the deportation to Hungary of 1,822 Bosnian Muslims; three suspects remained at large.

On 14 May, former police officer Goran Veselinović was convicted at Kraljevo District Court of war crimes and sentenced to 40 years' imprisonment for the murder of two Serb and two Albanian civilians in Mitrovica in 1999.

On 17 May, Saša Cvetjan, a member of the "Scorpions", was again sentenced to 20 years' imprisonment at Belgrade District court for the killing of 14 Albanian civilians in Podujevo in 1999. The Supreme Court had ordered a retrial in January.

On 23 May, the Montenegro Supreme Court confirmed the conviction and sentence of Nebojša Ranisavljević for the abduction of 20 mainly Muslim civilians from a train at Štrpci railway station in February 1993.

'Disappearances'

Investigations opened in January into the alleged mass cremation of the bodies of ethnic Albanians at the Mačkatica factory in Surdulica in 1999. The Humanitarian Law Centre alleged that witnesses were intimidated by local police officers.

By November, Serbia had handed over to UNMIK 836 bodies of ethnic Albanians killed in Kosovo, who had been transferred to Serbia in refrigerated trucks and buried in mass graves in Batajnica near Belgrade, Petrovo Selo and Bajina Bašta. No indictments had been issued by the end of the year; investigations had opened in 2000. On 25 October, six serving Serbian police officers and three former officers were indicted on suspicion of the murder of 48 ethnic Albanians in Suva Reka in Kosovo in March 1999; some of the bodies identified at Batajnica originated from Suva Reka.

Possible extrajudicial executions

Slavoljub Šćekić, Head of the General Criminal Division of the Montenegrin police, was murdered on 30 August. His family alleged official complicity and opened their own investigation.

The trial continued of Damir Mandić, the sole suspect – despite allegations of official complicity – in the murder in May 2004 of Duško Jovanović, editor-in-chief of the Montenegrin daily *Dan*.

Army of SCG

The Belgrade District Court opened investigations on 14 March into the unresolved deaths of two conscript sentries – Dražen Milovanović and Dragan Jakovljević – in October 2004 at a Belgrade military complex. Investigations continued with the German Wiesbaden Criminological Institute invited to assist in September, and the US Federal Bureau of Investigations in December.

In October, the period of compulsory military service was reduced from nine to six months; alternative service was cut from 13 to nine months. Amendments to legislation allowing for conscientious objection, introduced in February, breached Council of Europe standards allowing for application for conscientious objector status at any time.

Past political murders

On 29 June, Milorad "Legija" Ulemek-Luković was sentenced to 15 years' imprisonment for his part in the murder of four people during the attempted murder of current SCG Foreign Minister Vuk Drašković in 1999. Former head of Serbian state security Radomir Marković was also sentenced to 10 years' imprisonment, along with eight other security officials. In July Milorad Ulemek-Luković was sentenced to 40 years' imprisonment for the murder of former Serbian President Ivan Stambolić in August 2000; Radomir Marković was sentenced to 15 years in prison for failing to prevent the murder.

The trial continued of Milorad Ulemek-Luković, accused of involvement in the murder in March 2003 of Prime Minister Zoran Đinđić. In April another suspect, Dejan "Bagsy" Malenković, was extradited from Greece and in July was given witness-associate status (became a prosecution witness) by the court.

Police torture and ill-treatment

Reports of police torture or ill-treatment apparently fell, but investigations into previous cases remained seriously flawed, and in a number of trials testimony allegedly obtained under torture was admitted in evidence. In May a Ministry of Interior report confirmed six cases of torture during "Operation Sabre" in 2003, although the Ministry was reportedly unable to identify the police officers concerned.

The UN Committee against Torture in both May and November found SCG to be in violation of the Convention against Torture in relation to complaints submitted on behalf of two Romani men, Jovica Dimitrov and Danilo Dimitrijević. In December, Belgrade District Court found the Republic of Serbia in violation of its obligations under the Convention, in connection with the Committee against Torture's decision of 2001 in the case of Milan Ristić.

Minorities

In May the UN Committee on Economic, Social and Cultural Rights expressed concern over the lack of anti-discrimination legislation, reported incidents of inter-ethnic violence and widespread discrimination against Roma. They urged SCG to take special measures to alleviate poverty among Roma, and ensure that Roma had access to adequate, affordable and secure housing, adequate sanitation and safe drinking water, and affordable primary health care. The Committee also expressed concern at the continuing uncertain residence status of refugees, returnees and internally displaced people, including Roma.

Attacks on Roma individuals and communities were regularly reported but few perpetrators were brought to justice.

Attacks in the Vojvodina region continued, predominantly against the Hungarian minority.

In July, eight men were sentenced to between three and five months' imprisonment for the burning of the Hadrović mosque in Niš in March 2004. The attack was one of several that month targeting minorities in Serbia which took place in the wake of widespread attacks on Serb communities in Kosovo.

Attacks on human rights defenders

Human rights defenders and non-governmental organizations seeking to challenge impunity for war crimes were subjected to increased threats and attacks. Repeated and apparently systematic intimidation took the form of public threats, apparent "burglaries" and what appeared to be malicious prosecutions, as well as physical attacks. There was increasing concern about the independence of the media. Few perpetrators were brought to justice.

Violence against women

Research conducted in 2003 by the Belgrade Autonomous Women's Centre, and published by the World Health Organization (WHO) in November, showed that intimate partner violence remained widespread. Some 24 per cent of the 1,456 respondents surveyed had experienced physical or sexual violence, but only four per cent had reported this to the police; some 78 per cent had never sought assistance from any agency.

A Family Law introducing protective measures for victims of domestic violence came into force in July.

SCG remained a source, transit and destination country for women and girls trafficked for forced prostitution.

Kosovo

War crimes: domestic prosecutions

In May, three members of the "Kačanik" (Kaçanik) group accused of war crimes were convicted by an international panel at Priština District Court, and sentenced to between six and eight years' imprisonment. Four former members of the KLA known as the "Llap group", convicted and sentenced in 2003, were released in July after the Supreme Court annulled the verdict and ordered a retrial. In September, four Serb men were arrested in Gračanica (Ulpiana) for war crimes.

'Disappearances' and abductions

In April, a mass grave, reportedly containing the remains of non-Albanians killed in 1998, was found in Klina. Despite the resumption of talks, little progress was made in bringing to justice those responsible for both the "disappearances" of ethnic Albanians and the abduction of Serbs, Roma and other minorities.

Ethnically motivated crimes

There were regular reports of attacks on Serbian communities, including the use of tear gas, hand grenades and other explosive devices, arson, beatings and shootings.

According to the Organization for Security and Co-operation in Europe (OSCE), 426 people were charged with criminal offences in connection with the March 2004 violence in which 19 people died and 954 civilians and 184 police and security personnel were injured. As of November, some 209 people had been convicted and 12 acquitted, with 110 cases still pending and 95 charges dropped. The OSCE reported in December that criminal investigations had been hindered by problems including witness intimidation, loss of material evidence and poor co-operation between the police and the prosecution.

▭ In May, six Albanians were sentenced to a total of 38 years' imprisonment at Gnjilane (Gnilanë) District Court for the murder of Slobodan Perić and his mother, Anka Perić, in March 2004.

▭ On 7 April, 12 ethnic Albanians were convicted and sentenced for the murder of former police officer Hamez Hajra, his wife and three children in 2001; four received 30-year sentences.

▭ On 13 April, Florim Ejupi was arrested in Albania, and charged with the murder of 12 Serbs and six other offences in connection with the bombing of the Niš Express bus in March 2001; he was also charged with the murder of UNMIK and Kosovo Police Service (KPS) officers in February 2004.

Politically motivated crimes

Sadik Musa, a former protected witness, was shot on 31 January in Peć (Peja), and died on 1 February.

On 4 June Abdhyl Ayeti, a journalist associated with the Democratic League of Kosovo, was shot and wounded; he died on 25 June. A suspect was arrested on 15 June.

UNMIK and KPS officers were targeted in shootings and explosive devices were placed under police vehicles.

▭ Umar Ali Karya, a Nigerian UNMIK police officer, was killed by a car bomb on 13 January in Prizren.

Discrimination against minorities

In April a Memorandum of Understanding between the German government and UNMIK allowed the forcible return of Ashkali and "Egyptian" individuals from Germany. Voluntary returns remained low.

On 2 June, UNMIK submitted a report to the Council of Europe on measures taken to implement the Framework Convention for the Protection of National Minorities. This failed to note that internally displaced Roma, Ashkali and "Egyptian" people living near the former Trepča Mines lead-smelting site in Zvečan (Zveçan) municipality had been found by the WHO in 2004 to have dangerous levels of lead in their blood. There was grave concern at the failure of UNMIK and the PISG to respect and fulfil their right to health; despite international calls for their urgent relocation, they had not been moved by the end of the year.

Trafficking of women and girls for forced prostitution

An Administrative Directive implementing the 2001 trafficking regulation promulgated in February failed to guarantee trafficked women and girls an automatic right to protection and assistance. A trafficking action plan published in May failed to fully meet AI's 2004 recommendations on protecting the human rights of trafficked women and girls.

Arrests of groups of suspected traffickers were reported in March and May.

▭ In May a senior member of the UN High Commissioner for Refugees was convicted and sentenced for sexual exploitation of minors under 16 years, but charges related to trafficking were dropped.

AI country reports/ visits
Reports

- Amnesty International's concerns on the implementation of the "completion strategy" of the International Criminal Tribunal for the former Yugoslavia (AI Index: EUR 05/001/2005)
- Serbia and Montenegro: A wasted year – The continuing failure to fulfil key human rights commitments made to the Council of Europe (AI Index: EUR 70/005/2005)

SIERRA LEONE

REPUBLIC OF SIERRA LEONE
Head of state and government: Ahmad Tejan Kabbah
Death penalty: retentionist
International Criminal Court: ratified
UN Women's Convention: ratified
Optional Protocol to UN Women's Convention: signed

Trials continued before the Special Court for Sierra Leone. The Nigerian government refused to surrender former Liberian President Charles Taylor to the Special Court for Sierra Leone to be tried on charges of crimes against humanity and war crimes committed during the armed conflict in Sierra Leone. The trials before national courts of former combatants charged with murder and other offences in 2002 continued. Weaknesses, such as staff shortages, remained in the judicial sector. The acting editor of the leading newspaper *For Di People* died after a severe beating, amid fears that a member of parliament had been involved in his death. The Truth and Reconciliation Commission's 2004 report was distributed as part of a nationwide programme to raise awareness of human rights, including of women and children. However, a recommendation by the Commission to abolish the death penalty was not implemented.

Background

The security situation remained generally stable. The government assumed further responsibilities for maintaining security and consolidating the peace, and extended its authority. Some 9,500 police officers were deployed throughout the country, and international military advisers supported strengthening of the army.

Sierra Leone remained one of the poorest countries in the world, with 70 per cent of the population living on less than US$1 a day and high illiteracy rates. There was little progress in addressing other factors contributing to human rights violations, particularly widespread poverty, severe youth unemployment and the lack of basic services.

The UN High Commissioner for Human Rights visited Sierra Leone in July, primarily to support the establishment of the National Human Rights Commission. Later in July Parliament approved the law setting up the National Human Rights Commission, which was to start functioning from early 2006.

An August UN Security Council resolution replaced the UN peacekeeping office in Sierra Leone (UNAMSIL) with a peace building office, the UN Integrated Office in Sierra Leone (UNIOSIL), to focus on human rights and the rule of law from January 2006. The human rights section of UNAMSIL held a national conference in December to formulate a human rights action plan for the new mission.

The Special Court for Sierra Leone

Former Liberian President Charles Taylor continued to enjoy impunity despite international pressure, including from the European Parliament and the US Congress, for Nigeria to surrender him to the Special Court for Sierra Leone to face charges of crimes against humanity, war crimes and other serious violations of international law. The Campaign Against Impunity, a coalition of international human rights organizations, was formed to press the Nigerian government and other African Union member states for Charles Taylor's surrender to the Special Court.

President Olusegun Obasanjo of Nigeria maintained his refusal to surrender Charles Taylor, on the grounds that it would disrupt Liberia's transition. In July member states of the Mano River Union – Guinea, Liberia and Sierra Leone – called for Nigeria to review the terms under which Charles Taylor had been granted asylum in 2003, as he was allegedly breaking a commitment not to interfere in Liberian politics. In November the federal High Court in Nigeria ruled that two Nigerian victims of torture had legal standing to challenge the asylum given to Charles Taylor.

The Special Court established a second trial chamber in January, enabling a third trial to start in March. Three trials involving nine suspects indicted in 2003 continued throughout the year. In April the second trial chamber ordered the prosecution of a defence lawyer for allegedly revealing the identity of, and threatening, a protected witness. In July the prosecution closed its case in the trial of three members of pro-government Civil Defence Force (CDF) militias, and in October the first trial chamber unanimously dismissed a motion for acquittal. In November the trial began of three members of the former armed opposition Revolutionary United Front (RUF). The trial of three members of the Armed Forces Revolutionary Council (AFRC) had not concluded by the end of 2005. Reports of the death of Johnny Paul Koroma, the former AFRC Chairman, were not confirmed, and he remained at large.

The Special Court remained without sufficient guarantees of international funding to enable it to continue operating effectively until the end of 2006.

High Court treason trials

At the beginning of 2005, 57 former RUF and AFRC members and 31 former West Side boys, renegade soldiers, were on trial before the High Court in the capital, Freetown. They were charged with treason for allegedly overthrowing or seeking to overthrow an elected government by force. One of the accused, the daughter of former RUF leader Foday Sankoh, died in prison in 2005. There were repeated adjournments of the trials.

Nine former members of the RUF and AFRC and one civilian, sentenced to death for treason in December 2004, planned to lodge an appeal but did not have access to lawyers. The charges related to an armed attack in January 2003 on a military armoury in Freetown in an apparent attempt to overthrow the government.

Other former combatants were held in safe custody for periods mid-year, reportedly because they were testifying for the prosecution in the trials. Three former RUF members spent a month in July and August in the custody of the criminal investigation police.

Truth and Reconciliation Commission

The Truth and Reconciliation Commission distributed its report, published in 2004, which contributed to raising awareness of human rights concerns it highlighted. Key recommendations included the abolition of the death penalty, a moratorium on executions pending abolition, and commutation of pending death sentences.

Inspired by the example set by the Special Court for Sierra Leone, where the maximum sentence was a term of life imprisonment, civil society groups organized events throughout the year to raise concern about the death penalty.

The government's response to the report, published mid-year, made no commitment to abolish the death penalty, however. In November, a non-governmental follow-up committee presented a draft law to Parliament to adopt the Commission's recommendations as law.

Protracted justice reforms

Reform of the justice sector was slow. There were improvements to infrastructure with the building of court houses and prisons. Shortage of legal staff resulted in delays in the finalization of draft laws to protect women's human rights, including laws on marriage, succession, inheritance and sexual offences drafted by the Law Reform Commission. The Law Reform Commission carried out consultations on domestic violence legislation, for a draft bill to be presented to Parliament in 2006.

In the formal legal system, court adjournments and long delays in trials remained common. There was little opportunity for convicted prisoners to lodge appeals. Some legal aid was available in district towns but not in Freetown. Local courts, in which lay judges administered customary law, were functioning. However, chiefs and local court officials often gave rulings and adjudications in cases outside their jurisdiction, contributing to the denial of justice to a large proportion of the population. The Attorney General's Office provided training to local court officials during the year.

Press freedom under attack

Journalists and editors were targeted, giving rise to fears of a concerted attack on press freedoms.

☐ Paul Kamara, former editor of *For Di People*, was released from prison on appeal in November after serving 13 months of two concurrent two-year prison terms in the Central Prison, Freetown. He was convicted of seditious libel in 2004, after the paper claimed that a 1967 commission of inquiry had "convicted" President Kabbah, then a ministerial official, of fraud.

☐ In May, Sidney Pratt and Dennis Jones, journalists for the *Trumpet* newspaper, were arrested by police and accused of seditious libel. They were subsequently released without charge.

☐ On 10 May, Harry Yansaneh, acting editor of *For Di People*, was assaulted on the newspaper's premises by a group of men. He was hospitalized but died from his injuries in July. The coroner's inquest found that the death was caused by the assault. Eight people, including a senior government official, were arrested and charged with involuntary manslaughter. They were released on bail to await trial, which had not started by the end of 2005. There were concerns about government interference in the case after the Attorney General had the initial charges withdrawn because of a procedural error by the coroner.

AI country reports/visits

Reports

- Special Court for Sierra Leone: Statement to the National Victims Commemoration Conference, Freetown, 1 and 2 March 2005 (AI Index: AFR 51/002/2005)
- Sierra Leone: No one to turn to — Women's lack of access to justice in rural Sierra Leone (AI Index: AFR 51/011/2005)

Visits

AI delegates visited Sierra Leone for research in October and for lobbying in December.

SINGAPORE

REPUBLIC OF SINGAPORE
Head of state: S.R. Nathan
Head of government: Lee Hsien Loong
Death penalty: retentionist
International Criminal Court: not signed
UN Women's Convention: ratified with reservations
Optional Protocol to UN Women's Convention: not signed

Freedom of expression and assembly continued to be curbed. Thirty-six men were held without charge or trial under the Internal Security Act (ISA). Death sentences were imposed and eight people were executed. Jehovah's Witnesses continued to be imprisoned for conscientious objection to military service. Criminal offenders were sentenced to caning.

Background
The ruling People's Action Party (PAP), in power since 1959, maintained a dominating hold over political life and wider society. Official statements encouraging a more participatory, inclusive society were countered in practice by an array of laws restricting rights to freedom of expression, association and assembly.

Restrictions on freedom of expression and assembly
The threat of potentially ruinous civil defamation suits against opponents of the PAP continued to inhibit political life.

In March, the leader of the opposition Singapore Democratic Party, Chee Soon Juan, was unable to pay damages of 500,000 Singapore dollars (approximately US$306,000) awarded against him in defamation suits lodged in 2001 by two PAP leaders. He was at risk of being declared bankrupt and therefore unable to stand for election.

In September, the High Court rejected a second application to be discharged from bankruptcy lodged by former leader of the opposition Workers' Party, J. B. Jeyaretnam. Declared bankrupt after a series defamation suits by PAP leaders and others, he was expelled from Parliament in 2001 and remained unable to stand for election.

The threat of prosecution, and uncertainty over the boundaries of permissible public debate, contributed to a climate of self-censorship.

In March, government censors required film maker Martyn See to remove a documentary on Chee Soon Juan from Singapore's international film festival. He was then subjected to a criminal investigation and required to surrender equipment and material. No charges had been filed by the end of the year.

In May, the authorities threatened to sue a Singaporean student in the USA who criticized the government's scholarship system on his personal Internet blog.

Restrictions on freedom of assembly also inhibited peaceful civil society activity. In August, riot police ordered the dispersal of a group of four people holding a silent protest outside a government building to urge greater official accountability. A High Court judge subsequently dismissed their petition that the dispersal violated their constitutional right to peaceful protest.

In September police questioned local activists who had set up placards protesting at delays in opening a train station. No charges were filed.

In March, the authorities banned a weekend concert by a local AIDS support group, stating that the event, organized by a Christian gay organization, was against the public interest.

Detention without trial
At least 36 men remained in detention without charge or trial under the ISA. Seventeen other former ISA detainees were reportedly under orders restricting their freedom of movement and association. The authorities claimed the men were involved with Islamist groups, including Jemaah Islamiah, held responsible for planning or carrying out bomb attacks in the region.

Death penalty
Eight people were executed. Singapore was believed to have the highest rate of executions per capita in the world.

The hanging in May of Shanmugam s/o Murugesu, sentenced to death in 2004 for possession of just over 1kg of cannabis, sparked unprecedented public discussion. From April to August, local activists organized a public forum, petitions, vigils and other events to campaign against the death penalty. The authorities refused to allow an AI representative to address the public forum in May, while in August police banned the use of Shanmugam's face on posters on the grounds that it would "glorify" an executed convict.

In December Australian Van Tuong Nguyen, convicted in 2004 of smuggling heroin, was executed.

Conscientious objectors
At least two conscientious objectors to military service were imprisoned in 2005, and 12 others continued to serve prison sentences. All were members of the banned Jehovah's Witnesses religious group. There was no alternative to military service in practice for conscientious objectors in Singapore.

AI country reports/ visits
Visit
In May an AI representative met local activists and attended a public forum against the death penalty, but was denied permission to speak.

SLOVAKIA

SLOVAK REPUBLIC
Head of state: Ivan Gasparovič
Head of government: Mikuláš Dzurinda
Death penalty: abolitionist for all crimes
International Criminal Court: ratified
UN Women's Convention and its Optional Protocol:
ratified

There were continuing reports of discrimination against Roma in both public and private sectors; concerns included the lack of access to education and housing for Roma.

Discrimination against Roma

In January, the government produced its comments on the Concluding Observations of the UN Human Rights Committee, which had been published in 2003 and which expressed concern about discrimination against Slovakia's 500,000 Roma in the fields of education, employment, housing, health, social care and access to services. Among other issues the government addressed the placement in special schools of Roma children. In the context of Roma children often failing school entry tests, the government stated that they "come to school without pre-school education and sufficient knowledge of Slovak, lack basic hygiene and cultural and working skills, have limited concentration, patience and perseverance, and have underdeveloped fine motor coordination, different experience and knowledge of the world, and different interests and felt needs." The government reported that it would prepare differential school tests for Roma children from a socially disadvantaged environment by the end of 2005.

In April, the government official in charge of Roma affairs, Klára Orgovánová, announced the adoption of a National Action Plan for a "Decade of Roma Inclusion 2005-2015". The main areas of discrimination targeted in the National Action Plan are education, employment, health and housing.

Housing rights

In March, the UN Committee on Elimination of Racial Discrimination found that Slovakia had discriminated against a group of Roma with regard to housing rights. The case was brought by 27 Slovak citizens of Roma origin from Dobšiná, and followed a decision not to proceed with a previously announced project to set up low-cost housing for the Roma population in Dobšina, after an anti-Roma petition was received from certain politicians with nationalist agendas. The Committee stated that once a policy towards realization of the right to housing had been adopted by the authorities, its revocation and replacement with a weaker measure amounted to a violation of the Convention on the Elimination of All Forms of Racial Discrimination.

Záhorská Ves – update

In 2004 the Roma family of Štefan and Olga Šarkozi were reportedly ordered by the mayor of Záhorská Ves to leave their land and the village, after their house had been burned down by a racist mob in December 2003. The mayor was also reported to have confronted the Šarkozi family with private security guards, who assaulted Štefan and other members of the family with baseball bats. In 2005, Klára Orgovánová, the senior official for Roma affairs, was told by the mayor that the Šarkozi family had been offered compensation to leave the village, which it had initially accepted and later declined. AI was unable to confirm this.

Ban on affirmative action

In October, the Constitutional Court declared unconstitutional any affirmative action for ethnic minorities, such as Roma. The Court ruled that such action clashed with the Slovak constitution, as it "violated full equality before law".

In practice, the decision appeared to ban special measures, including those designed to improve access to education and employment for members of ethnic minorities. Under its international human rights obligations, Slovakia may be required to take special measures to redress historical discrimination and the conditions that cause or help to perpetuate discrimination.

Forced sterilizations

A new comprehensive Public Health Law, including provisions on sterilizations, informed consent and access to medical records, entered into force on 1 January. The law was drafted after civil society organizations highlighted substantial gaps in the previous legislation, which did not accord sufficient protection against forced sterilizations of women.

Citing this new law, the UN Committee on the Elimination of Discrimination against Women declined to conduct an inquiry into allegations of forced sterilizations of Romani women submitted by the European Roma Rights Centre. The Committee nevertheless expressed concern about possible individual cases of forced sterilizations in Slovakia and recommended that the Slovak authorities pursue the issue.

A case against Slovakia brought by three alleged victims of forced sterilization was heard by the European Court of Human Rights in Strasbourg. The decision was pending at the end of 2005.

AI wins case against Slovak police

In June, the Supreme Court announced that the police had not acted in line with the law when, in June 2004, they prevented 30 AI activists from gathering in front of the Belarus Embassy in Bratislava to protest against the detention of prisoner of conscience Professor Yury Bandazhevsky. Although AI notified the authorities of the demonstration in accordance with existing regulations, the police prevented demonstrators from entering the street where the Belarus Embassy is located. The Supreme Court decided that only the municipality, not the police, has the legal power to prevent people exercising the right to assemble. The police can only intervene if public order is disturbed or other illegal acts are linked to the event.

AI country reports/ visits
Report
- Europe and Central Asia: Summary of Amnesty International's concerns in the region, January-June 2005: Slovakia (AI Index: EUR 01/012/2005)

SLOVENIA

REPUBLIC OF SLOVENIA
Head of state: Janez Drnovšek
Head of government: Janez Janša
Death penalty: abolitionist for all crimes
International Criminal Court: ratified
UN Women's Convention and its Optional Protocol: ratified

There was continued concern about the status of thousands of people whose names were removed from the registry of permanent residents in 1992 (known as the "erased"). Members of Romani communities faced discrimination including in access to education.

The 'erased'
The Slovenian authorities failed to resolve the status of the so-called "erased" — some 18,305 individuals unlawfully removed from the Slovenian registry of permanent residents in 1992. The "erased" were mainly people from other former Yugoslav republics who had been living in Slovenia but had not acquired Slovenian citizenship after Slovenia became independent. The Slovenian authorities failed to ensure that the "erased" had full access to economic and social rights, including access to work, health care and, in some cases, education.

Although the Slovenian Constitutional Court had ruled in 1999 and 2003 that the removal of these individuals from the registry of permanent residents was unlawful, approximately 6,000 of the "erased" still did not have Slovenian citizenship or a permanent residence permit at the end of 2005.

Following the 2003 Constitutional Court decision, the Slovenian Ministry of Interior had issued approximately 4,100 decrees retroactively restoring the status of permanent residents to the individuals concerned. However, the Slovenian authorities stopped issuing such decrees in July 2004 and no new steps were taken to implement the Constitutional Court decision and to restore the rights of the "erased".

Many of the "erased" continued to live in Slovenia "illegally" as foreign nationals or stateless persons; others were forced to leave the country. Many of the

12,000 who had managed to obtain Slovenian citizenship or permanent residency — in many cases after years of bureaucratic and legal struggle — continued to suffer from the ongoing consequences of their past unregulated status and had no access to full reparation, including compensation.

Lack of access to education for Romani children
The Slovenian authorities failed to fully integrate Romani children into the education system and tolerated or promoted the creation of special classes for Romani children in certain primary schools. In some cases the children in the special classes were taught a reduced or simplified curriculum.

Concern was expressed in July by the UN Human Rights Committee that members of Romani communities continued to suffer prejudice and discrimination, including in access to education.

In March, after protests by parents of non-Romani children against the "large share" of Romani pupils attending the Bršljin primary school, the Slovenian Minister of Education and Sport proposed to create at that school special separate classes in certain subjects for Romani children. This proposal was subsequently retracted following protests by Romani parents and non-governmental organizations, including AI.

AI country reports/ visits
Reports
- Europe and Central Asia: Summary of Amnesty International's concerns in the region, January-June 2005: Slovenia (AI Index: EUR 01/012/2005)
- Slovenia: The "erased" — Briefing to the UN Committee on Economic, Social and Cultural Rights (AI Index: EUR 68/002/2005)
Visit
An AI delegate visited Slovenia in September.

SOLOMON ISLANDS

SOLOMON ISLANDS
Head of state: Queen Elizabeth II, represented by Nathaniel Waena
Head of government: Allan Kemakeza
Death penalty: abolitionist for all crimes
International Criminal Court: signed
UN Women's Convention and its Optional Protocol: ratified

Reconstruction and development efforts continued following five years of armed conflict that ended in 2003. Potentially divisive ethnic and regional differences remained to be addressed. In prosecutions for serious conflict-related crimes, at least 10 people were convicted, including the former leader of the Guadalcanal Liberation Front. Other former militants continued to await trial on remand, some after nearly two and a half years in pre-trial detention.

Post-conflict developments

Progress was reported on the reconstruction of infrastructure and key institutions affected by the conflict. However, significant development challenges remained, as more than 80 per cent of the population was still dependent on subsistence agriculture and fishing, with limited access to health and education services. The marked disparity in development between the capital, Honiara, and the provinces stirred tensions, as did reported corruption among political leaders.

With the continued presence of the Regional Assistance Mission to Solomon Islands (RAMSI) the security situation reportedly remained stable. However, in May a report by the Pacific Islands Forum found that entrenched provincialism and strong animosities between ethnic groups persisted. The report recommended establishing both a Truth and Reconciliation Commission and a commission of inquiry to investigate land issues and the underlying causes of ethnic conflict. Neither institution had been established by the end of 2005, although there were other community reconciliation initiatives. Concerns remained that proposed constitutional reforms designed to introduce a federal system of government could lead to further fragmentation.

Trials relating to the conflict

Although arrests relating to the conflict were still being made in December, most outstanding cases had proceeded to trial or were awaiting trial. In such cases, there were concerns about the length of time some detainees had been in custody. The courts decided that more than two years in pre-trial detention was reasonable in the circumstances.

During the year, the High Court convicted at least 10 people for their role in the violence and acquitted four. Among those convicted was Harold Keke, former leader of the Guadalcanal Liberation Front, who, with two others, was sentenced to life imprisonment for the 2002 murder of Augustine Geve, a former priest and government minister.

In two other murder trials, the court held that, despite possible evidence of threats and intimidation, the defence of duress was not available to former militia members who had voluntarily joined militant groups.

Militia members convicted in at least one trial lodged appeals on the grounds that they had been induced to make admissions as part of the peace process, without understanding that their statements would be used as evidence against them in criminal proceedings.

In October police used tear gas to quell a prison riot that reportedly started when suspects awaiting trial for conflict-related offences believed their appeal for amnesty had not been delivered.

Violence against women

In March the Christian Care Centre, the country's first purpose-built shelter for victims of family violence, opened near Honiara. In September, Centre staff and police officers received training on gender-based violence from the Fiji Women's Crisis Centre. However, a national policy on violence against women, including a coordinated, properly resourced inter-agency approach, was still outstanding. Women who experienced violence, particularly outside major town centres, were left without effective protection, health services or redress.

As the courts worked through their case backlog, a few historical cases of sexual assault came to trial. In May, former Deputy Police Commissioner Wilfred Akao was convicted and sentenced to two years' imprisonment for abducting and assaulting a woman in Honiara in 1996. Another man was sentenced to four and a half years on three counts of raping the same woman.

SOMALIA

SOMALIA
Head of state of Transitional Federal Government:
Abdullahi Yusuf Ahmed
**Head of government of Transitional Federal
Government:** Ali Mohamed Gedi
Head of Somaliland Republic: Dahir Riyaale Kahin
Death penalty: retentionist
International Criminal Court: not signed
UN Women's Convention and its Optional Protocol:
not signed

Thousands of civilians escaping human rights abuses fled the country or were displaced. There was no rule of law in the south. Journalists were arrested and human rights defenders threatened in several areas. Violence against women was widespread. In Somaliland, there were arbitrary detentions and unfair political trials and reports of torture. A 16-year-old girl imprisoned for espionage was released.

Background
Transitional Federal Government
In January, the Kenya-based Transitional Federal Parliament approved the appointment of a cabinet of ministers and assistant ministers by the Prime Minister, who had been appointed by the President of the Transitional Federal Government (TFG) in November 2004. The five-year TFG and other federal institutions were not, however, functional in Somalia by the end of 2005. This was the result of an internal division between, on the one hand, President Abdullahi Yusuf Ahmed and his associated clan-based factions, who mostly relocated from Kenya to Jowhar town in central Somalia, and, on the other hand, faction leaders who had returned to their base in the capital, Mogadishu. Open fighting between the two groupings was narrowly averted. The UN Secretary-General called again in October for a comprehensive ceasefire agreement.

An African Union peace-support force, proposed in 2004 at the conclusion of a two-year peace and reconciliation conference in Kenya, was not deployed for security reasons, and there was very little demobilization of faction militias as required by the Transitional Federal Charter (the interim Constitution).

There were continuing periodic outbursts of faction fighting and clan-militia violence in most of the central and southern regions. Police General Yusuf Ahmed Sarinle was assassinated in Mogadishu in January, apparently for supporting the TFG. Generally, humanitarian access was severely impeded, humanitarian supplies were often looted, and employees of UN agencies and international aid organizations were at risk of being killed or kidnapped for ransom.

Several warlords and others who were alleged to have committed war crimes, crimes against humanity or gross human rights violations, either under the pre-1991 Siad Barre government or during the subsequent civil wars, were appointed as ministers in the TFG or to other federal posts and continued to benefit from impunity.

The international community suspended commencement of reconstruction aid to Somalia until the TFG was united and functional, although the UN and World Bank began a joint needs assessment. A humanitarian emergency affected up to a million people in need of urgent assistance.

Somaliland
The self-declared Somaliland Republic in the north-west continued to press its demand for international recognition after 14 years of de facto independence. It remained the only part of the former Somali Republic to have a government and functioning administration. Its dispute with neighbouring Puntland over the contested Sool and Sanaag border regions remained unresolved, but 36 "prisoners of war" on both sides who had been captured in 2004 were exchanged in December.

Parliamentary elections were held in September. President Dahir Riyaale Kahin's ruling United Democratic People's Party gained 33 seats, while the opposition Unity (Kulmiye) and Justice and Welfare parties gained 28 and 21 seats respectively.

UN arms embargo
In October the UN Security Council condemned increasingly serious violations of its 1992 international arms embargo on Somalia. The report by a panel of experts identified violations by the governments of Ethiopia and Yemen and a third unnamed government, and also by certain Somali warlords and businesspeople in the fishing, charcoal and drugs industries. The monitoring group's report expressed concern that these illegal flows of small weapons to the TFG and opposition factions contributed to general insecurity and problems in establishing the transitional government.

Justice and rule of law
There was no rule of law or justice system in the central and southern regions of Somalia, apart from a number of Islamic (Sharia) courts, which did not follow recognized international standards of fair trial.

In September, Jama Aden Dheere, a pro-TFG faction-leader, was detained in Jowhar for political reasons and allegedly ill-treated.

In Somaliland there were cases of unfair political trials and detention without trial.

In January, Zamzam Ahmed Dualeh, aged 16, was pardoned and allowed to return home to Puntland under the care of the UN Independent Expert on human rights in Somalia. She had been convicted in 2004 of espionage and sentenced to five years' imprisonment after a grossly unfair trial. The Somaliland authorities continued to reject her allegations of rape and torture by police officers.

In September, dozens of people, including Muslim teachers, were arrested after a shoot-out between an armed group and police. They were accused of being part of an Islamist group linked to al-Qa'ida who were allegedly planning to attack government officials and foreigners. They were detained without charge or trial at the end of the year. Some were allegedly tortured.

◻ Twenty-nine elders of the Ogaden clan from Ethiopia who had been detained in November 2003 and convicted of armed conspiracy as alleged members of the Ogaden National Liberation Front (ONLF), which was in conflict with the Ethiopian government, were acquitted on appeal by the Supreme Court in 2005. However, they remained in detention in poor health in Hargeisa prison where two died in late 2005.

Journalists

Several journalists in Somalia (including Puntland) and also in Somaliland were threatened or detained, and two were killed. In August at a conference on Freedom and Rights of Journalists held in Mogadishu, despite death threats to the organizers, a National Union of Somali Journalists was established.

◻ A *British Broadcasting Corporation* (BBC) journalist, Kate Peyton, was assassinated in Mogadishu in February.

◻ In February, *HornAfrik* radio station in Mogadishu was bombed and a *HornAfrik* journalist, Duniya Muhyadin Nur, was killed by faction militias at a roadblock in June.

◻ In Puntland, Abdi Farah Nur, editor of the *Shacab* newspaper which had been banned by the Puntland authorities, was briefly detained in June in Garowe, his third arrest in the year.

Human rights defenders

Despite death threats, Somali human rights organizations continued to monitor and report on human rights violations, and to campaign for better protection of human rights, including the establishment of an independent National Human Rights Commission for Somalia, and similar human rights commissions in Somaliland and Puntland. Somaliland human rights defenders criticized prison conditions in Hargeisa, Berbera and Burao.

◻ A prominent peace activist, Abdulqadir Yahya Ali, director of the Centre for Research and Dialogue, was assassinated in Mogadishu in July by unidentified assailants.

The UN Independent Expert on human rights in Somalia reiterated concerns about human rights violations and welcomed the increasingly visible role played by civil society in promoting human rights.

Women's rights

Several women's rights organizations were active in reconciliation, militia disarmament, child rights protection and development initiatives. Women's organizations, including in Somaliland, also campaigned against violence against women, including female genital mutilation, rape — especially of internally displaced women — and domestic violence. There was deep concern that women's representation in Somalia's Transitional Federal Parliament fell short of an agreed quota of 12 per cent of seats.

Minority rights

Members of minorities continued to be subjected to social discrimination and abuses, including murder and rape, by clan members acting with impunity. Minority rights issues were debated publicly and minorities were allocated 31 seats in the Transitional Federal Parliament.

In Somaliland in May, dozens of minority rights activists and supporters were briefly detained at a demonstration in Hargeisa at the trial of a police officer, who was given a prison sentence for killing Khadar Aden Osman of the Gaboye minority.

Refugees and internally displaced people

Refugees continued to flee from faction-fighting, kidnappings, threats to human rights defenders and other human rights abuses. Conditions of 400,000 people in internal displacement camps were extremely poor. There were scores of deaths at sea of people trying to reach Yemen from Puntland in trafficking operations.

Death penalty

Eight men, including one tried in his absence, were sentenced to death in Somaliland in November for the murders of two British aid workers in 2003 and a Kenyan aid worker in 2004. They were alleged to be members of a group linked to al-Qa'ida. Their appeals were pending at the end of the year.

AI country reports/ visits
Report
· Somalia: Urgent need for effective human rights protection under the new transitional government (AI Index: AFR 52/001/2005)

SOUTH AFRICA

REPUBLIC OF SOUTH AFRICA
Head of state and government: Thabo Mbeki
Death penalty: abolitionist for all crimes
International Criminal Court: ratified
UN Women's Convention and its Optional Protocol:
ratified

There were incidents of police use of excessive force against demonstrators and ill-treatment of arrested suspects. The conduct of presiding magistrates and police investigators undermined the right to fair trial in several cases involving social movement protesters. Department of Home Affairs practices denied the majority of asylum-seekers access to refugee status determination procedures. Conditions in prison fell below international standards, largely as a result of acute overcrowding. Although an increased number of people clinically needing antiretroviral therapy for HIV/AIDS received treatment, the majority still had no access to treatment at public facilities. There was an increase in reported rapes and concern at delays in legal reforms affecting access to justice for survivors.

Background

Deputy President Jacob Zuma resigned under pressure in June, following the conviction on corruption charges of Schabir Shaik, his financial adviser. In November Jacob Zuma was indicted on corruption charges. These developments brought into the open differences within the ruling African National Congress (ANC) and between the ANC and its Alliance partners. With local government elections pending, ANC-dominated councils were increasingly targets of public protests for corrupt practices and their failure to deliver improvements in living standards. There was concern that municipal authorities misused their powers under the 1993 Gatherings Act in an attempt to suppress demonstrations by groups critical of their performance.

Human rights violations by police

Police responded to the wave of public protests in most cases without resorting to the use of excessive force. However, there were incidents in which they misused rubber bullets — the weapon of "last resort" under South African Police Service (SAPS) regulations — in their response to demonstrations in the Cape Town and Durban areas, in Delmas, Queenstown and Johannesburg. There was also misuse of pepper spray, in particular by members of the Municipal Police Services in Cape Town where they used it to break up peaceful protests against local government authorities, and against criminal suspects under arrest.
On 12 July unarmed members of the Treatment Action Campaign (TAC), who were involved in a

protest over the slow roll-out of antiretroviral treatment, were baton-charged, tear-gassed and shot at with rubber bullets by police. The majority of the protesters were HIV-positive women. The police did not warn protesters before they forcibly dispersed them from the Frontier Hospital in the Eastern Cape. Fifty-four people were seriously injured. The National Commissioner of Police ordered a departmental investigation and the retraining of the police unit involved. The TAC lodged a complaint with the Independent Complaints Directorate (ICD) which was still investigating the incident at the end of the year.
On 26 May, three Free State police officers were charged in the Harrismith regional court with murder and 16 counts of assault with intent to cause grievous bodily harm in connection with the fatal shooting of 17-year-old Teboho Mkhonza and the wounding of scores of other demonstrators on 30 August 2004.

Unfair trials

Fifty-one supporters of the Landless People's Movement (LPM) remained on trial in the Lenasia Magistrate's Court on a charge of breaching the Electoral Act by taking part in a demonstration on election day in April 2004. In June the magistrate rejected a defence application for her recusal (withdrawal from the case) on the grounds of bias after she made comments in open court that she had to report to the Minister of Justice about the trial. AI representatives attending trial proceedings in August observed that the magistrate behaved in a hostile manner towards the accused. On 29 November the magistrate rejected a defence application for the dismissal of the charges. The magistrate did not give reasons for the ruling. The proceedings were postponed until March 2006.

In November in the Protea Magistrate's Court, the presiding magistrate dismissed charges against a police officer in connection with the alleged torture of two LPM activists in April 2004. The magistrate, in acquitting the accused, reportedly attacked the complainants' organization as "disrespectful" of the government and also accused the complainants of being motivated by a desire to "undermine state authority".
In February, 13 officials and supporters of the Greater Harrismith Concerned Residents' Association from Intabazwe were charged with public violence and sedition in connection with a demonstration in August 2004. Five defendants were subjected to bail conditions which restricted their public political activities. On 10 February police allegedly arrested and assaulted Malefu Molaba, a local resident, while questioning her about the whereabouts of one of the accused, Neo Motaung. She lodged a complaint at Harrismith police station. In June, another accused, Sam Radebe, was allegedly assaulted and threatened by the police Investigating Officer. He laid a charge against the police officer at the Harrismith police station. In August the state withdrew the sedition charge and the court postponed the trial on the remaining charge until January 2006.

Prisoners' rights

On 15 December the Jali Commission of Inquiry handed its report to the President after a four-year inquiry into corruption and violence in prisons; the report had not been made public by the end of the year.

The UN Working Group on Arbitrary Detention visited the country in September and expressed alarm at the "rate of overcrowding in detention facilities". The overcrowding, in some cases by over 300 per cent of capacity, and the resulting poor prison conditions led the Judicial Inspectorate of Prisons to recommend that minimum sentence legislation be allowed to lapse. The UN delegates noted, in respect of prisoners awaiting trial or sentence, a "lack of adequate facilities so blatant that they fall short of international guarantees". The Civil Society Prison Reform Initiative urged Parliament in November to support the development of rehabilitation programmes and non-custodial alternatives to imprisonment.

In November a non-governmental organization, the AIDS Law Project, began legal proceedings against the Head of Westville Correctional Centre, Durban, on behalf of 20 prisoners who were urgently in need of antiretroviral treatment but were effectively denied access to it because of the alleged failure by the Department of Health to equip prison hospitals for this task. The problem had not been resolved by the end of the year.

On 25 May the Constitutional Court confirmed the validity of the 1997 Criminal Law Amendment Act provisions which enabled the replacement of all death sentences. Forty of the original 465 prisoners who were under sentence of death at the time of the abolition of the death penalty in 1995 were still awaiting replacement sentences at the time of a further Constitutional Court hearing in October.

Violations of refugee rights

The UN High Commissioner for Refugees, the courts, the South African Human Rights Commission and non-governmental organizations criticized the Department of Home Affairs (DHA) for failing to address organizational issues and arbitrary practices which prevented the majority of asylum-seekers from obtaining access to refugee status determination procedures and documentation in a timely manner. The closure in April of the Johannesburg area Refugee Reception Office (RRO) exacerbated the crisis. The effective denial of access to documentation left asylum-seekers at risk of arbitrary arrest, detention in police stations and in the Lindela Holding Facility, and deportation. It also meant that they were denied the right to work legally and to obtain health care or access to education. In August, the Minister of Home Affairs confirmed the government's determination to tackle these problems.

In October the report of the Ministerial Committee of Inquiry into deaths at the Lindela Holding Facility recommended urgent steps to address failures in the health care system and overcrowding at the facility. Lindela, which was run by a private company on behalf of the DHA, handled over 4,000 people per month awaiting deportation. Its clinic was found to have insufficient skilled staff and medicines and no emergency care procedures. On 28 October the Minister of Home Affairs stated that a new health care facility would be established.

On 1 March asylum-seekers, frustrated with repeatedly queuing outside the Cape Town RRO, pushed their way into the office and refused to leave the premises. They were kicked and hit with batons by officials, according to witnesses and the testimony of the asylum-seekers. The Minister of Home Affairs concluded, on the basis of an inquiry into the incident, that "no excessive force was used" and that one of the officials had been threatened with a knife by an asylum-seeker. The Minister instructed that changes should be made in the system for managing applications.

On 10 May, the Johannesburg High Court ordered the DHA to facilitate access to asylum determination procedures for 14 Ethiopians wrongly arrested and detained at Lindela. In October lawyers secured the release from Lindela of a recognized refugee who was due to be deported to Rwanda.

In a case brought by the Somali Refugee Forum, the Pretoria High Court on 11 November ordered the Minister and the DHA urgently to implement specific measures, including the reopening of the Johannesburg RRO, to ensure asylum-seekers had access without delay to asylum procedures. The government was ordered to file a report before 28 February 2006 on the extent of its compliance with the court order.

Access to health care for those living with HIV/AIDS

In July the Department of Health's HIV and Syphilis Antenatal Sero-prevalence Survey stated that between 5.7 and 6.2 million South Africans had been infected with HIV by 2004. It noted an increase in prevalence among women attending antenatal clinics, the highest rates being at 38.5 per cent of women aged between 25 and 29. A report of the South African Human Sciences Research Council in November concluded from its household survey that women were disproportionately infected, particularly women aged between 15 and 24, who had an HIV incidence rate eight times higher than men of the same age.

By the end of the year there were 229 "accredited" public health facilities providing treatment. However, the World Health Organization expressed concern at the slow progress in the roll-out of the antiretroviral treatment programme and at official statements that alternative therapies alone could prolong the lives of those living with HIV/AIDS. In September the Department of Health reported that 86,000 people had access to antiretroviral treatment in public sector facilities, although this was still less than 20 per cent of those estimated to need this treatment. About 10 per cent of children needing treatment were receiving it. Obstacles to access to treatment included severe shortages of skilled medical staff. The Joint Civil Society Monitoring Forum reported in November that additional obstacles included "under-spending" of HIV/AIDS budgets by provincial departments of health, a scarcity of appropriate drugs and treatment programmes for HIV-positive children, and a lack of national political leadership.

Violence against women
Police statistics for the year April 2004 to March 2005 recorded 55,114 reported rapes, an increase of 4.5 per cent over the previous year. Nationally, 40.8 per cent of the reported rapes were committed against minors and children.

In the period 2004/2005 the National Prosecuting Authority continued to develop dedicated sexual offences courts. The conviction rate in rape cases heard in these courts was at least 62 per cent, about 20 per cent higher than in the ordinary courts, which heard the bulk of cases.

Organizations involved in assisting survivors of sexual violence expressed concern at the continuing delays in the finalization of the Sexual Offences Bill, introduced in parliament in 2003 but referred back to the Department of Justice in early 2004.

On 6 December, former Deputy President Jacob Zuma was charged in the Johannesburg Magistrate's Court with the rape of a 31-year-old woman. He was released on bail and the trial postponed until February 2006.

On 8 December, Ncedile Ntumbukana was convicted of the rape and murder of Lorna Mlofana, a member of the TAC executive committee in Khayelitsha, Cape Town, in December 2003. She was beaten to death after telling him that she was HIV positive.

At the end of the year a Free State police officer was still on trial for the repeated rape of a woman detainee in custody at Smithfield police station; the woman became pregnant as a result.

Two rulings by the Constitutional Court strengthened the protection of women's rights.

On 13 June the Court ruled that a woman, referred to as N.K., who had been raped by three police officers while on duty, could sue the Minister of Safety and Security for damages. The Court held that in "committing the crime, the policemen not only did not protect the applicant, they infringed her rights to dignity and security of the person. In so doing, their employer's [the Minister's] obligation (and theirs) to prevent crime was not met".

On 7 November the Court upheld the constitutionality of Section 8 in the Domestic Violence Act which allows a court issuing a protection order to authorize a warrant of arrest in the absence and without the knowledge of the respondent.

Impunity
In September the Constitutional Court confirmed the State's right to re-indict Dr Wouter Basson, the former head of the military's covert chemical and biological warfare programme in the 1980s. The charges related to conspiracies to murder "enemies" of the then government outside the borders of the country. The charges had been quashed in 1999 by the trial judge.

In November the Butterworth Circuit Court sentenced two former members of the Security Police, Pumelele Gumengu and Aron Tyani, to 20 years' imprisonment each for the murder of an ANC supporter, Sthembele Zokwe, in January 1988. They were also convicted of the attempted murder of Sthembele Zokwe in 1987. On 27 March 2000 the Amnesty Committee of the Truth and Reconciliation Commission had rejected their applications for amnesty on the grounds that they had failed to make full disclosure, as required under the legislation, in relation to both incidents.

Discrimination and sexual identity
On 1 December the Constitutional Court ruled that the definition of marriage under the common law was inconsistent with the Constitution and invalid to the extent that it does not permit same-sex couples to enjoy the same rights accorded to heterosexual couples. Section 30 (1) of the 1961 Marriage Act was invalid also to the extent that it omits the gender-neutral term "or spouse". The effect of the ruling was suspended for 12 months to allow Parliament to correct the defects.

AI reports/visits
Visits
AI representatives visited the country in April, July and August.

SPAIN

KINGDOM OF SPAIN
Head of state: King Juan Carlos I de Borbón
Head of government: José Luis Rodríguez Zapatero
Death penalty: abolitionist for all crimes
International Criminal Court: ratified
UN Women's Convention and its Optional Protocol: ratified

Special courts were established to protect women from violence, but the law still failed to require the state to initiate investigations and prosecutions when violent crimes were committed in the home. While migrants already living in Spain were offered the opportunity to regularize their residency, most of those who succeeded in crossing Spain's southern borders in North Africa and the Canary Islands were denied assistance to seek asylum. Many were unlawfully expelled. At least 13 migrants from sub-Saharan Africa died and scores were injured trying to enter the Spanish enclaves of Ceuta and Melilla in North Africa, most reportedly as a result of excessive force or ill-treatment by the Spanish and Moroccan security forces. Conditions in some detention centres for minors were so poor as to amount to "institutional ill-treatment".

Background

The Basque armed group Euskadi ta Askatasuna (ETA) claimed responsibility for 24 attacks on business and tourist interests in Spain during 2005. In most cases, it used small explosive devices, causing minor injuries and damage to property. At least 42 people were injured at a convention centre in Madrid on 9 February, including at least five police officers, when a car bomb exploded hours before a scheduled visit by King Juan Carlos I and Queen Sofia. ETA had given a 30-minute warning by telephone to a newspaper. On 25 May, a car bomb planted by ETA in a Madrid street left 52 people injured. On 21 November a mass trial of 56 defendants (initiated in 1998 by judge Baltasar Garzón) opened before the National Criminal Court. The defendants were accused of being members of groups that provided financial, informational, political and other support to ETA.

On 17 May the lower chamber of parliament authorized the government to open talks with ETA if it abandoned its armed struggle.

On 7 February a programme was launched to grant amnesty to up to 800,000 undocumented migrants. Under regulations introduced in December 2004, migrants who could prove they were in Spain before August 2004, and who had a job contract and no criminal record, had three months to sign up as taxpayers and obtain rights of residence.

On 30 June parliament passed a law allowing same-sex marriages. The new law also gave all married same-sex couples the rights of inheritance previously allowed only to married men and women, and the right to adopt children.

On 9 November the Council of Europe's Commissioner for Human Rights presented the report on his March visit to Spain. He criticized the restriction that prevented lawyers interviewing some prisoners in private and the mechanisms for compensating victims of torture or ill-treatment.

In December Spain ratified the Optional Protocol to the UN Convention against Torture and Other Cruel, Inhuman or Degrading Treatment or Punishment, which it had signed in April.

Violence against women

In January a law on gender-based violence, adopted in December 2004, came into force. The law sought to bring together in a single instrument measures to prevent, assist and protect victims of violence as well as measures to prosecute, investigate and punish any offence committed. The law ensured the right for victims who lodge formal complaints to receive comprehensive assistance, including legal aid and access to health services and housing. For the first time, the law recognized that there are certain groups of women who are at greater risk of suffering gender-based violence.

In June, 17 courts dedicated solely to cases of gender-based violence began hearing cases, with an additional 433 courts empowered to hear domestic abuse cases. However, while strengthening protections against violence in the family, implementation of the new law was not as effective as had been hoped, resulting in an additional burden placed on the victim to actively pursue their formal complaint and demand formal measures for their own protection be set in motion. Further, only 5 per cent of women who suffered gender-based violence registered complaints, and many of those faced indifference by government authorities or suffered insensitive interrogations discouraging them from pursuing their case.

Survivors of domestic violence continued to experience considerable obstacles in obtaining assistance, protection and justice. Prejudice and discriminatory practices in public institutions and a lack of coordination between responsible government bodies increased the impediments for the most vulnerable groups, particularly undocumented migrant women, Roma women, and women with disabilities, mental disorders or addictions.

During 2005 the Ministry of the Interior introduced a protocol that provided, in conjunction with the Law on Aliens, that the immigration authorities should proceed with administrative sanctions and expulsion proceedings in the case of female irregular migrants who had sought protection as victims of gender-based violence after their claims were registered. In November, AI asked for the protocol to be withdrawn on the grounds that it constituted unlawful discrimination.

Killing and ill-treatment of migrants

People fleeing violence, injustice and deprivation who succeeded in crossing Spain's southern borders in North Africa, the Canary Islands and Andalusia continued to face obstacles in accessing asylum processes. Asylum-seekers were denied the necessary guidance and legal support. In Ceuta and Melilla, migrants were held in overcrowded holding centres and many were unlawfully returned to Morocco.

Harassment of migrants in unofficial camps in Morocco and moves to raise the height of perimeter fencing around Ceuta and Melilla prompted mass attempts to cross the border into Spanish territory from late August. At least 13 migrants died and scores were injured, many of them reportedly as a result of excessive force or ill-treatment by Spanish and Moroccan security forces. Despite President Zapatero's announcement of a joint investigation by the authorities in both countries, this appeared not to have started by the end of 2005.

In late September, Spanish authorities deployed 480 additional soldiers to guard the borders. During that same period, nearly 2,000 migrants and asylum-seekers who succeeded in entering Ceuta and Melilla were held in temporary holding facilities. Others were unlawfully expelled. In October, the Moroccan authorities reportedly bussed hundreds of men, women and children to the border with Algeria. In that same month, the international aid organization Médecins Sans Frontières reported finding more than 500 migrants, some handcuffed together, abandoned in the desert by the Moroccan authorities without food or water.

☐ Ayukabang Joseph Abunaw, aged 31, was reportedly killed when forces of the Civil Guard fired rubber bullets at close range at several hundred migrants climbing over perimeter fencing at Melilla at about 3am on 29 August. Eyewitnesses said that Civil Guard officers beat Ayukabang Joseph Abunaw with rifle butts and dragged him back into Moroccan territory. He reportedly died several hours later. Médecins Sans Frontières, in a preliminary examination, found a bruise on his chest typical of injuries caused by rubber bullets. According to an autopsy by the Moroccan authorities, the cause of death was internal bleeding from an injury to the liver.

☐ Four men from sub-Saharan Africa died and several others were seriously injured during the night of 28 September when several hundred people were confronted by Spanish and Moroccan security forces as they climbed razor-wire fencing around Ceuta. According to reports, two bodies on the Spanish side and two on the Moroccan side all had bullet wounds. The Civil Guard said bullets in the bodies on Spanish territory were not of the type used by their forces.

☐ On 28 December 2004, several people were illegally expelled, including asylum-seekers who had already entered Spain, one of whom was a 15-year-old minor from Guinea Conakry who suffered abuse. In May 2005 the Interior Ministry admitted that the minor had been summarily expelled because he was found between the two fences in Ceuta.

Use of tasers: death in custody

In February the Civil Guard stated that taser guns and other electro-shock weapons were not in official use. The Interior Ministry said in April that no such weapon had been acquired, but conceded that "there [were] no specific rules regulating the possible abuses of this type of weapon".

However, such weapons were reported to have been imported and used by the Civil Guard Special Intervention Unit, and local police forces in the Canary Islands, Espartinas (Seville) and Alcalà de Xivert (Castellón). One detainee allegedly died as a result of excessive force that included inappropriate use of a taser.

☐ Juan Martínez Galdeano died while detained by the Civil Guard in Roquetas de Mar (Almería) on 24 July. An internal investigation reported that closed circuit television footage showed that a baton and a taser had been used to restrain him. An autopsy revealed a causal link between the detainee's death from "acute respiratory or cardio-respiratory insufficiency" and his treatment in detention. He had cuffs on both hands and feet, and his body bore numerous injuries consistent with being struck by a baton. Two officers were indicted on charges including causing death by negligence and inhuman and degrading treatment.

Ill-treatment of minors in detention

Concerns about the conditions in detention centres for minors were raised in a report of the national Ombudsperson. The decrepit and unhealthy state of many centres did not comply with national law and regulations on the imprisonment of children. The Educational Centre for Child Offenders in Melilla was recommended for immediate closure in the report. It had a dilapidated structure, small and poorly lit cells, and only one small outdoor courtyard. Conditions in child detention facilities around Madrid were little better. They were overcrowded, had poor sanitary facilities and lacked basic furniture such as beds and tables.

In April the Ombudsperson for the Autonomous Community of the Canary Islands condemned "institutional ill-treatment" of minors in the Canary Islands. In June the first assistant to the national Ombudsperson requested the immediate closure of the detention centre in Gáldar on Gran Canaria, where conditions were particularly insanitary. The same recommendation was made by the Council of Europe's Commissioner for Human Rights.

Universal jurisdiction

Adolfo Scilingo, an Argentine former naval officer who had admitted to being aboard planes carrying detainees who were drugged, stripped naked and thrown into the sea during the military governments in Argentina, was convicted in Spain in April on charges that included crimes against humanity (see Argentina entry). He was sentenced to 640 years' imprisonment.

A ruling by the Constitutional Court in Spain in September opened the way for former Guatemalan President Rios Montt and other former military officers to be tried for human rights violations (see Guatemala entry).

Victims of the Civil War and Francoism

The government failed to present a report on the situation of victims of the 1936-39 civil war and of Francoism, despite the 2004 request by parliament for the authorities to submit such a report to allow reparations for the victims. An inter-ministerial commission had been set up in November 2004 to this end. In December 2005 President Zapatero promised to present the results of the commission's work within six months.

AI country reports/ visits
Reports
- Spain: More than words – Making protection and justice a reality for women who suffer gender-based violence in the home (AI Index: EUR 41/005/2005)
- Spain: The southern border – The State turns its back on the human rights of refugees and immigrants (AI Index: EUR 41/008/2005)

Visits
In May and October AI delegates visited Spain to carry out research and to raise with government officials concerns about violence against women in the home and the treatment of migrants and asylum-seekers, particularly in Ceuta and Melilla.

SRI LANKA

DEMOCRATIC SOCIALIST REPUBLIC OF SRI LANKA
Head of state: Mahinda Rajapakse (replaced Chandrika
Bandaranaike Kumaratunga in November)
Head of government: Ratnasiri Wickremanayake
(replaced Mahinda Rajapakse in November)
Death penalty: abolitionist in practice
International Criminal Court: not signed
UN Women's Convention and its Optional Protocol:
ratified

The ceasefire between the government and the
Liberation Tigers of Tamil Eelam (LTTE) remained in
place despite numerous violations and a
deteriorating relationship between the two parties.
Escalating political killings, child recruitment,
abductions and armed clashes created a climate of
fear in the east, spreading to the north by the end of
the year, while a nationwide state of emergency was
in place for much of 2005. Hundreds of thousands of
people remained displaced. Violence against women
was reported, including from displaced people's
camps. There were threats to reintroduce the death
penalty and numerous reports of torture in police
custody.

Background
The year began with massive efforts to provide
emergency relief to the 1 million people displaced by
the tsunami. However, initial co-operation gave way
to wrangling, as the LTTE accused the government of
discriminating against the north and east in the
distribution of aid and allegations emerged that
various parties were obstructing and diverting aid. In
January the government declared a state of
emergency and a coastal buffer zone in which
rebuilding was not permitted, resulting in thousands
of coastal communities being relocated inland.

Despite growing violence in the east, hopes for a
return to peace negotiations rose as, in May, the
government and the LTTE reached an agreement to
jointly manage the distribution of tsunami aid. In June
the People's Liberation Front (Janatha Vimukthi
Peramuna, JVP) withdrew from the government
coalition in protest at the agreement. Following a
petition lodged by the JVP in July, the Supreme Court
put a stay order on some elements of the agreement,
effectively blocking its implementation and resulting in
a further deterioration in the relationship between the
LTTE and the government.

There was an escalation of violence and insecurity in
the east and north throughout 2005, with a large
number of killings and frequent ambushes and
skirmishes, involving the LTTE, a breakaway LTTE
faction led by Colonel Karuna, and the Sri Lankan Army.

On 12 August the foreign minister, Lakshman
Kadirgamar, was assassinated, reportedly by the LTTE.
In response the government announced a state of
emergency and asked the LTTE to discuss the ceasefire
agreement. However, the talks did not take place.

Presidential elections on 17 November brought to
power the former Prime Minister, Mahinda Rajapakse.

Politically motivated killings
There were large numbers of politically motivated
killings, primarily in the east but increasingly also in the
north. The majority were apparently committed by the
LTTE, which assassinated civilians, members of rival
paramilitary groups and security force personnel.
Members of the breakaway Karuna faction also killed
civilians and LTTE cadres. The LTTE accused the security
forces of supporting the Karuna faction. The security
forces were reportedly responsible for a number of
extrajudicial executions of civilians.

In addition to targeted assassinations, there were
numerous attacks on security force posts, LTTE offices
and other sensitive targets. The high level of violence
created an atmosphere of fear and insecurity for
civilians.

A number of high-profile individuals were
assassinated. Foreign Minister Lakshman Kadirgamar
was killed in Colombo on 12 August, reportedly by the
LTTE. Ariyanayagam Chandra Nehru, a member of the
North East Secretariat on Human Rights (NESOHR) and
a former Tamil National Alliance (TNA) member of
parliament, and Kaushalyan, the LTTE political head for
Batticaloa and Ampara, were killed during an ambush
on 7 February, reportedly by the Karuna faction. Joseph
Pararajasingam, a member of parliament and of the
NESOHR, was shot dead by unknown assailants on 24
December in Batticaloa.

In December, during a visit to Sri Lanka, the UN
Special Rapporteur on extrajudicial, summary or
arbitrary executions stated that extrajudicial killings
were "violating the right to life of a large number of Sri
Lankans from all ethnic groups, and by undermining the
peace process, putting at risk the lives of many more."

▢ Dharmeratnam Sivaram, a Tamil journalist close to
the LTTE, was abducted and killed in Colombo on 28
April. He had been gagged and shot in the head.

▢ Kanapathy Rajadurai, Principal of Jaffna Central
College, was shot and killed on 12 October in Jaffna
town. He was reportedly killed by the LTTE.

Internally displaced people
At the beginning of 2005, an estimated 1 million people
were displaced by the tsunami and by September
approximately 450,000 of these remained displaced,
living in temporary shelters.

In response to the tsunami the government
established a coastal buffer zone, set at 100 metres from
the average high water line in the south and west, and
200 metres in the north and east. It was announced that
no rebuilding was permitted in this buffer zone apart
from certain exceptions (including tourist facilities) and
that communities who had lived in the buffer zone would
be relocated inland. By the middle of 2005 most of these
communities remained in temporary shelters awaiting
land to be identified for relocation. Coastal communities
expressed concern that the forced relocation would

erode their livelihoods and way of life. In addition, the large-scale relocation that followed the tsunami increased existing ethnic conflicts over land. Concerns were also raised that people displaced by the tsunami were treated differently on the basis of their ethnicity and regional location.

Approximately 350,000 people remained displaced by the conflict. These internally displaced persons (IDPs) had been unable to return home following the 2002 ceasefire for a number of reasons, including high-security zones, lack of available land for resettlement and landmines. Many were living in government-run camps in very cramped conditions with little privacy. Concern was expressed by the National Human Rights Commission in April at the lack of support and solutions available for people displaced by the conflict in comparison with people displaced by the tsunami. However, there were some indications that the focus on displacement following the tsunami helped to increase support for conflict IDPs.

Child soldiers
Following a short lull after the tsunami, reports of child recruitment by the LTTE rose, peaking in July, when 97 cases were reported to the UN Children's Fund (UNICEF). Although a small number of children were released by the LTTE during 2005, the LTTE failed to live up to its commitments under the Action Plan for Children Affected by War to end recruitment and comprehensively release the children within its ranks. In the face of these challenges, UNICEF began a review of the Action Plan.

It was reported mid-year that the LTTE was forcing all villagers within its territory between the ages of 15 and 50 to participate in military training.

Torture by police
Despite the announcement by the National Police Commission (NPC) in August 2004 that addressing torture by police would be its top priority, during 2005 there were numerous reports of torture in police custody, sometimes resulting in deaths. There was little attempt to prosecute police officers responsible for torture or to provide compensation for torture victims. Some torture victims who brought complaints were reportedly threatened by police. The terms of office of the current commissioners of the NPC expired at the end of November.

In November, the UN Committee against Torture considered Sri Lanka's second periodic report and expressed concern about "continued well-documented allegations of widespread torture and ill-treatment as well as disappearances mainly committed by the State's police forces".

🖝 Hettiarachchige Abeysiri was detained and reportedly tortured at Peliyagoda police station on 13 July. He was taken to hospital where he died from injuries caused by a blunt instrument.

Death penalty
There were no executions, despite an announcement in 2004 that the death penalty would be reactivated for certain crimes. However, in July, the Justice Ministry and Attorney General recommended that the death penalty be implemented in the case of three men convicted of the rape and murder of Rita John. These death sentences were not carried out by the end of the year.

In July, the Commissioner General of Prisons reported that there were approximately 100 prisoners on death row.

Violence against women
Incidents of sexual and domestic violence were reported throughout 2005, including sexual and domestic violence against women living in tsunami IDP camps. Women's groups expressed concern that the facilities in these camps did not provide security and made women vulnerable to violence. High levels of domestic violence were reported in some camps.

The Prevention of Domestic Violence Bill was passed in parliament, bringing in laws to arrest the growing trend of domestic violence in the country.

AI country reports/ visits
Statements
- Sri Lanka: Amnesty International urges President not to resume executions (AI Index: ASA 37/001/2005)
- Sri Lanka: Launch independent inquiry into attack on National Human Rights Commission (AI Index: ASA 37/002/2005)

Visits
AI delegates, including AI's Secretary General, visited Sri Lanka in August and December. Delegates met senior government and opposition politicians, local human rights activists and members of civil society and representatives of the LTTE.

SUDAN

REPUBLIC OF SUDAN
Head of state and government: Omar Hassan Ahmad
al-Bashir
Death penalty: retentionist
International Criminal Court: signed
UN Women's Convention and its Optional Protocol:
not signed

Grave abuses of human rights by government forces,
government-allied militias and armed political
groups continued in Darfur, western Sudan. Both
government-allied forces and, at times, armed
political groups attacked humanitarian workers and
other civilians. Suspected sympathizers of armed
political groups in Darfur were arbitrarily detained,
as were human rights activists and members of
political groups throughout northern Sudan. The new
Government of National Unity, formed in July
following a comprehensive peace agreement in
January, lifted the state of emergency, in force since
1989, except in eastern Sudan and Darfur. A new
Interim Constitution, in effect from July,
incorporated many positive human rights provisions
but retained the death penalty, including for minors,
and failed to remove immunity from prosecution for
senior officials responsible for war crimes or crimes
against humanity. Hundreds of political prisoners
continued to be held arbitrarily in Khartoum.
Arbitrary arrests, incommunicado detention, torture
and restrictions on freedom of expression persisted,
aimed in particular at human rights defenders,
student activists and internally displaced people in
and around Khartoum.

Background
There was continuing conflict in Darfur. The
government agreed a Declaration of Principles to
resolve the conflict with two armed political groups in
July, but the ceasefire was widely breached and a
lasting settlement remained remote. African Union
(AU) forces deployed in the region were still not at full
strength.

The International Criminal Court (ICC), based on a
referral by the UN Security Council, began to
investigate the situation in Darfur, but by the end of
2005 had not been granted access to Sudan. Sudan
established a national court for conflict-related crimes
in Darfur, claiming this would obviate the need for the
ICC. However, the authorities failed to investigate or
prosecute more than a few of those suspected of crimes
against humanity and war crimes in Darfur. The AU did
not enter into a co-operation agreement with the ICC,
and the Security Council did not take any further action
to implement Resolution 1593 (see below).

A Comprehensive Peace Agreement, ending decades
of civil war between the north and south, was signed on
9 January. The peace held, although certain southern

militias excluded from the peace agreement continued
to fight. The presence of the Ugandan armed political
group the Lord's Resistance Army increased in south
Sudan, as did the number of attacks it mounted against
civilians and, occasionally, humanitarian workers.
More than three million internally displaced people
(IDPs) and half a million refugees were expected to
return to the south.

On 24 March the UN Security Council established the
UN Mission in Sudan (UNMIS), with the task of
supporting the Comprehensive Peace Agreement and
providing support to the AU mission in Darfur.

The death in late July of John Garang de Mabior, head
of the government of South Sudan and first Vice-
President in the new Government of National Unity,
resulted in widespread rioting in Khartoum and Juba.
He was succeeded by Salva Kiir. As many as 130 people
died in the violence and over 1,500 people were
arrested in Khartoum.

In the east, where unrest continued to simmer, two
armed political groups, the Beja Congress and the Free
Lions, merged in February to form the Eastern Front.

Darfur
War crimes and crimes against humanity continued to
be committed by the government and government-
aligned nomadic militias known as the Janjawid. War
crimes were also committed by armed political groups
opposed to the government. Civilians were killed and
injured by government troops, who sometimes bombed
villages from the air, by Janjawid militias and in attacks
by armed political groups. Women and girls continued
to be sexually assaulted and abducted by government-
aligned militias and, occasionally, government forces.

After a major government offensive in January,
violence declined until April, then stabilized before
rising again in late August. Government human rights
violations against human rights activists continued.
Abuses by armed political groups increased as their
command structures broke down as a result of growing
factionalism and in-fighting. Such groups also
increasingly harassed humanitarian workers.
Peacekeeping troops of the AU Mission in Sudan (AMIS)
suffered attacks, including kidnappings, by
government-backed militias and some factions of the
armed political groups.

▭ On 7 April more than 350 militiamen attacked and
destroyed the village of Khor Abeche in south Darfur.
An unknown number of unarmed civilians were killed
or injured.

▭ On 30 May the authorities briefly detained Paul
Foreman, head of the international non-
governmental organization (NGO) Médecins Sans
Frontières-Holland. They charged him with crimes
against the state for publishing an allegedly false
report on rape in Darfur, and sought to compel him to
disclose the names of confidential sources.

▭ On 29 September, three members of the
national NGO, the Sudan Social Development
Organization, were abducted from Zam Zam IDP camp,
north Darfur, by the Sudan Liberation Army, an armed
political group.

Torture was widespread. In particular, suspected supporters of armed political groups and people within IDP camps were arbitrarily detained and tortured.

▢ On 14 March, military intelligence arrested Bakheet Alhaj from Sanya Afondu IDP camp. He was reportedly held in a hole in the ground for 13 days, flogged and beaten with gun butts. On 7 April he was remanded in custody to await trial.

Internally displaced people

More than 1.8 million people remained forcibly displaced internally, and 220,000 refugees were still in Chad. IDPs travelled from rural areas to settlements around towns and villages in Darfur fleeing attacks. Even within IDP camps, security was jeopardized by Janjawid militias and government forces.

▢ On 19 May police shot dead three people and injured 10 others in Kalma IDP camp in Nyala, south Darfur. The next day there were violent clashes between police and people living in the camp.

▢ On 25 May the security forces attacked Zam Zam IDP camp near El Fasher town in north Darfur. They reportedly fired indiscriminately, killing Mohamed Adam Khatir and injuring seven others.

▢ On 28 September, Janjawid militia forces attacked the IDP camp of Aro Sharow, killing 35 people and wounding 10, which forced over 4,000 to flee.

International initiatives on Darfur

A UN-appointed commission of inquiry reported in January that crimes against humanity and war crimes had been committed in Darfur by government and government-aligned militia, and that the Sudanese justice system was unable and unwilling to address the situation.

On 31 March the UN Security Council passed Resolution 1593, referring the situation in Darfur to the ICC. The resolution required Sudan and all other parties to the conflict to co-operate with the court. However, as a result of US pressure, a provision was inserted in the resolution to exempt nationals of states not party to the Rome Statute of the ICC (other than Sudan) from the jurisdiction of the ICC.

The African Commission on Human and Peoples' Rights did not make public the report of its July 2004 mission to Sudan, apparently because it was waiting for the Sudanese government to respond, despite the government's previous failure to co-operate on this issue.

Arbitrary arrests, torture and use of force

Freedom of expression continued to be repressed, with widespread arbitrary arrests, incommunicado detention and torture. Prominent among the victims were political activists, human rights defenders, student leaders and IDPs in and around Khartoum.

Members of the political opposition

▢ Following demonstrations in Port Sudan in which more than 20 people were reportedly killed, 17 members of the political wing of the Beja Congress were detained in January and February. They were released without charge in May and June.

▢ Supporters of the Popular Congress party arrested in September 2004 remained imprisoned. The government did not make public the findings of inquiries promised after the deaths of two Popular Congress student activists in 2004, reportedly as a result of being beaten after arrest.

▢ The Umma National Party headquarters in Omdurman was raided and temporarily closed in April. On 15 April, three student members of the party – Idriss Mohamed Idriss, Abu Bakr Dafallah Musa and Omar Dafallah Musa – were arrested by the security forces near Al Kalaklah central market, Khartoum, and reportedly badly beaten. They had been putting up posters. They were charged with causing a public disturbance and denied bail.

Human rights defenders

Human rights defenders and their organizations continued to face harassment and repression.

▢ The government initiated legal proceedings against one of the country's leading human rights groups, the Sudan Organisation Against Torture (SOAT), in an apparent attempt to silence it. The Bureau of Crimes Against the State reportedly began proceedings for spreading false information at the end of August, but did not inform the organization. Its members, charged with disclosing military information, propagating false news and public order offences, could face more than five years' imprisonment.

▢ Prominent human rights activist Mudawi Ibrahim was arrested on 24 January, went on hunger strike and was detained without charge until 3 March. On 8 May he was again arrested while leaving Sudan to receive a Front Line Defenders award from the President of Ireland. After considerable international pressure, he was released uncharged on 17 May.

▢ Adil Abdallah Nasr al-Din, the Director of a branch of the non-governmental Sudan Social Development Organization in Zalengei, west Darfur, was released on 19 April. He had been arrested in September 2004 and detained without charge or trial for four months, first in an unofficial detention centre near Kober prison in Khartoum and then for two months in Debek prison, north of Khartoum. He was reported to have been regularly beaten and tied up during his detention.

Students

Many student activists were arrested and beaten by police and other security forces. At least one was shot dead by police.

▢ On 11 April, Nagmeldin Gafar Adam Eisa, a student activist at Dilling University in Kordofan, died after being shot by the police on university premises during a protest against the conduct of student union elections. Police fired tear gas and live ammunition at the demonstrating students.

▢ On 19 April students demonstrating at El Fasher University in favour of UN Security Council Resolution 1593, were attacked by police and other security forces using tear gas and stun grenades and firing shots in the air. Four students were arrested, charged with public order offences, tried and acquitted. Another demonstration at the university, on 21 April, culminated in two students being injured, one seriously, as a result of police firing gunshots to disperse the crowd. Police reportedly refused to allow the seriously injured student, who was accompanied by AU personnel, passage to a hospital.

Restrictions on freedom of the press

Newspapers continued to be heavily censored, particularly in relation to Darfur. The news media were instructed not to comment on UN Security Council Resolution 1593. Several newspapers were suspended temporarily or permanently after publishing articles considered critical of the authorities. Journalists were harassed.

◻ In June the *Khartoum Monitor* was notified that its licence had been revoked by the High Court in 2003. The newspaper had successfully appealed against the closure at the time, but the National Security Services had appealed to have that decision overturned on four separate occasions without informing the newspaper.

◻ On 9 May the authorities briefly suspended *al-Wifaq* daily newspaper and fined the publication 8 million Sudanese pounds (about US$3,500) for publishing articles deemed blasphemous. The capital charge of blasphemy was brought against the editor, Mohamed Taha Mohamed Ahmed, but withdrawn soon afterwards.

Displaced people in and around Khartoum

The government forcibly relocated large numbers of IDPs living in and around Khartoum. Many had fled conflict and extreme deprivation in the south and Darfur; others were from marginalized communities throughout Sudan. The involuntary relocations sometimes led to violent clashes and mass arrests. Despite promises in July by the Governor of Khartoum State to consult with donors and UN agencies before relocating camps, settlements and groups of people, forcible relocation without warning continued.

◻ On 18 May fighting broke out between IDPs and police over the proposed relocation of the Soba Aradi IDP camp. Fourteen police officers and up to 30 IDPs were killed. On 24 May police arrested large numbers of IDPs. Mohammed Daw al Beit and three others arrested reportedly died in police custody.

◻ On 17 August armed police surrounded the Shikan IDP camp located in Omdurman, Khartoum. They arrived with lorries and emptied the entire camp of its residents. The majority of residents were moved to Fatah III camp, where basic services were lacking. Those relocated reported abuses by security forces during the relocation.

The east

Civilians were killed by the security forces following protests in eastern Sudan about underdevelopment and marginalization of the region.

◻ On 26 January peaceful demonstrators from the Beja ethnic community in Port Sudan presented a list of demands to the Red Sea State Governor. On 29 January the security forces reportedly used live ammunition against demonstrators allegedly armed with sticks and stones, attacked houses in nearby areas, and wounded residents, including children, by throwing grenades inside homes. At least 20 people were killed. A similar protest in Kassala town reportedly resulted in arrests and the beating of two students by the security forces. Two investigations were set up, but their findings were not made public.

◻ The Eastern Front, an armed political group, abducted three ruling party politicians on 24 May. They were released in early September.

AI country reports/ visits
Reports
- Sudan: Who will answer for the crimes? (AI Index: AFR 54/006/2005)
- Open letter to the President of Nigeria as Chairman of the African Union regarding Sudan referral to the ICC (AI Index: IOR 63/001/2005)
- Open letter to the members of the United Nations Security Council: The situation in the Sudan (AI Index: AFR 54/024/2005)
- Sudan: Amnesty International's recommendations on the deployment of a United Nations peace support operation (AI Index: AFR 54/025/2005)
- Sudan: Recommendations to donors funding Sudan (AI Index: AFR 54/036/2005)
- Sudan: Political repression in Eastern Sudan (AI Index: AFR 54/051/2005)
- Sudan: Memorandum to the National Constitutional Review Commission (AI Index: AFR 54/049/2005)
- Sudan: List of political detainees (AI Index: AFR 54/062/2005)

Visit
AI delegates visited southern Sudan in October.

SWAZILAND

KINGDOM OF SWAZILAND
Head of state: King Mswati III
Head of government: Absalom Themba Dlamini
Death penalty: retentionist
International Criminal Court: not signed
UN Women's Convention: ratified
Optional Protocol to UN Women's Convention: not signed

Over a quarter of the population faced severe food shortages. Three quarters of those in clinical need of antiretroviral therapy were not receiving it. A new Constitution was adopted amid continuing political tensions. Victims of forced evictions were still unable to access their rights. Reported rapes and other forms of sexual abuse of women and girls increased, but the government proposed legislative reforms to improve access to justice. Reports of torture, ill-treatment and misuse of lethal force by members of the police persisted, and there was a lack of redress for the victims. Limitations on freedoms of assembly and association included the suppression of demonstrations by force. Three people were under sentence of death. A draft law proposed creating 14 new death penalty offences.

Legal and constitutional developments
In June a new Constitution was adopted by parliament. Civil society organizations expressed concern at obstacles to public involvement in the drafting and adoption of the Constitution and at provisions entrenching the King's extensive powers and limiting the exercise of certain rights.

On 26 July the King assented to the new Constitution, which was then published in the *Government Gazette* as law. However, the King failed to issue a decree repealing the Proclamation of 12 April 1973, which vested all legislative, executive and judicial powers in the King and banned political parties. Government officials claimed that the Constitution was not yet in force. In a test case heard in the High Court in December, lawyers representing members of the Industrial Court argued that the Constitution was the applicable and supreme law in this case. The High Court had not given a ruling by the end of 2005.

The operations of the Judicial Services Commission were revived, and on its advice the King appointed three new judges on an "acting" basis and for one year only.

The government's obligations under a key 2002 Court of Appeal ruling remained partly unfulfilled. The forcible eviction of Chief Mtfuso Dlamini and his family from their home in KaMkhweli in 2000, along with that of other families from Macetjeni, had triggered a four-year rule of law crisis. In August the government refused to accept a petition from the Dlamini clan of KaMkhweli for the unconditional return of Chief Mtfuso, in exile in South Africa, as required under the Court ruling.

Violence against women and girls
In November a draft Sexual Offences and Domestic Violence Bill was issued in response to increasing concerns about sexual violence against women and young children. The Bill sought to redefine the crime of rape, criminalize marital rape, and introduce protection for "vulnerable witnesses" as well as new civil law remedies for those at risk of domestic violence. However, it also proposed 14 new capital offences.

In October police officials confirmed an increase since 2002 in reported rapes of women and children below 12 years of age. Over half the 544 rape cases reported to police by July involved minors under 18 years and young children. The Swaziland Action Group Against Abuse (SWAGAA), a non-governmental organization, dealt with an average of 21 cases of rape and sexual abuse a month in the first 10 months of the year. Perpetrators included family members and teachers. The Commissioner of Police established the Domestic Violence and Child Sexual Abuse unit in an attempt to improve police response to these crimes.

The new Constitution guaranteed women equality under the law, except in the "cultural" sphere. However, in a separate clause, which failed to fully protect women's rights, a woman could "not be compelled to undergo or uphold any custom to which she is in conscience opposed".

Access to health care
An HIV prevalence rate of 42.6 per cent was reported among women attending antenatal clinics. The UN Programme on HIV/AIDS (UNAIDS) and the Ministry of Health and Social Welfare reported that 56 per cent of pregnant women aged 25 to 29 were HIV-positive. In March, 8,373 people were receiving antiretroviral therapy, 23 per cent of those estimated to need it, according to the World Health Organization and UNAIDS. The drug treatment was free, but shortages were reported at certain hospitals. Access to voluntary counselling and testing improved.

There were concerns that the proposal in the Sexual Offences and Domestic Violence Bill, to provide a mandatory death penalty for "intentionally" transmitting HIV through "unprotected sex with another person", would increase the stigma associated with HIV/AIDS and discourage people from learning their status.

Children's rights
School students were subjected to whippings and forced labour as a form of collective punishment.

▭ In a two-week period, 59 per cent of 2,750 Swazi children surveyed said they were beaten at school, including with sticks, canes and sjamboks (whips), a report by the international aid organization, Save the Children, revealed in May.

▭ In February, 16-year-old Sandile Melusi Mthethwa was sentenced to "six strokes" by the High Court for culpable homicide.

Torture and misuse of lethal force

▭ In January the Prime Minister released the Coroner's report into the death in custody of Madlenkhosi Ngubeni on 22 May 2004. The Coroner concluded that he had been tortured, possibly by suffocation methods, by the police, who had also negligently failed to obtain urgent medical care. The Coroner also recommended that police officers who had tortured him and other detainees be investigated for possible prosecution, and that measures were taken to improve police professionalism. In November, in response to a civil claim for damages instituted by Madlenkhosi Ngubeni's family, the government denied in court papers any responsibility for his death.

There were further reports of torture, beatings and the misuse of lethal force by the police against crime suspects and political activists, and by game rangers, who have immunity from prosecution under the Game Amendment Act, against members of rural communities accused of illegal hunting.

▭ Zwelithini Mamba and Andreas Tsabedze, charged with contravening the Game Amendment Act, alleged in the Mbabane Magistrate's court that they had been severely caned and beaten by game rangers when they were arrested in Mlilwane Game Park in July.

▭ Steven Thwala, arrested on 17 August and convicted a week later of assaulting a police officer, alleged in court that he had been handcuffed and subjected to suffocation torture. He instituted a civil action against the police for the assault.

▭ Police investigating petrol bombings of three police officers' homes arrested supporters of banned organizations. Mabandla Gama, a member of the Swaziland Youth Congress (SWAYOCO), was questioned at Mbabane police station on the evening of 2 November. After returning home later that night, he was reportedly taken again from his Nkwalini home by six plain-clothes officers, and beaten and interrogated for several hours before being left at a bus station. He required treatment in hospital for his injuries.

▭ On 24 May, Charles Mabuza was shot dead by police who had come to his home to arrest his brother, Mfanzile Mabuza, for illegal possession of a pistol. Mfanzile Mabuza and a police officer, Sergeant Mfanasibili Dlamini, died in an exchange of gunfire. Initially the police said Charles Mabuza had been shot dead by his brother, and arranged a hasty official post-mortem without the presence of a family representative. After intervention by the family's lawyer, a second post-mortem was conducted by an independent forensic pathologist. The physical and ballistic evidence confirmed that Charles Mabuza died from injuries caused by high velocity gunshot consistent with that used in a police-issue R4/R5 assault rifle. No criminal or disciplinary steps against any police officer had been taken by the end of 2005.

▭ In December the Siteki Magistrate's Court ordered the police to take detainee Mdudusi Mamba to hospital for examination and treatment after he complained in court that he had been subjected to suffocation torture and beaten while suspended. He was charged with treason and attempted murder in connection with petrol bombings of government infrastructure, and remanded in custody.

Freedom of assembly attacked

▭ In August, Roland Rudd and Lynn Dingani Mazibuko, members of the Swaziland Agricultural and Plantation Workers Union, were acquitted of charges under the Arms and Ammunition Act in connection with a trade union demonstration in August 2003. Another accused, Alex Langwenya (see below), had been acquitted in December 2004.

Police used excessive force against unarmed demonstrators in a number of incidents.

▭ On 8 September police fired tear gas without sufficient warning at university students, injuring at least 10, including Khumbuzile Nkambule, who was hit in the face by a tear gas canister. The students had gathered outside the government's Cabinet Offices to protest at drastic reductions in the number of student scholarships. Khumbuzile Nkambule and others required hospital treatment. On 12 September the Deputy Commissioner of Police announced an inquiry by the police Complaints and Discipline Unit. No results were announced by the end of 2005. The student complainants expressed concern that no inquiry had been conducted by an independent body.

Demonstrations by opposition organizations were broken up by police on the grounds that they remained prohibited under the 1973 Proclamation.

▭ On 1 October tear gas and rubber bullets were used to disperse a SWAYOCO rally in the Manzini area. Police arrested seven SWAYOCO officials and members, including its president Alex Langwenya, who was beaten with batons. On 3 October, Alex Langwenya and six others were charged with malicious damage to property. After several court appearances, they were released on bail and the case was remanded but no trial date was set.

Death penalty

No new death sentences were imposed. Three prisoners remained under sentence of death awaiting the outcome of clemency appeals.

The new Constitution retained the death penalty but stated that the punishment could not be mandatory. However, the Sexual Offences and Domestic Violence Bill proposed 14 new offences carrying a mandatory death penalty.

AI country reports/ visits
Visit

In February, AI delegates met the Prime Minister and other government officials visiting the UK to discuss a range of concerns.

SWEDEN

KINGDOM OF SWEDEN
Head of state: King Carl XVI Gustaf
Head of government: Göran Persson
Death penalty: abolitionist for all crimes
International Criminal Court: ratified
UN Women's Convention and its Optional Protocol: ratified

Decisions by the Swedish authorities to deport foreign nationals were criticized by international human rights bodies. Asylum-determination procedures continued to fall below international standards.

International scrutiny

In May the UN Committee against Torture concluded that the Swedish authorities' decision to deport a Bangladeshi woman and her daughter to Bangladesh would amount to a breach of Sweden's obligation not to forcibly return a person to another state where they would be at risk of torture. The woman and her then four-year-old daughter had applied for asylum in Sweden in 2000. The Committee noted that the Swedish authorities had not contested the fact that she had been persecuted, detained and tortured, including by being raped. However, the Swedish immigration authorities considered that she had been raped by individual police officers, and had thus concluded that the culprits' actions were not sufficient to establish the responsibility of the Bangladeshi authorities.

In November, the European Court of Human Rights held unanimously that the deportation of four members of a Syrian family to Syria would amount to a violation of their right to life and of the prohibition of inhuman or degrading treatment. The case concerned a Syrian national and his family who had been refused asylum in Sweden on several occasions. In 2003 the principal applicant had been convicted in absentia by a Syrian court of complicity in a murder, and sentenced to death. Citing AI and other sources the European Court of Human Rights stressed that the death penalty was enforced for serious crimes in Syria. In spite of this, the Swedish authorities had considered that, upon his return to Syria, his case would be reopened and a retrial granted and had thus concluded that the family were not in need of protection.

'War on terror' deportations

In May the UN Committee against Torture concluded that the Swedish government's expulsion of Ahmed Hussein Mustafa Kamil Agiza from Sweden to Egypt in 2001 breached the prohibition of *refoulement*. The Committee considered that the Swedish government knew, or should have known, at the time of the complainant's removal that the Egyptian authorities resorted to consistent and widespread use of torture against detainees and that the risk of such treatment was particularly high in the case of detainees held for political and security reasons.

The Committee noted that the diplomatic assurances procured by the Swedish government provided no mechanism for their enforcement, and concluded that they did not suffice to protect against the manifest risk of torture. The Committee recalled that the prohibition of *refoulement* was absolute, even in the context of counter-terrorism measures. The Committee further stated that the Swedish government had also breached its obligations under the Convention by neither disclosing to the Committee relevant information nor presenting its concerns to the Committee for an appropriate procedural decision.

The parliamentary Constitutional Committee concluded in September that the Swedish government should not have accepted the Egyptian authorities' diplomatic assurances, and that therefore it should not have expelled Muhammad Muhammad Suleiman Ibrahim El-Zari and Ahmed Hussein Mustafa Kamil Agiza to Egypt in December 2001. Hanan Attia, Ahmed Hussein Mustafa Kamil Agiza's wife, and her five children were granted refugee status according to the UN Convention relating to the Status of Refugees.

Refugees and asylum-seekers

The Swedish authorities continued to consider a broad range of asylum applications to be "manifestly unfounded", including those from Romani applicants. The accelerated asylum-determination procedures fell far short of international standards for refugee protection. The asylum applicants were not given a full asylum interview and were, among other things, denied access to legal aid. In addition, those whose claims had been rejected could be forcibly returned to their home countries or a third country pending appeal against an initial rejection of their claim.

Violence against women

In March, the government decided to establish a commission to investigate why certain municipalities had action plans for addressing violence against women while others did not. The commission was also to consider ways in which to make the municipalities assume responsibility for supporting women who had been subjected to violence, including women with special needs. The results of the commission's work were to be announced in June 2006.

Prison conditions

Overcrowding in remand detention continued to be of concern despite several measures taken by the Swedish authorities to improve the situation. Reports of detainees having to share cells intended for single occupancy continued. The number of complaints received by the Justice Ombudsman regarding the treatment of detainees was higher than in recent years.

AI country reports/visits
Report
- Sweden: Refugee rights undermined in "War on Terror" (AI Index: EUR 42/001/2005)

SWITZERLAND

SWISS CONFEDERATION
Head of state and government: Samuel Schmid
Death penalty: abolitionist for all crimes
International Criminal Court: ratified
UN Women's Convention: ratified with reservations
Optional Protocol to UN Women's Convention: not signed

Allegations of ill-treatment, use of excessive force and racist abuse by police officers continued. A federal amendment to the asylum law was proposed which would violate the UN Refugee Convention by limiting asylum-seekers' access to an effective asylum and appeals procedures. Although important steps were taken by the legislature and police in several cantons, domestic violence against women remained a significant problem.

Police racism, ill-treatment and use of excessive force

The UN Committee against Torture (CAT) and the Council of Europe's Commissioner for Human Rights published their recommendations on Switzerland in May and June respectively. Both recommended the creation of an independent regional (cantonal) appeal commission that could examine complaints against police forces. CAT also recommended that victims and their families should be informed of their right to pursue compensation and that procedures should be made more transparent. In this regard CAT requested information about what steps Switzerland had taken to compensate the families of two people who had died during forcible deportation. The Commissioner proposed that an observer should be present during deportations of foreign nationals and insisted that private security agencies should not be permitted to manage deportations.

Following protests by a large number of international and national institutions and organizations, the government prohibited the use of electro-shock weapons, including tasers, during forced deportations of foreign citizens.

Some cantons took significant steps to prevent human rights violations and introduced high human rights standards in policing.

Asylum

In December, parliament proposed an amendment to the federal asylum law, limiting access to an effective asylum and appeal procedure for people who did not have identity documents. It also proposed limiting access to social welfare for rejected asylum-seekers, even if they could not leave Switzerland immediately. This amendment, if approved, risked exacerbating the criminalization and inhuman treatment of asylum-seekers whose applications for asylum have been rejected. Asylum-seekers have consistently complained about abuse and inhuman treatment by cantonal migration offices and cantonal police corps. In the canton of Solothurn, for example, asylum-seekers whose applications were rejected were unable to access social welfare services until the Federal court ruled that this practice was unconstitutional.

Violence against women

Domestic violence remained prevalent throughout Switzerland, despite the fact that the Swiss Penal Code allows for the prosecution of crimes of domestic violence, including rape, without an official complaint from the victim. Other aspects of domestic legislation regarding violence in the home varied between cantons.

A new federal law concerning foreign nationals gave rise to concerns as it failed to protect victims of domestic violence who were classified as non-nationals. They had a right to stay in Switzerland independently of continued marriage or cohabitation only if certain conditions were fulfilled, such as if they had been resident in Switzerland for at least three years and had important personal reasons to remain in the country. There were also concerns about the impact of this law on non-nationals who were victims or witnesses in cases of human trafficking, as the law did not give these individuals the right to stay in Switzerland. Cantons were, however, free to give them permission to stay on humanitarian grounds.

SYRIA

SYRIAN ARAB REPUBLIC
Head of state: Bashar al-Assad
Head of government: Muhammad Naji 'Otri
Death penalty: retentionist
International Criminal Court: signed
UN Women's Convention: ratified with reservations
Optional Protocol to UN Women's Convention: not signed

Freedom of expression and association remained severely restricted. Scores of people were arrested and hundreds remained imprisoned for political reasons, including prisoners of conscience and others sentenced after unfair trials. However, about 500 political prisoners were released under two amnesties. Torture and ill-treatment were common. Human rights defenders continued to face harassment. Women and members of the Kurdish minority continued to face discrimination.

Background

Syria became increasingly isolated after the assassination of former Lebanese Prime Minister Rafiq al-Hariri in Beirut on 14 February. In May the UN confirmed that Syria had withdrawn its forces from Lebanon. The state of emergency imposed in 1962 remained in force. The Association Agreement between Syria and the European Union, which was initialled in October 2004 and contains a human rights clause, remained frozen at the final approval stage.

Releases of political prisoners

Up to 312 political prisoners, including prisoners of conscience, were ordered to be released on 30 March under a presidential amnesty. Most were Kurds who had been detained following violent disturbances in north-eastern Syria in March 2004.

Some 190 political prisoners, including prisoners of conscience, were released under a presidential amnesty on 2 November. They included: 'Abd al-'Aziz al-Khayyir, arrested in February 1992 and sentenced after an unfair trial before the Supreme State Security Court (SSSC) in August 1995 to 22 years' imprisonment for membership of the Party for Communist Action; Haythem al-Hamwi, Muhammed Shehada, Yahya Shurbajee and Mu'atez Murad, community activists from Darya arrested in May 2003 and sentenced to between three and four years' imprisonment after unfair trials before Field Military Courts; and Mus'ab al-Hariri, who was arrested on 24 July 2002, aged 14 or 15, shortly after he and his mother returned to Syria after living in exile in Saudi Arabia. Mus'ab al-Hariri had been sentenced by the SSSC on 19 June 2005 to six years' imprisonment for alleged membership of the Muslim Brotherhood.

Imprisonment for political reasons

Scores of people were arrested during the year for political reasons, including tens of prisoners of conscience. At least several hundred people, including prisoners of conscience, remained imprisoned for political reasons. Scores were brought to trial before the SSSC and Military Courts, all of which suffer from a gross lack of independence and impartiality. Many of those facing trial were suspected members or affiliates of banned political parties such as the Kurdish Democratic Union Party, the Muslim Brotherhood, Hizb al-Tahrir, and the pro-Iraqi Arab Socialist Democratic Ba'th Party.

Prisoners of conscience included:

☐ Six men, who were arrested in 2001 and sentenced to up to 10 years' imprisonment after unfair trials in 2002 for their involvement in the "Damascus Spring" pro-reform movement, remained in prison.

☐ Former "Damascus Spring" detainee Kamal al-Labwani, who was released in September 2004 after three years' imprisonment, was rearrested on 8 November upon arrival in Damascus after several months in Europe and the USA. Charges against him, which related to his peaceful activities promoting democracy and human rights, included "weakening national morale", "inciting strife" and "belonging to a secret organization".

☐ 'Ali al-'Abdullah was arrested on 15 May, a week after he read a statement on behalf of the exiled Muslim Brotherhood leader at the unauthorized Jamal al-Atassi Forum. The Forum was then closed down by the authorities. He was charged with "promoting an illegal organization". He was released under the presidential amnesty on 2 November.

☐ Riad Drar was arrested on 4 June after he made a speech at the funeral of Islamic scholar Sheikh Muhammad Ma'shuq al-Khiznawi. He faced charges before the SSSC of "inciting sectarian strife", a charge commonly used against people promoting the rights of Syrian Kurds. He remained held in solitary confinement.

'War on terror' detentions and torture

Scores of Syrians remained in detention and were being tried before the SSSC for alleged membership of a Salafi Islamist organization and for alleged plans to carry out acts of terrorism, including in Iraq. The detainees included 16 men from al-'Otaybe, who were arrested in April 2004, and 24 men from Qatana, aged between 17 and 25, who were arrested in July 2004. They were reportedly tortured and ill-treated during long periods of incommunicado detention. There were widespread concerns that the arrests and trials were attempts by the authorities to portray the country as under threat from terrorism.

According to unconfirmed media reports emanating from government sources, in 2005 the Syrian authorities arrested up to 1,500 people allegedly seeking to fight alongside anti-US forces in Iraq. Many were reportedly returned to their country of origin. Saudi Arabian media and human rights activists stated from July that Saudi nationals had been detained and tortured in Syria, from October 2003, before being returned to Saudi Arabia.

☐ Pregnant sisters Heba al-Khaled, 17, and Rola al-Khaled, 20, and Nadia al-Satour and her baby, were arrested on 3 September and held hostage by the authorities to put pressure on their husbands, alleged Islamist militants, to give themselves up. They were first detained in the town of Hama, then transferred to the Palestine Branch of Military Intelligence in Damascus where they remained at the end of the year.

☐ Muhammad Haydar Zammar, a German national of Syrian origin, remained detained incommunicado, at an unknown location and without charge, for a fourth year, apparently on account of alleged links to al-Qa'ida. The US security forces were reportedly involved in his arrest and interrogation in Morocco in 2001, and in his secret transfer to Syria one or two weeks later. He was reportedly interrogated in Syria in November 2002 by agents of German intelligence and criminal investigation agencies.

In August and October, information was released during an inquiry in Canada on the actions of Canadian officials in relation to Syrian/Canadian national Maher Arar. It indicated that, like him, at least three other Canadian nationals of Arab origin had been detained, interrogated and tortured in Syria in previous years with the possible complicity or involvement of Canadian and other foreign intelligence agencies. All three claimed they were forced to sign statements without being permitted to read them. They were:

☐ Ahmed Abou El-Maati was detained for 11 weeks after he arrived in Syria on 12 November 2001. He alleged that during this time he was beaten with electric cables, burned with cigarettes and had ice-cold water poured over him. He was then transferred to Egypt where he suffered further torture.

☐ 'Abdullah Almalki said he was beaten on the soles of his feet, hung in a tyre and beaten, and suspended by his hands from a metal frame and beaten while detained at the Palestine Branch of Military Intelligence in Damascus for 22 months from May 2002.

☐ Muayyed Nureddin said he was beaten repeatedly on the soles of his feet with a cable and had cold water poured on him while detained in Syria from 11 December 2003 to 13 January 2004.

Human rights defenders under threat

Syrian human rights defenders became increasingly active, but faced arrest and harassment. Several unauthorized human rights organizations were operating. At least 10 human rights defenders were forbidden from travelling outside the country.

☐ Nizar Ristnawi, a founding member of the unauthorized Arab Organization for Human Rights-Syria (AOHR-S), was arrested on 18 April. He remained in detention on unknown charges at the end of the year.

☐ Muhammad Ra'dun, head of the AOHR-S, was arrested on 22 May in connection with statements he had made about human rights in Syria. He was charged with "spreading false news" and "involvement in an illegal organization of an international nature". He was released under a presidential amnesty on 2 November.

'Disappearances'

The government provided no information about thousands of Syrians, Lebanese and other nationals who "disappeared" in the custody of Syrian forces in previous years. These included some 17,000 people, mostly Islamists who "disappeared" after they were detained in the late 1970s and early 1980s, and hundreds of Lebanese and Palestinians who were detained in Syria or abducted from Lebanon by Syrian forces or Lebanese and Palestinian militias. In September, however, the government named one judge and two generals as its representatives on a joint Syrian-Lebanese committee intended to address the "disappearances" issue. Local human rights groups welcomed this but questioned the lack of independence and the limited powers of the committee.

Torture and ill-treatment

Torture and ill-treatment of political and criminal detainees continued to be widely reported, particularly during incommunicado, pre-trial detention. At least two deaths as a result of such treatment were reported.

☐ Ahmad 'Ali al-Masalma, a Muslim Brotherhood member, died at the end of March, two weeks after he was released from four weeks in detention. He was

arrested on his return from 26 years' exile in Saudi Arabia. He was allegedly tortured in detention and denied essential medication.

☐ Sheikh Muhammad Ma'shuq al-Khiznawi, an Islamic religious leader and outspoken figure within the Kurdish community, died on 30 May, 20 days after he "disappeared", apparently in the custody of Military Intelligence agents. His nose and teeth were broken and there was a wound on his forehead.

☐ Seraj Khalbous became seriously ill probably as a result of torture while detained incommunicado in September at al-Mezze and al-Fayha Political Security Branches in Damascus. He was beaten, stamped on, struck with large sticks, threatened with anal rape, subjected to extreme cold, sleep deprivation and humiliation, and witnessed others being tortured with electric shocks. He was released on 25 October.

Most allegations of torture were not investigated. However, in June it was reported that two senior officials at the Ma'dan Court building in Raqqa were each sentenced to two months in prison for torturing Amna al-'Allush in March 2002 to force her to "confess" to a murder. Despite this, Amna al-'Allush continued serving the 12-year prison sentence she received in April 2004.

Discrimination against Kurds

Syrian Kurds continued to suffer from identity-based discrimination, including restrictions on the use of the Kurdish language and culture. Tens of thousands of Syrian Kurds remained effectively stateless. As a result, they were denied full access to education, employment, health and other rights enjoyed by Syrian nationals, as well as the right to have a nationality and passport. In June, at its first meeting for 10 years, the ruling Ba'th Party Congress ordered a review of a 1962 census which could result in stateless Kurds obtaining Syrian citizenship.

Discrimination and violence against women

Women remained subject to discrimination under a range of laws including in the areas of marriage, divorce, the family, inheritance and nationality. They were also inadequately protected against domestic and other forms of violence. For example, men who commit rape can escape possible punishment if they marry the victim, and men who murder a female relative on grounds of her alleged "adultery" or "extra-marital sexual relations" can also escape punishment or be treated more leniently than other murderers.

The scale of violence against women remained poorly documented and few cases were publicized during the year.

☐ At her wedding party in al-Suweida in August, Huda Abu 'Assali, a Druze, was reportedly killed by her father and brother for having married a Kurdish man while away from home at university in Damascus. No prosecution was known to have been brought.

Death penalty

The death penalty remained in force for a wide range of crimes but the authorities disclosed little information about its use. It was not known how many people were sentenced to death or executed in 2005. However, the government informed the UN Human Rights Committee (HRC) that 27 executions were carried out during 2002 and 2003, although it was unclear whether this was the total or it excluded executions carried out after trials before the SSSC or military courts. In an interview published in August, former Defence Minister Mustafa Tlas claimed that he had authorized the hanging of 150 political opponents a week throughout the 1980s and that he had signed execution orders for thousands of detainees whose families were not notified.

UN Human Rights Committee
The HRC, commenting on Syria's third periodic report, criticized the government's failure to implement human rights reforms recommended by the HRC in 2001. It expressed concern about the continuing state of emergency; restrictions on freedom of expression and other basic rights; discrimination and violence against women; the targeting of human rights defenders; and Syria's use of the death penalty.

AI country reports/ visits
Report
- Syria: Kurds in the Syrian Arabic Republic one year after the March 2004 events (AI Index: MDE 24/002/2005)

Visits
AI and the Syrian authorities discussed the possibility of an AI visit to the country but no decision was reached. AI has not been permitted into Syria since 1997.

TAIWAN

TAIWAN
Head of state: Chen Shui-bian
Head of government: Frank Hsieh Chang-ting
Death penalty: retentionist

The government was reported to be drafting legal amendments to remove mandatory death penalty provisions from the Criminal Code. However, the death penalty remained as a discretionary punishment for murder, kidnapping leading to murder and other serious crimes. Three men were executed during the year and 17 sentenced to death. Migrant workers were reportedly subjected to violence while protesting against denial of their basic human rights.

Death penalty
Seventeen people were sentenced to death and three men were executed during 2005.

◻ Wang Chung-hsing was executed in January. He had been convicted of causing the deaths by drowning of six Chinese women in the Taiwan Straits. The execution order was signed by then Minister of Justice Chen Ding-nan, who in 2000 had promised to take steps towards total abolition of the death penalty.
◻ Two brothers, Lin Meng-kai and Lin Hsin-hung, were executed in December following convictions for murder.
◻ The 11th retrial of three men known as the "Hsichih Trio" was pending at the end of 2005, as the procurator appealed to the Supreme Court against their acquittal.
◻ In November a district court began hearing the sixth retrial of Hsu Tzu-Chiang, who had been convicted of kidnapping and murder and sentenced to death by the Supreme Court in April 2000.

Migrant workers
Large numbers of migrant workers continued to live in inhuman conditions in dormitories, with limited freedom of movement. Several protests were reported of migrant workers complaining about poor living conditions, lack of freedom of movement outside dormitories and payment below the official minimum wage.
◻ In August, about 300 Thai nationals who had been hired by a company involved in the construction of Kaohsiung mass transit railway protested against their pay and working conditions. In the course of their protests they reportedly set fire to company property.
◻ In August, at least four Filipino migrant labourers working at a chemical factory in Mailiao Yunlin County who were involved in a strike over deductions from salaries and other grievances were severely beaten by company security guards near Hsinchu. They were reportedly taken to the airport for deportation, and at least one was carried onto the plane semi-conscious and in need of medical attention. The four were accompanied by two more Filipino colleagues who were allegedly beaten by company security guards before their forcible deportation.

Legislation
Significant laws addressing human rights were passed in January, including the Aboriginal Basic Law and the Sexual Harassment Prevention Act. A law addressing freedom of expression — The Organic Law of the National Communications Commission — was passed in October.

TAJIKISTAN

REPUBLIC OF TAJIKISTAN
Head of state: Imomali Rakhmonov
Head of government: Akil Akilov
Death penalty: retentionist
International Criminal Court: ratified
UN Women's Convention: ratified
Optional Protocol to UN Women's Convention: signed

Torture and ill-treatment by law enforcement officers were reported. The location of the burial sites of prisoners sentenced to death and executed in previous years remained secret, subjecting relatives to cruel and inhuman treatment. Independent journalists faced increasing intimidation, including criminal prosecutions, by the authorities. Five Afghan refugees were forcibly returned to Afghanistan.

Background

The ruling People's Democratic Party won a large majority in parliamentary elections in February. The leaders of two opposition parties were banned from standing on the grounds that criminal cases had been opened against them, even though no trial had taken place. The Organization for Security and Co-operation in Europe (OSCE) observed the elections and concluded that they "failed to meet many of the key OSCE commitments for democratic elections".

In September, during his visit to Tajikistan, the UN Special Rapporteur on the independence of judges and lawyers raised concern about the lack of independence of the judiciary.

Torture, ill-treatment and impunity

There were continuing reports of torture and ill-treatment by law enforcement officers. It appeared that in most cases no investigation was conducted and the perpetrators enjoyed impunity.

The UN Human Rights Committee (HRC), after considering Tajikistan's first report to the Committee, raised concern about the "widespread use of ill-treatment and torture by investigation and other officials to obtain information, testimony or self-incriminating evidence from suspects, witnesses or arrested persons". It also reported on "poor conditions and overcrowding" in places of detention and the "limited access" to penitentiary institutions by civil society and international bodies.

Death penalty

Relatives of people executed before the moratorium on death sentences and executions took effect in 2004 continued to have no right to know where their loved ones were buried. The HRC urged the authorities to "take urgent measures to inform families of the burial sites". It also issued rulings on the cases of three former death row prisoners. In all cases it found serious violations of the International Covenant on Civil and Political Rights and urged Tajikistan to provide appropriate compensation. In the case of Valijon Khalilov, for example, who was executed on 2 July 2001, the HRC ruled that the execution was "in violation of the right to a fair trial". It said Tajikistan was obliged to provide Valijon Khalilov's mother with an appropriate remedy, including to inform her of the location of her son's grave.

Refugees

Five Afghan refugees – a mother and her four children – were forcibly returned to Afghanistan in September, in violation of Tajikistan's obligations as a party to the 1951 Refugee Convention and other human rights treaties. In 2004 they had applied for resettlement; three were subsequently accepted by Canada. In early 2005 the Refugee Status Determination Commission of Tajikistan annulled the mother's refugee status; her appeal against the decision was still pending before Dushanbe city court when the five were detained and then deported.

Trafficking of human beings

Trafficking of human beings remained a grave concern. The HRC urged Tajikistan to "redouble its efforts" in tackling trafficking and "rigorously review the activities of responsible governmental agencies to ensure that no State actors are involved".

TANZANIA

UNITED REPUBLIC OF TANZANIA
Head of state: Jakaya Kikwete (replaced Benjamin Mkapa in December)
Head of government: Edward Lowassa (replaced Frederick Sumaye in December)
Head of Zanzibar government: Amani Abeid Karume
Death penalty: retentionist
International Criminal Court: ratified
UN Women's Convention: ratified
Optional Protocol to UN Women's Convention: not signed

There were reports of human rights abuses during elections in Zanzibar. Female genital mutilation continued. Up to 400 people were under sentence of death; there were no executions.

Background

Elections for the Union (national) President and parliament scheduled for October were postponed until December. Jakaya Kikwete, candidate of the ruling Party of the Revolution (Chama Cha Mapinduzi, CCM), was sworn in as President after defeating the Civic United Front (CUF) and other opposition candidates. The CCM won 206 of the 232 parliamentary seats.

Zanzibar elections
Elections in semi-autonomous Zanzibar for the Zanzibar President, parliament and local councils were held in October. Amani Abeid Karume, the CCM candidate, was re-elected as President, defeating the CUF candidate. The CCM won 30 seats in the parliament, as against 19 for the CUF.

The CUF alleged that numerous human rights abuses, including beatings and arbitrary arrests of their supporters, were carried out by security forces and pro-CCM youth militias (known as "Janjaweed") during the voter registration process in early 2005.

Later there were violent clashes between CCM and CUF supporters in the weeks before the October elections, with scores of people injured. Police shot and wounded eight opposition supporters at a reportedly peaceful rally which took place on 9 October despite a ban.

For three days after the poll, CUF supporters alleging election fraud – some throwing stones and burning tyres, others protesting peacefully – confronted the security forces, who used tear gas and water-cannon to disperse protesters. Dozens of people were arrested, and two protesters reportedly died. Some detainees were charged with criminal offences but none had been tried by the end of the year.

There were allegations of widespread beatings and looting by the security forces targeting CUF supporters on Pemba island, including a reported shooting.

In November, several CUF leaders were briefly detained.

Violence against women
Female genital mutilation continued to be practised in many mainland areas, although the practice is illegal for girls under 18 years. There were no prosecutions reported.

Human rights defenders
Christopher Kidanka, an official of the Legal and Human Rights Centre, and Mpoki Bukuku, a photographer of the Citizen newspaper, were among dozens of people severely beaten by prison officers in Dar es Salaam on 10 September. The two men were investigating the forcible eviction of illegal tenants on Ukonga Prison property. Several prison officers involved were subsequently charged with assault.

Death penalty
Several death sentences were imposed by courts. There were no executions. Up to 400 people were under sentence of death at the end of the year.

THAILAND

KINGDOM OF THAILAND
Head of state: King Bhumibol Adulyadej
Head of government: Thaksin Shinawatra
Death penalty: retentionist
International Criminal Court: signed
UN Women's Convention and its Optional Protocol: ratified

Violence continued in the Muslim-majority southern provinces. Unidentified Muslim armed groups bombed, beheaded or shot Muslim and Buddhist civilians and members of the security forces. The authorities arbitrarily detained people and failed to investigate human rights abuses. Human rights defenders in the south were subjected to surveillance, harassment and anonymous death threats. Those in other regions also faced abuses. Torture and ill-treatment continued to be reported. Some 1,000 people remained under sentence of death. No executions were known to have taken place. Migrant workers continued to be denied basic labour rights.

Background
In February Prime Minister Thaksin Shinawatra's party, Thai Rak Thai, won a majority of parliamentary seats and formed a one-party government.

The violence in the south continued; more than 1,100 people died between January 2004 and the end of 2005. In July a new Emergency Decree empowered the Prime Minister to declare a state of emergency. Also in July the UN Human Rights Committee expressed concern about the new Emergency Decree; about persistent allegations of extrajudicial killings and ill-treatment by the police and army, particularly in the south during 2004; and about reports of the widespread use of torture and ill-treatment of detainees by law enforcement officials.

Legal developments
The Prime Minister used the new Emergency Decree, enacted by the Cabinet on 15 July, one day after a major attack by insurgents on Yala town, to declare a state of emergency in Yala, Narathiwat and Pattani provinces. It replaced the 1914 Martial Law Act previously in force there and was renewed in October for a further three months. The Emergency Decree's provisions include: detention without charge or trial for up to 30 days; the use of unofficial detention centres; press censorship; and legal immunity from prosecution for law enforcement officers.

Violence in the south
Violence in Songkla, Pattani, Yala, and Narathiwat provinces in the far south continued, characterized by bombings, beheadings and "drive-by" shootings of Muslim and Buddhist civilians and members of the security forces. The armed groups responsible did not

identify themselves and did not publicly state their demands, nor did they indicate any willingness to negotiate with the government. However, from August onwards, anonymous leaflets were found threatening anyone who opened their businesses on Fridays. Anonymous notes were also found at the scene of several attacks by armed groups which stated that the killings were in revenge for the security forces' arresting and killing "innocent people". The victims of the violence included members of the security forces and militias, civilian government officials, Buddhist and Muslim civilians, and members of Muslim armed groups.

The authorities' response to the violence was marked by arbitrary detentions and lack of investigations into human rights abuses. In February the government established the National Reconciliation Commission (NRC), chaired by former Prime Minister Anand Panyarachun, to help resolve the violence. In April the NRC made public two reports by government-appointed commissions investigating the security forces' violent suppression of a demonstration in Tak Bai in October 2004 and the military siege of Krue Se Mosque in April 2004. In October the NRC said that the government verged on "administrative bankruptcy" in the south because of its inability to protect people.

Human rights violations
⮂ Several Muslim political detainees were held continuously in heavy shackles in Yala Prison. An unknown number of detainees were held at the Yala Police Training Centre under the provisions of the Emergency Decree; they were not permitted full access to legal counsel or to their families.

⮂ Reports emerged in August in Narathiwat Province that the authorities had established a blacklist of people thought to be members of or sympathetic to armed opposition groups. Scores of young Muslim men were coerced into reporting to the provincial government to clear their names; some were required to attend a residential camp in what amounted to arbitrary detention. None were known to have been charged with any offence.

The government failed to conduct proper investigations into political killings and abductions and it remained unclear who was responsible for the violence.

⮂ In June Riduan Waemano, a Muslim student, and two of his friends were shot dead while praying in a house in Pattani Province. No forensic investigation was known to have been carried out and no one was brought to justice.

Abuses by armed opposition groups
Armed opposition groups killed Buddhist villagers, Muslim members of government-sponsored volunteer militias, Buddhist monks and civilian local government employees. Between January 2004 and September 2005, 60 teachers, principals, and employees of the school system were shot dead by unidentified armed groups.

⮂ In April Ma Rike Samae and his uncle Mat Samae, both Muslim volunteer militia members, were shot dead while they patrolled their village in Narathiwat province at night.

⮂ In October armed insurgents attacked a Buddhist temple in Pattani Province, beheading a Buddhist monk and killing two boys.

Impunity
Almost 200 people were killed or died from ill-treatment during the violent suppression of attacks by armed groups in April 2004 and a demonstration in Tak Bai in October 2004. No members of the security forces responsible were brought to justice.

The trial of five police officers accused of an assault on and theft from Muslim lawyer and human rights defender Somchai Neelapaijit in 2004 continued throughout 2005; his whereabouts remained unknown.

Human rights defenders
In the south, human rights defenders, including students, lawyers and academics, were subjected to surveillance, harassment, and anonymous death threats. Those in other regions also faced abuses.
⮂ In June Phra Supoj Suvacano, a Buddhist monk at a forest temple in Fang District, Chiang Mai Province, was hacked to death. He had been working to protect an area belonging to a Buddhist foundation from influential local land developers attempting to encroach on the land. The Ministry of Justice Department of Special Investigations conducted an investigation but no one was brought to justice for his murder.

Refugees and migrant workers
Refugees from Myanmar continued to arrive in Thailand, fleeing forced labour, relocation, extortion, and arrest. Almost 143,000 Karen and Karenni refugees remained in camps along the Thai-Myanmar border; refugees from the Shan ethnic minority continued to be denied access to refugee camps. More than 2,400 refugees were resettled to third countries during 2005.

A total of 705,293 migrant workers, 539,416 of them from Myanmar, registered for work permits while an unknown number of migrants remained in the country illegally. In July and August migrants from Myanmar, Laos and Cambodia were registered, entitling them to the same labour rights as Thai workers, including a legal minimum wage and safe working conditions. In practice, working and living conditions for migrant workers, most of whom did not receive the legal minimum wage, were poor. Migrant workers in garment factories in Tak Province received little more than half the legal minimum wage.

⮂ In September, more than 200 legally registered migrant workers from Myanmar were arrested and deported to Myanmar after protesting to the Ministry of Labour about long working hours and payment below the legal minimum wage in a fishing net factory in Khon Kaen Province.

Death penalty
Some 1,000 people remained under sentence of death, many of them held continuously in heavy metal shackles. The government told the UN Human Rights Committee that shackling was necessary because there

was not enough space to hold all the death row prisoners in solitary confinement.

AI country reports/ visits
Report
- Thailand: The plight of Burmese migrant workers (AI Index: ASA 39/001/2005)

Visit
AI delegates visited Thailand in September/October to investigate the violence in the south.

TIMOR-LESTE

DEMOCRATIC REPUBLIC OF TIMOR-LESTE
Head of state: Jose Alexandre "Xanana" Gusmão
Head of government: Di Marí Dim Amude Alkatiri
Death penalty: abolitionist for all crimes
International Criminal Court: acceded
UN Women's Convention and its Optional Protocol: ratified

Despite efforts to strengthen human rights and the rule of law, the administration of justice was weak and there were allegations of police abuses, including arbitrary detention and ill-treatment. Impunity for perpetrators of serious human rights violations in 1999 continued despite the completion of the UN-sponsored serious crimes process in May.

Background
In March parliament appointed Sebastião Dias Ximenes as Provedor for Human Rights and Justice (Ombudsman). His mandate was to combat corruption, prevent maladministration, and protect and promote human rights by making recommendations to relevant institutions, including the government. In July he expressed concern about his insufficient budget.

The UN Mission in Support of East Timor (UNMISET) was replaced in May by the UN Office in Timor-Leste (UNOTIL), which was mandated to support the development of critical state institutions until May 2006.

Justice system weaknesses
A severe shortage of national judges, prosecutors and defence lawyers in district courts limited the judiciary's ability to function and ensure the right to a fair trial within a reasonable time. This inadequacy discouraged access by the population to the formal justice system, and perpetuated reliance on traditional justice mechanisms that do not guarantee fair trial standards.

Freedom of expression and association
Concerns were expressed throughout the year by local and international organizations about provisions on "defamation" in the draft criminal code that would restrict freedom of expression.

In May, the Court of Appeal found that some provisions in the Law on Freedom of Assembly and Demonstrations were unconstitutional as they did not respect the principle of proportionality. The law, which was revised by parliament in July after eliminating the articles declared unconstitutional, was awaiting promulgation.

Police violations
Despite progress by the National Police of Timor-Leste in dealing with demonstrations without excessive use of force, reports of arbitrary detention and ill-treatment continued to occur.

Past human rights violations
The UN-sponsored serious crimes process, which was mandated to investigate and try those responsible for serious crimes committed in Timor-Leste (then East Timor) during 1999, terminated in May, although the job had not been completed. The UN Special Panels convicted a total of 84 people of serious crimes, including crimes against humanity, and acquitted three. Over 300 people indicted for serious crimes were not tried because they could not be brought within the jurisdiction of the Special Panels before the mandate ended. By the end of the year, there were serious concerns that indictees living in West Timor, Indonesia, were returning to Timor-Leste, and that there were no clear arrangements within the under-resourced judiciary to replace the Special Panels.

🗁 In August, Manuel Maia, who was indicted for crimes against humanity committed in Bobonara District in March and April 1999, entered Timor-Leste from West Timor. He was immediately detained by members of the community and handed over to the national police. He remained in detention pending trial for serious crimes at the end of the year.

In June, the report of a UN-sponsored Commission of Experts (CoE) mandated to review the prosecution of serious violations of human rights committed in 1999 in Timor-Leste was submitted to the UN Security Council. It concluded that accountability of those who bore the "greatest responsibility" for the violations had not been achieved, and recommended the continuation of the serious crimes process.

The CoE report expressed concerns about the terms of reference of the Truth and Friendship Commission, a truth-seeking mechanism officially established in March by Indonesia and Timor-Leste to review the 1999 crimes. The report was concerned that certain provisions may not comply with international standards on denial of impunity (see Indonesia entry), and recommended "clarification, re-assessment and revision" of those provisions. Despite these criticisms, the Truth and Friendship Commission was set up in August. The provisions relating to impunity remained in the Commission's mandate. The Security Council had not acted on the CoE's recommendations by the end of 2005.

In October, the Commission for Reception, Truth and Reconciliation in Timor-Leste handed in its final report to the Timor-Leste President. It contained a detailed account of human rights violations in Timor-Leste between 1974 and 1999. Its recommendations echoed those of the CoE report and called for the continuation of the UN-sponsored crime process and consideration of the setting up of an international tribunal under UN auspices if justice failed to be delivered.

AI country reports/ visits
Report
- Democratic Republic of Timor-Leste: Open letter to all members of the Security Council (AI Index: ASA 57/003/2005)

TOGO

REPUBLIC OF TOGO
Head of state: Faure Gnassingbé (replaced Gnassingbé Eyadéma in February and Abass Bonfoh in May)
Head of government: Edem Kodjo (replaced Koffi Sama in June)
Death penalty: abolitionist in practice
International Criminal Court: not signed
UN Women's Convention: ratified
Optional Protocol to UN Women's Convention: not signed

A UN fact-finding mission concluded that hundreds of people were extrajudicially executed and thousands wounded by the security forces and armed militia groups close to the ruling party before, during and after the presidential election which brought Faure Gnassingbé to power in April. Widespread arbitrary detentions, torture and violence against women were reported. Throughout the year critics of the government and human rights defenders faced harassment and intimidation.

Background
President Gnassingbé Eyadéma, who had ruled Togo for 37 years, died on 5 February. The Togolese Armed Forces (Forces armées togolaises, FAT) then proclaimed Faure Gnassingbé, his son, as President. The following day, the President of the National Assembly who, according to the Constitution, should have become interim President pending elections, was dismissed and replaced by Faure Gnassingbé. The Constitution was modified to allow the new head of state to serve the rest of his father's term, until 2008. This unconstitutional transfer of power was condemned by the main opposition parties and by the international community including the African Union (AU) and the European Union (EU). The AU and the Economic Community of the West African States

(ECOWAS) imposed sanctions and Togo was suspended from the International Francophone Organisation (Organisation Internationale de la Francophonie, OIF).

In the face of international pressure, Faure Gnassingbé stepped down and called presidential elections in April. He won the elections amid widespread violence and allegations by opposition parties of vote-rigging and law-breaking. The European Parliament considered that the elections were not free and fair.

Attacks on civilians by the FAT and militia groups during and after the presidential election led to the displacement and flight of tens of thousands of people. Humanitarian agencies reported that by August, more than 40,000 people had sought refuge in neighbouring Benin and Ghana. At the end of 2005, several thousand refugees were still in neighbouring countries.

In October, Togo ratified the Protocol to the African Charter on Human and Peoples' Rights on the Rights of Women in Africa.

Unlawful killings and 'disappearances'
Both government forces and armed militia groups close to the ruling party, the Rally of the Togolese People (Rassemblement du peuple togolais, RPT), unlawfully killed civilians between February and April. Some were killed in indiscriminate attacks, others were deliberately targeted and extrajudicially executed.

In the days following President Gnassingbé Eyadéma's death and during the presidential election, the security forces and members of the militias fired indiscriminately at opposition supporters on protest demonstrations. These attacks were particularly violent in Lomé and the towns of Atakapmé and Aného. Thousands of people were reportedly injured, with gunshot wounds to the upper parts of the body and head. Some people reportedly "disappeared" after their arrest by the FAT.

◻ On the day of the election, soldiers burst into several polling stations firing their weapons and tear gas grenades. According to an election observer from the opposition Union of Forces for Change (Union des Forces de Changement, UFC), assigned to the polling station at Be Plage, Lomé, two military vehicles containing members of the Presidential guard's commando regiment arrived, firing in the air as the votes were being counted. Many people panicked and tried to leave, but there was only one exit. The soldiers entered the room, fired tear gas grenades and live rounds and took the ballot boxes. The observer said he had to step over about 30 bodies to escape.

◻ On 26 April, the day on which the provisional election results were announced, soldiers and militiamen reportedly entered the home of an apprentice driver who lived in the Ablogamé district of Lomé, firing bullets. He said that they shot at people as they tried to flee, killing his mother and one of his friends.

◻ Kogbe Koffi, a 28-year-old sheet metal worker, was reportedly shot in the back in Atakpamé, on 26 April, when the security forces fired live ammunition at demonstrators protesting against the election results.

UN report
In September a fact-finding mission set up by the UN High Commissioner for Human Rights concluded that between 400 and 500 people were killed and thousands wounded at the time of the presidential election. The report found the state security forces and militia groups responsible for the political violence and the violations of human rights, and noted evidence that commando units within the FAT had been primed "not only to crush the demonstrators and militants but also to round up the corpses and systematically dispose of them so that they could not be counted." The report also criticized opposition groups for their part in serious violence.

Arbitrary arrests and detentions
Dozens of people were arrested during 2005, most apparently for their peaceful political opposition activities. Some were released within hours or days but others remained in detention without charge or trial for more than two months.

A woman shopkeeper named Dalas was arrested on 7 May in Aklakou, suspected of preparing food for people who demonstrated in Aného shortly after the presidential election. She remained in detention without charge or trial until 15 July.

In Aklakou, at least seven school students were arrested and accused of demonstrating after the presidential election. They were detained for more than two months without charge or trial at Vogan prison.

Torture
Dozens of people were tortured or ill-treated by the FAT and militia groups between February and April. Some people were beaten to death in front of their family.

At Bé Chateau in Lomé, in front of witnesses including foreign journalists, a motorcyclist trying to cross town was stopped by soldiers. A soldier hit him several times with a stick, made him pull down his trousers and kicked him in the testicles.

At Tokoin Séminaire, 15 soldiers entered the house of an opposition member and dragged him outside. They made him lie down, then held his arms and feet while others hit him with cudgels and thin cord. He was unconscious when they left.

In May the UN Committee against Torture postponed its consideration of the report of Togo, given the absence of a Togolese government delegation.

Violence against women
Gender-based violence, in particular rape of women, was reported, including cases from Atakpamé where FAT members and militia groups allegedly raped women suspected of supporting the opposition.

On 26 April, members of a militia group entered a house and beat the husband, the wife and three children. They then held the arms and feet of the woman while one of them raped her.

Attacks on freedom of expression
Repressive measures against the media, particularly those critical of government policies and the FAT, increased during 2005. Media workers were harassed and journalists were beaten for criticizing the government or trying to disseminate information about the repression that followed the death of President Gnassingbé Eyadéma.

A senior official intervened several times to prevent the radio station *Nana FM* broadcasting certain programmes, including a roundtable discussion which was suspended while on air three days after the President's death. In a meeting, in the presence of the FAT communications officer, the official reportedly threatened some private radio stations including *Nana FM, Kanal FM* and *Radio Nostalgia*.

The transmitters of *Radio France Internationale* (RFI) stopped broadcasting on FM for several months. The Minister of Communications publicly accused RFI of having launched "disinformation and destabilization campaigns".

Thierry Tchukriel, a radio journalist with *Rd'autan*, who went to Togo to cover the presidential election, was beaten by four soldiers on the night of 24 April, after being detained by the Togolese police. His press card and camera were confiscated.

Human rights defenders
Members of human rights organizations continued to face harassment, intimidation and to be at risk of attacks. Perpetrators were believed to be linked with the ruling party and to criminal gangs.

On 13 May, a group of young people associated with the ruling party prevented the Togolese Human Rights League (Ligue togolaise des droits de l'homme, LTDH) from holding a press conference. The LTDH had planned to publicize human rights violations since the death of President Eyadéma.

On 9 October, Dimas Dzikodo, an outspoken human rights defender and journalist, was assaulted by a group of unidentified men on his way back from work.

AI country reports/visits
Reports
- Togo: Radio Silence (AI Index: AFR 57/003/2005)
- Togo: AI memorandum on the human rights situation in Togo and recommendations to the African Union (AI Index: AFR 57/007/2005)
- Togo: A high risk transition (AI Index: AFR 57/008/2005)
- Togo: Will history repeat itself? (AI Index: AFR 57/012/2005)

Visit
AI delegates visited Benin in August to carry out research on human rights violations in Togo.

TRINIDAD AND TOBAGO

REPUBLIC OF TRINIDAD AND TOBAGO
Head of state: George Maxwell Richards
Head of government: Patrick Manning
Death penalty: retentionist
International Criminal Court: ratified
UN Women's Convention: ratified
Optional Protocol to UN Women's Convention: not signed

Death sentences continued to be imposed and officials threatened to resume executions. There were continuing reports of abuses by the police. Prison conditions remained poor and in some instances amounted to cruel, inhuman or degrading treatment.

Background

The Caribbean Court of Justice, a Trinidad and Tobago-based final court of appeal intended to replace the Judicial Committee of the Privy Council (JCPC), opened in April. By the end of 2005, Barbados and Guyana had altered their constitutions to enable the court to hear their cases.

More than 10,000 people took part in a protest in October against the high rate of violent crime. There were reportedly 382 murders in 2005, out of a population of 1.3 million.

Death penalty

Senior officials repeatedly expressed their intention to resume executions – the last executions in Trinidad and Tobago were in 1999. The mandatory death penalty continued to be the only sentence available for those convicted of murder.

Eighty-six people on death row whose sentences were commuted to terms of imprisonment by the JCPC in 2004 remained under sentence of death, as the government apparently ignored the ruling.

In June, a warrant was issued for the execution of Lester Pitman, even though he had an appeal pending. He was later granted a stay of execution pending the outcome of appeals. Lester Pitman was convicted of murder in 2004.

Abuses by police

Abuses by police, including unlawful killings, torture and ill-treatment, continued to be reported. At least 14 people were reportedly shot dead by police during 2005.

In January, 37-year-old Kevin Wallace was shot dead by police. Eyewitnesses said that he was shot in the back as he tried to run away, and that police kicked him as he lay bleeding, before taking him to hospital.

In August, 20-year-old Kendell Hamilton was shot dead by members of the Inter-Agency Task Force in Laventille. Police alleged that they fired in self-defence, but relatives claimed Kendell Hamilton was an innocent bystander. After community protests, police announced the death would be investigated.

Poor conditions of detention

Conditions in places of detention caused grave concern and in some cases amounted to cruel, inhuman and degrading treatment. Overcrowding in prisons, remand centres and court cell blocks was rife. Conditions were often unsanitary and medical care was inadequate. Death row prisoners alleged that they were denied necessary medicines.

Incidents of sexual assault in prison were allegedly frequent. Young offenders and people convicted of petty offences were reportedly held in crowded cells with prisoners convicted of serious offences.

Corporal punishment

Laws allowing corporal punishment for crimes including rape remained. Sentences of flogging continued to be passed, but were not apparently carried out.

Rawle Bekaroo was sentenced to 15 strokes of the birch and 20 years' imprisonment for kidnapping, rape and sexual assault by the First Criminal Court in Port of Spain in June.

TUNISIA

REPUBLIC OF TUNISIA
Head of state: Zine El 'Abidine Ben 'Ali
Head of government: Mohamed Ghannouchi
Death penalty: abolitionist in practice
International Criminal Court: not signed
UN Women's Convention: ratified with reservations
Optional Protocol to UN Women's Convention: not signed

Dozens of people were sentenced to lengthy prison terms following unfair trials on terrorism-related charges. Torture and ill-treatment continued to be reported. Hundreds of political prisoners, including prisoners of conscience, remained in prison. Many had been held for more than a decade. Solitary confinement and denial of medical care in prisons continued to be reported despite government promises to end long-term solitary confinement. Freedom of expression and association remained severely restricted.

Background

In July the ruling Democratic Constitutional Rally won 71 of the available 85 seats in the country's first ever indirect elections to the new 126-member upper house, the House of Councillors. The remaining 41 seats were appointed by President Ben 'Ali in August. The Tunisian Workers' General Union (Union Générale des Travailleurs Tunisiens) boycotted the elections.

In November, Tunisia hosted the World Summit on the Information Society, an intergovernmental and civil society meeting held under the auspices of the UN. The choice of Tunisia to host the meeting was criticized by national and international human rights organizations because of its wide-ranging restrictions on freedom of expression and association. In September, 11 governments and the European Union issued a joint statement raising concerns about restrictions on the participation of civil society groups at the Summit by the Tunisian authorities. Human rights defenders were intimidated and a French journalist was stabbed. AI delegates were prevented from meeting representatives of the National Council for Liberties in Tunisia (Conseil national pour les libertés en Tunisie, CNLT) at its Tunis office, by Tunisian security officers.

The Tunisia Action Plan, part of the European Neighbourhood Policy, came into force in July. It set out a series of actions and initiatives, and a regular review mechanism, on issues including human rights, migration and the fight against terrorism.

Violations in the 'war on terror'

Dozens of people were reportedly arrested and charged under anti-terrorism legislation passed in December 2003; at least 30 people were tried and sentenced. Detainees were often held incommunicado, sometimes for weeks, and there were allegations of torture to extract confessions or to force detainees to sign statements.

◻ At least 13 prisoners, known as the Bizerte group, were sentenced in April to prison terms of between five and 30 years, reduced to a maximum of 20 years on appeal in July. The accused were allegedly tortured and ill-treated during their detention in premises of the Ministry of the Interior. They had been arrested in April 2004 and charged under the anti-terrorism law of December 2003.

◻ In September, Tawfik Selmi, a Tunisian-Bosnian dual national, appeared before a military court in Tunis on charges of membership of a terrorist organization abroad. The court reportedly refused to allow the defence team access to the case file. The trial was due to recommence in February 2006. Tawfik Selmi had been expelled from Luxembourg in March 2003.

Update

◻ In March, Adil Rahali was sentenced under anti-terrorism legislation to 10 years' imprisonment, reduced to five years on appeal in October. A Tunisian national, he had been extradited from Ireland in April 2004 after his application for asylum was refused, and arrested upon arrival in Tunisia. He was secretly detained in the offices of the State Security Department of the Ministry of the Interior, where he was reportedly tortured.

Freedom of expression

Freedom of expression remained severely curtailed. In October, the UN Special Rapporteur on the promotion and protection of the right to freedom of opinion and expression publicly expressed concern at the lack of freedom of expression in Tunisia. In his statement he called on the Tunisian government to take action to increase freedom of expression and press freedom, and to release unconditionally all those imprisoned because of their beliefs or for their work as journalists.

The first congress of the Union of Tunisian Journalists (Syndicat des journalistes tunisiens, SJT), scheduled to be held in September, was banned without explanation after its president, Lotfi Hajji, had been repeatedly summoned for questioning by the State Security Department. The SJT was formed in 2004 in response to widespread censorship, to defend the rights of journalists and promote media freedom.

Human rights activists and organizations

Human rights defenders continued to face harassment and sometimes physical violence. Many human rights defenders, their families and friends were subjected to surveillance by the authorities, and their activities were severely restricted.

◻ In January, large numbers of police officers surrounded the CNLT headquarters, preventing members from attending the organization's general assembly. The police allegedly said they were under strict instructions not to allow the meeting to take place. On 3 and 4 September, the entrance to the building was again obstructed by plain-clothes police officers, who refused entry to members of the board. In addition, Sihem Ben Sedrine, the CNLT spokesperson, was subjected to a smear campaign in the state-controlled media, in which she was accused of "acting like a prostitute" and serving the interests of the US and Israeli governments.

◻ In March, lawyer and human rights defender Radhia Nasraoui was beaten up in the street by police officers. She was on her way to a demonstration to protest at the Tunisian government's invitation to Israeli Prime Minister Ariel Sharon to attend the World Summit on the Information Society. She sustained a broken nose, cuts to her forehead and extensive bruising. No action was known to have been taken against those responsible.

◻ As human rights organizations organized activities in the run-up to the World Summit on the Information Society, one group particularly targeted was the Tunisian Human Rights League (Ligue tunisienne pour la défense des droits de l'homme, LTDH). In September a court order effectively prevented the LTDH from carrying out preparatory activities two days before its national congress. The order was in response to a complaint by 22 people, reportedly close to the authorities, who said they had been unfairly dismissed as members from the LTDH.

Attacks on the independence of the judiciary

In a series of intimidatory measures, judges' activities and right to freedom of expression were further restricted.

In August, members were barred from the office of the Association of Tunisian Judges (Association des Magistrats Tunisiens, AMT), under orders from the Ministry of Justice and Human Rights. After calls for more independence for the judiciary, the AMT's telephone, fax and Internet access were increasingly disrupted, then effectively shut down. According to reports, judges were arbitrarily transferred to isolated areas, far from their families, in an attempt to intimidate and silence them.

Prisoners of conscience
People continued to be at risk of imprisonment, harassment and intimidation because of their non-violent beliefs.

Mohamed Abbou, a lawyer and human rights defender, was sentenced in April to three and a half years in prison, largely for publishing articles critical of the authorities on the Internet. Tunisian lawyers and civil society activists who protested at his trial were subjected to harassment and intimidation by the police on several occasions. His lawyers were reportedly denied permission to visit him in prison despite repeated attempts. His sentence was confirmed on appeal in June. At the end of 2005 he was imprisoned in El-Kef, 200 kilometres from his family home in Tunis, making visits difficult. The UN Working Group on Arbitrary Detention adopted the opinion in November that his detention was arbitrary.

Prison conditions
In April the authorities signed an agreement with the International Committee of the Red Cross (ICRC), which allowed it to visit prisons regularly to assess conditions of detention and the treatment of prisoners. The ICRC started visiting prisons in June.

Also in April the government said it would no longer hold prisoners in solitary confinement for more than 10 days. This commitment was given in a meeting with Human Rights Watch, which alleged that up to 40 political prisoners were held in solitary confinement or in small groups isolated from the general prisoner population. The government also said that Human Rights Watch would be allowed access to prisons when it next sent representatives to Tunisia.

However, throughout the year large numbers of political prisoners went on repeated hunger strikes to protest against the continuing denial of medical care and harsh prison conditions.

Torture and death in custody
In June, Houcine Louhichi, a taxi driver from Tabarka in the north-west province of Jendouba, died shortly after his transfer to Rabta Hospital in Tunis. A few days earlier, he had been released by the State Security Department in Tabarka, where he was detained incommunicado for almost two days and allegedly tortured until he lost consciousness. On his release, there were bruises all over his body. The reason for his detention was reportedly that he had carried in his taxi a Tunisian national wanted in connection with an alleged terrorist offence.

AI country reports/visits
Report
· Tunisia: Human rights abuses in the run-up to the WSIS (AI Index: MDE 30/019/2005)
Visits
An AI delegate visited Tunisia in June to observe the appeal of lawyer and human rights defender Mohammed Abbou. In November, AI delegates attended the World Summit on the Information Society.

TURKEY

REPUBLIC OF TURKEY
Head of state: Ahmet Necdet Sezer
Head of government: Recep Tayyip Erdoğan
Death penalty: abolitionist for all crimes
International Criminal Court: not signed
UN Women's Convention and its Optional Protocol: ratified

The Council of Ministers of the European Union (EU) formally opened negotiations for Turkey's membership of the EU. Practical implementation of reforms intended to bring Turkish law into line with international standards slowed in 2005. The law provided for continuing restrictions on the exercise of fundamental rights. Those expressing peaceful dissent on certain issues faced criminal prosecution and sanctions after the introduction of the new Turkish Penal Code. Torture and ill-treatment continued to be reported, with those detained for ordinary crimes particularly at risk. Law enforcement officers continued to use excessive force in the policing of demonstrations; four demonstrators were shot dead in November. Investigations of such incidents were inadequate and law enforcement officers responsible for violations were rarely brought to justice. Human rights deteriorated in the eastern and south-eastern provinces in the context of a rise in armed clashes between the Turkish security services and the armed opposition Kurdistan Workers' Party (PKK).

Background
In June, the new Turkish Penal Code (TPC), Code of Criminal Procedure and Law on the Enforcement of Sentences (LES) entered into force. The laws contained positive aspects, with the TPC offering greater protection from violence to women. However, the TPC in particular also included restrictions to the right to freedom of expression. Human rights defenders in Turkey also raised objections to the punishment regime

for prisoners envisaged by the LES. A revised draft of the Anti-Terror Law was being discussed by a parliamentary sub-commission at the end of the year; human rights groups had commented critically on earlier drafts.

In September Turkey signed the Optional Protocol to the UN Convention against Torture and Other Cruel, Inhuman or Degrading Treatment or Punishment.

In October the Council of Ministers of the EU formally opened negotiations for Turkey's membership of the EU.

Freedom of expression

A wide range of laws containing fundamental restrictions on freedom of expression remained in force. These resulted in the prosecution of individuals for the peaceful expression of opinions in many areas of public life. The pattern of prosecutions and judgments also often demonstrated prosecutors' and judges' lack of knowledge of international human rights law. In some cases comments by senior government officials demonstrated an intolerance of dissenting opinion or open debate and seemed to sanction prosecution.

Article 301, on the denigration of Turkishness, the Republic, and the foundation and institutions of the state, was introduced in June and replaced Article 159 of the old penal code. Article 159 and Article 301 were frequently applied arbitrarily to target a wide range of critical opinion. Journalists, writers, publishers, human rights defenders and academics were prosecuted under this law. Among the many prosecuted were journalist Hrant Dink, novelist Orhan Pamuk, Deputy Chair of the Mazlum Der human rights organization Şehmüs Ülek, and academics Baskın Oran and İbrahim Kaboğlu .

An international academic conference on perceptions of the historical fate of the Armenians in the late Ottoman period, to be held in May at Bosphorus University in Istanbul was postponed after comments made by the Minister of Justice, Cemil Çiçek, which fundamentally challenged the notion of academic freedom by portraying the initiative as treacherous. The conference eventually took place at Bilgi University in September. However, in December legal proceedings under TPC Articles 301 and 288 were initiated against five journalists who reported on attempts to prevent the conference.

A further restriction on freedom of expression remained in the broad restrictions on the use of minority languages in public life. Frequent prosecutions for speaking or uttering single words in Kurdish continued to be brought under Article 81 of the Law on Political Parties.

In May the Court of Appeal ordered the closure of the teachers' union, Eğitim-Sen, on the grounds that a clause in its statute defending the right to "mother-tongue education" violated Articles 3 and 42 of the Constitution which emphasize that no language other than Turkish may be taught as a mother tongue. Eğitim-Sen later revoked the relevant article of its statute in order to avoid closure.

⌷ In October the prosecutor initiated a case to close down permanently the Diyarbakır Kurdish Assocation (Kürd-Der) on various counts, including the decision to adopt a "non-Turkish" spelling of the word Kurdish in the association's name and statute, and provisions in the association's statute defending the right to Kurdish-language education. The association had previously been warned to adjust the disputed elements in its statute and name.

Provisions in the Press Law restricting press coverage of cases under judicial process were used in an arbitrary and overly restrictive way to hinder independent investigation and public comment by journalists on human rights violations. These provisions were also used to hinder human rights defenders.

Legal proceedings were begun against the Chairperson of the Diyarbakır branch of the Human Rights Association (HRA), Selahattin Demirtaş, and Mihdi Perinçek, HRA Regional Representative, in connection with a report they co-authored with others on the killing of Ahmet Kaymaz and Uğur Kaymaz (see below). The indictment alleged that the report violated Article 19 of the Press Law, undermining the prosecutor's preparatory investigation into the killings, despite the fact that the authors had no access to the contents of files on the case which, by court order and for reasons of security, were unavailable for inspection. The first hearing against the two began in July.

Torture and ill-treatment

Torture and ill-treatment by law enforcement officials continued to be reported, with detainees allegedly being beaten; stripped naked and threatened with death; deprived of food, water and sleep during detention; and beaten during arrest or in places of unofficial detention. Reports of torture or ill-treatment of individuals detained for political offences decreased. However, people detained on suspicion of committing ordinary crimes such as theft or for public disorder offences were particularly at risk of ill-treatment. Reports suggested that there were still many cases of law enforcement officials completely failing to follow lawful detention and investigative procedures and of prosecutors failing to ascertain that law enforcement officials had complied with procedures. Police also regularly used disproportionate force against demonstrators, particularly targeting leftists, supporters of the pro-Kurdish party DEHAP, students and trade unionists (see Killings in disputed circumstances below). Often those alleging ill-treatment, particularly during demonstrations, were charged with resisting arrest while their injuries were explained away as having occurred as police attempted to restrain them.

⌷ In October in Ordu, five teenagers aged between 15 and 18 were detained at the opening of a new shopping centre. The five reported being beaten, verbally abused, threatened and having their testicles squeezed while being taken into custody and while in custody at the Ordu Central Police Station. They were later released. Two reported that they were stripped and threatened with rape. Three were not recorded as having been in police detention. One was subsequently charged with violently resisting arrest. Beyond the alleged ill-treatment, which was documented in medical reports and photographs, other irregularities in the handling of the detained teenagers by the police and prosecutor demonstrated a failure to follow legal procedures at any point from the moment of detention onwards.

⬦ In March, in the Saraçhane area of Istanbul, demonstrators gathering to celebrate International Women's Day were violently dispersed by police, beaten with truncheons and sprayed with pepper gas at close range. Three women were reportedly hospitalized. The scenes drew international condemnation. In December, 54 police officers were charged with using excessive force; senior officers were not charged, but three received a "reprimand" for the incident.

Impunity

Investigations into torture and ill-treatment continued to be marked by deeply flawed procedures and supported suggestions of an unwillingness on the part of the judiciary to bring perpetrators of human rights violations to justice. An overwhelming climate of impunity persisted.

⬦ In April, four police officers accused of the torture and rape with a truncheon of two teenagers, Nazime Ceren Salmanoğlu and Fatma Deniz Polattaş, in 1999 were acquitted. More than six years after the judicial process had begun and after the case had been delayed more than 30 times, a court in İskenderun acquitted the officers due to "insufficient evidence". Lawyers for the young women announced that they would appeal against the decision. The two women had been sentenced to long prison terms on the basis of "confessions" allegedly obtained under torture.

⬦ Fifteen years after the death of university student Birtan Altınbaş, the trial of four police officers accused of killing him continued in the Ankara Heavy Penal Court No. 2. Birtan Altınbaş died on 15 January 1991 following six days in police custody, during which he was interrogated on suspicion of being a member of an illegal organization. The case, which received international condemnation and was widely reported in the Turkish press, demonstrated many aspects of the flawed judicial process.

⬦ The trial of four police officers charged with killing Ahmet Kaymaz and his 12-year-old son Uğur Kaymaz on 21 November 2004 in the Kızıltepe district of Mardin began in February. The four officers on trial were not under arrest and were still on active duty. It was significant that senior officers responsible for the police operation during which the two individuals were killed were excluded from the investigation and not charged, supporting the view that in cases of this kind prosecutors rarely examined the chain of command.

Fair trial concerns

The continuing inequality between prosecution and defence and the influence of the executive on the appointment of judges and prosecutors prevented the full independence of the judiciary. While from 1 June detainees enjoyed the right to legal counsel and statements made in the absence of lawyers were not admissible as evidence in court, few prosecutors in the new Heavy Penal Courts (which replaced the State Security Courts in 2004) attempted to review ongoing cases where statements were originally made without the presence of legal counsel and where defendants alleged that their testimony had been extracted under torture. Little effort was made to collect evidence in favour of the defendant and most demands of the defence to have witnesses testify were not met.

Imprisonment for conscientious objection

Conscientious objection was not recognized and no civilian alternative to military service was available.

⬦ In August, Sivas Military Court sentenced conscientious objector Mehmet Tarhan to four years' imprisonment on charges of "disobeying orders" and refusing to perform military service. He was a prisoner of conscience.

Killings in disputed circumstances

On 9 November in the Şemdinli district of Hakkâri, a bookshop was bombed, killing one man and injuring others. Three men were charged in connection with the incident. The alleged bomber was subsequently revealed to be a former PKK guerrilla turned informant and his alleged accomplices were two members of the security services, with identity cards indicating that they were plain-clothes gendarmerie intelligence officers. Subsequently, as the prosecutor carried out a scene-of-crime investigation, the assembled crowd was fired upon from a car, resulting in the death of one civilian and injury of others. The prosecutor's crime-scene investigation was postponed. A gendarmerie specialist sergeant was charged with disproportionate use of force resulting in death. AI called upon the government to establish an independent commission of inquiry to investigate all dimensions of these incidents including allegations of direct official involvement. During subsequent protests at the events in Şemdinli, three people in the Yüksekova district of Hakkâri and one person in Mersin were shot dead by police.

During 2005 approximately 50 people were shot dead by the security forces, over half of them in the south-eastern and eastern provinces. Many may have been victims of extrajudicial executions or the use of excessive force. "Failure to obey a warning to stop" was a common explanation provided by the security forces for these deaths.

At least two individuals were alleged to have been assassinated by the PKK. On 17 February, Kemal Şahin, who split from the PKK to found an organization allied with the Patriotic Democratic Party of Kurdistan, was killed near Suleimaniyeh in northern Iraq. On 6 July, Hikmet Fidan, former DEHAP deputy chair, was killed in Diyarbakır.

An organization calling itself the Kurdistan Freedom Falcons claimed responsibility for a bomb attack in July on a bus in the Aegean town of Kuşadası that killed five civillians.

Violence against women

Positive provisions in the new TPC offered an improved level of protection for women against violence in the family. The new Law on Municipalities required municipalities to provide shelters for women in towns with populations of more than 50,000 individuals. Implementation of this law will require adequate funding for the establishment of shelters from central government and full co-operation with women's organizations in civil society. Further efforts were needed to ensure that law enforcement officials, prosecutors and the medical profession were fully versed in the still little-known Law on the Protection of the Family.

Official human rights mechanisms

Official human rights monitoring mechanisms attached to the Prime Ministry failed to function adequately and had insufficient powers to report on and investigate violations. The work of the Prime Ministry Human Rights Advisory Board, encompassing civil society organizations, was obstructed and the Board became effectively inactive. Moreover, in November, former Chair İbrahim Kaboğlu, and Baskın Oran, a board member, were prosecuted for the contents of a report on the question of minorities in Turkey commissioned by the Board and authored by Baskın Oran. The Provincial and Human Rights Boards, set up by the Human Rights Presidency and also attached to the Prime Ministry, failed to conduct adequate investigations of human rights violations. Draft legislation on the creation of an ombudsman failed to advance.

AI country reports/visits
Reports
- Turkey: Memorandum on AI's recommendations to the government to address human rights violations (AI Index: EUR 44/027/2005)
- Concerns in Europe and Central Asia: January-June 2005: Turkey (AI Index: EUR 01/012/2005)
Visit
AI delegates visited Turkey in November.

TURKMENISTAN

TURKMENISTAN
Head of state and government: Saparmurad Niyazov
Death penalty: abolitionist for all crimes
International Criminal Court: not signed
UN Women's Convention: ratified
Optional Protocol to UN Women's Convention: not signed

Measures taken by Turkmenistan to counter international criticism of its human rights record failed to halt human rights violations. Religious minorities, civil society activists and relatives of dissenters were among those who faced harassment or imprisonment or were forced into exile for exercising their right to freedom of expression. At least 60 prisoners, serving prison terms in connection with an alleged assassination attempt on the head of state in 2002, remained incommunicado. In a further trial in the series of secret and unfair trials since the 2002 events, an unknown number of men were sentenced to life and other long terms of imprisonment.

International scrutiny

The UN Commission on Human Rights, at its 61st session in March and April, failed to follow up resolutions in 2003 and 2004 raising grave concerns about the human rights situation in Turkmenistan.

In December the UN General Assembly expressed "grave concern at continuing human rights violations", and, among other things, called on Turkmenistan to respond positively to requests by UN Special Rapporteurs to visit the country.

In August the UN Committee on the Elimination of Racial Discrimination considered Turkmenistan's first report to a UN committee. Among issues raised by the Committee were reports of hate speech, including by senior officials and public figures, against national and ethnic minorities and in favour of Turkmen "ethnic purity". The Committee expressed concern at reports that members of minorities were denied state employment or access to higher education, and that minority cultural institutions and numerous schools teaching in minority languages had been closed.

The authorities continued to deny that human rights were violated. On 23 March, President Saparmurad Niyazov was reported as saying that nobody was arrested on political grounds but that "wanted criminals" living abroad spread false reports.

However, to avoid being classified as a "country of particular concern" under the USA's International Religious Freedom Act – which could incur measures such as targeted trade sanctions – some concessions were made. The authorities released four conscientious objectors on 16 April, one of whom – Begench Shakhmuradov – had been sentenced to one year's imprisonment on 10 February for evading regular call-ups to active military service. Legal restrictions on registering religious communities were relaxed, and several religious minority congregations registered. However, conscientious objection remained a criminal offence, punishable by imprisonment, and harassment and intimidation of registered and unregistered religious minorities continued.

The risk remained that asylum-seekers forcibly returned to Turkmenistan might be arbitrarily detained, tortured or ill-treated, or imprisoned after unfair trials, including under a 2003 People's Council decree that increased the number of activities deemed treasonable in law.

Repression of dissent

Civil society activists, political dissidents and members of religious minority groups were subjected to harassment, arbitrary detention, torture and ill-treatment.

☐ Jehovah's Witnesses Durdygul Ereshova and Annajemal Tuylieva were detained by police on 7 October and taken to Niyazov district police station in Ashgabat. A senior officer allegedly insulted them, beat and kicked Annajemal Tuylieva, and threatened to rape them. Police were said to have accused them of "illegal religious activity" and "vagrancy", and to have confiscated the passport of Durdygul Ereshova's husband and threatened her with forcible resettlement to Lebap region in the east.

Relatives of exiled dissidents were targeted in an attempt to silence critics abroad speaking out about abuses in Turkmenistan.

☐ Ruslan Tukhbatullin, a senior postholder in the military administration of Dashoguz region, was reportedly forced to resign from his post in March and refused further military employment because of his family relationship to his brother Farid Tukhbatullin, an exiled human rights activist and director of the non-governmental group Turkmen Initiative for Human Rights.

Political prisoners

Dozens of prisoners sentenced following unfair trials in connection with a November 2002 alleged assassination attempt on President Niyazov continued to be held incommunicado. Many had allegedly been tortured and ill-treated following their arrests. They were denied access to families, lawyers and independent bodies including the International Committee of the Red Cross.

In a further secret trial in connection with the November 2002 events, several men were convicted and sentenced to imprisonment, bringing the number of those convicted in the case to at least 60.

☐ Major Begench Beknazarov, an armed forces officer who had gone into hiding following the alleged assassination attempt, was arrested in Ashgabat in May. He and several other men were subsequently tried and sentenced to prison terms in a closed trial in the first half of June. Their relatives were unable to visit them or obtain official trial documents. Begench Beknazarov was reportedly sentenced to life imprisonment. His parents, Raisa and Amandurdy Beknazarov, and one of his sisters, Dzheren

Beknazarova, were said to have been detained for 20 days at the Ministry of National Security building after the November 2002 events in an attempt to obtain information about his whereabouts and to put pressure on him to turn himself in. The three were reported to have been physically and psychologically ill-treated in detention. Their passports were subsequently confiscated. Raisa Beknazarova was dismissed from her job, and Dzheren Beknazarova expelled from university. Ayna Shikhmuradova, an aunt of Begench Beknazarov and sister-in-law of prominent opposition leader Boris Shikhmuradov, who was sentenced to life imprisonment following the alleged assassination attempt, was reportedly threatened with a beating by police at Ashgabat city police station in February 2003 unless she disclosed her nephew's whereabouts.

AI country reports/ visits
Reports
· Turkmenistan: The clampdown on dissent and religious freedom continues (AI Index: EUR 61/003/2005)
· Europe and Central Asia: Summary of Amnesty International's concerns in the region, January-June 2005: Turkmenistan (AI Index: EUR 01/012/2005)

UGANDA

REPUBLIC OF UGANDA
Head of state and government: Yoweri Kaguta Museveni
Death penalty: retentionist
International Criminal Court: ratified
UN Women's Convention: ratified
Optional Protocol to UN Women's Convention: not signed

The independence of the judiciary, freedom of expression and press freedom came under attack. Violence against women and girls was widespread. Torture by state security agents persisted.

Background

On 28 June Parliament voted to amend the Constitution and lifted the limit of two terms that a president could serve. Demonstrators protesting against this vote clashed with riot police. A national referendum on 28 July brought a return to a multi-party system of politics.

Abuses against civilians by all parties to the conflict in northern Uganda continued. In October the International Criminal Court (ICC) issued arrest warrants for five senior leaders of the armed opposition group, the Lord's Resistance Army (LRA). The accused were Joseph Kony, leader of the LRA; Vincent Otti, the second in command; Okot Odhiambo,

Dominic Ongwen and Raska Lukwiya. They were charged with crimes against humanity and war crimes committed in Uganda since July 2002.

Independence of the judiciary

Retired army colonel Dr Kizza Besigye, presidential candidate of the opposition party Forum for Democratic Change (FDC) in the 2006 elections, was arrested on 14 November. He was charged with rape and, together with 22 other people, treason and concealment of treason.

On 16 November, the High Court granted bail to 14 of the co-accused facing charges of treason. However, heavily armed state security agents were deployed in the courtyard of the High Court, reportedly ready to re-arrest the 14 once they emerged. Consequently, they were not released on bail but returned to prison. The 14 appeared before a military court on 18 November, charged with terrorism. Lawyers across Uganda staged a one-day strike on 28 November in protest at this siege of the High Court.

Thousands of people demonstrated in Kampala city centre against the arrest of Dr Besigye. Riot police used live ammunition, tear gas and water cannons against demonstrators. During the two-day protests, at least one person was killed and dozens were arrested. The Internal Affairs Minister banned demonstrations and processions ahead of Dr Besigye's bail application and court case.

On 24 November, Dr Besigye was charged before the military court with terrorism and unlawful possession of firearms. On the same day, he was scheduled to appear before the High Court for his bail application. Two lawyers representing Dr Besigye before the military court were charged with contempt of court and held for seven hours as they attempted to explain that their client was due to appear before the High Court. They were convicted and fined.

Dr Besigye was granted bail by the High Court on 25 November, but that morning, he had been remanded back to Luzira Maximum Security Prison by the military court and therefore he did not regain his freedom. The High Court ordered the military to suspend its trial until the Constitutional Court ruled on its legality, but the military court said the trial would go ahead. On 19 December Dr Besigye appeared before the High Court — his trial before the military court was scheduled for the same day. Dr Besigye's treason and rape cases were adjourned to January 2006 and he remained in prison until the end of the year.

Attacks on freedom of expression

Freedom of expression and press freedom came under attack and continued to be threatened. Journalists faced criminal charges because of their work.

In February the Media Council banned the play *The Vagina Monologues* by the US playwright Eve Ensler, which several women's organizations had planned to stage to raise awareness about violence against women.

In August the Uganda Broadcasting Council suspended the licence of *K FM 93.3 Radio* for a week after it broadcast a programme discussing the fatal helicopter crash that killed John Garang de Mabior, the Sudanese Vice President and Southern Sudanese leader, and seven Ugandan crew members. Andrew Mwenda, the programme's host, was charged with sedition and released on bail. His trial had not been fixed by the end of the year, pending the outcome of a constitutional petition challenging the sedition laws.

On 17 November, policemen and intelligence personnel raided the offices of Monitor Publications, newspaper publishers and owners of *K FM 93.3 Radio*. The *Monitor* daily newspaper had run a paid advertisement from the FDC calling for contributions to a fund for the legal defence of political prisoners in Uganda. Police claimed the advertisement breached the law because the FDC had not obtained permission to fundraise.

On 22 November, the State Minister for Information and Broadcasting issued a directive to revoke the licence of any media outlet hosting discussion of cases before the courts. He added that as the trial of Dr Besigye had started, all talk shows or debates "in respect of or incidental to that case and other cases" were banned.

Conflict in northern Uganda

The 19-year conflict between the government and the LRA persisted throughout 2005. There were clashes between the Uganda People's Defence Force (UPDF) and the LRA in Gulu, Pader, Kitgum, Lira and Apac districts.

At the end of August an estimated 1.4 million people were confined to Internally Displaced Persons (IDP) camps across northern Uganda. Overcrowding and poor sanitation rendered them vulnerable to outbreaks of disease, including cholera, while insecurity put them at risk of human rights abuses. In February, the government officially launched a National Policy for IDPs, which it said was based on international humanitarian law, human rights instruments and national laws.

The LRA extended its operations to daylight hours, contrary to its earlier practice, and continued to use road ambushes to attack civilians.

On 21 November, between seven and 10 LRA fighters ambushed a minibus taxi between Pader and Paiula in Pader district. Two civilians were killed instantly. Ten other civilians were removed from the vehicle, laid on the ground and executed. The vehicle was set on fire.

The LRA attacked the staff of non-governmental organizations (NGOs) in conflict-affected areas, making humanitarian access hazardous.

On 26 October, in an LRA ambush on the Pader Pajule road, one staff member of the NGO Agency for Co-operation and Research in Development (ACORD) was killed and two others were wounded. In a separate incident on the same day, the LRA killed a staff member of the NGO CARITAS about eight kilometres from Kitgum town.

Civilians also suffered human rights violations at the hands of government soldiers.

⊟ On 16 October, a family of four was shot dead by a member of the UPDF at the main entrance to the 4th Division Headquarters in Gulu Town. The soldier was reportedly a former LRA combatant.

Torture

Allegations of torture and ill-treatment committed by state security agents persisted throughout 2005. Uganda submitted its initial report on the implementation of the UN Convention against Torture to the Committee against Torture after a delay of 16 years. The Committee noted with concern "the lack of proportion between the high number of reports of torture and the very small number of convictions for such offences" which contributed to impunity. While acknowledging the difficult situation of internal conflict in northern Uganda, the Committee stressed that there were "no exceptional circumstances, whatsoever, which may be invoked as a justification of torture".

⊟ In July, the High Court sitting at Arua in the north-west ordered the government to pay compensation of Uganda Shillings 20,000,000 (approximately US$11,000) to Justine Okot, following his arrest and torture by UPDF soldiers who accused him of being a "rebel collaborator". He had been beaten with clubs and iron bars and molten plastic was poured on his body. He sustained severe injuries and permanent impairment. By the end of the year, he had not received payment.

Violence against women and girls

Women and girls continued to face widespread violence both in the public and private spheres of life, being subjected to beatings, killings, acid attacks and rapes. In northern Uganda, women and girls were raped and killed by all parties to the conflict. While police expressed concern about the growing number of rapes, especially of young girls, acts of violence were little reported for fear of reprisals. Between January and June, the rapes of 292 girls were reported in mid-western Uganda (Kabarole, Kamwenge, Bundibugyo, Kyenjojo and Kasese districts).

In September the UN Committee on the Rights of the Child recommended that the country adopt legislative measures to prohibit the persistent practice of female genital mutilation (FGM). It also recommended awareness-raising campaigns to combat FGM and other traditional practices harmful to the health, survival and development of children, especially girls.

Death penalty

In a landmark judgment delivered on 10 June, the Constitutional Court ruled in favour of ending laws that stipulate a mandatory death sentence. It ruled that the death penalty as such was not unconstitutional when it was defined as the maximum sentence for a crime, but that laws imposing a mandatory death sentence interfered with a judge's discretion in dispensing justice. The court stated that such laws were unconstitutional and must be amended by Parliament. The Attorney General appealed against the ruling and

by the end of 2005, the parties were awaiting the hearing of the appeal before the Supreme Court.

Death sentences continued to be imposed. At Luzira Maximum Security Prison, at the end of June, there were 555 prisoners on death row, 27 of whom were women. No executions were reported during the year.

AI country reports/visits

Reports/statements

- Uganda: Independent media and the right to information under threat (AI Index: AFR 59/006/2005)
- Uganda: First ever arrest warrants by International Criminal Court – a first step towards addressing impunity (AI Index: AFR 59/008/2005)
- Uganda: Call for a fair, prompt and public trial of arrested opposition leader and co-accused (AI Index: AFR 59/015/2005)
- Uganda: Attack on the independence of the courts (AI Index AFR 59/017/2005)

Visits

AI delegates visited northern Uganda in May and June to conduct research. An AI representative met President Museveni in October during his visit to the UK.

UKRAINE

UKRAINE
Head of state: Viktor Yushchenko (replaced Leonid Kuchma in January)
Head of government: Yuriy Yekhanurov (replaced Yuliya Timoshenko in September, who replaced Viktor Yanukovych in January)
Death penalty: abolitionist for all crimes
International Criminal Court: signed
UN Women's Convention and its Optional Protocol: ratified

Torture and ill-treatment in police detention continued to be routine. Anti-Semitic and racist attacks were reported throughout the country. Ukraine continued to be a major source of men, women and children trafficked abroad.

Background

After contested elections, Viktor Yushchenko took office as President on 23 January. In his inaugural speech he promised a "democratic government, a free press and an independent judiciary". On 8 September, after his chief of staff resigned alleging corruption in the government, Viktor Yushchenko dismissed Prime Minister Yuliya Timoshenko and other cabinet members, and formed a new government headed by Yuriy Yekhanurov.

Torture and ill-treatment

The new government acknowledged that torture and ill-treatment were a problem and took some positive steps. In January, amendments to Article 127 of the Criminal Code concerning torture made it possible to charge state officials with this crime. The General Prosecutor stated in September that 226 cases had been opened against police officers for torture and ill-treatment and that there had been more than 1,000 complaints during the past year. In September Ukraine signed the Optional Protocol to the UN Convention against Torture and Other Cruel, Inhuman or Degrading Treatment or Punishment.

Despite these measures, reports indicated that law enforcement officers continued to use torture and ill-treatment routinely and with impunity to extract confessions and information from detainees. Police officers were not adequately trained or equipped to gather evidence and therefore depended on confessions to solve crimes. Cases of torture and ill-treatment were rarely followed up and victims rarely received compensation.

Maksim Kalinin, aged 16, was allegedly beaten by police on 6 June in Kerch. According to reports, a girl he had argued with telephoned friends in the police to say that he had insulted her. Three police officers arrived shortly after and beat Maksim Kalinin. They then handcuffed him and took him to the local police station where they allegedly beat and threatened him. He was held for 24 hours and then driven home. He required hospital treatment for his injuries. His parents reported the ill-treatment to the prosecutor's office and a court case was started in June against the police officers involved. In December the officers were sentenced to three and four years in prison under Article 365 of the Criminal Code for exceeding their authority.

Poor conditions in pre-trial detention

Conditions in most pre-trial detention facilities failed to meet international standards. Most of the temporary holding facilities (ITTs) of the Ministry of the Interior dated from the 19th century or earlier and were not equipped with adequate sanitary facilities, ventilation or exercise yards. Tuberculosis continued to be widespread. However, a programme of renovation and reconstruction was started. According to the parliamentary Ombudsperson, by February, 139 of the 500 ITTs had been renovated and new ITTs had been built in Kharkiv, Dnipropetrovsk, Kirovohrad, Kyiv and Mariupul.

Racist attacks

There were continuing reports of anti-Semitic and racist attacks across the country. The Union of Councils for Jews in the former Soviet Union reported at least eight attacks against Jews and defacement of synagogues in Ukraine. Synagogues and Jewish community centres were vandalized in Ivano-Frankivsk, Izmail, Zhytomyr, Kyiv and Vinnytsya, and an Armenian church was daubed with anti-Semitic and anti-Armenian graffiti in Lviv. On several occasions during the year President Yushchenko condemned anti-Semitism and pledged to end it.

On 26 February Robert Simmons, an African-American US diplomat, was attacked by a group of skinheads in Kiev. His white companion was not touched. A formal complaint was lodged and the Ukrainian authorities initiated an investigation.

On 28 August Mordechai Molozhenov, a 32-year-old student of Judaism, and another student were attacked by skinheads in an underground passage in Kiev. The skinheads allegedly shouted anti-Semitic abuse during the attack. Mordechai Molozhenov was left in a coma and required brain surgery. He was later treated in hospital in Israel. Three suspects were detained for "hooliganism". The Deputy Minister of Internal Affairs told the Israeli ambassador that the attack had not been motivated by anti-Semitism. President Yushchenko, in a written statement, condemned all forms of racism and xenophobia, and called the incident shameful.

Trafficking in human beings

Ukraine continued to be a major source of men, women and children trafficked abroad, despite government efforts to address the problem. Article 149 of the Criminal Code, which came into force in 2001, criminalizes trafficking. The comprehensive anti-trafficking programme for 2002-2005, which included measures for prevention, prosecution and protection, continued to be implemented. However, a report published in April by the UN Children's Fund (UNICEF), the Organization for Security and Co-operation in Europe, the US Agency for International Aid and the British Council identified weaknesses in the steps being taken to stop trafficking. The report recommended amendments to domestic legislation to address internal trafficking, which was not included in Article 149. It also drew attention to the increasing number of minors being trafficked, and identified domestic violence as a major factor in forcing women to seek work abroad.

Update: 'disappearance' of Georgiy Gongadze

In January President Yushchenko promised that those responsible for the "disappearance" in September 2000 of investigative journalist Georgiy Gongadze would be brought before a court within two months. In March, two suspects were detained and allegedly confessed. On 5 March former Minister of Internal Affairs, Yuryi Kravchenko, committed suicide. He was due to be questioned that day in connection with the investigation. On 20 September parliament heard the long-delayed report of the investigating committee, which concluded that Georgiy Gongadze had been murdered, that the crime had been organized by former President Leonid Kuchma and Yuryi Kravchenko, and that other high ranking officials had been involved. On 8 November the European Court of Human Rights ruled that Ukraine had violated three articles of the European Convention for the Protection of Human Rights and Fundamental Freedoms in the case of Georgiy Gongadze.

AI country reports/ visits

Reports

- Ukraine: Time for Action – Torture and ill-treatment in police detention (AI Index: EUR 50/004/2005)
- Europe and Central Asia: Summary of Amnesty International's concerns in the region, January-June 2005: Ukraine (AI Index: EUR 01/012/2005)

Visits

AI delegates visited Ukraine in February, April, September and November to conduct research and meet government officials.

UNITED ARAB EMIRATES

UNITED ARAB EMIRATES
Head of state: Al-Sheikh Khalifa bin Zayed Al-Nahyan
Head of government: Al-Sheikh Maktoum bin Rashid Al Maktoum
Death penalty: retentionist
International Criminal Court: signed
UN Women's Convention: acceded
Optional Protocol to UN Women's Convention: not signed

Several political suspects were detained and held incommunicado at undisclosed locations, in some cases for months. A criminal suspect was alleged to have been tortured and at least one person, a foreign domestic worker, was sentenced to flogging. An application submitted in 2004 to establish an independent human rights organization was still not granted.

Background

In July a new federal law was introduced to prohibit the use of boys under the age of 18 as jockeys in camel races. In May the government agreed to establish a joint programme with the UN Children's Fund (UNICEF) to repatriate to their home countries children who had been brought to the United Arab Emirates (UAE) to be used as camel jockeys.

In Dubai Emirate, hundreds of mostly Asian migrant workers demonstrated outside the Labour and Social Affairs Ministry in September in protest at their working conditions and their employers' failure to pay their wages. In response, ministry officials were said to be pursuing these issues with the employers.

Incommunicado detention

At least three political suspects were detained incommunicado and without charge for several months. Political detainees were mostly held by State Security (Amn al-Dawla) officials, apparently on suspicion of holding Islamist views or calling for political reforms, although no reasons were given. They were held in solitary confinement and denied visitors, but allowed to make brief, usually monthly, telephone calls to their families.

🗁 'Abdullah Sultan al-Subaihat, Mohammad Ahmad Saif al-Ghufli and Sa'eed 'Ali Hamid al-Kutbi, were arrested on 2 August, and their homes and offices were searched. They were held incommunicado, reportedly in Abu Dhabi, but released without charge on 25 October.

🗁 Humeid Salem al-Ghawas al-Za'abi, a high-ranking officer in the UAE air force who was arrested in March 2004, continued to be held incommunicado throughout 2005. No charges were known to have been brought against him.

Torture and cruel judicial punishments

A foreign national was reported to have been tortured in May by police. 'Abdul Hameed Abu Fayad, an Irish national of Libyan origin, was said to have been beaten and threatened with rape by police in Sharjah in order to force him to confess to embezzlement.

Courts in some UAE Emirates continued to impose floggings for a range of offences.

🗁 In October a foreign woman employed as a domestic worker was sentenced to 150 lashes for becoming pregnant outside marriage by a Sharia (Islamic law) Court in the Emirate of Ras al-Khaimah. It was not known whether the sentence was carried out.

Discrimination against women

Women continued to be subject to discrimination under UAE laws, including the nationality law. This specifies that women, unlike men, cannot pass on their UAE nationality to their children if their spouses are foreign nationals. These children, in consequence, suffer serious restrictions on their residency, employment and education rights. They are considered migrant workers for employment purposes and required to pay higher fees for higher education.

Freedom of expression and human rights organizations

In Fujairah Emirate, the authorities intervened at the last minute to ban a conference on civil rights, women's rights and democracy due to take place on 21 September. It was to be attended by local rights advocates, intellectuals and members of the UAE's Jurists' Association. The authorities gave no reasons for the ban.

By the end of 2005, the Ministry of Labour and Social Affairs had still not responded to an application submitted in July 2004 by the UAE Association for Human Rights for legal registration as UAE's first independent human rights organization. It gave no explanation for the delay.

AI country reports/ visits
Report
- Gulf Cooperation Council (GCC) countries: Women deserve dignity and respect (AI Index: MDE 04/004/2005)
Visit
In May AI and the UAE's Jurists' Association held a joint seminar to promote the Stop Violence against Women campaign in the Gulf States.

UNITED KINGDOM

UNITED KINGDOM OF GREAT BRITAIN AND NORTHERN IRELAND
Head of state: Queen Elizabeth II
Head of government: Tony Blair
Death penalty: abolitionist for all crimes
International Criminal Court: ratified
UN Women's Convention: ratified with reservations
Optional Protocol to UN Women's Convention: ratified

The government continued to erode fundamental human rights, the rule of law and the independence of the judiciary, including by persisting with attempts to undermine the ban on torture at home and abroad, and by enacting and seeking to enact legislation inconsistent with domestic and international human rights law. Nonetheless, it lost its legal battle to reverse the ban on the admissibility in judicial proceedings of information obtained through torture as evidence. In July, 52 people were killed and hundreds wounded as a result of bomb attacks on the London transport system. Measures purporting to counter terrorism led to serious human rights violations, and concern was widespread about the impact of these measures on Muslims and other minority communities. Public judicial inquiries into cases of alleged state collusion in past killings in Northern Ireland began, but the government continued to fail to establish an inquiry into the killing of Patrick Finucane. Proposed legislation that would impact on past human rights abuses in Northern Ireland gave rise to serious concern.

'Anti-terrorism' measures
Serious human rights violations continued, including the persecution of men labelled by the government as "suspected international terrorists" on the basis of secret intelligence. Proposed and enacted measures involved punishment of people whom the authorities deemed a threat but against whom they said there was insufficient evidence to present to a court.

In the aftermath of the December 2004 ruling of the Appellate Committee of the House of Lords (the Law Lords) that indefinite detention was incompatible with the right to liberty and the prohibition of discrimination, the government failed to provide prompt redress to the victims. Instead, it waited until March for the relevant legislative provision to lapse. Simultaneously, the government passed the Prevention of Terrorism Act 2005 (PTA), which was inconsistent with the spirit of the Law Lords' ruling and allowed for violations of a wide range of human rights. The PTA gave a government minister unprecedented powers to issue "control orders" to restrict the liberty, movement and activities of people purportedly suspected of involvement in terrorism, again on the basis of secret intelligence. The imposition of "control orders" was tantamount to the executive "charging", "trying" and "sentencing" a person without the fair trial guarantees required in criminal cases.

In March the government imposed "control orders" on people interned under the previous legislation, subjecting them to severe restrictions and violating their human rights. "Control orders" were later imposed on other people, including at least one UK national.

In June the European Committee for the Prevention of Torture (CPT) published a report on its March 2004 visit. It found that detention under the Anti-terrorism Crime and Security Act 2001 had caused mental disorders in most of those interned, and that detention had been even more detrimental to their health because of its indefinite character and the lack of knowledge about the evidence against them. The CPT considered that the situation of some of them at the time of the visit amounted to inhuman and degrading treatment.

Also in June the Commissioner for Human Rights of the Council of Europe published a report of his November 2004 visit. This expressed concern about the PTA; the admission, as evidence, of information obtained through torture in judicial proceedings; prison conditions; the treatment of asylum-seekers; the low age of criminal responsibility; discrimination; and the need to set up public inquiries capable of establishing the full circumstances surrounding cases of alleged state collusion in killings in Northern Ireland.

In August the Prime Minister proposed new measures to counter terrorism. Most of them were inconsistent with the UK's obligations under domestic and international human rights law and many targeted non-UK citizens.

The government concluded Memorandums of Understanding with Jordan, Libya and Lebanon. It asserted that the "diplomatic assurances" featured in these memorandums could be relied on to relieve the UK of its domestic and international obligation not to send anyone to a country where they would be at risk of torture or other ill-treatment.

In August, most of the former internees were rearrested and, together with others newly arrested, were imprisoned under immigration legislation pending deportation on national security grounds. The government maintained it could forcibly remove the men, relying on the Memorandums of Understanding. The detainees were held in prisons far from their families, lawyers and doctors. Some of those detained had recently been acquitted by a UK court of terrorism-related charges. In October, partly as a result of their seriously deteriorating mental and physical health, a number of former internees were granted bail on conditions amounting to house arrest.

In October, a new Terrorism Bill was published. It contained sweeping and vague provisions that, if enacted, would undermine the rights to freedom of expression, association, liberty and fair trial. In November the Bill's proposal to extend the maximum period of police detention without charge from 14 to 90 days was rejected in parliament; a provision of 28 days was agreed. The Bill underwent further parliamentary scrutiny.

In December the government faced mounting accusations that it had allowed the USA to use UK territory in the context of secret transfers of individuals without any judicial process ("renditions") to countries where they were reportedly tortured and to various US detention centres around the world.

Police shootings
🗁 In July, after police shot dead Jean Charles de Menezes, an unarmed Brazilian man on his way to work in London, there were crucial delays in initiating an independent investigation into the killing. Evidence emerged giving rise to suspicion of an early attempt at a cover-up by the police.
🗁 In October the prosecuting authorities declined to bring charges against the police officers involved in shooting dead an unarmed man, Harry Stanley, as he was walking down a street in London in 1999.

Torture 'evidence'
In December, seven Law Lords unanimously confirmed the inadmissibility as evidence in judicial proceedings of information extracted under torture. They also ruled that there was a duty to investigate whether torture had taken place, and to exclude any evidence if the conclusion was that, on the balance of probabilities, it had been obtained through torture. AI coordinated a coalition of 14 organizations that jointly intervened in the case.

The case had been brought by 10 foreign nationals against being labelled "suspected international terrorists" by the UK authorities. As a result of the judgment, their cases were to be referred back to the court of first instance for its reconsideration of the "evidence".

Guantánamo Bay
In January the last four remaining UK nationals were released from US detention in Guantánamo Bay, Cuba. However, at least seven UK residents continued to be held there, including Bisher al-Rawi, an Iraqi national legally resident in the UK, and Jamil Al-Banna, a Jordanian national with refugee status in the UK. The UK authorities were implicated in their unlawful transfer to US custody, and continued to refuse to make representations on behalf of the UK residents to the US authorities.
🗁 In December, a UK court ruled that David Hicks, an Australian national detained in Guantánamo Bay, was entitled to be registered as a UK citizen and therefore to receive assistance by UK authorities.

UK armed forces in Iraq
The UK breached international and domestic human rights law through its role in the internment without charge of at least 10,000 people in Iraq. UK officials sat, along with US and Iraqi officials, on the Joint Detention Review Board, which reviewed the cases of all those interned by members of the Multinational Force in Iraq (in most cases, by US troops). At the end of October, the UK was itself holding 33 "security internees" in Iraq without charge or trial.
🗁 Hilal Abdul-Razzaq Ali Al-Jedda, a dual Iraqi-UK national who was arrested in October 2004, continued to be detained without charge in Iraq by UK forces.
🗁 In December the Court of Appeal of England and Wales ruled in the case of Al-Skeini that the Human Rights Act 1998 in principle had extra-territorial effect, and that the system for investigating deaths at the hands of UK armed forces personnel was seriously deficient, including in its lack of independence from the commanding officer.

Refugees and asylum-seekers
The Immigration, Asylum and Nationality Bill continued to be discussed in parliament. Provisions in the Bill, if enacted, would undermine one of the core purposes of the UN Refugee Convention – to provide protection for people seeking asylum on grounds of political persecution.

An increasing number of people who sought asylum in the UK were detained under Immigration Act powers at the beginning and end of the asylum process. Those detained included families with children, torture survivors and other vulnerable people. They were held in grim prison-like establishments and some complained of racist and other verbal abuse in detention.

There was no maximum time limit to such detention, nor was there an automatic and regular review by a court or a similar competent body as to the lawfulness of the decision to detain. In most cases, detention was arbitrary and other measures short of detention would have sufficed.

Prisons
Martin Narey, the outgoing chief executive in charge of prison and probation services, criticized the record-breaking increase in the prison population, which had led to severe overcrowding. He also said it was "gross" that about 16,000 prisoners were held in conditions in which they had to share a toilet in a cell in which they also ate. The number of self-inflicted deaths continued to be high.

Inquiries Act 2005
The Inquiries Act 2005 came into force in June. It undermined the rule of law, the independence of the judiciary and human rights protection. It therefore

failed to provide for effective, independent, impartial or thorough public judicial inquiries into serious human rights violations. AI called for its repeal.

Northern Ireland

Direct rule continued. In December the prosecuting authorities dropped all charges in the criminal prosecution which, in October 2002, had precipitated the suspension of the Northern Ireland Assembly and the reintroduction of direct rule by the UK government. Shortly after, one of the people against whom charges had been dropped, a senior Sinn Féin politician, confessed publicly that he was a British agent.

Collusion and political killings

Three separate public judicial inquiries into allegations of state collusion in the killings of Robert Hamill, Billy Wright and Rosemary Nelson began under Northern Ireland legislation. However, in November the Secretary of State for Northern Ireland converted the Billy Wright Inquiry into an inquiry to be held under the Inquiries Act, a move opposed by AI.

The government stated that it was making arrangements to establish an inquiry into the 1989 killing of prominent human rights lawyer Patrick Finucane under the Inquiries Act. It added that it was likely that a large proportion of the evidence would be considered in private since it involved issues "at the heart of the national security infrastructure in Northern Ireland". AI denounced as a sham the prospect of a Finucane inquiry under the Inquiries Act.

Legacy of the past

The government took two initiatives described as moves to address the legacy of past human rights abuses. In April a Historical Enquiry Team (HET) was set up with the view to the Police Service of Northern Ireland investigating unresolved conflict-related deaths. This gave rise to concern about a lack of independence in the investigation. In November the Northern Ireland (Offences) Bill was introduced in parliament which, if enacted, would sanction impunity for past human rights abuses committed by state agents and paramilitaries, and deprive victims of effective redress. In light of this, there was concern about the relevance of the HET's work.

Abuses by non-state actors

Abuses by members of paramilitary organizations, including killings, shootings and beatings, continued. Seven killings were attributed to members of Loyalist groups, two to members of Republican groups, and one pointed to Loyalist involvement.

▭ In January, Robert McCartney, a Catholic, was killed and another man seriously injured in the same attack. According to the police, the attack was carried out by members of the Provisional Irish Republican Army, although not sanctioned by the organization. In their search for justice, the McCartney family and their supporters were intimidated and threatened. In June, two people were charged in connection with the attack.

▭ In March, Stephen Nelson died as a result of injuries sustained during an assault in September 2004. The Independent Monitoring Commission attributed his death to members of the Ulster Defence Association, a Loyalist paramilitary organization.

Violence against women

An opinion poll commissioned by AIUK about attitudes towards sexual assault against women revealed widespread discriminatory and stereotypical views in the UK. Two women each week on average were killed by a partner or former partner. The UK continued to have very low conviction rates for the crime of rape with only 5.6 per cent of rapes reported to the police resulting in conviction.

AI country reports/ visits

Reports

- United Kingdom: Seeking asylum is not a crime — detention of people who have sought asylum (AI Index: EUR 45/015/2005)
- United Kingdom: Amnesty International's briefing on the draft Terrorism Bill 2005 (AI Index: EUR 45/038/2005)
- United Kingdom: Case for the Interveners on Appeal (AI Index: EUR 45/041/2005)
- United Kingdom: Human rights are not a game (AI Index: EUR 45/043/2005)
- United Kingdom: Amnesty International's briefing for the House of Commons' second reading of the Terrorism Bill (AI Index: EUR 45/047/2005)
- United Kingdom: Amnesty International's submission of 14 October to the UK Parliament's Joint Committee on Human Rights in connection with the Committee's inquiry into the subject of "counter-terrorism policy and human rights" (AI Index: EUR 45/050/2005)
- United Kingdom: Amnesty International's Briefing for the House of Lords' second reading of the Terrorism Bill (AI Index: EUR 45/055/2005)
- United Kingdom: "I want justice" (AI Index: EUR 45/056/2005)

Visits

AI delegates visited several immigration detention centres throughout the UK. AI delegates observed judicial hearings, including under counter-terrorism legislation.

UNITED STATES OF AMERICA

UNITED STATES OF AMERICA
Head of state and government: George W. Bush
Death penalty: retentionist
International Criminal Court: signed but declared
intention not to ratify
UN Women's Convention: signed
Optional Protocol to UN Women's Convention: not signed

Thousands of detainees continued to be held in US custody without charge or trial in Iraq, Afghanistan and the US naval base in Guantánamo Bay, Cuba. There were reports of secret US-run detention centres in undisclosed locations where detainees were held in circumstances amounting to "disappearances". Dozens of Guantánamo detainees went on hunger strike to protest against their harsh treatment and lack of access to the courts; some were reported to be seriously ill. Reports of deaths in custody, torture and ill-treatment by US forces in Iraq, Afghanistan and Guantánamo continued to emerge. Despite evidence that the US government had sanctioned interrogation techniques constituting torture or ill-treatment, and "disappearances", there was a failure to hold officials at the highest levels accountable, including individuals who may have been guilty of war crimes or crimes against humanity. Several trials took place of low-ranking soldiers charged with abusing detainees; in most cases sentences were light. There were reports of police brutality and use of excessive force in the USA. Sixty-one people died after being struck by police tasers, a huge rise over previous years. Sixty people were executed, taking the total to over 1,000 since executions resumed in 1977.

Guantánamo Bay

At the end of 2005 around 500 detainees of around 35 nationalities continued to be held without charge or trial at the US naval base in Guantánamo Bay; most had been captured during the international armed conflict in Afghanistan in 2001 and were held for alleged links to al-Qa'ida or the former Taleban government. They included at least two juveniles who were under 16 when they were taken into custody.

Legislation passed in December (the Detainee Treatment Act of 2005) removed the right of Guantánamo detainees to file habeas corpus claims in the US federal courts against their detention or treatment, allowing instead only limited appeals against the decisions of the Combatant Status Review Tribunals (see below) and military commissions. The legislation called into question the future of some 200 pending cases in which detainees had challenged the legality of their detention following a US Supreme Court ruling in 2004 that they had the right to file such claims.

By March, the Combatant Status Review Tribunals (CSRT), administrative panels set up in 2004, had determined that 93 per cent of the 554 detainees then being held were "enemy combatants". The detainees had no legal representation and many declined to attend the CSRT hearings, which could consider secret evidence and evidence extracted under torture.

In August an unknown number of detainees resumed a hunger strike, initiated in June, to protest against their continued lack of access to the courts and alleged harsh treatment, including beatings, by guards. More than 200 detainees were said to be taking part at one stage, although the US Department of Defense said the number was much lower. Several detainees alleged they had been verbally and physically abused while being force-fed, sustaining injuries when guards roughly inserted feeding tubes through their noses. The government denied any ill-treatment. The hunger strike was continuing at the end of the year.

In November, three UN human rights experts declined an offer by the US government to visit Guantánamo as it had placed restrictions inconsistent with the standard terms of reference for such visits.

Military commissions

In November the US Supreme Court, ruling in the case of Salim Ahmed Hamdan, agreed to review the legality of the military commissions set up under a presidential order to try foreign terror suspects. However, a further five Guantánamo detainees were named to stand trial before the commissions, which are executive bodies, not impartial or independent courts, bringing the total number designated to appear before them to nine. The government scheduled arraignment hearings before the commissions for January for two of those charged. One of them was Omar Khadr, who was 15 when taken into custody and whose mental health and alleged ill-treatment remained a particular cause for concern.

Detentions in Iraq and Afghanistan

During the year, thousands of "security internees" were held without charge or trial by US forces in Iraq. Regulations governing detentions stipulated that internees must either be released or transferred to Iraqi criminal jurisdiction within 18 months. They also provided that detainees could continue to be interned by the US-led Multi-National Force indefinitely for "continued imperative reasons of security". The International Committee of the Red Cross (ICRC) visited detainees in internment facilities but not those held in US division or brigade holding facilities immediately after arrest.

In Afghanistan, hundreds of detainees continued to be held in US military custody without charge or trial or access to families or lawyers at Bagram airbase, some for more than a year. Although the ICRC had access to detainees at Bagram, it had no access to detainees held in an unknown number of US forward operating bases. There were reports of ill-treatment in such facilities, including detainees being stripped naked during interrogation and deprived of food and sleep.

Detentions in undisclosed locations

There were continued reports that the US Central Intelligence Agency (CIA) operated a network of secret detention facilities in various countries. Such facilities were alleged to detain individuals incommunicado outside the protection of the law in circumstances amounting to "disappearances". Three Yemeni detainees told AI that they had been held in isolation for between 16 and 18 months in three detention facilities apparently run by the USA in unknown locations; their cases suggested that such detentions were not confined to a small number of "high value" detainees as previously suspected. In November the Council of Europe launched an investigation into reports that the network of US secret prisons included sites in Eastern Europe. The US authorities refused to confirm or deny the allegations.

Allegations of US involvement in the secret and illegal transfer of detainees between countries, exposing them to the risk of torture and ill-treatment, continued.

Torture and ill-treatment outside the USA

Evidence continued to emerge of the torture and ill-treatment of detainees in Guantánamo, Afghanistan and Iraq, before and after the abuses in Abu Ghraib prison, Iraq, which came to light in April 2004. Further information was published describing interrogation techniques officially approved at various periods for "war on terror" detainees, which included the use of dogs to inspire fear, stress positions, exposure to extremes of heat or cold, sleep deprivation and isolation.

There was continued failure to hold senior officials accountable for abuses. The final report of Naval Inspector General Vice-Admiral Church into Department of Defense interrogation operations worldwide, a summary of which was published in March, found "no link between approved interrogation techniques and detainee abuse". This was despite the fact that many such techniques violate international standards that prohibit torture and ill-treatment. The Church investigation did not interview a single detainee or former detainee, nor did it interview Secretary of Defense Donald Rumsfeld. No inquiries examined the CIA whose activities remained shrouded in secrecy.

The US Army reported in March that 27 deaths of detainees in US custody in Iraq and Afghanistan during raids, capture or in detention facilities had been listed as confirmed or suspected homicides. Some cases were under investigation while others had been referred to other agencies or were recommended for prosecution.

Other sources, including court records and autopsy reports, strongly indicated that some detainees had died after torture during or after interrogations. There was also evidence to suggest that delays and deficiencies in investigations had hampered prosecutions.

In March the American Civil Liberties Union (ACLU) and Human Rights First filed a federal lawsuit on behalf of eight men who had been tortured and ill-treated in US military detention facilities in Iraq and Afghanistan, seeking a declaration that Secretary Rumsfeld was responsible for violating US and international laws. The lawsuit, which was still pending at the end of the year, also sought compensatory damages for the victims.

Several trials of US military personnel accused of abusing detainees took place during the year, mainly involving low-ranking soldiers. Many received sentences that did not reflect the gravity of the crimes.

In March the government rescinded an April 2003 Pentagon Working Group Report on Detainee Interrogations which stated, among other things, that the President had authority during military operations to override the international prohibition against torture with regard to interrogations. In November the Pentagon approved a new policy directive governing interrogations, which would allow the army to issue a long-delayed revised field manual. The directive stated that "acts of physical or mental torture are prohibited". However, it did not elaborate other than to order that detainees be treated humanely "in accordance with applicable law and policy". In December the Army announced it had approved a new classified set of interrogation methods to be added to the revised Army Field Manual. Although the manual would specifically prohibit stripping, prolonged stress positions, sleep deprivation and use of dogs in interrogations, there was concern that the classified addendum may still include abusive techniques.

In December, Congress passed legislation prohibiting the cruel, inhuman or degrading treatment of people in the custody or control of the US government anywhere in the world. However, concern remained that a statement attached by President Bush when signing the bill into law effectively reserved the right of the executive to bypass the provision on national security grounds.

▭ In August and September, trials took place in a military court of US soldiers accused of abusing two Afghan detainees, Dilawar and Habibullah, who died from multiple blunt force injuries while being interrogated in an isolation section of the Bagram airbase in December 2002. As of December 2005, seven low-ranking soldiers had been convicted and received sentences ranging from five months' imprisonment to reprimand, loss of pay and reduction in rank. No one had been found responsible for serious offences such as torture or other war crimes.

Detention of 'enemy combatants' in the USA

▭ Jose Padilla — a US national held for more than three years without charge in US military detention — was among five people indicted in a US federal court in November on charges of conspiracy to murder US nationals overseas and supporting terrorists. The charges made no mention of the alleged conspiracy to detonate a "dirty bomb" in a US city for which he was originally detained. The Justice Department sought permission from the Appeals Court to transfer him to the federal prison system. However, the court did not agree and instead issued an order requiring both the government and his lawyers to submit briefs on whether it should withdraw its earlier ruling upholding the President's power to detain Jose Padilla indefinitely as an "enemy combatant". The issue had not been decided on by the end of the year.

▭ Ali Saleh Kahlah al-Marri, a Qatari national, remained detained without charge or trial as an "enemy combatant" in military custody. A lawsuit was filed in August alleging that he was suffering from severe physical and mental health problems as a result of his treatment, which included sleep deprivation, sensory deprivation, punitive shackling, exposure to cold, and disrespectful handling of the Qu'ran.

Prisoners of conscience

▭ Kevin Benderman, a US army sergeant, was sentenced to 15 months' imprisonment in July for refusing to redeploy to Iraq on grounds of his conscientious objection to the war, developed during a first term of service there. His application for conscientious objector status was refused on the ground that his objection was not to war in general but to a particular war.

▭ Camilo Mejia Castillo, Abdullah Webster and Pablo Paredes, three former soldiers imprisoned for their conscientious objection to serving in Iraq, were released during the year.

Trial of Ahmed Omar Abu Ali

Ahmed Omar Abu Ali, a US national, was convicted in a US federal court in November on charges of conspiracy to commit acts of terrorism. The trial was flawed as the jury was not allowed to hear evidence supporting claims by Ahmed Abu Ali that his videotaped confession, on which the prosecution relied almost exclusively, had been obtained following torture in Saudi Arabia. Ahmed Abu Ali alleged that he was flogged and threatened with death by the Interior Ministry's General Intelligence (al-Mabahith al-Amma) while being held incommunicado in Saudi Arabia in 2003. During the trial, general statements on the treatment of detainees from Saudi Arabian officials were used to undermine Ahmed Abu Ali's allegations, while the defence lawyers were not allowed to present any evidence pertaining to Saudi Arabia's human rights record on torture.

Ill-treatment and excessive use of force

There were continued reports of ill-treatment and deaths in custody involving tasers – electro-shock weapons deployed by some 7,000 US police and correctional agencies.

Sixty-one people died after being struck by police tasers, bringing to 142 the total number of such deaths since 2001. Coroners found tasers had caused or contributed to at least 10 of the deaths in 2005, increasing concerns about the safety of such weapons.

Most of those who died were unarmed men who reportedly did not pose a serious threat when they were electro-shocked. Many were given multiple or prolonged shocks, potentially harmful acts highlighted in a Department of Defense preliminary study into taser safety published in April 2005.

Several police departments suspended the use of tasers, others tightened the rules for taser use. However, most departments continued to authorize tasers in a wide range of situations, including against unarmed people who resisted arrest or refused to obey police commands. Mentally disturbed and intoxicated individuals, children and the elderly were among those shocked.

AI renewed its call on the US authorities to suspend use and sales of tasers and other stun weapons pending a rigorous, independent inquiry into their use and effects.

▭ In February police in Florida tasered a 13-year-old girl who had been fighting with her mother. The girl was handcuffed in the back of a police patrol car when she was shocked.

▭ In February, a 14-year-old developmentally disabled boy went into cardiac arrest after being shocked with a police taser in Chicago, Illinois, as he was sitting on a sofa in a care home and, according to police, attempted to stand up "in an aggressive stance". Doctors who treated him said the taser shocks had caused a potentially fatal disturbance of the heart rhythm and that he would have died had he not been immediately resuscitated by medical staff at the scene.

▭ Seventeen-year-old Kevin Omar, who was acting erratically under the influence of drugs, lapsed into a coma after being shocked three times by police officers from Waco, Texas; he died two days later. The medical examiner said he believed the taser was a contributory factor in the death.

Abuses of lesbian, gay, bisexual and transgender people

In September AIUSA published a report, *Stonewalled: police abuse and misconduct against lesbian, gay, bisexual and transgender people in the United States.* The report found that, although there was greater recognition of the rights of LGBT people, many still faced discriminatory treatment and verbal and physical abuse by police. It also showed that within the LGBT community, transgender individuals, people of colour, youth, immigrants, homeless individuals and sex workers experienced a heightened risk of abuse. The report found that police often failed to respond adequately to hate crimes or domestic violence against LGBT people.

Death penalty

In 2005, 60 people were executed, bringing to 1,005 the total number of prisoners put to death since executions resumed in the USA in 1977 following a moratorium. Two people were released from death row on grounds of innocence, bringing to 122 the total number of such cases since 1973.

On 1 March the US Supreme Court banned the execution of child offenders – those aged under 18 at the time of the crime – bringing the USA into line with international standards prohibiting such executions. Twenty-two child offenders had been executed in the USA since 1977.

Executions continued of people with mental illness and disorders, of prisoners who had been denied adequate legal representation at trial, and in cases where the reliability of evidence had been questioned.

☐ Troy Kunkle was executed in Texas on 25 January, despite suffering from serious mental illness, including schizophrenia, evidence of which was not presented to the jury that sentenced him to death. He was just over 18 at the time of the crime and had suffered a childhood of deprivation and abuse.

☐ Frances Newton was executed in Texas on 14 September, despite doubts over the reliability of her conviction. She was found guilty on the basis of circumstantial evidence, and always maintained that she was innocent.

Hurricane Katrina

In August Hurricane Katrina swept across Louisiana, killing more than 1,000 people and leaving hundreds of thousands of others homeless or temporarily displaced without their basic needs for food, clean water and medicines met. There was widespread anger at the federal government's slow response to the humanitarian disaster.

Scores of inmates in New Orleans Parish Prison were allegedly abandoned by guards following the hurricane. Prisoners reported being left locked in cells for days without food or drinking water as flood waters rose. There were reports, denied by the Louisiana authorities, that some prisoners had drowned. AI called for a full inquiry and for the authorities to ensure that all prisoners were fully accounted for. It also called for an investigation into allegations that evacuated inmates were ill-treated.

Other concerns

A joint study published in October by AI and Human Rights Watch, *The Rest of Their Lives: Life without Parole for Child Offenders in the United States*, reported that at least 2,225 child offenders under 18 at the time of the crime were serving sentences of life without parole. Such a sentence for child offenders is prohibited under the UN Convention on the Rights of the Child, signed but not ratified by the USA. Of the cases examined, 16 per cent of the offenders were aged between 13 and 15 at the time of the crime and 59 per cent received the sentence for their first conviction. Many were convicted of "felony murder" based on evidence of their participation in a crime during which a murder took place, but without direct evidence of their involvement in the killing. The report called on the US authorities to stop sentencing children to life without parole and to grant child offenders serving such sentences immediate access to parole procedures.

Daniel Strauss and Shanti Sellz, volunteers with a group called No More Deaths, were stopped by the US Border Patrol in July while they were taking three Mexican migrants found in the Arizona desert for urgent medical treatment. The volunteers were charged with offences linked to illegally transporting aliens and faced up to 15 years' imprisonment. Hundreds of irregular or undocumented migrants die in the desert each year after crossing from Mexico into the USA, many from exposure to extreme temperatures which reached record levels in Arizona in July. AI called for the charges against the two volunteers to be dropped on the ground that they had not assisted the migrants to evade immigration controls but were acting solely to protect life.

AI country reports/ visits

Reports

- USA: Guantánamo and beyond – The continuing pursuit of unchecked executive power (AI Index: AMR 51/063/2005)
- USA: US detentions in Afghanistan – an aide-memoire for continued action (AI Index: AMR 51/093/2005)
- USA/Jordan/Yemen: Torture and Secret Detention – Testimony of the "disappeared" in the "war on terror" (AI Index: AMR 51/108/2005)
- USA/Yemen: Secret detention in CIA "Black Sites" (AI Index: AMR 51/177/2005)
- USA: Killing possibility – The imminent execution of Stanley Williams in California (AI Index: AMR 51/187/2005)
- USA: The trial of Ahmed Abu Ali – Findings of Amnesty International's trial observation (AI Index: AMR 51/192/2005)
- Stonewalled: Police abuse and misconduct against lesbian, gay, bisexual and transgender people in the U.S. (AI Index: AMR 51/122/2005)

Visits

AI delegates visited Yemen in June and September/ October to visit former US "war on terror" detainees.

In November an AI observer attended the trial of Ahmed Omar Abu Ali.

URUGUAY

EASTERN REPUBLIC OF URUGUAY
Head of state and government: Tabaré Vázquez Rosas
(replaced Jorge Batlle Ibáñez in March)
Death penalty: abolitionist for all crimes
International Criminal Court: ratified
UN Women's Convention and its Optional Protocol:
ratified

Progress was made in dealing with human rights
violations committed in the 1970s and 1980s.
However, in most cases justice remained obstructed
by the 1986 Expiry Law, which prevented legal
proceedings against those involved in violations in
this period. There were reports of the ill-treatment of
detainees and of harsh conditions in prisons.

Impunity under the Expiry Law
The government of President Tabaré Vázquez Rosas
initiated a number of investigations to establish the
fate and burial places of victims of "disappearances"
from the period of military government (1973-1985). The
investigation sites included military barracks where a
number of human remains were discovered. Three
cases of past human rights violations were taken before
the courts. However, no attempts were made to abolish
the Expiry Law.

The government of Tabaré Vázquez Rosas
interpreted the scope of the Expiry Law as limited to
human rights violations committed under the military
governments after the June 1973 military coup. This
interpretation opened up the possibility of legal action
against some 600 active and former members of the
armed forces in connection with crimes committed
before the coup.

The new government also excluded from the Expiry
Law three cases that took place in Argentina, allegedly
with the co-operation of Uruguayan and Argentine
armed forces. The three cases were subsequently
brought before the courts.

▭ In June, former President Juan Maria Bordaberry
and former Minister of Foreign Affairs Juan Carlos
Blanco were charged with involvement in the
murders of legislators Zelmar Michelini and Héctor
Gutiérrez Ruiz and activists Rosario Barredo and
William Whitelaw. All four were killed in Argentina
in 1976.

▭ In August the armed forces revealed that the
remains of Maria Claudia Garcia de Gelman, who
"disappeared" with her husband in 1976, were almost
certainly buried in the grounds of the army's 14th
Battalion near the capital, Montevideo. However, in
November the Appeals Court shelved the case on the
grounds that it was covered by the Expiry Law.

Ill-treatment of prisoners
There were reports of detainees, including minors,
being ill-treated in police stations.

Harsh conditions and other ill-treatment were
reported at Libertad Prison, in the department of San
José, 50km from Montevideo. In June, hundreds of
prisoners staged a hunger strike in protest at
overcrowding at the prison and at the lack of food,
medical assistance, hot water or electricity. They also
demanded that Congress urgently introduce legislation
to ease prison overcrowding.

In September, the Senate passed the Humanization
and Modernization of the Prison System Law. The law
aimed to relieve overcrowding in prisons by granting
provisional or early release to certain categories of
prisoners.

AI country reports/visits
Statements
· Uruguay: Concrete reforms need to be made if there
  is to be effective human rights protection (AI Index:
  AMR 52/001/2005)
· Uruguay: Open letter to the President of the Oriental
  Republic of Uruguay, Dr Tabaré Vázquez Rosas (AI
  Index: AMR 52/002/2005)

UZBEKISTAN

REPUBLIC OF UZBEKISTAN
Head of state: Islam Karimov
Head of government: Shavkat Mirzioiev
Death penalty: retentionist
International Criminal Court: signed
UN Women's Convention: ratified
Optional Protocol to UN Women's Convention: not signed

**The security forces allegedly killed hundreds of
unarmed men, women and children when they fired
indiscriminately and without warning on a crowd in
the eastern city of Andizhan in May. The government
rejected international calls for an independent
international investigation and attempted to block
all but official reports of the killings. Hundreds of
demonstrators were detained and reportedly ill-
treated, and witnesses were intimidated. Journalists
and human rights defenders were harassed, beaten
and detained and some were prisoners of conscience
held on serious criminal charges. Following unfair
trials, at least 73 people were convicted of "terrorist"
offences and sentenced to between 12 and 22 years'
imprisonment for their alleged participation in the
unrest. Dozens of people were believed to have been
sentenced to death and executed. A presidential
decree promised abolition of the death penalty
in 2008.**

Background

In response to Uzbekistan's refusal to allow an independent international investigation of the May killings in Andizhan, the European Union (EU) in November announced an embargo on EU arms sales and military transfers to Uzbekistan, and a one-year visa ban on 12 senior government ministers and officials. However, the Minister of Internal Affairs was granted an exception on humanitarian grounds to receive medical treatment in Germany. In turn the authorities in Uzbekistan banned European members of the North Atlantic Treaty Organization (NATO) from using their airspace and asked all, apart from Germany, to withdraw their troops from Termez airbase. The UN General Assembly adopted a resolution, put forward by the EU, expressing deep regret over Uzbekistan's refusal to allow an international investigation and urging the authorities to stop their "harassment and detention of eyewitnesses".

Also in November the US military completed its withdrawal from Khanabad airbase, as requested by the Uzbekistani authorities. The airbase had been leased since October 2001 as part of the US-led "war on terror". On 14 November, the government signed a mutual defence agreement with the Russian Federation that would allow Russian use of military facilities in Uzbekistan.

'Akramia' trials

On 11 February, 23 business entrepreneurs prominent in Islamic charitable work went on trial at the Altinkul District Court, Andizhan. They were charged with attempting to overthrow the constitutional order, membership of an illegal religious organization, and possessing or distributing literature that threatened public safety. Arrested between June and August 2004, the men were accused of being members of a group seeking to establish an Islamic state and linked to the banned Islamist opposition party Hizb-ut-Tahrir, categorized as a "terrorist" organization in Uzbekistan. The authorities named the supposed group "Akramia" after its alleged founder, Akram Yuldashev, serving a 17-year prison sentence for "terrorism" and other anti-state charges imposed in 1999. The 23 consistently denied the charges or membership of any group. They appeared to have been held almost completely incommunicado in pre-trial detention. They said they were repeatedly threatened, subjected to physical, sexual and mental torture and ill-treatment, and forced to sign incriminating statements under duress.

Other individuals were arrested and charged in connected cases.

⌂ In February, nine men – all employees of one of the 23 entrepreneurs, who owned a furniture company in Tashkent – were charged with attempting to overthrow the constitutional order and membership of an illegal religious organization. In July, three of them were sentenced to between 15 and a half and 16 years in prison after an unfair trial. They were among 20 employees detained in September 2004 and reportedly coerced into saying they were Akramia leaders in Tashkent. The fate of the remaining detainees was not known.

⌂ In another case, a group of 13 men were reportedly arrested in Andizhan on 23 and 24 January, and charged with similar offences.

13 May killings

During the night of 12 to 13 May, unidentified armed men broke into military barracks and the prison in Andizhan, reportedly freeing the 23 entrepreneurs and hundreds of other prisoners, and occupying the regional government building. In the course of the day, thousands of people gathered in the main square, reportedly to demand justice and an end to poverty. According to the authorities, civilians took hostage a number of officials, and gunfire was exchanged between armed men and the security forces. Throughout 13 May the security forces reportedly fired sporadically on the mostly unarmed and peaceful crowd. In the early evening, after surrounding the protesters with buses, armed personnel carriers and other barriers, the troops fired indiscriminately and without warning, killing and wounding as many as 300 and possibly up to 500 people, eyewitnesses said. Relatives were not allowed to visit the wounded taken to hospital.

The same night, hundreds of people fled across the border to neighbouring Kyrgyzstan, walking in large groups. The authorities said most did not go voluntarily but were forced at gunpoint to be human shields for the armed insurgents. Refugees in Kyrgyzstan insisted they had not been coerced, and reported that Uzbekistani troops opened fire without warning as they approached the border village of Teshik Tosh, killing at least eight people and wounding others, including women (see Kyrgyzstan entry).

The authorities said that 187 people were killed on 13 May, and denied that troops had used excessive force or killed civilians, including women and children. At the end of 2005, the government had yet to publish the names of those killed. Although a parliamentary commission of inquiry was established, its members were closely allied to President Karimov, and reportedly did not carry out their own investigation but simply reviewed the findings of the criminal investigation. The inquiry failed to meet international standards for a thorough, independent and impartial investigation, and the government refused demands for an international inquiry. Although the trial began in December of 12 police officers charged with negligence in connection with the Andizhan events, by the end of 2005 no members of the security forces responsible for human rights abuses had been brought to justice.

Extradition requests and forcible returns

Following the 13 May killings, the authorities requested the extradition of suspected supporters of Akramia and Hizb-ut-Tahrir from Kazakstan, Kyrgyzstan and the Russian Federation. On 16 June the Prosecutor General's Office said it was seeking the extradition from Kyrgyzstan of 131 refugees who were "direct participants in the acts of terrorism [in Andizhan]".

☐ On 9 June, Dilshod Gadzhiev, Tavakkal Gadzhiev, Muhammad Kadirov and Abdubais (Gasan) Shakirov were forcibly taken from a refugee camp at Besh-Kana to a detention centre in the city of Osh in Kyrgyzstan, and handed over to Uzbekistani security forces. The four men were reportedly detained incommunicado, and at least one of them was tortured, in Andizhan prison after their return to Uzbekistan. The Uzbekistani authorities told the UN High Commissioner for Refugees (UNHCR) that the four had returned "voluntarily" and were held in a detention facility in Tashkent, but denied the UNHCR access to them.

☐ Russian law enforcement officers detained 14 ethnic Uzbek men in Ivanovo in the Russian Federation on 18 June, allegedly for swearing and refusing to show their identity documents. The Uzbekistani authorities requested their extradition for involvement in the 13 May events, supporting Akramia, and financing "terrorist" activities. All the men denied the accusations. A Russian citizen among them said he had visited Uzbekistan in May only to renew his Uzbekistani passport, and was released on 11 October. The other 13, a Kyrgyzstani national and 12 Uzbekistani nationals, applied for asylum in the Russian Federation in August but were still in custody at the end of 2005.

Unfair trials of 13 May suspects

Hundreds of people suspected of involvement in the 13 May events were detained, and many were allegedly ill-treated or tortured. In June, the Prosecutor General said that 102 detainees had been charged. The charges included "terrorism" and premeditated, aggravated murder — capital offences — as well as attempting to overthrow the constitutional order and organizing mass disturbances.

The first group of 15 defendants went on trial on 20 September. Access to the courtroom was restricted: a local independent human rights organization was allowed an observer, but the government refused a request by the UN High Commissioner for Human Rights to send observers. Subsequently, at least four closed trials reportedly started in November. All were unfair. Most detainees were believed to have been held incommunicado before trial and denied access to lawyers of their choice, relatives or medical assistance. The identity of the defendants, the charges against them, and the dates and locations of their trials were not notified to their relatives. International observers, human rights activists and families were denied access to all four trials, which were held in different locations outside Tashkent. In early December, 58 defendants were sentenced to terms of imprisonment from 12 to 22 years.

☐ The first trial, of 15 defendants including Tavakkal Gadzhiev, opened on 20 September before the Supreme Court in Tashkent. Access to the court was restricted. Relatives of the defendants, without notice of the trial, had not been able to apply to attend. The defendants pleaded guilty to charges of "terrorism" and asked for forgiveness, but there were concerns that their confessions, which followed closely the wording of the charges, had been extracted under duress. Government officials and the national media made prejudicial statements that presumed the guilt of the defendants. Most defendants had been held incommunicado and none was granted adequate access to a lawyer of his choice in pre-trial detention. There was no cross-examination of defendants or witnesses, and contradictions in the testimonies were not addressed. Witnesses for the defence faced intimidation. Out of hundreds of witnesses who testified, only one, Makhbuba Zokirova, told the court she had seen the security forces firing indiscriminately at mostly unarmed civilians, including women and children, even as they ran for safety. She asked the prosecutor whether she would be arrested for telling the truth. National newspapers subsequently denounced her as a traitor and an accomplice to terrorists. On 14 November the 15 defendants were sentenced to terms of imprisonment ranging from 14 to 20 years. Their appeals against their sentences were pending at the end of 2005.

Clampdown on dissent

The events in Andizhan were used as a pretext for a further clampdown on political freedoms in the name of national security and the "war on terror". Scores of civil society activists, including human rights activists and journalists who had tried to document the 13 May killings, were threatened, assaulted, detained, forcibly confined to their homes, and had their telephone connections cut. A number of human rights defenders considered to be prisoners of conscience were held on serious criminal charges. The authorities denounced as traitors and hypocrites those who questioned the official version of events, restricted access to websites linked with opposition groups in exile, and blocked the broadcasts of Russian television stations critical of Uzbekistan.

☐ Prominent human rights defender and prisoner of conscience Saidzhakhon Zainabitdinov was arrested on 21 May and detained. Initially held in police custody at the Andizhan Regional Department of Internal Affairs, he was reportedly transferred to Tashkent in July. His family and lawyer were denied information about his whereabouts. In November he was reportedly in an isolation unit at Tashkent prison, still incommunicado. Initially charged with defamation, punishable by up to three years in prison, in relation to an open letter about the case of the 23 entrepreneurs, he was subsequently charged with "terrorism" and other more serious charges. The real reason for his detention appeared to be his representation in court of one of the 23, and his reporting of the 13 May events, which received international media coverage.

The death penalty and flawed justice

Dozens of death sentences were believed to have been passed and executions carried out, but the government did not publish comprehensive statistics. The criminal justice system was flawed throughout with widespread corruption and a failure to investigate allegations of torture. The authorities carried out executions in secrecy, not informing relatives of the date of execution in advance or revealing the place of burial.

The EU strongly encouraged abolition of the death penalty at a meeting of the EU-Uzbekistan Cooperation Council in February. In March the UN Human Rights Committee deplored the execution of death row prisoners while their cases were still pending before the Committee.

📁 On 14 March, the father of Akhrorkhuzha Tolipkhuzhaev, sentenced to death on 19 February 2004, was turned away when he tried to visit his son. The following day, when a lawyer asked to see Akhrorkhuzha Tolipkhuzhaev, prison guards said he was no longer registered on death row. On 21 March the authorities assured the UN Human Rights Committee, which had been considering human rights violations in the case since May 2004, that he was still alive. On 6 April, his father received a death certificate stating the execution had taken place on 1 March. The Human Rights Committee described Uzbekistan's actions as a "grave breach" of its international legal obligations.

Under a presidential decree on 1 August the death penalty was to be abolished from 1 January 2008. However, without any moratorium on the death penalty or commutation of death sentences, scores of people remained at risk of execution.

AI country reports/ visits
Reports
- Uzbekistan: Questions of life and death cannot wait until 2008 – A briefing on the death penalty (AI Index: EUR 62/020/2005)
- Uzbekistan: Lifting the siege on the truth about Andizhan (AI Index: EUR 62/021/2005)
Visits
AI representatives visited Kyrgyzstan in May, June and July to interview refugees from Uzbekistan.

VENEZUELA

BOLIVARIAN REPUBLIC OF VENEZUELA
Head of state and government: Hugo Chávez Frías
Death penalty: abolitionist for all crimes
International Criminal Court: ratified
UN Women's Convention: ratified with reservations
Optional Protocol to UN Women's Convention: ratified

There were reports of unlawful killings of criminal suspects by police. Most cases were not investigated and the perpetrators remained unpunished. The lack of independence of the judiciary remained a concern. Persistent social and economic inequalities continued to limit access to the economic and social rights of Afro-descendants and indigenous peoples.

Background
Political polarization continued to be a destabilizing factor. There were continued concerns that critics of the government were being harassed, including through the criminal justice system. Some confrontations between supporters of President Chávez and the opposition took place before August municipal elections, which were won by President Chávez' party, Movimiento V República.

Congressional elections in December resulted in a landslide victory for President Chávez' party, after opposition parties refused to take part, accusing the electoral body of bias. The elections were largely regarded as fair by international observers.

International relations with the USA remained tense as US officials continued to accuse President Chávez' government of threatening the stability of the region. President Chávez continued to increase its co-operation with Latin American nations, including trade and energy links.

Police brutality
There were continuing reports of human rights violations by the police, including unlawful killings of criminal suspects. In most cases an investigation was not opened and the alleged perpetrators were not brought to justice. According to statistics published by the Public Prosecutor's Office in July, between 2000 and mid-2005, more than 6,100 people were killed by police in 5,500 incidents. Of the nearly 6,000 police officers implicated, only 517 were charged and fewer than 250 were under arrest.

The Commission of Internal Affairs of the National Assembly, the Human Rights Ombudsman and the Public Prosecutor's Office received reports of killings by the police in Guárico, Aragua, Falcón and Carabobo states. The National Assembly expressed its commitment to investigate these allegations. In a report published in July, local human rights organizations warned of a pattern of killings, possible "disappearances" and kidnappings in six states (Anzoategui, Capital District, Falcón, Miranda, Portuguesa and Yaracay).

Victims of human rights violations, and their relatives, were reportedly threatened and intimidated by police.

☐ In January, 16-year-old Rigoberto Barrios died in hospital after being shot eight times by the police in Guanayen town, Aragua State. He was the third member of his family allegedly killed by the police since they reported the killing of Narciso Barrios in December 2003, following an argument with Aragua State police officers. In June an attempt was made on the life of Óscar Barrios. He escaped unharmed. In August, Juan Barrios was threatened by two uniformed police officers. The family was granted police protection in May, following instructions from the Inter-American Court of Human Rights. However, by the end of 2005, none of the police officers implicated in the killings and threats had been prosecuted.

☐ Carmen Alicia Mota de Hernández and her family in Valle de la Pascua town, Guárico State, were reportedly subjected to a campaign of intimidation by police officers after reporting the killing of her husband, Arturo Hernández, in April 2004.

Lack of independence of the judiciary
The failure of the judiciary and the Public Prosecutor's Office to guarantee impartial and effective redress mechanisms for victims of human rights violations undermined their credibility. According to reports, 98 per cent of human rights violations remained unpunished. Only a small proportion of judges and prosecutors were reportedly in permanent employment.

Human rights defenders
Human rights defenders continued to face harassment and intimidation.

There were concerns over the safety of members of the human rights organization COFAVIC (Comité de Familiares de Víctimas de los Sucesos de Febrero-Marzo de 1989), after their police protection was withdrawn in March. The organization had made a public statement which criticized the authorities for not bringing to justice the perpetrators of human rights violations committed during confrontations in 1989 between the opposition, the police and the military. In November 2002, the Inter-American Court of Human Rights had ordered Venezuela to protect members of COFAVIC after they suffered threats and acts of intimidation.

Freedom of expression
Administrative and tax proceedings were allegedly used to restrict freedom of expression. The Office of the Special Rapporteur for Freedom of Expression of the Inter-American Commission on Human Rights expressed concern over the decision of the National Agency for the Administration of Taxes and Customs to impose a fine and order a 24-hour closure of the regional newspaper *El Impulso*, reportedly because it had criticized restrictions on freedom of expression in Venezuela.

Economic, social and cultural rights
In August the UN Committee on the Elimination of Racial Discrimination expressed concern that persistent social and economic inequalities continued to restrict the enjoyment of economic and social rights by Afro-descendants and indigenous peoples. It noted that indigenous lands and resources continued to be threatened by outsiders. The Committee also expressed concern about child labour, child prostitution, and about slavery in illegal gold prospecting sites in the upper Orinoco and Casiquiare and Guainia-Río Negro basins.

VIET NAM

SOCIALIST REPUBLIC OF VIET NAM
Head of state: Tran Duc Luong
Head of government: Phan Van Khai
Death penalty: retentionist
International Criminal Court: not signed
UN Women's Convention: ratified with reservations
Optional Protocol to UN Women's Convention: not signed

Freedom of expression, association and religious practice continued to be restricted by the authorities. Despite sizeable prisoner amnesties, political dissidents remained in prison. The human rights situation in the Central Highlands and limited access to the area continued to cause concern. More than 180 ethnic minority Montagnards continued to be imprisoned throughout 2005 and at least 45 faced unfair trials. At least 65 death sentences and 21 executions were reported.

Background
More than 26,500 people, including eight prisoners of conscience, were released under three large prisoner amnesties marking major national anniversaries. Released political and religious dissidents faced varying degrees of restriction and harassment.

In March the Prime Minister signed a Decree on Public Order tightly restricting public gatherings and specifying the authorization required. In July additional regulations were issued in an attempt to further control access to the Internet. New legislation was adopted by the National Assembly, including a new Civil Code in May and laws on National Security and Prevention and Control of Corruption in November.

In May the US Department of State and Viet Nam came to an agreement on enhancing religious freedom. The first Prime Ministerial visit to the USA since the end of the Viet Nam war in 1975 took place in June.

Viet Nam continued to deny access to independent human rights monitors.

Central Highlands
At least 45 members of Montagnard ethnic minority groups were sentenced to long terms of imprisonment during 2005. They were charged in connection with the 2001 and April 2004 protests about land ownership and religious freedom, and for assisting people to leave for Cambodia. The true figure was believed to be much higher. Despite severe restrictions on freedom of expression and on access to the area, reports of arrests, ill-treatment and forced renunciations of religion continued to emerge. The human rights situation caused more Montagnard people to seek asylum in Cambodia.

A six-month tripartite Memorandum of Understanding (MOU) was signed in January by Viet Nam, Cambodia and the UN High Commissioner for Refugees (UNHCR) aimed at resolving the situation of around 750 Montagnard asylum-seekers in sites in Cambodia (see Cambodia entry). The MOU contained significant gaps that reduced the protection of asylum-seekers returning to Viet Nam. Viet Nam agreed not to punish returnees for illegally leaving the country, but this did not preclude punishment for their religious or political beliefs. UNHCR was allowed several brief monitoring visits to returnees, apparently accompanied by Vietnamese officials.

▭ Y Jim Eban, Y Tuna H'Dok and seven other Montagnards of the Ede ethnic group were sentenced to between eight and 13 years' imprisonment in July for "undermining the national unity policy" by organizing anti-government protests and helping asylum-seekers.

Political imprisonment
Dissidents continued to be held on espionage charges for sharing information and opinions on political reform and human rights via the Internet. Nguyen Vu Binh, Nguyen Khac Toan and Dr Pham Hong Son, arrested in 2002 and sentenced to between five and 12 years' imprisonment, remained in prison at the end of 2005. Dr Pham Hong Son suffered serious health problems for which he did not receive appropriate medical treatment.

▭ Prisoner of conscience Nguyen Dinh Huy, 73, a former English and history professor, was released under the prisoner amnesty to mark Lunar New Year in February. He was arrested in November 1993 and sentenced to 15 years' imprisonment for planning an international conference on democracy and human rights. He had previously spent 17 years in prison without charge or trial for "re-education".

Suppression of religious freedom
Religious practice remained under the strict control of the authorities, despite the release of several religious dissidents and the issuing of instructions intended to facilitate official recognition of churches. Members of churches seen as opposing state policies were harassed, arrested and imprisoned, and church property was destroyed.

The senior leadership of the Unified Buddhist Church of Vietnam (UBCV) remained under house arrest, including 86-year-old Supreme Patriarch Thich Huyen Quang, and his deputy Thich Quang Do. In August, one member of the Hoa Hao Buddhist church burned himself alive in protest at religious persecution, following which at least seven other church members were arrested.

Religious dissidents and prisoners of conscience released during 2005 included UBCV Buddhist monk Thich Thien Mien, detained for 26 years; Father Pham Ngoc Lien (Tri) and Brother Nguyen Thien Phung (Huang), members of the Congregation of the Mother Coredemptrix, detained for 18 years; Catholic priest Father Thadeus Nguyen Van Ly, imprisoned since 2001; and Vietnamese Mennonite Christian Church members, Le Thi Hong Lien and Pastor Nguyen Hong Quang.

▭ Vo Van Thanh Liem, a Hoa Hao Buddhist monk, was arrested in August following harassment by local police authorities of a temple in An Giang province. He was sentenced to seven years' imprisonment for "opposing the public authorities".

Death penalty
Despite previous indications that the number of capital offences would be reduced, the death penalty was retained for 29 crimes, including economic offences. Large numbers of death sentences and executions were reported. According to official media sources, at least 21 people were executed and 65 people including six women were sentenced to death. The true figures were believed to be much higher. Almost all were accused of drug trafficking offences. Statistics on the death penalty remained classified as a "state secret".

In June the Ministry of Justice announced a proposal to change the method of execution from firing squad to lethal injection. By the end of 2005 this had not been implemented.

▭ Duong Quang Tri was sentenced to death by Ho Chi Minh City People's Court in January for tax fraud, allegedly involving up to US$382,000.

▭ In January Tran Van Le, a former narcotics police officer, and 16 others were sentenced to death following a major drug-trafficking trial. The sentences of 16 of the convicted were upheld on appeal in May; one sentence was commuted to life imprisonment.

AI country reports/visits
Reports
- Viet Nam: Freedom for elderly prisoners of conscience (AI Index: ASA 41/003/2005)
- Socialist Republic of Viet Nam: Appeal for Cyber-dissident – Dr Pham Hong Son (AI Index: ASA 41/018/2005)
- Socialist Republic of Viet Nam: Appeal for Cyber-dissident – Nguyen Vu Binh (AI Index: ASA 41/019/2005)
- Socialist Republic of Viet Nam: Appeal for Cyber-dissident – Nguyen Khac Toan (AI Index: ASA 41/020/2005)

YEMEN

REPUBLIC OF YEMEN
Head of state: 'Ali 'Abdullah Saleh
Head of government: 'Abdul Qader Bajammal
Death penalty: retentionist
International Criminal Court: signed
UN Women's Convention: ratified with reservations
Optional Protocol to UN Women's Convention: not signed

Hundreds of people were killed in Sa'da Province amid armed clashes between the security forces and followers of Hussain Badr al-Din al-Huthi, a cleric from the Zaidi community. Police also apparently used excessive force during violent protests in July against fuel price rises. More than 1,000 alleged followers of Hussain Badr al-Din al-Huthi were detained without charge or trial, as were hundreds of people arrested in previous years in the context of the "war on terror". In the rare cases where political prisoners were brought to trial, the proceedings fell far short of international standards. Press freedom was further restricted and journalists were frequently attacked by police and others. The government continued to forcibly return people to countries where they risked serious human rights violations. Dozens of people were reportedly executed and several hundred people remained under sentence of death.

Fuel protests

More than 30 people, including children, were reported to have been killed, and hundreds of others injured when a government decision to double fuel prices resulted in violent protests across the country on 19/20 July. Several soldiers and police were also among those killed. It was reported that protesters used firearms and the military used heavy weaponry, including helicopter fire and tanks.

'War on terror'

At least 200 people continued to be detained without charge or trial throughout 2005 as suspects in the "war on terror". More than 100 others were released after they agreed to engage in religious dialogue with Islamic figures and signed a pledge renouncing "extremist" views. However, dozens of those released were later rearrested after it was reported that some of those freed had gone to Iraq to fight against US-led forces.
◻ At least three Yemeni nationals who were returned to the country from secret, apparently US-run, detention camps abroad continued to be detained unlawfully and without trial apparently at the behest of the US authorities. The Yemeni authorities told AI in October that they had no basis for detaining Muhammad Faraj Ahmed Bashmilah, Salah Nasser Salim 'Ali and Mohammed Abdullah Salah al-Assad, following their return to Yemen in May 2005, but had been

requested to do so by the US authorities. Two other men, Walid Muhammad Shahir Muhammad al-Qadasi and Karama Khamis Khamisan, were returned to Yemen in April 2004 and August 2005 respectively. By the end of the year, the former was detained without charge or trial and the latter was standing trial on drug charges.
◻ In March, six Yemeni nationals accused of being al-Qa'ida members were sentenced to two years' imprisonment for forging travel documents. Five others were acquitted. All 11 were acquitted of another charge of establishing an armed group to carry out attacks in Yemen. Six of the defendants had been forcibly returned to Yemen from Saudi Arabia.
◻ In May, two suspected al-Qa'ida members, both Yemeni nationals who had been forcibly returned from Qatar, were reportedly convicted of forging documents. Al-Khadar Salam Abdullah al-Hatami was sentenced to three years and four months in prison. Abdullah Ahmed Saleh al-Raimi received a four-year sentence and lodged an appeal.

The Sana'a Committee

The Sana'a Committee, established in 2004 by Yemeni human rights defenders, AI activists, lawyers and others, met for a second time in June. The Committee widened its mandate to provide legal and other assistance to detainees' families and called on governments in the Gulf region to ensure that people detained in the context of the "war on terror" were treated humanely and in accordance with international human rights standards.

Unrest in Sa'da Province

Hundreds of people were reportedly killed in Sa'da Province where there were armed clashes between government security forces and followers of cleric Hussain Badr al-Din al-Huthi. Intense fighting broke out in the area in late March after the authorities launched a search for followers of the cleric, who was killed in September 2004. The area was closed to journalists and human rights activists on grounds of security. Some 400 people were reported to have been killed in a two-week period, many allegedly as a result of excessive use of force by government troops. Hundreds of local men were rounded up and detained. The government also closed hundreds of religious schools within the Zaidi community and in October ordered the closure of 1,400 charities which it said were contravening the law.

Arrests and trial of members of the Zaidi community

More than 1,000 followers of Zaidi cleric Hussain Badr al-Din al-Huthi were reported to have been detained. The crackdown was prompted by their continued chanting of anti-US and anti-Israeli slogans after Friday prayers.
In May, dozens of Zaidis, including children, were arrested. At the end of the year most remained in incommunicado detention without charge or trial and were at risk of torture and ill-treatment.
◻ Fourteen-year-old Ibrahim al-Saiani was detained in May. He was reportedly arrested after the security

forces stormed his family home in the capital, Sana'a. He remained in detention at the end of the year, reportedly in the Political Security prison in Sana'a. There were fears that he was at risk of torture and ill-treatment. According to reports, he sustained serious injuries in the clashes in Sa'da: his right arm was amputated, a piece of shrapnel was lodged in his skull and his right leg was injured. It was unclear whether he was receiving adequate medical treatment.

On 25 September, the President announced a pardon for followers of Hussain al-Huthi. However, it was not clear who was covered by the pardon and most of those held reportedly remained in detention.

▭ In August the trial began of 36 members of the Zaidi community, eight of them in absentia. They were accused of plotting to kill the President and senior army officers. The trial was adjourned after it was disrupted by defendants shouting verses from the Qur'an and political slogans. A subsequent hearing in November was also adjourned to seek clarification whether the suspects were covered by the presidential pardon.

▭ Zaidi cleric Yahia al-Dailami was sentenced to death on 29 May after an unfair trial. Another Zaidi cleric, Mohammed Muftah, who was also tried with Yahia al-Dailami, was sentenced to eight years' imprisonment. The prosecution lodged an appeal against the sentence and called for the death penalty to be imposed. On 3 December the Court of Appeal upheld the sentences. The two men were charged with vaguely worded offences including "communicating with Iran" and "supporting Hussain Badr al-Din al-Huthi". Both were prisoners of conscience.

▭ In June, the Special Criminal Court for terrorism in Sana'a reduced Judge Muhammad Ali Luqman's sentence from 10 to five years' imprisonment. His sentence was reduced on the grounds that there was insufficient evidence in relation to one of the charges. He had been arrested for his alleged support for Hussain al-Huthi and reportedly charged with "sedition, fanning sectarian discord and forming an armed gang".

Restrictions on media freedom

Media freedom was restricted and journalists who criticized the government were harassed, attacked and had their property confiscated. In May, the authorities introduced a draft press law which was strongly criticized by journalists as posing an even greater threat to press freedom than the existing Press and Publication Law (1990). New offences would include "criticizing heads of state" and some, such as "communicating classified information or documentation to foreign bodies", would be punishable by death.

Journalists attempting to report on the July fuel protests were arrested and attacked by police and security forces. Several were banned from covering the protests or had their equipment confiscated.

▭ Abdul Karim al-Khaiwani, chief editor of the opposition publication *al-Shura*, was released on 23 March following a presidential pardon. A prisoner of conscience, he had been sentenced to one year's imprisonment in September 2004 for his alleged support for Hussain al-Huthi. During his appeal hearing in March, defence lawyers Mohammed Naji Allow and Jamal al-Ju'bi, as well as the Secretary General of the Union of Journalists, Hafez al-Bukari, were badly beaten by the security forces. Other people attending the hearing were also allegedly beaten when they tried to leave the courtroom in protest.

▭ Jamal Amer, chief editor of the independent *al-Wassat* newspaper, was reportedly abducted outside his home on 23 August, taken to an unknown destination and beaten and threatened with death. Shortly before, his newspaper had accused government officials of corruption. A day later the office of Ahmed al-Hajj, an *Associated Press* journalist, was reportedly raided by the security forces, who confiscated files and two computers.

Women's rights

Women's organizations continued to campaign against discrimination and violence against women. Women's rights activists called on the government to reserve at least 30 per cent of parliamentary seats for women. In September the National Women's Committee announced that it would establish a coordination council to press political parties to support women in forthcoming presidential and local elections.

On 8 March, International Women's Day, a group of women journalists established a new organization, Women Journalists Without Borders, to promote human rights, including women's rights, across the Middle East, but the government revoked its licence after members of the organization reported on the July fuel protests.

In December a conference on the rights of Arab women was held in Sana'a, continuing the work of a similar conference in 2004.

Forcible returns

The Yemeni authorities forcibly returned at least 25 people to countries where they would be at risk of torture and other human rights violations, in contravention of international human rights standards.

▭ Twenty-five Saudi Arabian nationals considered to be suspects in the "war on terror" were reportedly returned involuntarily to Saudi Arabia on 28 March. In previous months, Saudi Arabia had returned at least 27 unnamed Yemenis to Yemen. Their fate was not known at the end of the year.

▭ Abdul Rahman Ameur and Kamal Berkane, both Algerian nationals, were believed to have been deported in May. They had completed prison sentences in Yemen in December 2003. Their whereabouts remained unknown at the end of the year and it was feared that they had "disappeared".

Death penalty

Death sentences continued to be passed and dozens of people were reportedly executed. Hundreds of people were believed to remain under sentence of death.

▭ Fuad 'Ali Mohsen al-Shahari, whose death sentence was ratified by President Saleh on 6 September, was executed on 29 November. He had been on death row for more than nine years. He had been sentenced to death for murder in 1996 at the end of a grossly unfair trial that may have been politically motivated or influenced by tribal factors.

◻ Fatima Hussein al-Badi, who was sentenced to death in February 2001 for the murder of her husband, was at risk of imminent execution. Her brother, who was sentenced at the same time, was executed in May.

◻ In February the Appeal Court upheld the death sentence on Hizam Saleh Mejalli, who was convicted of the 2002 bombing of the French oil tanker *Limburg* and other attacks. It also imposed a death sentence on Fawaz Yahya al-Rabi'ee who had previously been sentenced to 10 years in prison.

◻ Hafez Ibrahim's death sentence for a murder committed when he was 16, was stayed in April.

◻ Amina Ali Abdulatif's execution, scheduled for 2 May, was stayed to allow a review of her case. She was sentenced to death at 16 for the murder of her husband. The Attorney General reportedly appointed a special committee to review her case and confirm whether she was under 18 at the time of the crime.

Refugees

Around 80,000 refugees registered with UN High Commissioner for Refugees, including more than 68,000 refugees from Somalia, were living in Yemen. Around 7,000 were housed in Al-Kharaz refugee camp.

Throughout the year, hundreds of refugees drowned off the coast of Yemen either because they were forced to jump from smugglers' boats or because the boats became unseaworthy.

Refugees in Yemen faced poor economic conditions and a lack of work opportunities. There were reports of rapes of refugee women; the justice system failed to ensure that survivors had access to justice.

Oromo refugees from Ethiopia repeatedly complained of harassment by the Yemeni authorities, including arbitrary arrests.

AI country reports/ visits
Reports
- USA/Jordan/Yemen: Torture and secret detention — Testimony of the "disappeared" in the "war on terror" (AI Index: AMR 51/108/2005)
- USA/Yemen: Secret Detention in CIA "Black Sites" (AI Index: AMR 51/177/2005)
Visits
AI delegates visited Yemen in June to attend the Sana'a Committee meeting, and in September/October.

ZAMBIA

REPUBLIC OF ZAMBIA
Head of state and government: Levy Mwanawasa
Death penalty: retentionist
International Criminal Court: ratified
UN Women's Convention: ratified
Optional Protocol to UN Women's Convention: not signed

Human rights violations by the police remained common. Independent journalists were harassed and arrested. Opposition politicians were detained. No death sentences were carried out. In November, President Mwanawasa commuted 12 death sentences to life imprisonment.

Background

The Constitutional Review Commission reported in June. If implemented, its recommendations would strengthen freedom of expression by empowering parliament, reducing presidential powers, and introducing a Bill of Rights. Its recommendation that the new Constitution be adopted by a Constituent Assembly — a demand of civil society organizations — was rejected by President Mwanawasa. The President also opposed popular demands that the new Constitution be implemented before elections due in December 2006. Peaceful nationwide demonstrations over these demands took place in November.

In February, the Supreme Court dismissed a case brought by opposition politicians challenging the results of the 2001 elections.

A corruption case against former President Frederick Chiluba dragged on without resolution. In September, agreement was reached for a UK court to sit in Lusaka to hear charges against the former President. This was seen as a de facto recognition of the Zambian legal system's failure to deliver prompt and effective justice.

Legislation was tabled to create 60 paralegal posts across the country, which would strengthen popular access to legal advice. The Legal Aid Board had been effectively inoperative since its establishment in 2000 due to a lack of funds.

Threats to freedom of expression

Opposition party officials were arrested and denied equal access to state-controlled media. Independent journalists were harassed and arrested.

◻ On 24 July, opposition leader Michael Sata was arrested and charged with sedition and espionage after supporting striking mineworkers. The Minister of Mines stated publicly that Michael Sata was a "terrorist" who sought to make Zambia ungovernable. Michael Sata was released on 8 August. By the end of the year he had not been tried. The Chief of Police, Inspector General Zunga Siakalima, was dismissed by the President for initially refusing to arrest Michael Sata.

◻ In June Fred M'membe, editor of the independent newspaper *The Post*, was questioned by police about a series of editorials critical of the President which appeared in *The Post*. In November Fred M'membe was arrested for allegedly defaming the President, the charge relating to another editorial in the newspaper. He was released on bail after a few hours in custody. The case remained pending at the end of the year.

Violence against women

Sexual violence against women continued to be a major cause of HIV/AIDS. Widespread poverty continued to force many women into economically dependent sexual relations. The belief that HIV can be cured by sex with a virgin persisted, contributing to a high incidence of rape of girls.

In January, President Mwanawasa declared that new legislation would incorporate the UN Convention on the Elimination of All Forms of Discrimination against Women into Zambian law. However, no such legislation had been introduced by the end of 2005.

A Bill to amend the Penal Code, including by widening the scope of what the law considers a sexual offence and increasing the severity of punishments for sexual offences, received its second reading in December.

Abuses by police

Torture of suspects in police custody and excessive use of force by police continued. Low-paid police officers regularly detained people in order to recover debts owed by them to third parties.

▭ In June, police in Livingstone beat Catherine Mubiana for refusing to reveal the whereabouts of her brother. No one was charged or disciplined in connection with the assault.

▭ In September, Kennedy Zulu died in police custody in Lusaka after he was arrested in connection with a theft at his workplace. Relatives believed that police were paid by his employer to torture him so he would reveal the whereabouts of the stolen goods. A post mortem established that death was a consequence of injuries sustained during a beating with a blunt object. Police promised an inquest into the death, but this had not happened by the end of the year.

ZIMBABWE

REPUBLIC OF ZIMBABWE
Head of state and government: Robert Mugabe
Death penalty: retentionist
International Criminal Court: signed
UN Women's Convention: ratified
Optional Protocol to UN Women's Convention: not signed

The government engaged in widespread and systematic violations of the rights to shelter, food, freedom of movement and residence, and the protection of the law. Hundreds of thousands of people were forcibly evicted during winter and their homes demolished as part of Operation Murambatsvina (Restore Order). Tens of thousands of informal traders and vendors lost their livelihoods and their ability to support their families as part of the operation. Despite overwhelming evidence of humanitarian need the government repeatedly obstructed the humanitarian efforts of the UN and civil society groups. The police continued to operate in a politically biased manner and police officers were implicated in numerous human rights violations, including arbitrary arrest and detention, assault, ill-treatment of detainees and excessive use of force. Freedom of expression, association and assembly continued to be severely curtailed. Hundreds of people were arrested for holding meetings or participating in peaceful protests.

Background

In parliamentary elections held on 31 March, President Mugabe's Zimbabwe African National Union-Patriotic Front (ZANU-PF) party won 78 out of 120 contested seats. This gave ZANU-PF an effective two-thirds majority in parliament, where a further 30 seats go to people who are not elected, including traditional leaders sympathetic to ZANU-PF and direct Presidential appointees. There were fewer reports of politically motivated violence surrounding the elections than in previous elections. However, AI was concerned by the levels of non-violent intimidation and harassment, systematic repression of the rights to freedom of expression, association and assembly, and the manipulation of food distribution by the government-controlled Grain Marketing Board that took place before, during and after the parliamentary elections. Supporters of the main opposition party, the Movement for Democratic Change (MDC), suffered acts of reprisal following the March elections, including assault and destruction of property.

Voter turn-out for Senate elections in November was extremely low, reported to be less than 20 per cent of eligible voters. The MDC was split over a decision by its leader, Morgan Tsvangirai, not to contest the Senate elections and some MDC candidates stood for election. ZANU-PF won the majority of the seats.

A report by the African Commission on Human and Peoples' Rights (ACHPR) of a fact-finding mission to Zimbabwe in 2002, which was officially made public in February 2005, concluded that human rights violations had occurred in Zimbabwe. The ACHPR made several recommendations, but by the end of the year almost nothing had been done to implement them. Government ministers and officials made disparaging comments about the report and the ACHPR. In December the ACHPR adopted a resolution on Zimbabwe for the first time, condemning human rights violations and calling on the government to implement ACHPR and UN recommendations including an end to forced evictions and respect for freedoms of expression, association and assembly and the principle of separation of powers.

Despite a poor harvest, the government again decided not to appeal for food aid. Supplies of maize via the government's Grain Marketing Board were extremely erratic, particularly towards the end of the year, and many areas were without maize for long periods. World Food Programme reports repeatedly highlighted serious food insecurity in many areas, with incidence of hunger increasing towards the end of the year as Zimbabwe entered the traditional "hungry season".

Mass forced evictions and demolitions

In May the government embarked on Operation Murambatsvina, a programme of mass forced evictions and demolition of homes and informal businesses. The operation, which was carried out against a backdrop of severe food shortages, targeted poor urban and surrounding (peri-urban) areas nationwide. The evictions and demolitions were carried out without adequate notice, court orders, due process, legal protection, redress or appropriate relocation measures, in violation of Zimbabwe's obligations under international human rights law. During the operation police used excessive force: property was destroyed and people were beaten.

In June the UN Secretary-General appointed Anna Tibaijuka as Special Envoy on Human Settlement Issues in Zimbabwe to examine the impact of Operation Murambatsvina. In a report released on 22 July, she estimated that some 700,000 people had lost their homes, their livelihoods or both between May and July and that at least 2 million more people were indirectly affected by the operation. She stated that Operation Murambatsvina "was carried out in an indiscriminate and unjustified manner, with indifference to human suffering, and, in repeated cases, with disregard to several provisions of national and international legal frameworks".

The police, who carried out most of the evictions, and the government stated publicly that those evicted should "return to their rural areas". This was despite widely acknowledged food shortages and hunger in the rural areas. Moreover, many people evicted during Operation Murambatsvina had fled these areas because of political violence in previous years. People were forcibly put on police and government trucks and taken to rural areas. In numerous cases the authorities simply abandoned groups of people at rural bus stops or local authority offices, without access to shelter, food, water or sanitation.

On 28 June heavily armed police arrived at Porta Farm, an informal settlement of approximately 10,000 people established in 1991 on the outskirts of Harare, and began demolishing homes. The police were acting in defiance of two court orders prohibiting evictions from Porta Farm unless alternative accommodation was provided for the community. The police reportedly told residents that they were not going to obey the court orders as they were acting on orders "from above". Demolitions continued throughout the day and on 29 and 30 June police forcibly removed people by truck. Local human rights monitors reported that during the chaos several people were injured. At least three people reportedly died on 30 June. The deaths were raised with the authorities by the UN and civic groups, but no investigation had taken place by the end of the year. Some of those forcibly removed from Porta Farm were abandoned outside Harare, apparently left to make their own way to a rural village where they might be received by relatives. Others were taken to Caledonia Farm Transit Camp, established by the government to temporarily accommodate victims of the mass evictions. Conditions at Caledonia Camp were extremely poor.

In July the government launched Operation Garikai/Hlalani Kuhle (Reconstruction), under which it was implied that thousands of new homes would be built to address the needs of those made homeless by Operation Murambatsvina. However, no proper plans were made public and, although the government stated that 3 trillion Zimbabwe dollars had been allocated to the operation, it did not appear in the national budget. Given the grave economic crisis affecting Zimbabwe, there was widespread scepticism about the operation. By the end of the year the state and independent media as well as non-governmental organizations (NGOs) were reporting that the rebuilding operation was significantly behind schedule. Many of those houses designated as "built" remained incomplete, without access to services such as water and sanitation, and appeared to be uninhabited. The criteria used for allocating new houses were unclear, but appeared to include proof of employment or income, effectively excluding the majority of Operation Murambatsvina victims. Reports in the media, as well as from NGOs, stated that some of the new houses were allocated to civil servants and government officials, and there were several reports of corruption in relation to the operation.

While the majority of the evictions and demolitions took place between May and July, the government continued to evict people during the remainder of the year. In several cases, families endured repeated evictions as the government sought to drive people back to the rural areas.

Humanitarian crisis

Operation Murambatsvina resulted in enormous internal displacement of people. The UN described the aftermath as a "humanitarian crisis of immense proportions". Although the UN Special Envoy recommended that there should be full and unfettered access to humanitarian assistance for the victims of the forced evictions and house demolitions, the Zimbabwean authorities repeatedly obstructed and curtailed the humanitarian operations of the UN and civil society groups.

Humanitarian groups reported that in some cases negotiations with the authorities enabled them to supply food, water and other relief items to internally displaced people, but that their access was constrained and subject to arbitrary changes by the authorities, and they were generally prevented from providing temporary shelter, particularly tents, to those living in the open. Many humanitarian actors maintained that this was because the government thought tents were too visible a sign of the humanitarian crisis created by Operation Murambatsvina.

On 20 July the police conducted a series of night-time raids on churches in Bulawayo sheltering more than 1,000 of the most vulnerable victims of forced evictions, including elderly and ill people, and children. According to witnesses, the police arrived after midnight wearing riot gear and forced their way into the churches. Sleeping people were poked with batons and kicked to wake them up. They were forced onto trucks and transported to a transit camp outside Bulawayo. Within days the transit camp was closed and people were again forced to board trucks, in most cases at night, and were transported to various rural areas where they were left without shelter, food, water or sanitation. Following the raids the churches were told that they could no longer provide shelter to those made homeless as a result of Operation Murambatsvina. Police subsequently checked to make sure the churches were complying with this directive.

At the end of July more than 1,000 people – many from Porta Farm – were taken by police and government agencies to Hopley Farm, where they were left on open land with no shelter, no access to sanitation and insufficient food and clean water. The government did not provide humanitarian assistance, nor did it inform the humanitarian community that people were stranded there. On the contrary, when the plight of those at Hopley Farm began to be known in Harare, organizations that went to the camp to help were turned away by police. Some humanitarian access to Hopley Farm was subsequently negotiated by the UN and civic groups, but at the end of the year living conditions at Hopley Farm remained extremely poor.

On 31 October the UN Secretary-General expressed great concern about the humanitarian situation in Zimbabwe and the failure of the government to ensure proper humanitarian assistance for those in need. In November the government agreed to allow the UN to provide shelters, but continued to refuse the UN permission to use tents to provide immediate shelter for the homeless. By the end of the year the UN shelter programme had not been implemented and its future was unclear after the Minister for Local Government, Public Works and National Housing reportedly rejected

as sub-standard a model structure prepared by the UN in collaboration with government technicians. Meanwhile, thousands of people, including children, the ill, the elderly and other vulnerable people, continued to live without shelter and in conditions of extreme hardship. Overall, humanitarian access remained highly constrained.

Freedom of association and assembly curtailed

The Public Order and Security Act (POSA) and the Miscellaneous Offences Act continued to be used selectively to prevent the political opposition and civil society groups from meeting or engaging in peaceful protest. Hundreds of human rights activists and opposition supporters were arrested or detained under these laws during the year. Dozens of people were assaulted during arrest or while in police custody. Police repeatedly obstructed or denied detainees' access to lawyers, food and medical care.

On the evening of 31 March, the day of the parliamentary elections, police arrested approximately 260 women, some carrying babies, when the activist group Women of Zimbabwe Arise (WOZA) attempted to hold a peaceful post-election prayer vigil at Africa Unity Square in Harare. During and after the arrests, several of the women were beaten. Some were forced to lie on the ground and were beaten on the buttocks by police. Several were seriously injured and needed hospital treatment. None was given access to adequate medical treatment during their detention. The women and children were detained overnight in an open-air courtyard at Harare Central police station under armed guard. They were initially denied access to lawyers. Police reportedly told the women that they could pay a fine and be released if they pleaded guilty to minor offences under the Miscellaneous Offences Act; otherwise they would remain in detention over the weekend to face charges under the POSA. The women – several of whom were elderly, injured or with their children – decided to pay fines, fearing further abuses in detention.

On 8 November more than 100 people were arrested in Harare when the Zimbabwe Congress of Trade Unions tried to hold a peaceful demonstration protesting against the grave economic situation in Zimbabwe. Lawyers were initially denied access to the detainees, who were moved by police from one police station to another in an apparent attempt to prevent access to lawyers. Neither the detainees nor their lawyers were informed of the charges against them until the second day of their detention, when police said they would be charged under the POSA. However, the Attorney General refused to prosecute and all the detainees were released on 11 November.

Repressive laws including the Access to Information and Protection of Privacy Act and the Broadcasting Services Act were used to curtail freedom of expression.

On 15 December armed police in Harare raided *Voice of the People*, an independent radio station that broadcast from outside Zimbabwe but maintained offices in the country. Three staff members were detained. Police initially told lawyers that the three would be held until *Voice of the People* executive director John Masuku presented himself at the police station, and then said they would be charged under the Broadcasting Services Act. However, the Attorney General refused to prosecute, reportedly on grounds that there was no evidence of any offence. The three were released on 19 December. The same day John Masuku and *Voice of the People* board chairman David Masunda presented themselves at Harare Central police station and were detained. David Masunda was released later that day. John Masuku was held until 23 December and was charged under the Broadcasting Services Act with illegal possession and use of broadcasting equipment.

Human rights defenders under threat
Legislation passed by parliament in December 2004 governing the operation of NGOs, which was strongly criticized for targeting human rights groups, was not signed into law by the President. However, the government continued to use the Private Voluntary Organisations Act to intimidate and harass NGOs. Following the March elections, the government used provisions in the Act to investigate numerous NGOs. Investigation teams made unannounced visits to NGOs, and demanded to see documents relating to activities and funding. The investigation process was reported to be intimidating and intrusive.

The ever-present threat of closure created a climate of fear and compromised the effectiveness of many NGOs. Human rights activists continued to face harassment, arbitrary arrest and detention and assault, most frequently at the hands of the police.

Repressive legislation
On 30 August parliament passed the Constitution of Zimbabwe Amendment Act (No.17), which was subsequently signed into law by the President. The Act violated internationally recognized rights, including the right to equal protection of the law and the right to freedom of movement. Clause 2 of the Act removed the power of courts to hear any challenge or appeal against the acquisition by the state of agricultural land under Section 16 of the Constitution. Land owners and anyone with an interest or right in agricultural land so acquired can no longer challenge the lawfulness of the acquisition. Clause 3 of the Act extended the grounds under which it is possible to limit the right to freedom of movement enshrined in Section 22 of the Constitution. Freedom of movement can now be limited in "the public interest" and in "the economic interests of the State". Moreover, the Constitutional Amendment Act restricts the right to leave Zimbabwe. The new limitations on the right to freedom of movement breach international human rights standards.

In December the authorities seized the passports of Trevor Ncube, publisher of independent newspapers *The Standard* and the *Zimbabwe Independent*, opposition politician Paul Themba Nyathi and trade unionist Raymond Majongwe. The passports of Trevor Ncube and Paul Themba Nyathi were returned and the High Court subsequently ruled that the passport seizures were illegal. However, by the end of the year the passport of Raymond Majongwe had not been returned.

Update: Roy Bennett
Former opposition member of parliament (MP) Roy Bennett was released from prison on 28 June, having served eight months of an effective one-year prison sentence. It remained standard policy to commute a third of any sentence for good behaviour. Roy Bennett had been convicted of assaulting the Minister for Justice, Legal and Parliamentary Affairs during a heated exchange in parliament on 18 May. He was convicted by a parliamentary committee acting under the Privileges, Immunities and Powers of Parliament Act. The procedure was politically biased and failed to meet international standards for fair trial, including the requirement that a punishment be proportionate to the gravity of an offence. Roy Bennett was also denied the right of appeal. During his detention Roy Bennett suffered humiliating and degrading treatment.

AI country reports/ visits
Reports and other material
- Zimbabwe: Human rights defenders under siege (AI Index: AFR 46/001/2005)
- Zimbabwe: An assessment of human rights violations in the run-up to the March 2005 parliamentary elections (AI Index: AFR 46/003/2005)
- Zimbabwe: Unprecedented call for UN and AU action over evictions by 200 rights groups (AI Index: AFR 46/017/2005)
- Zimbabwe: Secret footage reveals desperate plight of homeless (AI Index: AFR 46/026/2005)
- Zimbabwe: A Joint Appeal to African Leaders to address the human rights situation in Zimbabwe (AI Index: AFR 46/030/2005)

Visits
Amnesty International delegates visited Zimbabwe in February, July/August and December.

AI Report 2006

PART 3

WHAT DOES AI DO?

Amnesty International (AI) mobilizes volunteer activists – people who give freely of their time and energy in solidarity with the victims of human rights abuses. At the latest count there were more than 1.8 million AI members and supporters in over 150 countries and territories in every region of the world. AI is funded largely by its worldwide membership and public donations.

AI members are women, men and children who come from many different backgrounds and hold widely different beliefs, but who are united by a determination to work for a world where everyone enjoys all human rights. Some members are organized in groups in local communities, schools and colleges. Others participate in networks focused on particular countries, issues or campaigning activities.

AI's Urgent Action network consists of thousands of AI members around the world who take immediate action in response to threats of execution, killing, torture or ill-treatment. Prisoners, human rights defenders and others at risk have testified to the impact of one of AI's most effective and enduring action techniques, which contributes to some improvement in nearly half of its appeal cases.

Through a range of campaigning methods, varying from country to country, AI members take up human rights issues with governments and businesses, sending appeals, collecting signatures for petitions, and making their voices heard in protests against abuses in their own and other countries. They raise general awareness about human rights by giving platforms to human rights defenders from around the world; organizing musical and other artistic events; providing education activities in schools and local communities; and offering human rights training for criminal justice professionals.

"We slept eight at a time as the cell was so cramped. As soon as the Urgent Actions began to arrive the authorities immediately offered to transfer me to a cell where I would be held alone."
Student leader Gagan Thapa chose not to receive preferential treatment, in protest at the detention of 16 detainees in a single police cell in Kathmandu, Nepal, in July. First arrested in April, he was released in May by order of the Supreme Court but was immediately redetained, then released again after another Supreme Court intervention. He was arrested in July, accused of shouting anti-monarchist slogans at a demonstration, and in August charged with sedition. He was released on bail to await trial before a special court.

Campaigning in 2005

In 2005, AI campaigns aimed in particular to stop violence against women, control the arms trade, and eradicate torture in the "war on terror".

At the World Social Forum in Brazil in January, AI activists joined non-governmental organizations and grassroots groups calling for a better world. The Forum tackled a range of issues, including social struggle and democratic alternatives, demilitarization, economic independence, and human rights and dignity. AI delegates cooperated with other activist and campaigning groups at the Forum in organizing seminars on women human rights defenders and on

Young letter-writers in Australia show replies from the children of Papua independence activist Amelia Yiggibalom, imprisoned in Indonesia and in August 2005 transferred to house arrest. AI involves children in adapted Urgent Actions or in sending postcard messages of support to prisoners of conscience, human rights defenders and their families.

PERSON TO PERSON

AI campaigns constantly confront new challenges and adapt to a changing world and developing concerns. However, AI members remain loyal to their commitment to work with and for individuals at risk of human rights abuse, and to exposing the impact of human rights abuses. The testimonies of individuals bear powerful witness to violations in countries worldwide. More than any statistics, the accounts of men, women and children who have experienced the horror of killings, torture or armed conflict can move and motivate other individuals to offer support and solidarity. By seeking to right the wrongs done to individuals, AI ensures that the personal remains at the heart of its campaigning.

CRUEL. INHUMAN. DEGRADES US ALL.
Torture and other ill-treatment are prohibited under customary international law, which applies to all states and permits no exceptions, including in times of war or public emergency. Now that consensus is under threat. The US government has argued that people rounded up in the "war on terror" can be denied the protection of that law.

With the collusion of other states, the USA has snatched people from other parts of the world, held them in secret, unlawfully transferred them between countries ("renditions"), and subjected them to torture and ill-treatment. Senior US officials have authorized the use of interrogation techniques that are cruel, inhuman or degrading and can amount to torture.

AI has campaigned for the US and other governments to *stop* torture and other ill-treatment, to close Guantánamo Bay and open all other "war on terror" detention sites to international and independent scrutiny, and to end the unlawful transfer of detainees across borders. AI also called for the *investigation* of US detention and interrogation practices throughout the world, and the *prosecution* of those responsible for torture and other ill-treatment, wherever it has occurred.

In the "war on terror", torture has gained a new acceptability in US government circles. The UK government has colluded in attacking human rights, the rule of law and the independence of the judiciary. Action appeals and more information can be found on line at www.amnesty.org/torture

corporate abuses, and encouraged people to sign up to the Control Arms campaign.

AI campaigning remained firmly rooted in the power of individuals working in support of other individuals. AI sections and members in 35 countries celebrated International Human Rights Day on 10 December by sending over 80,000 letters in a Global Letter-Writing Marathon, an annual event started by AI Poland in 2001. Once a year, AI supporters get together to write letters, e-mails and faxes to governments. They call for death sentences to be commuted, torture to be halted, prisoners of conscience to be released and other individuals to be protected from a range of human rights violations. Some people join the marathon for just a few minutes. Others keep going for the full 24 hours. More and more sections have found the marathon effective in attracting new supporters.

In December, AI launched its Make Some Noise campaign, a mix of music, celebration and action in support of AI's work. Thanks to an extraordinary gift from Yoko Ono – the recording rights to "Imagine" and John Lennon's entire solo songbook – AI was able to harness the power of music to inspire a new generation to stand up for human rights. Classic tracks about injustice, poverty and war, as relevant today as when they were first written, were recorded in new interpretations by international music artists for downloading exclusively for one year at www.amnesty.org/noise. In 2005, Make Some Noise campaigned for tighter controls on the weapons trade.

Whatever the particular focus, the activities of AI's members, supporters and staff aim to support the victims of human rights abuses and people working on their behalf, and to influence those who have the power to make a difference.

Torture and the 'war on terror'

As the international ban on torture and other cruel, inhuman or degrading treatment was flouted and challenged by the US and other governments, AI contested the arguments of those who sought to justify brutal and long-outlawed methods of interrogation in the particular circumstances of the "war on terror". AI's report *Cruel. Inhuman. Degrades us all – Stop torture and ill-treatment in the "war on terror"* (AI Index: ACT 40/010/2005) challenged states that claimed no longer to be bound by previously agreed human rights standards in the face of terrorist threats. Governments around the world agreed many years ago that torture and other ill-treatment are always wrong, and wrote into international law that there is never any circumstance that justified their use.

Yet over a year after the scandal of torture in Abu Ghraib prison in Iraq was exposed, the conditions remained in place for such treatment to occur at US

"What we are doing is too tough without the cooperation of Amnesty International",
Bangladeshi journalist and human rights defender Sumi Khan told AI activists in March. She was beaten unconscious and stabbed in the face and hands after exposing corruption and abuses such as child-trafficking.

"I would like to send a huge thank you to all Amnesty International members across the world, whose support I could feel."

Professor Yury Bandazhevsky, a prisoner of conscience for four years in Belarus, had been convicted on trumped-up charges because of his vocal criticism of the authorities' response to the Chernobyl nuclear disaster. He was conditionally released from an eight-year sentence in August.

detention facilities in Afghanistan, Iraq, Guantánamo Bay and beyond. Over a year after the US Supreme Court ruled that US courts had the jurisdiction to consider appeals from detainees in Guantánamo Bay, the US administration had ensured that not a single detention was judicially reviewed.

A gathering of former "war on terror" detainees was held in November in London, UK, by AI and the UK-based non-governmental organization Reprieve, as part of AI's campaign against torture and other ill-treatment committed in the name of security. The accounts of former detainees and their families confirmed growing numbers of reports that detainees were being held illegally, secretly flown across borders, and tortured and ill-treated at US detention facilities around the world. Former detainees spoke of being shackled in painful stress positions, of their extreme fear and exhaustion, of the lack of medical care, and of beatings and broken bones.

AI's response to the erosion of human rights, the rule of law and the role of the judiciary by the UK government was simple. In a report in November, *United Kingdom: Human rights are not a game* (AI Index: EUR 45/043/2005), AI's message was that respect for human rights is the route to security, not an obstacle to it. AI opposed anti-terrorism measures introduced following the attacks in the USA on 11 September 2001 and the London bombings on 7 July 2005, including a draft Terrorism Bill in 2005 that would extend the maximum period of police detention without charge from 14 to 28 days. AI called on the UK government to live up to its international obligations under human rights law.

Violence against women

In 2005, AI's Stop Violence against Women campaign highlighted the marginalization, prejudice and danger faced by women human rights defenders in the front line.

A conference organized by AI in Bahrain in early 2005 was the first aimed at combating violence and discrimination against women in Bahrain, Kuwait, Oman, Qatar, Saudi Arabia and the United Arab Emirates. Migrant domestic workers in particular are unable to access the protection of the law from violence at the hands of employers. Among those attending the conference were survivors of discrimination and violence, women human rights defenders, lawyers, academics, journalists, religious scholars and government officials.

In 2005 AI highlighted the impact on Palestinian women of the unprecedented levels of poverty, unemployment and health problems in the Occupied Territories caused by decades of Israeli military occupation, compounded by constraints imposed in a traditional patriarchal society. AI called on the Israeli government to end human rights violations in the Occupied Territories, and on the Palestinian Authority to take action to prevent, investigate and punish violence against women.

AI members in Turkey and the Netherlands worked with Turkish municipalities and architects in creating tulip gardens to raise public awareness about violence against women. Women's groups in Turkey use tulips to represent women who have died or suffered as a result of family and community violence. Legal discrimination against women, including the reduction or eradication of sentences of rapists if they married their victims, was removed in a new penal code.

AI called on the Japanese government to accept full responsibility for crimes committed against girls and women condemned to sexual slavery — so-called "comfort women" — in countries occupied by Japan before and during World War II. For over 60 years, the now elderly survivors of an estimated 200,000 victims have been denied justice and adequate reparation from the Japanese government, which only belatedly acknowledged responsibility for the crimes.

AI called on the Russian government to give higher priority to tackling domestic violence, including by publishing statistics on the incidence of violence against women in the home and the prosecution of perpetrators; by special training for police, judges and other professionals; by working with women's groups to counter common perceptions that domestic violence is a private matter; and by systematically setting up shelters and crisis centres to protect victims.

In collaboration with the Control Arms campaign, AI's campaign to Stop Violence against Women

"The whole time on the plane I was thinking: what is the best way to avoid torture, what is the best way to avoid torture?"

The human cost of unlawful transfers across borders was highlighted in 2005 in the public inquiry into Canada's role in the case of Maher Arar, who was only released after a long campaign by his family, AI and other human rights organizations. A Syrian-born Canadian national, he was detained in the USA in 2002 while returning to Canada from a family holiday in Tunisia. He was forcibly sent by the US authorities to Jordan and then on to Syria where he said he was severely beaten and threatened with other forms of torture during interrogation sessions up to 18 hours long. He was detained for almost a year in a tiny, unlit basement cell which he described as "a grave".

WOMEN UNDER FIRE

Every year half a million men, women and children are killed by armed violence – one person a minute. There are an estimated 639 million small arms in the world today. All governments have a responsibility to tighten controls on the arms trade.

Countless women and girls have been shot and killed or injured worldwide. Millions live in fear of armed violence in the home, in the community and in times of war. At the heart of these abuses against women lie the proliferation and misuse of small arms and deep-rooted discrimination against women.

AI members campaigned in support of the individual women and women's human rights organizations around the world that have become powerful forces for peace and human rights in their communities. Their actions show how real change can happen and women's lives can be made safer.

launched a report, *The Impact of Guns on Women's Lives* (AI Index: ACT 30/001/2005), in the USA and South Africa in March. The report showed the ways in which women are subjected to violence because of the growing availability of small arms, in times of peace as well as war. Studies and examples from several countries illustrated that women are more likely to be murdered than other members of households where there are guns.

Control Arms

AI called for tougher arms controls, better implementation of existing gun control laws and action to break the cycles of violence that threaten to brutalize successive generations.

The Million Faces petition, launched by AI and its partner organizations in the Control Arms campaign – Oxfam and the International Action Network on Small Arms – more than met its halfway target in 2005. The action was part of AI's campaign for an international Arms Trade Treaty that would oblige governments not to transfer arms internationally if they are likely to be used to commit serious violations of human rights and war crimes. Over half a million supporters signed up and posted their photos on line. The number of governments pledging support for the Treaty grew five-fold to 50 in 2005. They included the UK, one of the world's largest exporters of weapons. The Treaty, if implemented, would stem the proliferation of arms and save lives.

As civilians' lives were claimed daily in Haiti in political violence between armed groups and gangs, and by unlawful use of force by police, AI urged the international community to ensure adequate funding for the protection of human rights, and in particular for disarmament. A huge quantity of arms and small weapons, in the hands of former rebels and former

AI's repeated appeals for the hundreds of prisoners under sentence of death in the USA can have a powerful effect on those who have to make the decisions. The state governor of Virginia commuted the death sentence on Robin Lovitt to life imprisonment in November after receiving some 1,500 phone calls, letters and e-mails, nearly all of them urging clemency.

soldiers, criminal gangs with and without political affiliation, security guards and civilians, has exacerbated recurring political crises.

AI called on the UN Security Council to strengthen the UN embargo on arms exports to the Democratic Republic of the Congo (DRC) and ensure monitoring of airports in eastern DRC. AI called on the governments of Albania, Bosnia and Herzegovina, Croatia, Czech Republic, Israel, Russia, Serbia and Montenegro, South Africa, the UK and the USA to investigate reports of arms being illegally transferred to the governments of the DRC, Rwanda and Uganda for onward distribution to armed groups in eastern DRC.

The death penalty

The campaign against the death penalty gained strength in the course of 2005. AI members in more than 40 countries participated in the third World Day against the Death Penalty in October, which focused on Africa and which saw demonstrations, petitions, concerts and televised debates to campaign against capital punishment around the world.

In a long-overdue victory for campaigners against the death penalty, the execution of child offenders in the USA was declared unconstitutional by the US Supreme Court in March. The landmark decision by the Court, by five votes to four, followed years of campaigning by AI and other human rights groups to stop the execution of offenders under 18 at the time of the crime. The ruling was given in the case of Christopher Simmons, who was sentenced to death for a murder committed when he was 17 years old. AI joined 16 other Nobel Peace laureates in supplementing the legal appeals before the Court. The brief was cited in the majority opinion. Following the decision, more than 70 child offenders under sentence of death had their sentences commuted.

Progress towards abolition in a number of countries in Europe and Central Asia followed intensified campaigning by AI in recent years. The last provisions for the death penalty were removed from the Constitution in Moldova, and similar constitutional amendments were proposed in Kyrgyzstan. However, despite an announcement in Uzbekistan that the death penalty would be abolished in 2008, executions were reportedly still carried out and death sentences passed after trials that fell far short of international fair trial standards.

"Thank you all for your actions... a victory such as this one... has enormous significance! Now we need to continue, so that we can attain the full legal guarantee of their right to the land."

A human rights defender in Brazil thanked AI after a federal court in August overturned an order evicting 100 Guarani-Kaiowá people from land they had peacefully occupied on the Floresta ranch in the Sombrerito indigenous territory. Cattle ranchers shot one man dead before seeking their removal through the courts. Pictured are Guarani-Kaiowá leaders at a roadside camp by the Passo Piraju indigenous territory in August. They have waited years for preliminary identification studies of their ancestral land. Despite some progress in 2005, the campaign to protect the land rights of indigenous people is a long term and complex process. The Ñanderu Marangatu community was evicted from ancestral land in December despite presidential ratification earlier in 2005.

Economic, social and cultural rights

2005 saw an increase in AI campaigning at a global level for economic, social and cultural rights. The focus was on opposing grave abuses against marginalized people. In *Human rights for human dignity – A primer on economic, social and cultural rights* (AI Index: POL 34/009/2005), AI highlighted the obligations of governments not only within their own countries but also worldwide to take immediate actions to address hunger, homelessness and preventable disease.

AI joined the Centre on Housing Rights and Evictions and Zimbabwe Lawyers for Human Rights to coordinate a global call for the international community, including the UN and African Union, to stand up for human rights and against the mass forced evictions of hundreds of thousands of people in Zimbabwe. Over 200 mostly African human rights non-governmental organizations joined the call. In December the African Commission on Human and Peoples' Rights adopted – for the first time – a resolution condemning the human rights situation in Zimbabwe, including the mass evictions, and calling for humanitarian aid.

In Europe, AI campaigned to eliminate the targeting of minorities for racism, abuse and discrimination.

Together with other national and international human rights groups, AI denounced patterns of forced evictions against Roma, and denial of their right to adequate housing in Bulgaria, Greece, and Serbia and Montenegro (Kosovo). From July, AI campaigned for the relocation of around 530 Roma, Ashkali and Egyptiani internally displaced people in Kosovo, including 138 young children, who were living in camps contaminated by lead from a disused smelting site and at serious risk to their health.

AI continued to urge states to ensure that the poorest people could enjoy physical security and their civil and political freedoms, a necessary precondition for the exercise of economic, social and cultural rights. In *Claiming rights and resources – Injustice, oil and violence in Nigeria* (AI Index: AFR 44/020/2005), AI launched appeals to the government and oil companies aimed at ending killings and attacks on communities that continue 10 years after the executions of Ken Saro-Wiwa and other Ogoni campaigners for economic and social rights.

In Brazil, millions of people living in the poorest communities are caught between powerful criminal gangs, a corrupt and confrontational police force, and

In Nigeria, the ability of the people of the Niger Delta to campaign for their economic and social rights is impeded by threats to their civil and political rights. Pollution of the environment and extreme exploitation continue unchecked, and local communities' demands for their rights are suppressed with armed force.

PRISONERS OF POVERTY

Across the world, millions of women, men and children are denied decent education, housing and health care, and face levels of deprivation which undermine the right to live with dignity. Yet the world's wealth has never been greater. Hunger, homelessness and preventable disease are not inevitable social problems or just the result of natural disasters – they are a human rights scandal.

There are many more prisoners of poverty than prisoners of conscience, and AI has adapted to address the most pressing human rights issues of the day. AI members join local communities and activists worldwide in campaigning for economic, social and cultural rights.

Governments often blame a lack of resources, but even the wealthiest fail to address systematic discrimination, or pollution affecting the health of communities, or to ensure adequate housing or other economic, social and cultural rights. Violations of these rights are the result of policies, negligence, discrimination or ill will.

vigilante "death squads". In 2005, AI campaigning highlighted aggressive police operations in which the inhabitants of *favelas* (shanty towns), branded as criminals, are killed with impunity. In one terrifying attack in March, police officers shot at random at residents of a district of Rio de Janeiro, killing 29 people in a matter of hours. AI called for the government to implement human rights-based policing and ensure the effective protection of all Brazilians.

Human rights defenders
AI works to protect the right to promote and defend human rights, and takes action to ensure human rights defenders are able to carry out their work unimpeded.

As part of AI's work to defend those on the front line in the defence of human rights, AI called on the Chinese authorities to stop the detention and harassment of the Tiananmen Mothers, a group of 130 human rights defenders – mainly women – seeking accountability and redress for the killing of their children and other close relatives during the suppression of peaceful protests around Tiananmen Square in June 1989. They have distributed humanitarian aid to victims' families and helped to set up a fund for the education of the children of those killed or injured during the crackdown.

AI called on the Serbian authorities to stop the campaign of harassment of human rights defenders by individual political leaders, some of whom were members of the government or of allied political parties, and by members of the security forces. Activists, journalists and lawyers were assaulted, burgled and threatened with prosecution, especially around the 10th anniversary in July of the massacre at Srebrenica during the war in Bosnia and Herzegovina. Those under attack were primarily defenders – and in particular women leaders of targeted organizations – whose campaigning exposed

Dr Kamal al-Labwani, a human rights activist and prisoner of conscience in Syria for three years, urged AI to continue working for the release of people imprisoned in Syria simply for **"trying to help people obtain their rights"**. He told AI members in September how important it had been to him to learn that AI was working for his release.

In July AI's campaign to release migrant and refugee children from detention was successful when all children in Australian immigration detention centres were transferred with their families to homes in the community where they were required to live.

"Kids don't belong in detention centres" says the t-shirt of one young campaigner in Australia.

official failures to investigate human rights violations and address impunity for war crimes.

In February, Viet Nam released four prominent and long-standing prisoners of conscience, one of whom had been in prison for 25 years. AI appeals continued, however, for the release of cyber dissidents serving lengthy prison terms after being convicted of espionage for criticizing government policies, circulating petitions and making contact on the Internet with opposition groups in exile.

In Zimbabwe, AI called for an end to state detention, ill-treatment and harassment of human rights defenders and for the repeal of legislation that undermines their work. Human rights organizations work in a climate of fear and with the ever-present threat of closure. AI joined human rights groups in countries including Botswana, Namibia, Nigeria, Senegal, South Africa and Zambia in publicizing the condemnation by the African Commission on Human and Peoples' Rights of human rights violations in Zimbabwe. An awareness-raising tour of Europe by the women's activist group Women of Zimbabwe Arise (WOZA) was hosted by AI sections in October.

Refugees and migrants
Action to defend the rights of refugees, asylum-seekers, internally displaced people and migrants played a large part in the campaigning activities of AI sections and members around the world. AI opposed the return of people to countries where they faced persecution, the death penalty, torture or other ill-treatment, and campaigned for states to uphold their international obligations and respect all rights of displaced people and migrants.

AI members highlighted the cases of four men detained in Kyrgyzstan and at risk of forcible return to neighbouring Uzbekistan. They were among more than 500 people who fled Uzbekistan after the security forces fired on thousands of mainly peaceful demonstrators during protests in Andizhan in May.

Greece was the target of appeals for investigations into overcrowded and insanitary conditions for detained refugees and migrants, where children were held with adults and where some women were allegedly sexually abused.

On World Refugee Day on 20 June, AI drew attention to the plight of asylum-seekers and refugees, in particular those in arbitrary detention in Australia and a number of European countries, including Italy, Spain and the UK.

AI marked International Migrants Day on 18 December with appeals to states to ratify or implement the International Convention on the Protection of the Rights of All Migrant Workers and Members of Their Families, which only 34 states had ratified. An estimated 200 million migrants lived and worked outside their country of origin. They faced a range of human rights abuses, from having their salaries routinely withheld or their identity documents confiscated by their employers, to verbal and physical abuse at the hands of employers or a lack of access to proper housing and health care.

Justice and the rule of law

Threats to the right to justice and to the rule of law remained central to many areas of AI campaigning across a spectrum of countries.

In Colombia, AI called for an effective legal framework for the demobilization of illegal armed groups that fully respected the right of victims to truth, justice and reparation. More than 2,300 killings and "disappearances" were attributed to army-backed paramilitaries, despite their engagement in a demobilization process and their declaration of a unilateral ceasefire in 2002.

AI addressed a range of long-standing abuses by French police – fatal shootings, deaths in custody and torture and ill-treatment – and in the criminal justice system, most of them against foreign nationals or people of foreign origin. Complaints against the police soared in France but officers enjoyed effective impunity.

AI appeals continued for an end to the killings in the internal conflict in Nepal in which more than 12,000 people have died. An escalation in the fighting in 2005 resulted in hundreds more deaths of civilians and widespread detentions, rape and other torture by both government and insurgent forces. Children have been abducted and recruited as child soldiers.

Accountability for war crimes and crimes against humanity in Darfur, Sudan, remained a major focus of AI campaigning in 2005 as government forces, government-aligned militias and armed political groups targeted civilians. AI called for action by the international community to end the rape and abduction of women and girls, and attacks on human rights defenders.

How AI works

AI is a democratic, self-governing movement. Major policy decisions are taken by an International Council made up of representatives from all sections. The Council meets every two years, and has the power to amend the Statute which governs AI's work and methods. (The Statute is available from the International Secretariat or on the AI website, www.amnesty.org.) The Council elects an International Executive Committee of volunteers which carries out its decisions and appoints the movement's Secretary General, who heads the International Secretariat and is the movement's chief spokesperson.

AI's sections and local volunteer groups and networks are primarily responsible for funding the movement through donations from members and the public. No funds are sought or accepted from governments for AI's work investigating and campaigning against human rights violations. Information about AI's finances is published annually in the *Amnesty International Review*.

Information about AI is available from national section offices, on the AI website, and from the International Secretariat, Peter Benenson House, 1 Easton Street, London WC1X 0DW, United Kingdom.

AI's guiding principles

AI is independent of any government, political persuasion or religious creed. AI does not support or oppose the views of the victims whose rights it seeks to protect. It is concerned solely with the impartial protection of human rights.

AI forms a global community of human rights defenders whose principles include international solidarity, effective action for the individual victim, the universality and indivisibility of human rights, impartiality and independence, and democracy and mutual respect.

AI's vision is of a world in which every person enjoys all the human rights enshrined in the Universal Declaration of Human Rights and other international human rights standards. Its ambition is to promote ethical globalization to strengthen the forces of justice – the forces that provide hope for the many

"I spent two years incommunicado and was allowed to leave my cell for 10 minutes in 45 days. Thanks to the many thousands of letters written by AI members, my detention conditions changed. I could see my children once a month and I received medical treatment."

Rebiya Kadeer, released from five and a half years as a prisoner of conscience in China in March. A successful entrepreneur and women's rights advocate before her imprisonment, Rebiya Kadeer vowed to continue campaigning for the rights of the predominantly Muslim Uighur ethnic minority in China. She had been tried and convicted in secret for giving copies of local newspapers to relatives abroad. Following her release, the authorities continued to target her family in an apparent attempt to counter her influence as a Uighur activist overseas.

people worldwide whose rights have been abused.

AI's mission is to undertake research and action focused on preventing and ending grave abuses of the rights to physical and mental integrity, freedom of conscience and expression, and freedom from discrimination, within the context of its work to promote all human rights.

AI's goals

In 2005, AI's work to build a better world was organized around eight global goals.

Reform and strengthen the justice sector

The central importance of the rule of law for any field of human activity is widely recognized across societies and governing systems. Yet many of the domestic institutions which are meant to uphold the rule of law are seriously flawed, resulting in continuing widespread human rights violations, committed with impunity. Such human rights violations include the imprisonment of prisoners of conscience, unfair political trials, torture and other ill-treatment, "disappearances" and unlawful killings. International mechanisms to compensate for national failures have evolved rapidly in the last decade, but remain embryonic and contested.

In 2005, AI's objectives were to:
- Reform police practice and strengthen the judiciary.
- Address discrimination in the justice sector, particularly with regard to lesbian, gay, bisexual and transgender people (LGBT) and ethnic and religious minorities.
- Consolidate international criminal justice, specifically by supporting the International Criminal Court and universal jurisdiction.
- Ensure human rights in transitional justice.

Saleh Mahmud Osman thanked AI in April for campaigning for his release while he was in detention for seven months in 2004. He was arrested because of his human rights work as a lawyer at the Amal Centre in Nyala in the Darfur region of Sudan, which provides legal aid, medical treatment and rehabilitation for survivors of torture. © AI

"I would like to express my gratitude that the support you extended to me was the reason for my release... It is very important to tell you that all these [AI] reports are read by the government and by the authorities."

- Strengthen national, regional and international mechanisms of state accountability, focusing in particular on UN reform.
- Further develop international standards, for example on "disappearances" and with regard to companies.
- Study the impact of corruption on the administration of justice.

Abolish the death penalty

The momentum for abolition of the death penalty continues, particularly at the level of non-governmental organizations, through the emergence of a World Coalition against the Death Penalty, and the work of dedicated national organizations. However, a sizeable number of countries remain opposed to abolition, and the threats of terrorism, drugs and organized crime are being used to justify the retention or even in some cases the reinstatement of capital punishment.

In 2005, AI's objectives were to:
- Promote abolition of the death penalty in all countries and internationally, especially by showing the impact of discrimination.
- Monitor death penalty developments globally and respond quickly to events with action, particularly on cases that illustrate systemic problems in the application of the death penalty.
- Produce global statistics, thematic reports and action.
- End the use of the death penalty for child offenders.

Protect the rights of defenders

Human rights defenders are at the front line of work on human rights, and there is increasing recognition of the important role that activists play. Throughout the world, however, they are deliberately targeted in a variety of ways. Governments use many pretexts, including security and the "war on terror", to stifle legitimate criticism of their policies. Women human rights defenders in particular risk social stigma within their communities and attempts to discredit their work if they challenge the political order or social, religious, gender or sexual conventions.

Prisoner of conscience and environmental activist Felipe Arreaga Sánchez was released in September after spending more than 10 months in prison in Mexico. He had been prosecuted in retaliation for his peaceful struggle to prevent excessive logging of forests. Following his release, he said he would continue his environmental activism and he thanked national and international human rights organizations for their support.

> **"Amnesty International came to our aid at a time when a lot of doors were closing."**
> Sue Webster fought a lonely battle on behalf of her husband, Abdullah, until AI adopted him as a prisoner of conscience. A US armed forces officer at the time of his arrest, he served 11 months' imprisonment for his conscientious objection to the war in Iraq.

In 2005, AI's objectives were to:

■ Engage defenders from all sectors of society, including by building coalitions, skills and greater visibility for the work of women defenders.

■ Highlight the contribution of defenders to the security of society at large and address abuses impacting on their rights.

■ Promote the protection and safety of human rights defenders and counter the misuses of the judicial system to persecute them.

■ Widen and deepen the use of the UN Declaration on Human Rights Defenders, and support the work of UN and regional protection mechanisms.

Resist human rights abuses in the 'war on terror'

The framework of international law and multilateral action is undergoing the most sustained attack since its establishment. International human rights and humanitarian law are being challenged by governments as ineffective in responding to security issues. Armed groups continue to carry out abuses, and some operate in a loose global alliance. Public opinion is polarized.

In 2005, AI's objectives were to:

■ Address the human rights impact of counter-terrorism measures, focusing specifically on detention and trial safeguards, torture, killings and discriminatory laws and practices.

■ Address the impact of cooperation agreements among states on human rights protection.

■ Engage with the development of treaties on terrorism.

■ Promote international and regional mechanisms for state accountability.

■ Report on abuses by armed groups, and explore strategies for raising human rights concerns with these groups.

■ Advance progressive interpretations of international human rights and humanitarian law as relevant to the "war on terror".

Uphold the rights of refugees and migrants

The debate relating to the rights of refugees, migrants and the internally displaced has become increasingly high profile and politicized. People continue to move across borders seeking protection from persecution or driven by the prospects of economic opportunities. Demand for cheap migrant labour and exploitative labour practices continue. Xenophobic and racist responses to refugees, asylum-seekers and migrants continue in both developed and developing countries. Restrictive migration control measures and security measures targeting non-nationals increase the vulnerability of non-nationals to a wide variety of human rights abuses.

In 2005, AI's objectives were to:

■ Defend refugees' right not to be returned to countries where they might suffer abuses of their human rights.

■ Defend the right of asylum-seekers to access fair and satisfactory asylum procedures.

■ Ensure a human rights approach to durable solutions to refugee problems.

■ Promote the human rights of migrants.

■ Monitor and address arbitrary detention practices applied to refugees and migrants.

■ Enhance the access of refugees and migrants to their economic, social and cultural rights.

■ Improve protection of refugee and displaced girls and women at risk of sexual exploitation and abuse.

Promote economic, social and cultural rights for marginalized communities

Growing global inequalities, and the failure of governments to significantly reduce the number of people living in extreme poverty, are among the defining human rights issues of our times. There is still little acceptance that poverty raises fundamental issues of human rights. However, mass social movements are beginning to use the language of rights in global campaigns on issues including trade, aid, investment, debt and access to medicines.

In 2005, AI's objectives were to:

- Promote economic, social and cultural rights as human rights, including by participating in global processes such as those on trade.
- Strengthen legal recognition of economic, social and cultural rights, through national law reform initiatives and development of international standards and mechanisms.
- Address severe abuses of economic, social and cultural rights suffered by marginalized communities.
- Address abuses arising from HIV/AIDS.
- Highlight the obligations of economic actors such as companies and expose abuses, for example discrimination in employment.
- Promote human rights principles for privatization and in investment and trade agreements.

Stop violence against women

Violence against women is one of the most widespread and pervasive human rights violations. It is also one of the most hidden. It cuts across cultural, regional, religious and economic boundaries. It is manifested in the context of the family, in the community, in state institutions and in conflict and post-conflict situations. Thanks in particular to the women's movement, there have been significant advances in the promotion of women's rights in international law, including criminal law. However, such advances have made little difference for women on the ground and much remains to be done.

In 2005, AI's objectives were to:

- Demand that governments criminalize rape and ratify the UN Women's Convention without reservations.
- Challenge impunity for rape and other forms of violence against women, including by armed groups, in conflict and post-conflict situations.
- Ensure that states respect, protect and fulfil women's rights, using the standard of due diligence nationally and internationally to hold states accountable to their obligations.
- Challenge the tolerance within society of violence against women and urge traditional and informal authorities to take effective action to fight it.

"The Mauritanian authorities would probably not have given us official recognition without your campaign."
Fatimata Mbaye, Chair of the Mauritanian Human Rights Association. She thanked AI members after the Association and an organization campaigning for an end to slavery in Mauritania, SOS Esclaves, were officially recognized and allowed to operate legally in June 2005. Leading members of these organizations had all been detained in 1998.

Journalist Marielos Monzon is at risk from armed gangs because of her reporting of corruption and other human rights abuses. Human rights defenders in Guatemala have been killed or abducted. © AI

"When you receive all these letters from thousands of people all over the world…it is great to have that solidarity and support, because you have really tough moments when you are getting threats."

- Support women human rights defenders.
- Develop policies to address reproductive health rights and other related concerns.

Protect civilians and close the taps that fuel abuses in conflict

In parts of the world conflict appears chronic. Identity issues, poverty and mineral reserves are among the causes. Sometimes weak states are confronted with economically powerful armed groups; often conflict is prolonged by foreign governments, private companies and diaspora communities. Mass abuses against civilians persist, and despite significant international and national legal developments, impunity persists. Effective protection seems to depend too often on the presence of foreign troops.

In 2005, AI's objectives were to:

- Demand accountability for abuses in armed conflict by states and armed groups.
- Promote an agenda for protecting civilians, including through peacekeeping and peace-building.
- Campaign against the use of child soldiers.
- Demand accountability of external actors complicit in abuses, including second states and economic actors.
- Campaign to restrict the arms trade, including by promoting an Arms Trade Treaty.
- Campaign against indiscriminate weapons, such as cluster weapons.
- Advance the debate on the use of military force.

You can make a difference

AI works to improve human rights through the actions of ordinary people around the world. AI members and supporters have a record of real achievement. Prisoners of conscience have been released. Death sentences have been commuted. Torturers have been brought to justice. Governments have been persuaded to change their laws and practices. Sometimes solidarity keeps hope alive. Hope is a precious weapon for prisoners battling to survive, relatives trying to obtain justice or human rights defenders bravely continuing their work despite danger and isolation. However bleak the situation, AI's members and supporters, acting together, can make a difference.

CONTACT AI

AI SECTIONS

Algeria Amnesty International, 4 rue Idriss Bey (ex. Négrier), Alger 16004
email: amnestyalgeria@hotmail.com

Argentina Amnistía Internacional,
Av. Rivadavia 2206 - P4A,
C1032ACO Ciudad de Buenos Aires
e-mail: administracion@amnesty.org.ar
http://www.amnesty.org.ar

Australia Amnesty International, Locked Bag 23,
Broadway, New South Wales 2007
e-mail: hello@amnesty.org.au
http://www.amnesty.org.au

Austria Amnesty International, Moeringgasse 10,
A-1150 Vienna
e-mail: info@amnesty.at
http://www.amnesty.at

Belgium Amnesty International (Flemish-speaking),
Kerkstraat 156, 2060 Antwerpen
e-mail: directie@aivl.be
http://www.aivl.be
Belgium Amnesty International (francophone),
rue Berckmans 9, 1060 Bruxelles
e-mail: aibf@aibf.be
http://www.aibf.be

Benin Amnesty International, Sikècodji Carrefour
Marina, Immeuble Marina, 2ème étage, Cotonou
e-mail: aibenin@leland.bj

Bermuda Amnesty International, PO Box HM 2136,
Hamilton HM JX
e-mail: aibda@ibl.bm

Canada Amnesty International (English-speaking),
312 Laurier Avenue East, Ottawa, Ontario, K1N 1H9
e-mail: info@amnesty.ca
http://www.amnesty.ca
Canada Amnistie Internationale (francophone),
6250 boulevard Monk, Montréal, Québec, H4E 3H7
e-mail: info@amnistie.qc.ca
http://www.amnistie.qc.ca

Chile Amnistía Internacional, Oficina Nacional,
Huelén 188 A, 750-0617 Providencia, Santiago
e-mail: info@amnistia.cl
http://www.amnistia.cl

Côte d'Ivoire Amnesty International, 04 BP 895,
Abidjan 04
e-mail: aicotedivoire@yahoo.fr

Denmark Amnesty International, Gammeltorv 8, 5,
DK - 1457 Copenhagen K.
e-mail: amnesty@amnesty.dk
http://www.amnesty.dk

Faroe Islands Amnesty International, Hoydalsvegur 6,
FO-100 Tórshavn
e-mail: amnesty@amnesty.fo
http://www.amnesty.fo

Finland Amnesty International, Ruoholahdenkatu 24,
D 00180 Helsinki
e-mail: amnesty@amnesty.fi
http://www.amnesty.fi

France Amnesty International, 76 boulevard de
la Villette, 75940 Paris, Cédex 19
e-mail: info@amnesty.asso.fr
http://www.amnesty.asso.fr

Germany Amnesty International, Heerstrasse 178,
53111 Bonn
e-mail: info@amnesty.de
http://www.amnesty.de

Greece Amnesty International, Sina 30,
106 72 Athens
e-mail: info@amnesty.org.gr
http://www.amnesty.org.gr

Guyana Amnesty International,
Palm Court Building, 35 Main Street,
Georgetown
e-mail: rightsgy@yahoo.com

Hong Kong Amnesty International, Unit D, 3F,
Best-O-Best Commercial Centre, 32-36 Ferry Street,
Kowloon
e-mail: admin-hk@amnesty.org
http://www.amnesty.org.hk

Iceland Amnesty International, PO Box 618,
121 Reykjavík
e-mail: amnesty@amnesty.is
http://www.amnesty.is

Ireland Amnesty International,
Sean MacBride House, 48 Fleet Street,
Dublin 2
e-mail: info@amnesty.ie
http://www.amnesty.ie

Israel Amnesty International, PO Box 14179,
Tel Aviv 61141
e-mail: amnesty@netvision.net.il
http://www.amnesty.org.il

Italy Amnesty International,
Via Giovanni Battista De Rossi 10, 00161 Roma
e-mail: info@amnesty.it
http://www.amnesty.it

Japan Amnesty International, 4F Kyodo Bldg.,
2-2 Kandanishiki-cho, Chiyoda-ku,
Tokyo 101-0054
e-mail: info@amnesty.or.jp
http://www.amnesty.or.jp

Korea (Republic of) Amnesty International,
Gwangehwamun PO Box 2045, Chongno-gu,
Seoul, 110-620
e-mail: admin-kr@amnesty.org
http://www.amnesty.or.kr

Luxembourg Amnesty International,
Boîte Postale 1914, 1019 Luxembourg
e-mail: amnesty@pt.lu
http://www.amnesty.lu

Mauritius Amnesty International, BP 69,
Rose-Hill
e-mail: amnestymtius@intnet.mu

Mexico Amnistía Internacional, Zacatecas 230,
Oficina 605, Colonia Roma Norte Delegación,
Cuauhtémoc, CP 06700, Mexico DF
e-mail: informacion@amnistia.org.mx
http://www.amnistia.org.mx

Morocco Amnesty International, 281 avenue
Mohamed V, Apt. 23, Escalier A, Rabat
e-mail: admin-ma@amnesty.org

Nepal Amnesty International, PO Box 135,
Amnesty Marga, Basantanagar, Balaju,
Kathmandu
e-mail: info@amnestynepal.org
http://www.amnestynepal.org

Netherlands Amnesty International,
Keizersgracht 177, 1016 DR Amsterdam
e-mail: amnesty@amnesty.nl
http://www.amnesty.nl

New Zealand Amnesty International,
145 Nelson Street, Auckland
e-mail: campaign@amnesty.org.nz
http://www.amnesty.org.nz

Norway Amnesty International,
Tordenskioldsgate 6B, 0160 Oslo
e-mail: info@amnesty.no
http://www.amnesty.no

Peru Amnistía Internacional,
Enrique Palacios 735-A, Miraflores, Lima
e-mail: admin-pe@amnesty.org
http://www.amnistia.org.pe

Philippines Amnesty International, 17-B,
Kasing Kasing Street, Corner K-8th, Kamias,
Quezon City
e-mail: amnestypilipinas@meridiantelekoms.net

Poland Amnesty International, Piêkna 66 a lok.2,
00-672, Warszawa
e-mail: amnesty@amnesty.org.pl
http://www.amnesty.org.pl

Portugal Amnistia Internacional, Rua Fialho
de Almeida 13-1, PT-1070-128 Lisboa
e-mail: aiportugal@amnistia-internacional.pt
http://www.amnistia-internacional.pt

Puerto Rico Amnistía Internacional,
Calle El Roble 54-Altos, Oficina 11,
Río Piedras, 00925
e-mail: amnistiapr@amnestypr.org

Senegal Amnesty International, BP 269 Dakar
Colobane
e-mail: aisenegal@sentoo.sn

Sierra Leone Amnesty International, PMB 1021,
16 Pademba Road, Freetown
e-mail: aislf@sierratel.sl

Slovenia Amnesty International, Beethovnova 7,
1000 Ljubljana
e-mail: amnesty@amnesty.si
http://www.amnesty.si

Spain Amnistía Internacional, Fernando VI, 8,
1° izda, 28004 Madrid
e-mail: info@es.amnesty.org
http://www.es.amnesty.org

Sweden Amnesty International, PO Box 4719,
S-11692 Stockholm
e-mail: info@amnesty.se
http://www.amnesty.se

Switzerland Amnesty International, PO Box 3001,
Bern
e-mail: info@amnesty.ch
http://www.amnesty.ch

Taiwan Amnesty International, B1, No. 3, Sec. 1,
Dunhua S. Rd., Taipei 105
e-mail: aitaiwan@seed.net.tw
http://www.aitaiwan.org.tw

Togo Amnesty International, 2322 avenue du RPT,
quartier Casablanca, BP 20013, Lomé
e-mail: aitogo@cafe.tg

Tunisia Amnesty International,
67 rue Oum Kalthoum, 3ème étage, Escalier B,
1000 Tunis
e-mail: admin-tn@amnesty.org

United Kingdom Amnesty International,
The Human Rights Action Centre, 17-25 New Inn Yard,
London EC2A 3EA
e-mail: info@amnesty.org.uk
http://www.amnesty.org.uk

United States of America Amnesty International,
5 Penn Plaza, 16th floor, New York, NY 10001
e-mail: admin-us@aiusa.org
http://www.amnestyusa.org

Uruguay Amnistía Internacional, Colonia 871, apto. 5,
CP 11100, Montevideo
e-mail: amnistia@chasque.apc.org
http://www.amnistiauruguay.org.uy

Venezuela Amnistía Internacional,
Edificio Ateneo de Caracas, piso 6
Plaza Morelos Los Caobos, Caracas 1010A
e-mail: admin-ve@amnesty.org
http://www.amnistia.org.ve

AI STRUCTURES

Belarus Amnesty International, PO Box 10P,
246050 Gomel
e-mail: amnesty_by@gmx.net

Bolivia Amnistía Internacional, Casilla 10607, La Paz
e-mail: perescar@ceibo.entelnet.bo

Burkina Faso Amnesty International,
303 rue 9.08, 08 BP 11344,
Ouagadougou 08
e-mail: aburkina@fasonet.bf

Croatia Amnesty International, Martićeva 24,
10000 Zagreb
e-mail: admin@amnesty.hr
http://www.amnesty.hr

Curaçao Amnesty International, PO Box 3676,
Willemstad Kwartje Kavel 36, Curaçao,
Netherlands Antilles
e-mail: eisdencher@interneeds.net

Czech Republic Amnesty International,
Palackého 9, 110 00 Praha 1
e-mail: amnesty@amnesty.cz
http://www.amnesty.cz

Gambia Amnesty International,
49 Garba Gahumta Road, Bakau New Town, Banjul
e-mail: amnesty@gamtel.gm

Hungary Amnesty International, Rózsa u. 44, II/4,
1064 Budapest
e-mail: info@amnesty.hu
http://www.amnesty.hu

Malaysia Amnesty International, E6, 3rd floor,
Bangunan Khas, Jalan 8/1E, 46050 Petaling Jaya,
Selangor
e-mail: amnesty@tm.net.my
http://www.aimalaysia.org

Mali Amnesty International,
Immeuble Gossi Diawara, Rue 98, Porte 401,
BP E 3885, Badalabougou, Bamako
e-mail: amnesty.mali@ikatelnet.net

Moldova Amnesty International, PO Box 209,
MD-2012 Chișinău
e-mail: info@amnesty.md
http://www.amnesty.md

Mongolia Amnesty International,
Trade Union House, 4th floor, No. 410,
Sukh-Baater Square, Ulaanbaatar
e-mail: aimncc@magicnet.mn
http://www.amnesty.mn

Pakistan Amnesty International, B-12, Shelezon
Centre, Gulsan-E-Iqbal, Block 15, University Road,
Karachi - 75300
e-mail: amnesty@cyber.net.pk

Paraguay Amnistía Internacional,
Tte. Zotti No. 352 e/Hassler y Boggiani, Asunción
e-mail: ai-info@py.amnesty.org
http://www.py.amnesty.org

Slovakia Amnesty International, Benediktiho 5,
811 05 Bratislava
e-mail: amnesty@amnesty.sk
http://www.amnesty.sk

South Africa Amnesty International,
Kutlawanong Democracy Centre,
357 Visagie Street/cnr Prinsloo, Pretoria 0001,
Gauteng
e-mail: info@amnesty.org.za
http://www.amnesty.org.za

Thailand Amnesty International,
641/8 Ladprao Road, Ladyao Jatujak,
Bangkok 10900
e-mail: info@amnesty.or.th
http://www.amnesty.or.th

Turkey Amnesty International,
Muradiye Bayiri Sok, Acarman ap. 50/1,
Tesvikiye 80200, Istanbul
e-mail: posta@amnesty-turkiye.org
http://www.amnesty-turkiye.org

Ukraine Amnesty International, Ukrainskaia
Assotsiatsia "Mezhdunarodnaia Amnistia",
Chokolovsky bulvar, 1, kv. 12, Kiev
e-mail: office@amnesty.org.ua

Zambia Amnesty International, Room 108,
Zsic Building, Bueteco Road, Mufulira
e-mail: azambia@sections.amnesty.org

Zimbabwe Amnesty International,
Caspi House Block B, No. 6 Harare Street, Harare
e-mail: amnestyzimbabwe@yahoo.com

AI GROUPS

There are also AI groups in:
Angola, Aruba, Azerbaijan, Bahamas, Bahrain,
Barbados, Bosnia and Herzegovina, Botswana,
Cameroon, Cape Verde, Chad, Dominican Republic,
Egypt, Estonia, Grenada, India, Jamaica, Jordan, Kenya,
Kuwait, Kyrgyzstan, Lebanon, Liberia, Lithuania, Malta,
Mozambique, Palestinian Authority, Romania, Russian
Federation, Serbia and Montenegro, Trinidad and
Tobago, Uganda, Yemen

AI OFFICES

International Secretariat (IS)
Amnesty International, Peter Benenson House,
1 Easton Street, London WC1X 0DW,
United Kingdom
e-mail: amnestyis@amnesty.org
http://www.amnesty.org

ARABAI (Arabic translation unit)
c/o International Secretariat,
Peter Benenson House, 1 Easton Street,
London WC1X 0DW, United Kingdom
e-mail: arabai@amnesty.org
http://www.amnesty-arabic.org

Éditions Francophones d'Amnesty International (EFAI)
17 rue du Pont-aux-Choux, 75003 Paris, France
e-mail: ai-efai@amnesty.org
http://www.efai.org

Editorial de Amnistía Internacional (EDAI)
Calle Valderribas 13, 28007 Madrid, Spain
e-mail: mlleo@amnesty.org
http://www.edai.org

European Union (EU) Office
Amnesty International, Rue d'Arlon 37-41,
B-1000 Brussels, Belgium
e-mail: amnesty-eu@aieu.be
http://www.amnesty-eu.org

IS Beirut – Middle East and North Africa Regional Office
Amnesty International, PO Box 13-5696,
Chouran Beirut 1102 - 2060, Lebanon
e-mail: mena@amnesty.org

IS Dakar – Development Field Office
Amnesty International, SICAP Sacré Coeur Pyrotechnie,
Extension No. 25, BP 47582, Dakar, Senegal
e-mail: Kolaniya@amnesty.org

IS Geneva – UN Representative Office
Amnesty International, 22 rue du Cendrier,
4ème étage, CH-1201 Geneva, Switzerland
e-mail: gvunpost@amnesty.org

IS Hong Kong – Asia Pacific Regional Office
Amnesty International, 16/F Siu On Centre,
188 Lockhart Rd, Wanchai, Hong Kong
e-mail: admin-ap@amnesty.org

IS Kampala – Africa Regional Office
Amnesty International, Plot 20A, Kawalya Kaggwa
Close, Kololo, Uganda
e-mail: admin-kp@amnesty.org

IS Moscow – Russia Resource Centre
Amnesty International, PO Box 212,
Moscow 119019, Russian Federation
e-mail: msk@amnesty.org

IS New York – UN Representative Office
Amnesty International, 777 UN Plaza, 6th Floor,
New York, NY 10017, USA

IS Paris – Research Office
Amnesty International, 76 boulevard de la Villette,
75940 Paris, Cédex 19, France
e-mail: pro@amnesty.org

IS San José – Americas Regional Office
Amnistía Internacional,
Del ICE de Pavas 100 metros al Oeste,
50 metros al Norte y 25 metros al Este,
Apartamentos Cherito No. 4, Barrio Rohrmoser,
San José, Costa Rica
e-mail: admin-cr@amnesty.org

Selected international human rights treaties (AT 31 DECEMBER 2005)

States that have ratified or acceded to a convention are party to the treaty and are bound to observe its provisions. States that have signed but not yet ratified have expressed their intention to become a party at some future date; meanwhile, they are obliged to refrain from acts that would defeat the object and purpose of the treaty.

Treaty	Afghanistan	Albania	Algeria	Andorra	Angola	Antigua and Barbuda	Argentina	Armenia	Australia	Austria	Azerbaijan	Bahamas	Bahrain	Bangladesh	Barbados	Belarus	Belgium
International Covenant on Civil and Political Rights (ICCPR)	○	○		△	○		○	○	○	○	○	○		○	○	○	○
(first) Optional Protocol to the ICCPR			○	△	○		○	○	○	○	○			○	○	○	
Second Optional Protocol to the ICCPR, aiming at the abolition of the death penalty				△				○	○	○						○	○
International Covenant on Economic, Social and Cultural Rights	○	○		○	○		○	○	○	○	○		○		○	○	○
Convention on the Elimination of All Forms of Discrimination against Women (CEDAW)	○	○	○	○	○	○	○	○	○	○	○	○	○	○	○	○	○
Optional Protocol to CEDAW		○		○				△		○	○			○[10]		○	○
Convention on the Rights of the Child (CRC)	○	○	○	○	○	○	○	○	○	○	○	○	○	○	○	○	○
Optional Protocol to the CRC on the involvement of children in armed conflict	○			○			○	●	△	○	○		○				
International Convention on the Elimination of All Forms of Racial Discrimination	○	○	○	△		○	○	○	○	○	○		○	○	○	○	○
Convention against Torture and Other Cruel, Inhuman or Degrading Treatment or Punishment	○[28]	○	○[22]	△		○	○[22]	○	○[22]	○[22]	○[22]			○		○	○[22]
Optional Protocol to the Convention against Torture*		○					○			△	●						●
Convention relating to the Status of Refugees (1951)	●	○	○		○	○	○	○	○	○	○				○	○	○
Protocol relating to the Status of Refugees (1967)	●	○	○		○	○	○	○	○	○	○	○			○	○	○
Convention relating to the Status of Stateless Persons (1954)		○	○			○	○	○	○	○	○				○		○
Convention on the Reduction of Statelessness (1961)		○					○	○	○	○							
International Convention on the Protection of the Rights of All Migrant Workers and Members of Their Families (1990)			●				△				○			△			
Rome Statute of the International Criminal Court	○	○	△	○	△	○	○	△	○	○	○	△	△	△	○	○	○

LEGEND

● ratified in 2005
○ state is a party
◐ signed in 2005
△ signed but not yet ratified

10 Declaration under Article 10 not recognizing the competence of the CEDAW Committee to undertake confidential inquiries into allegations of grave or systematic violations

22 Declaration under Article 22 recognizing the competence of the Committee against Torture (CAT) to consider individual complaints

28 Reservation under Article 28 not recognizing the competence of the CAT to undertake confidential inquiries into allegations of systematic torture if warranted

* The Optional Protocol to the Convention against Torture will enter into force after 20 ratifications

12 Declaration under Article 12 (3) accepting the jurisdiction of the International Criminal Court (ICC) for crimes in its territory

124 Declaration under Article 124 not accepting the jurisdiction of the ICC over war crimes for seven years after ratification

** Signed the Rome Statute but have since formally declared their intention not to ratify

*** Acceded in 1962 but in 1965 denounced the Convention; denunciation took effect on 2 April 1966

Treaty	Belize	Benin	Bhutan	Bolivia	Bosnia and Herzegovina	Botswana	Brazil	Brunei Darussalam	Bulgaria	Burkina Faso	Burundi	Cambodia	Cameroon	Canada	Cape Verde	Central African Republic	Chad	Chile	China	Colombia	Comoros	Congo (Democratic Republic of the)
International Covenant on Civil and Political Rights (ICCPR)	●	○		○	●	○	●		●	○	●	○	●	○	●	●	○	●	◒	○		○
(first) Optional Protocol to the ICCPR		○		○	●				●	○		◐	●	○	●	●	○	●		○		○
Second Optional Protocol to the ICCPR, aiming at the abolition of the death penalty					●				●					●	○			◐		○		
International Covenant on Economic, Social and Cultural Rights	◐	○		○	●		●		●	○	●	○	●	○	●	○	●	○	●	○		○
Convention on the Elimination of All Forms of Discrimination against Women (CEDAW)	○	○	○	○	●	○	●		●	○	●	○	●	○	●	○	●	○	●	○	○	○
Optional Protocol to CEDAW	○[10]	◐		○	●		●		◐	●	◐	◐	●	○			◐		◐			
Convention on the Rights of the Child (CRC)	○	○	○	○	●	○	●	○	●	○	●	○	●	○	●	○	●	○	●	○	○	○
Optional Protocol to the CRC on the involvement of children in armed conflict	○	●	◐	○	●	○	●		●	◐	◐	○	◐	●	○		○	○	◐	●		○
International Convention on the Elimination of All Forms of Racial Discrimination	○	○	◐	○	●	○	●		●	○	●	○	●	○	●	○	○	●	○	●	○	○
Convention against Torture and Other Cruel, Inhuman or Degrading Treatment or Punishment	○	○		○	●[22]	○	●		●[22]	○	●[22]	○	○[22]	●[22]	●		●	○[22]	●[28]	○	◐	○
Optional Protocol to the Convention against Torture*		◐					◐		◐		◐		◐				◐					
Convention relating to the Status of Refugees (1951)	○	○		○	●	○	●		●	○	●	○	●	○		○	●	○		○		○
Protocol relating to the Status of Refugees (1967)	○	○		○	●	○	●		●	○	●	○	●	○	●	○	●	○	●	○		○
Convention relating to the Status of Stateless Persons (1954)				○	●	○	●							○				●		◐		
Convention on the Reduction of Statelessness (1961)					○	●							●				●					
International Convention on the Protection of the Rights of All Migrant Workers and Members of Their Families (1990)	○	◐		○	●					○	●	◐			●		◐	●		○	◐	
Rome Statute of the International Criminal Court	○	○		○	●	○	●		●	○	●	○	◐	○	◐	○	◐	◐	○[124]	◐		○

LEGEND

- ● ratified in 2005
- ○ state is a party
- ◐ signed but not yet ratified
- 10 signed in 2005
- 10 Declaration under Article 10 not recognizing the competence of the CEDAW Committee to undertake confidential inquiries into allegations of grave or systematic violations
- 22 Declaration under Article 22 recognizing the competence of the Committee against Torture (CAT) to consider individual complaints
- 28 Reservation under Article 28 not recognizing the competence of the CAT to undertake confidential inquiries into allegations of systematic torture if warranted
- * The Optional Protocol to the Convention against Torture will enter into force after 20 ratifications
- 12 Declaration under Article 12 (3) accepting the jurisdiction of the International Criminal Court (ICC) for crimes in its territory
- 124 Declaration under Article 124 not accepting the jurisdiction of the ICC over war crimes for seven years after ratification
- ** Signed the Rome Statute but have since formally declared their intention not to ratify
- *** Acceded in 1962 but in 1965 denounced the Convention; denunciation took effect on 2 April 1966

	Congo (Republic of the)	Cook Islands	Costa Rica	Côte d'Ivoire	Croatia	Cuba	Cyprus	Czech Republic	Denmark	Djibouti	Dominica	Dominican Republic	Ecuador	Egypt	El Salvador	Equatorial Guinea	Eritrea	Estonia	Ethiopia	Fiji	Finland	France
International Covenant on Civil and Political Rights (ICCPR)	○		○	○	○		○	○	○	○	○	○	○	○	○		○	○	○		○	○
(first) Optional Protocol to the ICCPR	○		○	○	○		○	○	○	○		○	○		○			○			○	○
Second Optional Protocol to the ICCPR, aiming at the abolition of the death penalty			○		○		○	○	○	○			○					○			○	○
International Covenant on Economic, Social and Cultural Rights	○		○	○	○		○	○	○	○	○	○	○	○	○	○	○	○	○		○	○
Convention on the Elimination of All Forms of Discrimination against Women (CEDAW)	○		○	○	○	○	○	○	○	○	○	○	○	○	○	○	○	○	○	○	○	○
Optional Protocol to CEDAW			○		○	◠	○	○	○			○	○		◠			○			○	○
Convention on the Rights of the Child (CRC)	○	○	○	○	○	○	○	○	○	○	○	○	○	○	○	○	○	○	○	○	○	○
Optional Protocol to the CRC on the involvement of children in armed conflict			○		○	◠		○		○		○	◠		○		●	◠		◐		○
International Convention on the Elimination of All Forms of Racial Discrimination	○		○	○	○		○	○	○			○	○	○				○	○	○	○	○
Convention against Torture and Other Cruel, Inhuman or Degrading Treatment or Punishment	○		○ [22]	○	○ [22]	○ [28]	○ [22]	○ [22]	○ [22]	○		◠	○ [22]	○	○ [28]			○	○	○ [22]	○ [22]	○ [27]
Optional Protocol to the Convention against Torture*			●		●		◠	◠	○									◠			◠	●
Convention relating to the Status of Refugees (1951)	○		○	○	○		○	○	○	○	○	○	○	○	○	○		○	○	○	○	○
Protocol relating to the Status of Refugees (1967)	○		○	○	○		○	○	○	○	○	○	○	○	○			○	○	○	○	○
Convention relating to the Status of Stateless Persons (1954)			○		○		○	○	○			○			◠			○	○		○	○
Convention on the Reduction of Statelessness (1961)			○		○		○	○				◠									◠	
International Convention on the Protection of the Rights of All Migrant Workers and Members of Their Families (1990)													○	○	○							
Rome Statute of the International Criminal Court	○		◠ [12]	○	○	◠	○	○	○		●	○	◠	◠			◠	○		○	○ [124] ○

LEGEND

● ratified in 2005
○ state is a party
◐ signed in 2005
◠ signed but not yet ratified

10 Declaration under Article 10 not recognizing the competence of the CEDAW Committee to undertake confidential inquiries into allegations of grave or systematic violations

22 Declaration under Article 22 recognizing the competence of the Committee against Torture (CAT) to consider individual complaints

28 Reservation under Article 28 not recognizing the competence of the CAT to undertake confidential inquiries into allegations of systematic torture if warranted

* The Optional Protocol to the Convention against Torture will enter into force after 20 ratifications

12 Declaration under Article 12 (3) accepting the jurisdiction of the International Criminal Court (ICC) for crimes in its territory

124 Declaration under Article 124 not accepting the jurisdiction of the ICC over war crimes for seven years after ratification

** Signed the Rome Statute but have since formally declared their intention not to ratify

*** Acceded in 1962 but in 1965 denounced the Convention; denunciation took effect on 2 April 1966

	Gabon	Gambia	Georgia	Germany	Ghana	Greece	Grenada	Guatemala	Guinea	Guinea-Bissau	Guyana	Haiti	Holy See	Honduras	Hungary	Iceland	India	Indonesia	Iran (Islamic Republic of)	Iraq	Ireland	Israel
International Covenant on Civil and Political Rights (ICCPR)	○	○	○	○	○	○	○	○	○	△	○	○		○	○	○	○			○	○	○	○
(first) Optional Protocol to the ICCPR		○	○	○	○	○		○	○	△	○			●	○	○					○	
Second Optional Protocol to the ICCPR, aiming at the abolition of the death penalty		○	○		○					△				△	○	○						
International Covenant on Economic, Social and Cultural Rights	○	○	○	○	○	○	○	○	○	○	○			○	○	○	○		○	○	○	○
Convention on the Elimination of All Forms of Discrimination against Women (CEDAW)	○	○	○	○	○	○	○	○	○	○	○	○		○	○	○	○	○		○	○	○
Optional Protocol to CEDAW	○		○	○	◓	○		○		△				○	○		△			○		
Convention on the Rights of the Child (CRC)	○	○	○	○	○	○	○	○	○	○	○	○		○	○	○	○	○	○	○	○	○
Optional Protocol to the CRC on the involvement of children in armed conflict	△	△		○	◓	○		○		△		△	○		○	○		●	△		○	●
International Convention on the Elimination of All Forms of Racial Discrimination	○	○	○	○	○	○	△	○	○	○	○	○		○	○	○	○	○	○	○	○	○
Convention against Torture and Other Cruel, Inhuman or Degrading Treatment or Punishment	○	△	○ [22]	○ [22]	○ [22]	○ [22]		○ [22]	○	△	○			○	○ [22]	○ [22]	△ [28]	○ [28]		○ [22]	○ [28]	
Optional Protocol to the Convention against Torture*	△		●			△		△	●					△		△						
Convention relating to the Status of Refugees (1951)	○	○	○	○	○	○		○	○	○		○			○	○					○	○
Protocol relating to the Status of Refugees (1967)	○	○	○	○	○	○		○	○	○		○			○	○	○			○	○	○
Convention relating to the Status of Stateless Persons (1954)			○		○			○	○					△	△	○					○	○
Convention on the Reduction of Statelessness (1961)			○		○			○						○	○						○	△
International Convention on the Protection of the Rights of All Migrant Workers and Members of Their Families (1990)	△				○			○	○	△	●			●				△				
Rome Statute of the International Criminal Court	○	○	○	○	○	○		○	○	△	○	△		○	○	○		△		△	○	△**

LEGEND

● ratified in 2005
○ state is a party
◓ signed in 2005
△ signed but not yet ratified

10 Declaration under Article 10 not recognizing the competence of the CEDAW Committee to undertake confidential inquiries into allegations of grave or systematic violations

22 Declaration under Article 22 recognizing the competence of the Committee against Torture (CAT) to consider individual complaints

28 Reservation under Article 28 not recognizing the competence of the CAT to undertake confidential inquiries into allegations of systematic torture if warranted

* The Optional Protocol to the Convention against Torture will enter into force after 20 ratifications

12 Declaration under Article 12 (3) accepting the jurisdiction of the International Criminal Court for crimes in its territory

124 Declaration under Article 124 not accepting the jurisdiction of the ICC over war crimes for seven years after ratification

** Signed the Rome Statute but have since formally declared their intention not to ratify

*** Acceded in 1962 but in 1965 denounced the Convention; denunciation took effect on 2 April 1966

Treaties (rows):

- International Covenant on Civil and Political Rights (ICCPR)
- (first) Optional Protocol to the ICCPR
- Second Optional Protocol to the ICCPR, aiming at the abolition of the death penalty
- International Covenant on Economic, Social and Cultural Rights
- Convention on the Elimination of All Forms of Discrimination against Women (CEDAW)
- Optional Protocol to CEDAW
- Convention on the Rights of the Child (CRC)
- Optional Protocol to the CRC on the involvement of children in armed conflict
- International Convention on the Elimination of All Forms of Racial Discrimination
- Convention against Torture and Other Cruel, Inhuman or Degrading Treatment or Punishment
- Optional Protocol to the Convention against Torture*
- Convention relating to the Status of Refugees (1951)
- Protocol relating to the Status of Refugees (1967)
- Convention relating to the Status of Stateless Persons (1954)
- Convention on the Reduction of Statelessness (1961)
- International Convention on the Protection of the Rights of All Migrant Workers and Members of Their Families (1990)
- Rome Statute of the International Criminal Court

Countries (columns):

Italy, Jamaica, Japan, Jordan, Kazakstan, Kenya, Kiribati, Korea (Democratic People's Republic of), Korea (Republic of), Kuwait, Kyrgyzstan, Lao People's Democratic Republic, Latvia, Lebanon, Lesotho, Liberia, Libyan Arab Jamahiriya, Liechtenstein, Lithuania, Luxembourg, Macedonia (former Yugoslav Republic of), Madagascar

Treaty	Malawi	Malaysia	Maldives	Mali	Malta	Marshall Islands	Mauritania	Mauritius	Mexico	Micronesia (Federated States of)	Moldova	Monaco	Mongolia	Morocco	Mozambique	Myanmar	Namibia	Nauru	Nepal	Netherlands	New Zealand	Nicaragua
International Covenant on Civil and Political Rights (ICCPR)	○		○	○	○		○	○	○		○	○	○	○	○		○	△	○	○	○	○
(first) Optional Protocol to the ICCPR	○		○	○	○		○	○	◐		○		○		○		○	△	△	○	○	○
Second Optional Protocol to the ICCPR, aiming at the abolition of the death penalty				○				○			○		○		○		○		○	○	○	△
International Covenant on Economic, Social and Cultural Rights	○		○	○	○		○	○	○		○	○	○	○	○		○		○	○	○	○
Convention on the Elimination of All Forms of Discrimination against Women (CEDAW)	○	○	○	○	○		○	○	●	○	○	○	○	○		○	○		○	○	○	○
Optional Protocol to CEDAW	△		○				△	○			○				○		○		△	○	○	
Convention on the Rights of the Child (CRC)	○	○	○	○	○		○	○	○	○	○	○	○	○		○	○		○	○	○	○
Optional Protocol to the CRC on the involvement of children in armed conflict	△		○	○			△		○	△	○		○		○	△	△		△	○	●	
International Convention on the Elimination of All Forms of Racial Discrimination	○		○	○	○		○	○	○		○	○	○	○	○		○	△	○	○	○	
Convention against Torture and Other Cruel, Inhuman or Degrading Treatment or Punishment	○		○	○	○²²		○²⁸	○	○²²		○	○²²	○	○²⁸	○		○	△	○	○²²	○²²	●
Optional Protocol to the Convention against Torture*			◑	●	○			●	●		◑									◑	◑	
Convention relating to the Status of Refugees (1951)	○			○	○		○	○	○		○	○	○	○		○	○			○	○	○
Protocol relating to the Status of Refugees (1967)	○			○	○		○	○	○		○	○	○	○		○	○			○	○	○
Convention relating to the Status of Stateless Persons (1954)									○											○		
Convention on the Reduction of Statelessness (1961)																				○		
International Convention on the Protection of the Rights of All Migrant Workers and Members of Their Families (1990)			○				○		○					○								●
Rome Statute of the International Criminal Court	○		○	○	○		○	●	△	△	○	△	△	○	○	○	○		○	○		

LEGEND

● ratified in 2005
● state is a party
◐ signed but not yet ratified
△ signed in 2005

10 Declaration under Article 10 not recognizing the competence of the CEDAW Committee to undertake confidential inquiries into allegations of grave or systematic violations

22 Declaration under Article 22 recognizing the competence of the Committee against Torture (CAT) to consider individual complaints

28 Reservation under Article 28 not recognizing the competence of the CAT to undertake confidential inquiries into allegations of systematic torture if warranted

* The Optional Protocol to the Convention against Torture will enter into force after 20 ratifications

12 Declaration under Article 12 (3) accepting the jurisdiction of the International Criminal Court (ICC) for crimes in its territory

124 Declaration under Article 124 not accepting the jurisdiction of the ICC over war crimes for seven years after ratification

** Signed the Rome Statute but have since formally declared their intention not to ratify

*** Acceded in 1962 but in 1965 denounced the Convention; denunciation took effect on 2 April 1966

	Niger	Nigeria	Niue	Norway	Oman	Pakistan	Palau	Panama	Papua New Guinea	Paraguay	Peru	Philippines	Poland	Portugal	Qatar	Romania	Russian Federation	Rwanda	Saint Kitts and Nevis	Saint Lucia	Saint Vincent and the Grenadines	Samoa
International Covenant on Civil and Political Rights (ICCPR)	○	○		○				○		○	○	○	○	○		○	○	○			○	○
(first) Optional Protocol to the ICCPR	○		○					○		○	○		○	○		○	○				○	○
Second Optional Protocol to the ICCPR, aiming at the abolition of the death penalty				○				○		○			△	○								
International Covenant on Economic, Social and Cultural Rights	○	○		○		△		○		○	○	○	○	○		○	○	○			○	○
Convention on the Elimination of All Forms of Discrimination against Women (CEDAW)	○	○	○	○		○		○	○	○	○	○	○	○		○	○	○	○	○	○	○
Optional Protocol to CEDAW	○	○	○					○		○	○		○	○		○	○				○	○
Convention on the Rights of the Child (CRC)	○	○	○	○	○	○	○	○	○	○	○	○	○	○	○	○	○	○	○	○	○	○
Optional Protocol to the CRC on the involvement of children in armed conflict		△		○	△	△		○		○	○	○	●	○		△	○	△				
International Convention on the Elimination of All Forms of Racial Discrimination	○	○		○		○		○	○	○	○	○	○	○	○	○	○	○		○		○
Convention against Torture and Other Cruel, Inhuman or Degrading Treatment or Punishment	○	○		○ [22]				○		○ [22]	○ [22]	○	○ [22][28]	○ [22]		○	○	○ [22]			○	
Optional Protocol to the Convention against Torture*				△						●			●			△						
Convention relating to the Status of Refugees (1951)	○	○		○			○	○	○	○	○	○	○	○		○	○	○	○		○	○
Protocol relating to the Status of Refugees (1967)	○	○		○				○	○	○	○	○	○	○		○	○	○			○	○
Convention relating to the Status of Stateless Persons (1954)				○							○	△									○	
Convention on the Reduction of Statelessness (1961)	○			○																		
International Convention on the Protection of the Rights of All Migrant Workers and Members of Their Families (1990)										△	●	○										
Rome Statute of the International Criminal Court	○	○		○	△			○		○	○	△	○	○		○	△	△		△	○	○

LEGEND

● ratified in 2005
○ state is a party
▲ signed in 2005
△ signed but not yet ratified

10 Declaration under Article 10 not recognizing the competence of the CEDAW Committee to undertake confidential inquiries into allegations of grave or systematic violations

22 Declaration under Article 22 recognizing the competence of the Committee against Torture (CAT) to consider individual complaints

28 Reservation under Article 28 not recognizing the competence of the CAT to undertake confidential inquiries into allegations of systematic torture if warranted

* The Optional Protocol to the Convention against Torture will enter into force after 20 ratifications

12 Declaration under Article 12 (3) accepting the jurisdiction of the International Criminal Court (ICC) for crimes in its territory

124 Declaration under Article 124 not accepting the jurisdiction of the ICC over war crimes for seven years after ratification

** Signed the Rome Statute but have since formally declared their intention not to ratify

*** Acceded in 1962 but in 1965 denounced the Convention; denunciation took effect on 2 April 1966

Treaty	San Marino	Sao Tome and Principe	Saudi Arabia	Senegal	Serbia and Montenegro	Seychelles	Sierra Leone	Singapore	Slovakia	Slovenia	Solomon Islands	Somalia	South Africa	Spain	Sri Lanka	Sudan	Suriname	Swaziland	Sweden	Switzerland	Syrian Arab Republic	Tajikistan
International Covenant on Civil and Political Rights (ICCPR)	○	△		○	○	○	○		○	○		○	○	○	○	○	○	○	○	○	○	○
(first) Optional Protocol to the ICCPR	○	△		○	○	○	○		○	○		○	○	○	○		○		○	○		○
Second Optional Protocol to the ICCPR, aiming at the abolition of the death penalty	○	△			○	○			○	○			○	○					○	○		
International Covenant on Economic, Social and Cultural Rights	○	△		○	○	○	○		○	○	○	○	△	○	○	○	○	○	○	○	○	○
Convention on the Elimination of All Forms of Discrimination against Women (CEDAW)	○	○	△	○	○	○	○	○	○	○	○		○	○	○	○	○	○	○	○	○	○
Optional Protocol to CEDAW	●	△		○	○	△	△		○	○	○		●	○	○				○			△
Convention on the Rights of the Child (CRC)	○	○	○	○	○	○	○	○	○	○	○	△	○	○	○	○	○	○	○	○	○	○
Optional Protocol to the CRC on the involvement of children in armed conflict	△			○	○	△	○	△	○	○		◖	△	○	●	△			○	○		○
International Convention on the Elimination of All Forms of Racial Discrimination	○	△	○	○	○	○	○		○	○	○	○	○	○	○	○	○	○	○	○	○	○
Convention against Torture and Other Cruel, Inhuman or Degrading Treatment or Punishment	△	△	○[28]	○[22]	○[22]	○[22]	○		○[22]	○[22]		○	○[22]	○[22]	△		○		○[22]	○[22]	○[28]	○
Optional Protocol to the Convention against Torture*		△		△	△		△						◖						●	△		
Convention relating to the Status of Refugees (1951)		○		○	○	○	○		○	○	○	○	○	○		○	○	○	○	○		○
Protocol relating to the Status of Refugees (1967)		○		○	○	○	○		○	○	○	○	○	○		○	○	○	○	○		○
Convention relating to the Status of Stateless Persons (1954)				●					○	○			○			○		○	○	○		
Convention on the Reduction of Statelessness (1961)				●					○									○	○			
International Convention on the Protection of the Rights of All Migrant Workers and Members of Their Families (1990)		△		○	△	○	△								○						●	○
Rome Statute of the International Criminal Court	○	△		○	○	△	○		○	○	△		○	○		△			○	○	△	○

Treaty	Tanzania	Thailand	Timor-Leste	Togo	Tonga	Trinidad and Tobago	Tunisia	Turkey	Turkmenistan	Tuvalu	Uganda	Ukraine	United Arab Emirates	United Kingdom	United States of America	Uruguay	Uzbekistan	Vanuatu	Venezuela	Viet Nam	Yemen	Zambia	Zimbabwe
International Covenant on Civil and Political Rights (ICCPR)	○	○	○	○			○	○	○		○	○		○	○	○	○		○	○	○	○	○
(first) Optional Protocol to the ICCPR			○	○				◒	◒		○	○				○	○		○			○	
Second Optional Protocol to the ICCPR, aiming at the abolition of the death penalty			○					◒	○					○					○				
International Covenant on Economic, Social and Cultural Rights	○	○	○	○		○	○	○	○		○	○		○	◒	○	○		○	○	○	○	○
Convention on the Elimination of All Forms of Discrimination against Women (CEDAW)	○	○	○	○	○	○	○	○	○	○	○	○	○	○	◒	○	○	○	○	○	○	○	○
Optional Protocol to CEDAW		○	○					○				○		○		○			○				
Convention on the Rights of the Child (CRC)	○	○	○	○	○	○	○	○	○	○	○	○		○	◒	○	○		○	○	○	○	○
Optional Protocol to the CRC on the involvement of children in armed conflict	○		○	●			○	○		●		●		○	○	○		◒	○	○			
International Convention on the Elimination of All Forms of Racial Discrimination	○	○	○	○	○	○	○	○	○		○	○		○	○	○	○		○	○	○	○	○
Convention against Torture and Other Cruel, Inhuman or Degrading Treatment or Punishment			○	○ [22]			○ [22]	○ [22]	○		○ [22]	○		○	○ [22]	○		○ [22]	○		○	○	
Optional Protocol to the Convention against Torture*			◒	◒				◒	●			◒		○		○							
Convention relating to the Status of Refugees (1951)	○		○	○		○	○	○	○		○	○		○		○	○		○		○	○	○
Protocol relating to the Status of Refugees (1967)	○		○	○		○	○	○	○		○	○		○	○	○	○		○		○	○	○
Convention relating to the Status of Stateless Persons (1954)					○	○					○			○		○						○	○
Convention on the Reduction of Statelessness (1961)						○								○		○							
International Convention on the Protection of the Rights of All Migrant Workers and Members of Their Families (1990)			○	◒				○			○					○							
Rome Statute of the International Criminal Court	○	◒	○		○			◒			○	◒	◒	○	◒**	○	◒		●	◒	◒	○	◒

Selected regional human rights treaties (AT 31 DECEMBER 2005)

African Union (formerly the Organization of African Unity)

States that have ratified or acceded to a convention are party to the treaty and are bound to observe its provisions. States that have signed but not yet ratified have expressed their intention to become a party at some future date; meanwhile, they are obliged to refrain from acts that would defeat the object and purpose of the treaty.

This chart lists countries that were members of the African Union at the end of 2005.

	Central African Republic	Chad	Comoros	Congo (Democratic Republic of the)	Congo (Republic of the)	Côte d'Ivoire	Djibouti	Egypt
African Charter on Human and Peoples' Rights (1981)	○	○	○	○	○	○	○	○
Protocol to the African Charter on the Establishment of an African Court on Human and Peoples' Rights (1998)	△	△	○	△	△	○	◐	△
African Charter on the Rights and Welfare of the Child (1990)	△	○	○		△	△	△	○
Convention Governing the Specific Aspects of Refugee Problems in Africa (1969)	○	○	○	○	○	○	◐	○
Protocol to the African Charter on Human and Peoples' Rights on the Rights of Women in Africa (2003)*		△	○	△	△	△	●	

	Algeria	Angola	Benin	Botswana	Burkina Faso	Burundi	Cameroon	Cape Verde
African Charter on Human and Peoples' Rights (1981)	○	○	○	○	○	○	○	○
Protocol to the African Charter on the Establishment of an African Court on Human and Peoples' Rights (1998)	○		△	△	○	○		
African Charter on the Rights and Welfare of the Child (1990)	○	○	○	○	○	○	○	○
Convention Governing the Specific Aspects of Refugee Problems in Africa (1969)	○	○	○		○	○	○	○
Protocol to the African Charter on Human and Peoples' Rights on the Rights of Women in Africa (2003)*	△		●		△	△		●

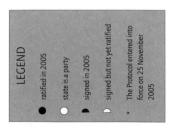

LEGEND

● ratified in 2005
○ state is a party
◐ signed in 2005
△ signed but not yet ratified
* The Protocol entered into force on 25 November 2005

	Niger	Nigeria	Rwanda	Sahrawi Arab Democratic Republic	Sao Tome and Principe	Senegal	Seychelles	Sierra Leone	Somalia	South Africa	Sudan	Swaziland	Tanzania	Togo	Tunisia	Uganda	Zambia	Zimbabwe
African Charter on Human and Peoples' Rights (1981)		○	●		●	○	●	○	●	○	●	○	●	○	●	○	●	○
Protocol to the African Charter on the Establishment of an African Court on Human and Peoples' Rights (1998)	○	○	●			○	◓	◒		○	◓	◒	◒	○	◒	○	◒	◒
African Charter on the Rights and Welfare of the Child (1990)	○	○	●	◒		○	○	◓	○		◒	●	◓	○		○		
Convention Governing the Specific Aspects of Refugee Problems in Africa (1969)	○	○	●		○	●	○	◓	○	●	○	●	○	●	○	○	●	○
Protocol to the African Charter on Human and Peoples' Rights on the Rights of Women in Africa (2003)*	◒	○	●		○		◓	◒		○		◒	◒	●		◒	◓	◒

	Equatorial Guinea	Eritrea	Ethiopia	Gabon	Gambia	Ghana	Guinea	Guinea-Bissau	Kenya	Lesotho	Liberia	Libya	Madagascar	Malawi	Mali	Mauritania	Mauritius	Mozambique	Namibia
African Charter on Human and Peoples' Rights (1981)	○	○	○	○	●	○	●	○	●	○	●	○	●	○	●	○	●	○	●
Protocol to the African Charter on the Establishment of an African Court on Human and Peoples' Rights (1998)	◒	○	◒	○	○	◒	◒	◓	○	○	◒	○	◒	○	◒	●	○	○	◒
African Charter on the Rights and Welfare of the Child (1990)	○	○	○	◒	○	●	○	◓	○	○	◒	○	●	○	○	●	○	○	○
Convention Governing the Specific Aspects of Refugee Problems in Africa (1969)	○		○	○	○	○	○	○	○	○	○	○	◒	○	○	◒	○		○
Protocol to the African Charter on Human and Peoples' Rights on the Rights of Women in Africa (2003)*	◓	◒	◓	●	◒	◒	◓	◒	○	◒	○	◒	●	●	●	◓	●	○	

LEGEND
- ● ratified in 2005
- ○ state is a party
- ◓ signed in 2005
- ◒ signed but not yet ratified
- * The Protocol entered into force on 25 November 2005

Organization of American States (OAS)

States that have ratified or acceded to a convention are party to the treaty and are bound to observe its provisions. States that have signed but not yet ratified have expressed their intention to become a party at some future date; meanwhile, they are obliged to refrain from acts that would defeat the object and purpose of the treaty. This chart lists countries that were members of the OAS at the end of 2005.

Treaty	Guyana	Haiti	Honduras	Jamaica	Mexico	Nicaragua	Panama	Paraguay	Peru	Saint Kitts and Nevis	Saint Lucia	Saint Vincent and the Grenadines	Suriname	Trinidad and Tobago	United States of America	Uruguay	Venezuela
American Convention on Human Rights (1969)		○[62]	●[62]	○	●[62]	○[62]	●[62]	○[62]	●[62]				●[62]			◐[62]	●[62]
Protocol to the American Convention on Human Rights to Abolish the Death Penalty (1990)						○	●	○								○	●
Additional Protocol to the American Convention on Human Rights in the Area of Economic, Social and Cultural Rights (1988)		△	△		●	△	●		●				●			○	△
Inter-American Convention to Prevent and Punish Torture (1985)		△	◐		●	△	●	○	●				●			○	●
Inter-American Convention on Forced Disappearance of Persons (1994)			●		●	△	●	○	●							○	●
Inter-American Convention on the Prevention, Punishment and Eradication of Violence against Women (1994)	●	○	●	●	●	●	○	●	○	●	○	●	○	●		●	●
Inter-American Convention on the Elimination of All Forms of Discrimination against Persons with Disabilities (1999)		△	△		●	○	●	○	●							○	△

Treaty	Antigua and Barbuda	Argentina	Bahamas	Barbados	Belize	Bolivia	Brazil	Canada	Chile	Colombia	Costa Rica	Cuba*	Dominica	Dominican Republic	Ecuador	El Salvador	Grenada	Guatemala
American Convention on Human Rights (1969)		○[62]	○	○[62]		○[62]	●[62]		●[62]	○[62]	●[62]		○	○[62]	●[62]	○[62]	○	○[62]
Protocol to the American Convention on Human Rights to Abolish the Death Penalty (1990)							●		△		●				●			
Additional Protocol to the American Convention on Human Rights in the Area of Economic, Social and Cultural Rights (1988)		○				△	●		△	○	●			△	○	○		○
Inter-American Convention to Prevent and Punish Torture (1985)		○				△	●		●	●	●				○	○		○
Inter-American Convention on Forced Disappearance of Persons (1994)		○				○	△		△	●	●				△			○
Inter-American Convention on the Prevention, Punishment and Eradication of Violence against Women (1994)	●	○	●	○	●	○	●		●	○	●		●	○	●	○	●	○
Inter-American Convention on the Elimination of All Forms of Discrimination against Persons with Disabilities (1999)		○					●		●	○	●		△	△	●	○		○

LEGEND

- ● ratified in 2005
- ○ state is a party
- ◐ signed in 2005
- △ signed but not yet ratified
- 62 Declaration under Article 62 recognizing the jurisdiction of the Inter-American Court of Human Rights on all matters relating to the interpretation or application of the American Convention and related treaties
- * In 1962, by resolution of the VIII Meeting of Consultation of Ministers of Foreign Affairs, the current government of Cuba was excluded from participation in the OAS

Council of Europe

States that have ratified or acceded to a convention are party to the treaty and are bound to observe its provisions. States that have signed but not yet ratified have expressed their intention to become a party at some future date; meanwhile, they are obliged to refrain from acts that would defeat the object and purpose of the treaty.

This chart lists countries that were members of the Council of Europe at the end of 2005.

	Denmark	Estonia	Finland	France	Georgia	Germany	Greece	Hungary	Iceland	Ireland	Italy
European Convention for the Protection of Human Rights and Fundamental Freedoms (ECHR) (1950)	●	○	●	○	●	○	●	○	●	○	●
Protocol No. 6 to the ECHR concerning the abolition of the death penalty in times of peace (1983)	●	○	●	○	●	○	●	○	●	○	●
Protocol No. 12 to the ECHR concerning the general prohibition of discrimination (2000)*		◿	●		●	◿	◢	◿	◢	◿	◢
Protocol No. 13 to the ECHR concerning the abolition of the death penalty in all circumstances	●	○	●	◿	●	○	●	○	●	○	◢
Framework Convention on the Protection of National Minorities	●	○	●		◢	○	◢	○	◢	○	●

	Albania	Andorra	Armenia	Austria	Azerbaijan	Belgium	Bosnia and Herzegovina	Bulgaria	Croatia	Cyprus	Czech Republic
European Convention for the Protection of Human Rights and Fundamental Freedoms (ECHR) (1950)	●	○	●	○	●	○	●	○	●	○	●
Protocol No. 6 to the ECHR concerning the abolition of the death penalty in times of peace (1983)	●	○	●	○	●	○	●	○	●	○	●
Protocol No. 12 to the ECHR concerning the general prohibition of discrimination (2000)*	●		●	◿	◢	◿	●		●	○	◢
Protocol No. 13 to the ECHR concerning the abolition of the death penalty in all circumstances	◢	○		○		○	●	○	●	○	●
Framework Convention on the Protection of National Minorities	●	●	●	○	●	◿	●	○	●	○	●

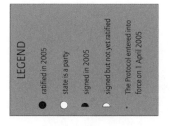

LEGEND
- ● ratified in 2005
- ○ state is a party
- ◢ signed in 2005
- ◿ signed but not yet ratified
- * The Protocol entered into force on 1 April 2005

SELECTED REGIONAL HUMAN RIGHTS TREATIES

	Romania	Russian Federation	San Marino	Serbia and Montenegro	Slovakia	Slovenia	Spain	Sweden	Switzerland	Turkey	Ukraine	United Kingdom
European Convention for the Protection of Human Rights and Fundamental Freedoms (ECHR) (1950)	●	○	●	○	●	○	●	○	●	○	●	○
Protocol No. 6 to the ECHR concerning the abolition of the death penalty in times of peace (1983)	●	△	●	○	●	○	●		●	○	●	○
Protocol No. 12 to the ECHR concerning the general prohibition of discrimination (2000)*	△	△	○	○	△	△	◐			△	△	
Protocol No. 13 to the ECHR concerning the abolition of the death penalty in all circumstances	●		●	○	●	○	△	○	●	△	●	○
Framework Convention on the Protection of National Minorities	●	○	●	○	●	○	●	○	●		●	○

	Latvia	Liechtenstein	Lithuania	Luxembourg	Macedonia (former Yugoslav Republic of)	Malta	Moldova	Monaco	Netherlands	Norway	Poland	Portugal
European Convention for the Protection of Human Rights and Fundamental Freedoms (ECHR) (1950)	○	○	○	○	○	○	○	●	○	○	○	○
Protocol No. 6 to the ECHR concerning the abolition of the death penalty in times of peace (1983)	○	○	○	○	○	○	●	●	○	○	○	○
Protocol No. 12 to the ECHR concerning the general prohibition of discrimination (2000)*	△	△		△	●		△		○	△		△
Protocol No. 13 to the ECHR concerning the abolition of the death penalty in all circumstances	△	○	●	△	●	○	△	●	△	●	◐	○
Framework Convention on the Protection of National Minorities	●	○	●	△	●	○	●	●	○	●	●	○

LEGEND

● ratified in 2005
○ state is a party
◐ signed in 2005
△ signed but not yet ratified
· The Protocol entered into force on 1 April 2005

WHETHER IN A HIGH-PROFILE CONFLICT OR A FORGOTTEN CORNER OF THE GLOBE, AMNESTY INTERNATIONAL CAMPAIGNS FOR JUSTICE AND FREEDOM FOR ALL AND SEEKS TO GALVANIZE PUBLIC SUPPORT TO BUILD A BETTER WORLD.

WHAT CAN YOU DO?

■ Join Amnesty International and become part of a worldwide movement campaigning for an end to human rights violations. Help us make a difference.

■ Make a donation to support Amnesty International's work.

Activists around the world have shown that it is possible to resist the dangerous forces that are undermining human rights. Be part of this movement. Combat those who peddle fear and hate. Join Amnesty International.

Together we can make our voices heard.

I WANT TO HELP

☐ I am interested in receiving further information on becoming a member of Amnesty International

name

address

country

email

☐ I wish to make a donation to Amnesty International

amount

Please debit my   Visa ☐   Mastercard ☐

number

expiry date

signature

Please return this form to the Amnesty International office in your country. (See pages 307-310 for further details of Amnesty International offices worldwide.) If there is not an Amnesty International office in your country, please return this form to Amnesty International's International Secretariat in London:

Peter Benenson House, 1 Easton Street, London WC1X 0DW, United Kingdom (donations will be taken in UK£, US$ or €)

www.amnesty.org